This g[...]
(288¹/[...]
630-m[...]
secon[...]
*Corn[...]
writte[...]
HENR[...]
who also researched and wrote the two other books in this SWCP series, plus several other Trailblazer guides. The fifth edition of the book was researched and written by Daniel McCrohan and Joel returned for this sixth edition.

Born in Poole, Dorset, **JOEL NEWTON**, first discovered the South-West Coast Path whilst on a family holiday to Cornwall in the spring of 2007. Later that same year, Joel found himself on a bus to Minehead with a bag that he would soon discover was far too heavy. Six weeks later he arrived in Falmouth sun-drunk, blistered, happy and with a newfound love for walking national trails. This passion led to Joel ambling along 10 more long-distance paths. Sitting in a café in Hastings, East Sussex, between walks in 2011, a stranger who was also there (stroking a puppy) admitted that he was the author of the guidebook Joel was reading: Trailblazer's *Hadrian's Wall Path*. They got talking and in 2012, Joel, Henry Stedman (the stranger) and Daisy (the puppy, by now a dog) walked, researched and co-authored Trailblazer's three-part series to the South-West Coast Path. Since then Joel has written the Trailblazer guide *Thames Path* and travelled and trekked in South-east Asia. This is Joel's eighth guidebook and when not walking he lives and works in Hastings.

Authors

Cornwall Coast Path (SWCP Part 2)
First edition: 2003, this sixth edition 2019

Publisher Trailblazer Publications
The Old Manse, Tower Rd, Hindhead, Surrey, GU26 6SU, UK ▯ trailblazer-guides.com

British Library Cataloguing in Publication Data
A catalogue record for this book is available from the British Library

ISBN 978-1-912716-05-0

© **Trailblazer** 2003, 2006, 2009, 2012, 2016, 2019: Text and maps

Series Editor: Anna Jacomb-Hood
Editor: Daniel McCrohan **Proof-reading**: Jane Thomas & Anna Jacomb-Hood
Cartography: Nick Hill **Layout**: Daniel McCrohan **Index**: Anna Jacomb-Hood
Photographs (flora): C5 Row 1 right, © Jane Thomas; all others © Bryn Thomas
Photographs (p114): © Philip Thomas **Additional material**: Patricia Major
All other photographs: © Joel Newton unless otherwise indicated

The maps in this guide were prepared from out-of-Crown-
copyright Ordnance Survey maps amended and updated by Trailblazer.

Dedication
For Michela

Acknowledgements
Thank you, Joy Salisbury, for the accommodation and lifts and for sharing your knowledge
of Cornwall, its beaches and cafés with me. Without your support walking the Cornish coast
would have thrown up many more challenges. And thank you for pointing me towards *The
Salt Path* by Raynor Winn – a tremendous book! Thanks to Michela Prescott for keeping me
company in St Ives and Lizard. (Henry's company wasn't quite the same!) I'm also grateful
to all of the campsites who put me up regardless of it being their peak season, and to the staff
in the numerous tourist information centres who patiently answered my questions. Thanks
also to Henry Stedman, who got me into this game in the first place, and is always willing
to offer help and advice when it comes to walking and writing about National Trails.
    A big thank you to all the readers who sent in suggestions for this new edition – Louise
Connell, Christine Evans, Joen Hermans, Chris Horn, Penny Jose, David Mallinson, Lena
Meyer, Andreas Niedermair, Guy De Pauw, Verena & Thomas Rhyner, Philip Scriver,
Stephen Smith, Frances Trenouth and Jon Wills. Lastly, and as ever, thanks to all at
Trailblazer: Daniel McCrohan for editing and layout, Nick Hill for maps, Jane Thomas and
Anna Jacomb-Hood for proofreading and Anna J-H for additional research and the index.

A request
The author and publisher have tried to ensure that this guide is as accurate and up to date
as possible. Nevertheless, things change. If you notice any changes or omissions that
should be included in the next edition of this book, please write to Trailblazer (address
above) or email us at ▯ info@trailblazer-guides.com. A free copy of the next edition
will be sent to persons making a significant contribution.

Updated information will be available on: ▯ **www.trailblazer-guides.com**

Photos – Cover & this page: Porthtowan Beach, looking north. **Previous page**: Whitesand Bay. A hiker heads north from Gwnver Beach. **Overleaf**: The beach at Gwythian.

Printed in China; print production by D'Print (☎ +65-6581 3832), Singapore

Cornwall
COAST PATH

SW COAST PATH PART 2 – BUDE TO PLYMOUTH

142 large-scale maps & guides to 81 towns and villages

PLANNING – PLACES TO STAY – PLACES TO EAT

HENRY STEDMAN & JOEL NEWTON

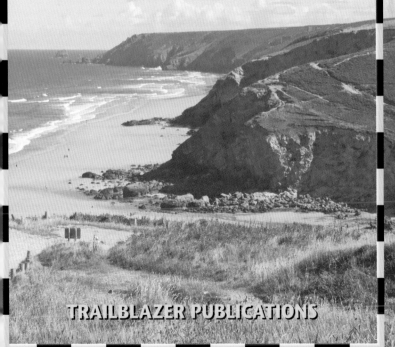

TRAILBLAZER PUBLICATIONS

INTRODUCTION

PART 1: PLANNING YOUR WALK

PART 2: THE ENVIRONMENT & NATURE

PART 3: MINIMUM IMPACT WALKING & OUTDOOR SAFETY

Contents

PART 4: ROUTE GUIDE & MAPS

Using this guide 78

APPENDICES

Contents

ABOUT THIS BOOK

This guidebook contains all the information you need. The hard work has been done for you so you can plan your trip without having to consult numerous websites and other books and maps. When you're all packed and ready to go, there's comprehensive public transport information to get you to and from the trail and detailed maps (1:20,000) to help you find your way along it.

● All standards of accommodation; reviews of campsites, hostels, B&Bs, hotels
● Walking companies if you want an organised tour and baggage-carrying services if you just want your luggage carried
● Itineraries for all levels of walkers
● Answers to all your questions: when to go, degree of difficulty, what to pack, and how much the whole walking holiday will cost
● Walking times in both directions and GPS waypoints
● Cafés, pubs, tearooms, takeaways, restaurants and shops for buying supplies
● Rail, bus & taxi information for all villages and towns along the path
● Street plans of the main towns both on and off the path
● Historical, cultural and geographical background information

❏ MINIMUM IMPACT FOR MAXIMUM INSIGHT

Man has suffered in his separation from the soil and from other living creatures ... and as yet he must still, for security, look long at some portion of the earth as it was before he tampered with it.
Gavin Maxwell, *Ring of Bright Water*, 1960

Why is walking in wild and solitary places so satisfying? Partly it is the sheer physical pleasure: sometimes pitting one's strength against the elements and the lie of the land. The beauty and wonder of the natural world and the fresh air restore our sense of proportion and the stresses and strains of everyday life slip away. Whatever the character of the countryside, walking in it benefits us mentally and physically, inducing a sense of well-being, an enrichment of life and an enhanced awareness of what lies around us. All this the countryside gives us and the least we can do is to safeguard it by supporting rural economies, local businesses, and low-impact methods of farming and land-management, and by using environmentally sensitive forms of transport – walking being pre-eminent.

In this book there is a detailed and illustrated chapter on the wildlife and conservation of the region and a chapter on minimum-impact walking, with ideas on how to tread lightly in this fragile environment; by following its principles we can help to preserve our natural heritage for future generations.

Warning: coastal and long-distance walking can be dangerous

Please read the notes on when to go (pp13-16) and outdoor safety (pp74-7). Every effort has been made by the author and publisher to ensure that the information contained herein is as accurate and up to date as possible. However, they are unable to accept responsibility for any inconvenience, loss or injury sustained by anyone as a result of the advice and information given in this guide.

INTRODUCTION

Synonymous with the sea and the sea's wild storms that created its dramatic coastline, Cornwall is a land of magic, myth and legend, of poetic writing and art. Its known history stretches back 5500 years and has witnessed Phoenician traders, pirates, smugglers and shipwrecks, the rise and fall of the tin-mining and fishing industries and a growing market

The Cornish coast is a holiday paradise that's easily accessible, where you'll enjoy some of the finest coastal walking Britain has to offer

in tourism which dates back to the days of Victorian villas built for long summer holidays.

The origins of the coast path lie in Cornwall's smuggling history. By the early 19th century smuggling had become so rife that in 1822 HM Coastguard was formed to patrol the entire British coastline. A coast-hugging footpath was created to enable the coastguards to see into every cove, inlet and creek and slowly but surely law and order prevailed and the smuggling decreased. By the beginning of the 20th century the foot patrols had been abandoned.

Walking the coast path is one of the best ways to experience fully the sights and sounds that make Cornwall unique and special. As well as the sheer physical pleasure of walking, the sea breeze in your hair, the taste of the salt spray on your lips, you are treated to the most beautiful and spectacular views of this beguiling and some-

(**Above**): The beach at Portreath. The path winds through numerous coves and passes many little villages and beaches on its 288¼-mile journey round Cornwall.

times hazardous coastline. The sky and the light change with the movement of even the smallest cloud over the sea that lies ultramarine and translucent on long hot summer days but becomes leaden and silver with mountainous white-crested waves in sudden storms. Watch for the seals that fool you by swimming under water for long periods, then bob up just when you'd thought they'd gone. You might see dolphins, too, or even a basking shark.

Walking allows you flexibility over the distances you want to cover, your speed depending on your level of fitness. You can be completely independent, carrying all the basics of life – food, shelter and clothes – on your back, or book B&Bs ahead and walk with the knowledge that your creature comforts, hot baths and comfortable beds, will be waiting for you at the end of the day.

As for rest stops, you'll be tempted time and time again. Explore quintessentially Cornish fishing villages or take a quick break on the Isles of Scilly. Try to identify some of Cornwall's profusion of wildflowers. Look into the little

(Below): The ruined engine houses of old tin mines, near Pendeen. You'll see evidence of the once great Cornish tin mining industry (see p181) in several places along the coast.

rock pools that are so full of life. Immerse yourself in contemporary art in St Ives. Investigate tin-mining history in a landscape so important that it has been declared a World Heritage Site. Try surfing or simply take a swim to cool off on a hot day.

For food, feast on Cornish pasties and crab sandwiches as you picnic on a clifftop or beach; in picturesque cottage tearooms gorge on scones piled high with strawberry jam and clotted cream. Above all eat fish fresh from the sea, superb shellfish, lobster, crab and scallops. As well as ubiquitous fish and chip shops and

There will be numerous chances every day to indulge in a cream tea. It's said that Cornish people will put the jam on first and the clotted cream on top of it whereas in Devon they do it the other way around. We say whatever floats your boat is fine.

beach cafés there are several top-class seafood restaurants in Cornwall, some run by famous TV chefs: Rick Stein has been in Padstow for many years and Jamie Oliver owns a restaurant in Watergate Bay.

The Cornish coast is a holiday paradise that's easily accessible, where you'll enjoy some of the finest coastal walking Britain has to offer.

This book covers the second section (288¼ miles) of the 630-mile South-West Coast Path

---

❏ **The South-West Coast Path**

Typing 'Minehead to South Haven Point, Dorset' into Googlemaps, reveals that travelling between the two can be completed in a matter of 3 hours 37 minutes by car, along a distance of 96.6 miles. Even walking, along the most direct route, takes only around 29 hours, so Googlemaps says, with the path an even shorter one at just 89.3 miles.

It is these two points that are connected by the South-West Coast Path (SWCP). This most famous – and infamous – of national trails is, however, a good deal longer than 89.3 miles. Though estimates as to its exact length vary – and to a large part are determined by which of the alternative paths one takes at various stages along the trail – the most widely accepted estimate of the path is that it is about 630 miles long (1014km). That figure, however, often changes due to necessary changes in the path caused by erosion and other factors.

So why, when you could walk from Minehead to South Haven Point in just 29 hours, do most people choose to take 6-8 weeks? The answer is simple: the SWCP is one of the most beautiful trails in the UK. Around 70% of those 630 miles are spent either in national parks or regions designated as Areas of Outstanding Natural Beauty. The variety of places crossed by the SWCP is extraordinary too: from sun-kissed beaches to sandy burrows, holiday parks to fishing harbours, esplanade to estuary, on top of windswept cliffs and under woodland canopy, the scenery that one travels through along the length of the SWCP has to be the most diverse of any of the national trails.

(cont'd overleaf)

INTRODUCTION

❏ The South-West Coast Path (cont'd from p9)

Of course, maintaining such a monumental route is no easy task. A survey in 2000 stated that the trail boasted 2473 signposts and waymarks, 302 bridges, 921 stiles, and 26,719 steps. Although out of date now, these figures do still give an idea of both how long the trail is, and how much is involved in building and maintaining it to such a high standard. The task of looking after the trail falls to a dedicated team from the official body, Natural England. Another particularly important organisation and one that looks after the rights of walkers is the South West Coast Path Association (see p46), a charity that fights for improvements to the path and offers advice, information and support to walkers. They also campaign against many of the proposed changes to the path, and help to ensure that England's right-of-way laws which ensure that the footpath is open to the public – even though it does, on occasion, pass through private property – are fully observed.

History of the path

In 1948 a government report recommended the creation of a footpath around the entire South-West peninsula to improve public access to the coast which, at that time, was pretty dire. It took until 1973 for the Cornwall Coast Path to be declared officially open and another five years for the rest of the South-West Coast Path to be completed. The last section to be completed, the North Devon and Exmoor stretch, is the first part that most coastal walkers complete, though it was actually the last section to be opened to the public, in 1978.

The origins of the path, however, are much older than its official designation. Originally, the paths were established – or at least adopted, there presumably being coastal paths from time immemorial that connected the coastal villages – by the local coastguard in the nineteenth century, who needed a path that hugged the shoreline closely to aid them in their attempts to spot and prevent smugglers from bringing contraband into the country. The coastguards were unpopular in the area as they prevented the locals from exploiting a lucrative if illegal activity, to the extent that it was considered too dangerous for them to stay in the villages; as a result, the authorities were obliged to build special cottages for the coastguards that stood (and, often, still stand) in splendid isolation near the path – but well away from the villages.

The lifeboat patrols also used the path to look out for craft in distress (and on one famous occasion used the path to drag their boat to a safe launch to rescue a floundering ship). When the coastguards' work ended in 1856, the Admiralty took over the task of protecting England's shoreline and thus the paths continued to be used.

The route – Minehead (Somerset) to Poole Harbour (Dorset)

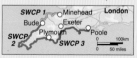

The SWCP officially begins at Minehead in Somerset (its exact starting point marked by a sculpture that celebrates the trail), heads west right round the bottom south-west corner of Britain then shuffles back along the south coast to South Haven Point, overlooking Poole Harbour in Dorset. On its lengthy journey around Britain's south-western corner the SWCP crosses national parks such as Exmoor as well as regions that have been designated as Areas of Outstanding Natural Beauty (including North, South and East Devon AONB and the Cornwall and Dorset AONBs), or Sites of Special Scientific Interest (Braunton Burrows being just one example – an area that also enjoys a privileged status as a UNESCO Biosphere Reserve), and even a couple of UNESCO World Heritage sites, too, including the Jurassic Coast of East Devon and Dorset and the old mining landscape of Cornwall and West Devon. Other features passed on the way include the highest cliffs on

How difficult is the path?

The South-West Coast Path (SWCP) is just a (very, very) long walk, so there's no need for crampons, ropes, ice axes, oxygen bottles or any other climbing paraphernalia. All you need to complete the walk is some suitable clothing, a bit of money, a rucksack full of determination and a half-decent pair of calf muscles.

No great level of experience is needed to walk the Cornwall section of the coast path as the walking is generally easy and you are never far from help. Villages and accommodation are reasonably close together so it is simple to adapt itineraries to suit all needs and levels of fitness.

Amongst the most challenging sections of the coast path in Cornwall are the stretches between Widemouth Bay and Crackington Haven, and between Port Isaac and Port Quin where the path never seems to be level, the difficult terrain from St Ives to Sennen Cove and the relentlessly steep undulations that immediately precede Polperro. However, as long as you plan ahead and are reasonably fit you should not experience difficulties on any of these stretches. Other points

mainland Britain (at Great Hangman – also the highest point on the coast path at 318m/1043ft, with a cliff-face of 244m), the largest sand-dune system in England (at Braunton Burrows), England's most westerly point (at Land's End) and Britain's most southerly (at the Lizard), the 18-mile barrier beach of Chesil Bank, one of the world's largest natural harbours at Poole, and even the National Trust's only official nudist beach at Studland! The path then ends at South Haven Point, its exact finish marked by a second SWCP sculpture. The path also takes in four counties – Somerset, Devon, Cornwall and Dorset – and connects with over fifteen other long-distance trails; the southern section from Plymouth to Poole also forms part of the 3125-mile long European E9 Coastal Path that runs on a convoluted route from Portugal to Estonia.

Walking the South-West Coast Path
In terms of difficulty, there are those people who, having never undertaken such a trail before, are under the illusion that coastal walking is a cinch; that all it involves is a simple stroll along mile after mile of golden, level beach, the walker needing to pause only to kick the sand out from his or her flipflop or buy another ice cream.

The truth, of course, is somewhat different, for coastal paths tend to stick to the cliffs above the beaches rather than the beaches themselves (which is actually something of a relief, given how hard it is to walk across sand or shingle). These cliffs make for some spectacular walking but – given the undulating nature of Britain's coastline, and the fact the course of the SWCP inevitably crosses innumerable river valleys, each of which forces the walker to descend rapidly before climbing back up again almost immediately afterwards – some exhausting walking too. Indeed, it has been estimated that anybody who completes the entire SWCP will have climbed more than four times the height of Everest (35,031m to be precise, or 114,931ft) by the time they finish!

Given these figures, it is perhaps hardly surprising that most people take around eight weeks to complete the whole route, and few do so in one go; indeed, it is not unusual for people to take years or even decades to complete the whole path, taking a week or two here and there to tackle various sections until the whole trail is complete.

to bear in mind are basically common sense: don't wander too close to either the top or bottom of cliffs; take care when swimming; be aware of the tides; and listen to weather forecasts. Your greatest danger on the walk is likely to be from the weather, which can be so unpredictable in this corner of the world, so it is vital that you dress for inclement conditions and always carry a set of dry clothes with you.

How long do you need?

If you're a fit walker who isn't carrying too much and who loves to spend all day on the trail you could manage Bude to Plymouth, or vice versa, a distance of around 288¼ miles (464km) depending on your exact route, in about 20 days. There's nothing wrong with this approach, of course – *chacun à son goût*, as the French probably say. However, **what you mustn't do is try to push yourself too fast, or too far**. That road leads only to exhaustion, injury or, at the absolute least, an unpleasant time.

> A fit walker could manage Bude to Plymouth in about 20 days ... but most walkers take roughly three and a half weeks

If you like your walking holiday to be a bit more relaxed with time to sit on the cliff tops, explore towns and villages, laze in the sun on the beaches, scoff scones in tearooms, visit an attraction or two, or sup local beers under the shade of a pub parasol – as well as have a few rest days – then you'll need to set aside at least one month. Most walkers will fit somewhere between these two extremes, taking roughly three and a half weeks which still allows time for exploring and one or two rest days.

When deciding how long to allow for the walk, those intending to **camp** and carry their own luggage shouldn't underestimate just how much a heavy pack can slow them down. On pp32-4 there are some suggested itineraries covering different walking speeds. For walkers with less time on their hands there are some superb day and weekend walks (see p35 & pp40-1) along parts of the coast path.

The practical information in this section will help you plan an excellent walk, covering every detail from what you need to do before you leave home to

designing an itinerary to meet your particular preferences. More detailed information about the day-to-day walking and towns and villages along the trail can be found in **Part 4**.

See pp32-4 for some suggested itineraries covering different walking speeds

INTRODUCTION

When to go

SEASONS

'My shoes are clean from walking in the rain.' **Jack Kerouac**

The decision of when to go may be out of your hands. However, if you are in a position to choose which time of the year to go, make your plans carefully. Do you prefer the vibrant colours of springtime wildflowers, or the rich tones of autumnal foliage and heather? Do you want weather warm enough for swimming? Do you like the buzz of big crowds, or do you prefer to walk in solitude? The following information should help you decide when is best for you.

April, May and June are possibly the best months to go walking in Cornwall

Spring and early summer
April, **May** and **June** are possibly the best months to go walking in Cornwall. The weather is warm enough without being too hot, the days are getting longer, the holiday crowds have yet to arrive and this is usually the driest time of the year. Perhaps the most beautiful advantage is the abundance of wildflowers which reach their peak in May. Cornwall starts to get busier in June as by now the sun is making an average appearance of seven hours a day.

Summer
July and **August** are the hottest months and also the busiest. This is the time of the school summer holidays when families and holidaymakers flock in their thousands to Cornwall. Demand for accommodation is high, particularly in

(Below): You'll pass numerous old harbours, some still quite busy such as here at Mevagissey.

INTRODUCTION

August, and many B&B owners and some campsites will only take bookings of at least two nights if not a full week. Surprisingly most of the coast path itself is not that busy, but you'll encounter the crowds at beaches, car parks and in towns, especially if the sun is out. The weather is generally good in July, although during particularly settled periods it can be very hot for walking. August can be wetter and overcast.

Autumn
September is often a wonderful month for walking. The days are still long, the temperature has not dropped noticeably and the summer crowds have long disappeared. The first signs of winter will be felt in **October** but there's nothing really to deter the walker. In fact there's still much to entice you, such as the colours of the heathland, which come into their own in autumn; a magnificent blaze of brilliant purples and pinks, splashed with the yellow flowers of gorse.

Winter
November can bring crisp clear days which are ideal for walking, although you'll definitely feel the chill when you stop on the cliff tops for a break. Winter temperatures rarely fall below freezing but the incidence of gales and storms definitely increases. You need to be fairly hardy to walk in **December** and **January** and you may have to alter your plans because of the weather. By **February** the daffodils and primroses are already appearing but even into **March** it can still be decidedly chilly if the sun is not out.

While winter is definitely the low season with many places closed, this can be more of an advantage than a disadvantage. Very few people walk at this time of year, giving you long stretches of the trail to yourself. When you do stumble across other walkers they are as happy as you to stop and chat. Finding B&B accommodation is easier as you will rarely have to book more than a night ahead (though it is still worth checking in advance as some B&Bs close out of season), but if you are camping, or on a small budget, you will find places to stay much more limited. Few campsites bother to stay open all year and many hostels will be closed.

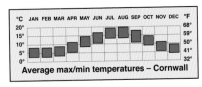

Average max/min temperatures – Cornwall

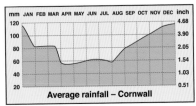

Average rainfall – Cornwall

WEATHER

The Cornish climate is considerably milder than that of the rest of Britain because of its southerly location and the influence of the Gulf Stream. Winter **temperatures** rarely fall below freezing and the mean maximum in summer is around 19°C. Sea temperatures range from about 9°C in February to about 17°C in August.

Rainfall is highest in the winter due to the regular procession of weather fronts moving east across the Atlantic. In the summer these fronts are weaker, less frequent and take a more northerly track.

Mean **wind speeds** are force 3-4 in summer and 4-5 in winter. Gales can be expected around ten days per month between December and February and less than one day per month from May to August.

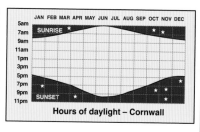

Hours of daylight – Cornwall

DAYLIGHT HOURS

If you are walking in autumn, winter or early spring you must take into account how far you can walk in the available light. It may not be possible to cover as many miles as you would in the summer.

The sunrise and sunset times in the table are based on information for the town of Penzance on the 15th of each month. This gives a rough picture for the rest of Cornwall. Please also bear in mind that you will get a further 30-45 minutes of usable light before sunrise and after sunset depending on the weather.

❑ FESTIVALS AND ANNUAL EVENTS

The events and festivities listed take place every year, though the dates may vary slightly. In addition to festivals you are likely to come across bands or groups of singers performing in pubs or in the open air in the main season. Be prepared to join in the Floral Dance if you are lucky enough to be in a village on the right evening.

March to May
● **St Piran's Day (5 March)** Festivities held throughout Cornwall (see box p144).
● **Giant Bolster Festival (May Day Bank Holiday)**, **St Agnes** Re-enactment of the legend of the Giant Bolster culminating in a torchlight procession of giant puppets to the cliff top where the wicked giant was tricked into killing himself whilst proving his love for Agnes.
● **'Obby 'Oss Day (May Day Bank Holiday)**, **Padstow** Festivities and procession as the hobby horse (see box p120) dances through the town.

June to August
● **Polperro Festival (mid June)** Nine days of events including comedy, live music and a fun-run (in case you're tempted)! (🖳 polperrofestivalsand lights.co.uk).
● **Golowan (mid to late June)**, **Penzance** Ten-day celebration of the midsummer Feast of St John and of west Cornwall's ancient Celtic traditions. Film, theatre, dance, traditional and contemporary music and a lively street procession (🖳 golowan.com).
● **Mevagissey Feast Week (late June)** Mevagissey adopted St Peter as its patron saint in 1752 and since then has always held a festival to celebrate the saint's day of 29 June. Considered the longest-running festival in Cornwall, it is a volunteer-run blend of traditional and modern events (🖳 mevagisseyfeastweek.org.uk).
● **Looe Festival by the Sea (mid July)** A celebration of the town's links with the sea, including music, food-tastings & boating (🖳 looefestivals.org).
● **Lafrowda Festival (mid July)**, **St Just** A week-long culture and music festival with all kinds of music (🖳 lafrowda-festival.co.uk). (cont'd overleaf)

❏ FESTIVALS AND ANNUAL EVENTS (cont'd from p15)

● **St Ives Biathlon (June/July)** An annual event that involves running along the coast path from St Ives to Carbis Bay then swimming back.

● **Padstow Carnival Week (end July)** Various events throughout the town and a carnival parade at the end of the week.

● **Barbican International Jazz and Blues festival, Plymouth (end July)** (🖳 barbicanjazzandbluesfestival.com) Four-day festival of music being played throughout the day in varying venues in The Barbican area.

● **Hayle Heritage Festival (late July to early August)** Events include a summer art show, horticultural show, Old Cornwall Society exhibition, traditional music and dancing, and Cornish wrestling.

● **Camel Sailing Week (early August)** Major regatta on the Camel Estuary.

● **Falmouth Classics and Regatta Week (first two weeks in August)** The highlight of Falmouth's sailing season catering for every class of boat including traditional classic yachts (🖳 falmouthweek.co.uk).

● **The British Firework Championships (mid August), The Hoe, Plymouth** Two-night competition between professional fireworks companies (🖳 britishfireworks.co.uk).

● **Bude Jazz Festival (last week of August), Bude** Eight days of jazz in 20 venues around the town (🖳 budejazzfestival.co.uk).

● **Newlyn Fish Festival (August bank holiday weekend)** The harbour is crammed with boats and the market filled with stalls, displays, cookery demonstrations and entertainment (🖳 newlynfishfestival.org.uk).

September to December

● **St Ives September Festival of Music and Art (mid September)** From classical music to jazz and folk, comedy, theatre and poetry (🖳 stivesseptemberfestival.co.uk).

● **Falmouth Oyster Festival and Fresh Seafood Week (mid to late October)** Celebrates one of the only remaining oyster fisheries still dredging under sail and oar. A must for lovers of the exquisite bivalve (🖳 falmouthoysterfestival.co.uk).

● **Lowender Peran Celtic Festival (mid to late October), Perranporth** Celtic dance and parade (🖳 lowenderperan.co.uk).

● **Tom Bawcock's Eve (23 December), Mousehole** In memory of a fisherman who put out to sea in a storm so that the starving population would not have a hungry Christmas. The event is celebrated with a carol concert, a torchlit procession and the consumption of an enormous stargazy pie (see box p23). Mousehole (see p196) is also illuminated with Christmas lights from mid December to early January.

● **C1 (Opposite) Top**: Godrevy Lighthouse, built in 1859, is one of many you'll see on your Cornish journey. **Bottom**: The cliffs stretch south from Porthtowan.

● **C2 Top**: Godrevy Beach, Point and Lighthouse. **Left, bottom**: The Rock–Padstow ferry. **Right, bottom**: Cape Cornwall (see p185), once thought to be Britain's most westerly point.

● **C3 Left**: Porthmeor Sands stretch north towards St Ives Head. **Right, top**: The internationally famous art gallery, Tate St Ives (see p164), overlooks Porthmeor Sands. **Middle, left**: Levant mine and engine house (see p181). **Middle, right**: The signpost at Land's End. **Right, bottom**: Fishing boats drawn up on the beach at Cadgwith Cove.

● **C4 Left, top**: On the path between Lizard Point and Cadgwith Cove, one of the finest stretches of the trail. **Left, bottom**: Idyllic Hemmick Bay. **Right** (clockwise from top left): **1.** The old signal station (see p229). **2.** A tall ship navigates Mevagissey Bay. **3.** Lizard Village is as quirky as the name suggests. **4.** The Mayflower Steps in Plymouth: where one epic journey began, yours ends. **5.** St Winwaloe Church (see p221).

PLANNING YOUR WALK

1

Practical information for the walker

ROUTE FINDING

For most of its length the coast path is well signposted. At confusing junctions the route is usually indicated by a finger-post sign with 'coast path' written on it. At other points, where there could be some confusion, there are wooden waymark posts with an acorn symbol and a yellow arrow to indicate in which direction you should head. The waymarking is the responsibility of the local authorities along the trail who have a duty to maintain the path. Generally they do a good job although occasionally you will come across sections of the trail where waymarking is ambiguous, or even non-existent, but with the detailed route maps and directions in this book and the fact that you always have the sea to one side it would be hard to get really lost.

Using GPS with this book

If you have a handheld **GPS receiver**, or GPS on your **smartphone**, you can take advantage of the waypoints marked on the maps and listed on pp330-5 of this book. Essentially a GPS (Global Positioning System) will calculate your position on the earth using a number of satellites and this will be accurate to a few metres. Some units may come with inbuilt mapping, but while it's possible to buy **digital mapping** (see p47) to import into a regular GPS unit or smartphone, it might be considered about as practical as having internet on a mobile phone – you still end up scrolling and zooming across a tiny screen.

Having said this, it is **by no means necessary** that you use a GPS in conjunction with this guide and you should be able to get by with simply the signposts on the trail and the maps in this book. However, a GPS can be useful if for some reason you do get lost, or if you decide to explore off the trail and can't find your way back. It can also prove handy if you find yourself on the trail after dark when you can't see further than your torch beam. If you do decide to use a GPS unit in conjunction with this book don't feel you need to be ticking off every waypoint as you reach it; you'll soon get bored; you should easily get by without turning on your GPS.

Opposite: Vault Beach (see p268), between Gorran Haven and Dodman Point.

You can either manually key the nearest presumed waypoint from the list in this book into your unit as and when the need arises or, much less laboriously and with less margin for keystroke error, download the complete list (but not the descriptions) for free as a GPS-readable file from the Trailblazer website. You'll need the right cable and adequate memory in your unit (typically the ability to store 500 waypoints or more). This file, as well as instructions on how to interpret an OS grid reference, can be found on the Trailblazer website (🖥 trailblazer-guides.com). See p47 for more on digital mapping.

ACCOMMODATION

There are plenty of places to stay all along the Cornwall Coast Path. It is always a good idea to book your accommodation in advance (see box p22), or at least phone ahead. National holidays and any major festivals and events (see pp15-16) are likely to fill up the available accommodation quite quickly so make sure you are aware of what is taking place in the region.

Camping

Camping can be good fun; modern tents are easy to erect and light, so carrying everything on your back need not be burdensome and will enable you to experience a greater sense of independence.

Most **campsites** are only open from Easter to October so camping in winter is not really practical. You will come across an enormous range of sites from a simple field on a farm with a toilet, shower and little else, to huge caravan and camping parks with restaurants, shops and swimming pools.

Prices range from £5 to about £15 per person and reach their peak in July and August when they can increase to as much as £20-25 per person. Note, prices are sometimes per pitch, which assumes two people sharing a tent, so in these cases single hikers can end up paying more than normal. It's advisable to book in advance where possible, although many campsites make special allowances for walkers and try to find space for them even if the campsite is officially full. Always call ahead in the morning to tell a campsite that you're planning to arrive that evening, and always tell them that you're a walker, hiking the coast path, and they'll normally find a space for you.

Officially, the coast path is not really suited to **wild camping**. If you want to camp wild you should ask permission from whoever owns the land, but finding out which farmhouse owns the field you want to camp in is no easy feat; you may find yourself trudging along miles of country lanes only to be told 'no'. Also, much of the coastline is owned by the National Trust who do not allow camping on their land. However, there will always be independent-minded souls who put up their tent as the spirit moves them. By pitching late in the day and leaving before anyone else is up, it is unlikely that you will be noticed.

Hostels

There is a reasonable scattering of hostels along the coast path providing budget accommodation for £15-25 per person per night (less for under 18s), usually in dormitories, although many now have private rooms available too. There are two types of hostels: **YHA hostels**, which are part of the Youth Hostel Association/Hostelling International (YHA/HI; see box below), and **independent hostels**, also referred to as backpacker hostels, which as the name suggests are independently owned. If you are planning to stay in hostels as often as possible you will have to make use of both types. Note, in almost all cases, **hostels require guests to show some form of photo ID when they check in**. A photocopy will suffice.

Hostels are not just for young travellers, the young at heart will be more than welcome at most places. In fact the YHA positively encourage the group referred to as the 'green greys', that is, conservation-minded older people who are an important market sector for them. If you find large groups of young people intimidating, you can always check if the hostel has any private rooms (this may be advisable in party towns such as Newquay, for example). Note, many hostels' dorms are mixed-sex, although some have single-sex dorms too.

One of the big advantages of staying in a hostel, aside from a cheap bed, is the option to cook your own food. Most hostels provide **well-equipped kitchens** and all they ask is that you clean up after yourself. There's also no need to carry a sleeping bag. All hostels recommended in this guide provide linen and may not even allow you to use your own sleeping bag. The YHA hostels are particularly clean and well equipped. Note that hostels very rarely provide towels (sometimes these can be bought at reception).

In some cases **camping** is available at YHA hostels for around £10-15 per tent per night, and campers can use the hostel's facilities.

Unfortunately, hostels aren't numerous enough or sufficiently well spaced to provide accommodation for every night of your walk so you will have to stay in B&Bs on several nights. The long stretch between Falmouth and Plymouth is particularly barren with only one hostel (at Boswinger, near Gorran Haven).

Most YHA hostels (but not independent hostels) are open only for group bookings between November and March; however, check the YHA website for up-to-date details.

❏ **Youth Hostel Association (YHA)**
You can join the YHA (☎ 0800-019 1700, ☎ 01629-592700, 💻 yha.org.uk) direct or at any hostel. However, you don't need to be a youth to stay in a YHA hostel. Nor do you need to be a member.

The annual membership fee is £20 (£15 if you pay by direct debit). If you are a member you get 10% off your entire booking (including food). Furthermore, a member can book for a group, and the whole group will get the discount as long as the member is part of that group (they check ID). Should at least one person be under-26 you will get a further 5% off the entire booking. As part of your membership you get a digital version of the YHA handbook.

If you are from a country other than Britain the equivalent organisation is Hostelling International; their website (💻 www.hihostels.com) has lists of each country's contact details. HI cards are accepted at all YHA hostels in Britain.

PLANNING YOUR WALK

Bed and breakfast (B&Bs) accommodation

B&Bs are a great British institution: for anyone unfamiliar with the concept you get a bedroom in someone's home along with a cooked breakfast the following morning; in many ways it is like being a guest of the family. However, the term B&B can apply equally to a night in someone's back bedroom in a suburban bungalow to one in a cliff-top farmhouse where every need is catered for, from a choice of herbal teas to free shampoos in the bathroom. It is an ideal way to walk in Cornwall as you can travel without too much clobber and relax in the evening in pleasant surroundings with the benefit of conversation with the proprietor. If you are struggling to find a room you could try **Airbnb** (🖳 airbnb.co.uk) but check carefully what you will be getting – standards can vary widely as these informal accommodation providers are unregulated.

Putting up at an **inn** (or pub) is a British tradition that goes back centuries and still appeals to many walkers. However, just because it's called an inn doesn't mean it will have old oak beams and a roaring log fire. Although there are some delightful traditional pubs, many places have been refurbished and have lost some of their character and charm. The biggest advantage of staying at an inn is convenience. Accommodation, meals and a bar are all provided under the same roof. If you've had a few too many pints of wonderful Cornish ale you don't have far to stagger home at closing time. On the other hand if you want an early night you may find the noise from the bar keeps you awake.

Guesthouses are often larger Victorian or Edwardian houses with rooms made en suite, filling the gap between B&Bs and hotels, although they may still be referred to as B&Bs. They are sometimes less personal and more expensive (£30-40 per person) but do offer more space and a lounge for guests. They are usually more geared to coping with holiday-makers and their owners are experienced in the hospitality trade, employing staff – if only young locals – to come in to do the bedrooms. They often take payment by credit and debit card and by cheque without quibble.

Most **hotels** along the coast are classier and more expensive than the above and therefore put many walkers off. The other problem for the walker is having suitably smart clothes to wear in the evening, unless of course, you have the panache to carry off designer fleece and walking boots in the restaurant. Once in a while you may feel you deserve a treat and at the end of a long day that Jacuzzi could be well worth paying extra for!

In general, hotels do not pay walkers any particular attention. They are simply one more guest who, if anything, requires rather more than the average guest when they arrive with pack, heavy boots and sometimes wet gear.

What to expect For the long-distance walker tourist-board recommendations and star-rating systems may be a starting point although by no means all the places on or near the Coast Path are registered. Many walkers rely on the tourist information centres to book their next night's lodging for them. There are numerous guides listing Best Places to Stay and it can be difficult to choose especially in places like St Ives and Penzance which are practically wall-to-wall with guesthouses. Bear in mind that walkers are only one of the many types of people on holiday and B&Bs are not there purely for our benefit. At the end of a long day you will simply be glad of a hot bath or shower and clean bed to lie down on. If they have somewhere to hang your wet and muddy clothes so much the better. It is these criteria that have been used for places included in this guide – televisions and tea- and coffee-making facilities are more or less standard these days.

Wi-fi is now generally the norm, although rural broadband speeds may be slow, and some older properties run by elderly hosts may not have it at all.

Bed and breakfast owners are often proud to boast that all rooms are **en suite** but this is sometimes merely a small shower and loo cubicle in the corner of the bedroom. Establishments without en suite rooms can be just as satisfactory as you may get sole use of a bathroom across the corridor and a hot bath is just what you need after a hard day on the trail, so accommodation descriptions indicate where a bath is available. Rooms without en suite facilities are generally cheaper.

Single rooms are sometimes rather cramped 'box' rooms with barely enough room for the bed which can be restricting if you are travelling with quite a big pack. **Twin** rooms have two single beds, while a **double** is supposed to have one double bed, although just to confuse things, twins are sometimes called doubles because the beds can be moved together to make a 'double' bed. This can lead to awkward moments so it is best to specify if you prefer two single beds. Some establishments have **family** rooms, which sleep three or more, although to confuse matters even further, others call these **triple** rooms and may also have a family room sleeping four people or more.

Some B&Bs provide an **evening meal**, particularly if there is no pub or restaurant nearby. Others may offer you a lift to a local eatery, while some will expect you make your own arrangements. Check what the procedure is when you book.

All accommodation listed should be open year-round (unless stated otherwise). Remember, however, that B&B owners can, and do, change their minds at a moment's notice, deciding to redecorate when it's quiet, or closing the business when they want to go away on holiday.

Smoking in enclosed public spaces is now banned so in effect every B&B is a non-smoking house. A tiny minority may set aside a room for smokers but few do.

Rates Proprietors quote their **tariffs** either on a **per person** (pp) basis or **per room**, assuming two people are sharing; rates are also sometimes given for single occupancy of a room where there are no single rooms. Accommodation **prices in this guide are quoted on a per person basis** and start at around £25pp for the most basic B&B-style accommodation rising to around £80pp for the most luxurious places. Most charge around £35-45pp. Guesthouses charge around £45-50pp and pubs around £30-40pp with breakfast included. Prices in hotels start at around the same but can rise to as much as £100pp or more; sometimes rates are for the room only and breakfast is additional. Solo walkers should take note: single rooms are not so easy to find so you will often end up

❏ **Booking accommodation in advance**

Booking ahead is a good idea for all types of accommodation as it guarantees you a bed for the night. If you are walking alone it also means someone is expecting you. During the high season (July and August) you may need to book a few weeks ahead, whereas in the winter a few days, or even the night before, should suffice. If you are walking in the low season check if the owner will provide an evening meal or that a local pub serves food. In high season, be aware that many B&Bs require a stay of at least two nights, or else charge a single-night supplement.

Many places have their own website and some offer online/email booking but for some places you will need to phone. Most places ask for a deposit (about 50%) if you book online, which is generally non-refundable if you cancel at short notice. Some places may ask for a 100% deposit if the booking is for one night only. Always let the owner know as soon as possible if you have to cancel your booking so they can offer the bed to someone else.

If the idea of booking all your accommodation fills you with dread, you may want to consider booking up with one of the self-guided walking holiday companies listed on pp28-30. They will happily do all the work for you, saving you a considerable amount of trouble and will also arrange for your baggage to be forwarded to the next night's accommodation.

occupying a double/twin room and are likely to have to pay a single occupancy supplement (£10-25).

Larger places take credit or debit cards. Most smaller B&Bs accept only cheques by post or payments by bank transfer for the deposit; the balance can be settled with cash or a cheque.

Self-catering holiday cottages

It is possible to walk a considerable part of the coast path from a fixed base using the excellent public transport to get to and from the trail each day; see box on p40 for more information and ideas.

Renting a self-catering cottage makes sense for a group of walkers as it will work out a lot cheaper and simpler than staying in B&Bs. Holiday cottages are normally let on a weekly basis but short breaks are often possible outside peak times. Cottages haven't been listed in this book, but they are numerous (more numerous than B&Bs these days it seems); search on the internet or contact the tourist information centre in the area where you want to stay for further details (see box on p46). Alternatively, contact the Landmark Trust (information ☎ 01628-825920, booking ☎ 01628-825925, 🖳 landmarktrust.org.uk) or the National Trust (☎ 0344-800 2070, 🖳 nationaltrustcottages.co.uk), both of which have several properties in Cornwall.

FOOD AND DRINK

Breakfast, lunch and evening meals

The traditional B&B **breakfast** is the celebrated 'full English' breakfast, or in Cornwall, the 'full Cornish': this consists of a choice of cereals and/or fruit juice followed by a plate of eggs, bacon, sausages, mushrooms, beans, fried bread and tomatoes, with toast and marmalade or jams to end and all washed down with tea or coffee. This is good for a day's walking, but after a week not so good for your cholesterol level. Sometimes B&B owners offer a continental breakfast option or will charge you less if all you want is a bowl of muesli or some toast. Alternatively, and also if you want an early start, it is worth asking if they would substitute the breakfast for a packed lunch. Most B&Bs will fill your flask with tea or coffee for the day, often without charge.

For **lunch** there are several options. The cheapest and easiest is to buy a picnic lunch or pasty at one of the many shops or bakeries you'll pass. Many B&Bs and hostels are happy to make a packed lunch for you for between £5 and £7. Otherwise you could eat out but you need to plan ahead to make sure the pub or restaurant or beach café is open and that you'll reach it in time for lunch. In

---

❑ **Traditional Cornish food**

● **The Cornish pasty** Visitors to Cornwall, whether walkers or not, cannot go home without having tried the ubiquitous pasty at least once. For some, once is enough whilst for others it becomes a lifetime's favourite. The pasty, for those who thought it was just a glorified meat pie, is shaped like a letter 'D', the pastry crimped on the curved side, with a filling of sliced beef with turnip (swede), potato and onion with a light peppery seasoning. The pastry is slow-cooked to a golden colour and is glazed with milk or egg.

Originally Cornish tin miners were sent off to work by their wives with their lunch in the form of a hot pasty containing a savoury filling at one end and fruit at the other – a complete meal that could be eaten without cutlery. Today they are mainly savoury. Pasties are eaten widely and available everywhere providing a meal on the run. Such is the iconic status of the pasty that the Cornish Pasty Makers Association was granted Protected Geographical Indication Status in February 2011, so that pasties are recognised as unique to Cornwall. Try one – you might get hooked.

● **Cornish cream tea** This is another walkers' favourite and you'll never be far from places offering this afternoon treat of scones, jam and clotted cream (thick, spreadable cream made by heating milk to evaporate the liquid) accompanied by a pot of tea; surely the cheapest decadent food available. Choose carefully and check that the scones are made on the premises or you may be disappointed. Prices start at around £5 and usually include two scones, a pot of tea, and plenty of jam and cream!

● **Fish** The fishing industry has been one of the biggest influences on the culinary traditions of Cornwall, and local favourites such as stargazy pie, sometimes referred to as 'starry gazey' pie, made with fish heads sticking out of the crust looking towards the sky, are on some menus. Fish pie is widely served, usually a good option washed down with a pint of the local ale. Even if you're on a tight budget the ubiquitous fish and chips can be satisfying if cooked with fresh fish. At the other end of the scale there are plenty of restaurants around the coast offering mouth-watering dishes concocted from locally caught fish. Species found in Cornwall's inshore waters include Dover sole, plaice, turbot, brill, gurnard, pollock, lemon sole, ray, cod, whiting, red mullet, John Dory, mackerel, sea bass and many more. There's also shellfish: lobsters, crabs, scallops, langoustines, clams and mussels, which are often fished for from the smaller coastal villages.

For further information about Cornish food and farmers' markets in Cornwall visit: 🖳 foodfromcornwall.co.uk.

recent times it has become quite the norm for walkers to travel light, taking only water and possibly a fruit bar or piece of fruit, confining their eating to the evening meal. Another option is to have a light lunch and then indulge in a **cream tea**.

During the summer you will also come across **seasonal snack shacks** by popular beaches and car parks serving light snacks such as filled sandwiches or baguettes, cakes, ice creams and soft drinks; the only trouble is not knowing exactly when they will be open. They tend to set up from around 10am-4pm, but sometimes they won't turn up if it's pouring with rain, so you can't rely on them being there every day, even in mid-summer.

For your **evening meal** the local pub is often the best place to head if your B&B does not provide a meal (most don't), or if you have not pre-booked one. Most pubs have a relatively standard 'pub-grub' menu featuring such regulars as fish and chips, steak and ale pie, and bangers (sausages) and mash, supplemented by one or two 'specials' such as fresh fish probably from a local source. Some pubs also have an attached à la carte restaurant with more elaborate meals. Most pub menus include at least two vegetarian options.

Most of the towns along the coast have Indian and Chinese takeaways/restaurants as well as fish and chip shops. If you want to splash out on fine-dining there are lots of nice restaurants along the coast path and local seafood is invariably on the menu. If they can't serve freshly caught fish in Cornwall they are just not trying.

Self-catering

The coast-path walker doesn't need to carry much food. Almost every village you pass through has a small shop or convenience store with plenty of food for snacks and picnic lunches and often cut sandwiches and pasties and a limited choice for cooking in the evening. Larger stores are well stocked with a range of groceries including lightweight campers' food such as instant mashed potato and pasta and sauce mixes and they'll usually have a selection of wine and beer too. **Fuel for camp stoves** requires a little more planning. Gas canisters are the easiest to come by with most general stores and campsite shops stocking them. Methylated spirit and Coleman fuel is sold in many outdoor shops and hardware stores and can occasionally be found in other shops too. Fuel canisters for stoves are now universally available.

Drinking water

We wouldn't recommend filling your water bottle or pouch from any stream or river on the coast path. Most streams run through farmland before reaching the coast. It may also have run off roads, housing or agricultural fields picking up heavy metals, pesticides and other chemical contaminants that we humans use liberally.

Tap water is safe to drink unless a sign specifies otherwise. Carry a two- or three-litre bottle or pouch and fill it up wherever you stay the night. During the day you could refill it in public toilets although not all meet reasonable standards of cleanliness and the taps are often awkward. As our use of endless plastic bottles becomes more of a problem and they continue to pollute the planet, many shops and cafés are now far more committed than they used to be to filling walkers' bottles up for them. A 3-litre 'platypus' style bag should be sufficient for all but the hottest days.

Real ales and cider

The process of brewing beer is believed to have been in Britain since the Neolithic period and is an art local brewers have been perfecting ever since. Real ale is beer that has been brewed using traditional methods. **Real ales** are not filtered or pasteurised, a process which removes and kills all the yeast cells, but instead undergo a secondary fermentation at the pub which enhances the natural flavours and brings out the individual characteristics of the beer. It's served at cellar temperature with no artificial fizz added unlike keg beer which is pasteurised and has the fizz added by injecting nitrogen dioxide.

There are plenty of pubs along the coast path serving an excellent range of real ales from around the country. The strength of beer is denoted by the initials ABV which means alcohol by volume followed by a percentage starting with the lowest at about 3.7%.

Distinctive Cornish beers worth watching out for include Betty Stoggs Bitter (4%), a strong hoppy beer, and Cornish Knocker Ale (4.5%) with its beautiful golden colour, both of which are brewed by **Skinner's** (🖥 skinners brewery.com) who have won a number of awards. **Sharp's** Brewery (🖥 sharps brewery.co.uk) also produces some fine ales, in particular Doom Bar Bitter (4%) named after the Doom Bar (see box on p116) near Padstow, and the citrusy Atlantic Pale Ale (4.2%). **St Austell** Brewery (🖥 staustellbrewery.co.uk) was first established in 1851 and several of their beers have won awards. The most popular brews are Tribute (4.2%) and Proper Job (4.5%), a powerful IPA. The most common of all these ales are St Austell's Tribute and Sharp's Doom Bar, both widely available.

Scrumpy (rough cider) is another Cornish favourite and well worth trying if you come across it on draught. You will immediately notice the difference from keg cider as it will be cloudy, with 'bits' floating in it and no fizz. You may also notice the difference afterwards; scrumpy is notorious for inducing wild nights out with subsequent periods of memory loss, sweating, dizziness, prolonged headaches, shaking, nausea and hot flushes. Another pint, anyone?

MONEY

A few campsites, hostels, B&Bs and small shops still require you to pay with cash, or by cheque from a British bank account, as they won't have credit/debit card facilities. You don't need to carry large amounts of money with you as all towns have banks with cash machines (ATMs) which are also found in convenience stores and supermarkets. Some ATMs charge (£1.50-1.95) for withdrawals though there are clear signs warning you of this before you actually withdraw the money. Alternatively, many supermarkets, some pubs, and a few smaller convenience stores will advance cash against a card (cashback).

Cashback is free of charge, although sometimes a minimum purchase of £5 or £10 is required.

Use the table of village and town facilities (see pp36-9) to plan how much money you'll need to withdraw at any one time. Travellers' cheques are rarely used now and can be cashed only at some banks and foreign exchange bureaus.

Using the Post Office for banking

Some UK banks have an agreement with the Post Office allowing customers to withdraw cash from branches using their debit card and pin number, or cheque-book and debit card. As many towns and villages have post offices, this is an extremely useful facility. Note, however, that many post offices along the

---

❏ Information for foreign visitors

● **Currency** The British pound (£) comes in notes of £50, £20, £10 and £5, and coins of £2 and £1. The pound is divided into 100 pence (usually referred to as 'p', pronounced 'pee') which comes in silver coins of 50p, 20p, 10p and 5p, and copper coins of 2p and 1p.

● **Money** Up-to-date **rates of exchange** can be found on ⌨ xe.com/ucc, at some post offices, or at any bank or travel agent.

● **Business hours** Most shops and main post offices are open at least from Monday to Friday 9am-5pm and Saturday 9am-12.30pm but many shops open earlier and close later, some open on Sunday as well. Occasionally, especially in rural areas, you'll come across a local shop that closes at midday during the week, usually a Wednesday or Thursday, a throwback to the days when all towns and villages had an 'early closing day'. Many supermarkets remain open 12 hours a day; the Spar chain usually displays '8 till late' on the door. Banks typically open at 9.30am Monday to Friday and close at 3.30pm or 4pm, but of course ATM machines are open all the time (if they are outside). Pub hours are less predictable; although many open daily 11am-11pm, often in rural areas, and particularly in winter months, opening hours are 11am-3pm and 6-11pm Mon-Sat, 11am/noon-3pm and 7-11pm on Sunday.

Last entry to most **museums** is usually an hour before the official closing time.

● **National holidays** Most businesses in the South-West are shut on 1 January, Good Friday (March/April), Easter Monday (March/April), first and last Monday in May, last Monday in August, 25 and 26 December.

● **School holidays** State-school holidays in England are generally as follows: a one-week break late October, two weeks over Christmas and the New Year, a week mid February, two weeks around Easter, one week at the end of May/early June (incorporating the last Monday in May) and five to six weeks from late July to early September. Private-school holidays fall at the same time, but are slightly longer.

● **Documents** If you are a member of a National Trust organisation in your country bring your membership card as you should be entitled to free entry to National Trust properties and sites in the UK. If you're staying in hostels, you will need to show some form of photo ID when you check in, although a photocopy will suffice.

● **EHICs and travel insurance** Although Britain's National Health Service (NHS) is free at the point of use, that is only the case for residents. All visitors to Britain should be properly insured, including comprehensive health coverage. The European Health Insurance Card (EHIC) entitles EU nationals (on production of the EHIC card so ensure you bring it with you) to necessary medical treatment under the NHS while on a temporary visit here. For details, contact your national social security institution,

Cornish coast are either under threat of closure or amalgamation into the one of the local shops, so if you're planning on using this facility it would be prudent to call ahead to ensure availability.

OTHER SERVICES

Almost all villages have a **general store**, a **post office** and **public telephone**.

Where they exist, special mention has also been made in Part 4 of other services that may be of use to walkers such as **banks**, **cash machines (ATMs)**, **launderettes**, **outdoor equipment shops**, **internet access**, **pharmacies**, **medical centres** and **tourist information centres**.

and note that things may change after Brexit. However, this is not a substitute for proper medical cover on your travel insurance for unforeseen bills and for getting you home should that be necessary. Also consider cover for loss and theft of personal belongings, especially if you are camping or staying in hostels, as there will be times when you'll have to leave your luggage unattended.

● **Weights and measures** In Britain, milk can still be sold in pints (1 pint = 568ml), as can beer in pubs, though most other liquid including petrol (gasoline) and diesel is sold in litres. Distances on road and path signs will continue to be given in miles (1 mile = 1.61km) rather than kilometres, and yards (1yd = 0.9m) rather than metres. The population remains divided between those who still use inches (1 inch = 2.5cm), feet (1ft = 0.3m) and yards and those who are happy with millimetres, centimetres and metres; you'll often be told that 'it's only a hundred yards or so' to somewhere, rather than a hundred metres or so.

Most food is sold in metric weights (g and kg) but the imperial weights of pounds (lb: 1lb = 453g) and ounces (oz: 1oz = 28g) are frequently displayed too. The weather – a frequent topic of conversation – is also an issue: while most forecasts predict temperatures in Celsius (C), many people continue to think in terms of Fahrenheit (F; see the temperature chart on p15 for conversions).

● **Smoking** The ban on smoking in public places relates not only to pubs and restaurants, but also to B&Bs, hostels and hotels. These latter have the right to designate one or more bedrooms where the occupants can smoke, but the ban is in force in all enclosed areas open to the public – even if they are in a private home such as a B&B. Should you be foolhardy enough to light up in a no-smoking area, which includes pretty much any indoor public place, you could be fined £50, but it's the owners of the premises who carry the can if they fail to stop you, with a potential fine of £2500.

● **Time** During the winter, the whole of Britain is on Greenwich Mean Time (GMT). The clocks move one hour forward on the last Sunday in March, remaining on British Summer Time (BST) until the last Sunday in October.

● **Telephone** From outside Britain the international country access code for Britain is ☎ 44 followed by the area code minus the first 0, and then the number you require. Within Britain, to call a landline number with the same code as the landline phone you are calling from, the code can be omitted: dial the number only. If you're using a mobile phone that is registered overseas, consider buying a local SIM card to keep costs down.

● **Emergency services** For police, ambulance, fire or coastguard dial either ☎ 999 or ☎ 112.

PLANNING YOUR WALK

Phones and wi-fi

The **mobile phone** reception along much of the coast path has improved in recent years; although it's still not unusual to walk for half a day without a signal, and in some small coastal villages you will have to climb up a nearby hill in order to make a phone call. Consequently **public telephone boxes** are marked on the maps wherever one is available. The minimum cost for making a call from a public telephone box is 60p.

Wi-fi is everywhere these days – in most pubs, cafés, restaurants, B&Bs, hotels, and even on some campsites – and it's almost always provided free of charge to customers. Having said that, those of you carrying smartphones may find you're able to get online more often through your mobile phone network in some areas.

WALKING COMPANIES

For walkers wanting to make their holiday as easy and trouble free as possible there are several specialist companies offering a range of services from accommodation booking to fully guided group tours.

Baggage carriers

The thought of carrying a large pack puts many people off walking long-distance trails. The main baggage company on the SWCP is the aptly named **Luggage Transfers** (☎ 01326-567247, 🖳 luggagetransfers.co.uk; Helston), who cover the whole of the path, charging from £9.50 per bag for a two-bag transfer. **WD Transfers** (☎ 01736-332894, 🖳 cornwallluggagetransfer.co.uk; Penzance) who operate along the stretch of coast between Padstow and Falmouth also offer a baggage-transfer service. Prices start at £14 per transfer, based on transferring two bags of no more than 20kg per bag, that's £7 per bag.

Alternatively, some of the **taxi firms** listed in this guide can provide a similar service within a local area if you want a break from carrying your bags for a day or so. LtTaxis (🖳 lttaxis.co.uk) provide pre-booked taxi services across the entire South-West Coast Path. See their website for quotes. Also, don't rule out the possibility of your **B&B/guesthouse owner** taking your bags ahead for you; plenty of them are glad to do so since it supplements their income and adds to the service they offer. Depending on the distance they may make no charge at all, or charge £10-15; this may be less than a taxi would charge.

Self-guided holidays

The following companies provide customised packages for walkers which usually include detailed advice and notes on itineraries and routes, maps, accommodation booking, daily baggage transfer and transport arrangements at the start and end of your walk. If you don't want the whole all-in package some of the companies may be able to arrange just accommodation booking or baggage carrying.

● **Celtic Trails** (☎ 01291-689774, 🖳 celtictrailswalkingholidays.co.uk; Chepstow) Organise walking holidays along particular sections of the footpath; length-of-time options are from four days to a week or more. They also offer tailor-made tours.

● **Compass Holidays** (☎ 01242-250642, 🖳 compass-holidays.com; Cheltenham) Organise walks of between three and eight days around the Lizard Peninsula (Helston to Mullion) and the entire Cornwall Coast Path.

● **Contours Walking Holidays** (☎ 01629-821900, 🖳 contours.co.uk; Derbyshire) Holidays include Westward Ho! to Padstow, Padstow to St Ives, St Ives to Penzance, Penzance to Falmouth and Falmouth to Plymouth in various combinations of three to ten days' walking plus tailor-made tours. Some dog-friendly itineraries.

● **Encounter Walking Holidays** (☎ 01208-871066, 🖳 encounterwalkingholi days.com; Fowey, Cornwall) Organise everything for the walker operating on every section of the path. Short breaks and week-long holidays through to two-month treks. Will help everyone from individual walkers to large groups and specialise in assisting overseas walkers along the route.

● **Explore Britain** (☎ 01740-650900, 🖳 explorebritain.com; Co Durham) Operate a variety of holidays including one based at Land's End, five to six days St Ives to Land's End, three days Bude to Tintagel, fourteen days Padstow to Frenchman's Creek, six days Newquay to Land's End.

● **Footpath Holidays** (☎ 01985-840049, 🖳 footpath-holidays.com; Wilts) Operate a range of walking holidays including inn-to-inn holidays for the whole path and single-centre holidays from Boscastle, Penzance and the Lizard. They also offer short breaks or one-week holidays plus tailor-made tours. Baggage transfer is included as part of inn-to-inn holidays.

● **Let's Go Walking** (☎ 01837-880075 or ☎ 020-7193 1252, 🖳 letsgowalking .com; Devon) Offer holidays covering the entire coast path with the length of stay to suit the distance walked.

● **Macs Adventure** (☎ 0141-530 8886, 🖳 macsadventure.com; Glasgow) Have walks covering the whole SWCP including Minehead to Westward Ho!, Westward Ho! to Padstow and Padstow to Poole.

● **Nearwater Walking Holidays** (☎ 01326-279278, 🖳 nearwaterwalkinghol idays.co.uk; Truro) Offer walks covering the whole path as well as sections from 5 days upwards.

● **Responsible Travel** (☎ 01273-823700; 🖳 responsibletravel.com; Brighton) Offer fully supported itineraries for 7 nights/8 days walking along sections of the path and can tailor-make according to requirements.

● **Sherpa Expeditions** (☎ 020-8875 5070, or freephone ☎ 0800-008 7741, 🖳 sherpaexpeditions.com; London) Offer eight-day holidays from Marazion to Mevagissey including the Lizard & Roseland peninsulas, Padstow to St Ives and St Ives to Penzance.

● **The Discerning Traveller** (☎ 01865-511330, 🖳 discerningtraveller.co.uk; Oxford) Offer three different week-long holidays along the path: 'Land's End and St Ives', 'Polperro to Mevagissey', and 'Tintagel Coast' which can be extended to include Bodmin Moor if desired.

● **The Walking Holiday Company** (☎ 01600-713008, 🖳 thewalkingholiday company.co.uk; Monmouth) Offer walks for the whole of the SWCP. Can create itineraries to suit whatever clients want.

- **Walk the Trail** (☎ 01326-567252, 🖥 walkthe trail.co.uk; Helston) Offers walking holidays of any itinerary from short breaks to the entire SWCP and anything in between.
- **Way2go4 Walking Holidays** (☎ 01288-331416, 🖥 way2go4.com; Cornwall/N Devon border) Offer walks at multiple locations on the coast path.
- **Westcountry Walking Holidays** (☎ 0330-350 1348, 🖥 westcountry-walk ing-holidays.com) Offer custom-made trips for any number of days to suit anywhere along the coast path.

Group/guided walking tours

Fully guided tours are ideal for individuals wanting to travel in the company of others and for groups of friends wanting to be guided. The packages usually include meals, accommodation, transport arrangements, minibus back-up, baggage transfer, as well as a qualified guide and are often for sections of the trail such as Padstow to St Ives, a popular route for a week's walking. The companies differ in terms of the size of the groups they take, the standards of accommodation, the age range of clients, the distances walked and the professionalism of the guides, so it's worth checking them all before making a booking.

- **Adventureline** (☎ 01209-820847, 🖥 adventureline.co.uk; Cornwall) Has a base in St Agnes and offers a variety of walks along different stretches of the coast path in most areas of Cornwall; seven nights.
- **Footpath Holidays** (see p29) Fully guided tours (short breaks or one week) are offered from their base in Boscastle.
- **HF Holidays** (☎ 020-8732 1250, 🖥 hfholidays.co.uk; Herts) Two itineraries (seven nights) based in St Ives: north and south Cornwall coast path.
- **Ramblers Walking Holidays** (☎ 01707-331133, 🖥 ramblersholidays.co.uk; Herts) Offer one week tours based in St Ives.
- **Walkitcornwall** (☎ 0771-408 4644, 🖥 walkitcornwall.co.uk; Cornwall) Offer guided walking holidays mainly along the Cornwall coast path.
- **Way2go4 Walking Holidays** (see above) Tours designed to be flexible, along the path on Cornwall/N Devon border, group size typically 6-12 people, short breaks & week holidays.

Budgeting

By **camping** and cooking your own meals you can get by on about £20-25pp per day outside the holiday season but a little more during it. If you envisage having the odd meal out and like to finish the day with a glass or two of wine or a pint at the pub £30-40 would be more realistic. Remember that the time of year you're walking will have a significant impact on your budget; during the height of the season campground charges can sometimes escalate dramatically.

As noted on p19, it isn't possible to stay in **hostels** every night. However, for the nights you do stay in one expect to pay £17-25pp. If you cook your own meals in the hostels, you will need about £30-35pp per day. If you eat the meals provided in some YHA hostels expect to pay around £6.50 for breakfast, about the same for a packed lunch, and approximately £10 for an evening meal.

On the nights when you have to stay in a **B&B** there won't be the facilities to cook for yourself, so you will have to eat out. For these days budget in the vicinity of £60-70pp if you can make do with a simple packed lunch and fish and chips for dinner, or £80-plus if you intend eating lunches and dinners at cafés, pubs and restaurants. (See also pp21-2).

Don't forget to set some money aside for the **inevitable extras**: postcards, stamps, washing and drying clothes, entrance fees for various attractions, cream teas, beer, buses and taxis, any changes of plan.

Itineraries

All walkers are individuals. Some like to cover large distances as quickly as possible, others are happy to stroll along, stopping whenever the fancy takes them. You may want to walk the coast path all in one go, tackle it over a series of weekends or use the trail for linear day walks; the choice is yours.

To accommodate these differences this book has not been divided into rigid daily stages which can lead to a fixed mindset of how you should walk. Instead, it's been designed to make it easy for you to plan your own perfect itinerary.

The **planning map** (opposite the inside back cover) and **table of village and town facilities** (pp36-9) summarise the essential information and make it straightforward to devise a plan of your own. Alternatively, to make it even easier, have a look at the **suggested itineraries** (pp32-4) and simply choose your preferred type of accommodation and speed of walking. There are also suggestions for those who want to experience the best of the trail over a day (see p35) or a weekend (see p40), or who want to plan a series of day walks from a fixed base (see box p40).

The **public transport maps** on pp52-3 and **service table** (pp54-5) may also be useful at this stage. Having made a rough plan, turn to Part 4 where you will find: summaries of the route, full descriptions of accommodation, places to eat and other services in each village and town; as well as detailed trail maps.

WHICH DIRECTION?

Although the route in this book has been described from Bude to Plymouth, it doesn't make much difference whether you walk the coast path in a clockwise or anti-clockwise direction. There is virtually the same amount of ascent and descent either way and the prevailing south-westerly wind will be in your face for one half of the walk and behind you for the other whichever way you go.

If you're walking solely on the north coast, or solely on the south, it may be worth walking west to east so that the wind is predominantly behind you.

SUGGESTED ITINERARIES

The itineraries that follow are suggestions only; feel free to adapt them to your needs. They have been divided into different accommodation types and each table has different itineraries to encompass different walking paces. **Don't forget to add your travelling time before and after the walk.**

Note that most campsites are open from Easter to October only; also there are not enough hostels along the coast path to allow you to stay in one every night and not all are open throughout the year.

STAYING IN HOSTELS (YHA AND INDEPENDENT)

		Medium pace				Fast pace		
Night	Place	Hostel	Approx Distance miles km		Place	Hostel	Approx Distance miles km	
0	Bude	H			Bude	H		
1	Crack'ton Haven		10	16	Crack'ton Haven		10	16
2	Boscastle§	YHA	7	11.5	Boscastle§	YHA	7	11.5
3	Port Isaac		14	22.5	Port Isaac		14	22.5
4	Padstow		12	19.5	Padstow		12	19.5
5	Treyarnon	YHA	10	16	Treyarnon	YHA	10	16
6	Newquay	H	13	21	Newquay	H	13	21
7	Perranporth	YHA	10	16	Perranporth	YHA	10	16
			(14	22.5*)			(14	22.5*)
8	Portreath	YHA	11	18	Portreath	YHA	11	18
9	Hayle		12	19.5	St Ives	H	17	27
10	St Ives	H	5	8	Zennor	H	6	9.5
11	Zennor	H	6	9.5	Sennen Cove		16	26
12	St Just	YHA	12	19.5	Penzance	YHA & H	17	27
13	Land's End	H	4	6.5	Porthleven		13	21
14	Porthcurno		6	9.5	Lizard	YHA	12	19.5
15	Penzance	YHA & H	11	18	Coverack	YHA	11	18
16	Porthleven		13	21	Falmouth	H	20	32**
17	Lizard	YHA	12	19.5	Boswinger	YHA	20	32
18	Coverack	YHA	11	18				
19	Mawnan Smith		11	18**	*No hostels between Boswinger and*			
20	Falmouth	H	9	14.5	*Plymouth. For continuation of these*			
21	Portloe		13	22	*routes see tables opposite and on p34.*			
22	Boswinger	YHA	7	10				

YHA = YHA hostel; H = independent hostel
Note: where there is no hostel, such as between Boswinger and Plymouth, it will be necessary to camp or stay in a B&B

§ YHA Tintagel is also a possibility but staying there would make the following day (Tintagel to Port Isaac) pretty short
* Depends on route across The Gannel (see pp137-8)
** Using ferry from Helford to Helford Passage (see p241)

CAMPING (EASTER TO OCTOBER ONLY)

Night	Relaxed pace Place	Approx Distance miles	km	Medium pace Place	Approx Distance miles	km	Fast pace Place	Approx Distance miles	km
0	Bude			Bude			Bude		
1	Widem'th Bay	3	5	Widem'th Bay	3	5	Widem'th Bay	3	5
2	Bossiney	18	29	Bossiney	18	29	Bossiney	18	29
3	Polzeath	19	30.5	Polzeath	19	30.5	Polzeath	19	30.5
4	Padstow	3	5	Padstow	3	5	Padstow	3	5
5	Mother Ivey's	8	13	Treyarnon	10	16	Treyarnon	10	16
6	Mawgan P'th	9	14.5	Mawgan P'th	7	11.5	Newquay	13	21
7	Newquay	6	9.5 (9.5	15*)	Crantock	8 (12	13- 19.5*)	St Agnes	13½ (17½	22- 28*)
8	Holywell	5½	9	St Agnes	11½	18.5	Gwithian	15½	25
9	St Agnes	8	13	Gwithian	15½	25	St Ives	9	14.5
10	Porthtowan	4½	7	St Ives	9	14.5	Pendeen	13	21
11	Gwithian	11	18	Zennor	6	9.5	Treen	15½	25
12	St Ives	9	14.5	Botallack	9	14.5	Marazion	13½	22
13	Zennor	6	9.5	Treen	13½	22	Praa Sands	6	9.5
14	Pendeen	7	11.5	Penzance	10½	17	Lizard	16	26
15	Sennen Cove	9	14.5	Praa Sands	9	14	Coverack	11	18
16	Treen	6½	10.5	Tenerife Farm (nr Mullion)	11	18	Gear Farm (nr Helford)	13	21
17	Penzance	10½	17	Kennack Sands (nr Cadgwith)	11	18	Falmouth	13	21**
18	Praa Sands	9	14.5	Coverack	5	8	Portscatho	6¼	10
19	Tenerife Farm (nr Mullion)	11	18	Gear Farm (nr Helford)	13	21	Gorran Haven	16½	26.5
20	Lizard	5	8	Falmouth	13	21**	Polruan	21	34
21	Coverack	11	18	Portscatho	6¼	10	Looe	12	19.5
22	Gear Farm (nr Helford)	13	21	Gorran Haven	16½	26.5	Cawsand	17½	28
23	Falmouth	13	21**	Charlestown	10¾	17.5	Plymouth (Barbican)	6	9.5
24	Portscatho	6¼	10	Polruan	10¼	16.5			
25	Gorran Haven	16½	26.5	Looe	12	19.5			
26	Charlestown	10¾	17.5	Cawsand	17½	28			
27	Polruan	10¼	16.5	Plymouth (Barbican)	6	9.5			
28	Polperro	7	11.5						
29	Looe	6	10						
30	Cawsand	17½	28						
31	Plymouth (Barbican)	6	9.5						

* Depends on route across The Gannel (see pp137-8)
** Using ferry from Helford to Helford Passage (see p241)

PLANNING YOUR WALK

PLANNING YOUR WALK

STAYING IN B&Bs

Night	Relaxed pace Place	Approx Distance miles	km	Medium pace Place	Approx Distance miles	km	Fast pace Place	Approx Distance miles	km
0	Bude			Bude			Bude		
1	C'ton Haven	10	16	C'ton Haven	10	16	Boscastle	17	27
2	Boscastle	7	11.5	Boscastle	7	11.5	Port Isaac	14	22.5
3	Tintagel	5	8	Port Isaac	14	22.5	Padstow	12	19.5
4	Port Isaac	14	22.5	Padstow	12	19.5	Porthcothan	12½	20
5	Padstow	12	19.5	C'stantine Bay	9½	15	Crantock	12½	20 (16½ 26.5*)
6	Mother Ivey's	8	13	Newquay	13½	22	St Agnes	11½	18.5
7	Mawgan Porth	9	14.5	Perranporth	10	16- (14 22.5*)	Gwithian	15½	25
8	Crantock	8 (12 19.5*)	13	Porthtowan	8	13	St Ives	9	14.5
9	Perranporth	8	13	Gwithian	11	18	Pendeen	13	21
10	Porthtowan	8	13	St Ives	9	14.5	Porthcurno	15	24
11	Portreath	3	5	Zennor	6	9.5	Marazion	14	22.5
12	Gwithian	8	13	St Just	11	18	Mullion	16	26
13	St Ives	9	14.5	Porthcurno	11	18	Coverack	17	27
14	Zennor	6	9.5	Penzance	11	18	Falmouth	20	32**
15	Pendeen	7	11.5	Porthleven	13	21	E Portholland	16½	26.5
16	Sennen Cove	9	14.5	Lizard	12	19.5	Charlestown	17	27
17	Porthcurno	6	9.5	Coverack	11	18	Polperro	17¼	27.5
18	Mousehole	7	11.5	Mawnan Smith	11	18**	Seaton	8¾	14.25
19	Marazion	7	11.5	Falmouth	9	14.5	Plymouth (Barbican)	19¾	31.5
20	Porthleven	10	16	Portloe	13¾	22.25			
21	Mullion	6	9.5	Mevagissey	12½	20			
22	Lizard	6	9.5	Charlestown	7¼	11.75			
23	Coverack	11	18	Fowey	10¼	16.5			
24	Helford	10	16	Looe	12	19.5			
25	Falmouth	10	16**	Cawsand	17½	28			
26	Portscatho	6¼	10	Plymouth (Barbican)	6	9.5			
27	Portloe	7½	12						
28	Mevagissey	12½	20						
29	Charlestown	7¼	11.75						
30	Fowey	10¼	16.5						
31	Polperro	7	11.5						
32	Looe	5	8						
33	Seaton	3¾	6.5						
34	Cawsand	13¾	21.5						
35	Plymouth (Barbican)	6	9.5						

* Depends which route across The Gannel (see pp137-8)
** Using ferry from Helford to Helford Passage (see p241)

THE BEST DAY AND WEEKEND WALKS

There's nothing quite like walking along a long-distance footpath for several days or even weeks but some people just don't have the time. The following highlights offer outstanding walking and scenery coupled with good public transport (see pp52-6) at the start and finish.

Day walks

● **Crackington Haven to Boscastle**　　　　**7 miles/11.5km (see pp86-90)**
A tough, but exhilarating day's walk along the top of beautiful green cliffs; some of the highest in Cornwall. Begin at the tiny hamlet of Crackington Haven and finish in the enchanting village of Boscastle with its pretty pubs, stone houses and witch museum!

● **Tintagel to Port Isaac**　　　　**9 miles/14.5km (see pp102-9)**
Another tough section, but despite the unforgiving ups and downs it is also one of the most enjoyable. Beginning at historic Tintagel with its castle and Arthurian legend, the path continues past historic mine workings and past the beautiful beaches of Trebarwith Strand and Tregardock before a roller-coaster cliff-top path leads eventually to the pretty white-washed buildings of Port Isaac.

● **Crantock to Perranporth**　　　　**8 miles/13km (see pp140-7)**
An excellent day's walk starting from the picturesque village of Crantock and finishing along the expansive sands of Perran Beach. Take a picnic to have at secluded Porth Joke, or stop for lunch in Holywell at the thatched Treguth Inn.

● **St Ives to Zennor**　　　　**6 miles/9.5km (see pp170-4)**
This walk offers a combination of wild Atlantic coastline, exquisite light and a feeling of remoteness that can't be matched by many other places on the coast path. It's also one of the trickiest parts of the whole trail with many rocky, uneven, boggy sections and some relentless ascents and descents. However, there is a good bus service so you can walk one way and take the bus back.

● **Porthcurno to Mousehole**　　　　**7 miles/11.5km (see pp192-8)**
A charming walk with lots of coves and headlands to explore.

● **Mullion Cove to the Lizard**　　　　**7 miles/11.5km (see p224-9)**
A cliff-top walk from a classic Cornish fishing village to the southernmost point in mainland Britain, taking in long stretches of windswept heath and beautiful Kynance Cove. This route can be very exposed in bad weather.

● **Mevagissey to Fowey**　　　　**18¼ miles/29.5km (see p273-85)**
You would need to leave early if contemplating this long but fulfilling day's walk. Featuring plenty of cliff-top walking, the beaches at Par, Pentewan & Polkerris, and the wonderful harbour village of Charlestown, such a hike would constitute a thorough introduction to what walking in Cornwall is all about.

● **Fowey/Polruan to Looe**　　　　**12¼ miles/19.75km (see pp286-99)**
Either starting in Polruan or with a short ferry journey across the River Fowey, this predominantly cliff-top route allows for a lunch-stop in Polperro – a small harbour village, full of character – before ending up in one of Cornwall's most bustling towns: Looe.　　　　*(cont'd on p40)*

PLANNING YOUR WALK

VILLAGE AND

Place name (Places in brackets are a short walk off the coast path)	Distance from previous place approx miles	km	Cash Machine (ATM)	Post Office	Tourist Information Centre/Point (TIC/TIP)/Visitor Centre (VC)
Bude & Upton			✔	✔	TIC
Widemouth Bay	3	5			
Crackington Haven	7	11.5			
Boscastle	7	11.5	✔	✔	VC
Bossiney	4	6.5			
Tintagel	1	1.5	✔	✔mobile	VC
Trebarwith Strand	2	3	✔		
Port Gaverne	6	9.5			
Port Isaac	1	1.5	✔		
Polzeath	9	14.5	✔		
Padstow	3	5	✔	✔	TIC
Trevone	5	8			
Harlyn Bay	1½	2.5			
Mother Ivey's Bay	1½	2.5			
Constantine Bay	2	3			
Treyarnon	½	1			
Porthcothan	2	3			
Mawgan Porth	4½	7	✔		
Watergate Bay	2	3			
Porth	2	3			
Newquay	4	6.5	✔	✔	TIC
Crantock	2	3 (or 6/9.5 on main road)			✔
Holywell	3½	5.5			
Perranporth	4½	7	✔	✔	TIC
(St Agnes)	3½	5.5 to Trevaunance Cove ✔		✔	
Porthtowan	4½	7		✔	
Portreath	3	5	✔	✔	
Gwithian	8	13			
Hayle	4	6.5	✔	✔	TIC
St Ives	6	9.5	✔	✔	TIC
(Zennor)	6	9.5 to Zennor Head			
(Gurnard's Head/Treen)	1	1.5 to Lean Point			
(Pendeen/Trewellard)	6	9.5 to Pendeen Watch		✔	
(Botallack)	2	3 to Zawn a Bal			
(St Just)	2	3 to Cape Cornwall ✔			TIP
Sennen Cove/Mayon	5	8	✔	✔	
Land's End	1	1.5	✔		VC
Porthcurno	5	8			
Treen	½	1			
Lamorna	4½	7			
Mousehole	2	3	✔	✔	
Newlyn	2½	4	✔		
Penzance	1½	2.5	✔	✔	TIC

(cont'd overleaf)

TOWN FACILITIES

Eating Place ✔= one ✔✔= a few ✔✔✔= three + (✔✔) = seasonal	Food Store	Campsite	Hostels YHA or H (Ind Hostel) (YHA)=seasonal	B&B-style accommodation ✔= one ✔✔= two ✔✔✔= three +	Place name (Places in brackets are a short walk off the coast path)
✔✔✔	✔✔	✔✔	H	✔✔✔	**Bude & Upton**
✔✔✔	✔	✔✔		✔✔	**Widemouth Bay**
✔(✔✔)		✔		✔✔	**Crackington Haven**
✔✔✔	✔	✔	(YHA)	✔✔✔	**Boscastle**
✔		✔		✔✔	**Bossiney**
✔✔✔	✔✔	✔	(YHA)	✔✔✔	**Tintagel**
✔✔	✔			✔	**Trebarwith Strand**
✔✔		✔		✔	**Port Gaverne**
✔✔✔	✔			✔✔✔	**Port Isaac**
✔✔✔	✔	✔✔		✔	**Polzeath**
✔✔✔	✔✔	✔		✔✔✔	**Padstow**
✔✔	✔			✔✔	**Trevone**
✔				✔	**Harlyn Bay**
		✔✔			**Mother Ivey's Bay**
(✔)	✔				**Constantine Bay**
✔		✔	YHA	✔	**Treyarnon**
	✔				**Porthcothan**
✔✔✔	✔	✔✔		✔✔✔	**Mawgan Porth**
✔✔✔		✔			**Watergate Bay**
✔✔✔		✔		✔✔✔	**Porth**
✔✔✔	✔✔✔	✔	H	✔✔✔	**Newquay**
✔✔✔	✔	✔		✔✔	**Crantock**
✔✔	(✔)	✔			**Holywell**
✔✔✔	✔✔✔	✔	(YHA)	✔✔✔	**Perranporth**
✔✔✔	✔✔	✔		✔✔✔	**(St Agnes)**
✔(✔)	✔	✔		✔	**Porthtowan**
✔✔✔	✔		YHA	✔✔	**Portreath**
✔✔✔		✔		✔	**Gwithian**
✔✔✔	✔✔✔	✔		✔✔✔	**Hayle**
✔✔✔	✔✔✔	✔	H	✔✔✔	**St Ives**
✔✔		✔		✔✔✔	**(Zennor)**
✔				✔✔	**(Gurnard's Head/Treen)**
✔✔✔	✔	✔		✔✔✔	**(Pendeen/Trewellard)**
✔		✔		✔	**(Botallack)**
✔✔✔	✔✔	✔ (Kelynack)	(YHA)	✔✔✔	**(St Just)**
✔✔✔	✔✔	✔	H	✔✔✔	**Sennen Cove/Mayon**
✔		✔	H	✔✔	**Land's End**
✔(✔)				✔✔✔	**Porthcurno**
✔✔		✔		✔	**Treen**
✔✔				✔✔	**Lamorna**
✔✔✔	✔snacks only	✔		✔✔✔	**Mousehole**
✔✔✔	✔			✔✔	**Newlyn**
✔✔✔	✔✔✔	✔	YHA/H	✔✔✔	**Penzance**

(cont'd overleaf)

PLANNING YOUR WALK

PLANNING YOUR WALK

VILLAGE AND

(cont'd from p36)

Place name (Places in brackets are a short walk off the coast path)	Distance from previous place approx miles	km	Cash Machine (ATM)	Post Office	Tourist Information Centre/Point (TIC/TIP)/Visitor Centre (VC)
Marazion	3	5	✔	✔	
Praa Sands	6¼	10		✔	
Porthleven	4½	7	✔	✔	
(Mullion Cove/Mullion)	6	9.5 to Mullion Cove	✔	✔	
(Lizard)	6	9.5 to Lizard Point	✔	✔	
Cadgwith	4	6.5			
Coverack	7	11.5			
Porthallow	5	8			
Helford	7¼	11.75			
Gweek	5	8		✔	
Helford Passage	5½	9 via Gweek; 0/0 by ferry			
(Mawnan Smith)	1	1.5 to Durgan		✔	
Falmouth	9	14.5	✔	✔	VC
St Mawes	ferry		✔	VC	
Place	ferry				
Portscatho/Gerrans	6¼	10 (from Falmouth)		✔	
Portloe	7½	12			
East Portholland	2½	4			
Gorran Haven	6½	10.5		✔	
Mevagissey	3½	5.5		✔	TIP
Pentewan	2¼	3.5		✔	
Charlestown	5	8	✔		
Par	4½	6.75	✔	✔	
Polkerris	2¼	3.5			
Fowey	4¾	7.5	✔	✔	TIC
Polruan	ferry		✔	✔	
Polperro	7¼	11.75	✔	✔	
Looe	5	8	✔	✔	TIC
Seaton	4	6.5			
Downderry	1¼	2		✔	
Portwrinkle	3	5			
Cawsand/Kingsand	10	16		✔	
Cremyll Ferry	3	5			
Plymouth (Mayflower Steps)	2¾	4.5	✔	✔	TIC

TOTAL DISTANCE **288¼ miles** (464km)

TOWN FACILITIES

(cont'd from p37)

Eating Place ✓ = one 𝓌 = a few 𝓌𝓌 = three + (𝓌) = seasonal	Food Store	Campsite	Hostels YHA or H (Ind Hostel) (YHA)=seasonal	B&B-style accommodation ✓ = one 𝓌 = two 𝓌𝓌 = three +	Place name (Places in brackets are a short walk off the coast path)
𝓌𝓌	✓	✓		𝓌𝓌	**Marazion**
(𝓌𝓌)	✓	✓		✓	**Praa Sands**
𝓌𝓌	𝓌	✓		𝓌𝓌	**Porthleven**
𝓌𝓌	𝓌𝓌	✓		𝓌𝓌	**(Mullion Cove/Mullion)**
		(Tenerife Farm)			
𝓌𝓌	𝓌	✓	(YHA)	𝓌𝓌	**(Lizard)**
✓		✓		✓	**Cadgwith**
		(Kennack Sands)			
𝓌𝓌	✓	✓	(YHA)	𝓌𝓌	**Coverack**
𝓌		✓		✓	**Porthallow**
𝓌	✓	𝓌			**Helford**
		(Gear Farm)			
✓	✓			✓	**Gweek**
✓					**Helford Passage**
𝓌	✓	✓		𝓌	**(Mawnan Smith)**
		(Pennance Mill Farm)			
𝓌𝓌	𝓌𝓌		H	𝓌𝓌	**Falmouth**
𝓌𝓌	✓			𝓌𝓌	**St Mawes**
					Place
𝓌𝓌	✓	✓		𝓌	**Portscatho/Gerrans**
𝓌				𝓌𝓌	**Portloe**
(✓)		YHA (Boswinger)		✓	**East Portholland**
𝓌𝓌	✓	✓		𝓌	**Gorran Haven**
𝓌𝓌	✓			𝓌𝓌	**Mevagissey**
𝓌𝓌	✓	✓		𝓌𝓌	**Pentewan**
𝓌𝓌	✓	✓		𝓌	**Charlestown**
𝓌	𝓌				**Par**
𝓌					**Polkerris**
𝓌𝓌	✓			𝓌𝓌	**Fowey**
𝓌𝓌	✓	✓		𝓌	**Polruan**
𝓌𝓌	✓	✓		𝓌𝓌	**Polperro**
𝓌𝓌	✓	✓		𝓌𝓌	**Looe**
		(Bay View Farm)			
𝓌𝓌	✓			✓	**Seaton**
𝓌	✓				**Downderry**
✓					**Portwrinkle**
𝓌𝓌	✓	✓		𝓌𝓌	**Cawsand/Kingsand**
		(Maker Heights)			
𝓌					**Cremyll Ferry**
𝓌𝓌	𝓌𝓌		H	𝓌𝓌	**Plymouth**
					(Mayflower Steps)

PLANNING YOUR WALK

Weekend walks

● **Crackington Haven to Port Isaac** **21 miles/34km (see pp86-109)**
This challenging walk combines the first two day walks as detailed above, with
the addition of the easy cliff-top section between Boscastle and Tintagel which
takes in some wonderful coves, inlets and the lovely beach at Bossiney Haven.

● **Padstow to Mawgan Porth** **17 miles/27km (see pp121-30)**
The highlights of this section include Pepper and Round Holes, Trevose Head
lighthouse, Park Head, Bedruthan Steps and a long section of coastline as wonderfully indented and eroded as the crooked man's crooked stile.

● **St Ives to Land's End** **23 miles/37km (see pp170-89)**
Pass through tough granite villages, head out onto Cape Cornwall and enjoy the
rugged atmosphere of this walk.

● **Sennen Cove to Mousehole** **13 miles/21km (see pp187-98)**
Start and finish in tiny fishing villages, walk to Land's End, the furthest point
west in England, and enjoy picnic lunches in beautiful coves crying out to be
explored.

● **Praa Sands to the Lizard** **17½ miles/28km (see pp214-29)**
Pack your camera for the scenic highlights of Mullion and Kynance coves and
enjoy striding out across the windswept heath and turf of the Lizard Peninsula.

● **Falmouth/Place to Mevagissey** **26 miles/42km (see pp255-73)**
Beginning in Place (see p270), this slightly tougher two-day wandering allows
for a night in Portloe as well as visits to such typical Cornish villages as
Portscatho and Portholland, rounded off with lunch of fish 'n' chips at Gorran
Haven. There are particularly good views from Nare Head and Dodman Point.

● **Mevagissey to Polperro** **26 miles/42km (see pp273-93)**
Providing the hiker with opportunities to stop overnight in Charlestown and
enjoy a lunch-stop in Fowey, this two-day stroll really does take in some of the
best Cornish towns. Parts of the path can be quite testing but a cream tea in
Pentewan and the views from Gribbin Head should easily divert your mind
away from any aching limbs.

● **Looe to Plymouth** **21¼ miles/34km (see p299-320)**
With the option of stopping in Portwrinkle, this relatively undemanding two-
day hike visits the small communities of Millendreath, Seaton and Downderry,

---

❑ **Walking from a fixed base**
An option to consider when making your plans is to stay at one place and use public
transport to get to and from different stretches of the coast path – rather than moving
on every day. This style of walking would particularly suit those on a short break, or
groups who wanted to rent a self-catering cottage (see p22).

When choosing a place to base yourself you need somewhere with good public
transport (see pp52-6), a variety of coast-path walks nearby and preferably somewhere with a bit of atmosphere so that you can enjoy yourself when you are not walking. Consider Boscastle (p90), Tintagel (p98), Port Isaac (p105), Padstow (p117), St
Ives (p164), St Just (p182), Mousehole (p196), Newlyn (p198), Penzance (p202),
Marazion (p208), Lizard Village (p224), Mevagissey (p270), Fowey (p283), Polperro
(p290) and Looe (p296).

PLANNING YOUR WALK

before rounding Rame Head and taking in the twin villages of Kingsand and Cawsand as well as the picturesque Mt Edgcumbe Country Park. There is plenty of cliff-top walking and a Napoleonic fort. In fact the particularly sturdy could achieve this in a single day – especially with the option of a ferry from Cawsand direct to Plymouth.

What to take

What and how much to take are very personal choices that take experience to get right. For those who are new to long-distance walking the suggestions below will help you reach a balance of comfort, safety and minimal weight.

KEEP IT LIGHT

When packing your rucksack it cannot be emphasised enough that the less weight you are carrying the more you will enjoy your walk. If you pack a lot of unnecessary items you will undoubtedly find yourself wanting to discard them as you go. If you are in any doubt about taking something, leave it at home.

RUCKSACK

If you are staying in B&Bs or hostels you will need a medium-sized pack of about 40-60 litres' capacity; just big enough to hold a change of clothes, a waterproof jacket, a few toiletries, a water bottle/pouch and a packed lunch. Hostellers may require a few extras such as a towel and food for cooking.

Those camping will need a rucksack big enough to carry a tent, sleeping bag, towel, cooking equipment and food. A pack of about 60-80 litres should be ample.

If you are walking with an organised tour or using a baggage-carrying service (see p28) you will be able to pack the bulk of your gear into a suitcase or holdall. While walking you need only a lightweight daypack for a spare jumper, waterproof jacket, water bottle/pouch and lunch but don't forget the camera, map and guide book... and some may also wish to bring walking poles, binoculars and a first-aid kit.

Pack everything inside a large plastic bag (or inside a number of smaller plastic bags for easier retrieval); there is nothing worse than discovering that all your clothes and sleeping bag have got wet. Most outdoor shops stock large bags made from tough plastic, or you can use two rubbish bags instead.

FOOTWEAR

A comfortable, sturdy pair of leather or fabric boots are ideal for walking the coast path. If you don't already own a pair and the cost of purchasing them is prohibitive you could get by with a lightweight pair of trainers or trail shoes between late spring and early autumn. However, they don't give as much support so on rough or slippery ground it can be easy to sprain or twist your ankle. They are also less waterproof, making it more difficult to keep your feet dry. Certainly, if you're carrying a heavy rucksack, walking boots rather than trainers are recommended.

If you are walking in the winter you'll be much more comfortable if your boots are waterproof; wet feet equals cold feet. To waterproof leather boots cover them in a layer of wax and take the wax with you so you can redo them a couple of times during your walk.

Gaiters are not really necessary but if you have a pair you may find them useful when it's wet and muddy, or to keep the sand out when walking across dunes and beaches.

CLOTHING

Even if you are setting out in good weather on just a day walk you should always have suitable clothing to keep you warm and dry should the weather change. Most walkers choose their clothes according to the versatile layering system, which consists of an outer layer or 'shell' to protect you from the wind and rain, a mid layer or two to keep you warm, and a base layer to transport sweat away from your skin.

The most important item is a **waterproof/windproof jacket**. Even in summer it can rain for a week and if the sun isn't out the sea breeze can make it feel distinctly chilly. The most comfortable jackets are those made from breathable fabrics that let moisture (your sweat) out, but don't let moisture (the rain) in.

A polyester **fleece**, or woollen jumper, makes a good middle layer as they remain warm even when wet. The advantage of fleece is that it is lightweight and dries relatively quickly. In winter you may want to carry an extra jumper to put on when you stop as you can get cold very quickly.

In summer cotton T-shirts are fine for a **base layer**, but at other times of the year you will be more comfortable wearing a thin thermal layer. Cotton absorbs sweat, trapping it next to the skin which will chill you rapidly when you stop exercising. Modern synthetic fabrics on the other hand, 'wick' sweat away from the body and dry rapidly although they can also quickly start to smell bad. More expensive but with far better odour control is Merino wool, which is lightweight, high-wicking, quick-drying and washable.

Shorts are great to walk in during the summer, although you'll probably want to bring a pair of **long trousers** for cooler days. Also, some sections of the path can become overgrown with stinging nettles and you may appreciate having your legs covered. Don't wear jeans; if they get wet they become incredibly heavy and stick uncomfortably to your skin. They also take forever to dry.

It is worth investing in good socks. There are many on the market that are designed with walkers in mind – check out the Thousand-Mile sock range. You will notice the difference particularly when they don't become hard and stiff after the first day of walking. How many pairs you take is a personal preference but assuming you'll want to change your socks daily, five pairs is about right.

Underwear goes without saying and how many pairs to take is a personal preference; five pairs normally suffice. Women may find a sports bra more comfortable because pack straps can cause bra straps to dig into your shoulders.

A **hat** with a brim is pretty much essential during the summer, keeping you cool and preventing sunburn (which can be a real danger in Cornwall in the summer months). In the cooler months you'll need a woolly hat and some **gloves**.

Don't forget your **swimming gear** and a **towel**; the white-sand beaches and crystal-clear aquamarine seas are extremely inviting.

You will also need a **change of clothing** for the evening. If you're staying in B&Bs and eating out you may feel more comfortable with something tidy. A spare pair of shoes such as lightweight sandals or trainers is also worth carrying, even if they do add a bit of weight. There's nothing worse than having to put wet, dirty (not to mention smelly) boots back on after you've showered and changed. If you're camping, early spring and late autumn nights can be decidedly chilly, so pack something warm.

❏ **Hiking with kids**
Being able to bring my kids along with me on trips is always a joy, but when it's a hiking trip, the main challenge is to keep them from dying of boredom! My five-year-old daughter Yoyo tagged along with me for part of my Cornwall Coast Path research for the last edition of this book. Here's how I managed to keep her excited about hiking along the same track for 10 days in a row:
● **Short walks** We aimed for 7km or 8km a day (more if not too hilly); so just a couple of hours in the morning, and a couple of hours in the afternoon.
● **Visible targets** 'We'll have a picnic when we get to the top of that hill' sounds much more encouraging to a five year old than 'We'll stop for lunch at 1 o'clock'.
● **Plenty of breaks** As well as stopping frequently for rests, we took a few mornings or afternoons off – mostly for beach time – and sometimes had the whole day off if it was raining.
● **Aiming for the beach** I also found it was a good idea to target something fun each day, like a beach or a swimming pool or a playground. When Yoyo knew there was going to be some play time up ahead, she was much more excited about getting to our destination.
● **Games** To make the walk more engaging Yoyo and I played games as we went along. Sometimes just something as simple as 'I spy', but she also enjoyed animal- and plant-spotting games – first person to spot 10 snails, for example.
● **Camping** We camped almost every day, and Yoyo absolutely loved it. There's nothing more exciting for a four- or five-year-old than sleeping in a tent!
● **Rucksack** It was great to have the option of my child-carrier rucksack although Yoyo hardly used it in the end. Most of the time it carried our tent rather than my daughter.
● **Scrapbook** It may sound strange, but having a plan to make a scrapbook together when you get back home makes the walk itself more fun. Yoyo loved collecting things for her scrapbook along the way (seashells, flowers, tickets, postcards etc).
● **Ice creams** If all else fails.

Daniel McCrohan

PLANNING YOUR WALK

❏ **Canine companions**
The South-West Coast Path is a dog-friendly path and many are the rewards that await those prepared to make the extra effort required to bring their best friend along the trail. However, you shouldn't underestimate the amount of work involved in bringing your pooch to the path. Indeed, just about every decision you make will be influenced by the fact that you've got a dog: how you plan to travel to the start of the trail, where you're going to stay, how far you're going to walk each day, where you're going to rest and where you're going to eat in the evening etc etc.

The decision-making begins well before you've set foot on the trail. For starters, you have to ask – and be honest with – yourself: can your dog really cope with walking ten-plus miles (16+km) a day, day after day, week after week? And just as importantly, will he or she actually enjoy it?!?

If you think the answer is yes to both, you need to start preparing accordingly. You'll certainly have to put extra thought into your itinerary. The best starting point is to study the advice on pp336-8 and the Village & town facilities table (pp36-9) to plan where you can stay and eat, and where to buy food for your mutt.

Henry Stedman

TOILETRIES

Only take the minimum. Essentials are **soap**, **shampoo**, **toothbrush**, **toothpaste**, any **medication** and, for women, **sanitary towels** and **tampons**. **Loo paper** is generally provided in public toilets, but bring a roll just in case and carry a small lightweight **trowel** for burying excrement if you get caught out far from a toilet (see p70-1 for the code of the outdoor loo). **Sunscreen is essential** and something to put on cracked lips is also a good idea. Deodorants, hair brushes, razors and so forth are up to you. If you are hostelling or camping you will also need a **towel**.

FIRST-AID KIT

Medical facilities in Britain are good so you only need to take a first-aid kit to deal with basic injuries. In a waterproof bag or container you should have: **scissors** for cutting tape and cutting away clothing; **aspirin** or **paracetamol** for treating mild to moderate pain; one or two **stretch bandages** for holding dressings or splints in place and for sprained ankles or sore knees; if you think your knees will give you trouble **elastic supports** are invaluable; a **triangular bandage** for broken/sprained arms; a small selection of **sterile dressings** for wounds; **porous adhesive tape** to hold them in place; **plasters/Band Aids** for minor cuts; a sturdier, preferably waterproof **adhesive tape** for blister prevention; **Compeed**, **Second Skin** or **Moleskin** for treating blisters; **safety pins**; **antiseptic cream** or liquid; **tweezers**; and treatment such as **Imodium** for acute diarrhoea – you never know when it might come in handy.

GENERAL ITEMS

Other essential items you should carry are: a **torch** (flashlight) in case you end up walking in the dark; a **whistle** to attract attention if you get lost or find yourself in trouble (see box p77); a **water bottle** or pouch (two litres is the best size); a **watch**; a current **tide chart** (available for about £1 from newsagents or TICs in coastal areas); and a **plastic bag** for carrying any rubbish you accumulate.

You should also carry some **emergency food** with you such as chocolate, dried fruit and biscuits.

Walking poles are now widely used (although opinions are divided on how much they really help). Using them requires some practice.

Useful items to carry are: a **pen-knife**; a **camera**; a **notebook** to record your impressions in a different way; **sunglasses** to protect your eyes from the glare off water and beaches on sunny days; **binoculars**; something to read; and a **vacuum flask** for hot drinks (worth the investment if you're on a budget as buying all those cups of tea or coffee can get expensive). A **map-case** can be a useful extra for protecting your map and guidebook in the rain, which can very quickly reduce both to pulp.

CAMPING GEAR

Campers will need a decent **tent** able to withstand wind and rain; a **sleeping mat**; a two- or three-season **sleeping bag** (you can always wear clothes inside your sleeping bag if you are cold); a **camping stove** and fuel; **cooking equipment** (a pot with a pot-grabber and a lid that can double as a frying pan is enough for two people); a **bowl**, **mug**, **cutlery** (don't forget a can-opener), **pen-knife** and a **scrubber** for washing up.

MONEY AND DOCUMENTS

It is most convenient to carry your money as **cash**. A debit **card** (with a PIN) is the easiest way to withdraw money either from banks, cash machines or post offices and, along with credit cards, can be used to pay in larger shops, restaurants and hotels. Remember to stock up on cash whenever you can, though, as there are numerous villages along the path that don't have facilities for withdrawing money. A **cheque book** is very useful for walkers with accounts in British banks as a cheque will often be accepted at a B&B where a card is not.

Always keep your money and documents in a safe place and in a waterproof container. In particular, those camping or staying in hostels should take care not to leave them lying around; it's much safer to carry them on you at all times.

MAPS

The hand-drawn maps in this book cover the trail at a scale of 1:20,000; plenty of detail and information to keep you on the right track. If you wish to explore inland, Ordnance Survey (☎ 0345-605 0505, 🖳 ordnancesurvey.co.uk) produce eight excellent maps covering the Cornish coast in their Explorer series; the ones with the orange cover. The numbers you'll require are: 111 Bude, Boscastle and Tintagel; 106 Newquay and Padstow; 104 Redruth and St Agnes; 102 Land's End, Penzance and St Ives; 103 The Lizard, Falmouth and Helston;

❑ SOURCES OF FURTHER INFORMATION

Trail information

● **South West Coast Path Association** (SWCPA; 💻 southwestcoastpath.org.uk) The SWCPA promotes the interests of users of the South-West Coast Path by, amongst other things, lobbying the numerous bodies responsible for the path in order to ensure it is maintained to a high standard. There are several places where the Association is actively seeking for the path to be re-routed so that it can genuinely be called a coast path. They publish an annual guide to the entire South West Coast Path (£15 to non-members) and are happy to provide advice and information to assist your coast-path walk. Membership, which includes a copy of the annual guide, costs £22 per year (£29 for non-UK residents).

Tourist information

● **Tourist information centres (TICs)** TICs provide locally specific information for visitors and may also provide an accommodation-booking service (for which there is usually a charge). Unfortunately many of the local council-run TICs in Cornwall have lost their funding. Some have managed to diversify or are now staffed by volunteers so remain open, while others have simply had to shut. There are TICs in: Bude (see p80), Padstow (p117), Newquay (p133), Perranporth (p144), Hayle (p160), St Ives (p165), Penzance (p203), Looe (p296) and Plymouth (p317).

● **Tourist information points (TIPs)** TIPs have leaflets about local attractions but they are unstaffed. There are TIPs at St Just (p183) and Mevagissey (p270). Many village shops, libraries or post offices also have local tourist information.

● **Visitor centres (VCs)** These generally provide information about their particular attraction, though they sometimes have general leaflets for other places of interest in the area but the staff will probably not be able to help with accommodation or similar queries. There are visitor centres at Boscastle (p90), Tintagel (p98), Land's End (p188), Falmouth (p250), and St Mawes (p255).

● **Tourist boards** For general information about the whole of Cornwall contact Cornwall Tourist Board (💻 visitcornwall.com).

Organisations for walkers

● **Backpackers' Club** (💻 backpackersclub.co.uk) A club for people who are involved or interested in lightweight camping through walking, cycling, skiing and canoeing. They produce a quarterly magazine, provide members with a comprehensive advisory and information service on all aspects of backpacking, organise weekend trips and also publish a farm-pitch directory. Membership costs £20 per year.

● **Long Distance Walkers' Association** (💻 ldwa.org.uk) An association of people with the common interest of long-distance walking. Membership includes a journal three times per year giving details of challenge events and local group walks as well as articles on the subject. Information on over 500 Long Distance Paths is presented in the LDWA's Long Distance Walkers' Handbook. Membership costs £18 per year, £25.50 for a family. International membership is £15/26 without/with the journal.

● **Ramblers** (formerly Ramblers' Association; 💻 ramblers.org.uk) Looks after the interests of walkers throughout Britain. They publish a large amount of useful information including their quarterly Walk magazine (£5.99 to non-members). The website also has a discussion forum. Annual membership costs £35.

● **Walking World** (💻 walkingworld.com) Online organisation. Membership fee of £18 allows access to pdf downloads of hundreds of walks throughout the UK including many in Cornwall, with a Find a walk feature.

105 Falmouth and Mevagissey; 107 St Austell and Liskeard; and 108 Lower Tamar Valley and Plymouth. These maps are also good for those with a particular interest in Cornwall's ancient sites as all sites, however minor, are shown.

AZ (🖥 az.co.uk) produce an adventure series of OS map booklets to the SWCP. Booklet 2 covers North Cornwall; booklet 3: South Cornwall.

Harvey Maps (☎ 01786-841202, 🖥 harveymaps.co.uk) produce a three-map series that covers the entire South West Coast Path: Map 1 and Map 2 cover the Cornwall sections.

Enthusiastic map buyers can reduce the often-considerable expense of purchasing them: Ramblers (see box opposite) has the complete range of OS Explorer and Landranger maps and members can borrow up to 10 maps for four weeks; all you have to pay for is return postage. Members of Backpackers' Club (see opposite) can purchase maps at a significant discount through the club.

Digital maps

There are numerous software packages now available that provide Ordnance Survey (OS) maps for a PC, smartphone, tablet or GPS. Maps are supplied by direct download over the Internet. The maps are then loaded into an application, also available by download, from where you can view them, print them and create routes on them. **Memory Map** (🖥 memory-map.co.uk) currently sell OS 1:25,000 mapping covering the whole of the UK for £65.

Both OS and Harvey maps can also be obtained online from **Anquet** (🖥 anquet.com).

For a subscription of £3.99 for one month or £19.99-25.99 for a year (on their current offer) **Ordnance Survey** (🖥 ordnancesurvey.co.uk) will let you download and then use their UK maps (1:25,000 scale) on a mobile or tablet without a data connection for a specific period.

USEFUL BOOKS

Flora and fauna

The following books are likely to be of interest to the enthusiast but may be too heavy to carry around.

● *Wildflowers of Britain and Europe* by W Lippert and D Podlech (Collins, £9.99) is a good compact book for beginners. It is organised by flower colour making it easy to flip immediately to the right section.

● *The Wild Flower Key* by Francis Rose and Clare O'Reilly (Frederick Warne, £19.99) is an excellent book for more serious botanists. It is very comprehensive and enables identification of plants whether in flower or not.

● *Birds of Cornwall* by Trevor and Endymion Beer (Tor Mark Press, £2.99) is an extremely lightweight book. Its low price makes it an excellent buy and it's usually stocked in TICs and local bookshops.

● *Birds of Britain and Europe* by J Nicolai, D Singer and K Wothe (Collins, £9.99) is a compact book. It features photographs and is organised by habitat making it easy to flip straight to the right section.

● The RSPB's *Pocket Guide to British Birds* by Simon Harrap and David Nurney (£4.99) identifies birds by their plumage and song.

● *Where to watch birds – Devon & Cornwall* by David Norman & Vic Tucker (A&C Black 2009, 5th ed, £16.99)

● *Collins Bird Guide* by Mullarney, Svensson, Zetterström & Grant (Harper Collins 1999, Pbk £16.99, Hbk £24.99)

● *Seashore Life of Britain and Europe* by Bob Gibbons, Denys Ovenden and Melanie Perkins (Michelin Green Guides, £2.50) is a conveniently sized guide to 150 species of seaweeds, molluscs, crustaceans and insects likely to be found along Britain's coastline.

● *Sea Shore of Britain and Europe* by Peter Hayward, Tony Nelson-Smith and Chris Shields (Collins, £16.99) is a more detailed guide to the seashore ecology.

● The Field Studies Council (🖳 www.field-studies-council.org) publishes a series of *Identification Guides* (fold-out charts) which are also practical.

There are also several field guide apps for smartphones, including those that can aid in identifying birds from their song as well as by their appearance.

Others

Good **non-fiction** reads include: *A History of Cornwall* by Ian Soulsby (Phillimore and Co, 1986); *King Arthur: The Dream of a Golden Age* by Geoffrey Ashe (Thames and Hudson, 1990); *The Lost Gardens of Heligan* by Tim Smit (Victor Gollancz, 1997) and *Poldark's Cornwall* by Winston Graham (Webb and Bower, 1983).

If you are interested in the ancient sites of Cornwall, *Ancient Cornwall* by Paul White (Tor Mark Press) is a slim volume that makes good night-time reading. It has a useful map of the sites.

The National Trust (NT) publish a series of leaflets titled *Coast of Cornwall* with history, information and maps about their coastal properties in each area. They cost £1 each (plus a charge for post and packing) and are available from NT shops in Cornwall or by post from the NT Regional Office (☎ 01208-265952; Lanhydrock House Shop, Bodmin, Cornwall PL30 5AD).

Recommended **fiction** includes: *To the Lighthouse* by Virginia Woolf (first published 1932); *Rebecca* (1938), *Jamaica Inn* (1936) and *Frenchman's Creek* (1941) by Daphne du Maurier; the *Poldark* novels by Winston Graham (12 volumes between 1945 and 2002); *The Minack Chronicles* by Derek Tangye (over 20 books describing the author's attempts to set up a flower farm in Cornwall though not all are relevant to Cornwall); *The Lamorna Wink* by Martha Grimes (Headline Books, 1999); *Zennor in Darkness* by Helen Dunmore (Viking Books, 1993); *The Mousehole Cat* by Antonia Barber (1990).

A recent memoir from the trail is *The Salt Path* by Raynor Winn (2018); well worth a read, although you may appreciate it more having walked the trail, rather than choosing to flick through its pages before setting off.

Getting to and from the Cornwall Coast Path

All the major towns along the coast path are reasonably well served by rail and/or coach services from the rest of Britain. Travelling by train or coach is the most convenient way to get to the trail as you do not need to worry about where to leave your car, how safe it will be while you're walking, or how to get back to it at the end of your holiday.

Choosing to travel by public transport is choosing to help the environment, a creative step in minimising your impact on the countryside. And it can be an

PLANNING YOUR WALK

❏ **GETTING TO BRITAIN**

By air
The best international gateway to Britain for the Cornwall Coast Path is London with its six airports: Heathrow (the main airport; 🖳 heathrowairport.com), Gatwick (🖳 gatwickairport.com), Stansted (🖳 stanstedairport.com), Luton (🖳 london-luton.co.uk) London City (🖳 londoncityairport.com) and Southend (🖳 southendairport.com). However, some charter and budget airlines also have flights to Newquay (🖳 cornwall airportnewquay.com), Exeter (🖳 exeter-airport.co.uk) and Bristol (🖳 bristolair port.co.uk) airports.

From Europe by train
Eurostar (🖳 eurostar.com) operates a high-speed passenger service via the Channel Tunnel between Paris, Brussels, Amsterdam, Lille and London. The Eurostar terminal in London is at St Pancras International station with connections to the London Underground and to all other main railway stations in London. Trains to Cornwall (and Plymouth) leave from Paddington station; see p50 for details.

For more information about rail services from your country contact your national rail company or Rail Europe (🖳 raileurope.com).

From Europe by coach
Eurolines (🖳 eurolines.com) have a wide network of long-distance bus services connecting over 500 destinations in 25 European countries to London (Victoria Coach Station). Visit the Eurolines website for details of services from your country.

From Europe by car
P&O (🖳 poferries.com) runs frequent passenger ferries from Calais to Dover; and from Rotterdam and Zeebrugge to Hull. Brittany Ferries (🖳 brittanyferries.com) has services from Santander and Roscoff to Plymouth; from Bilbao, St Malo, Cherbourg, Caen and Le Havre to Portsmouth; and from Cherbourg to Poole. There are also several other ferries plying routes between mainland Europe and ports on Britain's eastern coast. Look at 🖳 ferrysavers.com or 🖳 directferries.com for a full list of companies and services.

Eurotunnel (🖳 eurotunnel.com) operates a shuttle train service (Le Shuttle) for vehicles via the Channel Tunnel between Calais and Folkestone taking one hour between the motorway in France and the motorway in Britain.

❏ **Coach services**

Note: the services listed below operate daily but not all stops are included. Places in bold are on very near the coast path.

NX315 Eastbourne to Helston along the south coast via Brighton, Worthing, Southampton, Bournemouth, Exeter, **Plymouth**, Truro & **Falmouth**, 1/day

NX330 Nottingham to **Penzance** via Worcester, Bristol, **Plymouth**, Bodmin, Wadebridge, St Columb Major & Minor, **Newquay**, **Hayle**, **Lelant**, **Carbis Bay**, **St Ives**, St Erth & Crowlas, 1/day

NX404 London to **Penzance** via Heathrow Airport, Chippenham, Bath, Bristol Airport, Exeter, Paignton, **Plymouth**, Truro, **Hayle**, St Erth & Crowlas, 1/day

NX502 London Victoria to Westward Ho! via Heathrow Airport, Taunton, Wellington, Tiverton, Barnstaple & Bideford, 2/day (plus late May to early Sep Sat 1/day to **Bude**)

NX504 London to **Penzance** via Heathrow Airport, **Plymouth**, Bodmin, Wadebridge, St Columb Major & Minor, **Newquay**, Redruth, Pool, Camborne, **Hayle**, **Lelant**, **Carbis Bay**, **St Ives**, St Erth & Crowlas, 2/day

---

enjoyable experience in itself. How many of us have fond memories of relaxing to the clickerty-clack of the train wheels while sleepily watching the scenery pass by?

NATIONAL TRANSPORT

By rail

The main Cornwall line, operated by Great Western Railway (GWR, ☎ 0345-7000 125, 💻 gwr.com), runs from London Paddington through Exeter and Plymouth to finish at Penzance, with branch lines connecting major towns on the coast path. There are several services every day as well as a night train (the Night Riviera, Sun-Fri). Cross Country (☎ 0844-811 0124, 💻 crosscountry-trains.co.uk) operates services from Scotland, the North-East and the Midlands to Penzance.

To get to Bude it's best to take a train to Exeter St David's and then get one of the connecting buses (see pp52-5). However, the last train from London may arrive too late for the last bus to Bude so check in advance. Barnstaple, 35 miles to the north of Bude, and Okehampton, 30 miles to the east, are other possibilities though services only call at the latter in the summer months. In the summer GWR runs connecting buses regularly and daily from Okehampton to Bude. In contrast, from Barnstaple there are just one or two buses a day to Bude.

For Padstow get off the train at Bodmin Parkway station and catch First Kernow's Bus service No 11A (see box pp54-5) to Padstow, for Newquay you have to change at Par, for Falmouth you need to change at Truro, for St Ives change at St Erth.

National rail enquiries (☎ 03457-484950, 24hrs, 💻 nationalrail.co.uk) is the only number you need to find out all timetable and fare information.

Information is also available in the Cornwall public transport timetable booklets (see p56). Rail tickets are generally cheaper if you book them well in advance and also if you buy online. Most discounted tickets carry some restrictions so check what they are before you purchase them. Tickets can be bought through the relevant companies, or at any rail station. You can also get them online at 💻 thetrainline.com and 💻 qjump.co.uk.

If you want to book a **taxi** when you arrive visit 💻 traintaxi.co.uk for details of taxi companies operating at rail stations throughout England.

It is often possible to buy a train ticket that includes **bus travel** at your destination: for further information visit the Plusbus website (💻 plusbus.info).

By coach

National Express (☎ 0871-781 8181, lines open 24 hours a day; 💻 nationalexpress.com) is the principal coach (long-distance bus) operator in Britain. Travel by coach is usually cheaper than by rail but does take longer.

To get the cheapest fares you need to book seven days ahead. You can purchase tickets from coach and bus station ticket offices, National Express agents, directly from the driver (though not always, so do check with locals in advance), by telephone, or online. You need to allow at least four working days for posted tickets.

However, it is not easy to reach **Bude** by coach. There is a seasonal service (Saturday only) from London and several services to Westward Ho! but it is not easy to get to Bude from there. Your best bet is to travel to Exeter or Plymouth and from there take the local bus service to Bude (see box pp52-5).

Alternatively take a coach to **Barnstaple** and get Stagecoach's service from there to Bude. There are several coach services to other towns on the coast path and also services from **Falmouth** and **Plymouth** to London and elsewhere.

By car

The easiest way to drive into Cornwall is to join the M5 to Exeter and then take either the A30 or A38 depending on your final destination. Even if you're using a Sat Nav, a good road atlas is very useful for navigating Cornwall's country lanes. Sat Navs can send you the wrong way and, if you're using the one on your phone, are reliant upon your phone's battery and/or a strong signal. You can get detailed driving directions from the AA website (💻 theaa.com/route-planner/index.jsp) by clicking on the route planner.

Parking your car can be a problem. The safest place to leave it is in a garage that offers long-term parking or a long-stay car park, though these have no security and you can only purchase weekly tickets, necessitating a trip back to your car if you are going to be away longer. To avoid this hassle you may want to consider using public transport instead.

By air

Please bear in mind that air travel is by far the least environmentally sound option (see 💻 chooseclimate.org for the true costs of flying). However, if you prefer to fly see the box on p49.

PLANNING YOUR WALK

PLANNING YOUR WALK

Public Transport Map 1

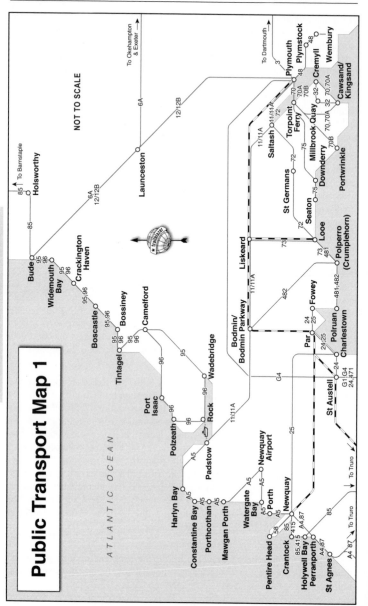

NOT TO SCALE

ATLANTIC OCEAN

To Barnstaple

To Okehampton & Exeter

To Dartmouth

To Truro

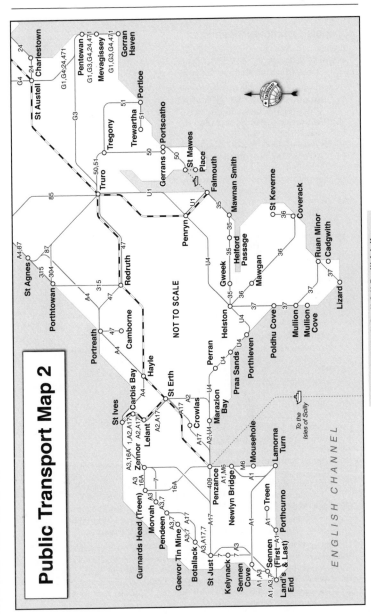

Public Transport Map 2

❏ PUBLIC TRANSPORT SERVICES

Buses

A-Line Coaches (☎ 01752-822740, 🖳 alinecoaches.co.uk)
32   **Cremyll** to **Cawsand** via Millbrook Quay, Mon-Fri 6-7/day

First Kernow (☎ 0345-646 0707, 🖳 firstgroup.com/cornwall)
A1 **Penzance** to **Land's End** via **Newlyn Bridge**, **Lamorna Turn**, **Sennen Cove/First & Last**, daily 1-2/hr (some continue to **Porthcurno & Treen**)
A2 **Penzance** to **St Ives** via **Marazion Bay**, St Erth & **Carbis Bay/Lelant**, daily 1/hr
A3 **St Ives** to **Land's End** via **Zennor, Gunnard's Head, Morvah, Pendeen, Geevor tin mine, Botallack, St Just, Sennen Cove & Sennen**, summer daily 1/hr, mid Apr to late May 3/day
A4 **Newquay** to **St Ives** via **Perranporth, St Agnes, Portreath & Hayle**, 1/day, 2/day between Perranporth & St Ives (summer only)
A5 **Newquay** to **Padstow** via **Porth, Watergate Bay**, Newquay Airport, **Mawgan Porth, Porthcothan, Constantine Bay & Harlyn Bay**, daily 1/hr, fewer out of season
A17 **Pendeen** to **St Ives** via **Botallack, St Just, Penzance**, Crowlas, St Erth, **Lelant & Carbis Bay**, daily 1-2/hr
M6 **Penzance** to **Mousehole** via **Newlyn**, daily 2/hr
U1 **Falmouth** to Truro via Penryn, daily 1-2/hr
U4 Penryn to Penzance via **Helston, Porthleven, Praa Sands, Perran & Marazion**, daily 1-2/hr
16A **Penzance** to **St Ives** via **Gurnard's Head** (3/day) & **Zennor** (3/day), Mon-Sat 1/hr
24 **Fowey** to **Mevagissey** via **Par, Charlestown**, St Austell & **Pentewan**, Mon-Sat 2/hr
25 **Newquay** to **Fowey** via **Charlestown & Par**, Mon-Sat 6/day
35 Helston to **Falmouth** via **Gweek, Helford Passage & Mawnan Smith**, Mon-Sat 4/day plus 1/hr Helford Passage to Falmouth
36 Helston to **St Keverne** via **Mawgan & Coverack**, Mon-Sat 6/day, Sun 3/day
37 Helston to **Lizard** via **Poldhu Cove, Mullion** & Ruan Minor (for **Cadgwith**), Mon-Sat 1/hr, Sun 4/day
47 Camborne to Truro via **Portreath** & Redruth, Mon-Sat 1/hr, Sun 5-6/day
50 Truro to **St Mawes** via Tregony, **Gerrans & Portscatho**, Mon-Sat 6-7/day, Sun 3/day
51 Truro to Trewartha via Tregony & **Portloe**, Mon-Fri 5/day, Sat 4/day
58 **Newquay** to **Pentire Head**, Mon-Sat 2/hr
85 Truro to Newquay via **Holywell Bay** & **Crantock**, Mon-Sat 8/day
87 **Newquay** to Truro via **Perranporth & St Agnes**, Mon-Sat 1/hr, Sun 5/day
95 Wadebridge to **Bude** via Camelford, **Tintagel, Bossiney, Boscastle, Crackington Haven & Widemouth Bay**, Mon-Sat 4/day
96 Camelford to Wadebridge via **Port Isaac, Polzeath & Rock**, daily 4-6/day (Sunday services in the summer start from **Bude** and go via **Widemouth Bay, Crackington Haven, Boscastle, Bossiney & Tintagel**)

Gorran and District Community Bus (☎ 01726-842733, 🖳 gorranbus.org)
Note: reservations (☎ 01726-844933) are recommended for these services.
G1 **Gorran Haven** to St Austell via **Mevagissey & Pentewan**, Wed & Fri 1/day
G3 **Gorran Haven** to Truro via **Mevagissey & Pentewan**, Tue 2/day & Thur 1/day
G4 **Gorran Haven** to **Plymouth** via **Mevagissey, Pentewan** & St Austell, third Monday in the month only

[See public transport maps on previous pages]

Buses (*cont'd*)
Hopley's Coaches (☎ 01872-553786, 🖳 hopleyscoaches.com)
304   Truro to **Porthtowan**, Mon-Sat 1/hr
315   Redruth to **St Agnes** via **Porthtowan**, Mon-Sat 5-6/day

Plymouth City Bus (☎ 01752 662271, 🖳 plymouthbus.co.uk)
11/11A **Plymouth** to **Padstow** via Saltash, Liskeard & Bodmin Parkway,
       Mon-Sat 2/hr, Sun 4/day
12/12B **Bude** to **Plymouth** via Launceston, Mon-Sat 6/day
       Bude to Launceston, Sun 6/day
48   **Plymouth** to Wembury via Plymstock, Mon-Sat 6/day
70/70A **Cremyll** to **Plymouth** via **Kingsand**, **Cawsand** & Torpoint Ferry,
       Mon-Sat 1/hr, Sun 6/day
70B   **Portwrinkle** to **Plymouth** via Torpoint Ferry, Mon-Sat 1/hr
72   **Plymouth** to **Looe** via Saltash & St Germans, Mon-Sat 7/day
       Looe to **Polperro**, Sun 5/day
73   **Polperro (Crumplehorn)** to Liskeard via **Looe**, Mon-Sat 1/hr, Sun 7/day
75   Seaton to Torpoint via **Downderry**, Mon-Sat, 6/day

Stagecoach (🖳 stagecoachbus.com)
3   **Plymouth** to Dartmouth, daily 1/hr
6A   **Bude** to Exeter via Launceston & Okehampton, Mon-Sat 2/day, Sun 1/day
85   Barnstaple to **Bude** via Holsworthy, Mon-Sat 1/day

St Ives Bus Company (🖳 stivesbuses.co.uk)
1   **St Ives** to **Carbis Bay**, Mon-Sat approx 1/hr

Travel Cornwall (Summercourt Travel; ☎ 01726-861108, 🖳 travelcornwall.uk.com)
409   **Penzance** to **St Just**, Mon-Sat 6-7/day
415   **Newquay** to **Holywell** via **Crantock**, Mon-Fri 3/day
471   St Austell to **Gorran Haven** via **Pentewan** & **Mevagissey**, Mon-Sat 1-2/day
481   **East Looe** to **Polruan** via **West Looe** & **Polperro (Crumplehorn)**,
       Mon-Fri 5/day
482   **Polruan** to Bodmin via **Polperro (Crumplehorn)**, Wed 1/day

West Penwith Community Bus Association
  (**WPCBA**; ☎ 01736-787385, 🖳 communitybus.co.uk)
7   **Land's End** to **Zennor** via **Sennen**, **Kelynack**, **St Just**, **Botallack**, **Geevor**,
      Pendeen & **Morvah**, Mon-Sat 5/day

Trains
GWR – Great Western Railway (☎ 0345-7000 125, 🖳 www.gwr.com)
● St Erth to **St Ives** via Lelant Saltings, **Lelant** & **Carbis Bay**, Mon-Sat 2/hr in
summer, Sun 1/hr, pm only in winter
● **Newquay** to **Par**, Mon-Sat 6/day, Sun 6/day in summer
● Truro to **Falmouth Docks**, Mon-Sat 1/hr, Sun 10/day
● Liskeard to **Looe** (Looe Valley Line), Mon-Sat 10/day, Sun 8/day
● **Plymouth** to **Penzance** via Liskeard, Bodmin Parkway, **Par**, St Austell, Truro,
Redruth, **Hayle** & St Erth, daily 1/hr

LOCAL TRANSPORT

Bus services

Cornwall has a comprehensive public transport network linking almost all the coastal villages with at least one bus per day in the summer, sometimes fewer in winter. This is great news for the walker as it opens up the possibility of linear day and weekend walks, or a series of walks from a fixed base (see box p40 for more ideas) without having to organise two cars: instead, you can just sit back and enjoy the ride along some of Britain's most scenic bus routes.

Note that between Falmouth and Plymouth the public transport system is not as kind to the walker as it is in the far west; however, with careful planning the buses can still be utilised to your advantage; just be aware that with coastal buses, it is common to have to make changes (and so inevitably wait) inland.

Timetables Cornwall Council produces a guide to all of Cornwall's public transport (bus, rail and ferry; 🖳 cornwall.gov.uk/publictransport) which comes as one booklet.

In Cornwall you can pick the timetable up for free from bus stations, train stations, and tourist information centres, or contact the Passenger Transport Unit (☎ 0300-123 4222) at Cornwall Council, New County Hall, Treyew Rd, Truro TR1 3AY. The service numbers of the most useful buses are given in the tables on pp54-5 so you can flip straight to the page you need in the actual timetable. A very useful **app** is 'Traveline SW'.

Bus companies and customer helplines If the contact details in the following tables prove unsatisfactory, you can contact traveline (☎ 0871-200 2233, 7am-10pm; 🖳 traveline.info) which has public transport information for the whole of the UK.

Tickets If you are going to be using the bus frequently over several days Explorer tickets are good value. They are valid for one, three or seven days and allow you unlimited travel within the county on the relevant company's services. Contact the bus operators for further details.

At the time of writing anyone over 60 could obtain a free NOW card which allows them to travel free on local buses after 9.30am.

Public transport at a glance The maps on p52-3 and the tables on pp54-5 are designed to make it easy for you to plan your day using public transport. Use the **public transport maps** to see which towns each service covers then turn to the **tables** to check the frequency of that service. Read the tables carefully; some services only run one day a week, or not on Saturdays or Sundays. The definition of a summer service depends on the company and the route; it may be Easter to October or May/July to September so do check.

Note, **bus services do change** from year to year. Use this information as a rough guide and confirm up-to-date details with bus operators before travelling.

Details about the various **ferry** services on the route are given in the relevant place in the text.

THE ENVIRONMENT AND NATURE

2

The Cornish coastline provides a diverse range of habitats – ocean, beaches, sand dunes, steep cliffs, cliff-top grasslands and heathland – resulting in a rich variety of wildlife. For the walker interested in the natural environment it is a feast for the senses.

It would take a book several times the size of this one to list the thousands of species which you could come across on your walk. What follows is a brief description of the more common species you may encounter as well as some of the more special plants and animals which are found in Cornwall. If you want to know more refer to the field guides listed on pp47-8.

Nature conservation arose tentatively in the middle of the 19th century out of concern for wild birds which were being slaughtered to provide feathers for the fashion industry. As commercial exploitation of land has increased over the intervening century, so too has the conservation movement. It now has a wide sphere of influence throughout the world and its ethos is upheld by international legislation, government agencies and voluntary organisations.

Conservation schemes (see box on pp66-7) are outlined on the premise that to really learn about a landscape you need to know more than the names of all the plants and animals in it. It is just as important to understand the interactions going on between them and man's relationship with this ecological balance.

Flora and fauna

FAUNA

In and around the fishing villages

The wild laugh of the **herring gull** (*Larus argentatus*) is the wake-up call of the coast path. Perched on the rooftops of the stone villages, they are a reminder of the link between people and wildlife, the rocky coast and our stone and concrete towns and cities. Shoreline scavengers, they've adapted to the increasing waste thrown out by human society. Despite their bad reputation it's worth taking a closer look at these fascinating, ubiquitous birds. How do they keep their pale grey and white plumage so beautiful feeding on rubbish?

❏ **Birding and birders**
Along with the Isles of Scilly, Cornwall is England's rare-bird capital. These rarities come from North America, Siberia and southern Europe and it takes an expert to tell them from more common species. The best way to find them is to look for a sea of telescopes. Birders are generally pretty friendly people and may well show you the bird, but they can be grumpy if they haven't seen the rarity – 'dipped out' in birder parlance!

Birdline South West (☎ 0906-870 0241) is the premium-rate phone line for up-to-the-minute rare bird news. Alternatively take a look at the regional birding website 🖳 cornwall-birding.co.uk.

Nobel-prize-winning animal behaviourist Nikko Tinbergen showed how the young pecking at the red dot on their bright yellow bills triggers the adult to regurgitate food. In August the newly fledged brown young follow their parents, begging for food. Over the next three years they'll go through a motley range of plumages, more grey and less brown each year till they reach adulthood. But please don't feed them and do watch your sandwiches and fish and chips – they are quite capable of grabbing food from your hand, especially in St Ives.

The village harbours are a good place for lunch or an evening drink after a hard day on the cliffs. Look out for the birds who are equally at home on a rocky shore or in villages, such as the beautiful little black-and-white **pied wagtail** (*Motacilla alba*) with its long, bobbing tail.

Also looking black from a distance as they strut the beach are **jackdaws** (*Corvus monedula*). Close up, however, they are beautiful with a grey nape giving them a hooded look and shining blue eyes. They are very sociable: you will often see them high up in the air in pairs or flocks playing tag or performing acrobatic tricks.

Small, dark brown and easy to miss, the **rock pipit** (*Anthus petrosus*) is one of our toughest birds, as it feeds whilst walking on the rocks between the land and the sea. They nest in crevices and caves along the rocky coastline.

Seen on or from the sea cliffs

Walking on the coastal path leads you into a world of rock and sea, high cliffs with bracken-clad slopes, exposed green pasture, dramatic drops and headlands, sweeping sandy beaches and softer country around the estuaries.

Stunning **stonechats** (*Saxicola torquata*) with black, white and orange colouring are common on heath and grassy plains where you may hear their distinctive song, which is not dissimilar to two stones being clacked together.

Twittering **linnets** (*Carduelis cannabina*) with their bright red breasts and grey heads fly ahead and perch on gorse and fences.

Green hairstreak butterflies (*Callophrys rubi*) emerge on gorse in May.

The vertiginous swoops of the path mean it's often possible to be at eye level or even look down on birds and mammals. Watch for **kestrels** (*Falco tinnunculus*), hovering on sharp brown wings, before plummeting onto their prey – **field voles** (*Microtus arvalis*).

At eye level the black 'moustache' of the powerful slate-grey-backed **peregrine** (*Falco peregrinus*) is sometimes visible. At a glance it can be mistaken for a pigeon, its main prey. But the power and speed of this, the world's fastest bird, soon sets it apart. In the late summer whole families fly over the cliffs. In mid winter look for them over estuaries where they hunt ducks and waders. Despite the remote fastness of the cliffs, peregrines have suffered terribly. Accidental poisoning by the pesticide DDT succeeded where WWII persecution for fear they would kill carrier pigeons failed, and they were almost extinct in Cornwall by the end of the 1960s. Their triumphant return means not only a thriving population on their traditional sea cliffs, but more and more nesting in our cities on man-made cliffs, such as tower blocks and cathedrals.

Cliff ledges, a kind of multi-storey block of flats for birds, provide nesting places safe from marauding land predators such as **foxes** (*Vulpes vulpes*) and rats. It's surprising just how close it's possible to get to **fulmars** (*Fulmarus glacialis*), which return to their nesting ledges in February for the start of the long breeding season that goes on into the autumn. Only in the depths of winter are the cliffs quiet. The Cornish nature reserve at Ropehaven near Black Head is one of the main breeding grounds for fulmars in the UK. Fulmars are related to albatrosses and like them are masters of the air. You can distinguish them from gulls by their ridged, flat wings as they sail the wind close to the waves with the occasional burst of fast flapping. Fulmars are incredibly tenacious at holding their nesting sites and vomit a stinking oily secretion over any intruders, including rock-climbers!

The elegant **kittiwake** (*Rissa tridactyla*), the one true seagull that never feeds on land, is another cliff nester, identified by its 'dipped in ink' black wingtips.

Black above, white below, **manx shearwaters** (*Puffinus puffinus*) make globe-encircling journeys as they sail effortlessly just above even the wildest sea. Small and fast on hard-beating wings, black and white **guillemots** (*Uria troile*) and **razorbills** (*Alca torda*) shoot out from their nesting ledges hidden in the cliffs. There are large colonies around the Godrevy–St Austell area. Guillemots have a long thin bill, razorbill a heavy half circle.

With their unmistakable parrot-shaped bills, **puffins** (*Fratercula arctica*) are a rare prize round these coasts.

Big, rapacious **great black-backed gulls** (*Larus marinus*) cruise the nesting colonies for prey. The second largest breeding colony in Cornwall nests on St George's Island just out to sea from Looe.

Stars of the sea show, however, must be the big, sharp-winged, Persil-white **gannets** (*Morus bassanus*) cruising slowly for fish, then suddenly plunging with folded wings into the sea. Their strengthened skulls protect them from the huge force of the impact with the water.

Two birds more familiar from the artificial cliffs of our cities can be seen here in their natural habitat – **house martins** (*Delichon urbica*), steely-blue backed like a **swallow** (*Hirundo rustica*), but with more V-shaped wings and a distinctive white rump, and **rock doves** (*Columba livia*). These are so mixed with town **pigeons** (*Columba livia domestica*) it's hard to say if any 'pure' wild birds remain, but many individuals with the characteristic grey back, small white rump and two black wing bars can be seen.

Where the path drops steeply to a rocky bay, **oystercatchers** (*Haematopus ostralegus*), with their black and white plumage and spectacular carrot-coloured bill, pipe in panic as they fly off.

This is also a good spot to get close to **shags** (*Phalacrocorax aristotelis*) and **cormorants** (*Phalacrocorax pygmeus*), common all round the coast, swimming low and black in the water. Shags are smaller and are always seen on the sea – cormorants are also on rivers and estuaries – and in the summer have a crest whilst cormorants have a white patch near their tail and white face. Close up, these oily birds shine iridescently; shags are green, cormorants are purple. They are a primitive species and as their feathers are not completely waterproof both must dry themselves after getting wet; their heraldic pose, standing upright with half-spread wings on drying rocks is one of the special sights of the coast path.

On or in the sea

The high cliffs are also a great place from which to look out over the sea. Searching for seals is an enjoyable and essential part of cliff walking. You'll spot lots of grey lobster-pot buoys before your first seal, but it's worth the effort. **Atlantic grey seals** (*Halichoerus grypus*) relax in the water, looking over their big Roman noses with doggy eyes, as interested in you as you are in them. Twice the weight of a red deer, a big bull can be over 200kg. On calm sunny days it's possible to follow them down through the clear water as they dive, as elegant in their element as they are clumsy on land.

Seals generally come ashore only to rest, moult their fur, or to breed. Seals 'haul out' – come up on the rocks – on Godrevy Island (Map 44, p158), the Carracks (Map 51, p171), near Zennor Head, and around Land's End (Map 61, p189) as well as on St George's Island near Looe and your walk to the town's harbour will introduce you to Nelson the seal, so named, unsurprisingly, as he only had one eye. The seal died in 2003, but was such a popular visitor to the harbour that 2008 saw a sculpture of the town's favourite sea-dweller unveiled.

Seal breeding takes place between September and December and the caves below Navax Point (Map 43, p157) are a popular breeding site. It is also possible to see them at the National Seal Sanctuary (see p241) in Gweek.

A cliff-top sighting of Britain's largest fish is also a real possibility, but is more chilling than endearing! **Basking sharks** (*Cetorhinus maximus*) can grow to a massive eleven metres and weigh seven tonnes, and their two fins, a large shark-like dorsal fin followed by a notched tail fin, are so far apart it takes a second look to be convinced it's one fish. But these are gentle giants, cruising slowly with open jaws, filtering microscopic plankton from the sea. You are most likely to see one during late spring and summer when they feed at the surface during calm, warm weather. Look out for coloured or numbered tags, put on for research into this sadly declining species and report them to the address given in the box on p70. Ironically, the Shark Angling Club of Great

THE ENVIRONMENT AND NATURE

❏ **Conservation and the fishing industry**
Small boats crowding sheltered harbours and the sea dotted with crab pot buoys are
constant reminders of this coast's fishing tradition. However, few people now work
full time in fishing. The great pilchard shoals are long gone, probably victims of
changing ocean currents rather than over fishing, but it is over fishing combined with
increasingly sophisticated catching methods that have left Newlyn as the only major
deep sea port. Strict quotas and an EU-sponsored scheme to take boats out of service
is further reducing the fleet. Controversy between different fishing methods focuses
on the damage done by bottom trawling, whilst the accidental catching of seabirds in
the miles-long gill nets catching sea bass has led to restrictions on their use in St Ives
Bay. There is also considerable resentment in Cornwall at the rights of EU partners,
especially the Spanish, to what many see as British waters. Now, for the smaller ports
crab fishing may be the main business with many exported to, ironically, the seafood-
hungry Spanish! Day boats fish inshore under the regulation of the Sea Fisheries'
Committees which make bye-laws within the six-mile limit and tourist boats take visitors fishing for the summer shoals of mackerel.

Britain (🖳 sharkanglingclubofgreatbritain.org.uk) is also based in Cornwall, in
Looe on the south coast.

Taking a longer view and with some good luck, watch the sea for dolphins,
porpoises or even a whale. **Harbour porpoises** (*Phocoena phocoena*) and **bot-
tlenose dolphins** (*Tursiops truncatus*) are the most likely to be seen, in places
like St Ives Bay, Mount's Bay and Falmouth Bay.

Other cetaceans you may catch a glimpse of are **Risso's dolphins**
(*Grampus griseus*), **common dolphins** (*Delphinus delphis*), **striped dolphins**
(*Stenella coeruleoalba*), orcas or **killer whales** (*Orcinus orca*) and **pilot whales**
(*Globicephala melaena*) but, be warned, they are fiendishly difficult to tell
apart: a brief glimpse of a fin is nothing like the 'whole animal' pictures shown
in field guides. Cetacean-spotting boat-trips are ubiquitous on the Cornish coast
and available from most harbour-based settlements.

In pastures, combes and woods
The path rises up onto rich green pasture. **Skylark** (*Alauda arvensis*) soar tune-
fully – almost disappearing into the spring sky, while in winter small green-
brown **meadow pipits** (*Anthus pratensis*) flit weakly, giving a small high-
pitched call. Spring also brings migrant **wheatears** (*Oenanthe oenanthe*): they
are beautiful with their grey and black feathers above, buff and white below, and
unmistakable when they fly and show their distinctive white rump. **Meadow
brown** (*Maniola jurtina*) butterflies flap weakly amongst the long grass.
Buzzard (*Buteo buteo*) soar up with their tilted, broad round wings, giving their
high, wild ke-oow cry. They are probably the most common bird of prey found
in Cornwall.

Rabbits (*Oryctolagus cuniculus*) are one of the few mammals you are likely to see. Prey for buzzard and foxes, they also play a vital role maintaining the
short turf habitat of a range of cliff-top species, including **small copper**

THE ENVIRONMENT AND NATURE

(*Lycaena phlaeas*) butterflies in September and **common blue** (*Polyommatus icarus*) and **small heath** (*Coenonympha pamphilus*) in May and August.

Ravens (*Corvus corax*) cronk-cronk over the cliffs and are distinguished from more common **carrion crows** (*Corvus corone*) by their huge size and wedge-shaped tail. One of the most exciting birds around the Cornish coast is the newly returned **chough** (see box opposite). The **corn bunting** (*Emberiza calandra*) is also a rare sight in Cornwall.

Rain and sun, cold and warmth are normal weather for most of us, but on the coast path the walker soon learns the overwhelming importance of the wind. Dip round a corner into a sheltered combe and suddenly the climate changes. Here are warm bracken slopes and small woodlands. Look out for the big holes and dug-out earth of **badger** (*Meles meles*) setts. Sadly the best chance of seeing a badger is dead on the roadside as they are so shy, and mostly nocturnal like foxes which are equally common, but much shyer than their urban cousins.

In spring familiar birds such as **robins** (*Erithacus rubecula*), **blackbirds** (*Turdus merula*), **blue** and **great tits** (*Parus major & caeruleus*), **chaffinches** (*Fringila coelebs*) and **dunnocks** (*Prunella modularis*) are joined by the small green **chiffchaff** (*Phylloscopus collybita*); it's not much to look at but is one of the earliest returning migrants and unmistakably calls its own name in two repeated notes. **Grey squirrels** (*Sciurus carolinensis*), introduced from North America in the late 19th century, are the other mammal you're most likely to see.

Butterflies such as the **small pearl-bordered fritillary** (*Boloria selene*) come out in May and August in brackeny combes rich in violets. Look out for the spectacular migrants **clouded yellow** (*Colias croceus*), **red admiral** (*Vanessa atalanta*) and **painted lady** (*Vanessa cardui*) in August and September, and the **wall brown** (*Lasiommata megera*) which has declined steeply and is now found almost exclusively near the coast.

In and around estuaries

Descending to the long walk round the estuaries is moving into a different, softer world of shelter and rich farmland. Best for birds in winter, they are a welcome refuge from the ferocity of the worst weather for wildlife and people. There are large flocks of ducks – whistling **wigeon** (*Anas penelope*), a combination of grey and pinky brown, with big white wing patches in flight – and waders like the brown **curlew** (*Numenius arquata*) with its impossibly long, down-curved beak and beautiful sad fluting call, evocative of summer moors.

The **redshank** (*Tringa totanus*), **greenshank** (*Tringa nebularia*), **golden** and **grey plover** (*Pluvialis sp.*) and **black-tailed** and **bar-tailed godwit** (*Limosa sp.*) can also be seen in winter. Look out for the big black, white and chestnut **shelduck** (*Tadorna tadorna*), and for the tall **grey heron** (*Ardea cinerea*), hunched at rest or extended to its full 175cm as it slowly, patiently stalks fish in the shallows. A real rarity 10 years ago, another species of heron, the stunning white **little egret** (*Egretta garzetta*) is now unmissable on Cornish estuaries. Here the more common gull is the nimble **black-headed gull** (*Larus ridibundus*), with its elegant cap, dark in summer but pale in winter. In summer, terns come: the big **sandwich tern** (*Sterna sandvicensis*) with its shaggy black cap and loud rasping call, and the smaller sleeker aerobatic **common tern** (*Sterna hirundo*). The Tamar, Looe River, Fal and Hayle estuaries are all good hunting grounds for numerous waders including the curlew, redshank and dunlin.

After near extinction, owing to pollution, **otters** (*Lutra lutra*) are returning to the rivers in Cornwall, though they are still very hard to see – look out for a slithering, lithe shape, or a dog-like head poking out from the water as they swim.

On sand dunes and heath and around mines
Sand dunes swarm with butterflies in high summer and the scarce **silver studded blue** (*Plebeius argus*) can be seen at Holywell Dunes west of Newquay in July and August. Dry heathland provides the warmth needed for reptiles such as **adders** (*Vipera berus*), **slow worms** (*Anguis fragilis*), a type of legless lizard that is commonly mistaken for a snake, and the **common lizard** (*Lacerta vivipara*) seen on the heath vegetation of cliff tops. They sun themselves on rocks or old mining spoil heaps. With their distinctive and beautiful brown, diamond-patterned backs, **adders** are our only poisonous snake, but they pose little risk to people in walking boots. Except in spring when the cold can make them sluggish, they quickly move off the path when they feel the vibration of feet.

You are very unlikely to see another beneficiary of mining, the **greater horseshoe bat** (*Rhinolophus ferrumequinum*). Old mine shafts where bats live have been covered with bat-friendly metal grilles rather than capped with concrete so they can still come and go. The most common bat is the smaller **pipistrelle** (*Pipistrellus pipistrellus*), but all bats are hard to tell apart in the dusk light.

FLORA

Cornwall is best known for its springtime flora when the cliff tops have spectacular displays of wildflowers. Being the most southerly county, flowers tend to come out in Cornwall earlier than in the rest of Britain; **daffodils** (*Narcissus sp.*) and **wild primroses** (*Primula vulgaris*) start to make an appearance as early

---

❏ **Choughs**
There is one very special and exciting thrill for walkers on The Lizard and West Penwith – against all the odds, Cornwall's emblem bird, the chough (Pyrrhocorax pyrrhocorax), has returned to nest! This stunning little crow, jet black with a bright red beak and legs, is packed with charisma; it's superbly agile in the air and charming on the ground as it pecks, in small flocks, for insects. The chough needs tight, low-grazed turf on the cliff edges. Over the years, flatter pastures were improved with fertiliser and the grass grew too long for choughs, and grazing was abandoned on the steep, rough slopes. Now, as you walk the cliff paths there's a good chance of seeing hardy Dartmoor ponies and Dexter cattle grazing the cliff edge. Pioneered by the National Trust, the improved habitat has allowed choughs to return.

From April to June there's a chough watchpoint most afternoons at the southerly point on the Lizard, from which choughs can be seen near the crevice in the cliff where they nest. All year round they can be seen between Mullion and this southerly point.

For updates on choughs visit Cornwall Bird Watching & Preservation Society's website (🖥 cbwps.org.uk).

as January. Trees find it difficult to grow on the coast except in sheltered valleys. **Blackthorn** (*Prunus spinosa*), **gorse** (*Ulex sp.*) and **elder** (*Sambucus nigra*) provide some windbreak.

When identifying wild plants it is best to identify the habitat first as this should considerably narrow your search.

Heathland

Heathland once used to stretch right across Cornwall from the Lizard to St Agnes and from Bodmin Moor in the east of the county to the Atlantic coast, covering an area of 80,000ha. Now just 7000ha remain of this internationally important habitat. Much of it has been destroyed by farming but there are still significant tracts around both St Agnes and the Lizard, as well as smaller coastal patches between St Ives and Land's End. Surprisingly, much of this has survived because of the mining industry (see box on p180).

Heather and associated species thrive on land contaminated by mine waste, preferring an acidic, nutrient-poor environment where there is little competition from other plants as few can tolerate such inhospitable territory. The unique nature of the Lizard is also a consequence of poor soil, caused by the underlying serpentine rock, which has similarly saved much of the area from the plough.

Heathland is at its best in August and September when it is ablaze with pinks, purples and yellow. Among the different types of heather found are **common heather** (*Calluna vulgaris*), **bell heather** (*Erica cinerea*), **cross-leaved heather** (*E. tetralix*) and **Dorset heather** (*E. ciliaris*), as well as **Cornish heath** (*E. vagans*), the Lizard being the only place in the world where it is found. **Common gorse** (*Ulex europaeus*) and **western gorse** (*U. gallii*) often grows amongst the heather. Other plants to look out for are **dyer's greenweed** (*Genista tinctoria*), **dwarf burnet** (*Rosa pimpinellifolia pumila*), **burnet rose** (*Rosa pimpinellifolia*), **betony** (*Betonica officinalis*), **bloody cranesbill** (*Geranium sanguineum*), **milkwort** (*Polygala sp.*), **dropwort** (*Filipendula vulgaris*), **heath-spotted orchid** (*Dactylorhiza maculata*) as well as **yellow bartsia** (*Parentucellia viscosa*) and **red bartsia** (*Odontites verna*).

Cropped turf

Traditionally farmed land is an important habitat for many wildflowers in Britain because the low-intensity grazing controls scrub and trees while allow-

> ❑ **Lizard flora**
> There are a number of rare plants found on the Lizard Peninsula growing in rough grassland and cropped turf. They include thyme broomrape (*Orobanche alba*), fringed rupturewort (*Herniaria ciliolata*), hairy greenweed (*Genista pilosa*), and green-winged orchid (*Orchis morio*). Cornish heath (*Erica vagans*) is a very special plant as it is unique to the area.

(Opposite) Top: Purple heather and orange crocosmia (an invasive garden escapee) brighten the trail between Porthtowan and Portreath. In the distance stands the ruin of an old mining tower. **Bottom**: A view from above – Land's End with Sennen Cove just visible to the north. (Photo © Bryn Thomas).

THE ENVIRONMENT AND NATURE

Above, clockwise from top left: **1**. Grey heron. **2**. Curlew. **3**. Shelduck. **4**. Chaffinch. **5**. Pied wagtail. **6**. Reed bunting. **7**. Redshank. (All ©BT).

Above, clockwise from top left : **1**. Herring gull. **2**. Oystercatchers. **3**. Puffin. **4**. Razorbill. **5**. Atlantic grey seal (© Joel Newton). **6**. Black headed gull. **7**. Great black-backed gull. (All ©BT).

Peacock
Inachis io

Small Tortoiseshell
Aglais urticae

Small Pearl-Bordered Fritillary
Boloria selene

Brimstone
Gonepteryx rhamni

Common Blue
Polyommatus icarus

Painted Lady
Vanessa cadui

Small Copper
Lycaena phlaeas

Red Admiral
Vanessa atalanta

Meadow
Brown
Maniola jurtina

Large Garden/
Cabbage White
Pieris brassicae

Clouded Yellow
Colias croceus

Mesembryanthemum

Tree Echium
Echium (species)

Sea Holly
Eryngium maritimum

Bell Heather
Erica cinerea

Heather (Ling)
Calluna vulgaris

Thrift (Sea Pink)
Armeria maritima

Rosebay Willowherb
Epilobium angustifolium

Common Vetch
Vicia sativa

Forget-me-not
Myosotis arvensis

Rowan (tree)
Sorbus aucuparia

Hottentot Fig
Carpobrutus edulis

Red Campion
Silene dioica

Common Dog Violet
Viola riviniana

Common Centaury
Centaurium erythraea

Common/Spear Thistle
Cirsium vulgare

Ramsons (Wild Garlic)
Allium ursinum

Germander Speedwell
Veronica chamaedrys

Herb-Robert
Geranium robertianum

Lousewort
Pedicularis sylvatica

Self-heal
Prunella vulgaris

Scarlet Pimpernel
Anagallis arvensis

Sea Campion
Silene maritima

Bluebell
Hyacinthoides non-scripta

Hogweed
Heracleum sphondylium

Dog Rose
Rosa canina

Meadow Buttercup
Ranunculis acris

Gorse
Ulex europaeus

Tormentil
Potentilla erecta

Birdsfoot-trefoil
Lotus corniculatus

Ox-eye Daisy
Leucanthemum vulgare

Common Ragwort
Senecio jacobaea

Primrose
Primula vulgaris

Cowslip
Primula veris

Yarrow
Achillea millefolium

Wall Pennywort
Umbilicus rupestris

Honeysuckle
Lonicera periclymemum

ing less aggressive plants to flourish. Unfortunately, traditional methods are being eroded by intensive farming practices such as heavy grazing and the widespread use of herbicides leading to a reduction, and even loss of, many species. However, in a few places low-intensity grazing has been reintroduced.

Short cropped turf is brilliant with flowers from early spring. The most common ones are **thrift**, or **sea pink** (*Armeria maritima*), **spring squill** (*Scilla verna*), **kidney vetch** (*Anthyllis vulneraria*) and **sea campion** (*Silene maritima*). Other wild flowers to look out for are **dyer's greenweed** (*Genista tinctoria*), **sheep's bit** (*Jasione montana*) and **bird's foot trefoil** (*Lotus corniculatus*). Rather unusually you may also come across swathes of **bluebells** (*Endymion non-scriptus*) on the cliff tops. Bluebells are more commonly associated with woodland, but can also be indicators of ancient woods.

Lime-rich grasslands
Soils in Cornwall are generally acidic, although in some areas coastal grasslands are 'limed' by windblown sand consisting of tiny shell fragments. Kelsey Head (Map 32, p141) is a good example of this type of habitat. **Cowslips** (*Primula veris*) grow in abundance and other lime-lovers are **salad burnet** (*Poterium sanguisorba*), **pyramidal orchids** (*Anacamptis pyramidalis*), **autumn lady's tresses orchids** (*Spiranthes spiralis*), **wild clary** (*Salvia horminoides*), **carline thistle** (*Carlina vulgaris*), **pale flax** (*Linum bienne*), **Cornish gentian** (*Gentianella anglica ssp. Cornubiensis*), and **hairy greenweed** (*Genista pilosa*).

Dunes
Dunes are formed by wind action creating a fragile, unstable environment. Among the first colonisers is **marram grass** (*Ammophila arenaria*) which is able to withstand drought, exposure to wind and salt spray and has an ability to grow up through new layers of sand that cover it. Other specialist plants are **sea holly** (*Eryngium maritimum*), **sea spurge** (*Euphorbia paralias*) and **sea bindweed** (*Calystegia soldanella*). The one thing that these seemingly indomitable plants can't tolerate is trampling by human feet; stay on the path which is nearly always well marked through dunes.

Hedges and field margins
Cornish hedges are not your stereotypical neat row of planted trees and shrubs. They are more like a wall than a hedge as they are constructed from stones and earth. In time, they provide a habitat for all types of vegetation ranging from simple mosses and grasses to fully fledged trees which are allowed to grow along the top of the hedges. Along with rough grassland at field edges these habitats provide a wildlife corridor and refuge for many species of wildflowers and small mammals such as voles and shrews.

Some flowers that you may see are **violets** (*Viola riviniana*), **lesser celandine** (*Ranunculus ficaria*), **red campion** (*Silene dioica*), **Alexanders** (*Smyrnium olusatrum*), **hogweed** (*Heracleum sphondylium*), **yarrow** (*Achillea millefolium*) and **foxgloves** (*Digitalis purpurea*).

THE ENVIRONMENT AND NATURE

(**Opposite**): Red hot poker display below St Michael's Mount. (Photo © Henry Stedman).

Gardens

The warm climate in Cornwall means that some plants not normally found in the British Isles thrive both in gardens and in sheltered areas in the wild as gar-

---

❏ CONSERVATION SCHEMES – WHAT'S AN AONB?

It is perhaps the chief joy of this walk that much of it is spent in an Area of Outstanding Natural Beauty (AONB). But what exactly is this, and other, designations and what protection do they actually confer?

National Parks

The highest level of landscape protection is the designation of land as a **National Park** (🖳 nationalparks.gov.uk). This designation recognises the national importance of an area in terms of landscape, biodiversity and as a recreational resource. However, it does not signify national ownership and they are not uninhabited wildernesses, making conservation a knife-edged balance between protecting the environment and the rights and livelihoods of those living in the park. There are 15 in Britain of which nine are in England but there are no national parks in Cornwall.

Areas of Outstanding Natural Beauty

The second level of protection is **Area of Outstanding Natural Beauty** (AONB; 🖳 landscapesforlife.org.uk); there are 48 AONBs in the UK; 33 wholly in England. Much of the South-West Coast Path crosses land covered by either this designation or its close relative **Heritage Coasts**, of which there are currently 32 in England. The primary objective of AONBs is conservation of the natural beauty of a landscape. As there is no statutory administrative framework for their management, this is the responsibility of the local authority within whose boundaries they fall.

    Cornwall AONB (🖳 cornwall-aonb.gov.uk) covers 958 sq km and covers 12 different areas including 10 stretches of the Cornish Coastline, the Camel Estuary and Bodmin Moor. One of the coastal areas, Hartland, is covered in the first guide (Exmoor and North Devon Coast Path) in this series. The others are in this guide: Pentire Point to Widemouth; Trevose Head to Stepper Point; St Agnes; Godrevy to Portreath; West Penwith; South Coast Western ie Lizard to Marazion & Helford River; South Coast Central ie Mylor and Roseland to Porthpean; South Coast Eastern ie Par Sands to Looe; and Rame Head which is from east of Whitsand Bay to east of Penlee Point.

National Nature Reserves and Sites of Special Scientific Interest

The next level of protection includes **National Nature Reserves** (NNRs) and **Sites of Special Scientific Interest** (SSSIs).

    There are 224 **NNRs** in England of which three are in Cornwall (the Lizard; Golitha Falls on the southern edge of Bodmin, and Goss Moor at the headwaters of the River Fal). The coast path passes through the Lizard NNR, an area of 1662 hectares, which was established to protect a rich collection of rare plant species.

    There are over 4100 **SSSIs** in England ranging in size from little pockets protecting wild flower meadows, important nesting sites (such as Loe Pool), or special geological features, to vast swathes of upland, moorland and wetland. SSSIs are a particularly important designation as they have some legal standing. They are managed in partnership with the owners and occupiers of the land who must give written notice before initiating any operations likely to damage the site and who cannot proceed without consent from **Natural England** (🖳 gov.uk/government/organisations/natural-england), the single body responsible for identifying, establishing and managing National Parks, Areas of Outstanding Natural Beauty, National Nature Reserves, Sites of Special Scientific Interest, and Special Areas of Conservation.

den escapees. These include the **tree echium** (from the Canary Islands), succulents such as the **aeonium** (Canary Islands) and **mesembryanthemum** (South Africa) species and purple **agapanthus** lilies, also from South Africa.

Special Area of Conservation (SAC) is an international designation which came into being as a result of the 1992 Earth Summit in Rio de Janeiro, Brazil. This European-wide network of sites is designed to promote the conservation of habitats, wild animals and plants, both on land and at sea. At the time of writing 236 land sites in England had been designated as SACs.

National Trails
The Cornwall coast path is a section of the South-West Coast Path, one of 15 National Trails in England and Wales. These are Britain's flagship long-distance paths which grew out of the post-war desire to protect the country's special places, a movement which also gave birth to National Parks and AONBs.

National Trails in England are largely funded by Natural England and are managed on the ground by a National Trail Officer. They coordinate the maintenance work undertaken by either the local highway authority, or the National Trust, where it crosses their land, and ensure that the trail is kept up to nationally agreed standards.

Conservation and campaigning organisations
These voluntary organisations started the conservation movement in the mid 19th century and are still at the forefront of developments. Independent of government and reliant on public support, they can concentrate their resources either on acquiring land which can then be managed purely for conservation purposes, or on influencing political decision-makers by lobbying and campaigning. Managers and owners of land include well-known bodies such as:

● **National Trust** (🖥 nationaltrust.org.uk) A charity with 3.4 million members which aims to protect, through ownership, threatened coastline, countryside, historic houses, castles and gardens, and archaeological remains for everyone to enjoy. The trust owns over 40% of the Cornish coastline, as well as sites such as the Old Post Office (see p98) in Tintagel and Godrevy Point (see p158).

● **English Heritage** (🖥 english-heritage.org.uk) Previously a statutory organisation, in 2015 English Heritage became a charity that looks after and conserves the National Heritage collection of over 400 historic buildings, including Tintagel Castle (see p98) and Pendennis Castle (see p258).

● **Royal Society for the Protection of Birds** (RSPB; 🖥 rspb.org.uk) The largest voluntary conservation body in Europe focusing on providing a healthy environment for birds and wildlife and with over a million members, and 150 reserves in the UK including two on the coast path: Hayle Estuary (p160) and Marazion Marsh (p208).

● The umbrella organisation for the 47 wildlife trusts in the UK is **The Wildlife Trusts** (🖥 wildlifetrusts.org). **Cornwall Wildlife Trust** (🖥 cornwallwildlifetrust .org.uk) is the largest voluntary organisation (800,000 members) in the county concerned with all aspects of nature conservation. They own over 55 nature reserves.

● **Marine Conservation Society** (🖥 mcsuk.org) A national charity dedicated solely to protecting the marine environment and its wildlife.

● **Butterfly Conservation** (🖥 butterfly-conservation.org) was formed in 1968 by some naturalists who were alarmed at the decline in the number of butterflies, and moths, and who aimed to reverse the situation. They have more than 30 branches throughout the British Isles and operate 33 nature reserves and also sites where butterflies are likely to be found. For further information contact the Cornwall branch.

THE ENVIRONMENT AND NATURE

3

MINIMUM IMPACT & OUTDOOR SAFETY

Minimum impact walking

By visiting Cornwall you are having a positive impact, not just on your own well-being, but on local communities as well. Your presence brings money and jobs into the local economy and also pride in and awareness of Cornwall's environment and culture. Cornwall receives over four million visitors annually (with the coast path attracting at least a quarter of those) who bring an estimated £1.8 billion into the regional economy.

However, the environment should not be considered only in terms of its value as a tourist asset. Its long-term survival and enjoyment by future generations will only be possible if both visitors and local communities protect it now. The following points are made to help you reduce your impact on the environment, encourage conservation and promote sustainable tourism in the area.

ECONOMIC IMPACT

Support local businesses

Rural businesses and communities in Britain have been hit hard in recent years by a seemingly endless series of crises. Most people are aware of the country code – not dropping litter and closing the gate behind you are still as pertinent as ever – but in light of the economic pressures there is something else you can do: **buy local**.

Look and ask for local produce to buy and eat; not only does this cut down on the amount of pollution and congestion that the transportation of food creates (the so-called 'food miles'), but also ensures that you are supporting local farmers and producers; the very people who have moulded the countryside you have come to see and who are in the best position to protect it. If you can find local food which is also organic so much the better.

It's a fact of life that money spent at local level – perhaps in a market, or at the greengrocer, or in an independent pub – has a far greater impact for good on that community than the equivalent spent in a branch of a national chain store or restaurant. While no-one would advocate that walkers should boycott the larger supermarkets, which after all do provide local employment, it's worth remembering that businesses in rural communities rely heavily on visitors for their very existence. If we want to keep these shops and post offices, we need to use them.

The website ⌨ foodfromcornwall.co.uk lists the various **farmers' markets** and farm shops in Cornwall.

ENVIRONMENTAL IMPACT

A walking holiday in itself is an environmentally friendly approach to tourism. The following are some ideas on how you can go a few steps further in helping to minimise your impact on the environment while walking the South-West Coast Path.

Use public transport whenever possible

More use of public transport encourages the provision of better services which benefits visitors, local people and the global environment. During peak periods traffic congestion in Cornwall is a major headache and you're doing yourself (and everyone else in the vehicle with you) a big favour by avoiding it. There's detailed information in this book on public transport services; turn to pp52-6 to make good use of it.

Never leave litter

Litter is a worldwide problem that is unsightly, pollutes the environment and kills wildlife. **Please** carry a rubbish bag with you so you can dispose of rubbish in a bin at the next town rather than dropping it. You can even help by picking up a few pieces of litter that other people leave behind.

● The lasting impact of litter You may think a small piece of rubbish has little effect but consider the following: silver foil lasts 18 months; textiles hang around for 15 years; a plastic bag lasts for 10 to 12 years and an aluminium drinks can will last for 85 years on the ground, or 75 years in the sea. An estimated one million seabirds and 100,000 marine mammals and sea turtles die every year from entanglement in, or ingestion of, plastics.

● Is it OK if it's biodegradable? Not really. Even a bit of orange peel takes six months to decompose. Apple cores, banana skins and the like are not only unsightly but they encourage flies, ants and wasps and can ruin a picnic spot for others.

Consider walking out of season

By walking the coast path at less busy times of the year you help to reduce overuse of the path at peak periods. Many fragile habitats, such as dunes, are unable to withstand the heavy use and consequent trampling. You also help to generate year-round income for local services and may find your holiday a more relaxing experience; there'll be less stress involved in finding accommodation and fewer people on the trail.

Erosion

Erosion is a natural process on any coastline, but it's accelerated by thousands of pairs of feet. Do your best to **stay on the main trail** and use managed footpaths wherever possible. If you are walking during the winter, or a particularly

MINIMUM IMPACT & OUTDOOR SAFETY

❏ **Reporting wildlife sightings**
Report basking shark sightings to the **Marine Conservation Society** (see box p67) by going to Species the Basking Shark where there is a report form to fill in, or send an A5 stamped addressed envelope to receive a basking shark report card. Remember to note any tags you've spotted. Reports are greatly appreciated.

If you see any of the other larger marine creatures such as dolphins, whales, seals and turtles you can report them online through **Seaquest South West Cornwall**, part of **Cornwall Wildlife Trust** (see box p67), giving the location, number and the direction they were heading in.

If you come across a stranded marine animal like a dolphin or porpoise, don't approach it but contact either **British Divers Marine Life Rescue** (office hours ☎ 01825-765546; out of office hours ☎ 07787-433412, 🖳 bdmlr.org.uk) or the RSPCA hotline (☎ 0300-123 4999, 🖳 rspca.org.uk).

---

wet period, be aware that braiding (the creation of more than one path) usually occurs when the path is muddy. Come prepared with good walking boots that don't mind a little dirt.

Respect all wildlife
Remember that all wildlife you come across on the coast path has just as much right to be there as you. Tempting as it may be to pick wild flowers you should leave all flora alone so the next people who pass can enjoy the sight as well. You never know if you may be inadvertently picking a rare flower, destroying its chances of future survival.

If you come across young animals or birds leave them alone. Every year hundreds of well-meaning but misguided people hand in supposedly abandoned young to the RSPCA, when in fact the only thing keeping the mother away was them.

The code of the outdoor loo
As more and more people discover the joys of walking in the natural environment issues such as how to go to the loo outdoors rapidly gain importance. How many of us have shaken our heads at the sight of toilet paper strewn beside the path, or even worse, someone's dump left in full view? Human excrement is not only offensive to our senses but, more importantly, can infect water sources.

Where to go The coast path is a high-use area and many habitats will not benefit from your fertilisation. As far as 'number twos' are concerned try whenever possible to **use public toilets**. There is no shortage of public toilets along the coast path and they are all marked on the trail maps. However, there are those times when the only time is now. If you have to go outdoors help the environment to deal with your deposit in the best possible way by following a few simple guidelines:

● **Choose your site carefully** It should be at least 30 metres away from running water, beyond the high tide mark and not on any site of historical or archaeological interest. Carry a small trowel or use a sturdy stick to **dig a small hole** about 15cm (6") deep to bury your faeces in. Faeces decompose quicker when in contact with the top layer of soil or leaf mould; by using a stick to stir loose soil into your deposit you will speed decomposition up even more. Do not squash it under rocks as this slows down the decomposition process. If you have to use rocks as a cover make sure they are not in contact with your faeces.

● **Pack out toilet paper and tampons** Toilet paper takes a long time to decompose whether buried or not. It is easily dug up by animals and may then blow into water sources or onto the trail. The best method for dealing with used toilet paper is to pack it out. Put it in a paper bag placed inside a plastic bag and then dispose of it at the next toilet. Tampons and sanitary towels also need to be packed out in a similar way. They take years to decompose and may be dug up and scattered about by animals.

ACCESS

Access to the countryside has always been a hot topic in Britain. In the 1940s soldiers coming back from World War II were horrified and disgruntled to find that landowners were denying them the right to walk across the moors; ironically the very country that they had been fighting to protect. After a long campaign to allow greater public access to areas of countryside in England and Wales, the Countryside & Rights of Way Act 2000 (CRoW), or 'Right to Roam' as dubbed by walkers, came into effect in 2005.

All those who enjoy access to the countryside must respect the land, its wildlife, the interests of those who live and work there and other users; we all share a common interest in the countryside. Knowing your rights and responsibilities gives you the information you need to act with minimal impact.

Rights of way

As a designated **National Trail** the coast path is a **public right of way**. A public right of way is either a footpath, a bridleway or a byway. The Cornwall coast path is a footpath for almost all its length which means that anyone has the legal right to use it on foot only.

Rights of way are theoretically established because the owner has dedicated them to public use. However, very few paths are formally dedicated in this way. If members of the public have been using a path without interference for 20 years or more the law assumes the owner has intended to dedicate it as a right of way. If a path has been unused for 20 years it does not cease to exist; the guiding principle is 'once a highway, always a highway'.

On a public right of way you have the right to 'pass and repass along the way' which includes stopping to rest or admire the view, or to consume refreshments. You can also take with you a 'natural accompaniment' (!) which includes a dog, but it must be kept under close control (see pp336-8).

Farmers and land managers must ensure that paths are not blocked by crops or other vegetation, or otherwise obstructed, that the route is identifiable and the surface is restored soon after cultivation. If crops are growing over the path you have every right to walk through them, following the line of the right of way as closely as possible. If you find a path blocked or impassable you should report it to the appropriate **highway authority**. Highway authorities are responsible for maintaining footpaths. In Cornwall the highway authority is **Cornwall Council**. The council is also the surveying authority with responsibility for maintaining the official definitive map of public rights of way.

Wider access

The access situation to land around the coast path is a little more complicated. Trying to unravel and understand the seemingly thousands of different laws and acts is never easy in any legal system. Parliamentary Acts give a right to walk

---

❏ THE COUNTRYSIDE CODE

The Countryside Code, originally described in the 1950s as the Country Code, was revised and relaunched in 2004, in part because of the changes brought about by the CRoW Act (see opposite); it was updated again in 2012, 2014 and also 2016. The Code seems like common sense but sadly some people still appear to have no understanding of how to treat the countryside they walk in. An adapted version of the 2016 Code, launched under the logo 'Respect. Protect. Enjoy.', is given below:

Respect other people
● **Consider the local community and other people enjoying the outdoors** Be sensitive to the needs and wishes of those who live and work there. If, for example, farm animals are being moved or gathered keep out of the way and follow the farmer's directions. Being courteous and friendly to those you meet will ensure a healthy future for all based on partnership and co-operation.
● **Leave gates and property as you find them and follow paths unless wider access is available** A farmer normally closes gates to keep farm animals in, but may sometimes leave them open so the animals can reach food and water. Leave machinery and farm animals alone – if you think an animal is in distress try to alert the farmer instead. Use gates, stiles or gaps in field boundaries if you can – climbing over walls, hedges and fences can damage them and increase the risk of farm animals escaping.

Protect the natural environment
● **Leave no trace of your visit and take your litter home** Take special care not to damage, destroy or remove features such as rocks, plants and trees. Take your litter with you. Litter and leftover food doesn't just spoil the beauty of the countryside, it can be dangerous to wildlife and farm animals. Fires can be as devastating to wildlife and habitats as they are to people and property – so be careful with naked flames and cigarettes at any time of the year.
● **Keep dogs under effective control** This means that you should keep your dog on a lead or keep it in sight at all times, be aware of what it's doing and be confident it will return to you promptly on command. Across farmland dogs should always be kept on a short lead. During lambing time they should not be taken with you at all (see pp336-8). Always clean up after your dog and get rid of the mess responsibly – 'bag it and bin it'.

Enjoy the outdoors
● **Plan ahead and be prepared** You're responsible for your own safety: be prepared for natural hazards, changes in weather and other events. Wild animals, farm animals and horses can behave unpredictably if you get too close, especially if they're with their young – so give them plenty of space.
● **Follow advice and local signs** In some areas there may be temporary diversions in place. Take notice of these and other local trail advice.

over certain areas of land such as some, but by no means all, common land and some specific places such as Dartmoor and the New Forest. However, in other places, such as Bodmin Moor and many British beaches, right of access is not written in law. It is merely tolerated by the landowner and could be terminated at any time.

Some landowners, such as the Forestry Commission, water companies and the National Trust, are obliged by law to allow some degree of access to their land. Land covered by schemes such as the Environmental Stewardship Scheme gives landowners a financial incentive to manage their land for conservation and to provide limited public access. There are also a few truly altruistic landowners who have allowed access over their land and these include organisations such as the RSPB, the Woodland Trust, and some local authorities. Overall, however, access to most of Britain's countryside is forbidden to the public, in marked contrast to the general rights of access that prevail in other European countries.

Right to roam

For many years groups such as **Ramblers** (see box p46) and **The British Mountaineering Council** (🖳 thebmc.co.uk) campaigned for new and wider access legislation. This finally bore fruit in the form of the Countryside and Rights of Way Act of November 2000, colloquially known as the CRoW Act, which granted access for 'recreation on foot' to mountain, moor, heath, down and registered common land in England and Wales. In essence it allows walkers the freedom to roam responsibly away from footpaths, without being accused of trespass, on about four million acres of open, uncultivated land.

On 28 August 2005 the South-West became the sixth region in England/Wales to be opened up under this act; however, restrictions may still be in place from time to time – check the situation on 🖳 openaccess.gov.uk.

Natural England (see p66) has mapped the new agreed areas of open access and they are also clearly marked on all the latest Ordnance Survey Explorer (1:25,000) maps. In the future it is hoped that the legislation can be extended to include other types of land such as cliff, foreshore, woodland, riverside and canal side.

❏ **Cornish words and place names**

Along the coast path you will come across many place names which are easily translated once you've become familiar with a few Cornish words. To get you started here are some of the most common words used in place names.

Boel/Voel – cliff	*Kellys* lost, hidden or	*Ros* – heath or moor
Bos/Bud – dwelling	grove	*Tol* – holed
Carrack – rock	*Men/Maen* – stone	*Towan* – sandhill
Chy – house	*Mor* – sea	*Tre* – hamlet or homestead
Cornovii – cliff castles	*oggy* – pastyl	*Treath* – beach
Dinas – hill fort	*Penn/Pen/Pedn* – headland	*Wheal* – mine
Dhu/Du – black	*Pol* – pool	*Zawn* – cleft
Enys – island	*Porth* – harbour or cove	

Health and outdoor safety

AVOIDANCE OF HAZARDS

Swimming

If you are not an experienced swimmer or familiar with the sea, plan ahead and swim at beaches where there is a lifeguard service; these beaches have all been marked on the trail maps. On such beaches you should swim between the red and yellow flags as this is the patrolled area. Don't swim between black-and-white chequered flags as these areas are only for surfboards. If there is a red flag flying this indicates that it is dangerous to enter the water. If you are not sure about anything ask one of the lifeguards; after all they are there to help you.

If you are going to swim at unsupervised beaches never do so alone and always take care. Some beaches are prone to strong rips. Never swim off headlands or near river mouths as there may be strong currents running. Always be aware of changing weather conditions and tidal movement. Cornwall has a huge tidal range and it can be very easy to get cut off by the tide.

If you see someone in difficulty do not attempt a rescue until you have contacted the coastguard (see box on p77). Once you know help is on the way try to assist the person by throwing something to help them stay afloat. Many beaches have rescue equipment located in red boxes; these are marked on the trail maps.

❑ Beware of the cow!

Most people are aware of the dangers of bulls – indeed, there are restrictions placed upon farmers who mustn't allow adult bulls to graze in fields that are crossed by a public right of way – but few people realise that cows can also be dangerous. Each year there are reports of people who have been attacked, or even trampled to death by cows; in the six years preceding 2015, 12 people in the UK were killed in such attacks and a study completed in January 2016 reported 54 cow attacks on walkers over the preceding 20 years.

Cows are particularly protective if there are young calves in the herd, but even without any calves around, a herd of cows can suddenly be spooked, either by a walker or, more likely, by a walker's dog. If you find yourself in a field of worryingly aggressive cattle, move away as carefully and quietly as possible, and if you feel threatened by them let go of your dog's lead and let it run free rather than try to protect it and risk endangering yourself. Your dog will outrun the cows. You might not be able to.

Those without canine companions should follow similar advice; move away calmly, do not panic and make no sudden noises. Chances are the cows will leave you alone once they establish that you pose no threat.

If you come to a field of cows with calves in the herd, think twice about crossing the field; if you can, go another way.

You can report incidents involving dangerous cattle at 🖥 killercows.co.uk.

Walking alone

If you are walking alone you must appreciate and be prepared for the increased risk. Take particular note of the safety guidelines below.

Safety on the Coast Path

Sadly every year people are injured walking along the trail, though usually it's nothing more than a badly twisted ankle. Parts of Cornwall can be pretty remote, however, and it certainly pays to take precautions when walking. Abiding by the following rules should minimise the risks:

- Avoid walking on your own if possible.
- Make sure that someone knows your plans for every day you are on the trail. This could be the place you plan to stay in at the end of each day's walk or a friend or relative whom you have promised to call every night. That way, if you fail to turn up or call, they can raise the alarm.
- If the weather closes in suddenly and fog or mist descends and you become uncertain of the correct trail, do not be tempted to continue. Just wait where you are and you'll find that mist often clears, at least for long enough to allow you to get your bearings. If you are still uncertain and the weather doesn't look like improving, return the way you came to the nearest point of civilisation and try again another time when conditions have improved.
- Always fill your water bottle or pouch at every available opportunity (don't empty it until you are certain you can fill it again) and ensure you have some food such as high-energy snacks.
- Always carry a torch, compass, map, whistle and wet-weather gear with you; a mobile phone can be useful though you cannot always rely on getting good reception, if any reception at all.
- Wear strong sturdy boots with good ankle support and a good grip, not trainers.
- Be extra vigilant with children.

Fitness

You will enjoy your walk more if you have a reasonable level of fitness. Carrying a pack for five to seven hours a day is demanding and any preparation you have done beforehand will pay off.

Water

You need to drink lots of water while you're walking; 3-5 litres per day depending on the weather. If you start to feel tired, lethargic or get a headache it may be that you are not drinking enough. Thirst is not a good indicator of when to drink; stop and have a drink every hour or two. A good indication of whether you are drinking enough is the colour of your urine, the lighter the better. If you are not needing to urinate much and your urine is dark yellow you need to increase your fluid intake.

Hypothermia

Hypothermia, or exposure, occurs when the body can't generate enough heat to maintain its core temperature. It's usually as a result of being wet, cold, unprotected from the wind, tired and hungry. It is easily avoided by wearing suitable clothing (see pp42-3), carrying and consuming enough food and drink and being aware of the weather conditions. Check the morale of your companions. Early signs to watch for are feeling cold and tired with involuntary shivering. Find some shelter as soon as possible and warm the person up with a hot drink and some chocolate or other high-energy food. If possible give them another warm layer of clothing and allow them to rest until feeling better.

If allowed to worsen, strange behaviour, slurring of speech and poor co-ordination will become apparent and the victim can quickly progress into unconsciousness, followed by coma and death. Quickly get the victim out of wind and rain, improvising a shelter if necessary. Rapid restoration of bodily warmth is essential and best achieved by bare-skin contact: someone should get into the same sleeping bag as the patient, both having stripped to their under-wear, any spare clothing under or over them to build up heat. Send urgently for help.

Hyperthermia
Heat exhaustion is often caused by water depletion and is a serious condition that could eventually lead to death. Symptoms include thirst, fatigue, giddiness, a rapid pulse, raised body temperature, low urine output and later on, delirium and coma. The only remedy is to re-establish water balance. If the victim is suffering severe muscle cramps it may be due to salt depletion.

Heatstroke is caused by failure of the body's temperature-regulating system and is extremely serious. It is associated with a very high body temperature and an absence of sweating. Early symptoms can be similar to those of hypothermia, such as aggressive behaviour, lack of co-ordination and so on. Later the victim goes into a coma or convulsions and death will follow if effective treatment is not given. To treat heatstroke sponge the victim down or cover with wet towels and vigorously fan them. Get help immediately.

Sunburn
Even on overcast days the sun still has the power to burn. Sunburn can be avoided by regularly applying sunscreen. Don't forget your lips and those areas affected by reflected light off the ground; under your nose, ears and chin. You should always wear a sun hat too, especially in mid-summer. If you have particularly fair skin wear a light, long-sleeved top and trousers.

Footcare
Caring for your feet is vital; you're not going to get far if they are out of action. Wash and dry them properly at the end of the day, change your socks frequently and if it is warm enough take your boots and socks off when you stop for lunch to allow your feet to dry out in the sun.

Blisters can make or break a walk and the best treatment for them really is prevention. All methods of prevention work on the idea of reducing friction between the skin and the boot. You need to take action as soon as you feel a rub developing, don't make the mistake of waiting just a little longer. There are many different ideas around, but one of the most effective is to strap the

❏ **Dealing with an accident**
● Use basic first aid to treat any injuries to the best of your ability.
● Try to attract the attention of anybody else who may be in the area. The **emergency signal** is six blasts on a whistle, or six flashes with a torch.
● If possible leave someone with the casualty while others go for help. If there is nobody else, you have a dilemma. If you decide to get help leave all spare clothing and food with the casualty.
● Telephone ☎ **999** and ask for the coastguard. They are responsible for dealing with any emergency that occurs on the coast or at sea. Make sure you know exactly where you are before you call.
● Report the exact position of the casualty and their condition.

affected area with tape; waterproof tape that has a smooth shiny surface works best. You may need to do this for a quite a few days until the skin toughens up.

If you've left it too late and you already have a blister one of the best ways to treat it is to cover it with Compeed or Second Skin (see p44 for first-aid kit). Another way is to build a layer of 'Moleskin' around the blister. Keep a careful eye on blisters to make sure they don't become infected.

WEATHER AND WEATHER FORECASTS

It is a good idea to listen to weather forecasts and in particular pay attention to wind and gale warnings. Winds on any coastline can get very strong and if the wind is high it is advisable not to walk. Walking in high winds is difficult particularly if you are carrying a pack which can act as a sail. If you are walking on a steep incline or above high cliffs it is dangerous. Even if the wind direction is inland it can literally blow you right over (unpleasant if there are gorse bushes around!), or if it suddenly stops or eddies (a common phenomenon when strong winds hit cliffs) it can cause you to lose your balance and stagger in the direction in which you have been leaning, ie towards the cliffs!

Another hazard on the coast is sea mist or fog which can dramatically decrease visibility. If a coastal fog blows over take extreme care where the path runs close to cliff edges.

Detailed weather forecasts for Cornwall and Devon are available through 🖥 bbc.co.uk/weather; 🖥 www.metcheck.com is also a useful source of information.

ROUTE GUIDE & MAPS

Using this guide

The trail guide and maps have not been divided into rigid daily stages since people walk at different speeds and have different interests. The **route summaries** below describe the trail between significant places and are written as if walking the coast path from Bude to Plymouth. To enable you to plan your own itinerary, **practical information** is presented clearly on the trail maps. This includes walking times, all places to stay, camp and eat, as well as shops where you can buy supplies. Further **service details** are given in the text under the entry for each place. For a condensed overview of this information see the **town and village facilities table** on pp36-9.

For **overview maps** and **profiles** see the colour pages at the end of the book.

TRAIL MAPS   [for map key see p338]

Scale and walking times
The trail maps are to a scale of 1:20,000 (1cm = 200m; 31/8 inches = one mile). Walking times are given along the side of each map and the arrow shows the direction to which the time refers. Black triangles indicate the points between which the times have been taken. **See important note below on walking times**.

The time-bars are a tool and are not there to judge your walking ability. There are so many variables that affect walking speed, from the weather conditions to how many beers you drank the previous evening. After the first hour or two of walking you will be able to see how your speed relates to the timings on the maps. Note also that time spent on ferry crossings is not included on time-bars.

Up or down?
The trail is shown as a dashed line. An arrow across the trail indicates the slope; two arrows show that it is steep. Note that the arrow points towards the higher part of the trail. If, for example, you are walking from A (at 80m) to B (at 200m) and the trail between the two is short

---

❏ **Important note – walking times** Unless otherwise specified, **all times in this book refer only to the time spent walking**. You will need to add 20-30% to allow for rests, photography, drinking water etc. When planning the day's hike count on 5-7 hours' actual walking.

and steep it would be shown thus: A— — — >> — — – B. Reversed arrow heads indicate downward gradient.

Other features

The numbered GPS waypoints refer to the list on pp330-5. Other features are marked on the map when pertinent to navigation. To avoid cluttering the maps and making them unusable not all features have been marked each time they occur.

ACCOMMODATION

Apart from in large towns where some selection of places has been necessary, the maps show almost every place to stay that is within easy reach of the trail and willing to take one-night stays. Details of each place are given in the accompanying text. For **B&B-style accommodation** the number and type of rooms is given after each entry: **S** = single room (one single bed), **T** = twin room (two single beds), **D** = double room (one double bed), **Tr** = triple room (three single beds or one double and one single) **F** = family room (usually a double and bunk beds, or a double and two singles). Thus family rooms can usually also be used as a double or twin.

Rates quoted are **per person** (pp) per night unless indicated otherwise; rates are usually discounted for longer stays. The rate for single occupancy (sgl occ) of a double/twin is also shown where appropriate. Some places either do not accept single-night bookings at peak times or they charge extra for them. Most B&Bs don't accept credit/debit cards but most guesthouses, hostels and hotels do, as do most of the large holiday parks. The text also mentions whether the premises have **wi-fi** (WI-FI); if a bath (◥) is available for at least one room; and whether **dogs** (🐾) are welcome. Most places will not take more than one dog in a room and only accept them subject to prior arrangement. Some make an additional charge (usually per night but occasionally per stay) while others may require a deposit which is refundable if the dog doesn't make a mess.

Prices for **camping** vary but for backpackers many sites charge for two people in a small tent although some charge per pitch and per person.

The route guide

[For the route guide from Devon along the coast path north of Bude see p321]

BUDE   [Map p81]

Bude is a small, compact seaside town with plenty of charm and character that sprawls out from its famous beach, Summerleaze.

Summer and bank holidays are when this normally sleepy little town springs into life and it can become quite hectic. However, arrive at any other time and you shouldn't have any trouble booking accommodation

and making your way around town. Built in 1830, the town's small **castle** (☎ 01288-357300, 🖳 thecastlebude.org.uk; 10am-5pm; free entrance) is worth exploring. Its heritage centre contains exhibitions on shipwrecks and lifeboats as well as displays on the Bude Canal and the geology of the Cornish coast. Inside too is the Willoughby

Gallery, which holds local art exhibitions, a gift shop and the pleasant Limelight Café (see Where to eat).

Pretty **Bude Canal** (see box on p83) runs from the beach past the castle and can be followed for a mile or so along the towpath or in boats. Also nearby is **Bude Light**, a Millennium project built to commemorate the life of Sir Goldsworthy Gurney, a Cornish scientist and inventor for whom the castle was originally built.

Bude Sea Pool (🖳 budeseapool.org) is a man-made tidal swimming pool, built in 1930 to provide a safe place for people to go sea swimming. It's free to use and open all year round.

Bude is also known for its **Jazz Festival** (🖳 budejazz.co.uk) which usually takes place over four days at the end of August or beginning of September, making rooms harder to come by at this time.

Services

Bude Tourist Information and Canal Centre (☎ 01288-354240, 🖳 visitbude .info; Mon-Sat 10am-5pm, to 6pm school summer holidays, Sun 10am-4pm; WI-FI) has a comprehensive listing of accommodation in the area (you can book accommodation through its website too) and the enthusiastic staff are willing to help. **Internet access** (first 15 mins free, then 60p/15 mins) is available as well.

There is also internet access at **Bude Library** (☎ 0300-123 4111; Mon, Wed & Fri 9.30am-5pm, Sat 10am-1pm; WI-FI), which has a good Cornish reference section. Most cafés, restaurants and pubs here have free WI-FI.

Bude's main **post office** (Mon-Fri 9am-5.30pm, Sat 9am-12.30pm) is at the top of Belle Vue, the main shopping street. There's also a **sub-post office** (same hours) which is part of a newsagent (daily 7am-5.30pm) opposite the tourist office.

For **food shopping**, there is a Sainsbury's (Mon-Sat 8am-8pm, Sun 10am-4pm) and a Co-op (Mon-Sat 8am-10pm, Sun 10am-4pm). There is also a Boots **pharmacy** (Mon-Sat 9am-5pm) while, for **walking and camping gear**, there's a branch of Mountain Warehouse

(Mon-Sat 9am-5.30pm, Sun 10am-4.30pm).

Spencer Thorn Bookshop (☎ 01288-352518; Mon-Sat 9am-5pm, Sun 4pm in summer) has a good selection of books on Cornwall.

There are **banks**: Barclays and TSB. Both have **ATMs** (cash machines); you will also find ATMs at all the town's supermarkets and convenience stores.

There's a **launderette** (Mon-Thur 8.30am-5pm, Fri 8.30am-8pm, Sat 9am-5pm, Sun 10am-5pm) off Lansdown Rd.

Where to stay

Campsites and hostels The 10-minute stroll out of town to *Upper Lynstone Caravan & Camping Park* (Map 1; ☎ 01288-352017, 🖳 upperlynstone.co.uk; Apr to end Sep; 🐾; walker & small tent £10, 2 people & tent £16-23) is well worth the effort. The quiet section is perfect for those continuing on the trail as it backs on to the cliffs and the coastal path to Upton and Widemouth Bay. There is a well-stocked shop, a laundry, and the free showers are roomy and spotlessly clean.

Another option is the fabulous *Cerenety Eco Campsite* (Map 1; ☎ 01288-356778, ☎ 07429-016962, 🖳 cerenety campsite.co.uk; tent pitch £4-5, caravan £4-6pp). It's in Upton, just off the coast path towards Crackington Haven, so not really in Bude itself, although not much further away than Upper Lynstone. It's basic (solar-heated showers, compost toilets) but friendly, well organised and genuinely eco-conscious. There's a caravan café, as well as open fires for self-caterers and marshmallow-toasters.

NorthShore Bude Backpackers (☎ 01288-354256, 🖳 northshorebude.com; ☎; WI-FI; 1 x 3-, 4 x 4-, 2 x 6-bed dorms, 4D/1T; £20-35pp; booking recommended) has everything a walker needs: internet access, wi-fi, a drying room and a laundry. It also benefits from a big and clean living area, kitchen (meals are not provided) and garden, and has Sky TV.

B&Bs and guesthouses B&B-style accommodation is scattered about the town,

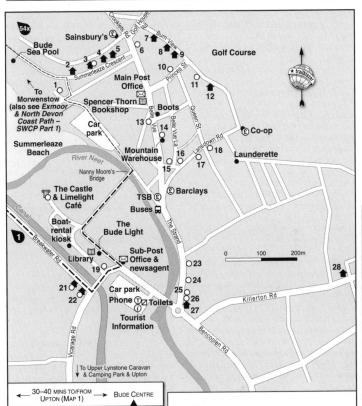

← 30–40 MINS TO/FROM → BUDE CENTRE
UPTON (MAP 1)

Bude

Where to stay
2 The Beach
3 The Edgcumbe
4 Atlantic House Hotel
5 The Grosvenor
7 Tee-Side
8 Sunrise
9 Links Side Guest House
12 Sea Jade Guest House
21 Falcon Hotel
22 Brendon Arms
27 Premier Inn
28 NorthShore Bude Backpackers

Where to eat and drink
1 Life's a Beach
3 The Deck
6 Coffee Pot Café
10 Sizzlers Fish & Chips
11 Bude Tandoori
13 A Taste of Cornwall
14 Butter Bun
15 Pengenna Pasties
16 Scrummies
17 Lansdown Bakery
18 Coffee Shop
19 Olive Tree Coffee House & Bistro
21 Falcon Hotel
22 Brendon Arms
23 Tiandi
24 Silver River Chinese Takeaway
25 Carriers Inn
26 La Bocca Pizza Kitchen

though traditional bed and breakfasts in family homes are less common than they used to be, so you may have to plump for a room in a pub or small hotel or guesthouse instead.

There is a clutch of these B&B guest-houses on or around Burn View: *Links Side Guest House* (☎ 01288-352410, 🖳 links sidebude.co.uk; 1S/5D/1T; WI-FI; £29-42.50pp, sgl/sgl occ from £53); *Sea Jade Guest House* (☎ 01288-353404, 🖳 seajade guesthouse.co.uk; 8D; WI-FI; from £35pp); *Sunrise* (☎ 01288-353214, 🖳 sunrise-bude .co.uk; 2S/1T/2D/2D or T; 🛏; WI-FI; 🐾; £35-45pp, sgl occ £40-60), and *Tee-Side Guest House* (☎ 01288-352351, 🖳 tee-side .co.uk; 1S/4D or T; WI-FI; from £37.50pp, sgl/sgl occ from £45-75). From the latter, as its name suggests, you can enjoy views overlooking the golf course while eating your breakfast.

Hotels Overlooking the beach from a great vantage point on the edge of Summerleaze Down, *The Beach* (☎ 01288-389800, 🖳 thebeachatbude.co.uk; 2T/14D; 🛏; WI-FI; £75-125pp) is Bude's most boutique-like hotel, with heated floors and very smart, modern rooms, half of which have sea views. The terraces from the bar and restaurant have sea views too. Single occupancy; dinner, bed and breakfast; and room-only rates are also available.

On the same road, *The Edgcumbe* (☎ 01288-353846, 🖳 edgcumbe-hotel.co.uk; Mar-Nov; 1S/11D or T; 🛏; WI-FI; £45-55pp, sgl occ £55-70) is a friendly place, with a young vibe to it. There's a small bar-restaurant with excellent meals, and a dry-ing room too; handy for wet tents and soggy walking boots. *Atlantic House Hotel* (☎ 01288-352451, 🖳 atlantichousehotel .com; 12D/3D or T; 🛏; WI-FI; £45-75pp,

sgl occ £70-150) has some nice sea-view rooms, although some of the rear rooms are a bit poky. Next door is *The Grosvenor* (☎ 01288-352062, 🖳 thegrosvenor-bude.co .uk; 1D/3D or T/1F; 🛏; WI-FI in public areas; well-behaved 🐾; £34.50-49pp, sgl occ from £65), the least welcoming of this bunch, and with no sea views.

On the other side of the canal, *Falcon Hotel* (☎ 01288-352005, 🖳 falconhotel .com; 4S/7T/18D; 🛏; WI-FI; £70-95pp but rates vary depending on demand) is an impressive place, and a more traditional, classier alternative to its main top-end rival, The Beach. Next door, *Brendon Arms* (☎ 01288-354542, 🖳 brendonarms.co.uk; 1S/ 5D/3T; 🛏; WI-FI; £39-50pp, sgl £39-47, sgl occ £39-62) is a popular pub which also has rooms.

Bude has a *Premier Inn* (☎ 08710-971078, 🖳 premierinn.com; The Strand). Rooms cost from £37, but it's worth check-ing online for offers.

Where to eat and drink
There are numerous options for food in Bude. Inside the castle is *Limelight Café* (10am-4pm), which does sandwiches, cream teas and coffee.

Pocket-sized *Butter Bun* (9.30am-4pm; WI-FI) has freshly made sandwiches and coffee. A couple of doors along, *A Taste of Cornwall* is Bude's best ice-cream parlour, with a range of unusual flavours as well as the classics. *The Coffee Shop* (☎ 01288-355973; Mar-Nov daily 10am-6.30pm, Dec-Feb 10.30am-5pm), on Lansdown Rd, sells fresh baked goods (from *Lansdown Bakery*), while nearby *Pengenna Pasties* (9am-5pm) does excel-lent pasties, scones and other baked goods.

On the outskirts of town, *Coffee Pot Café* (daily summer 8am-7pm, winter 8.30am-3pm; WI-FI) is a down-to-earth,

---

❑ **Where to stay: the details**
Unless specified, B&B-style accommodation is either en suite or has private facili-ties; 🛏 means at least one room has a bath; 🐾 signifies that dogs are welcome in at least one room but always by prior arrangement, an additional charge may also be payable (see pp336-8); WI-FI means wi-fi is available. See also pp79.

❏ **Bude Canal**

Bude Canal (🖳 bude-canal.co.uk) was dug to transport mainly sand inland from the seashore so that it could be spread on the fields to improve the soil which was rather poor in parts of north Cornwall. The Canal was the brainchild of one John Endyvean, the intention being to link up with the River Tamar at Calstock, thus providing a waterway between the Bristol Channel and the English Channel, 90 miles of canal to span just 28 miles as the crow flies.

The full scheme was never realised although by 1823 some 35 miles of canal were in operation. Once the railways were built the use of the canal began to decline and by World War II it became ineffective as a waterway. Today only a short stretch remains between Bude and Helebridge.

A project to restore the canal with the aid of a £45m grant from the Heritage Lottery Fund was completed in 2009. Whilst the lock-gates giving access to the open sea suffered damage in the early part of 2008 during some huge storms, the canal itself is currently in good working order. At the Helebridge end, **Weir Nature Centre** at Whalesborough Farm opened in 2011. It is a 40-minute walk along a flat tarmac path by the side of the canal.

Near the castle, a small **boat-rental kiosk** (Easter to end Sep 10am-5pm) has rowing boats (£10/hr), canoes and pedalos (£15/hr) for trips along the canal.

friendly café with cream teas, full English breakfasts, and some roadside patio seating.

Café by day, bistro by night, *Olive Tree Coffee House and Bistro* (☎ 01288-359577, 🖳 olivetreebude.co.uk; summer Tue & Sun 10am-5pm, Wed-Sat 10am-10pm, winter Tue-Sun 10am-4.30pm; WI-FI) serves a good variety of gluten-free and vegetarian dishes. It's a lovely spot beside the canal, but prices aren't cheap. More affordable, *Scrummies* (summer Mon-Sat 8am-9pm, Sun 9am-9pm; winter days/hours variable) is owned by local fisherman Cliff Bowden who catches, prepares and cooks 60-70% of the fish himself and offers a gigantic cod 'n' chips.

There are a few decent pubs. Next to the canal, *Brendon Arms* (see Where to stay; food daily noon-2pm & 6-9pm; summer noon-9pm) is a 150-year-old pub with plenty of garden seating out front. Meanwhile, at the bottom of The Strand, *Carriers Inn* (☎ 01288-352459; food daily noon-3pm & 6-9pm, summer daily noon-9pm; 🐾 on a lead in the bar) is even older, although less cheery. *Falcon Hotel* (see Where to stay) has a restaurant (daily noon-2pm & 6.30-9pm; booking preferred) but the menu is fairly standard pub grub. *The Deck* (🖳 thedeckbude.co.uk; May-Sep

daily 4-8.30pm, shorter hours in winter), which is the bar-restaurant at The Edgcumbe (see Where to stay) can also be recommended.

In terms of restaurants, *Life's a Beach* (☎ 01288-355222, 🖳 lifesabeach.info; mid Feb-Dec café daily 10.30am-3.30pm, evening bistro Mon-Sat 7-8.30pm, Jan-mid Feb Fri-Sun 11am-3pm) has the pick of locations, with fabulous beach views from its terrace. The lunchtime menu is good value (burgers and baguettes from £5.75). Evening is for fine dining, including good seafood (mains £17.50-24.50), and is indoors only.

The best Indian restaurant is *Bude Tandoori* (☎ 01288 359994, 🖳 budetandoori.co.uk; Sat-Thur noon-2pm, daily 5pm-11.30pm), which has some Bangladeshi dishes too, plus some outdoor seating by the roadside. *Tiandi* (☎ 01288-359686; Mon-Sat 11.30am-2.30pm & daily 5.30-10.30pm) advertises itself as 'East-Asian Fine Dining', and does a mix of mostly Chinese and Thai food.

On The Strand you'll find *Silver River Chinese Takeaway* (☎ 01288-352028; mid Feb to mid Jan Tue-Sun 5-10.30pm) and *La Bocca Pizza Kitchen* (☎ 01288-255855, 🖳 laboccabude.co.uk; daily 5-9pm, Fri & Sat noon-2.30pm).

ROUTE GUIDE AND MAPS

For classic British seaside fish 'n' chips you need look no further than *Sizzlers* (daily noon-3pm & 4.30-9pm).

Transport
[See also pp52-6] **Bus**-wise, for destinations north of Bude, Stagecoach's 85 goes from here to Barnstaple, where you'll find the nearest **railway station**. Alternatively, their 6A runs to the main rail hub at Exeter via Launceston and Okehampton. Plymouth City Bus No 12 heads to Launceston and Plymouth, while First Kernow's No 95 calls here en route between Wadebridge and Boscastle and their 96 between Wadebridge and Crackington Haven.

For a **taxi**, you could try contacting either Trev's Taxi (☎ 07799-663217, 🖳 trevstaxi.co.uk) or Bayside Taxis (01288-358076, 🖳 baysidetaxis.co.uk).

BUDE TO CRACKINGTON HAVEN   MAPS 1-5

The first **10 miles (16km, 4-5hrs)** start benignly enough following a grassy cliff-top for about a mile before unexpectedly meeting a road with a small cluster of houses, **Upton**.

The next port of call is **Widemouth Bay** (pronounced 'Widmouth') the first of many beaches popular with surfers and sun-seekers alike and adequately supplied with cafés and places to stay.

Once past these early distractions the hard work begins with a punishing ascent onto **Penhalt Cliff**, the first of several more ups and downs (Millook, Chipman Point and Castle Point) on the trek to **Crackington Haven**.

Despite these testing beginnings there is still time to appreciate the beautiful green cliffs that slope down to the waves below and, once you reach Crackington, you'll be rewarded with a lovely village tucked around a sheltered cove and a sense of satisfaction at completing what for most people will have been a strenuous first day's walk.

UPTON   [MAP 1]
Upton is a satellite village of Bude so it is not surprising to find several places to stay and thus is worth considering, especially if everywhere in Bude is fully booked. There is a handful of accommodation options including two excellent campsites: *Upper Lynstone Camping* and *Cerenety Eco Campsite* – for both see p80.

Advertised on a sign beside the road *Upton Cross Guest House* (☎ 01288-355310, 🖳 uptoncrossbandb.co.uk; 3D or T/1Tr; ➤; WI-FI; 🐾; from £35pp, £50 sgl occ) is a lovely B&B. The owner will run guests into Bude for an evening meal and is used to walkers.

Up on a hill a quarter of a mile further on but reached from the cliff path is *Elements* (☎ 01288-352386, 🖳 elements-life.co.uk; 1S/8D/2F; WI-FI; £40-80pp, sgl £55-65), a boutique hotel with well-equipped rooms and restaurant, which makes a great place to stop for lunch or a coffee. They have a small sauna and gym, and the **restaurant-café** (daily 10am-9.30pm) is very good.

❑ **Important note – walking times**
Unless otherwise specified, **all times in this book refer only to the time spent walking.** You will need to add 20-30% to allow for rests, photography, checking the map, drinking water etc. When planning the day's hike count on 5-7 hours' actual walking.

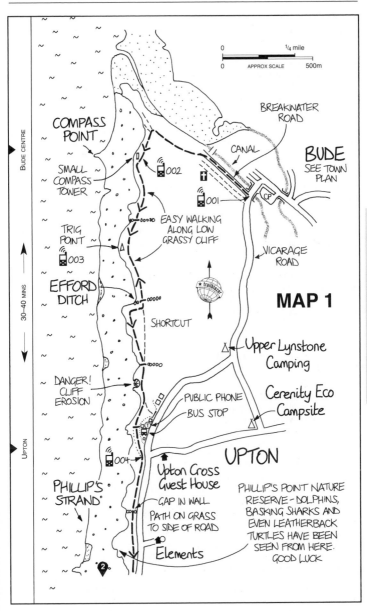

¼ mile

0   500m

APPROX SCALE

BREAKWATER ROAD

CANAL

BUDE
SEE TOWN PLAN

CP

COMPASS POINT

SMALL COMPASS TOWER

002

001

VICARAGE ROAD

EASY WALKING ALONG LOW GRASSY CLIFF

TRIG POINT
003

EFFORD DITCH

MAP 1

SHORTCUT

trailblazer

Upper Lynstone Camping

Cerenity Eco Campsite

DANGER! CLIFF EROSION

PUBLIC PHONE
BUS STOP

004

UPTON

PHILLIP'S STRAND

Upton Cross Guest House

GAP IN WALL
PATH ON GRASS TO SIDE OF ROAD

Elements

2

PHILLIP'S POINT NATURE RESERVE – DOLPHINS, BASKING SHARKS AND EVEN LEATHERBACK TURTLES HAVE BEEN SEEN FROM HERE. GOOD LUCK

BUDE CENTRE

30-40 MINS

UPTON

WIDEMOUTH BAY
[MAP 2 & MAP 3, p88]

The village, which gets very busy in the summer, is strung out rather randomly along the main road behind the long beach but it has a **general store** (daily 9am-5.30pm, shuts at 1pm on a Wed) selling all the essentials including alcohol.

There are two (seasonal) cafés if you need refreshment. *Café Widemouth* (9am-7pm, winter 10am-4pm) has a more extensive menu, more seating and better sea views. *Black Rock Café* is smaller, but serves similar fare.

Another option, and a good one if you're camping at Widemouth Bay Caravan Park, is *Widemouth Manor* (Map 3; ☎ 01288-361207, 🖥 widemouthmanor .co.uk; noon-2pm & 6-9pm). It has a good quality pub menu (mains £8.50-19.95) and the views from the back garden are lovely. Booking is advisable.

Campers have two options. The first requires a steep climb from the trail to the pleasant *Penhalt Farm Holiday Park* (Map 3; ☎ 01288-361210, 🖥 penhaltfarm.co.uk; WI-FI; 🐾) where pitches for a two-man tent cost £10-16 depending on the season. They have a small shop for essential foodstuffs and accept Visa, MasterCard and Switch. The second option, *Widemouth Bay Caravan Park* (Map 3; ☎ 01288-361208,

🖥 johnfowlerholidays.com; tent pitch £10-16; WI-FI; 🐾), is less of a hike from Widemouth Bay, but is a less endearing, oversized campsite, run by John Fowler Holiday Parks. The facilities are excellent – they even have an indoor swimming pool – but the atmosphere is more Butlins than South West Coast Path. Great if you have kids to entertain. Not so great if you don't.

Set back from the beach is *The Bay View Inn* (☎ 01288-361273, 🖥 bayview inn.co.uk; 1S/3D/2F; ☞; WI-FI; £55-65pp, sgl from £50, sgl occ rate on request). The pub is the heartbeat of the surfing community but is happy to welcome walkers. The bar is modern and opens to an extensive area of decking, a good place to sit out and enjoy a pint. **Food** (Mon-Fri noon-2.30pm & 5.30-9pm, Sat noon-9pm, Sun noon-8pm) is served. Next to the general store is the *Beach House* (☎ 01288-361256, 🖥 beachhousewidemouth.co.uk; 1S/6D/1T/2F; £33-80pp, sgl occ from £80; WI-FI), which has undergone an impressive-looking revamp. Rooms are small, but most come with sea views. There's a good restaurant, a more informal café and a bar, plus picnic tables scattered around the back garden, which leads down to the beach.

First Kernow's No 95 & (Sun only) 96 **bus** services stop here. [See also pp52-6].

CRACKINGTON HAVEN
[MAP 5, p91]

Crackington Haven lies at the head of the cove of the same name and can get busy in summer thanks to its lovely beach, which is ideal for families. Overlooking the beach, the friendly pub, *Coombe Barton Inn* (☎ 01840-230345, 🖥 coombebarton.co.uk; 5D/1T, some en suite; from £35pp, from £45 sgl occ; 🐾; WI-FI) is the focal point for the village. One en-suite room has a balcony. The restaurant (**food** served daily noon-2.30pm & 6.30-9.30pm) has an excellent pub-grub menu, including a mouthwatering lamb shank shepherd's pie. There's no ATM in the village, but you can get cash back from the pub.

For **B&B** try *Lower Tresmorn Farm* (☎ 01840-230667, 🖥 lowertresmorn.co.uk;

4D/2F; ☞; WI-FI; £35-55pp, sgl occ £50-78), a lovely old building up on the cliffs before you reach the Haven, only five minutes from the coast path. One room has a four-poster bed and views to Lundy Island. Two-night bookings are preferred. Closer to the village is *Trewartha B&B* (☎ 01840-230420, 🖥 trewarthabychy@gmail.com; 2D/1T; from £30pp, sgl occ £35; WI-FI), which has a double room in the main house, plus a self-contained two-room chalet at the bottom of the owner's peacock-filled garden. It's a bit of a hike uphill from the coast path, but they'll pick you up if you have a room booked.

Campers will need to walk half a mile beyond Trewartha B&B.

(cont'd on p90)

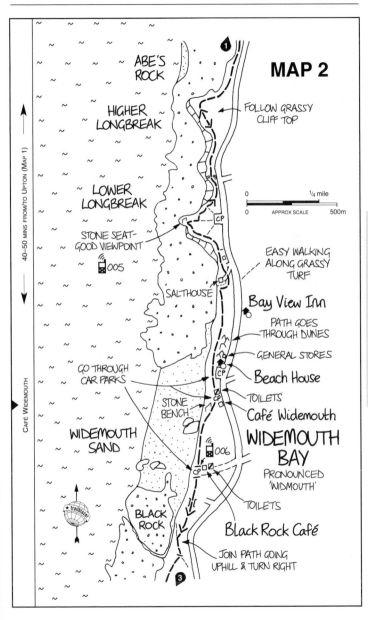

MAP 2

FOLLOW GRASSY CLIFF TOP

ABE'S ROCK

HIGHER LONGBREAK

LOWER LONGBREAK

STONE SEAT- GOOD VIEWPOINT

📱 005

SALTHOUSE

EASY WALKING ALONG GRASSY TURF

Bay View Inn

PATH GOES THROUGH DUNES

GENERAL STORES

Beach House

TOILETS

Café Widemouth

GO THROUGH CAR PARKS

STONE BENCH

WIDEMOUTH SAND

📱 006

WIDEMOUTH BAY

PRONOUNCED 'WIDMOUTH'

TOILETS

BLACK ROCK

Black Rock Café

JOIN PATH GOING UPHILL & TURN RIGHT

0 ¼ mile
0 APPROX SCALE 500m

40–50 MINS FROM/TO UPTON (MAP 1)

CAFÉ WIDEMOUTH

★ trailblazer

ROUTE GUIDE AND MAPS

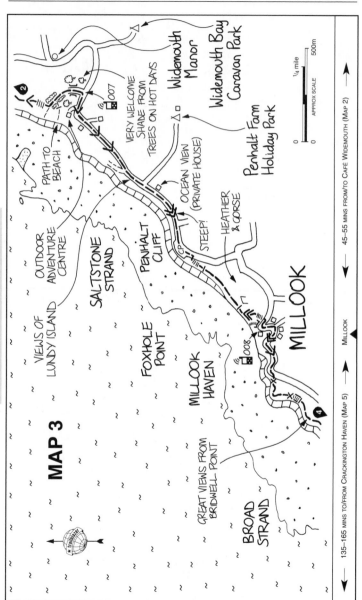

MAP 3

Widemouth Bay Caravan Park

Penhalt Farm Holiday Park

Widemouth Manor

△ Widemouth Bay

007

VERY WELCOME SHADE FROM TREES ON HOT DAYS

△ X

OCEAN VIEW (PRIVATE HOUSE)

PATH TO BEACH

HEATHER & GORSE

STEEP!

OUTDOOR ADVENTURE CENTRE

SALTSTONE STRAND

PENHALT CLIFF

VIEWS OF LUNDY ISLAND

FOXHOLE POINT

MILLOOK HAVEN

008

MILLOOK

GREAT VIEWS FROM BRIDWELL POINT

BROAD STRAND

APPROX SCALE

0 — 500m

0 — ¼ mile

ROUTE GUIDE AND MAPS

135–165 MINS TO/FROM CRACKINGTON HAVEN (MAP 5) ← — → MILLOOK — 45–55 MINS FROM/TO CAFÉ WIDEMOUTH (MAP 2)

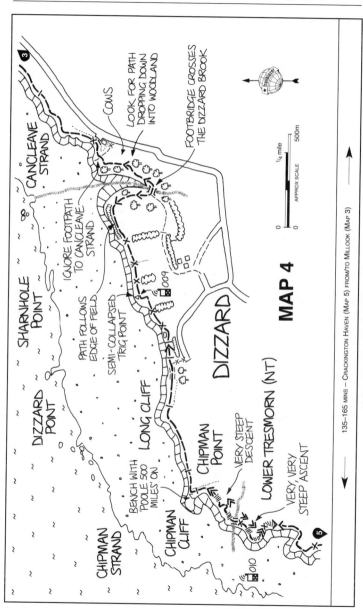

CANCLEAVE STRAND

LOOK FOR PATH DROPPING DOWN INTO WOODLAND

COWS

FOOTBRIDGE CROSSES THE DIZZARD BROOK

SHARNHOLE POINT

IGNORE FOOTPATH TO CANCLEAVE STRAND

DIZZARD POINT

PATH FOLLOWS EDGE OF FIELD

SEMI-COLLAPSED TRIG POINT

009

DIZZARD

LONG CLIFF

CHIPMAN STRAND

BENCH WITH 'POOLE 500 MILES' ON

CHIPMAN CLIFF

CHIPMAN POINT

VERY STEEP DESCENT

LOWER TRESMORN (NT)

VERY, VERY STEEP ASCENT

010

MAP 4

¼ mile

APPROX SCALE

500m

0

0

★ trailblazer

(cont'd from p86) **Coxford Meadow Campsite** (☎ 01840-230707, 🖳 north-corn wall-accommodation.com; £8pp); turn left when you get to Tremayna Methodist Church and the entrance to the campsite will be on your right. It's a small, family-run campsite with lovely countryside views, but no dogs allowed. Note you could take a short cut through St Gennys to get here.

There are two cafés competing to supply your need for a cup of tea and a scone: *Haven Café* (daily 9.30am-5.15pm in summer) and *Cabin Café* (summer 8am-8pm, winter 11am-4pm) stare uneasily at each other across the car park. The latter is a colourful and sunny place with surfboards hanging off the walls and pasties made on the premises. Both will make takeaway sandwiches for walkers.

By the bus stop, there's both a **public toilet** and an excellent interpretative panel with information on the history and geology of the area which you can read whilst waiting for the **bus**. The services are First Kernow's No 95 and 96, running on the Bude/Camelford to Wadebridge routes. [See also pp52-6].

CRACKINGTON HAVEN TO BOSCASTLE [MAPS 5-8]

The cliffs on this **7-mile (11km, 2½-3½hrs)** stretch are some of the highest in Cornwall (**High Cliff**, 731ft, is the highest point on the coast path in Cornwall and the highest sea cliff in the county); the path is careful to keep to the top of them.

If you feel the urge to head for the beach the only access is at **The Strangles** (Map 6) which can be reached by a detour down a steep path. There are some beautiful rugged coves and clefts on the approach to Boscastle, particularly at **Pentargon** (Map 8) where a small waterfall freefalls over a lip into the sea below.

BOSCASTLE [MAP 8, p95]

Beautiful Boscastle is tucked into a small but deep green valley that ends in a sheltered natural harbour. During the 18th and 19th centuries roads to the harbour were rough and narrow so the village relied on the sea for trade and transport. Leading away from the harbour is the medieval part of the village, based round the site of the 12th-century **Bottreaux Castle** from which the village derives its name, but of which there is little trace these days.

The village made headline news in 2004 when a spectacular and devastating flash flood swept through the streets carrying away houses and cars and creating chaos, although miraculously there were no fatalities. A year later most of the buildings had been faithfully restored to their original state and today the village looks smart and spruce.

Boscastle has plenty to offer the visitor. For starters there's the fascinating **Museum of Witchcraft and Magic**

(☎ 01840-250111, 🖳 museumofwitchcraft .com; Easter to Halloween Mon-Sat 10.30am-6pm, Sun 11.30am-6pm, last entry 5.30pm; admission £5).

The excellent **Visitor Centre** (☎ 01840-250010, 🖳 visitboscastleandtintagel .com; daily Mar-Oct 10am-5.30pm, Nov-Feb 10.30am-4pm), run by the National Trust, has stylish graphics and artwork describing the never-to-be-forgotten flood as well as the history and geology of the area and some of the characters who made it famous. It also has a gift shop and can help with finding accommodation.

Services

The village is well supplied with shops and places of refreshment all within a small area. The **post office** (daily 8am-5pm) and a free-to-use **cash machine** are in the Spar **supermarket** (6am-8pm), and there is a **public toilet** at the main car park where the buses stop.

ROUTE GUIDE AND MAPS

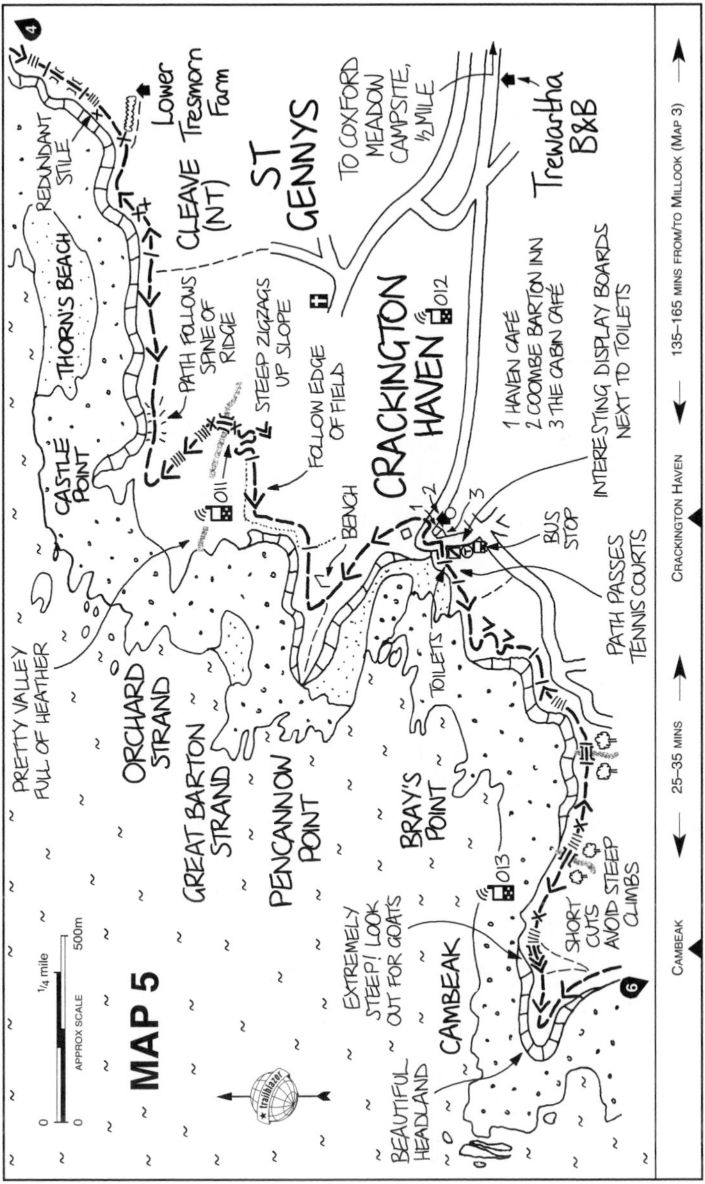

MAP 5

APPROX SCALE

0   500m

0   ¼ mile

PRETTY VALLEY FULL OF HEATHER

ORCHARD STRAND

GREAT BARTON STRAND

PENCANNOW POINT

BRAY'S POINT

EXTREMELY STEEP! LOOK OUT FOR GOATS

BEAUTIFUL HEADLAND

CAMBEAK

SHORT CUTS AVOID STEEP CLIMBS

6

013

THORN'S BEACH

REDUNDANT STILE

Lower Tresmorn Farm

CLEAVE (NT)

ST GENNYS

CASTLE POINT

PATH FOLLOWS SPINE OF RIDGE

STEEP ZIGZAGS UP SLOPE

FOLLOW EDGE OF FIELD

011

BENCH

CRACKINGTON HAVEN

012

4

TO COXFORD MEADOW CAMPSITE, ½ MILE

Trewartha B&B

1 HAVEN CAFÉ
2 COOMBE BARTON INN
3 THE CABIN CAFÉ

INTERESTING DISPLAY BOARDS NEXT TO TOILETS

BUS STOP

PATH PASSES TENNIS COURTS

TOILETS

1 2 3

CAMBEAK   ◀   25–35 MINS   ▶   CRACKINGTON HAVEN   ◀   135–165 MINS FROM/TO MILLOOK (MAP 3)   ▶

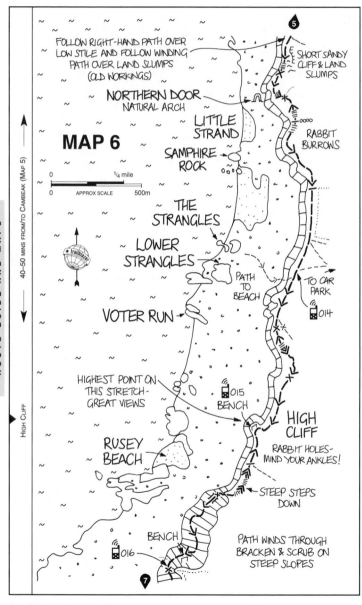

40–50 MINS FROM/TO CAMBEAK (MAP 5)

High Cliff

5

FOLLOW RIGHT-HAND PATH OVER
LOW STILE AND FOLLOW WINDING
PATH OVER LAND SLUMPS
(OLD WORKINGS)

SHORT SANDY
CLIFF & LAND
SLUMPS

NORTHERN DOOR
NATURAL ARCH

LITTLE
STRAND

RABBIT
BURROWS

MAP 6

SAMPHIRE
ROCK

0   ¼ mile
0   APPROX SCALE   500m

**THE
STRANGLES**

**LOWER
STRANGLES**

PATH
TO
BEACH

TO CAR
PARK

014

VOTER RUN

HIGHEST POINT ON
THIS STRETCH -
GREAT VIEWS

015
BENCH

**HIGH
CLIFF**

RABBIT HOLES -
MIND YOUR ANKLES!

**RUSEY
BEACH**

STEEP STEPS
DOWN

BENCH

016

PATH WINDS THROUGH
BRACKEN & SCRUB ON
STEEP SLOPES

7

Where to stay

For camping, the nearest option is *Trebyla Farm Caravan & Camping* (☎ 01840-250308, 🖳 boscastlecampsite.co.uk; £6-7 per adult), a simple, friendly, family-run campsite, about half a mile past Boscastle Farm Shop & Café.

YHA Boscastle (☎ 0845-371 9006, 🖳 yha.org.uk/hostel/boscastle; 20 bunk beds & 4 double beds; from £16pp; reception open 8-10am & 5-10pm) was extensively refurbished after having suffered severely in the flood. It has very helpful staff, self-catering facilities and a lovely location beside the canal leading down to the harbour.

Just past the Spar and highly recommended, *Lower Meadows* (☎ 01840-250570, 🖳 lowermeadows.co.uk; 3D/1T/1F; WI-FI; £41-45pp, sgl occ from £70) is a B&B which welcomes walkers and one-nighters.

Down the hill is *Bridge House* (☎ 01840-250011, 🖳 bridgehouse-boscastle.co.uk; 1D/2T, WI-FI; £30-35pp, sgl occ £45-70), right in the heart of the village in a typical stone-built house. Recently under new management this is a friendly place to spend the night and has a tea room attached.

Next to the bridge, *The Riverside* (☎ 01840-250216, 🖳 hotelriverside.co.uk; 1S/7D/3T/3T/2F; ☛; WI-FI; £47.50-55pp, sgl £50-55, sgl occ £72.50, plus £5 for 1-night stays) occupies a building built by Sir Richard Grenville of Revenge fame ('At Flores in the Azores Sir Richard Grenville lay...'), extensively refurbished since the flood and a lovely place to stay.

The premier hotel in the village is *The Wellington* (☎ 01840-250202, 🖳 welling tonhotelboscastle.com; 3S/7D/3T/1F; ☛; WI-FI; 🐾; £50-72.50pp, sgl £60-75, sgl occ rate on request). Dinner, bed and breakfast rates are also available.

Where to eat and drink

Right on the trail as you come into Boscastle is the award-winning *Boscastle Farm Shop & Café* (☎ 01840-250827, 🖳 boscastlefarmshop.co.uk; café 9am-4pm, shop 9am-5pm; WI-FI; 🐾) with a fabulous food menu, and a well-stocked shop and deli. The emphasis is on farm-grown or locally sourced food and drinks, and there's a large back garden with wonderful sea views and a children's play area.

There is a wide choice of sustenance in the town itself, from Cornish cream teas to

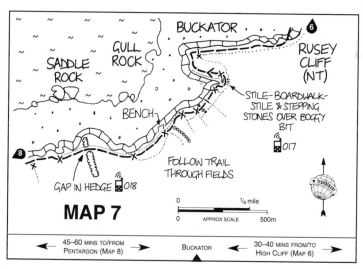

MAP 7

0 .... 1/4 mile
0 .... 500m
APPROX SCALE

45-60 MINS TO/FROM PENTARGON (Map 8) ←→   BUCKATOR   30-40 MINS FROM/TO HIGH CLIFF (Map 6)

pasties, fish & chips, pub grub and restaurants: there is something for everyone. If you need supplies for the trail, *Boscastle Bakery* (9am-4.30pm, winter 9am-3pm) does an excellent line in pasties as well as good-value rolls and sandwiches. Nearby there's also a grocery store, *Cornish Stores*, with fresh fruit and veg, and the small Spar supermarket (6am-8pm).

Harbour Light Tea Shop (☎ 01840-250953; daily Easter-Oct 10am-5pm) was originally housed in a 16th-century building – one of the many destroyed by the floods. Rebuilt in 2006, this is one of the most popular stops with walkers, with its location right on the path and lovely food. Another nice café option is *Pilchard Cellar Café* (summer 10am-5pm, winter 10.30am-4pm; 🐾), which is attached to the Visitor Centre. You can get a decent soup here plus good-value pasties, teacakes and scones, and they serve bottles of Tintagel Brewery Ale as well as tea and coffee. The tea room at *Bridge House* is another that will not let you down calorie-wise.

For pub food, the *Cobweb Inn* (☎ 01840-250278, 🖳 cobwebinn.com; food Mon-Sat 11.30am-2.30pm & 5.15-9.30pm, Sun noon-2.30pm & 6-9.30pm) is popular;

on Sundays they have a carvery. The pub is open all day and their range of beers includes Sharp's Doom Bar and St Austell's Tribute. Nearby *Old Manor House* (☎ 01840-250251; summer daily 11am-9pm, winter hours may vary) also does decent pub food, with the added attraction of some roadside garden seating.

Riverside Restaurant (see Where to stay; daily 8.30am-9pm, winter hours may vary) has a delightful spot by the stream which runs down to the harbour, and serves a good range of locally caught fish (evening mains £11.25-18.95). Its daytime-menu prices are more affordable.

At the top end of the market, *The Wellington* (see Where to stay) has a swanky restaurant (daily 6.30-9pm, booking advisable), where mains will cost £14-28. The bar is open all day.

Far cheaper is the smashing little takeaway *Sharon's Plaice* (daily noon-9pm).

Transport
[See also pp52-6] First Kernow's No 95 & (Sun only) 96 **bus** services run between here and Bude and also to Wadebridge and Tintagel. For a **taxi**, ring BosCars (☎ 07790-983911).

BOSCASTLE TO TINTAGEL   [MAPS 8-11]

For the next **5 miles (8km, 2-2½hrs)** you leave the high cliffs behind. You start by passing the site of the **Willapark Iron Age fort**, where there now stands a **National Coastwatch tower** (and where you may stumble across some very cute ponies), before following a convoluted and rugged section of coastline, decorated with small bays, coves and headlands. The walking is not too strenuous and there are plenty of tempting places for a break, not least the sheltered **Rocky Valley**, just before **Bossiney**, a narrow gorge that provides welcome shade on hot summer days.

At the end of this leg are the ruins of **Tintagel Castle**, a fittingly mystical spot for a fortress that is reputed to be the birthplace of the legendary King Arthur.

❏ **Important note – walking times**
Unless otherwise specified, **all times in this book refer only to the time spent walking**. You will need to add 20-30% to allow for rests, photography, checking the map, drinking water etc. When planning the day's hike count on 5-7 hours' actual walking.

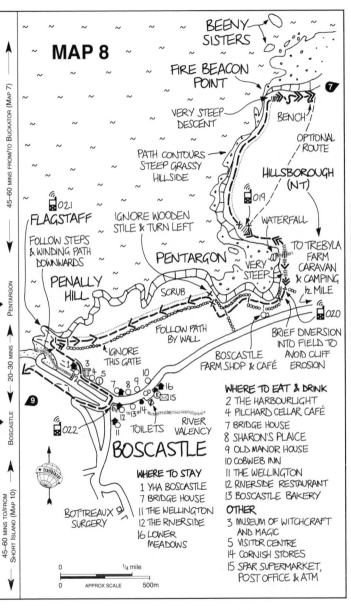

MAP 8

BEENY SISTERS

FIRE BEACON POINT

VERY STEEP DESCENT

BENCH

OPTIONAL ROUTE

PATH CONTOURS STEEP GRASSY HILLSIDE

HILLSBOROUGH (NT)

021
FLAGSTAFF

FOLLOW STEPS & WINDING PATH DOWNWARDS

IGNORE WOODEN STILE & TURN LEFT

019

WATERFALL

PENTARGON

TO TREBYLA FARM CARAVAN & CAMPING ½ MILE

PENALLY HILL

SCRUB

VERY STEEP

FOLLOW PATH BY WALL

020

BRIEF DIVERSION INTO FIELD TO AVOID CLIFF EROSION

IGNORE THIS GATE

BOSCASTLE FARM SHOP & CAFÉ

9

022

TOILETS

RIVER VALENCY

BOSCASTLE

BOTTREAUX SURGERY

WHERE TO STAY
1 YHA BOSCASTLE
7 BRIDGE HOUSE
11 THE WELLINGTON
12 THE RIVERSIDE
16 LOWER MEADOWS

WHERE TO EAT & DRINK
2 THE HARBOURLIGHT
4 PILCHARD CELLAR CAFÉ
7 BRIDGE HOUSE
8 SHARON'S PLAICE
9 OLD MANOR HOUSE
10 COBWEB INN
11 THE WELLINGTON
12 RIVERSIDE RESTAURANT
13 BOSCASTLE BAKERY

OTHER
3 MUSEUM OF WITCHCRAFT AND MAGIC
5 VISITOR CENTRE
14 CORNISH STORES
15 SPAR SUPERMARKET, POST OFFICE & ATM

0   ¼ mile
0   APPROX SCALE   500m

trailblaze

45–60 MINS FROM/TO BUCKATOR (MAP 7)

PENTARGON

20–30 MINS

BOSCASTLE

45–60 MINS TO/FROM SHORT ISLAND (MAP 10)

ROUTE GUIDE AND MAPS

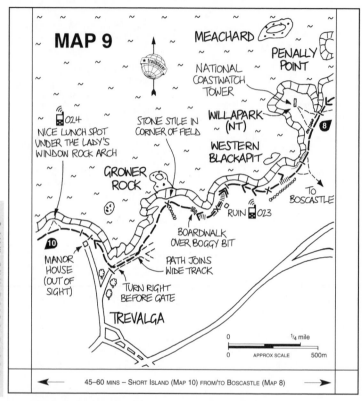

MAP 9

MEACHARD

PENALLY POINT

NATIONAL COASTWATCH TOWER

trailblazer

WILLAPARK (NT)

STONE STILE IN CORNER OF FIELD

024
NICE LUNCH SPOT UNDER THE LADY'S WINDOW ROCK ARCH

WESTERN BLACKAPIT

TO BOSCASTLE

8

GROWER ROCK

RUIN 023

BOARDWALK OVER BOGGY BIT

10

MANOR HOUSE (OUT OF SIGHT)

PATH JOINS WIDE TRACK

TURN RIGHT BEFORE GATE

TREVALGA

0   ¼ mile
0   APPROX SCALE   500m

45–60 MINS – SHORT ISLAND (MAP 10) FROM/TO BOSCASTLE (MAP 8)

BOSSINEY   [MAP 10]

The small village of Bossiney is essentially an offshoot of Tintagel and is only really worth the detour if you intend staying the night – take the path that runs off the coast path at Bossiney Haven. **Bossiney Mound**, an ancient earthen mound beside a small stone chapel, is thought to be the site of a former Norman castle. It is said to be where Arthur's Round Table lies buried. Sir Francis Drake, who lived in nearby **Old Borough House**, was elected MP for Bossiney in 1584 after giving his election speech from Bossiney Mound.

You can't really miss *Trewethett Farm Caravan and Campsite* (☎ 01840-770222; Mar-Oct; WI-FI; 🐾) right by the path, a

Caravan Club site with a shop (summer daily all day), and excellent shower facilities. A walker & tent costs £6.60-9.10.

Grange Cottage (☎ 01840-770487; 1S/1D/1D or T/1T; £34-36pp) is a decent B&B option. There's also the fairly upmarket *Bossiney House Hotel* (☎ 01840-770240, 🖥 bossineyhouse.com; 10D/6T/3F; 🛏; WI-FI; 🐾; £54-65pp, £72-85 sgl occ), which has a pool. Their smart restaurant, *Cedar Tree* (daily noon-2pm & 6.30-9pm), uses locally sourced produce including fresh fish direct from Port Isaac.

First Kernow's No 95 & 96 **bus** services between Boscastle and Wadebridge stop here; see also pp52-6.

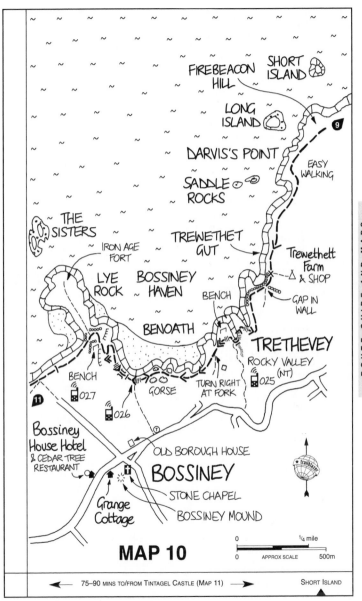

FIREBEACON HILL

SHORT ISLAND

LONG ISLAND

DARVIS'S POINT

SADDLE ROCKS

EASY WALKING

THE SISTERS

IRON AGE FORT

TREWETHET GUT

Trewethett Farm & SHOP

LYE ROCK

BOSSINEY HAVEN

BENCH

GAP IN WALL

BENOATH

TRETHEVEY

ROCKY VALLEY (NT)

025

BENCH

027

GORSE

TURN RIGHT AT FORK

026

Bossiney House Hotel & CEDAR TREE RESTAURANT

OLD BOROUGH HOUSE

BOSSINEY

STONE CHAPEL

Grange Cottage

BOSSINEY MOUND

★ trailblazer

MAP 10

0   ¼ mile

0   500m

APPROX SCALE

← 75–90 MINS TO/FROM TINTAGEL CASTLE (MAP 11) →

SHORT ISLAND

ROUTE GUIDE AND MAPS

TINTAGEL [Map p101]

There has been a settlement here since the Iron Age. However, Tintagel is associated in many minds with the legend of King Arthur who is supposed to have been born at the site of **Tintagel Castle** (Map 11; ☎ 01840-770328, ☐ english-heritage.org.uk; daily Apr-Sep 10am-6pm, Oct 10am-5pm, Nov-Apr Sat & Sun only 10am-4pm; £9.50), built in AD1236 and which, even in its ruined state, dominates the narrow inlet on its rocky promontory. Go up to the ruined castle at dusk and watch the sun set as the wind whistles about the ancient ramparts. There's a *café* (see Map 11; opens same time as castle, closes 30 mins earlier), serving locally sourced food and fresh coffee, and a shop close to the castle entrance. The castle was a stronghold of the dukes of Cornwall but whilst the position is stunning only a few walls remain.

There is more to find out about the Arthurian legend back in the town itself, at **King Arthur's Great Halls** (☎ 01840-770526; Mar-Oct Tue-Sun 10am-5pm, last entry 4pm; £5), which tells the story in detail with a laser light show and where you can shop for memorabilia to your heart's content.

Now owned by the National Trust and open to visitors, the **Old Post Office** (☎ 01840-770024, ☐ nationaltrust.org.uk; daily Mar & Oct 11am-5pm, Apr-Sep 10.30am-5.30pm; £4.60) is a 600-year-old medieval 'hall house' with a famously undulating slate roof. It hasn't been used as a post office since Victorian times.

Services

You'll find **Tintagel Visitor Centre** (☎ 01840-779084, ☐ visitboscastleandtintagel .com; 10am-4pm) beside the bus stop. There are **public toilets** behind it. There is no longer an actual **post office**, but there is a mobile one in the visitor centre (Tue, Wed & Fri 9.30-11.30am).

For provisions there is a Spar **supermarket** (daily 6.30am-9pm) and a Premier (Mon-Sat 7am-9pm, Sun 8am-8pm); both have free **ATMs**. Boots **pharmacy** (Mon-Sat 9am-5.30pm) is on Fore St.

❑ The King Arthur myth

Given the high profile accorded King Arthur in Tintagel where the name is purloined for pubs, pasties and pizzas it is worth pausing for a moment to ask exactly who he was. Disappointingly, it seems the answer is that he is a figure predominantly from the imagination.

Whether the saga in Geoffrey of Monmouth's *History of the Kings of Britain* from the 12th century was drawn from legend or not, this dubious work came out hundreds of years after the events described. It was Tennyson who popularised the myth drawing on Malory's *Morte d'Arthur* and the Victorians lapped it up thanks to its dreamy, romantic imagery and nostalgia for an era when good prevailed over evil but at a terrible cost.

The 20th century re-working of the story brought us *The Sword in the Stone* and *The Once and Future King* by TH White, later translated into film versions that help to keep the myth alive. Arthur's adoption by the hippie community ensures that the torch is passed on. Don't be disappointed. Somewhere back in the 6th century a real king called Arthur did actually exist although the stuff about knights and round tables and Merlin the Wizard is fiction. It's a great story and who could fail to be stirred by Tennyson's description of the last battle:

> *So all day long the noise of battle rolled*
> *Among the mountains by the winter sea*
> *Until King Arthur's table, man by man,*
> *Had fallen in Lyonesse about their Lord.*
> **Alfred, Lord Tennyson**, *Morte d'Arthur*, 1885

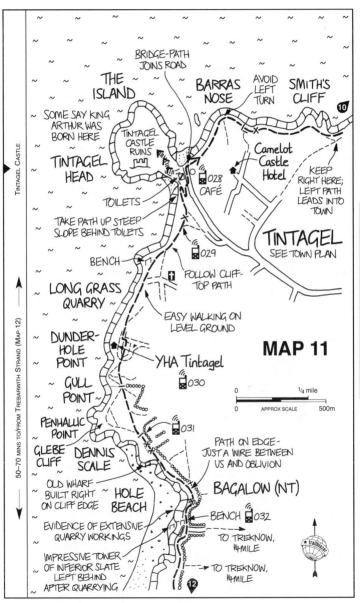

Where to stay

Campers should head for *Headland Caravan and Camping Park* (☎ 01840-770239, ⌨ headlandcaravanpark.co.uk; Easter/Apr-Oct; WI-FI; laundry); they charge £6.50-7.50 per walker. Annoyingly, the showers are on those 20p timers that all campers hate.

Those intending to stay at *YHA Tintagel* (Map 11; ☎ 01840-770334 or ☎ 0845-371 9145, ⌨ tintagel@yha.org.uk; Apr-Oct; 22 beds, from £15pp; self-catering only) will need to keep going past Tintagel for 30 minutes to Dunderhole Point. In a fantastic position perched right on the cliff top, the building was once the manager's office for the quarry workings on the cliffs. There are four bunk-bed dormitories, with communal bathroom facilities, plus one twin room in an annexe with a sink but no private bathroom.

For **B&B** accommodation, if money is tight you could do far worse than stay at *Castle View* (☎ 01840-770421, ⌨ castleviewbandb@aol.com; 1S/1D/1T, shared bathroom; ➼; £22.50-25pp, sgl occ £25-30); it may not be as chic as some of the others on offer in the village but the view is great, the service friendly and it's close to the path.

At the right-angle bend in the road, *Pendrin Guest House* (☎ 01840-770560, ⌨ pendrintintagel.co.uk; 2S/6D/1T; WI-FI; from £41pp, sgl from £45) accepts credit/debit cards. Practically next door is the more modern *Bosayne Guest House* (☎ 01840-770514, ⌨ bosayne.co.uk; 3S/3D/1T/1F; ➼; WI-FI; from £35pp, sgl £40). Both places welcome walkers and cyclists.

Trevenna Lodge (☎ 01840-770264, ⌨ trevennalodge.com; 3D/1F; ➼; WI-FI; £39.50-44.50pp, sgl occ from £70) is a well-run establishment that likes to source local ingredients for the tempting breakfast menu. Nearby is *The Avalon* (☎ 01840-770116, ⌨ theavalonhotel.co.uk; 7D; WI-FI; £47-58pp, sgl occ from £69). Some rooms have hand-crafted gothic beds. Walkers are welcome and they also provide luggage transfer.

A couple of the town's nice old pubs have rooms too. In the heart of things, *King Arthur's Arms* (☎ 01840-770628, ⌨ king arthursarms.co.uk; 5 flexible rooms; WI-FI; from £33pp) has decent rooms but it can get a bit hectic downstairs. On Fore St, *Ye Olde Malthouse* (☎ 01840-770461, ⌨ malt housetintagel.com; 1S/4D/1T/1Tr; ➼; WI-FI; ➿; £40-62.50pp, sgl from £60) boasts rooms befitting a building steeped in such character. Another pub on the same strip is *The Cornishman Inn* (☎ 01840-770238, ⌨ cornishmaninn.com; 1S/4D/3T/3F; WI-FI; £40-50pp, sgl from £60).

The Wootons Inn (☎ 01840-770170, ⌨ facebook.com/TheWootonsInn; 5D/3T/2F; ➼; WI-FI; ➿) is a pub with rooms that was being given a full refurb at the time of research. Room rates prior to the refurbishment were £50-55pp.

Amongst the several hotels in town is The *Tintagel Arms Hotel* (☎ 01840-770780, ⌨ thetintagelarmshotel.co.uk; 5D/1T; ➼; WI-FI; ➿; from £27.50pp, sgl occ from £45), on Fore St, provides pleasantly refurbished rooms, some with four-poster beds, and a small heated outdoor swimming pool.

The enormous *Camelot Castle Hotel* (☎ 01840-770202, ⌨ camelotcastle.com; approx 50 rooms, various sizes; ➼; WI-FI; ➿; £45-175pp) is impossible to miss and although it's more suitable for tour groups, the prices for the cheapest rooms aren't extortionate.

Where to eat and drink

Tintagel is full of pubs and cafés, pretty much all of which offer free WI-FI for customers.

One of the first places you'll come to is *The Cornish Bakery* (⌨ thecornishbak ery.com; daily 8am-6pm); bustling and busy. Fear not if there's a queue. It's a chain you'll come across again on the CCP; just wander along Fore St and Bossiney Rd and take your pick of the others.

On Fore St, you'll find the cute *Charlie's Café* (daily 10am-5pm) with breakfasts (£5-7), sandwiches (£3-6) and cream teas, plus a decent wine list; and *King Arthur's Café* (daily 10am-5pm): down-to-earth, with full-English breakfasts and the like, but also good coffee.

Next door is **Pengenna's Pasties** (daily 10am-5pm), a regional chain that crops up all along the coast; produce is prepared and cooked on the premises. The pasties are best bought freshly made so get there early. There is some outdoor seating in a back garden. Hunger allowing it's worth continuing to Bossiney Rd where you will find **Primrose Cottage Café** (summer daily 8.30am-6.30pm, winter closed) serving the omnipresent cream teas, as well as lunches, but also *Eats* (☎ 01840-770244;

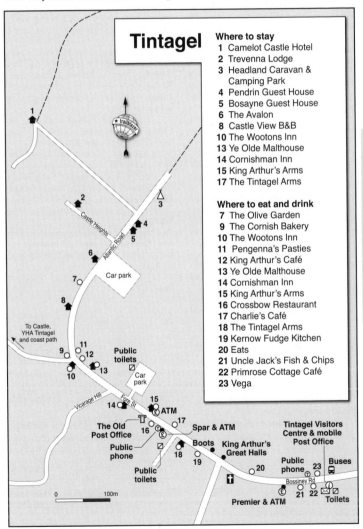

Tintagel

Where to stay
1 Camelot Castle Hotel
2 Trevenna Lodge
3 Headland Caravan & Camping Park
4 Pendrin Guest House
5 Bosayne Guest House
6 The Avalon
8 Castle View B&B
10 The Wootons Inn
13 Ye Olde Malthouse
14 Cornishman Inn
15 King Arthur's Arms
17 The Tintagel Arms

Where to eat and drink
7 The Olive Garden
9 The Cornish Bakery
10 The Wootons Inn
11 Pengenna's Pasties
12 King Arthur's Café
13 Ye Olde Malthouse
14 Cornishman Inn
15 King Arthur's Arms
16 Crossbow Restaurant
17 Charlie's Café
18 The Tintagel Arms
19 Kernow Fudge Kitchen
20 Eats
21 Uncle Jack's Fish & Chips
22 Primrose Cottage Café
23 Vega

★ trailblazer

Castle Heights

Atlantic Road

Car park

To Castle,
YHA Tintagel
and coast path

Public toilets

Car park

Vicarage Hill

Fore St

ATM

The Old Post Office

Public phone

Public toilets

Spar & ATM

Boots

King Arthur's Great Halls

Tintagel Visitors Centre & mobile Post Office

Public phone

Buses

Bossiney Rd

Premier & ATM

Toilets

0   100m

ROUTE GUIDE AND MAPS

summer daily when busy), where you'll discover decent food at very reasonable prices (curries, chilli, lasagne; all £7). The café has taken over the location of the old launderette, much to the locals' chagrin.

Opposite the visitor centre is the wonderful unique *Vega* (☎ 01840-770460, 🖳 vegatintagel.wordpress.com; Wed-Sun noon-3pm & 6-9pm; 🐾), which serves 100% vegan food and drinks and donates 50% of its profits to animal welfare charities. As well as a tapas menu – the idea being you can try numerous vegan dishes in order to sample how tasty they are – there are vegan curries, chillis, lasagnes and pasta dishes on offer (all £8).

Of the pubs, *King Arthur's Arms* (see Where to stay; summer daily 9am-9pm, winter 10am-3pm & 6-9pm; 🐾) does standard pub fare including their 'famous' big breakfast served all day from 9am onwards. There are also real ales, three of which are brewed in Tintagel.

The *Cornishman Inn* (see Where to stay; food daily 12.30-2.30pm & 6-9pm) has decent daily specials (mains £10-15), with steak and fish featuring highly. The main draught beer is Sharp's Doom Bar.

Ye Olde Malthouse (see Where to stay; Tue-Sat noon-3pm & 6-9pm) has new owners as of 2018 and the food they are serving is fabulous.

On Fore St *The Tintagel Arms Hotel* (see Where to stay) does standard pub food noon-3pm & 6.30-9pm; mains £10-15. *The Wootons Inn* (see Where to stay; daily noon-2.45pm & 6.30-8.45pm) has similar fare for similar prices.

Other restaurant options include *Crossbow* (Mar-Oct 10am-9pm daily), right on Fore St. It's a busy place but a great spot to soak up Cornwall's hectic tourist vibe. Burgers and steaks (£10-15) are the mainstays.

Slightly away from the main street, *The Olive Garden* (☎ 01840-779270; food daily 6-9.30pm) on Atlantic Rd is an unassuming place serving up a predominantly Italian menu (mains £9-16), including decent pizza.

If you've got a sweet tooth, why not treat yourself to some home-made fudge from *Kernow Fudge Kitchen* (Mon-Fri 11am-5pm, Sat 10am-5pm, Sun 11am-4pm) on Fore St. Just follow your nose.

For fish & chips head to *Uncle Jack's* (Mon-Thur 5-9pm, Fri & Sat 5-9.30pm, Sun 5-8.30pm).

Transport

[See also pp52-6] First Kernow's No 95 and (Sun only) 96 **bus** services between Bude/Camelford and Wadebridge stop here on Bossiney Rd.

For a **taxi**, call Camelot Taxis (☎ 01840-770172).

TINTAGEL TO PORT ISAAC   [MAPS 11-15]

This testing **9-mile (15km, 3½-4½hrs)** section begins with an easy stroll past old slate quarry workings (see box p104) and tin-mine workings (see box p180) on a level cliff-top. However, once past the attractive hamlet at **Trebarwith Strand** things get decidedly tougher.

Indeed the path between Trebarwith and Port Gaverne is one of the most challenging legs of the whole walk. The trail itself is well-trodden and easy to follow but there is a series of ascents and descents that may have the weak-willed swearing to hang up their boots. If your calf muscles are aching, take comfort in the dramatic views on this lonely coastline, kept hidden from most holidaymakers by its inaccessibility.

The hard work is over as soon as you reach the pretty twin villages of **Port Gaverne** and **Port Isaac**.

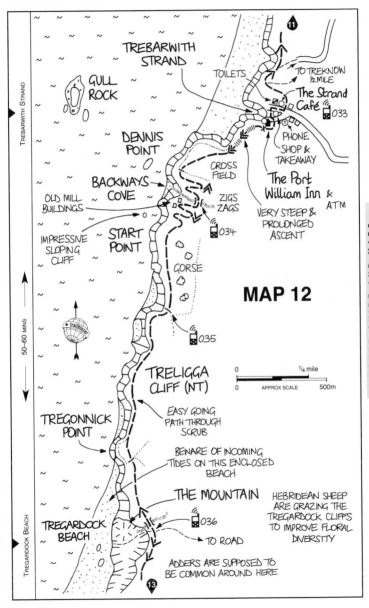

TREBARWITH STRAND

TREGARDOCK BEACH

50-60 MINS

TREBARWITH STRAND

GULL ROCK

TOILETS

TO TREKNOW ½ MILE

The Strand Café

033

DENNIS POINT

CROSS FIELD

PHONE SHOP & TAKEAWAY

BACKWAYS COVE

ZIGS ZAGS

The Port William Inn & ATM

OLD MILL BUILDINGS

034

VERY STEEP & PROLONGED ASCENT

IMPRESSIVE SLOPING CLIFF

START POINT

GORSE

MAP 12

035

trailblazer

TRELIGGA CLIFF (NT)

0   ¼ mile
0   APPROX SCALE   500m

TREGONNICK POINT

EASY GOING PATH THROUGH SCRUB

BEWARE OF INCOMING TIDES ON THIS ENCLOSED BEACH

THE MOUNTAIN

HEBRIDEAN SHEEP ARE GRAZING THE TREGARDOCK CLIFFS TO IMPROVE FLORAL DIVERSITY

TREGARDOCK BEACH

036

TO ROAD

ADDERS ARE SUPPOSED TO BE COMMON AROUND HERE

11

13

TREBARWITH STRAND
[MAP 12, p103]

This tiny settlement squeezed into a narrow defile overlooks a sandy beach and would be an ideal spot for lunch if it were not within an hour's walk from Tintagel, where most walkers will have stayed the night. There is a **shop** (9.30am-6pm) that sells ice-creams, drinks and snacks and an adjoining **takeaway** (10am-6pm) where you can pick-up pasties as well as hot drinks. Opening times for both are somewhat dependent on the tide as well as any water that may fall from above.

The Port William Inn (☎ 01840-770230, 🖳 theportwilliam.co.uk; 7D/1T; 🛏; WI-FI; 🐾; £45-85pp, sgl occ rate on request; food daily noon-9pm) sits in an elevated position above the cove. The bar, which has an **ATM**, has a certain nautical bias and the menu reflects this with several seafood specials including St Austell beer-battered haddock fillet. The rooms here are good, but expensive in the high season.

The other place for a pitstop is *The Strand Café* (☎ 01840-779482; Easter to Sep 10am-5pm, may close earlier in bad weather) right on the slipway to the beach. As well as coffee they do soups, fresh prawns, crab sandwiches, homemade burgers and cream teas.

❏ Slate quarries on the cliffs

Between Tintagel and Trebarwith Strand evidence of a once-thriving slate industry can still be seen on the cliffs. There were two ways of getting the slate: the first was by digging a hole in the ground in the area of known deposits and winching it to the surface; the other was by getting at the slate that had been exposed by cliff erosion.

Lanterdan and West quarries, both passed on the coastal path, are remarkable for the volume of slate extracted during the three hundred years they are known to have been worked. The isolated pinnacle of Lanterdan is thought to have been left as the fixing point for a cable necessary for winching the slate out of the cliff workings although another explanation is that it contains inferior slate and was left as not worth the effort to extract. The so-called 'wharf' at Penhallic Point was used as a loading gantry whereby cut slate could be lowered onto ships which were eased close in to the cliffs which would have been trimmed to allow the ships to approach as closely as possible.

Slate was split on the cliff tops by hand and the remains can be seen in the area around YHA Tintagel (see Map 11) on Glebe Cliff, which was formerly one of the quarry buildings.

PORT GAVERNE
[MAP 14, p106]

Port Gaverne is more peaceful than its near neighbour Port Isaac; it consists of a slipway, a café-cum-restaurant, and a hotel with a few cottages scattered nearby.

There's also a small campsite; the only one near Port Isaac: *Brooklands Farm Campsite* (☎ 01208-880259; £5pp; showers £1; Easter to Oct only) is a small, simple, single-field campsite run by the welcoming Ann Cleave and her husband Barry. It's only around 20 minutes' walk from the centre of Port Isaac.

If you have some cash to splash, *Port Gaverne Hotel* (☎ 01208-880244, 🖳 portgaverne-hotel.co.uk; 10D/3T/3F; 🛏; WI-FI; 🐾; £75-100pp; food daily noon-2.30pm & 6-9pm) has a lot of character. The food is excellent too, though not cheap. Starters cost £7.50-8.95, and mains £14.50-18.95.

Facing the harbour and owned by the hotel is *Pilchards Cafe* (☎ 01208-880891, 🖳 portgavernehotel.co.uk/restaurant/pilchards-cafe; closed during winter); the food is no less mouthwatering but slightly cheaper. There's a lovely little beer garden outside… and a tuk-tuk stop (!), which connects the café with Stargazy Inn in Port Isaac (see p108): don't be tempted to cheat on your coastal walk!

PORT ISAAC   [Map p108]

Over the hill from Port Gaverne is the picturesque village of Port Isaac. The steep lanes and alleyways are lined on each side by white-washed fishermen's cottages and down by the tiny cove are the still-thriving **fish cellars**.

If you are here for a night in the main season go down to The Platt and listen to either St Breward Silver Band (usually Thursdays) or Cornwall's most famous shanty singers Fisherman's Friends (🖳 the fishermansfriends.com; often Fridays).

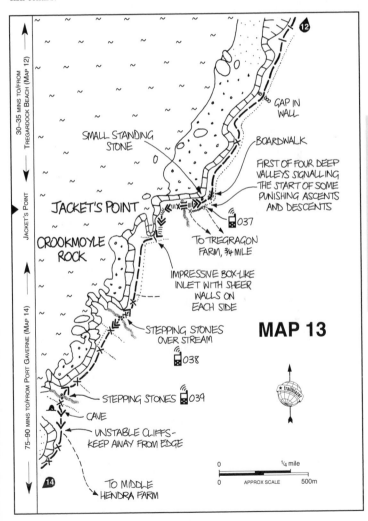

30-35 MINS TO/FROM TREGARDOCK BEACH (MAP 12)

◄ JACKET'S POINT ─

75-90 MINS TO/FROM PORT GAVERNE (MAP 14)

12

GAP IN WALL

SMALL STANDING STONE

BOARDWALK

FIRST OF FOUR DEEP VALLEYS SIGNALLING THE START OF SOME PUNISHING ASCENTS AND DESCENTS

JACKET'S POINT

037

CROOKMOYLE ROCK

TO TREGRAGON FARM, ¾ MILE

IMPRESSIVE BOX-LIKE INLET WITH SHEER WALLS ON EACH SIDE

STEPPING STONES OVER STREAM

038

MAP 13

STEPPING STONES 039

CAVE

UNSTABLE CLIFFS - KEEP AWAY FROM EDGE

14

TO MIDDLE HENDRA FARM

0   ¼ mile

0   APPROX SCALE   500m

ROUTE GUIDE AND MAPS

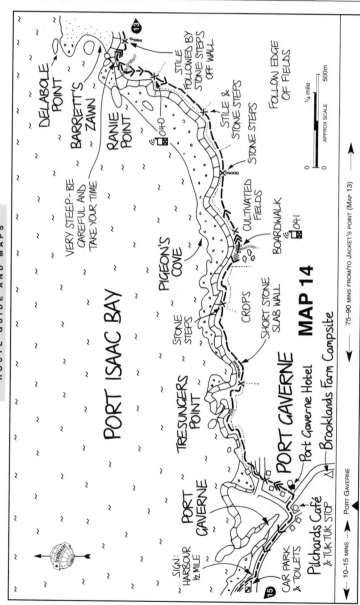

PORT ISAAC BAY

DELABOLE POINT

BARRETT'S ZAWN

RANIE POINT

STILE FOLLOWED BY STONE STEPS OFF WALL

FOLLOW EDGE OF FIELDS

STILE & STONE STEPS

STONE STEPS

VERY STEEP - BE CAREFUL AND TAKE YOUR TIME

CULTIVATED FIELDS

BOARDWALK

PIGEON'S COVE

CROPS

STONE STEPS

SHORT STONE SLAB WALL

MAP 14

APPROX SCALE

0 — 500m

0 — ¼ mile

TRESUNGERS POINT

PORT GAVERNE

Port Gaverne Hotel

Brooklands Farm Campsite

PORT GAVERNE

SIGN: HARBOUR ½ MILE

Pilchards Café & TUK TUK STOP

CAR PARK & TOILETS

10–15 MINS → PORT GAVERNE

← 75–90 MINS FROM/TO JACKET'S POINT (MAP 13)

ROUTE GUIDE AND MAPS

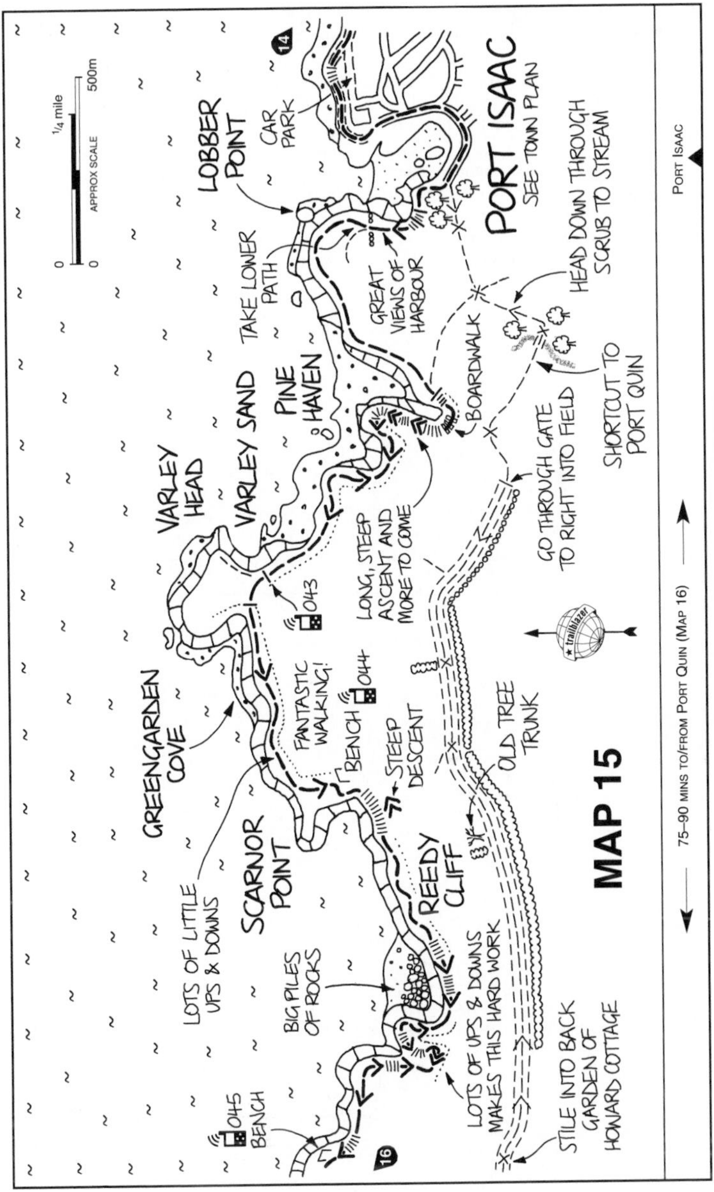

MAP 15

Port Isaac
PORT ISAAC
SEE TOWN PLAN

LOBBER POINT
CAR PARK
14

TAKE LOWER PATH
GREAT VIEWS OF HARBOUR
HEAD DOWN THROUGH SCRUB TO STREAM

VARLEY HEAD
VARLEY SAND
PINE HAVEN
BOARDWALK
SHORTCUT TO PORT QUIN

GREENGARDEN COVE
043
LONG, STEEP ASCENT AND MORE TO COME
GO THROUGH GATE TO RIGHT INTO FIELD

SCARNOR POINT
LOTS OF LITTLE UPS & DOWNS
FANTASTIC WALKING!
BENCH 044
STEEP DESCENT

BIG PILES OF ROCKS
REEDY CLIFF
OLD TREE TRUNK

045 BENCH
16
LOTS OF UPS & DOWNS MAKES THIS HARD WORK
STILE INTO BACK GARDEN OF HOWARD COTTAGE

¼ mile
APPROX SCALE
0   500m

75-90 MINS TO/FROM PORT QUIN (MAP 16)

trailblazer

ROUTE GUIDE AND MAPS

Services are mostly bucket-and-spade shops but there is a Co-op **supermarket** (7am-10pm daily), with an **ATM** inside, uphill from the harbour. Like other Cornish hideaways, artists have moved in and there are some informal galleries exhibiting their work. Port Isaac is the setting for the TV drama Doc Martin which can make the village very busy with 'TV location tourists' in the summer and also seems to have had a significant influence on the rather overinflated room rates in the village.

Where to stay

Campers should head to **Brooklands Farm Campsite** (see p104) in Port Gaverne.

B&Bs are thin on the ground in Port Isaac these days; many have been turned into more lucrative holiday homes it seems. **Gallery B&B** (☎ 01208-881032; 1T/2D; ✆; WI-FI; 🐾; £47.50-65pp), also known as Harbour View B&B, is nice, but pricey. It sits above an artist's studio with work in progress lying about. All rooms have sea views. **Three Gates Meadows B&B** (☎ 01208-880609, 🖥 cornwall-online.co.uk/ threegatesmeadow-portisaac; 1T/1D shared bathroom; WI-FI; from £40pp), cheaper but also more basic, is opposite the Co-op.

The **Old School Hotel & Restaurant** (☎ 01208-880721, 🖥 theoldschoolhotel.co .uk; 2S/9D/1F; ✆; WI-FI in bar; 🐾; £42.50-79pp, sgl £50-67) is a gorgeous building (c1875) with an excellent restaurant and well turned-out rooms. Likewise, **The Slipway Hotel & Restaurant** (☎ 01208-880264, 🖥 portisaachotel.com; 5D/ 1T/1F; ✆; WI-FI; £65-80pp).

Stargazy Inn (☎ 01208-811516, 🖥 stargazyinn.co.uk; 1T/4D/1 suite; WI-FI; £75-100pp), offers 'luxury' B&B, has a fine restaurant and featured as Wenn House in Doc Martin. The tuk-tuk which you may have seen on your trek up the hill to Port Isaac connects the inn with Pilchards Café in Port Gaverne.

Where to eat and drink

The first establishment you'll see (especially if you've arrived by tuk-tuk) will be the

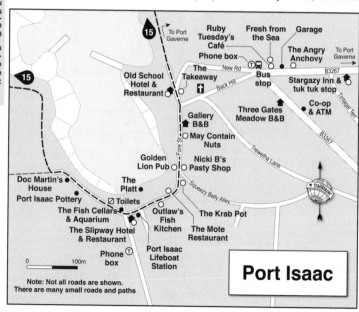

Port Isaac

Stargazy Inn (see Where to stay) which is open for lunch, dinner (mains £14-18.50; lobster £25/39.95 half/whole) and cocktails. On the opposite side of the road there are a couple of places worth considering. The excellent *Fresh from the Sea* (☎ 01208-880849, 🖥 freshfromthesea.co.uk; daily 9.30am-5pm) is unusual in that the fish is caught by the owner then cooked on site. They do sandwiches with crab, lobster or smoked salmon (£7.50-11.50), or else try the scrumptious mackerel paté on toast (£8). In the evening, *The Angry Anchovy* (☎ 01208-881384, 🖥 theangryanchovy .co.uk; daily from 6pm) specialises in pizza (£6-13) but has pasta dishes and pasties on the menu too.

Down the hill towards the harbour, *May Contain Nuts* (Mon-Sat 9.30am-4.30pm, Sun & bank holiday Mons 10am-4.30pm) sells pasties, as surprisingly, does *Nicki B's Pasty Shop* (Mon-Sat 8.30am to when sold out, usually 4.30-5pm, Sun 9.30am to when sold out), whilst, *The Krab Pot* (☎ 01208-880542; 🐾; Sat-Thur 10am-4pm) is a delightful seafood-based café (fish dishes £9.50-15.95).

For pub food, there are two fine options: decide between the 300-year-old *Golden Lion* (☎ 01208-880336, 🖥 the goldenlionportisaac.co.uk) serving bar meals daily (summer noon-2.30pm & 5.30-9pm, winter 6-8pm), with wonderful

views across the harbour from its second-floor restaurant, and *The Mote* (☎ 01208-880226, 🖥 the-mote.co.uk; Feb-Dec daily noon-9pm) which has been transformed into a top culinary venue for foodies, with fish dominating the menu (main dishes £13.50-29).

Outlaw's Fish Kitchen (☎ 01208-881183, 🖥 outlaws.co.uk/fishkitchen; daily noon-3pm & 6-9pm; Feb-Jun Tue-Sat only) is Port Isaac's standout seafood restaurant. It serves up small tapas-like servings of seafood (£7.50-14) and has an impressive wine list to boot.

Nearby, *The Slipway Hotel & Restaurant* (see Where to stay; food served daily noon-2.30pm & from 6.30pm) serves locally sourced ingredients where possible and the fish (including crab and lobster and the catch of the day) comes from the fish cellar over the road. Equally refined, the *Old School Hotel & Restaurant* (see Where to stay; daily noon-2.30pm & 6-9.30pm, cream teas and sandwiches available all day), serves some fantastic food. Mains here cost £11.95-22.50.

For Fish 'n' Chips, head to *The Takeaway*.

Transport

[See also pp52-6] First Kernow's No 96 **bus** stops by the Central Garage in the upper village.

PORT ISAAC TO PADSTOW [MAPS 15-20]

If medals were ever to be given out for the toughest section of the SWCP then the initial three miles of this winding **12-mile (19km, 4-5hrs)** stage would certainly stand somewhere on the podium. Indeed, you may want to prepare for it by buying a pasty before you set off, especially since the first chance of refreshment is nine miles away in Polzeath. (Note, you can actually avoid this difficult section by taking the signposted diversion off left, just past Doc Martin's house, (see opposite) which takes you through farmland to Port Quin, see Map 15.)

Taken as a whole, this stage is fairly wild and lonely, though once past Port Quin the stage poses few difficulties. Add to this the pretty beaches tucked between sheer cliffs and the very attractive hamlet of **Port Quin**, with its tiny cove housing a sheltered beach, and you have the ingredients for a very enjoyable day's walking. Note, Port Quin has a small car park where, during the summer, unless it's pouring with rain, you'll find the friendly *Fiona's Café* (Map 16; ☎ 07879-476431; 11am-4pm Easter-Oct). It is run out of the back of a vintage Citroën, lovingly dubbed the 'tin-can van'. *(cont'd on p112)*

ROUTE GUIDE AND MAPS

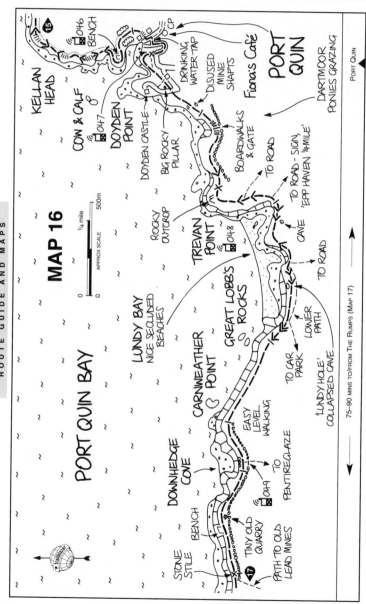

MAP 16

Port Quin

75-90 MINS TO/FROM THE RUMPS (MAP 17)

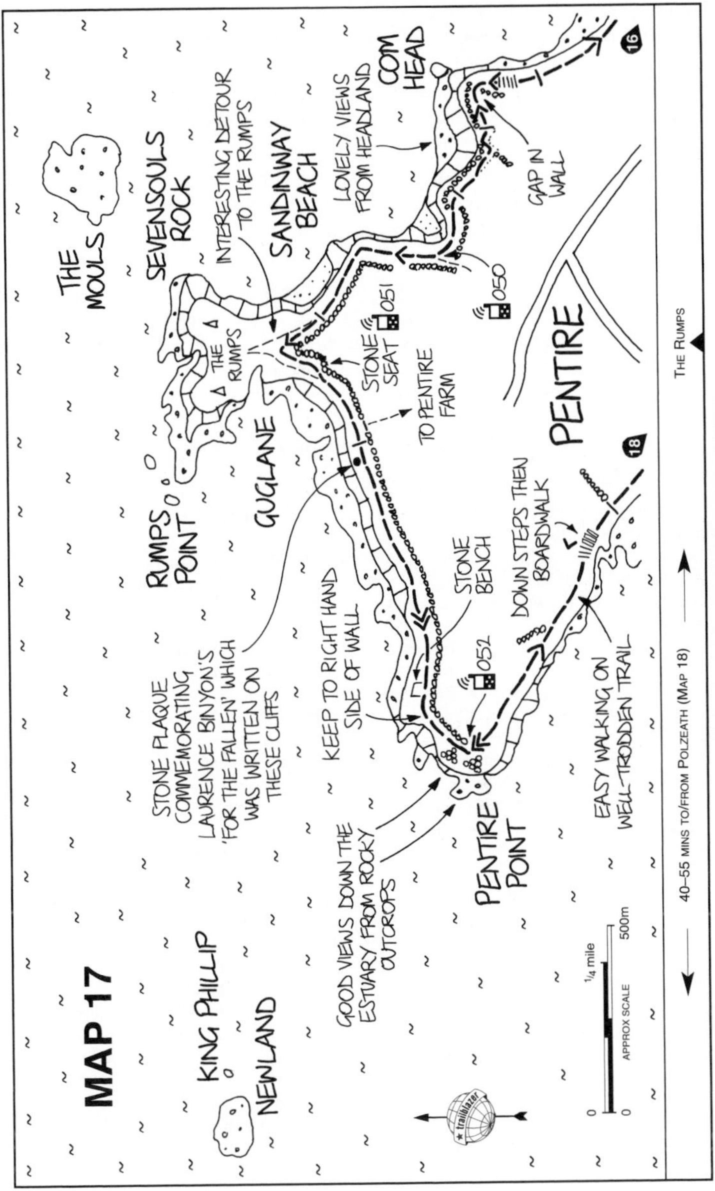

MAP 17

THE MOULS

KING PHILLIP

NEWLAND

SEVENSOULS ROCK

RUMPS POINT

THE RUMPS

GUGLANE

SANDINWAY BEACH

COM HEAD

16

LONELY VIEWS FROM HEADLAND

INTERESTING DETOUR TO THE RUMPS

GAP IN WALL

050

051

STONE SEAT

TO PENTIRE FARM

PENTIRE

18

STONE PLAQUE COMMEMORATING LAURENCE BINYON'S 'FOR THE FALLEN' WHICH WAS WRITTEN ON THESE CLIFFS

KEEP TO RIGHT HAND SIDE OF WALL

STONE BENCH

052

DOWN STEPS THEN BOARDWALK

GOOD VIEWS DOWN THE ESTUARY FROM ROCKY OUTCROPS

PENTIRE POINT

EASY WALKING ON WELL-TRODDEN TRAIL

APPROX SCALE

¼ mile

500m

0

0

40–55 MINS TO/FROM POLZEATH (MAP 18)

THE RUMPS

ROUTE GUIDE AND MAPS

(cont'd from p109) After the windswept and beautiful headland at **The Rumps** the path swings by **Pentire Point** and the vast **Padstow Bay** comes into view. Along the stretch between The Rumps and Pentire Point is a small plaque commemorating the moving war poem For the Fallen, written somewhere on this point by Laurence Binyon in 1914 at the start of WWI. The plaque bears the poem's fourth (and most famous) stanza:

> *They shall grow not old, as we that are left grow old*
> *Age shall not weary them, nor the years condemn*
> *At the going down of the sun and in the morning*
> *We will remember them.*

From Pentire Point, if the tide is out you will be able to marvel at the acres and acres of sand filling the **Camel Estuary** as it sweeps back to Padstow. At the holiday town of **Polzeath** you leave the cliffs behind and follow an easy path by the beach and through the dunes via **Trebetherick** where there is a seasonal **café** (Map 18; Easter to Oct 10.30am-5.30pm) to **Rock**, where a passenger ferry leaves regularly for Padstow. It is worth making a detour to **St Enodoc Church** (see Map 18 and box on p114) where John Betjeman is buried.

POLZEATH   [MAP 18]

Polzeath (pronounced Pol-zeth) is a seaside resort, a place for holidaymakers, for families, days on the beach, sand between the toes and rock pools. It is also a place for the surfer and along the strip during the season wetsuits and boards can be hired by the hour, half day or day. There is less reason for the walker to stop here, although Polzeath does provide an alternative should all accommodation be fully booked in Padstow.

All the services are concentrated along the strip facing Hayle Bay including a Spar **supermarket** (daily 7.30am-9pm). The **ATM** near Ann's Cottage surf shop charges £1.85 per transaction; better perhaps to use the cashback facility offered by Spar.

Where to stay, eat & drink

Campers have two options: *Valley Caravan Park* (☎ 01208-862391, 🖳 valley caravanpark.co.uk; walker & tent £8-14; WI-FI), set back from the beach and welcoming walkers, and the sprawling *Tristram Caravan and Camping Park* (☎ 01208-862215, 🖳 polzeathcamping.co.uk; Apr to late Oct; 🐾; walker & tent £10-12) which looks out over the beach.

Most of the **B&Bs** cater for holidaymakers and tend to turn away walkers during the summer, particularly one-nighters.

An exception is *Seaways* (☎ 01208-862382, 🖳 seaways-polzeath.co.uk; 1S/2T or D/1F; ➥; WI-FI; from £42pp, sgl £50-55), less than five minutes from the beach.

For **food**, as you enter Polzeath you are welcomed by *Granny's Café* (hot food 9am-2pm, cakes and hot drinks 9am-5pm) where you'll get a hot drink for £1 or a full English for as little as £5. Closer to the beach, *Vanilla* (daily 10.30am-5.30pm, until 7pm on sunny evenings) does simply sumptuous ice-creams.

Opening earlier than the others (from 8am weather permitting) and right on the beach is *Wave Hunters*, a beach shack selling perky coffee and bacon baps. *The Tube Station* (☎ 01208 869200, 🖳 tubestation .org; WI-FI; Tue-Sat 10am-4pm), on your left just before you leave the seafront road to rejoin the path, is a café, art gallery and community church.

Nearby, *The Waterfront* (☎ 01208-869655, 🖳 waterfrontpolzeath.co.uk; daily Easter to Sep/Oct 10am-10.30pm, winter Thur-Sun lunch and supper only; 🐾; WI-FI; mains £10-20) is a first-floor bar-restaurant serving pizza, burgers and the like. Downstairs they operate *Sand Bar*, a café serving hungry surfers.

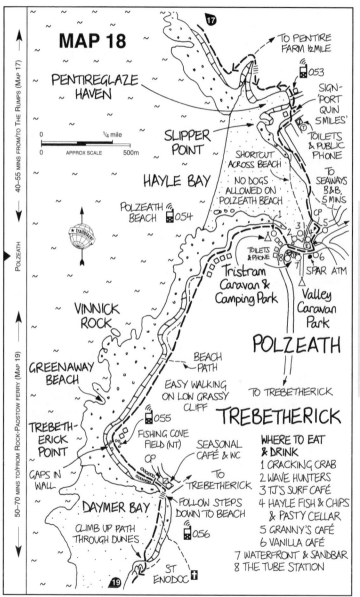

MAP 18

TO PENTIRE FARM ½ MILE

📱 053

SIGN-'PORT QUIN 5 MILES'

TOILETS & PUBLIC PHONE

PENTIREGLAZE HAVEN

SLIPPER POINT

SHORTCUT ACROSS BEACH

NO DOGS ALLOWED ON POLZEATH BEACH

TO SEAWAYS B&B, 5 MINS

HAYLE BAY

POLZEATH BEACH 📱 054

CP

1
2 3 1
5
E
4

TOILETS & PHONE 8 B 6
7
SPAR ATM

Tristram Caravan & Camping Park

VINNICK ROCK

Valley Caravan Park

POLZEATH

GREENAWAY BEACH

BEACH PATH

EASY WALKING ON LOW GRASSY CLIFF

TO TREBETHERICK

TREBETHERICK

📱 055

TREBETH-ERICK POINT

FISHING COVE FIELD (NT)

CP

SEASONAL CAFÉ & WC

TO TREBETHERICK

WHERE TO EAT & DRINK

1 CRACKING CRAB
2 WAVE HUNTERS
3 TJ'S SURF CAFÉ
4 HAYLE FISH & CHIPS & PASTY CELLAR
5 GRANNY'S CAFÉ
6 VANILLA CAFÉ
7 WATERFRONT & SANDBAR
8 THE TUBE STATION

GAPS IN WALL

DAYMER BAY

FOLLOW STEPS DOWN TO BEACH

📱 056

CLIMB UP PATH THROUGH DUNES

ST ENODOC

trailblaze

0   ¼ mile
0   500m
APPROX SCALE

40–55 MINS FROM/to THE RUMPS (MAP 17)

POLZEATH

50–70 MINS TO/FROM ROCK-PADSTOW FERRY (MAP 19)

ROUTE GUIDE AND MAPS

❑ Church of St Enodoc and John Betjeman's grave

A worthwhile and easy detour since it's only a few hundred yards off the coast path, the Church of St Enodoc is named like most Cornish churches after an obscure Celtic saint. The approach from the beach across the golf course brings you to the church path that crosses the fairway, a delightful walk.

© Philip Thomas

Protected now by tamarisk the church is set in a hollow, its 13th-century spire visible above the sand dunes of Daymer Bay. Battered by storms over the centuries it slowly succumbed to the advancing sand which piled high against the walls, blocked the door and began to fill the aisles. By the early 1800s the church had been almost abandoned and the only access was through the roof. Restoration began in the mid-19th century by local craftsmen using as much of the original stone as possible so it has retained an atmosphere of earliest Christianity even in its final Victorian, basically Norman-style, restoration.

John Betjeman (Poet Laureate 1972-84) is best known for his poetry but he was also a journalist and broadcaster. There is a memorial to his father, his mother is buried here and he had his own grave so placed that the ornate headstone is set looking out to sea over the view he loved.

The Trebetherick area and Betjeman

John Betjeman's love of Cornwall and in particular North Cornwall went back to early childhood when every year his family made the day-long journey by the Great Western Railway from London's Waterloo station to Wadebridge where they'd be met by horse-drawn brake 'out of Derry's stables'; its carriage lamps lighting their uphill way

© Philip Thomas

'past haunted wood and on
To far Trebetherick by the sandy sea.'
Soon he'd 'safe in bed' be watching the insects
  'drawn to the candle flame
While through the open window came the roar
Of full Atlantic rollers on the beach.'

Before breakfast he'd run alone 'monarch of miles of sand
Its shining stretches satin-smooth and vein'd.
I felt beneath bare feet the lugworm casts
And walked where only gulls and oyster-catchers
Had stepped before me to the water's edge.'

He writes of 'fan-shaped scallop shells, the backs of crabs, bits of old driftwood worn to reptile shapes' and how the sandhoppers leapt around him if he lifted up 'heaps of bladder wrack' left by the outgoing tide. He felt they all welcomed him back and he returned almost annually throughout his life until, staying for longer than usual, he died at Trebetherick in 1984.

Patricia Major

Across the road, *TJ's Surf Café* (🖥 tjssurfshop.co.uk/surf-cafe; Sun-Wed 10am-4pm, Thur-Sat 10am-8.30pm) does similar fare, but has the added attraction of being right on the beach. Also overlooking the beach, from its cliff-top perch beside Tristram Caravan and Camping Park, is Polzeath's best restaurant, *Cracking Crab* (☎ 01208-862333, 🖥 winkingprawngroup .co.uk/cracking-crab; 8.45am-4pm & 6-9pm), a seafood specialist with big breakfasts, lunchtime baguettes (£5.10-8.95),

Doom Bar ale on tap and a quality evening menu (mains from £16.75). The sunsets from here are spectacular.

For **takeaway**, try either *Hayle Fish 'n' Chips* (daily noon-9pm), where you can also get pizza (5-9pm), or *Pasty Cellar*.

Transport
[See also pp52-6] First Kernow's No 96 **bus** service (between Bude/Camelford and Wadebridge) stops at the beach.

ROCK   [MAP 19, p116]
Originally a small fishing village, these days Rock has a reputation for being exclusive and pricey. It's true that second-homers have snapped up all the available property and in the summer the Porsche count is high, but for the rest of the year, it's a quiet residential neighbourhood with a wonderful waterfront.

Keen ale drinkers might like to sample a pint of Doom Bar, the UK's best-selling

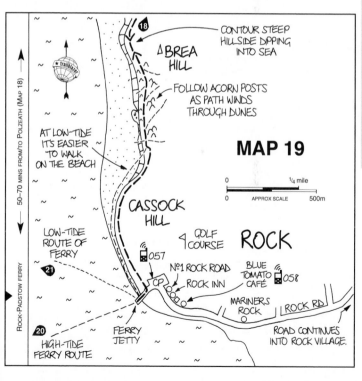

ROUTE GUIDE AND MAPS

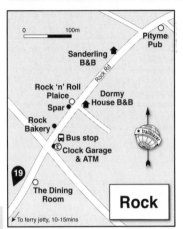

cask ale, on its home turf. But note, only the cask version is still brewed at the Sharp's Brewery here in Rock. Bottled Doom Bar is now brewed in Burton upon Trent.

As with many popular Cornish villages you may find it difficult to book a room here for a single night in peak season.

Where to stay
Rock maybe small but it has a couple of good B&Bs. The relaxed *Dormy House* (☎ 01208-863845, 🖳 dormyhouserock.co.uk; 5D or T; WI-FI; from £55pp, sgl occ £90) is run with Scandinavian flair and efficiency by the Anglo-Swedish owners. At the smaller *Sanderling* (☎ 01208-862420, 🖳 sander ling-rock.co.uk; 2D, T or F; 🛏; WI-FI; 🐾; £40-45pp plus £20 single-night supplement), the rooms each have their own private fridge and dining facilities.

Where to eat and drink
Just back from the ferry jetty (see Map 19), the first place you see is *No 1 Rock Road* (Map 19; ☎ 01208-863008, 🖳 no1rockroad

.com; summer daily 10.30am-10pm, winter Tue-Sat 10am-9.30pm; mains £20-26), although next door *Rock Inn* (summer daily 10am-9.30pm, winter Tue-Sat 10am-9.30pm; mains £10-20) is cheaper. Both have sea-view terrace seating.

Nearby, *Blue Tomato* (Map 19; ☎ 01208-863841, 🖳 bluetomatocafe.co.uk; daily 9am-5pm; 🐾; WI-FI) is more of a café, although the food is restaurant quality; there is even a menu for dogs.

Just along Rock Rd is the pub-restaurant *Mariners Rock* (Map 19; ☎ 01208-863679, 🖳 themarinersrock.com; food noon-3pm & 6-9pm, Sun noon-4pm; WI-FI; 🐾) with sea-view terrace seating, and Doom Bar on tap. Note, they were changing management at the time of research and were closed for maintenance.

About a mile from the ferry is a row of shops (see map opposite). Also here is *The Dining Room* (☎ 01208-862622, 🖳 thedin ingroomrock.co.uk; Wed-Sun 7-9pm & bank holiday Mons), with mains on their à la carte menu from £23.95. Carrying on past Clock Garage, where there is an **ATM** (£1.70 charge), *Rock Bakery* (aka *Malcolm Barnecutt*, 🖳 barnecutt.co.uk; Mon-Wed 7.30am-3pm, Thur & Fri to 3.30pm, Sat to 2.30pm) is on the left; a superb sandwich shop that also sells fruit. Further on there's the Spar **supermarket** (daily 8am-7pm), next door to chippy *Rock'n'Roll Plaice* (Sun & Mon 5-8pm, Tue 5-9pm, Wed-Sat noon-1.30pm & 5-9pm; also serves breakfast baps 8-11.30am); and if you keep going you'll come to a pub with the curious name of *The Pityme Inn* (☎ 01208-862228; 🐾; food served daily noon-2pm & 6.30-9pm).

Transport
[See also pp52-6] First Kernow's **bus** No 96 stops near the Clock Garage. For the ferry to Padstow, see box opposite.

❏ The Doom Bar
The Camel Estuary forms a rare natural harbour guarded by a particularly dangerous sand bar across its entrance known as the Doom Bar, created by the Celtic Sea meeting the River Camel. Over 300 vessels have been wrecked or stranded on the bar which you can see at low tide.

❏ **Rock to Padstow ferry**

Black Tor Ferry (☎ 01841-532239) operates daily between Padstow and Rock. The service starts at 7.50am from Padstow and runs every 20 minutes. The times for the last ferry of the day from Padstow (20 mins earlier for last ferry from Rock) are: Nov-Mar 4.50pm; Apr-May 5.50pm; June to mid July 6.50pm; mid July to Aug 7.50pm; 1st Sep to mid Sep 6.50pm; mid Sep to end Oct 5.50pm. No Sunday service early Nov to mid Feb. The fare is £2 single, £4 return. In Padstow passengers embark at North Quay when the tide is in but at low tide the ferry operates from the lower beach (see Map 21), clearly signposted. Dogs (£1 return) can be taken on the ferry.

In addition to this, an evening service is maintained by **Rock Water Taxi** (☎ 07778-105297, 🖳 rock-watertaxi.co.uk; Easter-Oct 7pm-midnight weather and tide permitting, from 7.30pm mid July to end Aug; £4 single, £7 return), although in winter the service operates on Sundays only 9.30am-4.30pm.

PADSTOW [MAP 20, p119]

Originally called Petrocstow, after St Petroc established a monastery here in the 6th century, pretty Padstow clusters around the harbour; cosy and sheltered from the prevailing wind. The parish church of **St Petroc's** was built between 1425 and 1450 but the lower part of the tower was built even earlier. The pulpit is decorated with carved scallop shells to honour pilgrims to the shrine of St James in Santiago, Spain.

Padstow is the most important and the most sheltered port on the north coast although large vessels are prevented from getting in by the **Doom Bar** (see box opposite).

This is definitely a place to dawdle, eat fish & chips and watch the goings-on in the harbour. Boat trips are advertised by men calling out as you pass 'Pay when you come back. If you don't come back you don't pay!' Padstow has become synonymous with the TV chef Rick Stein who has made the place his own with numerous establishments under his name.

For a bit of history visit **Padstow Museum** (☎ 01841-532752, 🖳 padstow museum.co.uk; free admission; daily 10.30am-4.30pm), now housed inside the town's former railway station, Old Station House, on Station Rd.

Another option for a rainy day is the **National Lobster Hatchery** (☎ 01841-533877, 🖳 nationallobsterhatchery.co.uk; £4.50; 10am-5pm); it is a conservation research centre where you can see tiny

juvenile lobsters being reared, before they are released into the seas.

Padstow is the start/end-point of the very popular cycle route, the Camel Trail, which runs for 18 miles along a disused railway track between Padstow and Wenfordbridge via Wadebridge and Bodmin. It can easily be done in a day, there and back. If you want to rent bikes, **Padstow Cycle Hire** (☎ 01841 533533, 🖳 padstowcyclehire.com; 9am-5pm; bike rental per day £17-26, helmets free) has everything you need, even dog trailers.

'**Obby 'Oss Day** (see box on p120) is held here every May, and Carnival Week is in July (see p15).

Services

The town centre is compact with everything you need within a few paces of the harbour. The **tourist information centre** (TIC ☎ 01841-533449, 🖳 padstowlive.com; Easter-Oct Mon-Fri 9am-5.30pm, Sat & Sun 10am-4pm, winter 10am-4pm, closed on Sundays), situated on the North Quay, is very useful. You can get **internet access** (£1/15 mins) here and they'll find you a room even when the town is at bursting point. Most cafés, pubs and restaurants have free wi-fi.

Around Market Place you will find Barclays **bank**, and the **post office** (Mon-Fri 9am-5.30pm, Sat to 12.30pm) in the Spar **shop** (Mon-Sat 7am-9pm, Sun 8am-9pm; winter Mon-Sat 7am-6pm, Sun 8am-6pm).

There is a branch of Boots **pharmacy** (Mon-Sat 8.30am-7pm, Sun 10am-6pm) centrally too.

Up the hill above the town is **Padstow Surgery** (☎ 01841-532346; daily 8.30am-6pm) on Boyd Avenue and a big Tesco **supermarket** (Mon-Sat 7am-9pm, Sun 10am-4pm), which has an **ATM** outside.

For **camping necessities**, including fuel for stoves, Mountain Warehouse (9am-5.30pm), near the tourist information centre, is well stocked.

Where to stay

You can camp at the very welcoming *Dennis Cove Camping* (☎ 01841-532349, 🖳 denniscovecampsite.co.uk; walkers £11-12) about ten minutes from the harbour and close to the Camel Cycle Trail. It's best to call ahead in July and August though they will always try to accommodate walkers if they possibly can.

There are numerous places to stay since Padstow is an exceedingly busy resort but B&Bs frequently get booked up during the height of the season, especially at weekends, meaning one-nighters are rarely welcomed with open arms. Book well ahead at these times and be prepared for a two- or three-night stay, using the buses to take you out to the coast path and back again at night. At other times of the year this will not be a problem.

Close to the harbour is the fabulously central *South Quay B&B* (☎ 01841-532383, 🖳 southquaybedandbreakfastpadstow.co.uk; 2D; WI-FI; 🐾; £37.50-47.50pp, sgl occ £60), also known as Cullinan's B&B. One of the rooms is on the top floor, with a balcony overlooking the harbour.

Up the hill leading away from South Quay is *Treverbyn House* (☎ 01841-532855, 🖳 treverbynhouse.com, Station Rd; 3D; ▼; WI-FI; £65-67.50pp, sgl occ from £115), a large turreted house with spacious rooms and period furniture. Single-night bookings are usually only accepted outside the high season.

On colourful, pastel-painted Duke St, *Cyntwell B&B* (☎ 01841- 533447, 🖳 cyntwell.co.uk; 4D; WI-FI; ▼; £44-49pp, sgl

occ from £60) has four lovely doubles and a friendly welcome. It's pronounced 'Sintwell', in case you were wondering.

Plenty of Padstow's historic pubs have rooms too. *The Old Ship Hotel* (☎ 01841-532357, 🖳 oldshiphotel-padstow.co.uk; 3S/9D/3F; ▼; WI-FI; 🐾; £60-75pp) is central and gives discounts for stays of more than one night. *The London Inn* (☎ 01841-532554, 🖳 staustellbrewery.co.uk/pub/padstow/london-inn; 3D/1T; WI-FI; from £40pp), at 6 Lanadwell St, is a proper locals' pub with good food, great ale and rooms up top. *Old Custom House* (☎ 01841-532359, 🖳 oldcustomhousepadstow.co.uk; 23D or F; ▼; WI-FI; £60-102.50pp) meanwhile, is a very slick, hotel-like operation, with smart rooms attached to the old pub, but with a separate reception area next door.

Also at the pricier end of the market, Rick Stein has a number of options, the most affordable being the rooms above *Rick Stein's Café* (central reservations ☎ 01841-532700, 🖳 rickstein.com; 3D; ▼; WI-FI; 🐾; from £55pp). Visit the website or phone for information about his other accommodation possibilities.

The iconic *Metropole Hotel* (☎ 01841-532486, 🖳 the-metropole.co.uk; 58 rooms; ▼; WI-FI; 🐾; £35-160pp, sgl occ from £59; food served daily till 9pm), built in 1904, is a very traditional kind of place, although it does have wi-fi throughout, a spa and an outdoor heated pool, which non-residents can use too (adults/children £6/4).

If you fancy a longer stay (3-night minimum or 7-night in summer) *50 Church Street* (☎ 01841-532121, 🖳 50churchstreet.co.uk; 1D; ▼; WI-FI; £42.50-45pp) is a homely one-bedroom flat with a kitchen. It overlooks the attractively ageing St Petroc's Church in the old town.

Where to eat and drink

Padstow Fish and Chip Café (☎ 01841-532915; daily summer 11.30am-9pm, winter 11.30am-4.30pm), on the harbour, and the more down-to-earth chippy, *Chip Ahoy* (☎ 01841-534753; noon-2.30pm & 4.30-9pm), on Broad St, are equally good. However, the fish & chip shops in Padstow

Padstow MAP 20

HIGH TIDE FERRY TERMINAL

Ferry to Rock

Harbour

Fish dock

National Lobster Hatchery

Padstow Cycle Hire

Public toilet

i@ TIC & internet

North Quay

Public toilet

Mountain Warehouse

West Quay

Market St

South Quay

Strand St

St Edmund's Lane

Car park

Public toilets

Bus stop

Padstow Museum & former railway station

Station Road

Trevorbyn Rd

Dennis Rd

Dennis Lane

New St

To Dennis Cove Camping, 500m

To the Camel Trail & Dennis Cove Camping

To Tesco & Padstow Surgery

Barclays £

Boots

Lanadwell St

Broad St

Duke St

Spar, ATM & Post Office £

Cross St

St Saviour's Lane

High Street

Church Street

St Petroc's

A389

B3276

B3276

100m

0

Trailblazer

Where to stay
1 50 Church Street
3 Cyntwell B&B
4 Old Ship Hotel
11 Rick Stein's Café
12 London Inn
15 Old Custom House
16 South Quay B&B
19 Metropole Hotel
20 Treverbyn House

Where to eat and drink
4 Old Ship Hotel
5 Rojano's
6 Shipwright's Inn
7 Cherry Tree Coffee House
8 Padstow Fish & Chip Café
9 Chough Bakery
10 Paul Ainsworth @ No 6
11 Rick Stein's Café
12 London Inn
13 Chip Ahoy
14 The Harbour Inn
15 Old Custom House
17 St Petroc's Bistro
18 Seafood Restaurant
21 Stein's Deli
22 Stein's Fish and Chips
23 Ben's Crib Box Café

ROUTE GUIDE AND MAPS

must feel permanently upstaged by *Stein's Fish and Chips* (see column opposite).

For something in the rucksack, try *Chough Bakery* (☎ 01841-532835, 🖳 the choughbakery.co.uk, 3 The Strand; daily Apr-Oct 8.30am-5pm, Nov-Mar 9am-4.30pm). For posh picnic supplies, try *Stein's Deli* (Sun-Thur 10am-5.30pm, Fri-Sat 9.30am-5.30pm).

Cute cafés are dotted around the harbour. *Cherry Tree Coffee House* (9am-5pm daily), with its range of breakfasts (£6-8) and lunchtime paninis (£6-7), is particularly popular. *Ben's Crib Box Café* (8am-2pm, Sun 9am-2pm) is the closest thing Padstow has to a builders' café, and is the cheapest place to get a decent breakfast.

There is no shortage of lovely old pubs. The two most popular are *Old Custom House* (see Where to stay; food served daily 10am-9.30pm), and the *Shipwright's Inn* (☎ 01841-532451; food daily noon-9pm), largely because of their harbour-side locations.

For a more down-to-earth local, though, try *The Harbour Inn* (food noon-9.30pm) or *The London Inn* (see Where to stay; food noon-3pm & 6-9pm) where the low-beamed ceilings and fine ales will keep your mind off the lack of a sea view.

The *Old Ship Hotel* (see Where to stay; open daily Easter-Oct 10am-10pm, Nov-Mar noon-9pm) is another pub option, with fairly standard pub grub, but the added attraction of lots of outdoor seating out front.

Rojano's (☎ 01841-532796, 🖳 paul-ainsworth.co.uk; Mar-Nov daily noon-

9.30pm), at 9 Mill Square, is a pleasant place with Italian tendencies. Under the same ownership, *Paul Ainsworth @ No 6* (☎ 01841-532093, 🖳 paul-ainsworth.co .uk; Tue-Sat noon-2.30pm & 6-10pm; open bank holiday Mondays) has an exotic menu (mains £31-45) including offerings such as pale ale chicken and fish of the day.

Few people would contemplate a visit to Padstow without giving some thought to trying one of Rick Stein's restaurants. The central reservation service (see Where to stay) covers all of them, although you can't book at *Stein's Fish and Chips* (South Quay; 11.30am-3pm & 5-9pm) which is the cheapest of them all (fish & chips £10.95). Also reasonably priced is *Rick Stein's Café* (see Where to stay; 8am-3pm & 4-9.45pm) where mains cost £12.95-19.95 (3 courses £23.95).

Stein's flagship *Seafood Restaurant* (peak season daily noon-2.30pm & 6.30-10pm, out of season noon-2pm & 7-10pm) is a mecca for foodies, but the cheapest meal on the menu is £20 (Cornish cod, chips and tartare sauce). The three-course lunch costs £41pp.

At *St Petroc's Bistro* (daily noon-3pm & 5.30-9.30pm) you can eat outdoors under awnings in fine weather. The food here is also superb and slightly cheaper.

Transport

[See also pp52-6] The **bus** terminus is at the bottom of Station Rd beside the former railway station, which now houses the town's museum. Plymouth City Bus's No 11/11A service goes to Bodmin Parkway

---

❏ The Hobby Horse celebration

On May Day bank holiday the **'Obby 'Oss**, a man wearing a head mask set on a circular wooden hoop about 6ft in diameter, dances through Padstow town. He is preceded by a Teazer who leads the dance with theatrical movements. The accompanying retinue are dressed in white with added ribbons and flowers.

This celebration has been performed for centuries and there are many theories about its origins. Some say it has pagan roots while others think it began during one of England's numerous wars with France, when the women of the town dressed up to frighten off an enemy landing while all the men were at sea. Or perhaps it is simply a welcome to the summer, a tradition that has both persisted and changed over the years.

Be aware that if you are passing through Padstow at this time of year you will have to book your accommodation well in advance.

station and Plymouth and the A5 follows the coast road to Newquay.

See the box on p117 for details of the **ferry** service between Rock and Padstow. If you need a **taxi** try the following: Ocean Taxis (☎ 07980-001323); Call-a-cab (☎ 01841-521184); or Padstow Taxi Services (☎ 01841-551021, 🖳 padstowtaxiservice .co.uk).

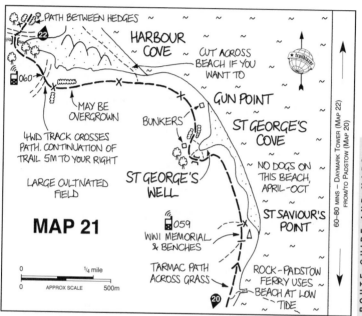

PATH BETWEEN HEDGES

HARBOUR COVE

CUT ACROSS BEACH IF YOU WANT TO

★ trailblazer

GUN POINT

MAY BE OVERGROWN

BUNKERS

ST GEORGE'S COVE

4WD TRACK CROSSES PATH. CONTINUATION OF TRAIL 5M TO YOUR RIGHT

LARGE CULTIVATED FIELD

ST GEORGE'S WELL

NO DOGS ON THIS BEACH, APRIL-OCT

MAP 21

059 WWI MEMORIAL & BENCHES

ST SAVIOUR'S POINT

0   ¼ mile
0   APPROX SCALE   500m

TARMAC PATH ACROSS GRASS

ROCK-PADSTOW FERRY USES BEACH AT LOW TIDE

60-80 MINS – DAYMARK TOWER (MAP 22) FROM/TO PADSTOW (MAP 20)

ROUTE GUIDE AND MAPS

PADSTOW TO TREVONE   [MAPS 20-23]

It's an easy and enjoyable **5 miles (8km, 1¾-2¼hrs)** to Trevone with cliff-top scenery at its best without the sharp ascents and descents characteristic of the path up to now.

The path soon leaves Padstow behind and we begin to experience what coastal walking is all about.

Two pretty little coves (Harbour and Hawker's) lead you to *Rest A While Tea Garden* (Map 22; ☎ 01841-532919; daily 10.30am-4.30pm, weather dependent) where morning coffees, light lunches and afternoon tea are on offer, should you not have replenished calories sufficiently in Padstow.

Past **Stepper Point** we head for a 19th-century stone Daymark Tower, an early aid to navigation, and a pause here gives time to take in the Camel Estuary behind and the rugged coastline ahead. Marvellous.

The **Merope Islands** are huge chunks of rock that have split away from the mainland like fragments of broken teeth. *(cont'd on p124)*

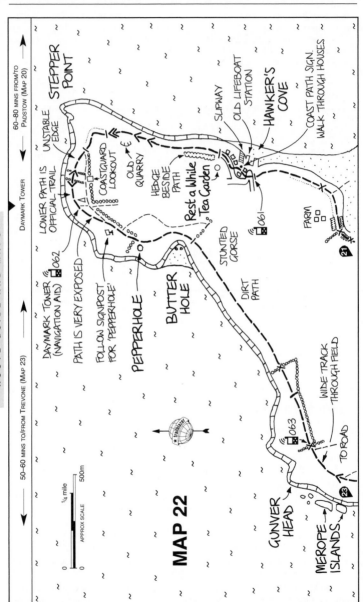

ROUTE GUIDE AND MAPS

50–60 MINS TO/FROM TREVONE (MAP 23)

DAYMARK TOWER

60–80 MINS FROM/TO PADSTOW (MAP 20)

STEPPER POINT

UNSTABLE EDGE

LOWER PATH IS OFFICIAL TRAIL

COASTGUARD LOOKOUT

OLD QUARRY

HEDGE BESIDE PATH

Rest a While Tea Garden

SLIPWAY

OLD LIFEBOAT STATION

HAWKER'S COVE

COAST PATH SIGN. WALK THROUGH HOUSES

061

FARM

21

DAYMARK TOWER (NAVIGATION AID) 062

PATH IS VERY EXPOSED

FOLLOW SIGNPOST FOR 'PEPPERHOLE'

PEPPERHOLE

BUTTER HOLE

STUNTED GORSE

DIRT PATH

WIDE TRACK THROUGH FIELD

063

TO ROAD

23

GUNVER HEAD

MEROPE ISLANDS

MAP 22

¼ mile

500m

0

APPROX SCALE

0

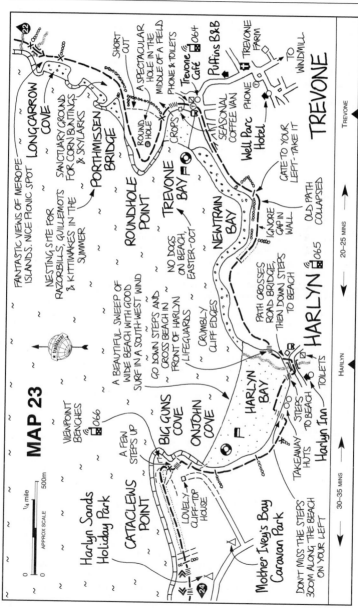

MAP 23

¼ mile

500m

0

0

APPROX SCALE

FANTASTIC VIEWS OF MEROPE ISLANDS. NICE PICNIC SPOT

LONGCARROW COVE

NESTING SITE FOR RAZORBILLS, GUILLEMOTS & KITTIWAKES IN THE SUMMER

SANCTUARY GROUND FOR CORN BUNTINGS & SKYLARKS

PORTHMISSEN BRIDGE

SHORT CUT

A SPECTACULAR HOLE IN THE MIDDLE OF A FIELD

TREVONE FARM

Puffins B&B

TO WINDMILL

Trevone Café 🏚064

PHONE & TOILETS

ROUND HOLE

CROPS

Well Parc Hotel

PHONE

SEASONAL COFFEE VAN

TREVONE

ROUNDHOLE POINT

TREVONE BAY

GATE TO YOUR LEFT- TAKE IT

NEWTRAIN BAY

IGNORE GAP IN WALL

OLD PATH COLLAPSED

NO DOGS ON BEACH, EASTER-OCT

TREVONE

HARLYN 🏚065

A BEAUTIFUL SWEEP OF WIDE BEACH WITH GOOD SURF IN A SOUTH-WEST WIND

GO DOWN STEPS AND CROSS BEACH IN FRONT OF HARLYN LIFEGUARDS

CRUMBLY CLIFF EDGES

PATH CROSSES ROAD BRIDGE, THEN DOWN STEPS TO BEACH

HARLYN

20-25 MINS

VIEWPOINT BENCHES 🏚066

A FEW STEPS UP

BIG GUNS COVE

ONJOHN COVE

HARLYN BAY

STEPS TO BEACH

TOILETS

Harlyn Inn

TAKEAWAY HUTS

30-35 MINS

Harlyn Sands Holiday Park

CATACLEWS POINT

LOVELY CLIFF-TOP HOUSE

Mother Ivey's Bay Caravan Park

DON'T MISS THE STEPS 300M ALONG THE BEACH ON YOUR LEFT

(cont'd from p121)   The sudden gaping holes that have opened up in the turf – terrifying to contemplate going near – are two of the strange features of the morning's walk.

Note the increase in the carpet of wild flowers – sea pinks, cornflowers, kidney vetch – particularly during May. Sometimes the flowers reach down the cliffs almost into the sea.

TREVONE   [MAP 23, p123]

This is the first bay after leaving Padstow with seasonal cafés and shops catering for the influx of holidaymakers who populate the place in the season. The **shop** (8.30am-6pm) attached to Trevone café sells essentials such as milk, eggs and newspapers.

Take the road away from the beach to find accommodation. You'll soon find *Puffins B&B* (☎ 01841-520684, 💻 www .cornwall-online.co.uk/puffinsbandb-tre vone; 1Tr; £45-50pp, plus £20 sgl occ) a self-contained studio loft at the top of a family home, complete with a lounge area. Further up into the village, *Well Parc Hotel* (☎ 01841-520318, 💻 wellparc.co.uk; 4D/ 3F; 👟; WI-FI; £30-45pp) is a pub-restaurant with B&B rooms. Food is served daily all

day Easter to September, and noon-2pm & 7-9.30pm the rest of the year.

More of a hub during the daytime, though, is *Trevone Café* (☎ 01841-520275; Easter-Oct daily 8am-6pm or later; Nov-Mar Sat & Sun 8am-6pm, Mon-Fri 8am-noon) where you can eat in, or sit at one of their outdoor tables overlooking the beach, or use the connected **takeaway** (noon-4pm). They serve booze here too. There's also a **seasonal coffee van** right on the path.

First Kernow's A5 **bus** service between Padstow and Newquay stops at Trevone but not at the beach: you have to walk just over a mile to the junction with the B3278 at Windmill. [See also pp52-6].

TREVONE TO TREYARNON   [MAPS 23-24]

This section of **5 miles (8km, 2-2½hrs)** is mostly fairly flat with a lovely spot of beach walking at **Harlyn Bay**, perfect for its kind, then out to Trevose Head past the lighthouse. The cliffs above **Mother Ivey's Bay** are great for a long picnic.

Booby's Bay and **Constantine Bay** are popular surf beaches with a scattering of houses along the low-lying foreshore. Constantine Bay in particular has a reputation as one of the best surf-pullers in North Cornwall.

HARLYN BAY & MOTHER IVEY'S
BAY   [MAP 23, p123]

Most walkers, if they stop here at all, will visit *Harlyn Inn* (☎ 01841-520207; 💻 har lyn-inn.com; 2D or T/3D or F/7D; 👟; WI-FI; 🐾; £35-50pp) for a pint and some lunch. The place lacks style and the food (served noon-2.30pm & 6-8.30pm) is your usual pub fare. An intact **Iron Age cemetery** was found on the site of the pub when it was built approximately 40 years ago; it contained over a hundred slate coffins with human remains and bronze and iron ornaments. The finds are in Truro Museum.

The stretch above Harlyn Bay and Mother Ivey's Bay (see Map 24) is rather

overwhelmed by two large caravan sites. *Harlyn Sands Holiday Park* (☎ 01841-520720, 💻 harlynsands.co.uk; WI-FI) is monstrous; facilities include restaurants and a leisure pool. It's pricey (£12-30 per tent pitch), and often fully-booked.

Mother Ivey's Bay Caravan Park (☎ 01841-520990, 💻 motheriveysbay.com; 2 walkers & tent £9-23; Apr-Oct) makes walkers feel more welcome, although it's still worth calling ahead to check they have space for a tent. There's a well-stocked shop here, which closes at 6pm, but no restaurant.

First Kernow's **bus** A5 (see pp52-6) stops at the bridge.

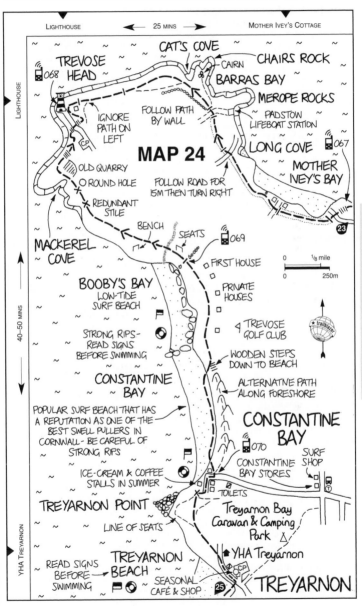

LIGHTHOUSE ←— 25 MINS —→ MOTHER IVEY'S COTTAGE

LIGHTHOUSE

068

TREVOSE HEAD

CAT'S COVE

CHAIRS ROCK

CAIRN

BARRAS BAY

MEROPE ROCKS

PADSTOW LIFEBOAT STATION

LONG COVE

067

MOTHER IVEY'S BAY

IGNORE PATH ON LEFT

FOLLOW PATH BY WALL

MAP 24

CP

OLD QUARRY

O ROUND HOLE

FOLLOW ROAD FOR 15M THEN TURN RIGHT

REDUNDANT STILE

BENCH

SEATS

069

MACKEREL COVE

FIRST HOUSE

PRIVATE HOUSES

BOOBY'S BAY

LOW-TIDE SURF BEACH

40–50 MINS

TREVOSE GOLF CLUB

STRONG RIPS – READ SIGNS BEFORE SWIMMING

WOODEN STEPS DOWN TO BEACH

CONSTANTINE BAY

ALTERNATIVE PATH ALONG FORESHORE

CONSTANTINE BAY

POPULAR SURF BEACH THAT HAS A REPUTATION AS ONE OF THE BEST SWELL PULLERS IN CORNWALL – BE CAREFUL OF STRONG RIPS

070

SURF SHOP

CONSTANTINE BAY STORES

ICE-CREAM & COFFEE STALLS IN SUMMER

TOILETS

TREYARNON POINT

LINE OF SEATS

Treyarnon Bay Caravan & Camping Park

YHA TREYARNON

YHA TREYARNON

READ SIGNS BEFORE SWIMMING

TREYARNON BEACH

TREYARNON

SEASONAL CAFÉ & SHOP

0   1/8 mile
0   250m

trailblazer

ROUTE GUIDE AND MAPS

23

25

CONSTANTINE BAY & TREYARNON
[MAP 24, p125]

YHA Treyarnon (☎ 0345-371 9664, 💻 yha.org.uk/hostel/treyarnon; 68 beds, some en suite rooms; from £15pp, camping £15 per tent, bell tent sleeps 5, £49-99; WI-FI) is a gem, and the heartbeat of this area. They have dorms and private rooms, and you can camp in their garden (in your own tent or one of their bell tents). The café (10am-9pm) meanwhile is open to all, and often pulls in a big crowd during summer weekends with its live music or sea-shanty singers. The garden terrace has fabulous sea views with some magical sunsets. They have real ale on tap, and evening meals are available too.

Behind the YHA, *Treyarnon Bay Caravan and Camping Park* (☎ 01841-520681, 💻 treyarnonbaycaravanpark.co.uk;

🐾 £2 Apr-Jun & Sep only; Apr to end Sep) charges £12-17 for a tent and two people.

The well-stocked **Constantine Bay Stores** (8am-5pm, till 7pm in high season) is a short walk inland and is perfect for picnic supplies. You can also get **cashback** here.

It's also where First Kernow's A5 **bus** service (between Padstow and Newquay) stops. [See also pp52-6].

In the summer there is often a **snack kiosk** at the far end of the bay bringing overpriced refreshments to holidaymakers.

Overlooking Treyarnon Beach is a seasonal **café** (Easter-Sep 10am-6pm at peak times; otherwise 10am-4.30pm) where you can get breakfast rolls and cups of tea, and seasonal **shop** (Easter-Sep 8am-6pm) for food supplies and buckets and spades.

TREYARNON TO MAWGAN PORTH [MAPS 24-27]

This **7 miles (11km, 2-2¾hrs)** of cliff-top walking is relatively easy with plenty of opportunity to enjoy the impressive scenery.

You first pass **Warren** and **Pepper** coves where weather and the sea have effectively split an **iron-age fort** into three parts. The ditches and ramparts are clearly visible and give you a good idea of what to look for at the numerous other forts and castles along the Cornish coast.

At **Porthcothan** (Map 25) there is a handy **shop**, Porthcothan Stores (daily 8am-6pm in summer; limited hours in the winter), which sells tea and snacks, and a **bus** stop: the No A5 bus service stops here en route between Padstow and Newquay. Then it's up to one of the most beautiful stretches of coast, **Park Head** to **Bedruthan Steps**, which gets quite crowded in summer. This area was a popular spot with the Victorians who were much taken with the wild sea cliffs.

Just beyond Bedruthan Steps, by the viewpoint for an iron-age fort, is a National Trust shop and **seasonal café**. Leaving the day trippers behind, you're then bound for **Mawgan Porth** where there are plenty of places to take a breather and refreshments.

MAWGAN PORTH   [MAP 27, p129]

Mawgan Porth is a cluster of old-fashioned retail shops and properties around the cove catering for visitors to its large beach. **Cornish Fresh Village Stores** (Mon-Sat 8am-9pm, Sun 8.30am-9pm) is a well-stocked mini-supermarket with pasties and coffee to boot. **Betty's News** (7.30am-5pm) has a **cashpoint** (£1.95 charge).

The beachfront is dominated by *The Merrymoor Inn* (☎ 01637-860258, 💻 merry

moorinn.com; 1S/1T/5D; 🐾; WI-FI; from £40-48.75pp, sgl occ £65-82.50), a no-nonsense pub serving good-value food (daily summer breakfast for non-residents from 10am, other meals noon-9pm; winter noon-2.30pm & 6-9pm), and local ales. There's sea-view terrace seating out at the front, and they have decent bed and breakfast rooms.

A little way out of the village is luxury B&B *Sea Vista* (☎ 01637-860276, 💻 sea

(sidebar) ROUTE GUIDE AND MAPS

vista.co.uk; 5D/1T/1F; ☻; wi-fi; £37.50-70pp, sgl occ from £65; summer minimum 2 nights). A little further up the road, *Bre-Pen Farm* (☎ 01637-860420, 💻 bre-pen farm.co.uk; 1T/3D; from £37.50pp, sgl occ £65) also has a well-stocked farm shop and a tearoom (summer daily 10am-4.30pm, winter Mon, Tue & Thur-Sat 10am-4.30pm), although sadly no camping.

The nearest campsite is *Magic Cove Touring Park* (☎ 01637-860263, 💻 magic cove.co.uk; tent & 2 people £16-25), just

300 yards from the beach. It's a well-appointed site with sparklingly clean toilets and level grassy pitches but can be booked up months in advance in peak season.

If so, about another mile up the road (turn left after Sun Haven Valley Country Holiday Park then bear right) is *Rettorick Mill* (☎ 01637-860460, 💻 retorrickmill.co .uk; camping £8pp), which is more likely to have space for hikers as there is no vehicular access to their camping field. *Scott & Babs* (10am-8pm), a barnhouse restaurant

(cont'd on p130)

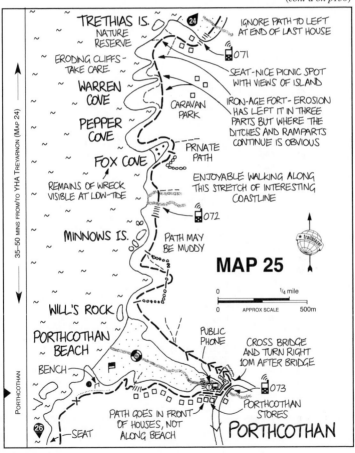

TRETHIAS IS.
NATURE RESERVE

IGNORE PATH TO LEFT AT END OF LAST HOUSE

📱 071

ERODING CLIFFS - TAKE CARE

WARREN COVE

CARAVAN PARK

SEAT - NICE PICNIC SPOT WITH VIEWS OF ISLAND

PEPPER COVE

IRON-AGE FORT - EROSION HAS LEFT IT IN THREE PARTS BUT WHERE THE DITCHES AND RAMPARTS CONTINUE IS OBVIOUS

FOX COVE

PRIVATE PATH

REMAINS OF WRECK VISIBLE AT LOW-TIDE

ENJOYABLE WALKING ALONG THIS STRETCH OF INTERESTING COASTLINE

📱 072

MINNOWS IS.

PATH MAY BE MUDDY

MAP 25

0   ¼ mile
0   APPROX SCALE   500m

WILL'S ROCK

PORTHCOTHAN BEACH

PUBLIC PHONE

CROSS BRIDGE AND TURN RIGHT 10M AFTER BRIDGE

BENCH

📱 073

PORTHCOTHAN STORES

PORTHCOTHAN

PATH GOES IN FRONT OF HOUSES, NOT ALONG BEACH

SEAT

26

35-50 MINS FROM/TO YHA TREYARNON (MAP 24)

PORTHCOTHAN

24

ROUTE GUIDE AND MAPS

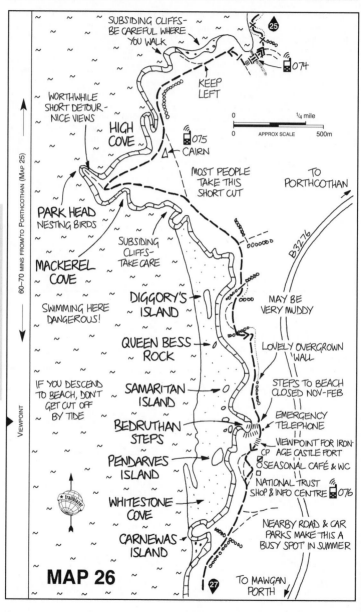

60-70 MINS FROM/to PORTHCOTHAN (MAP 25)

ROUTE GUIDE AND MAPS

VIEWPOINT

SUBSIDING CLIFFS-
BE CAREFUL WHERE
YOU WALK

25

074

KEEP
LEFT

WORTHWHILE
SHORT DETOUR-
NICE VIEWS

HIGH
COVE

075
CAIRN

MOST PEOPLE
TAKE THIS
SHORT CUT

TO
PORTHCOTHAN

0   ¼ mile

0   500m
APPROX SCALE

PARK HEAD
NESTING BIRDS

SUBSIDING
CLIFFS-
TAKE CARE

B3276

MACKEREL
COVE

DIGGORY'S
ISLAND

MAY BE
VERY MUDDY

SWIMMING HERE
DANGEROUS!

QUEEN BESS
ROCK

LOVELY OVERGROWN
WALL

IF YOU DESCEND
TO BEACH, DON'T
GET CUT OFF
BY TIDE

SAMARITAN
ISLAND

STEPS TO BEACH
CLOSED NOV-FEB

EMERGENCY
TELEPHONE

BEDRUTHAN
STEPS

VIEWPOINT FOR IRON-
AGE CASTLE FORT
CP
SEASONAL CAFÉ & WC

PENDARVES
ISLAND

NATIONAL TRUST
SHOP & INFO CENTRE   076

WHITESTONE
COVE

NEARBY ROAD & CAR
PARKS MAKE THIS A
BUSY SPOT IN SUMMER

CARNEWAS
ISLAND

trailblazer

MAP 26

27

TO MAWGAN
PORTH

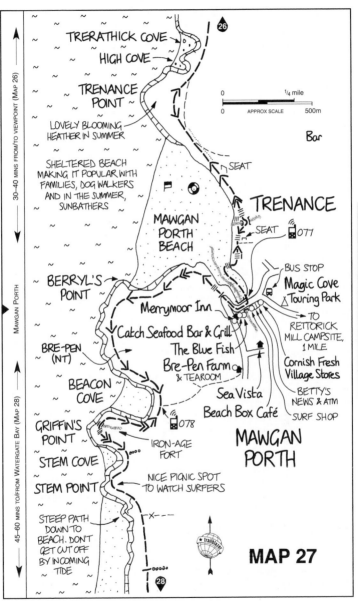

TRERATHICK COVE

HIGH COVE

TRENANCE POINT

LOVELY BLOOMING HEATHER IN SUMMER

SHELTERED BEACH MAKING IT POPULAR WITH FAMILIES, DOG WALKERS AND IN THE SUMMER, SUNBATHERS

MAWGAN PORTH BEACH

BERRYL'S POINT

BRE-PEN (NT)

BEACON COVE

GRIFFIN'S POINT

STEM COVE

STEM POINT

STEEP PATH DOWN TO BEACH. DON'T GET CUT OFF BY INCOMING TIDE

Bar

SEAT

TRENANCE

SEAT 077

BUS STOP

Magic Cove Touring Park

TO RETTORICK MILL CAMPSITE, 1 MILE

Merrymoor Inn

Catch Seafood Bar & Grill

The Blue Fish

Bre-Pen Farm & TEAROOM

Cornish Fresh Village Stores

BETTY'S NEWS & ATM

Sea Vista

Beach Box Café

SURF SHOP

MAWGAN PORTH

078

IRON-AGE FORT

NICE PICNIC SPOT TO WATCH SURFERS

0 ¼ mile
0 500m
APPROX SCALE

26

28

MAP 27

trailblazer

30-40 MINS FROM/TO VIEWPOINT (MAP 26)

MAWGAN PORTH

45-60 MINS TO/FROM WATERGATE BAY (MAP 28)

ROUTE GUIDE AND MAPS

(cont'd from p127) specialising in wood-fired food, is on site here, so you won't go hungry. It's worth phoning ahead to check they're open though, so you don't go hungry.

Beach Box Café (Mon-Sat 9am-7pm, Sun 9am-5pm) does smashing food and coffee (breakfast too, until 11am), and has terrace seating on the roof, while *The Blue Fish Bar* (noon-2pm & 5-8pm) is a traditional seaside chippy with plenty of seating

inside and out. Next door is *Catch Seafood Bar & Grill* (☎ 01637-860372, 🖥 catch mawganporthbeach.co.uk; daily 9.30am-11pm but advised to call ahead) where a main (seafood) will cost £14-23. Breakfast (from 9am-ish); brunch (until 2pm) and sandwiches (noon-5pm) are also served.

First Kernow's invaluable A5 **bus** service stops on Mawgan Rd. [See also pp52-6].

MAWGAN PORTH TO NEWQUAY [MAPS 27-30]

The first part of this **6-mile (10km, 1½-2hrs)** stretch is perfectly easy once the initial climb out of Mawgan Porth is over with, and apart from a minor descent to **Beacon Cove**, a climb to the Iron Age fort at **Griffin's Point** and a short descent to **Stem Cove**, it's plain sailing to **Watergate Bay**. Watergate Beach looks inviting but the path follows the cliffs above it to arrive at the bay. Where gaps in the gorse permit there are fine views over the beach and if there is a strong swell it is easy to while away an hour watching the crowds of surfers, some flying gracefully with the waves, others spectacularly wiping out. You may also be treated to a fly-past by the RAF who regularly practise manoeuvres over this stretch of coastline from their nearby base and you are likely to hear the planes going to and from Newquay airport.

It would be nice to walk along the beach from Watergate but the tide prevents it so the coast path remains on the cliffs until the first buildings (Sands Resort Hotel) begin to appear. You can walk on the pavement down the hill to **Porth Beach** but it's more pleasant to take the cliff path out to **Trevelgue Head** where a narrow footbridge leads across to the island on which was built one of Cornwall's largest Iron Age forts. As usual there is little of the fort remaining, though the walk to and around it is gentle, with plenty of benches for you to rest upon, nearly all dedicated to the memory of people 'who loved this spot'. It's not difficult to see why.

The route from Porth to Newquay is mostly on tarmac. Taking the bus would be a good option though there are some things of interest to look at including the sporting activities on the cliffs above **Lusty Glaze Beach** where groups can be seen abseiling from fixed lines on the cliffs kitted out in safety helmets and harnesses. Once into the town you can take the old tramway, now a pedestrian walkway and work your way along, above **Newquay's beaches** – Tolcarne, Great Western Sands and Towan Sands – to the little harbour that's still home to fishing boats.

WATERGATE BAY [MAP 28]

Surfing hotspot Watergate Bay is another gastronomic haven with two restaurants for foodies.

The more affordable of the two is *The Beach Hut* (☎ 01637-860877, 🖥 watergate bay.co.uk/thebeachhut.htm; Easter-Sep daily

9am-9pm; winter Sun-Thur noon-4pm, Fri & Sat noon-9pm), which is right on the beach and has a narrow balcony to sit out on for coffee and cakes. Mains cost £10-22 and include gourmet burgers and some excellent seafood.

Right above it, and accessed from the car park, is the more celebrated *Fifteen Cornwall* (☎ 01637-861000, 🖳 fifteen cornwall.co.uk; 8.30am-10am, noon-2.30pm & 6.15-9.15pm in peak season but hours vary so check in advance), part of Jamie Oliver's laudable operation to train young people in the catering trade. Booking some way ahead is essential in the summer; bear in mind there is a cancellation charge

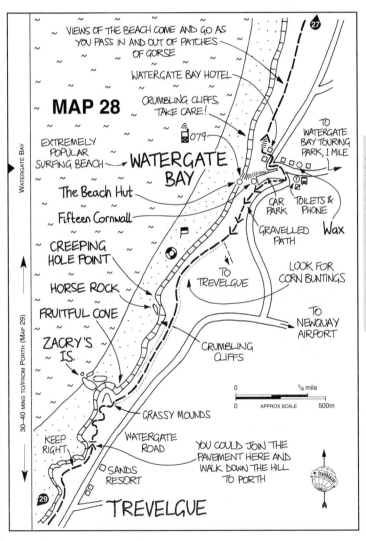

MAP 28

VIEWS OF THE BEACH COME AND GO AS YOU PASS IN AND OUT OF PATCHES OF GORSE

WATERGATE BAY HOTEL

CRUMBLING CLIFFS, TAKE CARE!

079

EXTREMELY POPULAR SURFING BEACH → WATERGATE BAY

The Beach Hut

Fifteen Cornwall

CREEPING HOLE POINT

HORSE ROCK

FRUITFUL COVE

ZACRY'S IS.

KEEP RIGHT

GRASSY MOUNDS

WATERGATE ROAD

SANDS RESORT

TREVELGUE

TO WATERGATE BAY TOURING PARK, 1 MILE

CAR PARK

TOILETS & PHONE

GRAVELLED PATH

Wax

LOOK FOR CORN BUNTINGS

TO TREVELGUE

TO NEWQUAY AIRPORT

CRUMBLING CLIFFS

YOU COULD JOIN THE PAVEMENT HERE AND WALK DOWN THE HILL TO PORTH

27

29

0   ¼ mile
0   APPROX SCALE   500m

WATERGATE BAY

30-40 MINS TO/FROM PORTH (MAP 29)

ROUTE GUIDE AND MAPS

if you fail to turn up. Mains on the dinner menu cost approximately £20-30.

For those who don't fancy fine dining, **Wax** (☎ 01637-860353, 🖳 waxwatergate .co.uk; food noon to late) is popular. It's open all year, is usually busy, and serves burgers, fish & chips and pizza for £10-15.

Camping is available at **Watergate Bay Touring Park** (☎ 01637-860387, 🖳 watergatebaytouringpark.co.uk; WI-FI; 🐾;

camping £7.75-18.75pp) which is about a mile inland. The park has a shop, café, launderette and swimming pool! There are also camping pods being built so it may be worth enquiring regarding these too.

It's a steep climb to get to the park; alternatively, First Kernow's A5 **bus** stops right outside. The A5 also stops opposite Wax. [See also pp52-6].

PORTH   [MAP 29]

Porth is an outpost of Newquay but has enough accommodation and eating possibilities to make it a popular choice among walkers reluctant to face the overly hedonistic tendencies of many of Newquay's visitors. It is quiet and has a lovely beach; who could ask for more?

Where to stay

Campers can try **Porth Beach Tourist Park** (☎ 01637-876531, 🖳 porthbeach .co.uk; pitch 2-man tent £16-46; WI-FI; 🐾; Mar to end Oct), an excellent, albeit pricy campsite, with a stream running down one side of the park. They also have four-man 'glamping pods' (£45-75).

For **B&B** try **Porth Beach Hotel** (☎ 01637-838225, 🖳 porthbeachhotel.co.uk; 1S/10D/2T; ☛; WI-FI; £55-95pp) or **The Cove** (☎ 01637-875311, 🖳 cornishwave .com/surf-and-stay/cove-guest-house; 1S/ 2D/ 3D, T or F; WI-FI; £45-75pp), where you can enjoy a beer and wonderful views from their front terrace, above Alexandra Rd.

Overlooking Lusty Glaze Beach before you hit Newquay is **Kallacliff** (☎ 01637-871704, 🖳 kallacliffhotel.co.uk; 4D/1T/3F; ☛; WI-FI; £40-55pp, sgl occ same rate), a friendly bed & breakfast with sea views. Passers-by can also have breakfast or lunch here, or even just a cream tea.

Where to eat and drink

Right on the beach is the colourful local pub, the **Mermaid Inn** (☎ 01637-872954; food served daily 11.30am-9pm; WI-FI), with Sharp's Doom Bar and Skinner's Betty Stogs on draught. The pub isn't the prettiest, but once inside it's friendly with a large outdoor seating area and an extensive and varied menu (mains £9-15). It also has an **ATM**. Right across the road from the pub is the **Estrella Morada Bar de Tapas** (☎ 01637-877271; summer daily 10.30am-3pm & 6.30-9pm) with good tapas (£4-7).

Down at the far end of the beach towards Newquay, **Café Coast** (☎ 01637-871962; daily Apr-Sep, 10.30am-4pm) sells hot and cold drinks, cream teas, cakes, ices and light meals, and has a garden overlooking the beach.

For something a bit different, climb down the steep flight of steps to **Lusty Glaze Restaurant** (☎ 01637-872444, 🖳 lustyglaze.co.uk; Easter-Oct, daily 10am till late in summer; earlier out of season; evening mains £9-24), nestled in a secluded, privately-owned cove.

Transport

[See also pp52-6]   First Kernow's A5 (Padstow to Newquay) **bus** service calls here.

NEWQUAY   [MAP 30, p135]

Newquay is the surf capital of Cornwall and the major UK competitions are held on Fistral Beach (see box p136). Not surprisingly therefore, there are numerous shops selling surfing equipment and the casual gear that surfers like to wear.

Since cheap flights to Newquay Airport became available, Newquay has also become a favourite venue for stag and hen parties, to the dismay of many. If a night out on streets filled with practically paralytic 20-somethings doesn't sound like

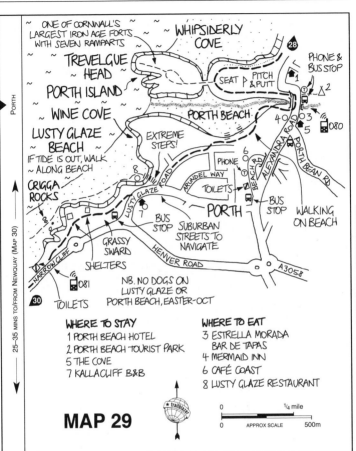

ONE OF CORNWALL'S LARGEST IRON AGE FORTS WITH SEVEN RAMPARTS

WHIPSIDERLY COVE

TREVELGUE HEAD

PORTH ISLAND

WINE COVE

LUSTY GLAZE BEACH

IF TIDE IS OUT, WALK ALONG BEACH

CRIGGA ROCKS

EXTREME STEPS!

SEAT PITCH & PUTT

PHONE & BUS STOP

PORTH BEACH

PHONE

ARUNDEL WAY

TOILETS

PORTH

BUS STOP

WALKING ON BEACH

BUS STOP

SUBURBAN STREETS TO NAVIGATE

GRASSY SWARD

SHELTERS

HENVER ROAD

A3058

TOILETS

NB. NO DOGS ON LUSTY GLAZE OR PORTH BEACH, EASTER-OCT

PORTH

25-35 MINS TO/FROM NEWQUAY (MAP 30)

WHERE TO STAY
1 PORTH BEACH HOTEL
2 PORTH BEACH TOURIST PARK
5 THE COVE
7 KALLACLIFF B&B

WHERE TO EAT
3 ESTRELLA MORADA BAR DE TAPAS
4 MERMAID INN
6 CAFÉ COAST
8 LUSTY GLAZE RESTAURANT

MAP 29

★ trailblazer

0   ¼ mile
0   500m
APPROX SCALE

ROUTE GUIDE AND MAPS

your cup of tea, then consider pushing on to Crantock, a lovely old village a couple of miles further on.

Services

The **tourist information centre** (☎ 01637-854020, 🖳 visitnewquay.org; Mon-Fri 9.15am-5.30pm, Sat & Sun 10am-4pm; winter Mon-Fri 9am-5pm, Sat & Sun) is on Marcus Hill. Bank St has branches of Barclays, HSBC and NatWest **banks**, all with **ATMs**, and a Boots **pharmacy**

(Mon-Sat 8.30am-7pm, Sun 9am-5pm), a WH Smith **newsagent** (Mon-Fri 8.45am-6.30pm, Sat 8.45am-5.30pm; Sun 10am-4pm) and a number of **bakeries** for pasties and filled rolls for the trail.

At 22a Cliff Rd, up towards the railway station, Newquay Camping (☎ 01637-877619, 🖳 newquaycampingshop.com; summer daily 9am-9pm, winter Mon-Sat 10am-4pm) stocks **camping gear** including fuel. There are **launderettes** on East St and Manor Rd.

Supermarkets include Sainsbury's (Mon-Sat 7am-9pm, Sun 10am-4pm) on Fore St, Aldi (8am-10pm) on Cliff Rd, and Asda (7am-11pm, Sun 11am-5pm), just off Cliff Rd. All have free-to-use **ATMs** outside. There's also a Spar on Tower Rd (daily 8am-10pm, 9am-10pm on Sun).

The main **post office** (Mon-Fri 9am-5.30pm, Sat 9am-12.30pm) is on East St.

Most cafés, pubs and restaurants offer free wi-fi.

Where to stay
Camping The nearest campsite to the town centre is *Trenance Holiday Park* (☎ 01637 873447, 🖳 trenanceholidaypark .co.uk) on Edgcumbe Ave; it's a hectic, popular site and is usually full during the season. They might squeeze in a tent (£8-9.50pp) though. They have an on-site **café** (Mon-Sat 8.30am-noon & 5-7pm, Sun 9am-noon), shop and launderette.

Hostels The hostel scene is changing in Newquay with the old scruffy bear-pit hostels being replaced by trendier establishments that could almost be called 'boutique-hostels'. Many, however, cater primarily to the stag-/hen-do crowds, so are by no means suitable for weary trekkers, concerned only with an uninterrupted night's sleep.

One old-style surfer haunt has survived: *Newquay International Backpackers* (☎ 01637-879366, 🖳 back packers.co.uk, 69-73 Tower Rd; 50 beds; dorm £12-26pp, sgl £21-35, T/D £22-36pp). Prices include a help-yourself toast-and-cereal breakfast.

Longbeach Hotel (☎ 01637-874751, 🖳 longbeachhotel.co.uk; 2D/1T/5D or F; WI-FI; from £20pp but check online for deals), at 11 Trevose Avenue, straddles the line between hostel and budget hotel with its basic, but clean rooms and seasonal dorms, and has pleasant views of the golf course and the sea.

B&Bs Newquay has a huge variety of places to stay but remember that this is a seaside town and the majority of visitors are on holiday rather than hiking the coast path. Although walkers are welcome, their muddy boots, rucksacks and wet gear can be an inconvenience. Some streets are lined with B&Bs so finding one with a vacancy should not be too difficult; the only problem being whether they are prepared to take you for a single night in high season.

St Bernard's (☎ 01637-872932, 🖳 st bernardsguesthouse.com; 5D/2D or T/1D or S; WI-FI; 🐾; £30-45pp, sgl occ from £48), at 9 Berry Rd, has hanging baskets and a licensed bar. They are environmentally aware and are keen on recycling. Almost next door, *Wenden Guest House* (☎ 01637-872604, 🖳 newquay-holidays .co.uk; 6D; WI-FI; 🐾 in winter; £32.50-40pp, sgl occ room rate) has a strict couples-only policy; a polite way of saying 'no children allowed'.

Towards the Headland as you leave the town, *Treheveras* (☎ 01637-874079, 🖳 tre heveras.co.uk; 3D or T/2F; WI-FI; £30-35pp), at 2a Dane Rd, guarantees at least seven items on your breakfast plate. A comfortable, welcoming establishment, walker friendly and right on the trail, this is a great choice if you want an early start the next day.

If you prefer to stay in a pub, try the *Griffin Inn* (☎ 01637-874067, 🖳 griffin-inn-newquay.co.uk; 1S/9D/4T/1F; WI-FI; £37.50-42.50pp, sgl occ £50-55) near the station. It's in a noisy part of town.

Hotels Next to Aldi supermarket, *Travelodge* (☎ 0871 9846244, 🖳 travelo dge.co.uk; 72 rooms; £23.50-60pp) offers dependable, if bland, accommodation.

The beautifully restored *Harbour Hotel* (☎ 01637-873040, 🖳 harbourhotel .co.uk; 4D/1T; 🍺; WI-FI; 🐾; £90-125pp) on North Quay Hill has five exquisitely decorated rooms, each with its own balcony overlooking the harbour.

Further round towards Beacon Cove, the large *Atlantic Hotel* (☎ 01637-872244, 🖳 atlantichotelnewquay.co.uk; 1S/4T/52D, all with sea view; WI-FI; £78-140pp), with its deep-pile carpets and mahogany panelling, exudes affluence and comfort from every pore. It also has a top-quality restaurant and a lovely outdoor pool.

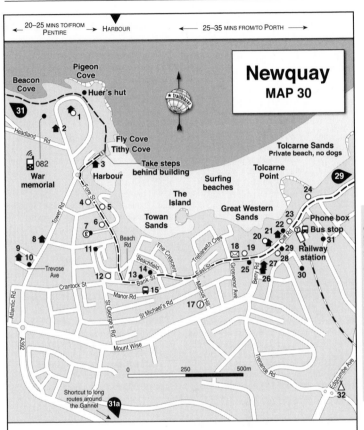

ROUTE GUIDE AND MAPS

Where to stay
1 Atlantic Hotel
2 Treheveras
3 Harbour Hotel
8 Newquay International
  Backpackers
9 Longbeach Hotel
20 Griffin Inn
21 Travelodge
26 Wenden Guest House
27 St Bernard's Guesthouse
32 Trenance Holiday Park

Where to eat/drink
1 Silks Bistro
3 Harbour Fish & Grill
4 The Beached
  Lamb Café
5 Fort Inn
6 Café Cloud
12 The Central
19 Senor Dick's
20 Griffin Inn
23 The Cod End
24 The Maharajah
28 Towan Blystra

Other
7 Sainsbury's
10 Spar
11 Launderette
13 Boots pharmacy
14 WH Smith
15 Bus station
17 Tourist Info
18 Post Office
22 Aldi Supermarket
25 Launderette
29 Newquay Camping
30 Asda
31 Police station

If that's not luxurious enough for you, consider treating yourself to a pampering at *The Headland* (Map 31; 01637-872211; headlandhotel.co.uk; 96 rooms; ☛; ✕; WI-FI; £69-150pp), Newquay's iconic, Grade II-listed, luxury hotel.

Where to eat and drink
Approaching from the railway station, the options come thick and fast with Chinese, Indian, Italian, Mexican and fast-food restaurants following one after another. On Cliff Rd, *The Maharajah* (☎ 01637-877377, ☐ maharajah-restaurant.co.uk; daily 5.30-10pm) is Newquay's most popular Indian restaurant, and has wonderful sea views. By the post office, *Señor Dick's* (☎ 01637-870350, ☐ senor-dicks.co.uk; daily 6-11, noon to late in summer) is a Mexican restaurant with mains from £9.95 to £12.95.

Back on Cliff Rd, *The Cod End* (11.30am-8.30pm) is arguably Newquay's best fish & chip restaurant. Cod & chips cost £8.95 and can be enjoyed with fabulous sea views from its backyard terrace.

For pub grub, *Fort Inn* (☎ 01637-875700, ☐ fortinnnewquay.co.uk; daily noon-9.30pm) is one of the better choices, with St Austell beers on tap, a good-value menu (mains £11-16) and sea-view terrace seating. Also owned by the St Austell Brewery, *The Central* (☎ 01637-873810, ☐ thecentralnewquay.co.uk; WI-FI; daily 11am-8pm, to 9pm in summer) is probably the main party pub in town, with crowds spilling out onto the pavement seating area which has space heaters on colder nights. The food menu is extensive, though nothing special.

Up towards the station on Cliff Rd, *Griffin Inn* (see Where to stay) serves food daily from noon to 9pm, while, directly opposite, *Towan Blystra*, (☎ 01637-852970, ☐ jdwetherspoon.co.uk; daily 8am-midnight) is a Wetherspoon's pub (so no dogs allowed) with popular roadside terrace seating.

Cute cafés are dotted around town too. *Café Cloud* (9.30am-5.30pm) has a cool-blue interior and a relaxing atmosphere in which to sample cream teas, coffees, cakes and scones. More Bohemian is *The Beached Lamb Café* (9am-4.30pm daily, to 11pm during summer holidays; ✕; WI-FI) which is licensed and serves bottled beers and cocktails. It does decent breakfasts and lunches, including veggie, vegan and gluten-free options, and is very chilled out and friendly.

For fine dining, the excellent *Harbour Fish & Grill* (☎ 01637 873040, ☐ theharbourfishandgrill.com; 10am-9pm) at Harbour Hotel (see Where to stay) has wonderful views over Newquay's harbour and beaches, especially from its terrace.

Silks Bistro and Champagne Bar at the Atlantic Hotel (see Where to stay; bar 11am-10.30pm; food served noon-3pm &

❏ **Surfing**
If you fancy a day on the waves there are loads of surf shops up and down the coast offering lessons and equipment hire. If you've never surfed before the best way to begin is with a lesson. They will start you off on a long (7-8ft), soft, foam board which is more buoyant than a normal board and easier to paddle thus making it easier to take off on a wave. You'll be taught the basics like how to leap to your feet but after that it's practice, and lots of it. Most places charge around £30 for a full day's lesson which includes all equipment and transport to the beach. However, it pays to shop around and ask lots of questions; the price may be for a one-to-one lesson or with a group of twenty people. Alternatively, try body surfing which is much more straightforward and the necessary equipment is also available for hire.

If you prefer to keep your feet dry you may be lucky enough to catch one of the major surf competitions held in Newquay each year, such as the English National Surfing Championships which take place over the May Day bank holiday and the British Cup Surfing over the Spring bank holiday (the last weekend of May).

6-10.30pm), is also top class, with an ambience just on the formal side of relaxed and daily specials with a seafood bias.

Beyond the Headland, *Rick Stein Fistral* (Map 31; ⌨ rickstein.com/eat-with-us/fistral; 9am-9pm) is the best of a cluster of café-restaurants overlooking Fistral Beach, and one of the few Rick Stein establishments that won't break the bank; you can get a breakfast bacon roll for £2.95, while cod and chips cost £9.45.

Transport

[See also pp52-6] The **bus station** is right in the centre of town. First Kernow operates a number of services from here: the No 85 to Truro via Crantock, the 87 to Truro via Perranporth and St Agnes, the A5 to Padstow via Newquay Airport and the 58 via a circular route to Pentire Head.

Newquay's **railway station**, just off Cliff Rd, has trains to Par from where you can change for Penzance and Bodmin Parkway. GWR's ticket office is open Mon-Fri 9am-3.30pm, Sat 8am-5pm and Sun 9am-4.30pm.

There are three National Express **coach** services (see box p50) a day. **Newquay Airport** (☎ 01637-860600, ⌨ newquaycornwallairport.com) has flights to a number of UK airports.

For a **taxi**, try calling A2B Taxis (☎ 01637-877777).

NEWQUAY TO CRANTOCK   [MAPS 30-31 & 31a]

This simple **2-mile (3km, 35-45 mins** if using ferry; longer for other options) stretch leaves Newquay by way of the headland, crosses inland of Fistral Beach through the dunes and becomes involved with suburban streets, most of them with Pentire in the name; choose your route. The only obstacle of the route is the crossing of the tidal **Gannel River** and how easy this is will depend on the state of the tide (see box on p138). You can cross by ferry at high tide, by the Penpol footbridge, or by walking the long way round by the Laurie footbridge at Trevemper (see options in detail below).

Once across the Gannel, you may decide to walk the short distance inland to the lovely old village of **Crantock** (see p138), or carry on the official route, or if it is low tide walk along the beach through the dunes.

Crossing the Gannel River   [Map 31, p139; Map 31a, p140]

If you haven't already bought a tide table it might be worth getting hold of one now. There are four ways to cross the Gannel; which one you take depends on the time of year and the state of the tide. On the **Pentire** side, light refreshments, including sandwiches, cakes and hot drinks, are available at *Fern Pit Café* (⌨ fernpit.co.uk; end May-mid Sep, daily 10am-6pm), open whether the ferry is running or not. There is also a **seasonal café** on the opposite side near the car park. Note all distances are Newquay–Crantock. See Map 31 (p139) for **timings** for each route.

● The official crossing (2 miles/3km) is via the **Fern Pit Ferry (A; Map 31)** (☎ 01637-873181, ⌨ fernpit.co.uk). This is the quickest and easiest option but the ferry (£1.20 each way) only operates from late May to mid September, daily 10am-6pm. If the tide is out you can walk across their footbridge (note this is also closed during the winter) for free.

● The second option (3 miles/5km) is to cross the **Penpol Footbridge (B; Map 31)**. This footbridge is tidal but you should be able to cross two to four hours

❏ **Tides**

Tides are the regular rise and fall of the ocean caused by the gravitational pull of the moon. They are actually very long waves which follow the path of the moon across the ocean. Twice a day there is a high tide and a low tide and there are approximately 6¼ hours between high and low water.

Spring tides (derived from the German word springan meaning to jump) are tides with a very large range that occur just after the full- and new-moon phases when the gravitational forces of the sun and the moon line up. High tides are higher and low tides lower than normal. Spring tides occur twice every month.

Neap tides occur halfway between each spring tide and are tides with the smallest range, so you get comparatively high low tides and low high tides. They occur at the first and third quarters of the moon when the sun, moon and earth are all at right angles to each other, hence the gravitational forces of the sun and the moon are weakened.

It is a good idea to carry a tide table with you; they can be purchased for about £1.50 from newsagents or TICs in coastal areas. Tide times are also available online at 🖳 tidetimes.org.uk, then select your location.

either side of low tide. If you are in any doubt whatsoever it is very easy to continue walking from here to the next bridge further up the Gannel.
● The third option (5 miles/8km) is the **Laurie Bridge (C; Map 31a)**, which is also a bridleway. The only time it's not possible to cross this bridge is one hour either side of a high spring tide.
● The final option (6 miles/9.5km) is to follow the **main road** (A392) right around the Gannel. However, this is a long and boring walk with the constant smell of exhaust fumes. You really would do much better to wait for the tides, plan ahead, or catch a bus (First Kernow's No 85; see box p54).

CRANTOCK   [MAP 31]

Crantock is a traditional Cornish village with thatched cottages clustered round a village green. It's a ten-minute walk uphill from Crantock Beach where there is a barely adequate **seasonal café** so if you need refreshments head into the village.

There is a curious enclosure known as **Crantock Round Garden**. It used to be a pound (a place to keep stray cattle in until they could be claimed). You can even check out the stocks, last used in the 19th century, round the back of the church.

Londis **store** (Mon-Sat 8am-8pm, Sun 8am-7pm) and **post office** (Mon-Fri 9am-5.30pm, Sat 9am-12.30pm) has a good range of essentials including sandwiches and fruit.

For **campers** there is *Quarryfield Caravan and Camping Park* (☎ 01637-872792, 🖳 quarryfield.co.uk; 🐾; £7-10pp; Easter-Oct), with a lovely hilltop location

between Crantock Beach and Crantock Village.

Most **B&Bs** have closed in recent years, or are now holiday apartments. One exception is the excellent *Carden Cottage* (☎ 01637-830806; 2D/1T; WI-FI; £40-45pp, sgl rate on request; baggage transfer), a charming cottage in a quiet location. Walkers are frequent guests here and are made to feel very welcome. To the west of the village is *Fairbank Hotel* (☎ 01637-830424, 🖳 fairbankhotel.co.uk, West Pentire Rd; 2S/10D/2T; ✆; WI-FI; £56-61pp, sgl/sgl occ from £57) which is licensed and has a restaurant (open from 7pm).

Two lovely old **pubs** stand opposite each other beside the church. *The Old Albion* (☎ 01637-830243, 🖳 oldalbioncrantock.com; 🐾; May-Sep food daily noon-9pm; rest of year daily noon-3pm & 6-9pm) is a 400-year-old traditional village pub

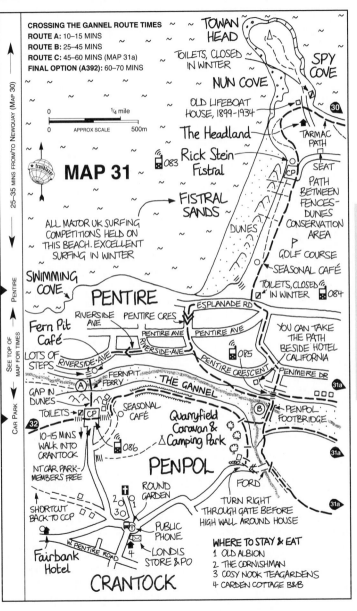

CROSSING THE GANNEL ROUTE TIMES
ROUTE A: 10–15 MINS
ROUTE B: 25–45 MINS
ROUTE C: 45–60 MINS (MAP 31a)
FINAL OPTION (A392): 60–70 MINS

0 ____ ¼ mile
0 ____ APPROX SCALE ____ 500m

MAP 31

TOWAN HEAD

TOILETS, CLOSED IN WINTER

SPY COVE

NUN COVE

OLD LIFEBOAT HOUSE, 1899-1934

The Headland

083 Rick Stein Fistral

FISTRAL SANDS

ALL MAJOR UK SURFING COMPETITIONS HELD ON THIS BEACH. EXCELLENT SURFING IN WINTER

DUNES

30

TARMAC PATH

SEAT

PATH BETWEEN FENCES-DUNES CONSERVATION AREA

GOLF COURSE

SEASONAL CAFÉ

TOILETS, CLOSED IN WINTER 084

SWIMMING COVE

PENTIRE

RIVERSIDE AVE   PENTIRE CRES

ESPLANADE RD

Fern Pit Café

PENTIRE AVE   PENTIRE AVE

RIVERSIDE AVE

085

YOU CAN TAKE THE PATH BESIDE HOTEL CALIFORNIA

LOTS OF STEPS   RIVERSIDE AVE

PENTIRE CRESCENT

PENMERE DR

FERNPIT

A   FERNPIT FERRY

THE GANNEL

31a

GAP IN DUNES

B   PENPOL FOOTBRIDGE

32   TOILETS   CP

SEASONAL CAFÉ

Quarryfield Caravan & Camping Park

086

31a

10-15 MINS WALK INTO CRANTOCK

NT CAR PARK– MEMBERS FREE

PENPOL

FORD

31a

SHORTCUT BACK TO CCP

ROUND GARDEN

2
3   1

TURN RIGHT THROUGH GATE BEFORE HIGH WALL AROUND HOUSE

Fairbank Hotel

W. PENTIRE ROAD

PUBLIC PHONE

LONDIS STORE & PO

4

CRANTOCK

WHERE TO STAY & EAT
1 OLD ALBION
2 THE CORNISHMAN
3 COSY NOOK TEAGARDENS
4 CARDEN COTTAGE B&B

25–35 MINS FROM/TO NEWQUAY (MAP 30)

PENTIRE

SEE TOP OF MAP FOR TIMES

CAR PARK

ROUTE GUIDE AND MAPS

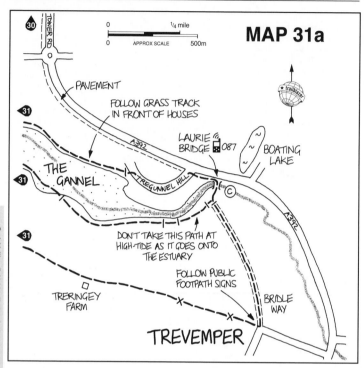

with a thatched roof. *The Cornishman* (☎ 01637-830869; food daily Easter-Oct noon-9pm; WI-FI) is also friendly and serves some superb food. Both have pleasant outdoor seating areas.

Alternatively, *Cosy Nook Tea Gardens* (☎ 01637-830324; Easter-Oct daily 10am-5pm; July & Aug Wed-Fri 6.30-8.30pm) is

as cute as it sounds, with all-day breakfasts (£5.50), lunches and cream teas (£6.20) all year, plus evening meals in summer. It's unlicensed, but you can bring your own booze.

Both First Kernow's No 85 and Travel Cornwall's No 415 **bus** services stop here. See also pp52-6.

CRANTOCK TO PERRANPORTH   [MAPS 31-34]

The next **8 miles (13km, 2-3hrs)** provide classic cliff-top walking with some sharp ups and downs soon after leaving Crantock including the descent to the secluded beach at **Porth Joke**, accessed only on foot.

For **campers** a short stroll inland (about half-a-mile) will see you arrive at the fabulous *Porth Joke Campsite* (☎ 01637-831207, 🖳 crantockholiday.co .uk/camping; May-Sep). Coastal walkers with small tents (£9 per night) are always welcomed. A little further inland, *Treago Farm Campsite* (☎ 01637-830277, 🖳 treagofarm.co.uk; hiker £8-10; 🐾) has a licensed bar and shop.

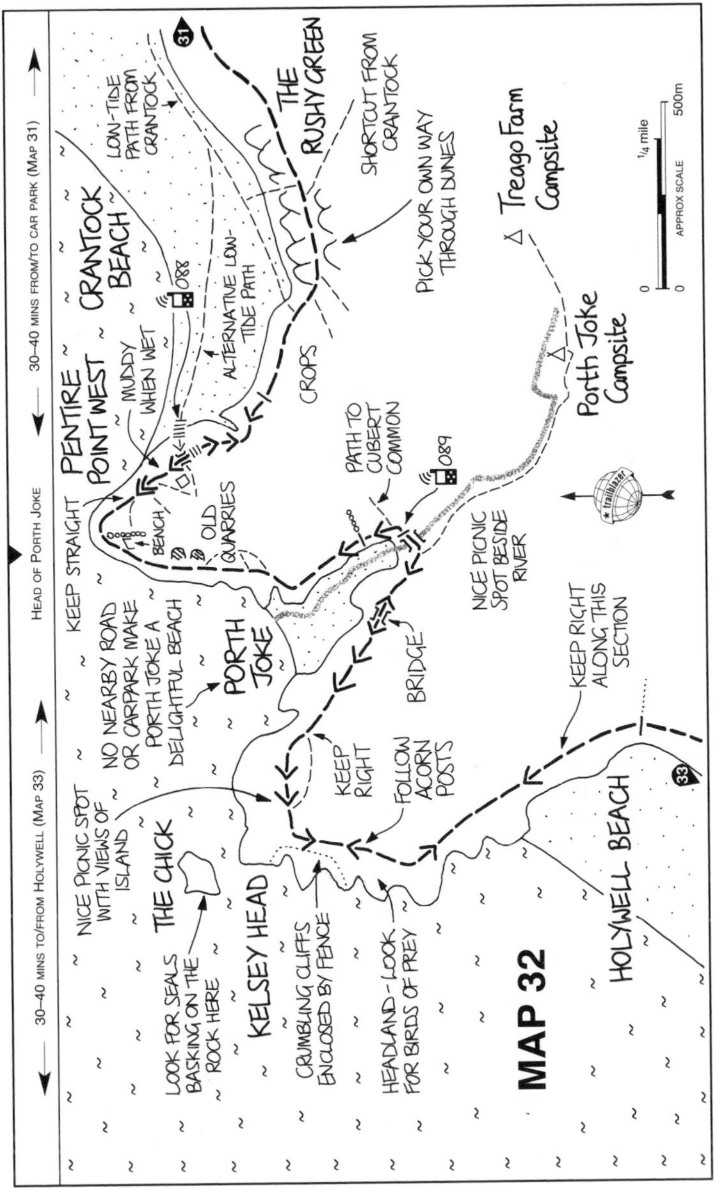

MAP 32

THE RUSHY GREEN

CRANTOCK BEACH

LOW-TIDE PATH FROM CRANTOCK

SHORTCUT FROM CRANTOCK

PICK YOUR OWN WAY THROUGH DUNES

△ Treago Farm Campsite

PENTIRE POINT WEST

ALTERNATIVE LOW-TIDE PATH

MUDDY WHEN WET

CROPS

△ Porth Joke Campsite

PATH TO CUBERT COMMON

KEEP STRAIGHT

BEACH

OLD QUARRIES

NICE PICNIC SPOT BESIDE RIVER

NO NEARBY ROAD OR CARPARK MAKE PORTH JOKE A DELIGHTFUL BEACH

PORTH JOKE

BRIDGE

KEEP RIGHT

FOLLOW ACORN POSTS

KEEP RIGHT ALONG THIS SECTION

NICE PICNIC SPOT WITH VIEWS OF ISLAND

THE CHICK

LOOK FOR SEALS BASKING ON THE ROCK HERE

KELSEY HEAD

CRUMBLING CLIFFS ENCLOSED BY FENCE

HEADLAND – LOOK FOR BIRDS OF PREY

HOLYWELL BEACH

APPROX SCALE

0   ¼ mile

0   500m

ROUTE GUIDE AND MAPS

Kelsey Head with its huge expanse of grass is a place to linger and savour so don't keep charging ahead. Slow the pace down a bit and make the most of an exquisite area.

Next comes **Holywell** with two pubs and a large holiday park after which the coast path skirts the scattered installations of **Penhale Camp**, MoD property, which is heavily fenced. You imagine that somebody has you under observation as you pass by the concrete barracks and communications masts and hear the noise of small-arms fire from the ranges. Once behind this, a narrow, heart-stopping path brings you by stages to the start of **Perran Beach**, a two-mile long stretch of golden sand bordered by dunes, the walk along the edge of the tide making a welcome change. You'll see dog walkers, families, horse-riders and, if the wind is up, sand yachts whistling across the beach; you'll probably want to take your boots off. The approach to Perranporth is exciting, the town coming into sight only as you round the rocky outcrop of **Cotty's Point**. At high tide it will be necessary to leave the beach at the lifeguard station and continue the last leg to Perranporth through the dunes.

Perranporth is the largest settlement between Newquay and St Ives.

HOLYWELL   [MAP 33]

Holywell's beach is very popular with families. It has **seasonal beach shops**, a grocery **store** (daily 9am-7pm, closed in winter) and two **pubs**, one of which offers **B&B**. There is some dispute over the exact site of the holy well this village is named after. Some say it's in the caves on the northern end of the beach, others that it's further inland along the road.

Of the two pubs, the *Treguth Inn* (☎ 01637-830248, 🖥 thetreguthinn.com; food daily noon-9pm) is the oldest; a converted 13th-century farmhouse with a thatched roof. It's open all day May to October and serves standard pub grub with some vegetarian options. Nearer the beach, so more convenient for walkers, is *St Piran's Inn*

(☎ 01637-830205, 🖥 stpiransinn.co.uk; wifi; food daily all day in summer, rest of year Wed-Sat noon-3pm & 5.30-9pm, Sun noon-4pm), where you can also opt to spend the night (4D; from £47.50pp).

Meadow Holiday Park (☎ 01872-572752, 🖥 holywellholidaypark.co.uk; Mar-Oct; hiker and tent £13-14) is quite small so it's wise to phone ahead to reserve a tent pitch. There are other, larger holiday parks here too, but you're less likely to snag a last-minute pitch at these in high season.

First Kernow's No 85 and 87 and Travel Cornwall's No 415 **bus** services all stop here. See also pp52-6. The bus stop is five minutes' walk from the beach near Treguth Inn.

PERRANPORTH   [MAP 34, p145]

Named after St Piran (see box on p144), the patron saint of Cornwall, Perranporth is a small, old-fashioned seaside town that depends for its existence on the holiday trade. Perran Beach is a major drawcard and a spell of nice weather sees it crowded with sun- and fun-seekers of all ages.

Perranzabuloe Museum (☎ 01872-573321, 🖥 perranzabuloemuseum.co.uk; Ponsmere Rd; Easter-Oct Mon-Fri 10.30am-4.30pm, Sat 11am-1pm; free) provides some

useful information on the area's industrial past with displays on mining, fishing and farming.

Both Co-op **shops** (daily 7am-10pm) have **ATMs**. For **groceries** there is also a Premier (daily summer 7am-10pm) on St George's Hill. The **post office** (closed Wed afternoons) is on St Piran's Rd, and there's **internet access** at the library (Tue 9.30am-5pm, Thur 1-5pm, Fri 10am-1pm), which is attached to the museum.

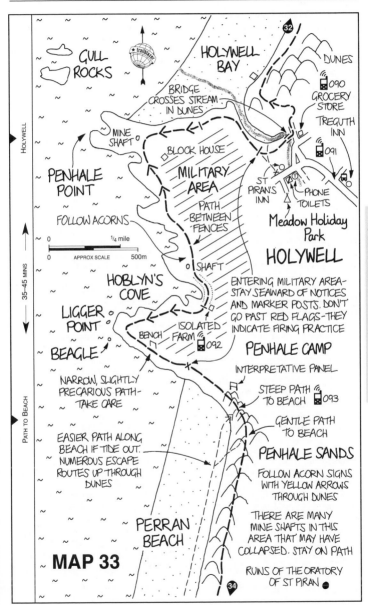

GULL ROCKS

HOLYWELL BAY

DUNES

BRIDGE CROSSES STREAM IN DUNES

📱 090 GROCERY STORE

TREGUTH INN

📱 091

MINE SHAFT

BLOCK HOUSE

PENHALE POINT

MILITARY AREA

ST PIRAN'S INN

PHONE TOILETS

FOLLOW ACORNS

PATH BETWEEN FENCES

Meadow Holiday Park

HOLYWELL

HOBLYN'S COVE

SHAFT

ENTERING MILITARY AREA - STAY SEAWARD OF NOTICES AND MARKER POSTS. DON'T GO PAST RED FLAGS - THEY INDICATE FIRING PRACTICE

LIGGER POINT

ISOLATED FARM 📱 092

BENCH

PENHALE CAMP

BEAGLE

INTERPRETATIVE PANEL

NARROW, SLIGHTLY PRECARIOUS PATH - TAKE CARE

STEEP PATH TO BEACH 📱 093

GENTLE PATH TO BEACH

EASIER PATH ALONG BEACH IF TIDE OUT. NUMEROUS ESCAPE ROUTES UP THROUGH DUNES

PENHALE SANDS

FOLLOW ACORN SIGNS WITH YELLOW ARROWS THROUGH DUNES

PERRAN BEACH

THERE ARE MANY MINE SHAFTS IN THIS AREA THAT MAY HAVE COLLAPSED. STAY ON PATH

MAP 33

RUINS OF THE ORATORY OF ST PIRAN ●

HOLYWELL

35-45 MINS

PATH TO BEACH

0   ¼ mile
APPROX SCALE
0   500m

★ trailblazer

32

34

ROUTE GUIDE AND MAPS

There is a **launderette** (summer daily 8am-10pm, winter 8am-8pm) on The Gounce. Nearby on Beach Rd is **Perranporth Surgery** with a Boots **pharmacy** (Mon-Fri 8.30am-6.15pm, Sat 9am-5.30pm) next door. The **tourist information centre** (☎ 01872-575254, 💻 perran porthinfo.co.uk; Mon-Sat 9am-5pm, Sun phone service only), staffed by volunteers, is on a side-street just off St Piran's Rd.

Where to stay

The hideously large Perran Sands Caravan & Camping Park dominates the dunes behind Perran Beach. It's like a small Disney-esque village with restaurants, rides and even its own 'high street'. Luckily, hikers can skip such nonsense and continue on to the excellent, family-run *Tollgate Farm Caravan and Camping Park* (off Map 34; ☎ 01872-572130, 💻 tollgatefarm.co.uk; Easter to end Sep; hiker & tent £7-11) at the other side of the

Perran Sands site. It has good shower facilities, a launderette, a farm shop selling beer and wine, and a great takeaway *café* (8.30-10.30am & 6-8pm, high season only) which knocks out coffee and bacon sandwiches for breakfast, and Indian curries and stone-baked pizzas for dinner. It's a fair walk to and from town from here, but First Kernow's A4 & 87 buses stop outside (the bus stop is called 'Perran Sands').

YHA Perranporth (Map 34; ☎ 0345-371 9755, 💻 yha.org.uk/hostel/perran porth; Mar-Nov; 24 beds; from £18pp; self-catering only) is up on the hill on the cliffs at Droskyn Point; a fantastic location overlooking Perran Beach, and a prime spot for watching the sunset, brew in hand. There are two 4-bed private rooms, and two 8-bed dorms. There is also **camping** (from £14) available.

B&B accommodation is thin on the ground. One option is *Trevian Lodge* (☎ 01872-572523, 💻 trevianlodge.co.uk; 2D;

❏ St Piran and the lost Oratory

St Piran, the patron saint of Cornwall, supposedly arrived in Perranporth in the 6th century having floated from Ireland on a millstone. In his old age he had been captured by pagan Irish and thrown over a cliff with this millstone round his neck. The stone floated and became a raft. He built a small chapel – the Oratory of St Piran – on Penhale Sands, and lived there for many years as a hermit performing miracles for the locals. When he died his relics were kept in a shrine nearby and became a major place of medieval pilgrimage. The forgotten Oratory was lost to the sand dunes during the Middle Ages, but rediscovered in the 18th century, and in 1910 was encased in a concrete structure to help protect it. However modern conservationists grew worried that a lack of public commitment to preserve the site might lead to its eventual demise so they took the unusual step of removing its protective structure and allowing the sand dunes to once again engulf the Oratory, for its own protection. All was not lost, though. Local campaigners recently won a 14-year-long battle to re-expose the remains of what is thought to be one of the oldest Christian edifices in the British Isles. The excavation work was finally completed in November 2014.

St Piran's popularity among the Cornish lies in the tradition that it was he who first discovered tin. He was cooking on a fireplace of black rock when he saw that the intense heat made a trickle of pure white metal ooze from the stones. He shared this knowledge with the locals and it was on this that the prosperity of Cornwall was based.

St Piran is not only remembered on St Piran's Day on 5 March, but also on the Cornish flag, a white cross on a black background symbolising the white tin seeping from the black rock, the triumph of good over evil and God's light shining out of the darkness.

For further details visit the St Piran's Trust website (💻 stpiran.org).

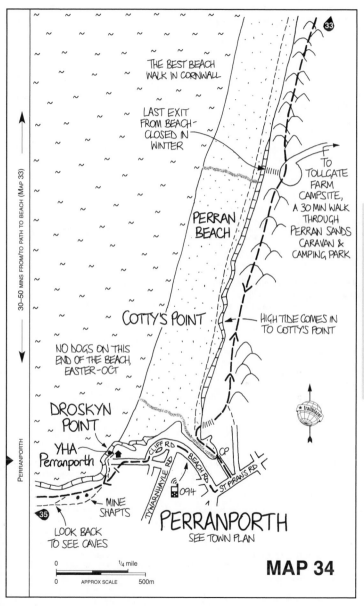

THE BEST BEACH
WALK IN CORNWALL

LAST EXIT
FROM BEACH -
CLOSED IN
WINTER

PERRAN
BEACH

TO
TOLLGATE
FARM
CAMPSITE,
A 30 MIN WALK
THROUGH
PERRAN SANDS
CARAVAN &
CAMPING PARK

COTTY'S POINT

HIGH TIDE COMES IN
TO COTTY'S POINT

NO DOGS ON THIS
END OF THE BEACH,
EASTER-OCT

DROSKYN
POINT

YHA
Perranporth

CLIFF RD

TYWARNHAYLE RD

BEACH RD

CP

ST PIRANS RD

094

MINE
SHAFTS

PERRANPORTH
SEE TOWN PLAN

LOOK BACK
TO SEE CAVES

35

30-50 MINS FROM/TO PATH TO BEACH (MAP 33)

PERRANPORTH

33

trailblazer

ROUTE GUIDE AND MAPS

0   1/4 mile
0   APPROX SCALE   500m

MAP 34

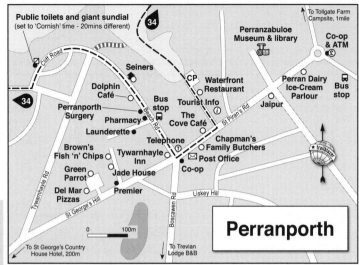

Perranporth

Public toilets and giant sundial (set to 'Cornish' time - 20mins different)

To Tollgate Farm Campsite, 1mile

Perranzabuloe Museum & library

Co-op & ATM

Cliff Road

Seiners

CP   Waterfront Restaurant

Perran Dairy Ice-Cream Parlour

Bus stop

Dolphin Café

Bus stop

Tourist Info

Jaipur

Perranporth Surgery

Pharmacy

Beach Rd

The Cove Café

St Piran's Rd

Launderette

Brown's Fish 'n' Chips

Telephone

Chapman's Family Butchers

trailblazer

Tywarnhayle Inn

Post Office

Green Parrot

Jade House

Co-op

Del Mar Pizzas

Premier

Liskey Hill

Tywarnhayle Rd

St George's Hill

Boscawen Rd

0   100m

To St George's Country House Hotel, 200m

To Trevian Lodge B&B

ROUTE GUIDE AND MAPS

£37.50-40pp), at 1 Trevian Close. From the town centre walk south down Boscawen Rd, left on to St Michael's Rd and Trevian Close is on your right. It's a nice place, but no dogs or young children are allowed. More accommodating, but a little further out of town, *St George's Country House Hotel* (☎ 01872-572184, 🖳 stgeorgescountryhouse hotel.com; 5D/1T/1F; 🛏; 🐾; £45-75pp, sgl occ from £90) is a grand, whitewashed, detached house with dormer windows and a friendly welcome. They keep their own hens, bake their own bread and have a **bistro-bar** attached (food is served all day and they can provide packed lunches).

For a pub with rooms, try *Seiners* (☎ 01872-573118, 🖳 seiners.co.uk; 2S/6T/13D/2F; 🛏; 🐾; £30-42.50pp, sgl £40-45, sgl occ £45-60), on the sea front.

If you are still struggling to find a place to stay you could try 🖳 airbnb.co.uk (see p20).

Where to eat and drink

For Indian cuisine, try *Jaipur* (☎ 01872-573625, 🖳 jaipurindiancuisine.co.uk; daily 5pm to late). For Chinese, *Jade House* (☎

01872-572880; Sun-Thur 5.30-10.30pm, Fri & Sat to 11pm). Next to Jade House is *Brown's Fish 'n' Chips* (Mon-Sat noon-9.30pm, Sun noon-8.30pm; limited hours out of main season), which has some restaurant seating as well as a takeaway.

Tywarnhayle Inn (aka the Tye; ☎ 01872-572215, 🖳 tywarnhayleinn.co.uk; summer daily 11.30am-9pm, winter noon-3pm & 6-8pm) does quality pub food for decent prices (mains £11-14.50, although steaks cost more). *Seiners* (see Where to stay; bar serves food daily noon-3pm & 6-9pm, restaurant 6pm to late) is like the lower deck of a sailing ship inside, with a range of piratical beers from Truro Brewery. Try the large bowl of mussels with chips (£13.50) or one of their fish specials.

The *Waterfront Restaurant* (☎ 01872-573167; Easter-Oct daily from 6.30pm to late, from 5pm in July & Aug) is pub-like, with a wooden cabin in the garden serving booze. The menu includes buffalo chicken wings, steak, fish and their crab special.

Green Parrot (☎ 01872-574990, St George's Hill; food daily 8am-10pm) is a Wetherspoon's serving standard pub fare at reasonable prices. Sharing the pub's car park is *Del Mar Italian Restaurant and Pizzeria* (☎ 01872-572878, 🖥 delmar restaurant.co.uk; daily summer noon-midnight, winter Sat & Sun noon-3pm, 5pm-midnight) specialising in pizzas.

Cove Café (☎ 01872-571487; daily summer 8.30am-5.30pm, winter hours vary) is on St Piran's Rd. They do a decent breakfast, paninis and cream teas.

All your Cornish ice-cream cravings can be met at *Perran Dairy Ice-Cream Parlour* (10am-5pm), which also does coffee and paninis. *Dolphin Café* (8am-4pm,

summer to 6pm), meanwhile, is more of a no-frills place, serving good value fry-up breakfasts as well as fish and chips. There's some outdoor seating with beach views.

For the best pasty in town, locals swear by *Chapman's Family Butcher's* (8am-5pm Mon-Sat).

Transport
[See also pp52-6] First Kernow's No 87 and A4 **bus** services stop on Beach Rd.

For a **taxi**, ring Atlantic Taxis (☎ 01872-571111).

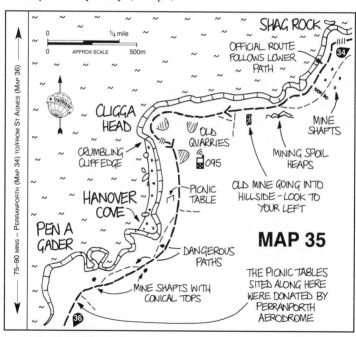

75-90 MINS – PERRANPORTH (MAP 34) TO/FROM ST AGNES (MAP 36)

SHAG ROCK

OFFICIAL ROUTE FOLLOWS LOWER PATH

34

CLIGGA HEAD

OLD QUARRIES

095

MINE SHAFTS

CRUMBLING CLIFF EDGE

MINING SPOIL HEAPS

HANOVER COVE

PICNIC TABLE

OLD MINE GOING INTO HILLSIDE - LOOK TO YOUR LEFT

PEN A GADER

MAP 35

DANGEROUS PATHS

MINE SHAFTS WITH CONICAL TOPS

THE PICNIC TABLES SITED ALONG HERE WERE DONATED BY PERRANPORTH AERODROME

36

trailblazer

0   1/4 mile
0   APPROX SCALE   500m

ROUTE GUIDE AND MAPS

PERRANPORTH TO PORTHTOWAN   [MAPS 34-38]

This **8-mile (13km, 2½-3hrs)** section passes through terrain that is mostly heathland which at one time covered the whole of the west of Cornwall. The walking is relatively easy and you should be able to crack on and make light of the few ups and downs, the most severe of which is down to **Chapel Porth**, where there is a seasonal **beach café** (Apr-Oct 10am-5pm). It is here that you first begin to encounter the remains of Cornwall's mining industry at **Wheal Coates** and

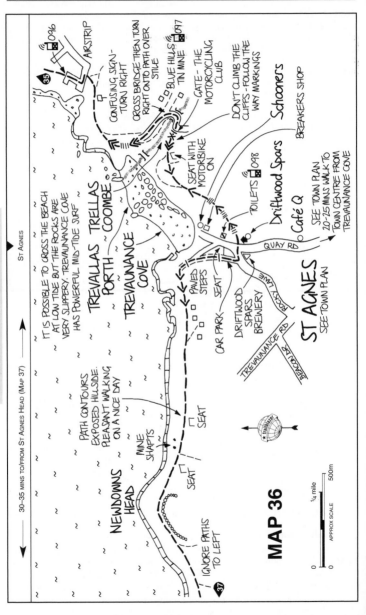

ROUTE GUIDE AND MAPS

St Agnes ▶

◀—— 30–35 MINS TO/FROM St Agnes Head (Map 37) ——▶

IT IS POSSIBLE TO CROSS THE BEACH AT LOW TIDE BUT THE ROCKS ARE VERY SLIPPERY. TREVAUNANCE COVE HAS POWERFUL MID-TIDE SURF

AIRSTRIP

📷 096

85

CONFUSING, SIGN-POST TURN RIGHT

CROSS BRIDGE THEN TURN RIGHT ONTO PATH OVER STILE

BLUE HILLS 📷 097 TIN MINE

GATE – THE MOTORCYCLING CLUB

DON'T CLIMB THE CLIFFS – FOLLOW THE WAY MARKINGS

Schooners

BREAKERS SHOP

TREVALLAS TRELLAS PORTH ~ COOMBE

TREVAUNANCE COVE

SEAT WITH MOTORBIKE ON

TOILETS 📷 098

Driftwood Spars

Café Q

QUAY RD

SEE TOWN PLAN 20–25 MINS WALK TO TOWN CENTRE FROM TREVAUNANCE COVE

ST AGNES
SEE TOWN PLAN

PAVED STEPS SEAT

CAR PARK SEAT

DRIFTWOOD SPARS BREWERY

ROCKY LANE

TREVAUNANCE RD

BEACON DR

PATH CONTOURS EXPOSED HILLSIDE. PLEASANT WALKING ON A NICE DAY

SEAT

MINE SHAFTS

SEAT

NEWDOWNS HEAD

IGNORE PATHS TO LEFT

37

MAP 36

¼ mile

0 · 500m

0 ·

APPROX SCALE

Towan Roath mines, the abandoned engine houses lonely relics of a once-thriving period. You'll also notice the heads of many shafts close to the path, most of them fenced and in some cases topped with a steel-wire pyramid-shaped cage for safety. They have become colonised by the greater horseshoe bat, an endangered species you are unlikely to see unless you are passing at dusk.

ST AGNES (Trevaunance Cove)

Trevaunance Cove is small and rocky with a sandy beach at low tide. At mid tide the surf can be powerful. The village of St Agnes itself is a 20- to 25-minute walk inland with houses and cottages dotted along the way. See p15 for details of the **Giant Bolster Festival** held here in May.

A well-known local landmark not to be missed is the **Stippy Stappy**, a row of mine workers' cottages that climb the hill-like steps. Also worth visiting is the small **St Agnes Museum** (☎ 01872-553228, 🖳 stagnesmuseum.org.uk; Penwinnick Rd; Easter-Oct daily 10.30am-5pm, free), housed inside the 19th-century Chapel of Rest. It has numerous exhibits on the area's rich mining and maritime history. For **groceries** there's Select Convenience (Mon-Sat 7.30am-10.30pm, Sun 8.30am-10.30pm), which also houses the local **post office** and an **ATM**, and Spar (daily 8am-10pm). There is also a Boots **pharmacy** (Mon-Fri 9am-6pm, Sat 9am-5.30pm).

Where to stay

Campers need to go a little way out of the village to find *Presingoll Farm Caravan and Camping Park* (☎ 01872-552333, 🖳 presingollfarm.co.uk, Penwinnick Rd; 🐾; walker & tent £8), a working farm with a well-run campsite. There's a small shop and a laundry. Alternatively, further along the coast path towards Porthtowan is *Beacon Cottage Farm* (Map 37; ☎ 01872-552347, 🖳 beaconcottagefarmholidays.co.uk; 🐾; £9 for walkers; Easter-Oct), another nicely run site with a lovely sea-view location and a small shop selling essentials.

Back in St Agnes, or more specifically at Trevaunance Cove, *Driftwood Spars* (Map 36; ☎ 01872-552428, 🖳 driftwood spars.co.uk; Quay Rd; 1S/9D/1T/4F; ⬤; WI-FI; 🐾; £45-70pp, sgl occ from £50) is a tastefully decorated and enthusiastically

run establishment with a pub, a restaurant and smart B&B rooms.

In the village proper, *Enysvilla* (☎ 01872-552137, 🖳 enysvilla.co.uk; 1D/2D, T or F; WI-FI, 🐾; £40-55, sgl occ £50-65) welcomes walkers.

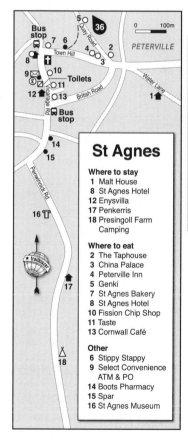

St Agnes

Where to stay
1 Malt House
8 St Agnes Hotel
12 Enysvilla
17 Penkerris
18 Presingoll Farm
  Camping

Where to eat
2 The Taphouse
3 China Palace
4 Peterville Inn
5 Genki
7 St Agnes Bakery
8 St Agnes Hotel
10 Fission Chip Shop
11 Taste
13 Cornwall Café

Other
6 Stippy Stappy
9 Select Convenience
  ATM & PO
14 Boots Pharmacy
15 Spar
16 St Agnes Museum

ROUTE GUIDE AND MAPS

In nearby Peterville, the ever-popular *Malt House* (☎ 01872-553318, 07808-030034, 🖳 themalthousestagnes.co.uk; 1D en suite/3D shared facilities; WI-FI; 🐾; £30-35pp) is the kind of B&B you seldom find now; a home from home.

Just out of the village on Penwinnick Rd is *Penkerris* (☎ 01872-552262, 🖳 penkerris.co.uk; 1D/3D or T en suite, 1S/2D/1T/1F shared facilities; ☛; WI-FI; £25-35pp, plus £5-10 sgl occ), a lovely detached Edwardian house with Virginia creeper climbing over it and a slightly fading ambience that only adds to the experience of staying here. It has been run by the same redoubtable lady for the past 20 years; she welcomes walkers and has written a book on local walks. Evening meals are available.

For pub accommodation, try *St Agnes Hotel* (☎ 01872-552307, 🖳 st-agnes-hotel.co.uk; 1T/4D/1F; ☛; WI-FI; 🐾; £50-65pp, sgl occ from £80), opposite the church. They are refreshingly dog-friendly.

Where to eat and drink

Down on the coast path, and housed in a whitewashed 17th-century building, welcoming *Driftwood Spars* (see Where to stay) is a popular pub with standard pub food (Mon-Sat noon-2.30pm & 6.30-9.30pm, Sun noon-8pm). They also own the small *Driftwood Spars Brewery* (☎ 01872-552591, 🖳 driftwoodsparsbrewery.co.uk; noon-5pm) opposite, which brews half a dozen beers on site, including the award-winning Alfie's Revenge.

Schooners (☎ 01872-553149, 🖳 schoonerscornwall.com; Mon-Sat breakfast 10-11.45am, lunch 12.30-3pm, dinner 6-9.30pm, Sun brunch 10am-3pm), meanwhile, peers down over the beach. There's an extensive, if not cheap, menu to choose from as well as daily specials.

Following Quay Rd towards St Agnes you'll pass *Café Q* (☎ 01872-857045), newly-opened after redevelopment, and *Genki* (☎ 01872-555858, 🖳 genkicornwall.co.uk), a small beach hut café, full of big flavours and fantastic food.

In Peterville, *The Taphouse* (☎ 01872-553095, 🖳 the-taphouse.com; Mon-Sat noon-2pm & 5.30-9pm) is a lively, unconventional, bright-orange pub with decent food, and live music some evenings. Nearby, *The Peterville Inn* (☎ 01872-552406; food Mon-Sat noon-2.30pm & 6-9pm) has a decent seafood restaurant.

Up in St Agnes itself, the pub restaurant at *St Agnes Hotel* (see Where to stay; food daily 8am-9pm) is open all day for non-residents too, even for breakfast. On the opposite side of the road, *Taste* (☎ 01872-552194; Tue-Sat noon-2pm & 6-9pm, Sun noon-2pm) is a good option for seafood as well as other locally sourced dishes (mains £14.50-25).

For cheaper eats there's *Fission Chip shop* (Tue-Sat 5-8.30pm) in the centre, the

China Palace Chinese (☎ 01872-552688; daily noon-2pm & 5-11pm), next to The Peterville Inn, and *Cornwall Café* (9.30am-4.30pm), a crockery-filled Aladdin's cave of tea cups and china plates; the perfect spot for a Cornish cream tea. For a more modern café, try *St Agnes Bakery* (7.30am-4.30pm).

Transport

[See also pp52-6] Hopley's No 315 and First's 87 and A4 **bus** services all call here.

For a **taxi** call St Agnes Taxis (☎ 01872-553795, 🖥 stagnestaxis.com).

PORTHTOWAN [MAP 38]

Porthtowan is a small settlement, hardly even a village, but it has a large car park to serve its fine beach, and **Porthtowan**

Village Stores (☎ 01209-891210; Mon-Fri 7.30am-8pm, Sat & Sun 8am-8pm), which stocks basic supplies, including bread and

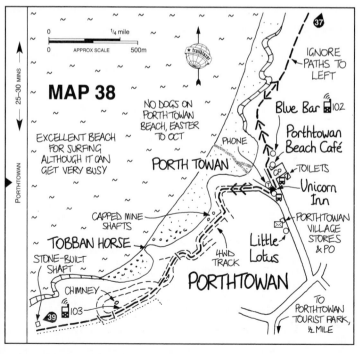

ROUTE GUIDE AND MAPS

pasties, and also houses the local **post office** (same hours as the store).

The nearest **campsite** to the beach is **Porthtowan Tourist Park** (☎ 01209-890256, 🖥 porthtowantouristpark.co.uk; hiker & tent £14.95-19.95; open Apr-Oct; WI-FI) about one mile away. It has a laundry room and a **shop** (daily 8.30-10.30am & 4.30-7.30pm) selling a few essentials such as bread, milk, eggs, bacon and some tinned food.

Apart from that, your only other choice is the local pub, **Unicorn Inn** (🖥 facebook.com/PorthtowanUnicorn), which serves standard pub food and may offer B&B too. However, the pub is now under new management and it is unclear what the situation will be regarding accommodation. Previously they had three en suite rooms plus an annexe with 18 dorm beds; check in advance.

A much better bet for food is either the hugely popular **Blue Bar** (☎ 01209-890329, 🖥 blue-bar.co.uk; 🐾; food summer daily 10am-9pm; WI-FI) which entices many walkers off the path with its unpretentious atmosphere, fine ales and no-nonsense menu (try the spice-tinged 'Dirty Chips' – chips with pulled pork, cheese and jalapeño peppers; £7.50-11), or **Porthtowan Beach Café** (🖥 porthtowanbeachcafe.com; daily 9.30am-4.30pm, and evenings in summer) next door.

Next to the shop, **Little Lotus** (☎ 07478-393693) sells coffee, and amongst other delights, organic burgers and falafels.

Bus services include Hopley's No 315 to St Agnes and 304 to Truro, and First's A4 travelling between Newquay and St Ives. See also pp52-6.

PORTHTOWAN TO PORTREATH [MAPS 38-40]

For most of these **3 miles (5km, 1-1¼hrs)** the walking is alongside heavily fenced **MoD land** with frequent signs warning of dire penalties for straying from the path. It keeps to the edge of the cliffs and on the sea side the views are spectacular but it is hard to ignore the concrete buildings and chain link fencing of Penhale Camp.

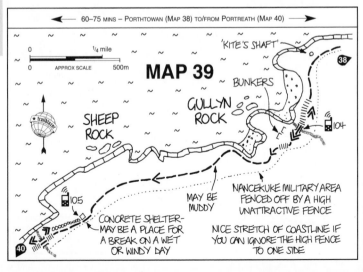

← 60–75 MINS – PORTHTOWAN (MAP 38) TO/FROM PORTREATH (MAP 40) →

MAP 39

'KITE'S SHAFT'

BUNKERS

GULLYN ROCK

SHEEP ROCK

NANCEKUKE MILITARY AREA FENCED OFF BY A HIGH UNATTRACTIVE FENCE

MAY BE MUDDY

NICE STRETCH OF COASTLINE IF YOU CAN IGNORE THE HIGH FENCE TO ONE SIDE

CONCRETE SHELTER– MAY BE A PLACE FOR A BREAK ON A WET OR WINDY DAY

0   ¼ mile
0   APPROX SCALE   500m

traillazer

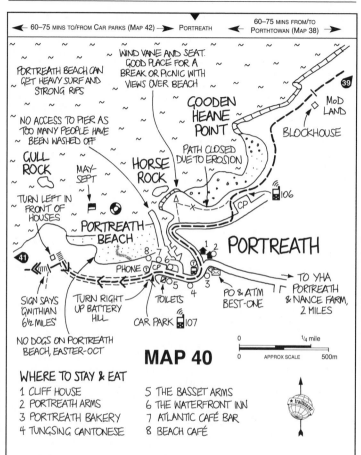

WIND VANE AND SEAT.
GOOD PLACE FOR A
BREAK OR PICNIC WITH
VIEWS OVER BEACH

PORTREATH BEACH CAN
GET HEAVY SURF AND
STRONG RIPS

GOODEN
HEANE
POINT

39

MoD
LAND

BLOCKHOUSE

NO ACCESS TO PIER AS
TOO MANY PEOPLE HAVE
BEEN WASHED OFF

PATH CLOSED
DUE TO EROSION

GULL
ROCK

MAY-
SEPT

HORSE
ROCK

CP

106

TURN LEFT IN
FRONT OF
HOUSES

PORTREATH
BEACH

PORTREATH

41

PHONE

CP

1 2

TO YHA
PORTREATH
& NANCE FARM,
2 MILES

8 7

PO & ATM
BEST-ONE

SIGN SAYS
'GWITHIAN
6½ MILES'

TURN RIGHT
UP BATTERY
HILL

TOILETS

6 5   4   3

NO DOGS ON PORTREATH
BEACH, EASTER-OCT

CAR PARK 107

0   ¼ mile

MAP 40

0
APPROX SCALE   500m

★ trailblazer

WHERE TO STAY & EAT

1 CLIFF HOUSE
2 PORTREATH ARMS
3 PORTREATH BAKERY
4 TUNGSING CANTONESE

5 THE BASSET ARMS
6 THE WATERFRONT INN
7 ATLANTIC CAFÉ BAR
8 BEACH CAFÉ

ROUTE GUIDE AND MAPS

PORTREATH   [MAP 40]

Portreath is a small community with just about all you might need in the way of refreshment or an overnight stop on the way to St Ives.

The row of shops opposite the Portreath Arms consists of a Best-One **store** (daily 8am-1pm, 1.30-9pm), which houses the **post office** (Mon-Fri 9am-1pm, 1.30-5.30pm, Sat 9am-12.30pm) and a **cash machine** (£1.85 charge), and **Portreath Bakery** (☎ 01209-842612; main season Mon-Sat 6.30am-6pm;

rest of year to 5pm Mon-Fri and to 4pm Sat) for fresh coffee, filled rolls, pasties and marvellous pastry goods.

Where to stay

YHA Portreath (off Map 40; ☎ 01209-842244, 🖳 yha.org.uk/hostel/portreath, or 🖳 mary.alway@btinternet.com; open all year; 20 beds; from £18pp), at Nance Farm, in **Illogan**, a village about two miles from Portreath, is a converted barn on a working farm, with a self-catering kitchen and dry-ing room. It's a bit of a pain to find; you'll probably need to call for directions. First Kernow's **bus** No 47 (see pp52-6) goes to Illogan, but it is a half-mile walk to the hostel from Paynters Lane End bus stop.

B&B is available at the attractive *Cliff House* (☎ 01209-843847, 🖳 cliffhouseportreath.co.uk; 2S/2D/1T; WI-FI; 🐾; from £40pp, sgl £50, sgl occ rate on request; luggage transfer), an ideal stopover and a great favourite with coast-path walkers. In the conservatory at the front of the house there are some fascinating old photos of Portreath when it was a thriving port for sailing ships.

Portreath Arms Hotel (☎ 01209-842259, 🖳 theportreatharms.co.uk; 2D/4T/1F; 🐾; £37.50-55pp, sgl occ from £55) can also organise luggage transfer.

Where to eat

The windswept *Beach Café* (10am-5pm) is the only place that's genuinely on the beach. It does all-day breakfasts (£6), plus tea, coffee, sandwiches and snacks.

The Atlantic café-bar (☎ 01209-843490; food Wed-Sat 10am-8.45pm, Sun-Tue to 6.15pm) is a good-looking modern place with fish dishes and pub grub, plus a takeaway window to one side, serving chips, pasties and the like.

Nearby, *The Waterfront Inn* (☎ 01209-842777, 🖳 thewaterfrontinn.webs .com; food Mon-Sat noon-3pm & 6-9pm, Sun noon-4pm) does standard pub food at reasonable prices although the *Basset Arms* (☎ 01209-842077; food daily noon-2pm & 6-9pm), set back from the road, is a better bet. The food is decent pub grub and the atmosphere more pleasant. Further down the same road is a Chinese restaurant, *Tungsing Cantonese* (☎ 01209-844672; Mon, Wed, Thur & Sun 5-9.30pm, Fri-Sat 5-10pm), which is closed on Tuesdays.

At *Portreath Arms Hotel* (see Where to stay; food daily noon-2pm & 6-9pm) mains cost from £8.

First Kernow's No 47 and the seasonal A4 **bus** services call here; see pp52-6.

PORTREATH TO GWITHIAN   [MAPS 40-44]

This **8-mile (13km, 2-2¾hrs)** leg is nearly all on the cliff top through gorse and shrub with only a narrow path to walk on. Once you reach Hudder Cove and the spectacularly named **Hell's Mouth** you are well rewarded as the cliffs are filled with nesting birds while grey seals breed in the caves below Navax Point. The path here has been surfaced to suit the heavy use that it now gets from dog walkers and joggers who are able to park in the car parks close to the cliff edge. The *Hell's Mouth Café* (Map 43; summer Mon-Fri 9am-5.30pm, Sat & Sun 9am-6pm) is worth a short diversion if you're thirsty.

Godrevy Point is in the care of the National Trust and is a popular place for picnics and recreation. The offshore lighthouse was the inspiration for Virginia Woolf's classic novel, *To the Lighthouse*. Written in 1927, it drew on her memories of holidays with her parents in St Ives; the lighthouse in the book is merely a device for the development of the plot. Plans to switch off the light

---

❏ **Beware, these cliffs are unstable...**
You are likely to see black and yellow triangular warning signs bearing these or similar words at several points along the South-West Coast Path, but they have particular significance at North Cliff, near Deadman's Cove (Map 42). On 23rd September 2011, geologist Richard Hocking captured video footage here of an estimated 200,000 tonnes of rock face collapsing into the sea, just days after the coastal path was diverted inland. So don't ignore those warning signs!

permanently were shelved after vocal protests by fishermen and Virginia Woolf fans. From the NT car park at Godrevy the path cuts off the coast and follows a long stretch of road into **Gwithian** so you may need a break at Godrevy Beach Café (p157), which is right on the coast path as you come into Gwithian.

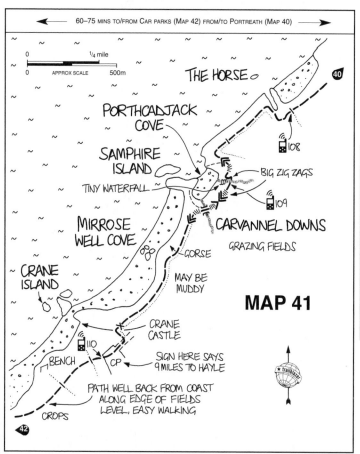

60–75 MINS TO/FROM CAR PARKS (MAP 42) FROM/TO PORTREATH (MAP 40)

0   1/4 mile
0   APPROX SCALE   500m

THE HORSE
40

PORTHCADJACK COVE

SAMPHIRE ISLAND

TINY WATERFALL

108

BIG ZIG ZAGS

109

MIRROSE WELL COVE

CARVANNEL DOWNS

GRAZING FIELDS

GORSE

MAY BE MUDDY

CRANE ISLAND

MAP 41

CRANE CASTLE

110

SIGN HERE SAYS 9 MILES TO HAYLE

BENCH   CP

PATH WELL BACK FROM COAST ALONG EDGE OF FIELDS LEVEL, EASY WALKING

CROPS

42

★ trailblazer

ROUTE GUIDE AND MAPS

❏ **Important note – walking times**
Unless otherwise specified, **all times in this book refer only to the time spent walk-ing.** You will need to add 20-30% to allow for rests, photography, checking the map, drinking water etc. When planning the day's hike count on 5-7 hours' actual walking.

GWITHIAN [MAP 44, p158]

Gwithian is a sandy sort of place just inland from the dunes with the main road running through it bordered by a few houses.

The best choice for campers is the family-run *Gwithian Farm Campsite* (☎

01736-753127, 🖳 gwithianfarm.co.uk; 🐕; WI-FI; hiker & tent £8-10), a welcoming, well-run site with a shop (including fresh coffee), laundry and a spotlessly clean shower block. They are happy to re-charge

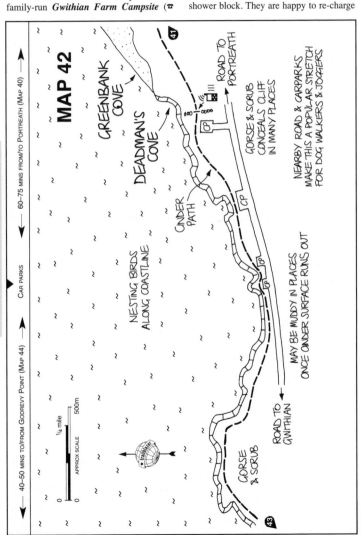

← 40–50 MINS TO/FROM GODREVY POINT (MAP 44) — — CAR PARKS — 60–75 MINS FROM/TO PORTREATH (MAP 40) →

MAP 42

GREENBANK COVE

DEADMAN'S COVE

CINDER PATH

NESTING BIRDS ALONG COASTLINE

ROAD TO PORTREATH

GORSE & SCRUB CONCEALS CLIFF IN MANY PLACES

NEARBY ROAD & CARPARKS MAKE THIS A POPULAR STRETCH FOR DOG WALKERS & JOGGERS

CP

CP

MAY BE MUDDY IN PLACES ONCE CINDER SURFACE RUNS OUT

ROAD TO GWITHIAN

GORSE & SCRUB

¼ mile
500m
APPROX SCALE
0

41

43

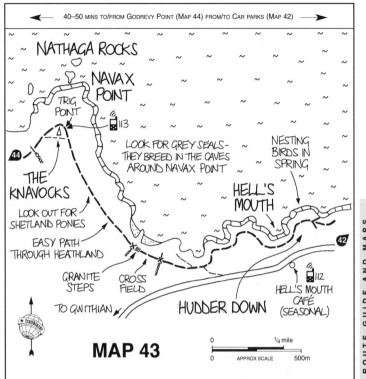

NATHAGA ROCKS

NAVAX POINT

TRIG POINT

113

44

THE KNAVOCKS

LOOK OUT FOR SHETLAND PONIES

EASY PATH THROUGH HEATHLAND

GRANITE STEPS

CROSS FIELD

TO GWITHIAN

LOOK FOR GREY SEALS— THEY BREED IN THE CAVES AROUND NAVAX POINT

NESTING BIRDS IN SPRING

HELL'S MOUTH

42

112

HELL'S MOUTH CAFÉ (SEASONAL)

HUDDER DOWN

★ trailblaze

MAP 43

0 _____ ¼ mile

0 _____ 500m

APPROX SCALE

ROUTE GUIDE AND MAPS

---

phones, and never turn walkers away. **B&B** can be found up the mile-long track at *Nanterrow Farm* (☎ 01209-712282, 💻 nan terrowfarm.co.uk; 1D/1F, shared bathroom; £29-39pp, sgl occ £32-45), a beautiful place with a lovely welcome.

For food, *Godrevy Beach Café* (☎ 01736-757999; 10am-5pm) is an enterprise with lots of imagination. Their street food evenings (Wed & Thur 5-8pm) bring themed specials to an already excellent café menu. They also operate *The Hut* (daily 9am-6pm weather dependent) next door, from which you can purchase snacks as well as hot and cold drinks. *The Rockpool* (☎ 01736-449990, 💻 therockpoolbar.co .uk; 10-11.30am, noon-3pm & 5-8.30pm) is

a bar and grill with a menu dominated by burgers, steaks and seafood.

Further into the beach, through the dunes, is *The Jampot* (summer daily 10am-5pm, winter Tue-Sun 10am-5pm), a café serving home-made cakes, snacks and drinks. The food is cheap and there's local art on the walls. Nearby, *Sunset Surf* (10am-4pm, plus Aug evenings) is a very popular, family-friendly café-bar, serving breakfasts, cream teas, burgers and pasta.

The Red River Inn (☎ 01736-753223, 💻 red-river-inn.com) used to be a very popular pub for evening meals and a beer, but had closed at the time of research, with no news on its future. Hopefully, it will reopen.

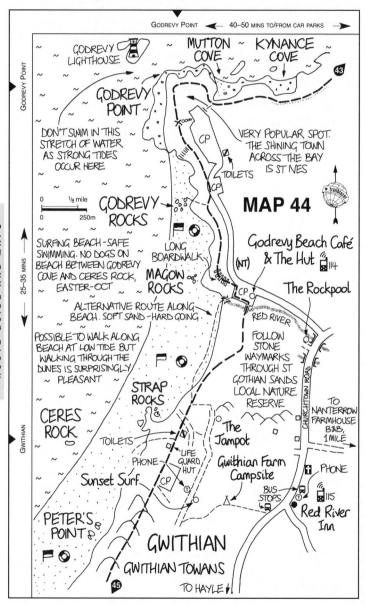

GODREVY POINT ← 40–50 MINS TO/FROM CAR PARKS →

GODREVY LIGHTHOUSE

MUTTON COVE

KYNANCE COVE

43

GODREVY POINT

GODREVY POINT

DON'T SWIM IN THIS STRETCH OF WATER AS STRONG TIDES OCCUR HERE

CP

VERY POPULAR SPOT. THE SHINING TOWN ACROSS THE BAY IS ST IVES

TOILETS

CP

MAP 44

GODREVY ROCKS

SURFING BEACH - SAFE SWIMMING. NO DOGS ON BEACH BETWEEN GODREVY COVE AND CERES ROCK, EASTER-OCT

LONG BOARDWALK

Godrevy Beach Café & The Hut 114

MAGON ROCKS

(NT)

The Rockpool

ALTERNATIVE ROUTE ALONG BEACH. SOFT SAND - HARD GOING.

CP

RED RIVER

25-35 MINS

POSSIBLE TO WALK ALONG BEACH AT LOW TIDE BUT WALKING THROUGH THE DUNES IS SURPRISINGLY PLEASANT

FOLLOW STONE WAYMARKS THROUGH ST GOTHIAN SANDS LOCAL NATURE RESERVE

STRAP ROCKS

CERES ROCK

CHURCHTOWN ROAD

TO NANTERROW FARMHOUSE B&B, 1 MILE

TOILETS

The Jampot

PHONE

PHONE

LIFE GUARD HUT

Gwithian Farm Campsite

Sunset Surf

CP

BUS STOPS

115

GWITHIAN

PETER'S POINT

Red River Inn

GWITHIAN TOWANS

45

TO HAYLE ↓

GODREVY POINT

GWITHIAN

GWITHIAN TO HAYLE [MAPS 44-46]

For these **4 miles (6km, 1-1¼hrs)** you have the choice of either walking along the beach or taking the official coast path through the dunes.

Although it is continually up and down, the walk through the dunes is actually quite pleasant. It's a game of connect the dots as you follow the acorn posts with their yellow arrows from dune to dune and the sleepy undemanding scenery allows your mind to wander. Though the posts are not always easy to find, if you keep to a roughly straight line you shouldn't go far wrong. Be aware, however, that if the sun is out, the dunes trap the heat and shelter you from the breeze; it can get very hot so take plenty of water.

The last part of this section, from **Hayle Towans** to **Hayle**, is through an industrial area.

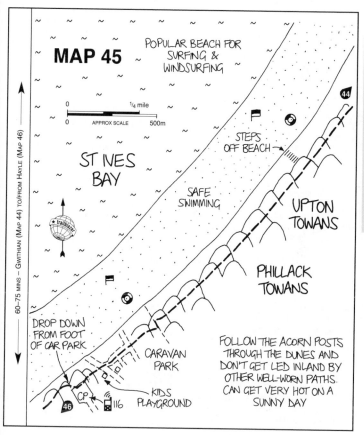

HAYLE [MAP 46]

Hayle (*heyl* meaning estuary in Cornish) is recorded as having supplied tin as early as 1500BC and the Romans sailed their ships up as far as St Erth. Today the estuary is home to lobster boats, their catch going mostly to the continent.

For keen birdwatchers the muddy flats are good twitching territory and the RSPB owns a **nature reserve** on the estuary. Autumn and winter are particularly good for migrating and wintering wild fowl such as widgeon, teal, shelduck and waders, including dunlin, curlew and grey plover.

Hayle has two centres: Copperhouse, around Fore Street, and Foundry Square, south of the railway station. It is a fair-sized town where walkers can find all the services they need including **banks** (Lloyds being the closest to the trail), with cash machines, and a **post office** (Mon-Fri 9am-5.30pm) at 13 Penpol Terrace inside McColl's **newsagent** (Mon-Sat 6am-8pm, Sun 7am-8pm), which also has a free-to-use ATM. The **tourist information centre** (☎ 01736-754399; Mon-Wed & Fri 9am-6pm, Sat 9.30am-12.30pm) is in the **library** (same hours) where **internet access** is available (£1.80/30 mins) for visitors.

There are numerous small shops along Penpol Terrace including a Spar **supermarket** (7am-10pm) and a Boots **pharmacy** (Mon-Fri 8.30am-6pm, Sat 9am-5.30pm). Alternatively, head to the huge **Asda supermarket** (Mon-Sat 7am-11pm, Sun 10am-4pm) by South Quay.

One surprise for walkers coming out of the dunes may be the open-air **swimming pool** (☎ 01736-755005; late May to late Sep daily 11am-6pm; adult/children £5/3), on East Quay, which has the cute **Café Riviere** (11.30am-4pm) beside its entrance. There's a **launderette** (Mon-Sat 8am-6pm) on Foundry Square.

The **Heritage Festival** (see p16) is held here every summer.

Where to stay

Campers can head to *Beachside Holiday Park* (☎ 01736-753080, 🖳 beachside.co .uk; tent pitch £12-38; WI-FI), one of a cluster of large holiday parks along the coast here. It's more set up for the caravan set, but walkers can pitch tents here too. Facilities include a shop, a bar and even an outdoor pool.

B&Bs include the *Mad Hatter* (☎ 01736-754241, 🖳 www.cornwall-online .co.uk/madhatter; 1D or T en suite/1D/1T/ 1S/1F share facilities; ✆; WI-FI; 🐾; from £40pp, sgl occ plus £5) at 73 Fore St, which has a tearoom (see Where to eat) downstairs; and family-run *Creekside* (☎ 01736-753969, 🖳 valsherris@hotmail.com; 3D; ✆; from £37.50pp, sgl occ £50) at 34 Penpol Terrace.

Alternatively try *White Hart Hotel* (☎ 01736-752322, 🖳 whitehearthotel-hayle.co .uk; 2S/15D/5T/2F; ✆; WI-FI; £43-70pp, sgl occ £75-95), an old coaching inn, housed in an elegant Regency building dating from 1838.

HAYLE – MAP KEY

Where to stay, eat and drink
1 Balti King
2 Mad Hatter
4 The Terrace
5 Eastern Empire
6 Café Riviere
7 Philp's Bakery
8 Lewy's Fish & Chips
9 Creekside B&B
10 Mr B's ice-creams
14 Warrens Bakery
16 Salt
19 White Hart Hotel

Other
3 Tourist Information, library & internet access
11 McColl's newsagent & post office
12 Pharmacy (Boots)
13 Spar supermarket
15 Asda supermarket
17 Launderette
18 Lloyds bank

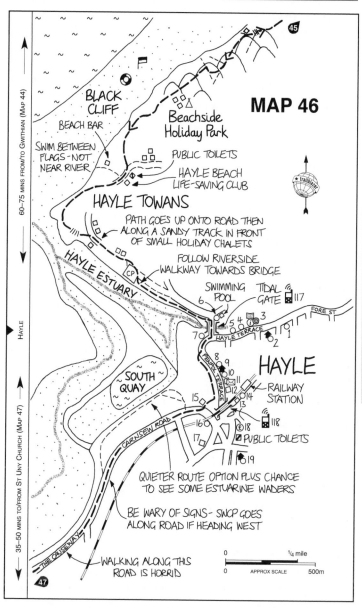

MAP 46

BLACK CLIFF

BEACH BAR

SWIM BETWEEN FLAGS - NOT NEAR RIVER

Beachside Holiday Park

PUBLIC TOILETS

HAYLE BEACH LIFE-SAVING CLUB

HAYLE TOWANS

PATH GOES UP ONTO ROAD THEN ALONG A SANDY TRACK IN FRONT OF SMALL HOLIDAY CHALETS

FOLLOW RIVERSIDE WALKWAY TOWARDS BRIDGE

HAYLE ESTUARY

CP

SWIMMING POOL

TIDAL GATE

117

FORE ST

6

5 4

i@ 3

7

HAYLE TERRACE

2 1

8 9

HAYLE

10

PENPOL TERRACE

11

12

RAILWAY STATION

SOUTH QUAY

15

14

13

118

16

18

17

PUBLIC TOILETS

19

CARNSEW ROAD

QUIETER ROUTE OPTION PLUS CHANCE TO SEE SOME ESTUARINE WADERS

BE WARY OF SIGNS- SWCP GOES ALONG ROAD IF HEADING WEST

THE CAUSEWAY

WALKING ALONG THIS ROAD IS HORRID

47

0   1/4 mile

0   500m

APPROX SCALE

60-75 MINS FROM/TO GWITHIAN (MAP 44)

HAYLE

35-50 MINS TO/FROM ST UNY CHURCH (MAP 47)

45

ROUTE GUIDE AND MAPS

Where to eat and drink

Grab pizza and other Mediterranean dishes at *The Terrace* (☎ 01736-753745, 🖳 theter racehayle.com; daily 5.30-9.30pm; pizza £8.95-£12.95), Indian at *Balti King* (☎ 01736-755300, 🖳 baltikingrestaurant.co .uk; daily 5.30-11.30pm), Chinese at *Eastern Empire* (☎ 01736-753272; daily 5.30-11pm) or fish & chips at *Lewy's Fish and Chips* (daily noon-2pm & 5-9pm).

For ice-cream, look no further than *Mr B's* (☎ 01736-755808, 🖳 mrbsicecream.co .uk; daily 11am-5.30pm).

One place that is very popular is *Philp's Bakery* (☎ 01736-755661, 🖳 philps bakery.co.uk; Mon-Sat 8.30am-6pm, Sun 10.30am-4.30pm), on East Quay, reckoned by some to bake the best pasties in Cornwall. The more central *Warrens Bakery* (Mon-Sat 8.30am-5pm, Sun 10am-4pm) is good for pastries and a coffee.

Food is also available in *White Hart Hotel* (see Where to stay; daily noon-2pm & 6-8.30pm) and at the little **tearoom** attached to *Mad Hatter* B&B (see Where to stay; Easter-Oct 10am-5pm); Cornish cream teas are, of course, available.

For a gastro pub experience, try *Salt* (☎ 01736-755862, 🖳 salt-hayle.co.uk; 10am to late), with steaks (£14-16) and gourmet burgers (£11-13) on an otherwise fairly standard pub-grub menu. They have cocktails and live music on Friday evenings.

Public transport

[see pp52-6] First Kernow's A4 **bus** service calls here as do some **coach** services (NX330, NX404 & NX504; see box p50). Hayle is also a stop on the **railway** line (operated by GWR) to Penzance. For a **taxi** ring Hayle Taxis (☎ 01736-753000), or St Erth & Hayle Cars (☎ 01736-754000).

HAYLE TO ST IVES   [MAPS 46-49]

This **6-mile (9.5km, 1¾-2½hrs)** stretch leaves Hayle along the busy Carnsew Rd and The Causeway crossing to the other side of the estuary. It's a delightful – if noisy – excursion in a stunning seascape.

Thankfully, the path leaves the busy roads behind and briefly follows the B3301 going beneath the branch line between St Erth and St Ives. From here the route follows The Saltings; a quiet suburban walk through the outskirts of **Lelant**.

From **St Uny Church** the coast path follows the railway line into St Ives, firstly through more dunes then past **Carbis Bay**. The path beyond Carbis Bay winds its way through wooded cliffs to arrive at the broad sands of **Porthminster Beach** where there is an upmarket beach café (see p169) complete with decking.

LELANT & CARBIS BAY
                          [MAPS 47 & 48]

In **Lelant** there's a seasonal **teashop** at Lelant station.

In **Carbis Bay** there's a Tesco **supermarket** (Mon-Sat 8am-8pm, Sun 10am-4pm) and a very smart B&B called *Chy-an-Gwedhen* (☎ 01736-798684, 🖳 chyangwed hen.com; 1S/3D/1T; WI-FI; £37.50-52.50pp,

sgl £60-80), although most walkers will push on to St Ives where food, drink and accommodation are plentiful.

First's A2 & A17 **bus** services stop at both places and St Ives Bus Co's No 1 stops at Tesco Carbis Bay; see pp52-6.

NX330 and NX504 **coach** services (see box p50) call at both places.

❑ **Important note – walking times**
Unless otherwise specified, **all times in this book refer only to the time spent walking**. You will need to add 20-30% to allow for rests, photography, checking the map, drinking water etc. When planning the day's hike count on 5-7 hours' actual walking.

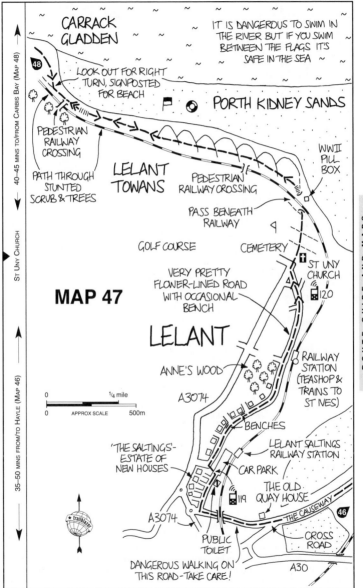

CARRACK GLADDEN

IT IS DANGEROUS TO SWIM IN THE RIVER BUT IF YOU SWIM BETWEEN THE FLAGS IT'S SAFE IN THE SEA

LOOK OUT FOR RIGHT TURN, SIGNPOSTED FOR BEACH

PORTH KIDNEY SANDS

PEDESTRIAN RAILWAY CROSSING

PATH THROUGH STUNTED SCRUB & TREES

LELANT TOWANS

PEDESTRIAN RAILWAY CROSSING

WWII PILL BOX

PASS BENEATH RAILWAY

GOLF COURSE

CEMETERY

ST UNY CHURCH

120

VERY PRETTY FLOWER-LINED ROAD WITH OCCASIONAL BENCH

MAP 47

LELANT

ANNE'S WOOD

A3074

RAILWAY STATION (TEASHOP & TRAINS TO ST IVES)

0   1/4 mile

0   APPROX SCALE   500m

BENCHES

LELANT SALTINGS RAILWAY STATION

'THE SALTINGS'- ESTATE OF NEW HOUSES

CAR PARK

119

THE OLD QUAY HOUSE

A3074

THE CAUSEWAY   46

trailblazer

PUBLIC TOILET

CROSS ROAD

DANGEROUS WALKING ON THIS ROAD-TAKE CARE!

A30

40-45 MINS TO/FROM CARBIS BAY (MAP 48)

ST UNY CHURCH

35-50 MINS FROM/TO HAYLE (MAP 46)

48

ROUTE GUIDE AND MAPS

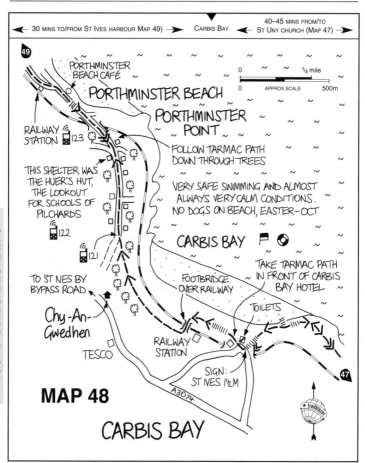

PORTHMINSTER BEACH CAFÉ

PORTHMINSTER BEACH

PORTHMINSTER POINT

RAILWAY STATION 123

THIS SHELTER WAS THE HUER'S HUT, THE LOOKOUT FOR SCHOOLS OF PILCHARDS
122

121

FOLLOW TARMAC PATH DOWN THROUGH TREES

VERY SAFE SWIMMING AND ALMOST ALWAYS VERY CALM CONDITIONS. NO DOGS ON BEACH, EASTER–OCT

CARBIS BAY

TAKE TARMAC PATH IN FRONT OF CARBIS BAY HOTEL

FOOTBRIDGE OVER RAILWAY

TOILETS

TO ST NES BY BYPASS ROAD

Chy-An-Gwedhen

TESCO

RAILWAY STATION

SIGN: ST IVES 1½M

A3074

MAP 48

CARBIS BAY

0   ¼ mile
0   APPROX SCALE   500m

★ trailblazer

47

49

ST IVES   [MAP 49, p167]

Pretty St Ives has attracted artists for years and is certainly a place worth spending some time in, even if it's just to chill out, and soak up the charms of its harbour and tightly packed fishermen's cottages. It is a very popular destination, though, so can get overcrowded with tourists in the height of summer. If you are coming in the main season (particularly July and August) it is advisable to book accommodation in advance.

The flagship gallery is **Tate St Ives**, Porthmeor Beach. It's well worth a visit and has a fine *café* (Mar-Oct daily 10am-4.20pm, Nov-Feb Tue-Sun 10am-4.20pm). If you're interested in art you should put an hour aside to visit the **Barbara Hepworth Museum**; see box opposite for both.

There are numerous small **galleries** in St Ives with art on display but also usually for sale with prices ranging from moderately expensive to ludicrous. Your wanders round the town might also bring you to the doors of the **St Ives Museum** (☎ 01736-796005; Easter-Oct Mon-Fri 10.30am-4.30pm, Sat 10.30am-3.30pm, last admission 30 mins before closing; £3), at Wheal Dream, by the harbour front. The exhibits include memorabilia of local significance such as the fishing industry, shipwrecks, lighthouses and lifeboats.

In addition to all this several **festivals** (see pp15-16) are held here every year.

Services

The **tourist information centre** (☎ 01736-796297 or 0905 2522250, ☐ visitstives.org .uk; daily Mon-Sat 10am-5pm, Sun 10am-4pm) in the Guildhall has helpful staff and a good range of material on what to see and do locally.

Various **banks,** including Barclays and HSBC, have branches with ATMs on High St. The main **post office** (Mon-Fri 9am-5.30pm, Sat 9am-12.30pm) is at the end of Fore St on the harbour front. A second post office (Mon-Fri 8.30am-6pm, Sat 9am-12.30pm) is on Tregenna Hill. On The Stennack is a **launderette** (daily 8.30am-

8.30pm). Further up the same road is a **medical centre** (Stennack Surgery; ☎ 01736-793333, ☐ thestennacksurgery.co .uk) which has a minor injuries unit (Mon-Fri 8am-8pm). There are several **pharmacies** including Leddra Chemist (Mon-Sat 9am-5.30pm) at 7 Fore St. There are also several **convenience stores** dotted around town, including two branches of the Co-op (7am-11pm), one on The Stennack and the other on Tregenna Hill.

For **camping gear**, there's a Mountain Warehouse (Mon-Sat 9am-5.30pm, Sun 11am-5pm) on Fore St.

St Ives Bookseller (☐ stives-bookseller.co.uk; Mon-Sat 9am-9pm, Sun 11am-4pm) has lots of local-interest books, including some St Ives-themed children's books. On Gabriel St the **library** (☎ 01736-795377, ☐ cornwall.gov.uk/library; Mon, Wed & Fri 9.30am-5pm, Sat 10am-1pm, WI-FI) offers **internet access** (£1.80 for 30 mins).

The **cinema** is opposite **St Ives Theatre** (☐ stives-cornwall.co.uk/st-ives-theatre), the venue used by an enterprising local drama company, Kidz-R-Us (☐ kidzrus.net).

❑ Art in St Ives

It was the quality of light and the landscape which first attracted artists to St Ives and is still inspiring them today. Most modern art histories of Cornwall start with Turner's visit in 1811; however, 1928 is when the development of St Ives as an artists' colony really began with a meeting of Alfred Wallis, Ben Nicholson and Christopher Wood.

Tate St Ives (☎ 01736-796226, ☐ tate.org.uk/visit/tate-st-ives; Mar-Oct daily 10am-5.20pm, last admission 5pm, Nov-Feb Tue-Sun 10am-4.20pm, last admission 4pm; £10.50) was built on the site of the town's old gas works. The gallery has no static collection and instead displays exhibitions of selected works from the national Tate collection. Even if you are not a supporter of modern art you are bound to find something of interest.

Barbara Hepworth Museum and Sculpture Garden (☎ 01736-796226, ☐ tate .org.uk/visit/tate-st-ives/barbara-hepworth-museum; same opening hours as the Tate; £7.70) is on the site of the former studio of Barbara Hepworth, a well-known sculptor who worked mainly with stone and bronze. Some of her sculptures are big enough to walk inside and around so that you can study every angle. Her studio has been preserved exactly as it was when she died in 1975 and there is a collection of her sculptures in the garden; a very peaceful place to spend a morning or afternoon watching each work change with the movement of the sun.

You can buy a joint ticket to both the Tate and Barbara Hepworth Museum for £14.50.

Where to stay

Campsites and hostels For **campers**, ***Ayr Holiday Park*** (off Map 49; ☎ 01736-795855, 🖳 ayrholidaypark.co.uk; tent & two adults £14.50-27) is about 10 to 15 minutes' walk from the harbour. Alternatively, consider Trevalgan Touring Park, see p172.

Hostel accommodation is available at ***Cohort Hostel*** (☎ 01736-791664, 🖳 stayatcohort.co.uk; 2T/1Tr/40 dorm beds; WI-FI; from £20pp), who have transformed the former St Ives International Backpackers building into a modern hostel that is clean, colourful and well-run. Common areas are large, comfortable and well-equipped (sofas, TVs, kitchen, outdoor courtyard), but some of the dorms, and the showers, are extremely cramped. There's no café, but they do sell coffee and booze in the common room.

B&Bs, pubs and guesthouses There are several B&Bs and guesthouses up by the bus terminus, overlooking the harbour.

The Rookery (☎ 01736-799401, 🖳 thestivesbandb.com; 1S/4D/1Tr/1F; ◡; WI-FI; £39.50-52.50pp, sgl £50-65), at 8 The Terrace, welcomes walkers and one-night stays. Most rooms have a sea view.

A few doors down, at No 5, ***The Belmont*** (☎ 01736-793401, 🖳 thebelmontstives.co.uk; 1S/3D; WI-FI; £45-50pp, sgl occ from £55) is a tidy, well-run house, although they prefer stays of at least two nights if possible. A couple of doors up from these two, at No 10, is ***Golden Hind B&B*** (☎ 01736-796632, 🖳 goldenhindstives.com; from £50pp, sgl from £65).

Just round the corner, at 7 Porthminster Terrace, is ***Rivendell*** (☎ 01736-794923, 🖳 rivendell-stives.co.uk; 1S/4D/1T, most en suite; WI-FI; £45-53pp), a smart Victorian villa which was used in the final episode of the 1990s TV series, *Wycliffe*, set in Cornwall. Next door, at No 9, is the slightly-less-stylish ***Carlill*** (☎ 01736-796738, 🖳 carlillguesthouse.co.uk; 1S/2D/1T/1F; WI-FI; £40-50pp), which also offers packed lunches and luggage transfer.

In the old part of town, down by the harbour, there are some lovely, intimate, fisherman's cottages, some of which offer B&B. On Bunker's Hill, a cobbled lane just off Fore St, is the best of the lot. ***Grey Mullet*** (☎ 01736-796635, 🖳 uktourismonline.co.uk/south-west-england/cornwall/st-ives/the-greymullet-gh; 1S/5D/1T; ◡; from £35pp), with hanging baskets festooning the front, and low wood-beamed ceilings inside, is housed in an old stone building that dates from 1776, and is an absolute pleasure to stay in. ***Downlong Cottage*** (☎ 01736-798107, 🖳 downlongcottage.co.uk; 3D/1T/1F; WI-FI; £37.50-47.50pp, sgl occ on request), meanwhile, is

ST IVES – MAP KEY

Where to stay
- **1** Downlong Cottage
- **3** Sloop Inn
- **5** Grey Mullet
- **21** Queens Hotel
- **24** Cohort Hostel
- **25** The Western Hotel
- **29** Regent Hotel
- **30** Pedn-Olva Hotel
- **31** Belmont
- **32** The Rookery
- **33** Golden Hind B&B
- **34** Carlill
- **35** Rivendell

Where to eat & drink
- **2** Mermaid Seafood Restaurant
- **3** Sloop Inn
- **4** Balancing Eel
- **6** Moomaid of Zennor
- **7** Porthmeor Café & Bar
- **8** The Beach Restaurant
- **9** St Ives Bakery
- **10** Myrings Fudge & Rock Shop
- **12** Peppers Pasta & Pizzeria
- **13** The Union Inn
- **14** The Castle Inn
- **15** Talay Thai Tapas
- **16** Lifeboat Inn
- **18** Harbour Fish & Chips
- **20** Scoff Troff Café
- **21** Queens Hotel
- **22** The Golden Lion
- **23** Coasters Café
- **26** Rajpoot
- **27** The Mex
- **28** Blas Burger Works

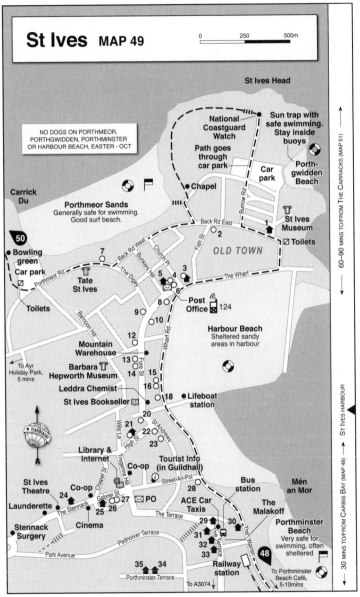

St Ives MAP 49

0   250   500m

St Ives Head

NO DOGS ON PORTHMEOR, PORTHGWIDDEN, PORTHMINSTER OR HARBOUR BEACH, EASTER - OCT

National Coastguard Watch

Sun trap with safe swimming. Stay inside buoys

Path goes through car park

Car park

Porthgwidden Beach

Burrow Rd

Chapel

Carrick Du

St Ives Museum

Porthmeor Sands
Generally safe for swimming.
Good surf beach.

Toilets

Back Rd East

Fish St

OLD TOWN

50

Bowling green Car park

7

Back Rd West

Bunkers Hill

Church Pl

2

The Digey

Porthmeor Rd

Tate St Ives

The Wharf

Toilets

5   4   3

6

8

9

Post Office 124

Barnoon Hill

10

Wharf Rd

Harbour Beach
Sheltered sandy areas in harbour

12

To Ayr Holiday Park, 5 mins

Mountain Warehouse

13

Fore St

Barbara Hepworth Museum

14

15

16

Leddra Chemist

St Ives Bookseller

18

Lifeboat station

20

21

St Andrews

22

Wills La

23

High St

Tregenna Hill

Library & Internet

Co-op

Tourist Info (in Guildhall)

Street-An-Pol

Bus station

Mén an Mor

St Ives Theatre

24

Co-op

25

Chapel St

Gabriel St

27

26

PO

28

ACE Car Taxis

The Malakoff

Launderette

The Stennack

Cinema

The Terrace

29   30

Porthminster Beach
Very safe for swimming, often sheltered

Stennack Surgery

Pednolver Terrace

The Warren

31

The Terrace

32

33

48

Park Avenue

35   34

Porthminster Terrace

Railway station

To A3074

To Porthminster Beach Café, 5-10mins

60-90 MINS TO/FROM THE CARRACKS (MAP 51)

ST IVES HARBOUR

30 MINS TO/FROM CARBIS BAY (MAP 48)

ROUTE GUIDE AND MAPS

★ trailblazer

at 95 Back Rd East and also welcomes one-night stays.

There are also B&B rooms at nearby *Sloop Inn* (☎ 01736-796584, ☐ sloop-inn .co.uk; 12D/3T/4F, most en suite; ▾; WI-FI; ✹; £57.50-75pp, sgl occ 25% discount from room rate), one of Cornwall's oldest pubs. However, in high season the minimum stay is three nights.

Another pub doing bed and breakfast is *The Queens Hotel* (☎ 01736-796468, ☐ queenshotelstives.com; 8D/2F; WI-FI; £35-£80pp but check online for offers) at 2 High St. It's a smart, central gastropub with bright, modern rooms.

Hotels At *The Western Hotel* (☎ 01736-795277, ☐ westernhotel-stives.co.uk; 2S/7D/2T/3Tr; ▾; WI-FI; £30-60pp, sgl £30-70), on Gabriel St, rooms are simple but smart enough, and breakfast costs an extra £5. The bar here is the lively Kettle 'n' Wink, known as the 'Kidleywink'; good for live music. The name comes from a time when ale houses kept smuggled brandy in a kettle; to order a glass, you needed to wink surreptitiously in the direction of the kettle.

Next to the bus station is *Regent Hotel* (☎ 01736-796195, ☐ regenthotel.com; 2S share facilities/5D/2T/1F en suite; WI-FI; £48-65pp, sgl from £53, sgl occ minus £5 from room rate), where most rooms have fabulous views of the harbour. They don't do meals here, but take most credit cards.

Close by, down the steps to The Warren, is a lovely hotel, *Pedn-Olva* (☎ 01736-796222, ☐ pednolva.co.uk; 2S/19D/4T/2Tr/3F; ▾; WI-FI; £90-165pp but check online for offers), albeit with eye-wateringly high room rates in peak season. It is owned by St Austell Brewery and has a bar/restaurant looking out over the bay.

Where to eat and drink

St Ives has a seemingly endless number of eateries, suiting all tastes and budgets. Of course, fresh fish is often the order of the day, with langoustine, crab, line-caught bass, bream, monkfish and scallops all featuring prominently on menus around the harbour.

Fast food For a gourmet take on traditional fish & chips, try *Harbour Fish & Chips* (11.30am-10pm), which has restaurant seating and sells beer and wine too. *The Beach Restaurant* (10am-10pm) is similar, with eat-in or takeaway options. For a traditional fish 'n' chip takeaway head to *Balancing Eel* (noon-2pm & 5-7.30pm).

Rajpoot (☎ 01736-795307; 5-6 Gabriel St; daily 5.30-10.30pm) is a good bet for Indian food, but bring your own booze as it's unlicensed. Practically next door is *The Mex* (☎ 01736-797658, ☐ the mex-stives.co.uk, daily 5.30-9.30pm, Mon-Sat only in winter) where Mexican mains cost £10.95-13.95.

Those with a sweet tooth shouldn't miss a visit to *Myrings Fudge & Rock Shop* (10am-5pm), a family-run Cornish fudge business that's been going for more than 30 years. If you want to thank the neighbour for feeding the cat while you're away, they also do mail order so you can send a box home rather than lugging it round with you.

There are nearly as many bakeries in St Ives as there are seagulls. Our favourite is *St Ives Bakery* on the corner of Fore St and The Digey.

Pubs There are numerous old pubs in the town. Most people gravitate to the harbour for an evening stroll, and the *Lifeboat Inn* (☎ 01736-794123; WI-FI; food daily noon-9pm) is right at the heart of things; there's a decent range of seafood here, as well as Sky TV. Established around 1312, the *Sloop Inn* (see Where to stay; food served 9-11am, noon-3pm & 5-10pm) is one of Cornwall's oldest pubs, and has plenty of character with low beams, slate floors and wooden benches. You can eat in the main pub (if you can find a table) or upstairs at *The Captain's Table* (☎ 01736-796584; daily 6-10pm), where booking would be advisable.

The Castle Inn (☎ 01736-796833; ✹; food Mon-Sat noon-2.30pm & 6-8.30pm), 16 Fore St, lies back from the seafront and feels a little off the tourist trail, though there is plenty to attract you here, including the building's old granite walls, stained-glass windows, fine real ales and reasonably priced food. Next door is ***The Union Inn*** (☎ 01736-796486, 🖳 unioninn-stives.co.uk; food daily noon-3pm & 5.30-9pm), where most main meals cost less than £10. ***The Golden Lion*** (☎ 01736-797935, 🖳 goldenlionstives.co.uk; food noon-9.30pm; WI-FI; 🐕) is central and is good value too. It's also the place to come in the town if you're after local cider. Up the road, ***The Queens Hotel*** (see Where to stay; food noon-9pm) serves some appetising dishes (mains; £10-16).

Cafés The friendliest café in town, and certainly the most family-focused, is ***Scoff Troff Café*** (☎ 01736-797341; 8am-late), where you'll be greeted with a warm welcome, good strong coffee and all-day breakfasts that include Welsh rarebit, Scottish salmon and eggs Benedict as well as the traditional full-English. There's pizza, pasta dishes and other delights in the evening too.

Down at the harbour, ***Moomaid of Zennor*** (10am-9.30pm) is a cute café, serving ice-cream made on a farm in nearby Zennor, and cakes as well as good coffee.

For proper beach-side cafés, you need to walk away from the harbour a short distance. With its greenhouse-like all-glass walls, ***Porthmeor Café & Bar*** (☎ 01736-793366, 🖳 porthmeor-beach.co.uk; summer 9am-10.30pm, winter 9am-5pm, Fri & Sat 6-9pm) offers unrivalled sea views from its perch overlooking Porthmeor beach. They do lunchtime tapas (£2.75-9.95) and evening meals (£12.95-18.50) as well as coffee, cream teas and breakfasts.

Even better, though, is the multi-award-winning ***Porthminster Beach Café*** (Map 48; ☎ 01736-795352, 🖳 porthminstercafe.co.uk; summer daily 9am-10pm, winter Tue-Sun noon-3pm & 6-9pm), 15 minutes walk south of the harbour. You can have coffee on the decked area right on the beach or dine inside on something more substantial, looking out over St Ives Bay.

Restaurants An absolute gem is ***Blas Burger Works*** (☎ 01736-797272, 🖳 blasburgerworks.co.uk, The Warren; Feb-Nov Tue-Sat 5-10pm; peak season daily noon-9.30pm) an intimate restaurant with only a small number of tables. Local organic produce is their focus, and their burgers (from £12.95) are stupendously tasty.

For Italian, head to ***Peppers Pasta & Pizzeria*** (☎ 01736-794014, 🖳 peppers-stives.co.uk, 22 Fore St; daily from 5.30pm; pizza £7.50-11.50).

A seafood restaurant quietly operating away from the mayhem surrounding the harbour is ***Mermaid Seafood Restaurant*** (☎ 01736-796816, 🖳 mermaidstives.co.uk; Mon-Sat 6-9pm), aptly located at 21 Fish St. The most expensive of the mains offered, The Mermaid seafood platter, costs £19.95.

There's Thai tapas (£2.95-9) amongst other spicy dishes back on the harbour at ***Talay Thai*** (☎ 01736-795157, 🖳 talaythai.kitchen; daily noon-3pm & 5-10pm).

Transport

[See also pp52-6] Services from the **bus station** at The Malakoff include First Kernow's A2, A3, A4, A17, and their 16A to Zennor. St Ives Bus No 1.

NX330 and NX504 **coach** services (see box p50) operate here.

The **railway station** is at Porthminster Beach. Trains (operated by GWR) run to St Erth where you must change for mainline services but the ride to Lelant Saltings is a delightful short journey. Many folk do the trip both ways for the sheer fun of it but you could walk to Lelant and get the train back in an afternoon; a great little excursion.

For a **taxi**, ACE Cars (☎ 01736-797799) have an office by the bus station.

❑ Where to stay – the details

Unless specified, B&B-style accommodation is either en suite or has private facilities; 🛁 means at least one room has a bath; 🐕 signifies that dogs are welcome in at least one room but always by prior arrangement, an additional charge may also be payable (see pp336-8); WI-FI means wi-fi is available. See also p79.

ST IVES TO ZENNOR HEAD   [MAPS 49-52]

Although the next **6 miles (10km, 1¾-2½hrs)** are pretty hard going, they are also amongst the most stunning. Often cited as the toughest section of the whole path, this is mostly due to what is underfoot rather than any particularly nasty ascent. The path hugs the contours of the coastline, sending you on an endless series of ups and downs as it travels through boggy fields and across rough and rocky terrain. But the gradients aren't as severe as the sections around Port Isaac or Crackington Haven. The problem is you need to keep your eyes on the ground, particularly in wet weather, which prolongs the section.

While the weathered and windblown landscape is reward enough, there's also much evidence of its ancient occupation, if you care to venture a little inland, in the form of ancient stone circles and quoits (see box on p172). It is little wonder that many artists found inspiration here.

Although the tiny village of **Zennor** is a 10- to 15-minute walk inland, walkers who don't visit are missing a treat. The museum is well worth checking out.

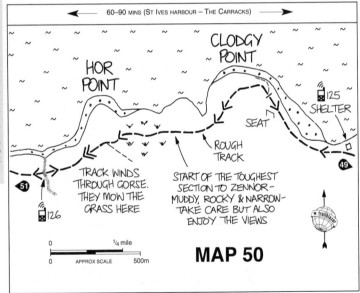

MAP 50

❏ **Important note – walking times**
Unless otherwise specified, **all times in this book refer only to the time spent walking**. You will need to add 20-30% to allow for rests, photography, checking the map, drinking water etc. When planning the day's hike count on 5-7 hours' actual walking.

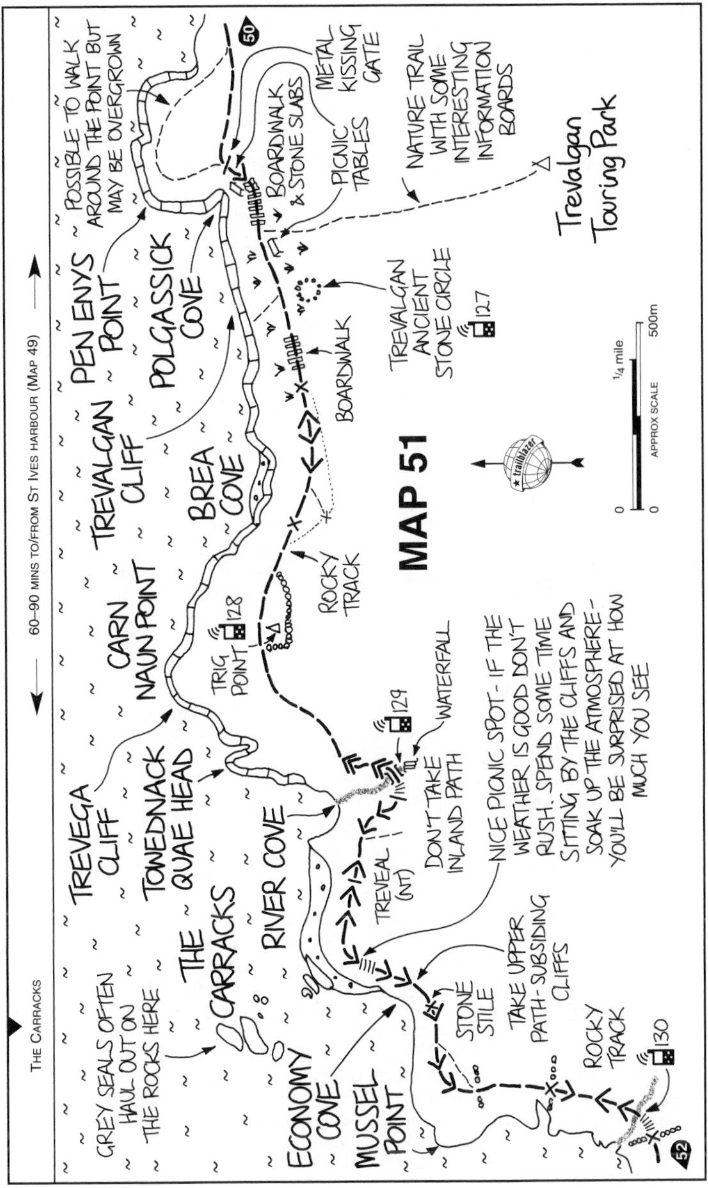

THE CARRACKS

← 60-90 MINS TO/FROM ST IVES HARBOUR (MAP 49) →

GREY SEALS OFTEN HAUL OUT ON THE ROCKS HERE

THE CARRACKS

TREVEGA CLIFF

TOWEDNACK QUAE HEAD

CARN NAUN POINT

TREVALGAN CLIFF

PEN ENYS POINT

POSSIBLE TO WALK AROUND THE POINT BUT MAY BE OVERGROWN

METAL KISSING GATE

NATURE TRAIL WITH SOME INTERESTING INFORMATION BOARDS

BOARDWALK & STONE SLABS

PICNIC TABLES

POLGASSICK COVE

BREA COVE

Trevalgan Touring Park

TREVALGAN ANCIENT STONE CIRCLE

127

BOARDWALK

TRIG POINT 128

ROCKY TRACK

MAP 51

APPROX SCALE

0   ¼ mile

0   500m

RIVER COVE

TREVEAL (NT)

WATERFALL

129

DON'T TAKE INLAND PATH

NICE PICNIC SPOT – IF THE WEATHER IS GOOD DON'T RUSH, SPEND SOME TIME SITTING BY THE CLIFFS AND SOAK UP THE ATMOSPHERE – YOU'LL BE SURPRISED AT HOW MUCH YOU SEE

ECONOMY COVE

MUSSEL POINT

STONE STILE

TAKE UPPER PATH– SUBSIDING CLIFFS

ROCKY TRACK

130

52

ZENNOR [MAP 52]

Zennor seems to emerge from the rocky landscape itself, surrounded as it is by granite tors and outcrops, boulder-strewn fields with their high stone walls and the slate and granite cliffs of the coastline. The village has attracted its share of outsiders for centuries, not least the author DH Lawrence and his wife Frieda who lived at Higher Tregerthen Farm, near Zennor, for a period during World War I.

Zennor is a tiny place with the few houses clustered together round the *Tinners Arms* pub (see Where to stay, eat and drink) and the 12th-century granite **church of St Senara**, neither of which should be missed. Take a moment to look inside the church and find the **Mermaid's Chair**, a 600-year-old carved chair whose dark wood has been polished by time. The mermaid is a pagan superstition and it's remarkable that its depiction in a Christian church should have been tolerated to the present day.

Where to stay, eat and drink

You can **camp** at *Trevalgan Touring Park* (Map 51; ☎ 01736-791892, 🖳 trevalgan touringpark.co.uk; hiker & small tent £12-28; May-Sep). It is reached from the cliff path by a series of signposts in the form of notices describing the flora and fauna of the area and by following them you come to the campsite which has consistently been voted Park of the Year by various organisations and magazines. You can also get here on Royal Buses No 44 service (🖳 royalbuses.co.uk; July-end Sep daily 1-2/hr) from Stennack Surgery in St Ives.

Zennor Chapel Café & Guesthouse (☎ 01736-798307, 🖳 zennorchapelguesthouse .com; 2D/3F; £40-60pp; WI-FI) has a large, welcoming café (daily 9am-5pm) with beautifully renovated B&B rooms above it. Staff are friendly and their sandwiches, cakes, teas and coffees are top notch.

The famous *Tinners Arms* (☎ 01736-796927, 🖳 tinnersarms.com; 2S share facilities/2D en suite; WI-FI; 🐕; from £60pp, sgl from £70) has accommodation in the White House adjoining the pub. The lovely, simple bedrooms are a pleasure with crisp white linen and plain white walls. They serve great **food** (Mon-Sat noon-3pm, Sun till 4pm, Mon-Sat 6-9pm,

---

❏ Ancient Cornwall

The history of Cornwall goes back a lot further than its churches and the arrival of the saints. There is another history which is far less tangible and more mysterious with most of its secrets yet to be unlocked by modern man.

Mesolithic nomadic hunters and gatherers were the first settlers after the Ice Age but they left few remains. Neolithic man arrived from across the Atlantic in 3500BC, bringing both the skills to rear crops and raise flocks *and* the art of building *quoits*, the stone chambers used for communal burials. **Zennor Quoit** is relatively easy to visit from the coast path and is signposted from Zennor church (see Map 52).

In 2000BC the Beaker Folk arrived and many believe it was they who erected the stone circles and standing stones, enigmas to modern science and thinking. The **Merry Maidens** and the **Pipers** (see box p194 and Map 65) are worth visiting.

It was Bronze-Age man, 1500-700BC, who made the discovery of adding tin to copper. **Ballowal Barrow** (see Map 58), right on the coast path, is thought to be late Bronze Age or early Iron Age. Its purpose is unknown, but one speculation is that the *barrows* were used for religious ceremonies.

The Iron Age Celts, 700BC, introduced the iron-making process from north-west Europe. They organised themselves into clans and formed alliances under kings. As you walk the coast path you pass many signs of Celtic occupation in the form of hill-forts and cliff castles. It has even been suggested that the name Cornwall was derived from the Cornish word *cornovii*, meaning cliff castles.

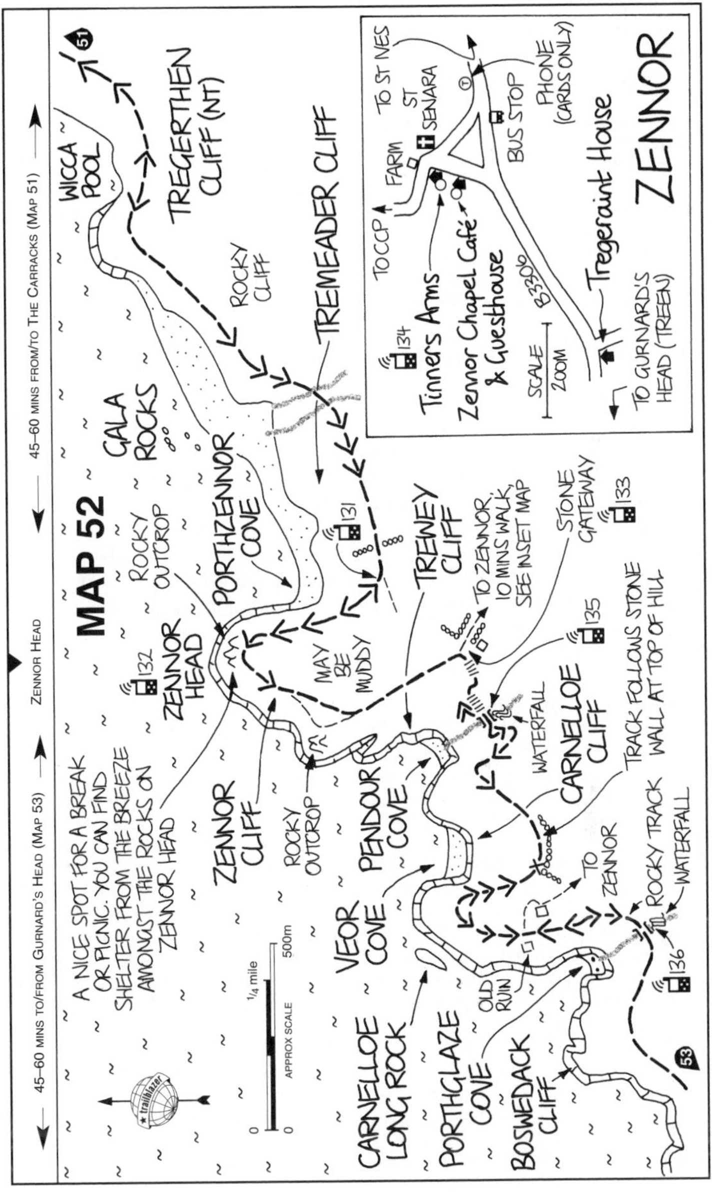

MAP 52

45–60 MINS TO/FROM GURNARD'S HEAD (Map 53) — ZENNOR HEAD — 45–60 MINS FROM/TO THE CARRACKS (Map 51)

ZENNOR

TO ST IVES
ST SENARA
FARM
TO CCP
PHONE (CARDS ONLY)
BUS STOP
Tinner's Arms
Zennor Chapel Cafe & Guesthouse
Tregeraint House
B3306
SCALE 200m
TO GURNARD'S HEAD (TREEN)

WICCA POOL
TREGERTHEN CLIFF (NT)
TREMEADER CLIFF
ROCKY CLIFF
GALA ROCKS
PORTHZENNOR COVE
ROCKY OUTCROP
ZENNOR HEAD
A NICE SPOT FOR A BREAK OR PICNIC. YOU CAN FIND SHELTER FROM THE BREEZE AMONGST THE ROCKS ON ZENNOR HEAD

ZENNOR CLIFF
ROCKY OUTCROP
MAY BE MUDDY
TRENEY CLIFF
STONE GATEWAY
TO ZENNOR, 10 MINS WALK, SEE INSET MAP
WATERFALL
CARNELLOE CLIFF
TRACK FOLLOWS STONE WALL AT TOP OF HILL
PENDOUR COVE
VEOR COVE
CARNELLOE LONG ROCK
PORTHGLAZE COVE
OLD RUIN
BOSWEDACK CLIFF
TO ZENNOR
ROCKY TRACK
WATERFALL

APPROX SCALE
0   500m
0   ¼ mile
True North

ROUTE GUIDE AND MAPS

Sun till 8.30pm); the menu changes frequently with choices such as braised Cornish beef cheek in red wine (£13.75), or creamy Mevagissey lemon sole (£13.95). The stone-flagged floors, oak benches and Cornish beer all add to the charm. On Thursday nights musicians gather in the pub (outside in summer) and sessions begin with fiddles, guitar and penny whistle until closing time; all in all, a fantastic Cornish experience.

About half a mile along the road, in the direction of Gurnard's Head (Treen), *Tregeraint House* (☎ 01736-797061, 🖳

www.cornwall-online.co.uk/tregeraint-house; 2D/1T, shared facilities; WI-FI; from £42.50pp, sgl occ £50) is a lovely B&B, artistically decorated and in a secluded setting. Walkers are made to feel very welcome here.

Transport
[See also pp52-6] The **bus** stop is on the main road, a sharp sprint from the pub if you have lingered too long over your pint. Zennor is on First Kernow's A3 St Ives to Land's End coastal route; their A17 and 16A also stop here as does WPCBA's No 7.

ZENNOR HEAD TO PENDEEN WATCH [MAPS 52-56]

For the next **7 miles (11km, 2¼-3hrs)** the going is sometimes rocky along this quite challenging stretch with some damp places unless there has been a particularly dry spell. The path cuts across the long, graceful neck of **Gurnard's Head**. The small settlement here, lying 10 minutes inland, is technically Treen but is generally referred to as Gurnard's Head.

The route-finding is easier now with improved waymarking across the boulder-strewn cliffs of **Bosigran**, a favourite haunt for rock-climbers.

Approaching the lighthouse of **Pendeen Watch** you meet a tarmac road which leads to the facilities at Pendeen village, a half-mile walk inland. It's more pleasant, though, to continue on the coast path, then take the footpath into the village just before Geevor Tin Mine museum.

GURNARD'S HEAD (TREEN)
[MAP 53]
This Treen should not be confused with the Treen (Map 63) on the south coast. In fact, it is possible that this is why the village is more commonly referred to as Gurnard's Head.

There are two much-talked-about places here: for bed and breakfast, *Cove Cottage* (☎ 01736-798317, 🖳 www.cornwall-online.co.uk/cove-cottage; 2D shared facilities; ➧; from £65pp) occupies one of the most remarkable positions not just on the coast but anywhere in the world; right on the cliff edge, with the waves crashing on to the rocks below. What a location! Off to one side you'll find the ruins of a long-abandoned fish packhouse; to the other side, steps leading down to the deserted sandy beach of Treen Cove. The owners always welcome walkers, but they do have

a two-day minimum stay policy in July and August.

Half a mile up the slope, by the road junction, is *The Gurnard's Head Hotel* (☎ 01736-796928, 🖳 gurnardshead.co.uk; 4D/3D or T; ➧; 🐾; WI-FI; £62.50-122.50pp, sgl occ from £90), a fine pub with seven very comfortable B&B rooms, This place has won awards for its **food** (daily noon-2.30pm & 6-9.30pm), and booking ahead is certainly recommended for evening meals. The menu changes regularly but is always sumptuous and features local produce wherever possible. A two/three-course set lunch costs £20/24; a two/three course supper will set you back around £22/27.50. The wine list is fittingly sophisticated; one of the best along the coast.

First Kernow's A3, A17 & 16A **bus** services stop here. See also pp52-6.

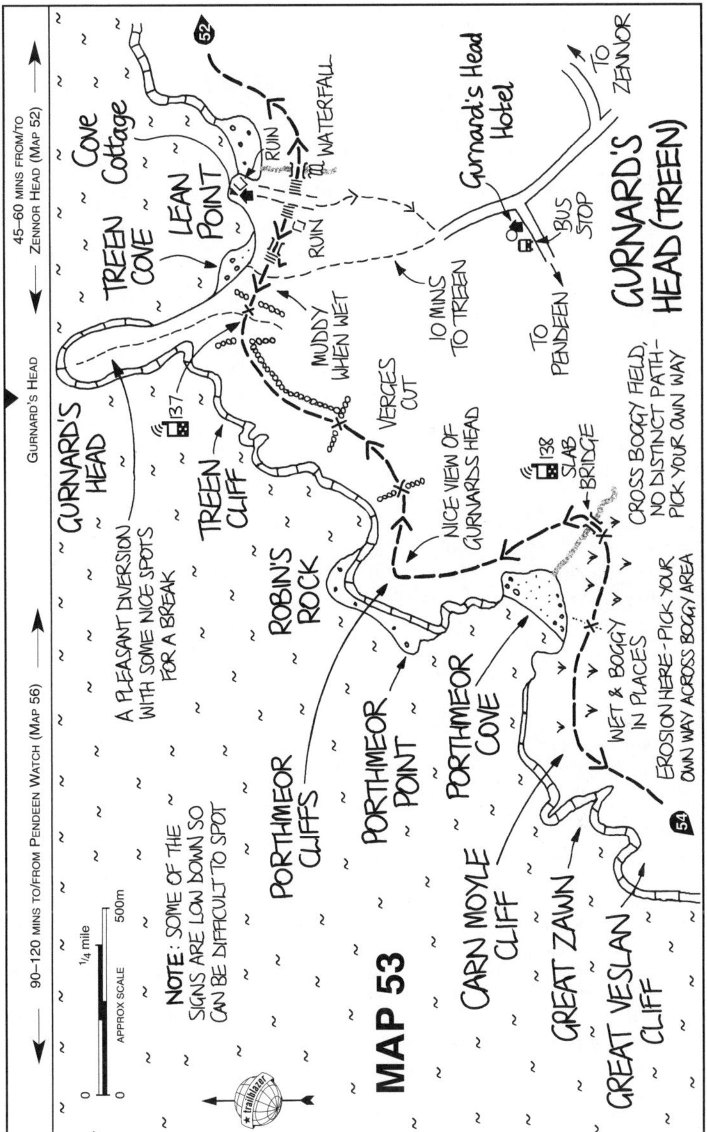
90–120 MINS TO/FROM PENDEEN WATCH (MAP 56)
GURNARD'S HEAD
45–60 MINS FROM/TO ZENNOR HEAD (MAP 52)
MAP 53
0
1/4 mile
500m
APPROX SCALE
NOTE: SOME OF THE SIGNS ARE LOW DOWN SO CAN BE DIFFICULT TO SPOT
A PLEASANT DIVERSION WITH SOME NICE SPOTS FOR A BREAK
GURNARD'S HEAD
TREEN CLIFF
137
ROBIN'S ROCK
PORTHMEOR CLIFFS
PORTHMEOR POINT
PORTHMEOR COVE
CARN MOYLE CLIFF
GREAT ZAWN
GREAT VESLAN CLIFF
TREEN COVE
LEAN POINT
Cove Cottage
RUIN
RUIN
WATERFALL
52
MUDDY WHEN WET
VERGES CUT
NICE VIEW OF GURNARDS HEAD
10 MINS TO TREEN
138
SLAB BRIDGE
WET & BOGGY IN PLACES
EROSION HERE - PICK YOUR OWN WAY ACROSS BOGGY AREA
CROSS BOGGY FIELD, NO DISTINCT PATH - PICK YOUR OWN WAY
54
TO PENDEEN
BUS STOP
Gurnard's Head Hotel
TO ZENNOR
GURNARD'S HEAD (TREEN)

← 90–120 MINS (GURNARD'S HEAD – PENDEEN WATCH) →

DON'T GET LED TO THE CLIFF TOP BY CLIMBERS' PATHS

HALLDRINE COVE

53

BOSIGRAN CLIFF
LOOK FOR ROCK CLIMBERS

BOSIGRAN CASTLE

PORTHMOINA COVE

139

PICK YOUR WAY ACROSS ROCKY FIELD. PATH INDISTINCT AND NOT MARKED

NESTING BIRDS INCLUDING KITTIWAKES

BRANDY'S ROCKS

RUIN

FOLLOW PATH ACROSS BRIDGE, NOT INLAND!

140

OLD MINES

TREVOWHAN CLIFF

WHIRL POOL

141

OLD MINE

55

TO TREEN

STEPPING STONES

B3306

REMEMBER TO LATCH GATE

NARROW & BOGGY

TO PENDEEN

TREVEAN CLIFF

PATH MEANDERS UP & DOWN, WELL ABOVE CLIFF

0   ¼ mile
0   500m
APPROX SCALE

trailblazer

MAP 54

ROUTE GUIDE AND MAPS

MORVAH [MAP 55]

This is one of the smallest parishes in Cornwall with about 70 residents but is a community bursting with energy. At its heart is **The Schoolhouse**; originally a chapel, dating from 1744, but now a gallery, craft centre and great-value *coffee shop* (☎ 01736-787808, 🖥 morvah.com; summer Tue-Sun 10.30am-4.30pm, winter Thur-Sun 11.30am-4pm). Have a look at the stained-glass door which the community created depicting scenes from daily life in the area.

First's A3 **bus** service stops here as does WPCBA's No 7. (See also pp52-6).

PENDEEN & TREWELLARD
[MAP 56, p178]

Pendeen

Pendeen has a **post office** (Mon-Wed & Fri 9am-1pm & 2-5.30pm, Thur 9am-1pm, Sat 9am-12.30pm) and a Costcutter **convenience store** (Boscaswell Stores; Mon-Sat 7am-8pm, Sun 8am-7pm) which sells hot pasties and sausage rolls.

Next door is friendly *Lil's Chippy* (Mon 8-11am, Tue 8-11am, noon-1.15pm & 5-7pm, Wed & Thur 8-11am & 5-7pm, Fri & Sat 8-11am, noon-1.15pm & 5-7.30pm) with complicated opening times, but delicious bacon butties for breakfast (Mon-Sat) as well as the usual chippy fare for the rest of the day.

Campers can stay in the back field belonging to *The North Inn* (☎ 01736-788417, 🖥 thenorthinnpendeen.co.uk; 3D or T/1D; 🛏; 🐕; WI-FI; campers £5, B&B from £40pp; food daily noon-2.30pm & 6.30-8.30pm), a traditional local with St Austell real ale and good-value pub grub, including curry specials. Campers get use of the showers attached to the pub. The four **B&B** rooms are in an annexe behind the main building.

Radjel Inn (☎ 01736-788446; 1S/1D/1T shared facilities; 🛏; 🐕; from £30pp) is a St Austell Brewery pub, also with rooms. Meals are served daily 11am-8.30pm.

B&B is also available at the ivy-clad *Old Count House* (☎ 01736-788058, 🖥 dymondep@aol.com; 2D, shared facilities; £30-40pp), while right opposite the

Costcutter store is *St John's B&B* (☎ 01736-786605, 🖥 stjohnshousebedand breakfast.co.uk; 1D en suite, 1T/1D shared bathroom; 🛏; £35-40pp).

First's A3 **bus** service stops at Boscaswell Stores and Geevor Tin Mine. WPCBA's No 7 also calls here [See pp52-6].

Trewellard

Trewellard, right next to Pendeen, has a few more options for food and accommodation, including possibly the most unusual place to stay on the whole coast path: *Gypsy Caravan B&B* (☎ 01736-787585, 🖥 gypsycaravanbandb.co.uk; 🐕; 1D; from £28pp) is a genuine gypsy caravan, permanently positioned in a private garden on Levant Rd, and just 300m from the coast path. It's cosy, to say the least, but has been renovated beautifully, and has oodles of character, plus a heater, a television and tea and coffee facilities. The toilet and shower are just outside, beside the

ROUTE GUIDE AND MAPS

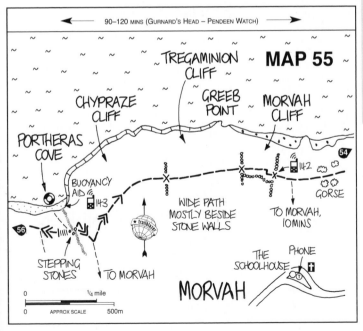

90–120 MINS (GURNARD'S HEAD – PENDEEN WATCH)

MAP 55

TREGAMINION CLIFF

CHYPRAZE CLIFF

GREEB POINT

MORVAH CLIFF

PORTHERAS COVE

BUOYANCY AID

54

GORSE

WIDE PATH MOSTLY BESIDE STONE WALLS

TO MORVAH, 10 MINS

STEPPING STONES

TO MORVAH

THE SCHOOLHOUSE

PHONE

MORVAH

0   ¼ mile

0   APPROX SCALE   500m

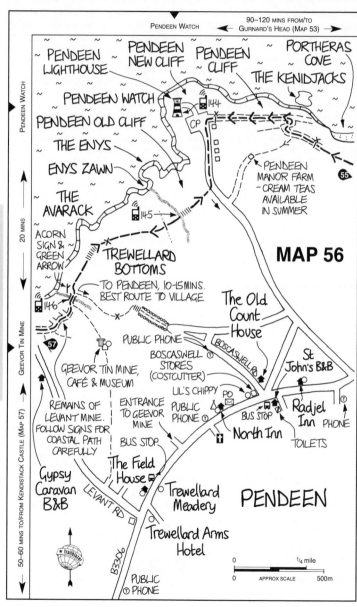

MAP 56

90–120 MINS FROM/TO GURNARD'S HEAD (MAP 53)

owner's house. You can choose to have your breakfast in the caravan, in the owner's conservatory or on the patio beside the caravan.

For a more conventional B&B, try *The Field House* (☎ 01736-788097, 🖥 www .cornwall-online.co.uk/field-house; 2D; WI-FI; £35-40pp), a lovely place boasting a sea view and a rooftop terrace with a private sitting room. Equally lovely here is the **food** (served April-Sep on Thur & Fri, from 7pm; take your own wine), which is available to non-residents too. The menu changes on a regular basis but often features delights such as Aga-baked Newlyn

hake fillet with mango, chilli and tomato salsa. You can also get a decent meal at *Trewellard Arms Hotel* (☎ 01736-788634; daily noon-3pm & 6-9pm; 🐾). It's standard pub fare, plus half a dozen real ales, including the ever-popular Doom Bar.

Another, more unusual option for dinner is the gothic-themed *Trewellard Meadery* (☎ 01736-788345; summer daily 6.30-9.30pm, winter Fri-Sun 6.30-9pm, booking recommended). The menu includes mead (honey wine), while the food is served 'in the rough' – that is, on wooden platters and eaten with fingers. They also do takeaways.

PENDEEN WATCH TO CAPE CORNWALL [MAPS 56-58]

There is a lot to see on this **4-mile (6km, 1½-1¾hrs)** section, scattered with tin-mining ruins, and with views from the cliff tops all the way. Just off the path and signposted from it are the remains of **Geevor Tin Mine** (see box 'Mining in Cornwall' on p180), closed in 1990 but now a museum where you can get a coffee or cream tea (entry to the café is free) and a tour underground if you have the time.

The surroundings here are post-industrial and offer a fascinating insight into what it must have been like when the mine was in full operation. The path then passes right by the remains of **Levant Mine** and on to the eyrie cliff-top location of **Crown Mine**, both of which had starring roles in the 2015 TV adaptation of Winston Graham's *Poldark*. The old engine houses appear dotted along the coast as if guarding it like sentinels.

The backdrop changes again by the time you reach the site of the Iron Age fort known as **Kenidjack Castle**, a nice place to take a break and admire the views towards Cape Cornwall. Once thought to be the most westerly point in the British Isles, **Cape Cornwall** (see box p185) is often referred to as 'the connoisseur's Land's End'. It is certainly everything that Land's End could have been in different hands. A cape is defined as a headland where two oceans or channels meet; in this case the English Channel and St George's Channel. There's a **snack caravan** in the car park during the season, open all day depending on the weather.

The coast path doesn't actually go out to the very point of the Cape but there's nothing to stop you from making the short diversion just to say you've done it, and perhaps to get a photo of the remains of the tiny **St Helen's chapel**.

The thriving community of **St Just** is another town popular with artists and is well worth the detour for lunch or a coffee, even if you're not scheduled to stay there. Take the road out of the car park – it should take you 15-20 minutes on foot. You can then rejoin the path near YHA Land's End.

BOTALLACK [MAP 57]

There's a good **campsite** here: *Trevaylor Caravan and Camping Park* (☎ 01736-787016, 🖳 trevaylor.com; 🐾; WI-FI; pitch for two people £12-14.50). There's an on-site bar and restaurant and a shop selling most essentials including camping gas.

The *Queen's Arms* (☎ 01736-788318, 🖳 queensarms-botallack.co.uk; WI-FI; daily noon-2.30pm & 6-9pm; mains £10.50-15.95) is a lively place for an evening, and the food is great too. They have Press Gang cider on tap, as well as real ales such as Tallack Tipple and Sharp's Doom Bar. Note the ornate ceiling above the stairs, which is thought to be around 150 years old and is one of the reasons this lovely 17th-century building is Grade II listed.

First's A3 **bus** service stops right outside the pub. WPCBA's No 7 also calls here. [See also pp52-6].

❏ Mining in Cornwall

For at least two thousand years tin, copper and lead have been extracted from the Cornish peninsula. Tin found in streams was first utilised by Bronze-Age people. As these sources became exhausted miners began to dig out veins of ore from solid rock. It wasn't until the early 19th century that the technology of steam-driven pumps allowed mines to be worked below the water table. With the invention of dynamite, mining literally exploded. Shafts could be constructed to depths of over 300m (1000ft) and could even be extended below the seabed. At Levant Mine it is said that miners could hear the rumble of boulders being rolled across the seabed during bad storms.

Life in the mines was tough. Poor pay and extreme conditions such as constant dampness and the intense heat given off by the rock itself led to an average life expectancy of less than forty years. When the market collapsed due to cheaper sources being discovered in South America and Australia many Cornishmen emigrated, taking their knowledge to these countries.

Today all that can be seen of this once huge industry are the engine houses left on the surface. The hundreds of miles of underground galleries and shafts lie forgotten, destined to become yet another secret clutched to the bosom of the earth.

Between Pendeen Watch and Cape Cornwall are two popular mining attractions. The first you pass is **Geevor Tin Mine** (Map 56; ☎ 01736-788662, 🖳 geevor.com; Apr-Oct Sun-Fri 9am-5pm, Nov-Mar Sun-Fri 9am-4pm; admission £14.60) which closed as a mine in 1990 and is now a museum where you can don a helmet to be guided on a half-hour underground tour. There's also a small *café* (open same hours as the mine, no mine ticket needed), the pasties and home-made soup are recommended.

The second place, well worth a visit, is the National Trust's **Levant Engine House** (Map 57; ☎ 01736-786156, 🖳 nationaltrust.org.uk/levant-mine; Mar 15-Nov 1 10.30am-5pm Sun-Fri, Nov 2-March 12 10.30am-4pm Fridays only; admission £8.10) where the cliff-top engine house and steam-powered beam engine have been restored to their former glory. The engine, which from 1840 to 1930 lifted copper and tin ore to the surface, is now steamed up for the public in the main season; phone beforehand to check opening. The Levant Mine was the site of a tragic disaster in 1919 when the lift collapsed killing 31 miners. For a mind-boggling insight into the harsh realities of life in the mines join one of the free tours here which really help to make sense of all the mines you see on your walk.

Cornwall and West Devon's industrial heritage is of international importance. For several centuries the region was the world's largest producer of tin and copper providing some of the main raw materials for the industrialisation of the world. In recognition of the importance of this, the mining sites of the region were granted World Heritage site status

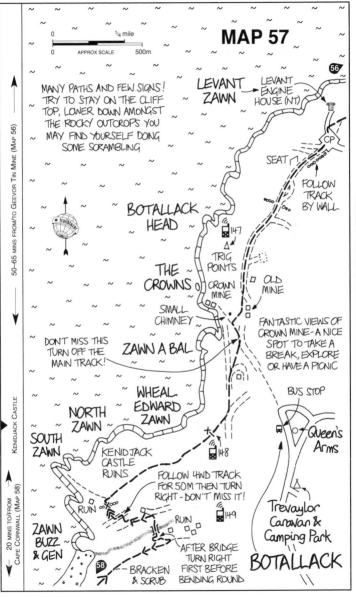

MAP 57

0 ——— ¼ mile
APPROX SCALE
0 ——— 500m

MANY PATHS AND FEW SIGNS!
TRY TO STAY ON THE CLIFF
TOP, LOWER DOWN AMONGST
THE ROCKY OUTCROPS YOU
MAY FIND YOURSELF DOING
SOME SCRAMBLING

LEVANT ZAWN

LEVANT ENGINE HOUSE (NT)

56

CP

SEAT

FOLLOW TRACK BY WALL

★ trailblazer

BOTALLACK HEAD

147
TRIG POINTS

THE CROWNS

CROWN MINE

OLD MINE

SMALL CHIMNEY

FANTASTIC VIEWS OF CROWN MINE - A NICE SPOT TO TAKE A BREAK, EXPLORE OR HAVE A PICNIC

DON'T MISS THIS TURN OFF THE MAIN TRACK!

ZAWN A BAL

WHEAL EDWARD ZAWN

BUS STOP

NORTH ZAWN

Queen's Arms

SOUTH ZAWN

KENIDJACK CASTLE RUINS

148

FOLLOW 4WD TRACK FOR 50M THEN TURN RIGHT - DON'T MISS IT!

149

Trevaylor Caravan & Camping Park

RUIN

RUIN

ZAWN BUZZ & GEN

58

AFTER BRIDGE TURN RIGHT FIRST BEFORE BENDING ROUND

BRACKEN & SCRUB

BOTALLACK

50-65 MINS FROM/TO GEEVOR TIN MINE (MAP 56)

KENIDJACK CASTLE

20 MINS TO/FROM CAPE CORNWALL (MAP 58)

ROUTE GUIDE AND MAPS

CAPE CORNWALL   [MAP 58]

If you're just passing through, a mobile **café** sells tea, coffee, sandwiches and cakes in the Cape car park from Easter to October.

Cape Cornwall Golf Club (☎ 01736-788611, 🖥 capecornwallgolfclub.co.uk; 7D/3T/1F; £32.50-65pp, sgl occ from £50; ☞; WI-FI; food daily 8am-9pm) has some lovely **B&B accommodation**, a good restaurant and a bar. Rooms are bright and modern with en suite bathrooms and iPod

docking stations. In the **restaurant**, mains cost £11-19 and include gourmet burgers, ribeye steak and wild mushroom risotto. The other option is *Boswedden House* (☎ 01736-788733, 🖥 boswedden.org.uk; 1S/5D or T/2F; WI-FI; £35-50pp), a retreat and healing centre with B&B too. Rooms are immaculate. There's also a heated indoor **pool** (open to public 8.30am-4.30pm; £5) and sauna to ease aching muscles.

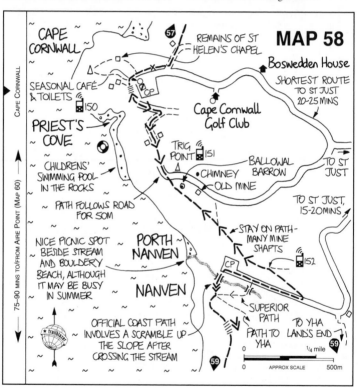

ST JUST

Dear Lord, we hope that there be no shipwrecks, but if there be, let them be in St Just for the benefit of the inhabitants.   Spoken in St Just Church by **Parson Amos Mason**, 1650

St Just is the most westerly town in England and, as if in deference to the Atlantic weather, built from granite

arranged in a charmingly rugged way. Despite its isolated location St Just is a surprisingly cosmopolitan place with art shops

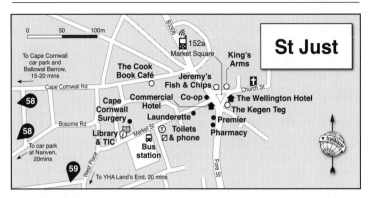

and an active social life throughout the year. Whereas most of the villages round here have only a weekend of events for their annual carnivals, St Just's Lafrowda Festival (see p15) lasts a whole week. More than 50 artists have made St Just their home and their work can be seen at the many **galleries** around the town. The **church** is worth a visit for its two splendid medieval frescoes, *St George* and *Christ of all Trades*. Also note the wooden plaque near the door listing all the vicars and rectors since 1297.

Services

Tourist information (☎ 01736-788165, 🖳 stjusttourist@cornwall.gov.uk) is based at the **library** (☎ 01736-788669; Mon-Sat 10am-1pm, Mon-Thur 2-5pm, Fri 2-6pm, winter closed Thur) where **internet access** (£1.80/30 mins, 60p/30mins with your library card from home) is available. Cape Cornwall **doctors' surgery** (☎ 01736-788306, 🖳 capecornwallsurgery.co.uk; Mon-Fri 8am-1pm & 2-6.30pm) is behind the library. The town also has a **pharmacy** (Mon-Fri 9am-1pm & 2-6pm, Sat 9am-12.30pm). For supplies, the Co-op **supermarket** (daily 7am-10pm), and Premier (7am-10pm), with **cashpoint** outside, are both by Market Square. There's a **launderette** (7am-8pm) on Market St.

Where to stay, eat and drink

Apart from the campsites at Botallack (p180) and Kelynack (p185), the only budget accommodation around here is at YHA Land's End (see p185).

You can stay and eat at two of the pubs in St Just. *Commercial Hotel* (☎ 01736-788455, 🖳 commercial-hotel.co .uk; 1S/4D/6T; WI-FI; 🐕; £32.50-44.50pp, sgl £39-59) has nice airy rooms and a lovely conservatory dining area (food noon-2pm & 6-9pm; mains £9.95-12.95). *Wellington Hotel* (☎ 01736-787319, 🖳 wellingtonhotelcornwall.co.uk; 2T/5D/4F; 🍺; WI-FI; £27.50-60pp; food daily noon-2pm & 6-9pm, winter to 8.30pm) is your other option.

St Just has a cluster of pleasant **cafés**. Amongst the more unusual is *The Cook Book* (☎ 01736-787266, 🖳 thecookbook stjust.co.uk; daily 9am-5pm, winter to 4pm; 🐕) which as well as serving excellent coffee and delicious cakes, sandwiches, soups and breakfasts, has more than 5000 rare and second-hand books on display for customers to browse and buy. It's a mobile phone-free zone. Another great little café is *Kegen Teg* (☎ 01736-788562; Mon-Sat 10am-5pm), right on the square, where all the food is freshly prepared and home made. You can get huge, all-day breakfasts, including veggie ones, for less than a tenner. They also have burgers made from locally sourced meat, though much of their menu is vegetarian.

For a **pub** oozing character look no further than *The King's Arms* (☎ 01736-788545; food Mon-Sat noon-2pm & 5-9pm, Sun noon-3pm; WI-FI, 🐕), on Market

ROUTE GUIDE AND MAPS

Square, which was constructed in the 14th century to house the builders of the church next door. The beer is from St Austell brewery, and the menu (mains £10-15) is standard pub grub, plus a range of burgers.

Next door to The King's Arms is *Jeremy's Fish and Chips* (Mon 4.30-8.30pm, Tue-Sat noon-2pm & 4.30-9pm), a

takeaway which has some seating upstairs.

Transport

[See also pp52-6] St Just is served by several **bus** services including First Kernow's A3 & A17, WPCBA's No 7 & Travel Cornwall's No 409. Buses stop at the large car park opposite the library.

CAPE CORNWALL TO SENNEN COVE [MAPS 58-61]

This is a fine walk of **5 miles (8km, 1¾-2hrs)** along the cliffs, gradually flattening out to provide a gentle approach through the dunes to **Whitesand Bay**. Practically everyone will find this walk a real pleasure and as a day walk it is very popular. The cliffs are honeycombed with old mine workings so it is best to keep to the path. Leaving Cape Cornwall the path climbs to the trig point on **Ballowal Barrow** then it wanders through fields to descend into the **Cot Valley** where a tarmac road leads to a car park for people going to the tiny, geologically significant beach of **Porth Nanven** with its curious round boulders.

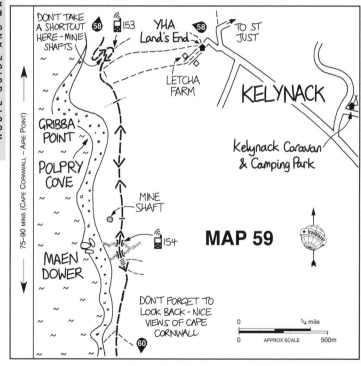

❏ **Cape Cornwall**
Cape Cornwall is a headland four miles north of Land's End which was thought at one time to be the most westerly point in mainland Britain. It turned out later not to be so after calculations proved Land's End to have that distinction. It is a place of stunning beauty once the crowds have left. The cape is the point at which the current divides, going south into the English Channel and north into St George's Channel. There is an old chimney at the highest point left over from the days when tin mining dominated the area and shafts extended right out under the sea. The chimney dates from 1850 and served the Cape Cornwall Mine extracting tin and copper from beneath the sea bed between 1836 and 1879 when the mine merged with the St Just United Mine further south.

In the early 20th century the Cape was owned by Captain Francis Oates: he had started work at 12 years old and worked his way up to become owner of the Cape and managing director of de Beers in South Africa. On retirement, in 1909, he returned to Cornwall and built Porthledden House near St Just as his family home.

The views back to Cape Cornwall are great and if you keep an eye on the rocks you may see seals popping their heads up for a look around. Dolphins are not an unusual sighting either, and basking sharks are occasionally seen. Look up and you may even catch a glimpse of that most iconic of Cornish birds, the red-legged Cornish chough (see p63).

Zig-zag paths take you round **Gribba Point** from where the path is quite easy and level, with one down and up at **Maen Dower**. **Sennen Cove** comes into sight and you may like to take to the beach as an alternative to the official route through the dunes.

KELYNACK   [MAP 59]
YHA Land's End (☎ 01736-788437, 🖳 yha.org.uk/hostel/lands-end; 28 dorm beds/ 1T/2D or F; from £21pp; WI-FI), at Letcha Vean in St Just-in-Penwith, is secreted away amongst the trees in the Cot Valley and, as with all the YHAs along the Cornwall coast path, is a lovely place to stay.

Camping (Apr-Sep; from £12pp) is available in the front garden. There are self-catering kitchen facilities, but breakfast and evening meals are available too – and there's a licensed bar.

An alternative is *Kelynack Caravan and Camping Park* (☎ 01736-787633, 🖳 kelynackcaravans.co.uk) but it's a slightly tiresome walk inland. However, a range of accommodation is available from **camping** (£7-8pp) to **B&B** (2D/1D or T; 🐾; from £35pp, sgl occ £45). The whole complex is very well run with a **shop** (open daily in season 8.30-10am & 5.30-7pm) selling groceries including fresh milk and fruit, and there's a sparkling clean toilet block.

WPCBA's No 7 **bus** service calls here; see pp52-6.

SENNEN & MAYON   [MAP 60, p186]
Most people will want to stay as close to Land's End as possible, but this small settlement on top of the hill above Sennen Cove, gives you some more options. It actually comprises Mayon and Sennen but tends to be known collectively as Sennen. It takes

around half an hour to climb up to here from places on the coast path such as Sennen Cove, Gwnver Beach or Land's End.

You can buy food for the day at the Costcutter **convenience store** (daily 8am-8pm), which also houses the **post office**

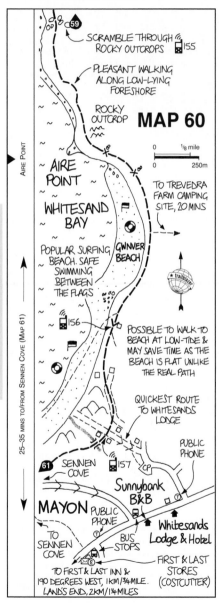

SCRAMBLE THROUGH ROCKY OUTCROPS 155

PLEASANT WALKING ALONG LOW-LYING FORESHORE

ROCKY OUTCROP

MAP 60

0 ⅛ mile
0 250m

AIRE POINT

AIRE POINT

WHITESAND BAY

TO TREVEDRA FARM CAMPING SITE, 20 MINS

POPULAR SURFING BEACH. SAFE SWIMMING BETWEEN THE FLAGS

GWNVER BEACH

156

POSSIBLE TO WALK TO BEACH AT LOW-TIDE & MAY SAVE TIME AS THE BEACH IS FLAT UNLIKE THE REAL PATH

QUICKEST ROUTE TO WHITESANDS LODGE

PUBLIC PHONE

61 SENNEN COVE 157 CP

Sunnybank B&B

MAYON PUBLIC PHONE

TO SENNEN COVE

BUS STOPS

Whitesands Lodge & Hotel

FIRST & LAST STORES (COSTCUTTER)

TO FIRST & LAST INN & 190 DEGREES WEST, 1KM/¾-MILE. LAND'S END, 2KM/1¼-MILES.

ROUTE GUIDE AND MAPS

25-35 MINS TO/FROM SENNEN COVE (MAP 61)

(same hours) and has an **ATM**. There's also a good **fish & chip shop** here, called *190 Degrees West* (☎ 01736-872723, 🖳 190 degreeswest.co.uk; Sun-Wed 5-8pm, Thur-Sat noon-2pm & 5-8.30pm).

If you are planning to **camp**, *Trevedra Farm* (off Map 60; ☎ 01736-871818, 🖳 trevedrafarm .co.uk; hiker & tent £10.50-14.50; 🐾; Easter to Oct) is a working farm with a campsite and **shop** (daily all day in peak season; limited hours at other times) selling fresh bread, milk and pasties. The campsite is about a mile inland: take the steps off Gwnver Beach, climb up, cross a lane, a stile and two fields.

To camp closer to Land's End, try the larger, less friendly Seaview Holiday Park (p188).

Whitesands Lodge (☎ 01736-871776 or ☎ 07375-514597, 🖳 whitesandslodge.co.uk; 18 beds, B&B from £25pp) is a well-known independent **hostel** with a loyal following, particularly among the surfing crowd. As well as rooms, they also have shared **yurts** and **tipis** (from £19pp) in the garden, but you'll need your own bedding. Under the same management and on the same plot of land, *Whitesands Hotel* (☎ as for Lodge, 🖳 whitesandshotel.co.uk; 1S/2D/1T/1D or F; £39-49pp) provides slightly better quality **B&B** accommodation. **Food** is available daily (8.30am-8.30pm) from the café-restaurant-bar.

Sunnybank B&B (☎ 01736-871278, 🖳 sunnybankhousebandb .com; 1S/1T shared facilities/3D en suite/1F private facilities; WI-FI; from £40pp, sgl £35, sgl occ £60-65) is a small, family-run guesthouse.

Standing alongside St **Sennen Church** (founded in AD520, although the oldest part of the current structure is 13th century), *The First and Last Inn* (☎ 01736-871680, 🖳 firstandlastinn.co.uk; 2D/1D or T; £35-40pp; food daily May-Sep noon-9pm; Oct-Apr noon-2pm & 6-9pm) dates from at least 1620 and is a famous old smugglers' haunt with a fascinating history. Beside the bar, a deep well (now covered with glass) is said to have once been the start of a smuggling

tunnel that led all the way to cliffs. Former landlady Ann Treeve was reportedly sentenced to death by drowning for her part in the illicit operation. As well as the steep road, there's a footpath that leads down to Sennen Cove from opposite Costcutter.

First's A1 & A3 **buses** stop at the First and Last Inn. WPCBA's No 7 also calls here. [See also pp52-6].

❏ **National Coastwatch**
Modern technology, such as accurate positioning systems, has made coastal waters much safer, but it can still fail in distress situations close to shore. The **National Coastwatch Institution** (🖳 nci.org.uk) was reformed in 1994 to re-instate a visual lookout along the British coastline and is manned by volunteers. If they see anybody in distress including yachtsmen, divers, walkers, climbers or people in difficulty the watchkeeper immediately informs the nearest HM Coastguard Rescue Centre to alert the rescue services. There are now 46 stations operating around the coast. The NCI is funded entirely by public donations and company sponsorships.

SENNEN COVE   [MAP 61, p189]
Sennen Cove is a small beach-side community where fishing and the tourist trade are the only source of employment. The winter weather is too wild for the boats to go out so from November onwards the quay is piled high with lobster pots and the fishermen spend their time maintaining their boats and nets. There is a **shop**, The Old Boathouse, which sells basics above the southern end of the beach.

The *Old Success Inn* (☎ 01736-871232, 🖳 oldsuccess.co.uk; 1S/2T/10D/1F; 🛏; WI-FI; £58-80pp, sgl occ £100-110) is under St Austell Brewery, so the beers are

Tribute, HSD and Proper Job. **Food** is served daily noon to 9pm in summer, and they have some smart **B&B** rooms above the pub. Further along the coast path, cute *Little Bo Café* (daily 10am-5pm) has terrace seating, hearty breakfasts, decent coffee and lunchtime toasties and baguettes. They also serve alcohol. Between the two, *Blue Lagoon* (daily noon-9pm) is a no-frills café where you can eat in or takeaway.

First's A1 & WPCBA's No 7 **buses** stop here. [See also pp52-6]. If you want a **taxi** ring Logan Rock Cars (☎ 01736-871786, 🖳 loganrockcars.co.uk).

SENNEN COVE TO PORTHCURNO   [MAPS 61-63]

This **6-mile (9.5km, 1¾-2½hrs)** section contains some spectacular cliff-top walking including the rounding of Land's End, a big milestone on the coast path. The mile from Sennen Cove to Land's End is an easy walk on a hard-packed path, virtually a stroll in the park, used by the whole spectrum of humanity. However, in bad weather it can be very exposed, particularly across Land's End and **Gwennap Head**, as there is barely a rock or bush to shelter behind. **Dr Syntax's Head** is the true most westerly point of mainland England; a Union Jack flagpole marks the spot.

A few hundred metres south of this is the **Land's End** complex, home of the much-photographed Land's End signpost, with distance markers for New York and John O'Groats. It's also where you'll find (perhaps to your horror), a theme park to rival any seaside town in England. Thankfully, there's also a bar and restaurant in the hotel here, so you can grab a beer to celebrate reaching this far.

As you leave the Land's End complex, you'll pass Greeb Animal Farm (adult/child £4/3), an 18th-century farm with pigs, goats, chickens and the like.

From here, the cliff architecture is full of arches and holes, such as the natural land-bridge of **Tol-Pedn-Penwith**, or holed headland, created by the ceaseless battering of the sea, and which you can walk across. If you keep on the alert, your chances of seeing grey seals are high, although your pace slows as you watch for them to pop up then disappear again. The path passes through **Porthgwarra** where there is a **seasonal café** (Map 62), phone and toilets.

LAND'S END [MAP 61]

Land's End stirs all sorts of emotions in coast-path walkers. No one who comes here can be unaffected by the beauty of the rugged coastline and the windswept heath; nor the sense of accomplishment at having come this far. However, the development of the West Country Shopping Village, and the abundance of children's theme-park rides, does tend to dispel one's sense of wonder. The **Visitor Centre** (☎ 0871-7200044, ⬜ landsend-landmark.co.uk; daily 10am-5pm, Tue & Thur to 9pm, limited hours in winter) is more of a ticket office for the attractions, some of which are quite interesting (the RSPB has a Wildlife Discovery Centre here), than a place for tourist information. There's an **ATM** in the shopping village, but it charges for withdrawals.

There are several places for refreshments of the tea, coffee and ice-cream type, including the **Old Bake House** (11am-4pm; takeaway kiosk open until 5.30pm) which also does pasties and jacket potatoes.

Land's End Hotel (☎ 01736-871844, ⬜ landsendhotel.co.uk; wi-fi; 3S/2T/19D /4F; £45-75pp, sgl occ from £60) would be a great venue for a celebration but is a little over-the-top for a simple overnight stay. The **restaurant-bar** is open for breakfasts (8-10am), lunches and cream teas (noon-6pm)

and evening meals (6.30-8.30pm) with an uninspiring menu but a fabulous view.

Hikers, backpackers and cyclists tend to prefer **Land's End Hostel** (☎ 07519-309908 or 07585-625774, ⬜ landsendholidays.co.uk; wi-fi; 14 beds/2D or T; from £30pp), a family-run hostel, housed in a converted barnhouse, which is about as close as you can be to Land's End without actually staying in the Land's End Hotel. For **YHA Land's End** see p185.

Camping is available at **Seaview Holiday Park** (☎ 01736-871266, ⬜ seaview.org.uk; hiker & tent £13-15; Apr-Oct; booking recommended in summer). It's well equipped, and the pitches are soft and flat, but the owners could be more welcoming to hikers, and, surprisingly for such a large operation, they only accept cash.

As it's the last conventional B&B before Land's End, **Treeve Moor House** (☎ 01736-871284, ⬜ www.treevemoorhouse .co.uk; 1D/1T; ☛; wi-fi; from £40pp, sgl occ £60) is in demand from cyclists about to start the End-to-End cycle ride to John O'Groats. Booking is essential here.

Buses (First Kernow's A1) travel regularly between Penzance and Land's End. Their A3 service to St Ives also calls here as does WPCBA's No 7. [See also pp52-6].

❏ **Important note – walking times**
Unless otherwise specified, **all times in this book refer only to the time spent walking.** You will need to add 20-30% to allow for rests, photography, checking the map, drinking water etc. When planning the day's hike count on 5-7 hours' actual walking.

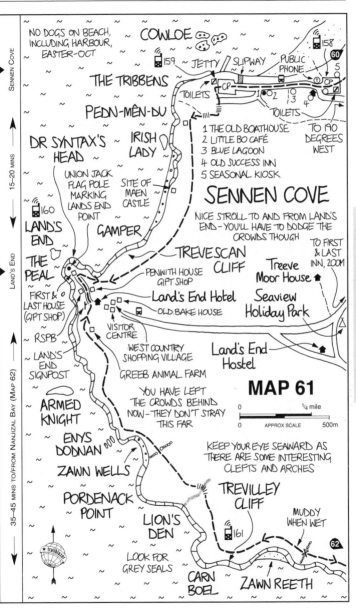

SENNEN COVE

15-20 MINS

LAND'S END

35-45 MINS TO/FROM NANJIZAL BAY (MAP 62)

NO DOGS ON BEACH, INCLUDING HARBOUR, EASTER-OCT

COWLOE

THE TRIBBENS

PEDN-MÊN-DU

DR SYNTAX'S HEAD

IRISH LADY

UNION JACK FLAG POLE MARKING LANDS END POINT

SITE OF MAEN CASTLE

LAND'S END

GAMPER

THE PEAL

FIRST & LAST HOUSE (GIFT SHOP)

RSPB

LAND'S END SIGNPOST

ARMED KNIGHT

ENYS DODNAN

ZAWN WELLS

PORDENACK POINT

159 — JETTY   SLIPWAY

PUBLIC PHONE

158

60

5

CP

TOILETS

CP

1 2   3

4

TOILETS

1 THE OLD BOATHOUSE
2 LITTLE BO CAFÉ
3 BLUE LAGOON
4 OLD SUCCESS INN
5 SEASONAL KIOSK

TO 190 DEGREES WEST

SENNEN COVE

NICE STROLL TO AND FROM LAND'S END - YOU'LL HAVE TO DODGE THE CROWDS THOUGH

160

TREVESCAN CLIFF

PENWITH HOUSE GIFT SHOP

Land's End Hotel

OLD BAKE HOUSE

VISITOR CENTRE

WEST COUNTRY SHOPPING VILLAGE

GREEB ANIMAL FARM

YOU HAVE LEFT THE CROWDS BEHIND NOW - THEY DON'T STRAY THIS FAR

TO FIRST & LAST INN, 200M

Treeve Moor House

Seaview Holiday Park

Land's End Hostel

MAP 61

0   1/4 mile
0   APPROX SCALE   500M

KEEP YOUR EYE SEAWARD AS THERE ARE SOME INTERESTING CLEFTS AND ARCHES

TREVILLEY CLIFF

MUDDY WHEN WET

62

161

LION'S DEN

LOOK FOR GREY SEALS

CARN BOEL

ZAWN REETH

trailblazer

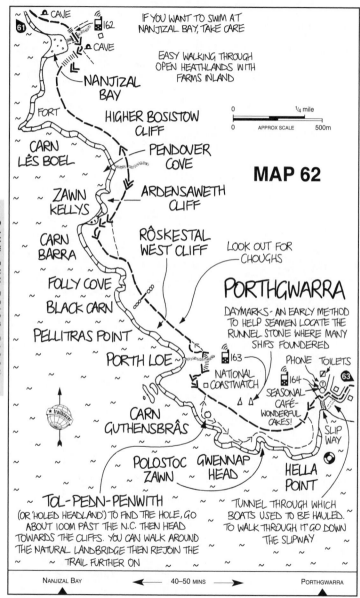

IF YOU WANT TO SWIM AT
NANJIZAL BAY, TAKE CARE

EASY WALKING THROUGH
OPEN HEATHLANDS WITH
FARMS INLAND

61

CAVE

162

CAVE

NANJIZAL
BAY

FORT

HIGHER BOSISTOW
CLIFF

CARN
LÊS BOEL

PENDOVER
COVE

ZAWN
KELLYS

ARDENSAWETH
CLIFF

RÔSKESTAL
WEST CLIFF

LOOK OUT FOR
CHOUGHS

CARN
BARRA

FOLLY COVE

BLACK CARN

PELLITRAS POINT

PORTH LOE

163

NATIONAL
COASTWATCH

MAP 62

0   ¼ mile
0   APPROX SCALE   500m

PORTHGWARRA

DAYMARKS - AN EARLY METHOD
TO HELP SEAMEN LOCATE THE
RUNNEL STONE WHERE MANY
SHIPS FOUNDERED

PHONE   TOILETS

164

63

SEASONAL
CAFÉ -
WONDERFUL
CAKES!

SLIP
WAY

CARN
GUTHENSBRÂS

★ trailblazer

POLOSTOC
ZAWN

GWENNAP
HEAD

HELLA
POINT

TOL-PEDN-PENWITH
(OR 'HOLED HEADLAND') TO FIND THE HOLE, GO
ABOUT 100M PAST THE N.C. THEN HEAD
TOWARDS THE CLIFFS. YOU CAN WALK AROUND
THE NATURAL LANDBRIDGE THEN REJOIN THE
TRAIL FURTHER ON

TUNNEL THROUGH WHICH
BOATS USED TO BE HAULED.
TO WALK THROUGH IT GO DOWN
THE SLIPWAY

NANJIZAL BAY   ◀—— 40–50 MINS ——▶   PORTHGWARRA

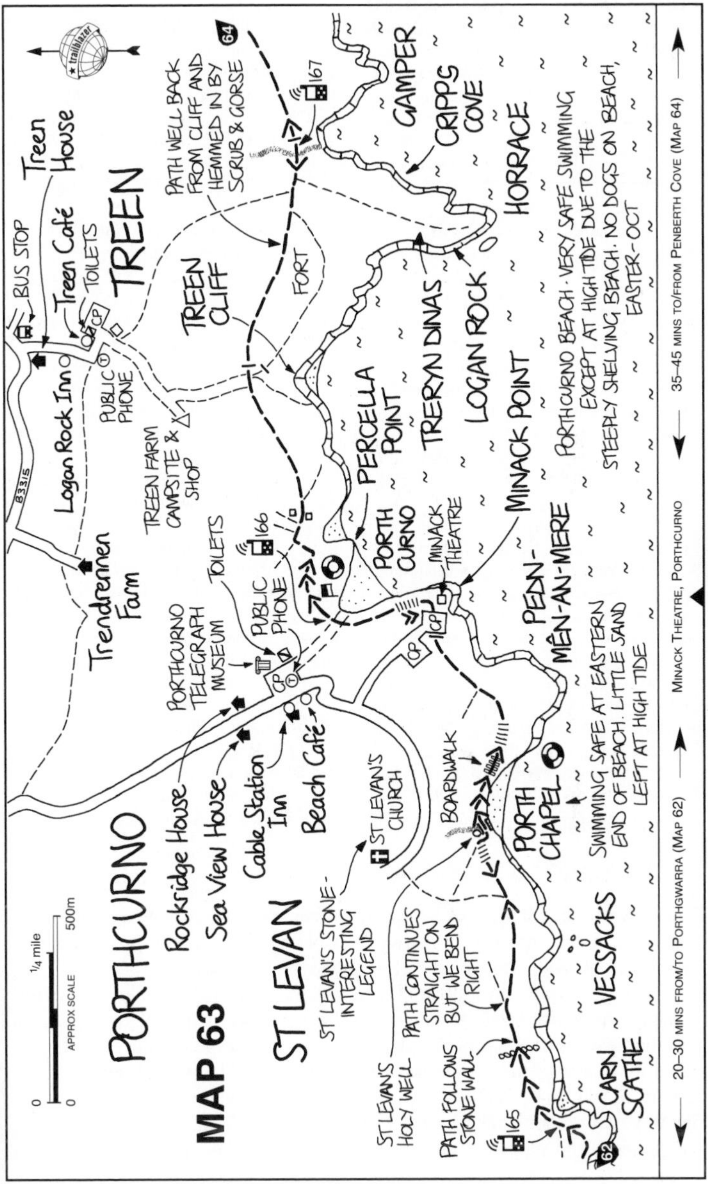

MAP 63

PORTHCURNO

ST LEVAN

TREEN

APPROX SCALE

0 ¼ mile
0 500m

Rockridge House
Sea View House

Cable Station Inn
Beach Café

St Levan's Stone –
interesting legend

St Levan's Holy Well

Path continues straight on
but we bend right

Path follows stone wall

ST LEVAN'S CHURCH

Boardwalk

CARN SCATHE

VESSACKS

PORTH CHAPEL

Swimming safe at eastern
end of beach. Little sand
left at high tide

PENN-MÊN-AN-MERE

Trendrennen Farm

Porthcurno Telegraph Museum

PUBLIC PHONE
TOILETS

Treen Farm Campsite & shop

Trendrennen
Farm

PORTH CURNO

PERCELLA POINT

TRERYN DINAS

LOGAN ROCK

MINACK POINT

MINACK THEATRE

Porthcurno Beach: very safe swimming
except at high tide due to the
steeply shelving beach. No dogs on beach,
Easter–Oct

Treen House

BUS STOP

Logan Rock Inn

Treen Café
TOILETS

PUBLIC PHONE

TREEN

TREEN CLIFF

FORT

Path well back
from cliff and
hemmed in by
scrub & gorse

GAMPER

CRIPPS COVE

HORRACE

B3315

ROUTE GUIDE AND MAPS

20–30 MINS FROM/TO PORTHGWARRA (MAP 62)   MINACK THEATRE, PORTHCURNO   35–45 MINS TO/FROM PENBERTH COVE (MAP 64)

PORTHCURNO [MAP 63, p191]

A visit to the spectacular open-air **Minack Theatre** (☎ 01736-810181, 🖳 minack .com; Apr-Sep daily 9.30am-5pm, Oct-Mar 10am-4.30pm; £5) is essential even if you are unable to see a performance (May-Sep, usually daily 2pm & 7.30pm). The theatre and fabulous sub-tropical gardens are open for visits throughout the year but the hours can vary so check in advance.

The theatre programme includes anything from musicals to Shakespeare and tickets cost £10-14. This remarkable place, perched on the top of the cliff, was the brainchild of the late Rowena Cade (1893-1983) who, in 1930, with the help of a couple of workman, transformed the gully above Minack Rock into a rudimentary stage and seating area, so that she could stage a performance of *The Tempest*. Over time, she developed the site into the stunning, Greek-style open-air theatre we see today.

Another interesting place is **Porthcurno Telegraph Museum** (☎ 01736-810966, 🖳 telegraphmuseum.org; daily Easter-Oct 10am-5pm, last entrance 4pm; £9.50; WI-FI). Porthcurno was the departure point for the first transatlantic cable and the museum tells the remarkable story of the men who overcame the obstacles to lay undersea telegraph cables, many of which come ashore here at Porthcurno. There's a **café** and **gift shop** inside.

It's also worth visiting **St Levan's Church** with its 12th-century font and medieval carvings in the Celtic style. On the pew ends are figures such as eagles, fish, a bishop and a shepherd, and in the churchyard is a large stone said to have been split in half by St Levan himself so that people would have something by which to remember him. Opinions vary as to its true origin but its supposed pagan significance was neutralised by the stone cross standing close by.

Sea View House (☎ 01736-810638, 🖳 seaviewhouseporthcurno.com; 1S/2D/2T; WI-FI; £40-45pp, sgl occ from £60) can provide packed lunches, luggage transfer and accepts credit cards. *Rockridge House* (☎ 01736-810410, 🖳 rockridgehouseporth curno.co.uk; 1T/2F; ♥; WI-FI; £25-37.50pp, sgl occ from £60), 5 Old Cable Lane, has rooms in the house plus a two-bedroomed self-contained flat available at the same rates.

The *Cable Station Inn* (☎ 01736-810479, 🖳 cablestationinn.co.uk; 1D/1F in cottage next door; WI-FI; from £40pp) is the only pub or restaurant in town. It has a strange layout, owing to the fact that it was originally an exiles club for overseas Cable and Wireless workers, but can't be changed as parts of the building are listed. It serves **food** (noon-9pm; mains £10-15) and has two rooms in a beautiful stone cottage next door.

Porthcurno Beach Café (☎ 01736-811108; daily 9.45am-7pm; 🐾) is a great spot for lunch; there's booze and tapas available as well as your normal paninis and sandwiches and jacket potatoes.

First's A1 **bus** calls here; see pp52-6.

PORTHCURNO TO LAMORNA [MAPS 63-66]

The next **5 miles (8km, 2-2½hrs)** of coastline are sometimes described as sub-tropical. The undergrowth is denser than previously, in some places growing overhead to provide a shady tunnel through which to walk.

After passing the turn-off to **Treen** you may like to make the short detour to the **Logan Rock** (see box opposite). From here you can make quick progress, one moment walking up high amongst the scrub and gorse, the next dipping down for a taste of the sea at numerous exquisite little coves, all tempting you to stop and explore. The cove at **Penberth** is usually entirely free of tourists, and to pass through it seems almost an intrusion on the people who make their living here from the sea. Look out for the now disused 19th-century capstan winch, which used to haul boats up onto the beach. Dogs are discouraged here, and dog-owners are asked to take a diversion inland to keep them from fouling the slipway.

Beyond **Trevedran Cliff** the path crosses an area of heathland with rough, dry-stone walls before turning down to the verdant valley of **St Loy**.

The path crosses the beach on boulders before regaining the cliffs and passing the lighthouse of **Tater-Du** (not open to the public) down to the right. Built in 1965 it was fully automated from the start. The name is Cornish for 'black loaf', after the rocks hereabouts.

Between the lighthouse and Lamorna is the unobtrusive entrance to the **Minack Chronicles Nature Reserve**, set up by the late authors Derek and Jeannie Tangye, who lived here in a cliff top daffodil farm called Dorminack. Derek was the author of *The Minack Chronicles* (p48), and they set up this small reserve, only accessible from the coast path, as a place for local wildlife to thrive. It wasn't intended for visitors, but those who wish to 'seek solitude, enjoy peace, and contemplate nature and the elements' are welcome to walk around it.

TREEN [MAP 63, p191]

A short jaunt up a dirt track, the tiny hamlet of Treen feels like a well-kept secret. Not to be confused with Treen near Gurnard's Head (Map 53) on the north coast, this Treen has a few farmhouses and the warm and homely *Logan Rock Inn* (☎ 01736-810495, ☐ theloganrockinn.co.uk). **Food** is served daily (noon-2.30pm & 5.30-9pm); the menu is standard pub fare but also includes locally sourced fish, lobster and other specials. Between 2.30pm and 6pm an afternoon menu and cream teas are served. Nearby *Treen Café* (10am-4pm) is good for coffee and snacks.

The very friendly folks at *Treen Farm Campsite* (☎ 01736-810273 or ☎ 07598-469322, ☐ treenfarmcampsite.com, hiker and tent £10; 🐾; Easter to Oct) don't take bookings, but never turn walkers away. Their **shop** (daily 8am-7pm in season) sells homemade pasties, bread, milk and booze.

Just past the pub, *Treen House* (☎ 01736-810379, ☐ treenhousebedandbreak fast.co.uk; ♥; WI-FI; 2D/1T; £45-50pp) is a **B&B** with lovely en suite rooms and very friendly welcome.

Further from the village, there's also a nice B&B at *Trendrennen Farm* (☎ 01736-810585, ☐ trendrennen.com; 3D; ♥; WI-FI; from £40pp, sgl occ supplement applicable). Sit out in the huge garden and admire the view.

About two miles (3km) further on, just past Porthguarnon, is another campsite at *Treverven Farm* (off Map 64; ☎ 01736-810200, ☐ trevervetntouringpark.co.uk; hiker & tent £12-15.50; Easter-Oct), which is signposted from the coast path.

First's A1 **bus** service stops in Treen; see also pp52-6.

For a **taxi** try Logan Rock Cars (☎ 01736-871786).

❑ **The Logan Rock** [Map 63]

Right out on the headland of **Treryn Dinas** sits a massive 70-tonne boulder that could once be rocked by pushing it gently. That is until Lieutenant Goldsmith succeeded in pushing it right off its perch in 1824. Villagers were incensed as two local people had been employed as guides to the stone. The lieutenant promised to restore it to its original position, but despite help from Admiralty lifting equipment, was unable to restore its fine balance, although it can still be rocked with some difficulty.

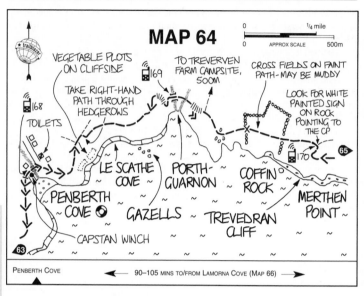

LAMORNA [MAP 66, p196]

Lamorna is one of the few wooded coves along the coast path. Note that it is privately owned so you must keep your dog on a lead here or risk a fine. There isn't much in the way of services but walkers will be glad to discover **Lamorna Cove Café** (daily 10.30am-5pm, later in peak season), with ice-cream, teas, pasties, and lunches served on the decking opposite. If your water bottle needs filling there's a tap outside the café.

You may prefer to head further up the cove road to the local pub, the **Lamorna Wink** (☎ 01736-731566, 🖥 lamornawink

.co; food 11.30am-2pm, meals 6-9pm), which serves food and a selection of ales, and has a nautical theme with charts and maps on the walls and a ship's wheel above the fireplace. The name goes back to a time when spirits were banned but smuggled brandy could be had with a wink to the publican. Martha Grimes' murder mystery *The Lamorna Wink* is set in the area and is a good read.

The closest **B&Bs** are a mile or two up the road. At **Lamorna Pottery** (off Map 66; ☎ 01736-810330, 🖥 lamornapottery.co.uk;

❑ Merry Maidens and Pipers

Inland from the coast are two ancient sites, the **Merry Maidens** stone circle and the **Pipers**, two large standing stones nearby. According to legend the Merry Maidens were nineteen young girls dancing in the fields to the tunes of the two nearby Pipers when they should have been attending vespers on the Sabbath. For their sins they were all turned to stone.

It is possible to visit these sites by walking inland (see Map 65) and then staying on the road and walking to Lamorna (see Map 66) but this involves walking along narrow roads which get busy in the summer. The alternative is to return on the same path.

2D/1T shared facilities/1F en suite; from £42.50pp, sgl occ £75), evening meals are available by arrangement, and they have a *café* (daily 10am-4.30pm) with a tasty lunchtime menu including salads, quiches and homemade soup. It first opened as a **pottery** in 1948, and you can still buy locally-crafted ceramics here. But note, due to refurbishments the twin and double rooms are not available for all of 2019. Nearby

Castallack Farm B&B (off Map 66; ☎ 01736-731969, 🖥 castallackfarm.co.uk; 1D/1T/1 apartment; ✻; from £40pp, sgl occ £80) is more modern.

First's A1 **bus** services stop at what they call Lamorna Turn, a junction about a one-mile walk uphill from the cove. Apparently, if buses drove all the way down to the cove they'd struggle to get back up to the main road. See pp52-6 for details.

LAMORNA TO MOUSEHOLE [MAPS 66-68]

This simple **2-mile (3km, 40-50 mins)** stretch passes through the pine forest of the **Kemyel Crease Nature Reserve**, then heads inland through scrub to arrive at the top of the hill above Mousehole. On reaching the road you turn right and walk down into the tiny village acclaimed by Dylan Thomas as 'the loveliest village in England'.

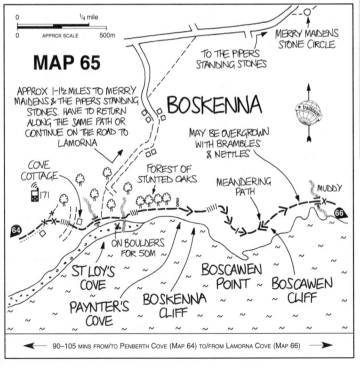

ROUTE GUIDE AND MAPS

0 ¼ mile
0 APPROX SCALE 500m

MAP 65

APPROX 1-1½ MILES TO MERRY MAIDENS & THE PIPERS STANDING STONES. HAVE TO RETURN ALONG THE SAME PATH OR CONTINUE ON THE ROAD TO LAMORNA

MERRY MAIDENS STONE CIRCLE

TO THE PIPERS STANDING STONES

BOSKENNA

★ trailblazer

MAY BE OVERGROWN WITH BRAMBLES & NETTLES

COVE COTTAGE
171

FOREST OF STUNTED OAKS

MEANDERING PATH

MUDDY

64

66

ON BOULDERS FOR 50m

ST LOY'S COVE

PAYNTER'S COVE

BOSKENNA CLIFF

BOSCAWEN POINT

BOSCAWEN CLIFF

← 90–105 MINS FROM/TO PENBERTH COVE (MAP 64) TO/FROM LAMORNA COVE (MAP 66) →

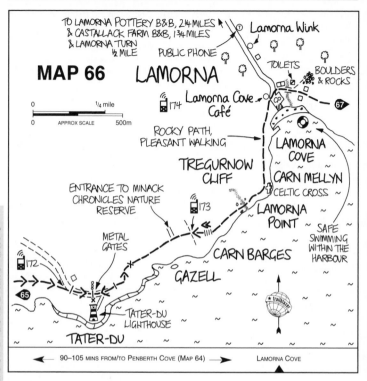

TO LAMORNA POTTERY B&B, 2¼ MILES
& CASTALLACK FARM B&B, 1¾ MILES
& LAMORNA TURN
½ MILE
PUBLIC PHONE

Lamorna Wink

MAP 66 LAMORNA

TOILETS

BOULDERS & ROCKS

0 ¼ mile
0 APPROX SCALE 500m

174 Lamorna Cove Café

67

ROCKY PATH, PLEASANT WALKING

LAMORNA COVE

TREGURNOW CLIFF

CARN MELLYN

ENTRANCE TO MINACK CHRONICLES NATURE RESERVE

CELTIC CROSS

173

LAMORNA POINT

SAFE SWIMMING WITHIN THE HARBOUR

METAL GATES

172

CARN BARGES

GAZELL

65

trailblazer

TATER-DU LIGHTHOUSE

TATER-DU

← 90–105 MINS FROM/TO PENBERTH COVE (MAP 64) →   LAMORNA COVE

ROUTE GUIDE AND MAPS

MOUSEHOLE
[MAP 68 p199 & map p198]

Pronounced 'mowzell', possibly from the Cornish *mouz hel* or 'maiden's brook' or alternatively because the entrance to the harbour was so tight that getting through it was like trying to sail through a mouse hole, Mousehole is a former pilchard-fishing village. The old stone quay and cottages are hardly equal to the volume of visitors that crowd in during the season. Traffic is the bane of the village and the time will have to come when cars are banned, leaving the narrow streets to pedestrians. The village is like a film-set; a romantic notion of what a Cornish village should look like and one of the most appealing on the coast path.

There are plenty of services available to the walker although with Penzance only five miles away, a couple of hours on foot or fifteen minutes on the bus, many will push on to the much bigger destination. Anyone walking the coast path in December may like to be here for **Mousehole Lights**, when the village is illuminated by a display of Christmas lights, and **Tom Bawcock's Eve** (see p16) on the 23rd.

Coming down the hill into the village you pass the **Wild Bird Hospital** (Map 68; ☎ 01736-731386; daily 10am-4.30pm) for injured, orphaned or oiled birds, which you might decide to visit. Entry is free although of course donations will always be greatly appreciated.

In the centre of the village is a **newsagent/post office** (Mon-Fri 8am-5.30pm, Sat 8.30am-5.30pm, Sun 9am-noon) with some limited groceries. **Hole Foods** (8am-5pm, Sun 9am-noon) is a café with a decent **deli**.

There's an **ATM** (£1.50 charge) in the Ship Inn (see Where to Stay).

Where to stay
Campers should head to Mousehole Camping (see p198), a mile uphill in the village of Paul.

B&Bs are thin on the ground these days. *Tremayne* (☎ 01736-731214, ☐ tremaynemousehole.co.uk; 2D/1F; WI-FI; ✼; £40-47.50pp, sgl occ from £75; Easter to Oct), at 1 The Parade, is one of the few that is left, and has three decent rooms plus an attached **café** (11am-5pm).

There are also some very smart B&B rooms, some with sea views, at *The Ship Inn* (☎ 01736-731234, ☐ shipinnmousehole.co.uk; 7D/1F, ✿; WI-FI; ✼; £39.50-69.50pp, sgl occ from £60; an old pub which celebrates the local festival, Tom

Bawcock's Eve (see p16) on 23rd December. For something much more upmarket, *The Old Coastguard Hotel* (☎ 01736-731222, ☐ oldcoastguardhotel.co.uk; 14D; ✿; ✼; WI-FI; £70-122.50pp, sgl occ from £105) has regal rooms and fabulous sea views across Mount's Bay.

Where to eat and drink
Old Pilchard Press Café (☎ 01736-731154, 8 Old Quay St; Easter-Dec daily 8.30am-6pm, Jan-Mar closes earlier) does breakfasts, cream teas (with scones freshly baked every day), ploughman's and salads.

For a traditional tearoom, the best in the village is *Four Teas Café* (☎ 01736-731532, ☐ fourteascafemousehole.co.uk; daily 9am-5pm) – inspired by the 1940s, hence the name. Tiny *Jessie's Dairy* (daily 9am-5pm) is difficult to pass by on a hot day. They have all sorts of ice-cream including gooseberry and wild cherry. They also serve Cornish pasties and takeaway sandwiches.

ROUTE GUIDE AND MAPS

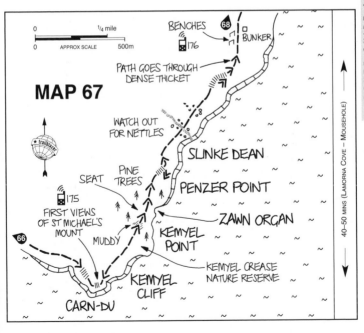

MAP 67

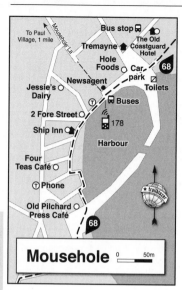

Mousehole

To Paul Village, 1 mile — Mousehole La.
Bus stop
Tremayne — The Old Coastguard Hotel
Hole Foods
Newsagent — Car park — 68
Jessie's Dairy — Toilets
2 Fore Street — Buses
Ship Inn — 178
Harbour
Four Teas Café
Phone
Old Pilchard Press Café
68
0 — 50m

For a good-value evening meal, try the pub-grub menu at *The Ship Inn* (see Where to stay; daily noon-2.30pm & 6-8.30pm), which includes home-made fish pie and Newlyn crabmeat sandwiches.

For more refined dining, seek out *2 Fore Street* (☎ 01736-731164, 🖳 2fore street.co.uk; Feb-Dec 10am-3.30pm & 5.30-9.30pm). Choose whether to eat inside at the plain wooden tables (with artwork by local artists adorning the walls), or in the garden if the weather is good. Evening mains (£15-20) feature venison, duck and monkfish.

Even classier is the restaurant at *The Old Coastguard Hotel* (see Where to stay; 12.30-2.30pm & 6-9pm; booking recommended; WI-FI). The food is fantastic, as are the sea views, and there are some fine real ales on tap too.

Transport
[See also pp52-6] First's M6 **bus** to Penzance runs throughout the day.

PAUL [MAP 68]
A mile to the north of Mousehole, this tiny village is where you'll find *Mousehole Camping* (Map 68; ☎ 07802-903073, 🖳 mouseholecamping.co.uk; tent £14-18) based at the local football club, Mousehole AFC. From Mousehole, walk north up Mousehole Lane and take the second left

after Paul Parish Church. Opposite the church is a good pub with rooms, *The King's Arms* (01736-731224, 🖳 thekings armspaul.com; 16D/1T, some rooms can be Tr; mix of en suite and shared facilities; £45-80pp, sgl occ from £60) that serves **food** (daily noon-2pm & 6-9pm, Sun to 8pm) and St Austell brewery ales.

MOUSEHOLE TO PENZANCE [MAPS 68-70]

The **4-mile (6km, 1-1¼hrs) section** between Mousehole and Penzance is all on tarmac. From the harbour car park the path stays close to the shore on the concrete sea wall but soon leaves it to join a cycle path all the way through **Newlyn** to **Penzance**. On the way you'll pass the memorial to the Penlee lifeboat, the *Solomon Browne*, lost with all hands in 1981 whilst trying to rescue the crew of the *Union Star*, an event of national importance at the time.

NEWLYN [MAP 69, p201]
Newlyn is a working fishing port that steadfastly refuses to be turned into a nostalgia trip for the benefit of the tourists. There is plenty to look at for those who like to lean on stone jetties watching the boats. The

Fish Festival (see p16) is held here in August.

Newlyn is famous in the art world for having given its name in the 19th century to a colony of artists who came here attracted

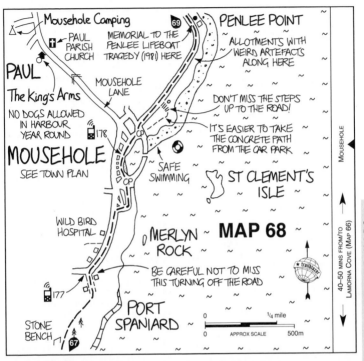

❏ Cornwall's fishing industry

One of Cornwall's oldest fishing industries is that of fishing for pilchard. Shoals containing millions of fish would appear seasonally off the Cornish coast and a lookout man, called a *huer*, would be stationed on top of the cliffs to alert the community of a sighting. When the pilchards were spotted he would cry 'hevva' (shoal) and then direct the waiting fishermen with semaphore signals using branches so that they could surround the fish with their nets.

Over-fishing brought the industry to an end by the 1920s, although recently pilchards have once again been caught off Cornwall. Pressing and salting of pilchards is still carried out by traditional methods in Newlyn with the end product being exported to Italy as was traditionally done.

Nowadays in Cornwall there are about 850 fishing vessels of which some 200 are over ten metres in length. About 2000 fishermen are directly employed on board and there are considerably more related jobs onshore.

In the smaller harbours most of the fishing boats you see are landing crabs and lobsters using various types of crab pot, although they may also use nets to fish for spider crabs, ray and anglerfish depending on the season. These vessels tend not to work more than five to ten miles away from their respective ports.

by the seascapes and its similarity to Brittany, in France. Most of their names will be unfamiliar to those not interested in art but in their day the work of Stanhope Forbes, Walter Langley and Edwin Harris was widely applauded. Their paintings can best be appreciated by a visit to Penlee House Gallery (see p202) in Penzance whilst here in Newlyn. **Newlyn Art Gallery** (☎ 01736-363715, 🖳 newlynart gallery.co.uk; Easter-Oct Mon-Sat 10am-5pm, Nov-Easter Tue-Sat 10am-5pm, bank hols 11am-4pm; £2.20) is a small but beautifully laid-out showcase for work by contemporary artists of local provenance. The galley's **café** is open from Tuesday to Saturday 11am-3pm.

For food supplies, the **Co-op** (daily 7am-10pm; free **ATM**) is well stocked with groceries including fruit and sandwiches. The **post office** here was closed at time of research. However, there is a highly active local campaign to save it, so by the time you arrive it may have re-opened.

Where to stay

There's a lovely **B&B** as you walk in to Newlyn from Mousehole: *The Smugglers* (☎ 01736-331501, 🖳 smugglersnewlyn.co .uk; 3D; W-FI; £45-50pp) overlooks the dock and beyond, across the curve of Mount's Bay to Penzance, and is actually a restaurant with rooms, but is arguably one of the best bed and breakfasts along the coast path. Named after different Newlyn artists, the rooms are large and comfortable with king-sized beds and sea views. The restaurant is top notch too (see Where to eat). They prefer two-night minimum stay during the high season, but it's still worth calling ahead to see if they have a single-night vacancy.

You could also try the *Swordfish Inn* (☎ 01736-362830, 🖳 swordfishinn.co.uk; 4D; from £50pp) for en suite accommodation. Rooms are nothing special, but the bonus here is that they charge the same £50 rate for single occupancy.

Where to eat and drink

For fast food, try *Lewis's Fish 'n' Chips* (Mon-Sat noon-2pm & 4.50-9pm, Sun 5-8pm) or *China Garden* (☎ 01736-367483; Sun-Thur 5.30-11pm, Fri & Sat to 11.30pm), a Chinese takeaway. There's also a decent Italian, *The Bridge* (☎ 01736-363446, 🖳 thebridgenewlyn.com; Thur-Sat noon-3pm, daily 5.30-9.30pm), which does pizza, pasta and various seafood specials. Takeaway is available too.

Aunty May's (Mon-Sat 9am-3pm), which has been going for over 20 years, is just the place for freshly-baked pasties. They do sandwiches and cakes too, as well as tea and coffee.

Pub-wise, the first one you come to, **The Fisherman's Arms** (☎ 01736-363399), was always a good bet for food, but it was completely gutted by a fire in early 2019, so its future was uncertain at the time of research. A little further along, the *Red Lion Inn* (☎ 01736-362012; food summer daily noon-2pm & 6-9pm, winter noon-2pm only) is renowned for its crab soup.

The Smugglers Restaurant (see Where to stay; summer Tue-Sat 7-9.30pm, winter hours may vary) has a wonderful view of the harbour; the very boats you are watching have probably brought in the fish you are eating. Mains cost from around £10 to £16, and they have Camel Valley wines available too.

On the bridge, *Mackerel Sky Seafood Bar* (☎ 01736-367199, 🖳 mackerelsky cafe.co.uk; daily noon-3pm & 6-9pm) is a charming riverside seafood restaurant, which doesn't take bookings. They serve tapas-style tasting plates (around £7-10) – mussels, crab claws, scallops, smoked mackerel pate etc – rather than large main dishes.

A mention must also go to *Jelbert's* (Mon-Fri 10.30am-5.30pm, Sat & Sun 10.30am-7pm), an ice-cream shop selling one flavour only (vanilla), but which has built up an international reputation over the years. Single-scoop cones with a flake cost just £1.25.

Transport

[See also pp52-6] First's A1 and M6 **bus** services pass through Newlyn.

For a **taxi** there's Stone's Taxis (☎ 01736-363400).

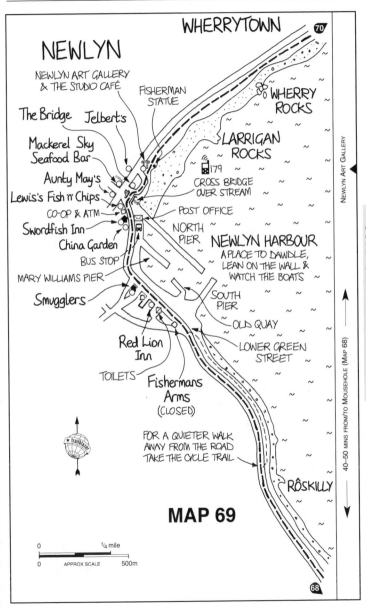

MAP 69

ROUTE GUIDE AND MAPS

40–50 MINS FROM/TO MOUSEHOLE (MAP 68)

PENZANCE [MAP 70, p204]

Penzance is a busy, bustling town whose heyday was in the 19th century when it was the commercial centre of the tin-mining industry. A statue of **Sir Humphry Davy**, born in the town and inventor of the miners' safety lamp, stands outside the Market House.

Penzance is a happy hunting ground for those who love galleries, rivalling St Ives in its artistic prominence. The flagship is **Penlee House Gallery** (☎ 01736-363625, 🖥 penleehouse.org.uk, Morrab Rd; Easter-Sep Mon-Sat 10am-5pm, Oct to Good Fri Mon-Sat 10am-4.30pm, open on bank holidays; £5), located inside a grand Victorian house in the leafy grounds of Penlee Park. The gallery has a wide-ranging collection from archaeology to photography documenting the life and history of west Cornwall, as well as an art collection from the late 19th century painted by well-known Newlyn artists. Last admission is 30 minutes before closing time. There's a nice café, called *The Orangery* (see Where to

eat), plus a shop with a selection of cards. A close second, under the same umbrella as the Newlyn Gallery, is **The Exchange** (☎ 01736-363715, 🖥 newlynartgallery.co.uk, Princes St; Easter-Oct Mon-Sat 10am-5pm, Nov-Easter Tue-Sat 10am-5pm; £2.20; café Tue-Sat 10am-4.30pm) in the town's former telephone exchange, showcasing the best of contemporary art. Of the many other galleries in Penzance there is sure to be something that appeals and a couple of hours mooching about looking at artwork can pass the time agreeably.

As well as housing the Penlee House Gallery, **Penlee Park**, which is free to enter, also contains a small **outdoor theatre** (☎ 01726-879500, 🖥 penleeparktheatre.com; tickets £6-14) which puts on performances in July and August. Shows range from Shakespeare plays to Cornish sea shanty concerts, and tend to start at 7.30pm, although children's shows start earlier. There are occasional matinées too. Check the website for upcoming shows.

❏ Visiting the Isles of Scilly

Penzance is one of the gateways to the Isles of Scilly, an archipelago of five inhabited islands and numerous small rocky islets, 28 miles off Cornwall, with a population of just over 2000. They are promoted for their peace and tranquillity, and can make a fantastic short break from the rigours of coast-path walking.

You can travel to the Isles of Scilly either by sea or air with **Isles of Scilly Travel** (☎ 01736-334220, 🖥 islesofscilly-travel.co.uk). *Scillonian III* (mid Mar to end Oct; sgl from £53) sails from Penzance once a day to the main island of St Mary's. Services operate daily except during the World Pilot Gig Championships (early May), although can be cancelled due to weather conditions. Departure times vary depending on the tides, but the boat leaves Penzance in the morning (between 8.30am and 10.30am) and returns in the afternoon (between 3pm and 4.30pm). The journey takes 2hrs 45mins.

The Skybus services operate from Land's End, Newquay, Exeter, Southampton and Bristol airports; single fares cost from £85 from Land's End and from £102.50 from Newquay. They fly from April to October, and there are at least half a dozen flights each day. Flights to/from Land's End Airport take just 20 minutes.

Their helicopters are now also in the air again between Land's End and the Isles of Scilly (one way/return from £107.50/215). They operate year-round, six days a week, with a maximum eight flights per day.

You can buy a helicopter or fly-sail combo return ticket from around £82 (helicopter/sail, approximately £130).

The Isles of Scilly Travel ticket office in Penzance is in the **Weighbridge Office** (8am-4pm Mon-Sat), over the road from the dock.

Don't miss a walk along historic **Chapel Street**, in some ways charmingly unchanged since the 19th century. The Grade 1 listed **Egyptian House**, with its extraordinary facade, dates back to 1835.

Built in 1935, the wonderful art-deco outdoor pool, the **Jubilee Swimming Pool** (☎ 01736 369224, 🖳 jubileepool.co.uk; daily 10.30am-6pm, £5) is also worth a visit.

Golowan Festival (see p15) in June, is a celebration of the arts that includes theatre, music, carnival and fireworks.

Services

The **tourist information centre** (☎ 01736-335530; Tue-Fri 10am-5pm, Sat 10am-4pm, Sun 10am-2pm) is right outside the train station. Behind it, in the same building, there is a **bus information office** (Mon-Fri 8.30am-4.45pm, Sat 8.30am 1.30pm).

The main shopping street is Market Jew St. On it you will find a couple of **supermarkets** including Co-op (Mon-Fri 8am-10pm, Sat 8am-9pm, Sun 10am-4.30pm), Tesco Express (daily 6am-11pm), the **newsagent-cum-stationer** WH Smith (Mon-Sat 8.30am-5.30pm, Sun 10am-4pm), and the main **post office** (Mon-Fri 9am-5.30pm, Sat 9am-12.30pm).

Millets Outdoor Shop (Mon-Sat 9am-5.30pm, Sun 10am-4pm) and Mountain Warehouse (Mon-Sat 9am-5.30pm, Sun 10am-4pm) both have plenty of **camping supplies** including camping gas.

There are several High Street **banks** including HSBC, Barclays and NatWest, all with **ATMs** and all on Market Jew St.

For **internet access** try Penzance Library (☎ 01736-363954, Alverton Rd; Mon-Fri 9am-5pm, Sat 10am-1pm; WI-FI; internet £3.60/hr or £1.80 with library card from home), on Alverton St.

There are some good **bookshops** including The Edge of the World Bookshop (Mon-Sat 9am-5.30pm) at 23 Market Jew St.

Suds & Surf **launderette** (☎ 01736-364815; daily 8am-8pm) is near the railway station.

The pedestrian-only Causeway Head is the best place to find fruit and vegetables; there's also a small **cinema** on this street.

This way also leads to **West Cornwall Hospital** (☎ 01736-874000), which has a 24hr Urgent Care Centre, while down Morrab Rd there's a **medical surgery** (☎ 01736-363866; Mon-Fri 8.30am-5.30pm) with a **dental surgery** next door.

Back on Market Jew St there are a couple of **pharmacies** including branches of Boots (Mon-Sat 9am-5.30pm, Sat 10am-4pm – with a second branch on Morrab Rd), and Superdrug (Mon-Sat 9am-7pm, Sun 10.30am-4.30pm).

Where to stay

YHA Penzance (☎ 0345-371 9653, 🖳 yha.org.uk/hostel/penzance; 100 beds; WI-FI; £17-25pp) is housed inside a lovely Georgian Mansion, but is a bit out of the way, over the A30 at Castle Horneck. There are dorm beds, private doubles and twins, and even some family rooms. You can **camp** (£12pp) in the grounds; campers have their own shower block but can use the other facilities in the hostel. They also have accommodation in bell tents. There's a games room, a barbecue area and a **bar-café** with real ales on tap, and food available three times a day. It's about a 15-minute walk from the coast path: to get here walk up Alexandra Rd, left onto Alverton Rd, then right on Castle Horneck Rd and across the A30.

There is a decent independent hostel, *Penzance Backpackers* (☎ 01736-363836, 🖳 pzbackpack.com; Alexandra Rd; 24 beds; WI-FI; from £17pp), which is smaller but also well run and friendly. They have self-catering facilities and private rooms as well as the dorms.

At 29 Lannoweth Rd is the newest hostel in town: *easyPZ Backpackers* (☎ 01736-368136, 🖳 easypz.info; 15 dorm beds, 1D; beds from £23pp, £58 for the double room).

For a **pub with rooms**, you could try *The Longboat Inn* (☎ 01736-364137, 🖳 longboatinn.co.uk; 1S/2T/3D/1F; WI-FI; £50-75pp, sgl from £65), opposite the railway station; there's also some smashing food to be considered (see Where to eat).

When it comes to **B&Bs** you have a very wide choice. However, be aware that many places do not accept advance bookings for one-night stays in the main season.

Alexandra Rd is lined with guesthouses. Built in the 19th century following the arrival of the trains, many of these buildings are known as 'gentlemen's residences' as they were built for the local professionals. The following are all of a reasonable standard: *Torwood House* (☎ 01736-360063, 🖥 torwoodhousehotel.co.uk; 1S/1T/2D/3F; ☕; WI-FI; 🐾; £35-37.50pp; sgl occ £45-55) is a nice cheerful place. *Tremont House* (☎ 01736-362614, 🖥 tremonthotel.co.uk; 2S/6D/2T; WI-FI; £35-50pp, sgl from £50) is a lovely friendly place with breakfasts so good they've won awards. They've also received a green tourism award for their eco-friendly approach to running their B&B.

On this same strip is *The Dunedin* (☎ 01736-362652, 🖥 dunedinhotel.co.uk; 1S/4D/1T/1F; £35-65pp, sgl occ £50-60); and

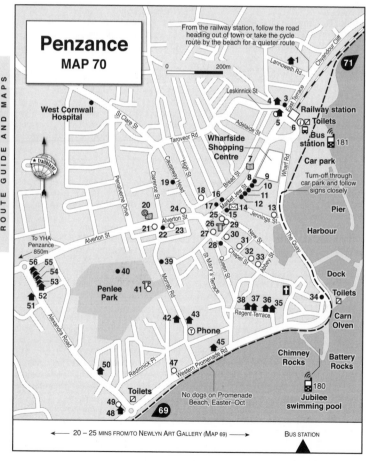

Penzance
MAP 70

0   200m

From the railway station, follow the road heading out of town or take the cycle route by the beach for a quieter route

Chyandour Cliff

71

Lannoweth Rd.

Leskinnick St

West Cornwall Hospital

St Clare St

Taroveor Rd

Adelaide St

East Terrace

Railway station

Toilets

Bus station 181

Car park

Turn-off through car park and follow signs closely

Wharfside Shopping Centre

Wharf Rd

Causeway Head

High St

Clarence St

Bread St

Market Jew St

Pier

Harbour

Penalverne Drive

Alverton St

Alverton St

Jennings St.

New St

The Quay

Dock

To YHA
Penzance
850m

St Mary's Terrace

Chapel St

Abbey St

Queen St

Toilets

Carn Olven

Penlee Park

Morrab Rd

Regent Terrace

Alexandra Road

Redinnick Pl

Western Promenade Rd

Phone

Chimney Rocks

Battery Rocks

No dogs on Promenade Beach, Easter–Oct

Toilets

69

180

Jubilee swimming pool

← 20 – 25 MINS FROM/TO NEWLYN ART GALLERY (MAP 69) →   BUS STATION

The Pendennis (☎ 01736-363823, 🖥 the pendennis.co.uk; 2S/3D/4D or T, most en suite; ☛; WI-FI; from £34pp, sgl from £53, sgl occ from £60.50).

At *Keigwin House* (☎ 01736-363930, 🖥 keigwinhouse.co.uk; 2S/1T/2T or D/3D/1F some en suite; ☛; WI-FI; £30-40pp) there is a warm welcome for walkers as the manageress is a keen walker herself.

Back down the bottom of the hill near the front, walkers are also very welcome at *Treventon Guest House* (☎ 01736-332730, 🖥 penzance-bed-and-breakfast.co.uk; 4D/1T; ☛; £37.50-42.50pp).

On the Promenade is smart-looking *Beachfield Hotel* (☎ 01736-362067, 🖥 beachfield.co.uk; 6S/4T/4D/4F; ☛; WI-FI; 🐾; £30-77pp) with sea views and a restaurant. Further along the Promenade is the less refined, but arguably more welcoming

Lugger Inn (☎ 01736-363236, 🖥 thelug ger.co.uk; 20 rooms; £43-70pp, sgl occ from £360) which also has a restaurant.

Nearby Morrab Rd also has some accommodation. *The Lynwood* (☎ 01736-365871, 🖥 lynwood-guesthouse.co.uk; 2S/2T/2D, some en suite; £35-50pp) at No 41 provides dressing gowns for standard rooms and they also have drying facilities. Across the road at No 29 is *Woodstock* (☎ 01736-369049, 🖥 woodstockguesthouse .co.uk; 2S/1D/2D/1T/1F, some en suite; £40-47.50pp, sgl/sgl occ from £50).

Continuing along Western Promenade you come to Regent Terrace with several guesthouses to choose from, including: *Lombard House* (☎ 01736-364897, 🖥 lom bardhousehotel.com; 6 flexible rooms, ☛; WI-FI; £40pp), at No 16: *Camilla House Hotel* (☎ 01736-363771, 🖥 camillahouse

ROUTE GUIDE AND MAPS

PENZANCE – MAP KEY

Where to stay
1 EasyPZ Backpackers
4 Cornerways Guest House
5 The Longboat Inn
35 Warwick House
36 Lombard House
37 Blue Seas
38 Camilla House Hotel
42 Lynwood
43 Woodstock
45 Lugger Inn
48 Beachfield Hotel
50 Treventon Guesthouse
51 Penzance Backpackers
52 Torwood House
53 Pendennis
54 Keigwin House
55 Tremont House
56 Dunedin Hotel

Where to eat & drink
5 The Longboat Inn
13 Old Lifeboat House Bistro
18 Archie Brown's
21 The Shore
23 Lavenders Café
24 New Hong Kong
25 Harris's Restaurant
27 Curry Corner
29 Mackerel Sky Café
30 Colyers Café
31 The Bakehouse
32 Turks Head
33 Admiral Benbow
41 Orangery Café
47 Fraser's
49 Thai Moon

Other
3 Suds & Surf Laundrette
6 Tourist Information
7 Edge of the World Books

Other (cont'd)
8 WH Smith
9 Superdrug
10 Mountain Warehouse
11 Tesco Express
12 Boots
14 Post Office
15 Co-op
16 Millets
17 Sir Humphrey Davy statue
19 Cinema
20 Library & internet access
22 Boots Pharmacy
26 The Exchange
28 The Egyptian House
34 Weighbridge Office (Scilly Isles tickets)
39 Medical & Dental Surgery
40 Open-air theatre
41 Penlee House Gallery

.co.uk; 2S/6D or T; WI-FI; £50-56.50pp, sgl from £60), at No 12; *Warwick House* (☎ 01736-363881, 🖳 warwickhousepenzance .co.uk; 2S/3D/2T; 🛏; WI-FI; £47.50-57.50pp, sgl from £65), at No 17; and *Blue Seas Hotel* (☎ 01736-364744, 🖳 blueseas hotel-penzance.co.uk; Mar to mid Dec; 1S/5D/2T; 🛏; WI-FI; from £40pp), at No 13.

Near the railway station, at *Cornerways Guest House* (☎ 01736-364645, 🖳 penzance.co.uk/cornerways; 2S/1T/1D; WI-FI; 🐾; from £42.50pp, plus £3 for one-night stays), 5 Leskinnick St.

Where to eat and drink

There are lots of tea shops and coffee houses in town including the stylish *Orangery* (☎ 01736-361325; Easter to Sep Mon-Sat 10am-5pm, rest of year to 4.30pm, lunch served noon-3pm), overlooking the gardens at Penlee House Gallery, which serves hot paninis and jacket potatoes with a choice of fillings.

Nearby, *Lavenders Café* (🖳 lavenders delibakery.co.uk; Mon-Sat 9am-6pm) is attached to a deli and bakery, and does good sandwiches, pasties, cream teas and the like, with the emphasis on local products. *Colyers Café* (daily 9am-4pm) is opposite The Exchange gallery (p202), and is a great-value, family-run affair with all-day breakfasts from just £3.95.

Perhaps the most environmentally conscious café in town is the all-vegetarian *Archie Brown's* (☎ 01736-362828, 🖳 archiebrownscornwall.co.uk; Mon-Sat 9am-5.30pm), on Bread St. The veggie breakfast here costs £6.85, and there are vegan and gluten-free options too. The ground floor is a shop selling health-food products.

More upmarket, but still good for a coffee and a cake, is the charming *Old Lifeboat House Bistro* (Tue-Sun 9.30am-11.30am, noon-2.30pm & 5.30-9pm) housed in the former lifeboat house with some outdoor seating. They have a range of tasty breakfasts (£5-8), plus sandwiches, soups and salads for lunch. Evening mains cost £12-20, with seafood the speciality.

There are lots of **fish & chip shops** in Penzance, but a nice choice is *Fraser's* (🖳

frasersfishandchips.co.uk; Sun-Thur noon-8.30pm, Fri & Sat noon-9pm) on the Promenade. Fish & chips cost £6.95/10.45 to takeaway/eat in the restaurant.

Next door to a small Chinese supermarket is the Chinese restaurant and takeaway, *New Hong Kong* (☎ 01736-362707, Alverton Rd; Sun-Thur 5.30-11pm, Fri & Sat 5pm-11.30pm, Sun noon-2.30pm). For Indian food, *Curry Corner* (☎ 01736-331558; Mon-Sat noon-2pm, Sun-Thur 5pm-midnight, Fri & Sat 5pm-1am) is a sound choice.

On the corner of Alexandra Rd and the Promenade, *Thai Moon* (☎ 01736-369699, 🖳 thaimoon.co.uk; Mon-Sat 5-10pm) is a friendly and popular Thai restaurant.

There are two wonderful old pubs on historic Chapel St: the swashbuckling *Admiral Benbow* (☎ 01736-363448, 🖳 the benbow.com; food daily noon-3pm, Mon-Sat 6-9.30pm, Sun 6-9pm) is named after a 17th-century seafarer whose story is told in notes included with the menu. The food is great for its kind (mains £10-15), and draught ales include Sharp's Doom Bar and St Austell's Tribute. No less nautical in theme and with similar food is the nearby *Turks Head* (☎ 01736-363093, 🖳 turks headpenzance.co.uk; daily noon-2.30pm & 6-9pm). You could also try *The Longboat Inn* (see Where to stay; food daily 7am-9pm; 🐾; WI-FI).

For something more chic, the *Bakehouse* (☎ 01736-331331, 🖳 bake houserestaurant.co.uk; Tue-Sat 6-9pm), through an archway off Chapel St, is an intimate little restaurant with a well-devised menu (mains £11-20), including a range of steaks.

Harris's Restaurant (☎ 01736-364408, 🖳 harrissrestaurant.co.uk; Tue-Sat noon-2pm & 7-9.30pm), at 46 New St, is bedecked with hanging baskets outside and is held by some to be the best restaurant in Penzance. The menu (mains £20-30) includes such culinary delights as roasted monkfish and loin of Cornish spring lamb. The lobster (£29.95) is pretty special too. Next door is the equally charming seafood restaurant *Mackerel Sky Café* (10am-3pm

& 6-9pm), whose sister restaurant is in nearby Newlyn.

Receiving rave reviews, another option for seafood is *The Shore* (☎ 01736-362444, 🖳 theshorerestaurant .uk; Tue-Sat 6.30-9pm; set menu £56), 13/14 Alverton St.

Transport

[See also pp52-6] **Train** services, operated by GWR, run roughly hourly to St Erth (change for St Ives), Par (for Newquay) and Plymouth.

First Kernow's A1, A2, A17, M6 & 16A and Travel Cornwall's 409 **bus** services call here. Penzance is also served by **coaches** (NX330, NX404 & NX504; see box p50).

For a **taxi**, try Bailey's Taxis on Lower Queen St (☎ 01736-363778), Roger Care Taxi Services at 35 Trevean Rd (☎ 01736-367433), or Carnes Taxis (☎ 01736-363572).

PENZANCE TO MARAZION [MAPS 70-73]

The walk to Marazion (**3 miles/ 5km, 45-50 mins**) is on a cycle path between the railway line and the beach and makes for quite a pleasant stroll with the whole prospect of Mount's Bay to add to the enjoyment.

On the way in to Marazion, at **Long Rock** you pass *Jordan's Café* (Map 71; ☎ 01736-360502, 🖳 jordanscafe.co.uk; daily 10am-5.30pm; WI-FI) serving freshly baked pizza, ciabattas, paninis and baguettes, to eat in or take away. You may also see one of the seasonal cafés which pop up annually along this stretch. Those who don't wish to walk along totally flat cycle tracks can always catch the **bus** (First Kernow's A2; see pp52-6).

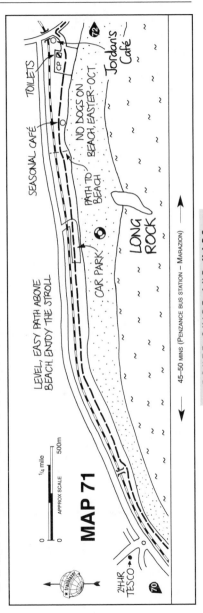

MAP 71

45-50 MINS (PENZANCE BUS STATION – MARAZION)

ROUTE GUIDE AND MAPS

MARAZION [MAPS 72 & 73]

The name derives from the Cornish *marghas byghan* or 'small market' from the days when the village held two markets, the marghas byghan and the *marghas yow* or 'Thursday market'. Over time these have become Marazion and Market Jew, the latter now the name of the main street in Penzance.

The iconic island of **St Michael's Mount** (see box p210) attracts huge numbers of visitors every year. The village itself is quaint and has much to satisfy the curious wanderer. The little **Marazion Museum** (Easter-Oct 10am-4pm; £1), inside the Town Hall building, was once the jail and a typical cell has been reconstructed. Of interest to nature lovers is the **RSPB Nature Reserve** (☎ 01736-711682; open 24hrs; free, but donations welcome) on Marazion Marsh, which has Cornwall's largest reed bed.

Cobble Corner Newsagents and **shop** (daily 7am-6.30pm) houses the **post office** (Mon-Fri 9am-5.30pm, Sat 9am-12.30pm) and has a free **cash machine** inside. Nearby, there's a **pharmacy** (Mon-Fri

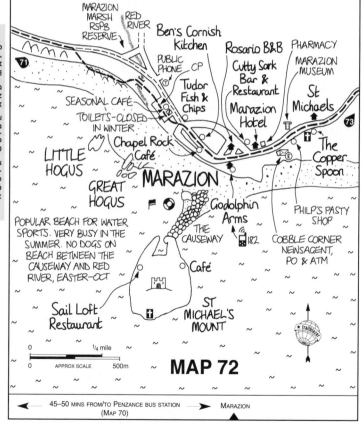

MARAZION MARSH RSPB RESERVE

RED RIVER

Ben's Cornish Kitchen

Rosario B&B

PHARMACY

MARAZION MUSEUM

PUBLIC PHONE CP

Cutty Sark Bar & Restaurant

St Michaels

SEASONAL CAFÉ

Tudor Fish & Chips

Marazion Hotel

TOILETS - CLOSED IN WINTER

The Copper Spoon

LITTLE HOGUS

Chapel Rock Café

MARAZION

GREAT HOGUS

Godolphin Arms

PHILP'S PASTY SHOP

POPULAR BEACH FOR WATER SPORTS. VERY BUSY IN THE SUMMER. NO DOGS ON BEACH BETWEEN THE CAUSEWAY AND RED RIVER, EASTER-OCT

THE CAUSEWAY 182

COBBLE CORNER NEWSAGENT, PO & ATM

Café

Sail Loft Restaurant

ST MICHAEL'S MOUNT

0   ¼ mile
0 APPROX SCALE 500m

MAP 72

71

73

trailblazer

45-50 MINS FROM/TO PENZANCE BUS STATION (MAP 70)   MARAZION

9am-1pm & 2-5.30pm, Sat 9am-noon), as well as **Philp's Pasty Shop** (Mon-Sat 9am-4pm, Sun 10am-4pm). Pasty fans will remember Philp's from Hayle; they're one of the best.

Where to stay

The nearest place to **camp** is *Wheal Rodney Holiday Park* (off Map 73; ☎ 01736-710605, 💻 whealrodney.co.uk; tent & 2 people £15-23; Easter-Oct), a 15-minute walk inland from the path. They have a **shop** (daily 9am-7.30pm) and an indoor pool on what is a nicely appointed site.

There are several options if you want to stay in Marazion. *Rosario B&B* (☎ 01736-711998, 💻 rosario-marazion.co.uk; 1S/2D/1T; 🐾; WI-FI; £45-50pp, sgl occ rate

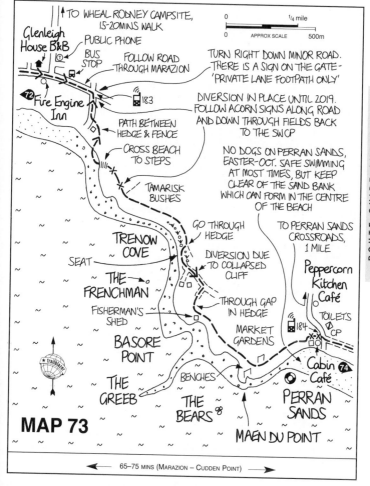

TO WHEAL RODNEY CAMPSITE, 15-20MINS WALK

Glenleigh House B&B

PUBLIC PHONE

BUS STOP

FOLLOW ROAD THROUGH MARAZION

72 Fire Engine Inn

📱 183

PATH BETWEEN HEDGE & FENCE

CROSS BEACH TO STEPS

TAMARISK BUSHES

TURN RIGHT DOWN MINOR ROAD. THERE IS A SIGN ON THE GATE - 'PRIVATE LANE FOOTPATH ONLY'

DIVERSION IN PLACE UNTIL 2019. FOLLOW ACORN SIGNS ALONG ROAD AND DOWN THROUGH FIELDS BACK TO THE SWCP

NO DOGS ON PERRAN SANDS, EASTER-OCT. SAFE SWIMMING AT MOST TIMES, BUT KEEP CLEAR OF THE SAND BANK WHICH CAN FORM IN THE CENTRE OF THE BEACH

TRENOW COVE

GO THROUGH HEDGE

DIVERSION DUE TO COLLAPSED CLIFF

SEAT

THE FRENCHMAN

FISHERMAN'S SHED

THROUGH GAP IN HEDGE

MARKET GARDENS

BASORE POINT

TO PERRAN SANDS CROSSROADS, 1 MILE

Peppercorn Kitchen Café

📱 184

TOILETS

CP

THE GREEB

BENCHES

THE BEARS

Cabin Café

74

PERRAN SANDS

MAEN DU POINT

MAP 73

trailblazer

0 — 1/4 mile
0 — 500m
APPROX SCALE

ROUTE GUIDE AND MAPS

◄— 65-75 MINS (MARAZION – CUDDEN POINT) —

❏ **St Michael's Mount** [Map 72, p208]

St Michael's Mount (☎ 01736-710507, or for tide and ferry information ☎ 01736-710265, 🖳 stmichaelsmount.co.uk) is steeped in history. In one of the earliest written records of Cornwall, Greek historian Diodorus Siculus wrote that in the 1st century BC tin was taken on wagons to Ictis (St Michael's Mount) at low tide, thence by sea to Brittany, France, and from there overland to the Mediterranean. Much later, in 1645 during the Civil War, it was one of the last Royalist strongholds and was only eventually taken after a long siege. The spectacular 14th-century castle surmounting the Mount was originally a Benedictine Priory dating from the 12th century, the daughter-house of the famous Mont St Michel in Normandy, France. It is now the home of the St Aubyn family.

The island with its **castle** is open late March to early November (Sun-Fri, 10.30am-5pm, to 5.30pm in July & Aug) but is closed on Saturday. The **gardens** are open from mid April to September (mid Apr to June Mon-Fri 10.30am-5pm, July to the end of Sep Thur & Fri only 10.30am-5pm, to 5.30pm in July & Aug); last admission 45 minutes before closing time.

Entry to the castle costs £10 and to the gardens £8 or a combined ticket is £15 (NT members get in free). The island has a **shop** and *café* and *Sail Loft Restaurant* (☎ 01736-710748); all are open the same hours as the castle. Dogs are not allowed in the castle or gardens.

To get to the island you can walk across the causeway from Marazion at low tide or catch one of the regular ferry boats which ply back and forth during the summer months. They charge £2 each way and leave from one of three slipways depending on the state of the tide. All visits are also subject to the weather.

Be prepared for a steep climb on cobbles.

on request), on The Square, is a charming establishment that offers luggage transfer. *St Michaels* (☎ 01736-711348, 🖳 st michaels-bedandbreakfast.co.uk; 1T/4D/1F; WI-FI; £50-60pp, sgl occ £90-110), on Fore St, is a little pricier and prefers minimum two-night stays.

On Fore St *Glenleigh House B&B* (Map 73; ☎ 01736-710308, 🖳 glenleigh-marazion.co.uk; 1S/5D/1T; WI-FI; 🐾; £42.50-57.50pp, sgl occ from £70) is full of Victorian-era charm.

Rather more up-market is *Marazion Hotel* (☎ 01736-710334, 🖳 marazionhotel .co.uk; 3T/5D/2D or T; ➴; WI-FI; 🐾; £66-115pp, sgl occ rate on request).

Equally salubrious, but with the choice location overlooking St Michael's Mount, is *The Godolphin Arms* (☎ 01736-888510, 🖳 godolphinarms.co.uk; 6D/2T /2F; WI-FI; 🐾; £60-115pp; sgl occ from £130), with modern rooms in immaculate condition.

Where to eat and drink

For snacks and quick bites, there's *Tudor Fish & Chips* (☎ 01736-711889; Mon-Sat noon-8pm, Sun noon-7.30pm); the slimline *Chapel Rock Café* (☎ 01736-719468; Apr-Oct daily 10am-6pm), which serves soups, Italian-bread sandwiches, pizza and coffee, plus a range of breakfasts; and *The Copper Spoon* (☎ 01736-711607; 🐾; WI-FI), which serves seasonal vegetarian food either to eat in or takeaway.

The award-winning *Ben's Cornish Kitchen* (☎ 01736-719200, 🖳 benscornish kitchen.com; food Tue-Sat noon-1.30pm & 7-8.30pm) serves excellent food (2/3 courses £29/35) and fine wine (£3-11 per glass) in refreshingly unpretentious surroundings.

The back terrace of *The Godolphin Arms* (see Where to stay; food noon-9pm) looks out over the causeway to St Michael's Mount; a fabulous vista in the setting sun, and a very popular spot with holidaymakers as well as thirsty walkers. Locally caught fish are well-represented on the menu, which also has the usual pub grub offerings. They serve breakfast here too (8-11am).

With an emphasis on local produce, The *Cutty Sark Bar & Restaurant* (food daily noon-3pm & 6-9pm) belongs to Marazion Hotel (see Where to stay) next door.

Up the hill as you leave the village is the ever-so-friendly *Fire Engine Inn* (Map 73; ☎ 01736-710771, 🖥 thefireengine marazion.pub; food Tue-Sat noon-2pm,

Mon-Sat 6-8.30pm, Sun noon-2.30pm & 6-7.30pm). The food they serve here is top-notch pub grub (mains £9-15), the location, perched above the crowds, overlooking St Michael's Mount, is impressive, and so too is the sign by the door: 'Walking boots welcome!'

Transport

First Kernow's U4 **bus** service calls here en route between Penryn and Penzance. See p52-6 for more details.

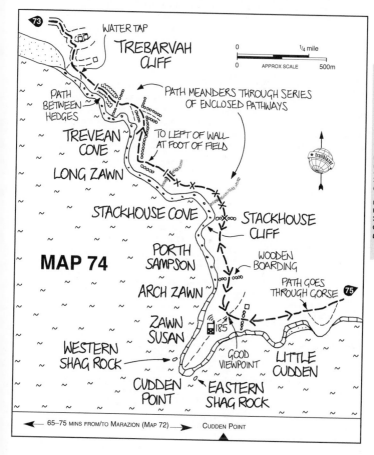

MARAZION TO PRAA SANDS [MAPS 73-76]

The first half of this **6¼ miles (10km, 1¾-2hrs)** provides fairly uninteresting walking on low-lying cliffs devoted to market gardening, and requires close attention in following the waymarker posts to avoid straying inland.

Things liven up at **Perran Sands** where there are some great cafés. *The Cabin Café* (Map 73; summer daily 9am-5.30pm; winter 10am-4pm; WI-FI) is down on the seafront with inside and outside seating, plus great coffee. The *Peppercorn Kitchen Café* (Map 73; Tue-Sun 10am-3pm) is well worth the short walk up the hill. All the food is freshly made, gluten-free meals are available and the coffee served is Origin, a local product originating from Constantine Bay. First Kernow's U4 **bus** (see pp52-6) calls at Perran (Crossroads).

From Perran Sands the walking gets a little more interesting. **Prussia Cove** (see box opposite), however, makes the effort worthwhile with Bessy's Cove below a real smugglers' landing place. From here good cliff-top walking takes you to the impressive beach at Praa Sands.

PRAA SANDS [MAP 76]

Praa (pronounced 'pray' locally) Sands is a mini holiday resort that gets very busy in the summer and is stone dead in winter.

A short walk from the beach, **Pengersick Castle** (☎ 01736-763973) is a Grade II-listed fortified manor house, dating from the late Middle Ages (14th century). It features one of the few towers of its type preserved in Britain. They do guided tours (£5), but you might need to call ahead, especially outside peak season. There is a **shop** (Mon-Fri 7.30am-6pm, Sat 8am-6pm, Sun

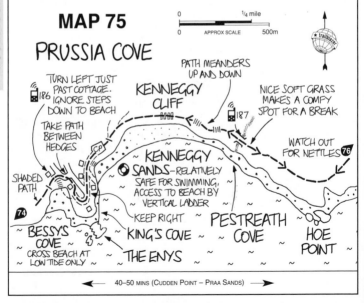

❏ **Prussia Cove** [Map 75]

Prussia Cove derives its name from the former King of Prussia Inn which stood on the cliff. It was run by the notorious Carter family whose smuggling exploits have guaranteed them a place in local folklore. The size of their operation was of such a scale that they needed to mount a small battery of guns to ward off the customs men. More recently, in 1979, a smuggling racket was busted by Customs and Excise who confiscated £3 million worth of marijuana.

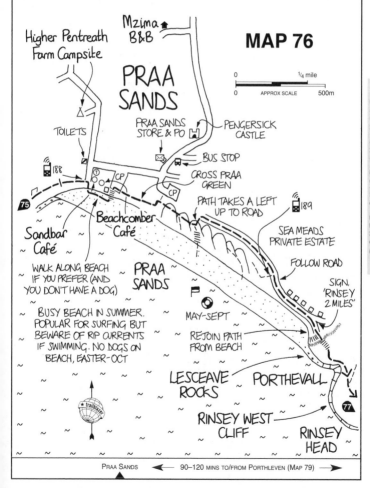

MAP 76

Mzima B&B

Higher Pentreath Farm Campsite

PRAA SANDS

0 — ¼ mile
0 — 500m
APPROX SCALE

TOILETS

PRAA SANDS STORE & PO

PENGERSICK CASTLE

188

BUS STOP

CROSS PRAA GREEN

PATH TAKES A LEFT UP TO ROAD

189

75

CP

CP

Beachcomber Café

SEA MEADS PRIVATE ESTATE

Sandbar Café

FOLLOW ROAD

WALK ALONG BEACH IF YOU PREFER (AND YOU DON'T HAVE A DOG)

PRAA SANDS

SIGN. 'RINSEY 2 MILES'

BUSY BEACH IN SUMMER. POPULAR FOR SURFING BUT BEWARE OF RIP CURRENTS IF SWIMMING. NO DOGS ON BEACH, EASTER-OCT

MAY-SEPT

REJOIN PATH FROM BEACH

★ trailblazer

LESCEAVE ROCKS

PORTHEVALL

77

RINSEY WEST CLIFF

RINSEY HEAD

PRAA SANDS ◀— 90–120 MINS TO/FROM PORTHLEVEN (MAP 79) —▶

9am-1pm), with an adequate stock of groceries, combined with a **post office** (Mon-Fri 9am-5.30pm, Sat to 12.30pm) on Pengersick Lane. Note, that at the time of research these times were subject to change.

If you want to camp, *Higher Pentreath Farm Campsite* (☎ 01736-763240, 🖥 higherpentreathcampsite.co.uk; two hikers & tent £13.50; May-Sep) is a small, family-run place with lovely sea views. It's uphill from the beach, but only a five-minute walk.

For **B&B**, about half a mile inland, and also uphill, *Mzima* (☎ 01736-763856, 🖳 marianfoy@hotmail.com; 1T/1F shared bathroom; 🛏; from £40pp) has reasonable rates and welcomes one-night-stay walkers.

The seasonal *Sandbar Café* (☎ 01736-763516, 🖳 sandbarpraasands.co.uk; WI-FI; 10am-11pm, food served until 9pm), is the focal point of Praa Sands, especially on summer evenings, when it becomes more like a bar-restaurant than a café, with occasional live music, real ales and decent pub grub.

Right next door is the more laid-back, and also seasonal, *Beachcomber Café* (☎ 01736-762977; 8.30am-7.30pm).

First Kernow's U4 **bus** stops outside the post office. [See also pp52-6].

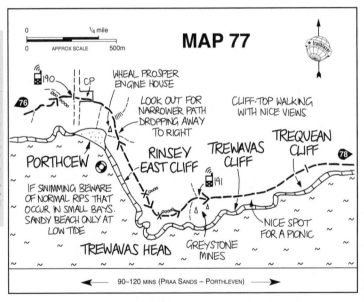

MAP 77

WHEAL PROSPER ENGINE HOUSE

LOOK OUT FOR NARROWER PATH DROPPING AWAY TO RIGHT

CLIFF-TOP WALKING WITH NICE VIEWS

PORTHCEW

RINSEY EAST CLIFF

TREWAVAS CLIFF

TREQUEAN CLIFF

IF SWIMMING BEWARE OF NORMAL RIPS THAT OCCUR IN SMALL BAYS. SANDY BEACH ONLY AT LOW TIDE

NICE SPOT FOR A PICNIC

TREWAVAS HEAD

GREYSTONE MINES

◄— 90–120 MINS (PRAA SANDS – PORTHLEVEN) —►

PRAA SANDS TO PORTHLEVEN   [MAPS 76-79]

This **4½-mile (7km, 1½-2hrs)** stretch of harder walking returns you to the clifftops again after the lower-level terrain between Marazion and Praa Sands. This is another area of old copper workings and you pass some weathered spoil tips that have begun to blend with their surroundings.

As you get nearer to **Porthleven** you'll find some of the cliffs are subsiding and the path has been fenced off to keep it well back from what is at present the edge. On the last headland there is a **memorial** (see Map 79, p216) to the many mariners drowned off these coasts.

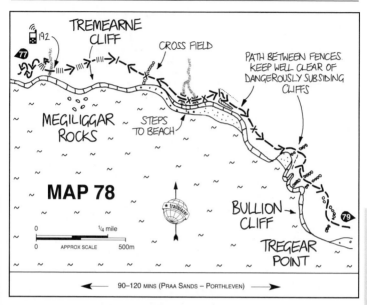

TREMEARNE CLIFF

CROSS FIELD

PATH BETWEEN FENCES.
KEEP WELL CLEAR OF
DANGEROUSLY SUBSIDING
CLIFFS

MEGILIGGAR ROCKS

STEPS TO BEACH

MAP 78

0   1/4 mile

0   APPROX SCALE   500m

BULLION CLIFF

TREGEAR POINT

79

90–120 MINS (PRAA SANDS – PORTHLEVEN)

ROUTE GUIDE AND MAPS

PORTHLEVEN [Map p217]

Porthleven Harbour was built using prisoners from the Napoleonic wars for manpower, and at one time housed a fishing fleet which harvested the huge shoals of pilchards and mackerel in the bay. Today its prosperity depends on tourism and the winters have to be endured. The coast is subject to ferocious storms and waves have been known to crash right over the harbour wall to wreck the boats sheltering within. What few fishing boats are left work the local reefs for crab and lobster during the summer months, some of the catch going to local restaurants and the rest to Newlyn for export abroad.

The shops and restaurants are smart and becoming increasingly chic. Amongst them there's a **supermarket** (8am-9pm), with an **ATM** inside it, and a Boots **pharmacy** (Mon-Fri 8.30am-6pm, Sat 8.30am-5.30pm) close to the harbour. On Fore St the **post office** (Mon-Fri 9am-5.30pm, Sat 9am-12.30pm) is inside Premier convenience store (Mon-Sat 6.30am-10pm, Sun 7am-10pm), which also has an ATM.

Where to stay

Mill Lane Campsite (☎ 01326-573881; £10-14 per tent) is a small campsite run by a local pub (called Out of the Blue) and situated beside Porthleven AFC's football ground. The toilets and showers are in the pub building, but can be used round the clock.

Also on Mill Lane, but back towards the harbour, is *Wellmore End Cottage B&B* (☎ 01326-569310; 1D/1F; £30-40pp, sgl occ from £60), with cosy rooms and cracking fruit-filled breakfast.

An Mordros Hotel (☎ 01326-562236, 🖳 anmordroshotel.com; 3D/1T; WI-FI; from £42pp, sgl occ rate on request) is a small hotel with views over the harbour, but you'll need to book for a minimum of two nights.

You can also find good-quality B&B accommodation at the St Austell Brewery owned *Harbour Inn* (☎ 01326-573876, 🖳 harbourinnporthleven.co.uk; 1S/1T/10D/3F; 🛆; WI-FI; £33-75pp, sgl occ from £110). It's worth checking online for offers.

On the harbour is *Kota* (☎ 01326-562407, 🖳 kotarestaurant.co.uk; 1D/1F;

from £30pp, sgl occ £40-50), a fine-dining restaurant with two lovely, spacious rooms. The harbour views are a treat, as is the home-smoked salmon for breakfast.

Where to eat and drink

It would be hard to go hungry in Porthleven. From chippies to bakeries, and pub grub to fine dining, it has most bases covered.

Philps Bakery (Mon-Sat 8am-4pm, Sun 9am-4pm) – yes, it's them again – is an excellent source of rucksack fillers, and neither *Porthleven Fish & Chips* (☎ 01326-554257; Mon-Sat 11.45am-8.30pm, Sun 4-8pm) nor *Top Chippy* (☎ 01326-554046; Mon 4.30-7pm, Tue 4.30-9pm, Wed-Thur 11.30am-2pm & 4.30-9pm, Fri-Sat 11.30am-9pm, Sun 4.30-8pm), will let you down. A few yards from the latter, you can get hot drinks and some smashing meals on the extensive menu at *Seadrift Café* (☎ 01326-558783, 🖵 seadriftporthleven.co.uk;

food daily 10am-9pm). For **Chinese** cuisine try *Moonflower* (☎ 01326-562973; daily 5.30-11.30pm; eat-in or takeaway).

Cafés are in abundance. *The Hideaway* (8am-4pm) is the most down-to-earth of the lot, offering great-value breakfasts (six items; £6.95). Practically next door, *Twisted Currant* (9am-5pm) is a very pleasant tearoom, offering goodies such as fish chowder (£8.30) and avocado on toast with poached eggs (£4.25/7.74 small/large). Popular *Nauti but Ice* (☎ 01326-573747, 🖵 www.nautibutice.co.uk; daily 9am-5pm) is a cross between a café, a sandwich shop and an ice-cream parlour, and has some terrace seating. More chic and modern is *The Brew House* (9am-5pm), with good strong coffee and a few cakes.

Of the two or three **pubs** near the harbour, the *Ship Inn* (☎ 01326-564204, 🖵 the shipinnporthleven.co.uk; daily noon-2.30pm & 6-9pm, winter no food Sun

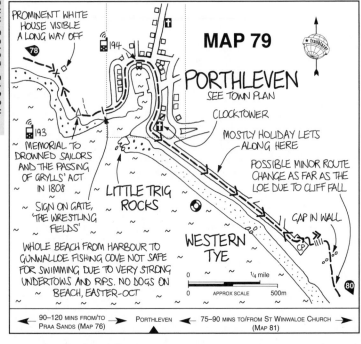

PROMINENT WHITE HOUSE VISIBLE A LONG WAY OFF

78

194

MAP 79

trailblazer

PORTHLEVEN
SEE TOWN PLAN

CLOCKTOWER

MOSTLY HOLIDAY LETS ALONG HERE

POSSIBLE MINOR ROUTE CHANGE AS FAR AS THE LOE DUE TO CLIFF FALL

193

MEMORIAL TO DROWNED SAILORS AND THE PASSING OF GRYLLS' ACT IN 1808

SIGN ON GATE, 'THE WRESTLING FIELDS'

LITTLE TRIG ROCKS

GAP IN WALL

WESTERN TYE

CP

WHOLE BEACH FROM HARBOUR TO GUNWALLOE FISHING COVE NOT SAFE FOR SWIMMING DUE TO VERY STRONG UNDERTOWS AND RIPS. NO DOGS ON BEACH, EASTER-OCT

0   ¼ mile

APPROX SCALE   500m

80

← 90-120 MINS FROM/TO PRAA SANDS (MAP 76) → PORTHLEVEN ← 75-90 MINS TO/FROM ST WINWALOE CHURCH (MAP 81) →

evenings) has the most atmosphere. If it's available don't pass up the crab thermidor. The Cornish fish pie is also very good. Beers include Doom Bar and Courage Bitter. *Harbour Inn* (see Where to stay; daily noon-9pm) always has plenty of punters dining from its pub menu (mains £8-14), which includes steak & Cornish ale pie (£11.50) and beer-battered cod & chips

(£10-17). There are vegetarian options too. Fine-dining options are also plentiful here, and Rick Stein has jumped on the bandwagon with *Rick Stein's Fish & Shellfish* (🖳 rickstein.com; Mon-Fri noon-2.45pm & 5.30-9.30pm, Sat-Sun noon-3.30pm & 5.30-9.30pm), a classy place right on the harbour. Mains cost £15-20. More established is the much-lauded *Kota* (see Where

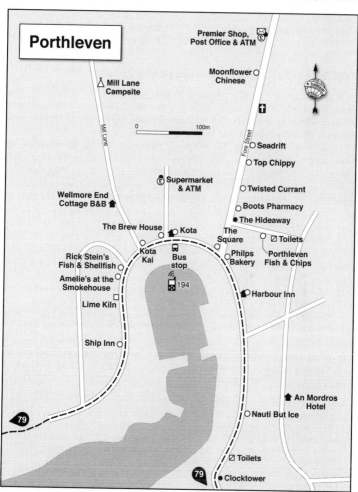

Porthleven

Premier Shop,
Post Office & ATM

Moonflower
Chinese

△ Mill Lane
Campsite

Mill Lane

0   100m

Fore Street

○ Seadrift

○ Top Chippy

£ Supermarket
& ATM

○ Twisted Currant

Wellmore End
Cottage B&B ↟

○ Boots Pharmacy

● The Hideaway

The Brew House ○ ↟ Kota

The
Square

☑ Toilets

Kota
Kai

Bus
stop

○ Philps
Bakery

Porthleven
Fish & Chips

Rick Stein's
Fish & Shellfish ○

Amelie's at the ○
Smokehouse

194

Lime Kiln □

↟○ Harbour Inn

Ship Inn ○

↟ An Mordros
Hotel

○ Nauti But Ice

☑ Toilets

79

79   ● Clocktower

to stay; Tue-Sat 6-9pm; mains £15-25), a multi-award-winning evening-only restaurant offering the likes of Cornish lamb rump, roast turbot, gnocchi and kale, and Cornish duck. A few doors down, their more affordable restaurant-café, *Kota Kai* (daily noon-2.30pm & 5-9pm) is open for lunch too.

Amelie's at the Smokehouse (☎ 01326-653653, 🖥 ameliesporthleven.co.uk; daily noon-2.30pm & 6-9pm) is another smart place with large glass doors, allowing customers to look over the harbour while they eat. The menu (most mains £10-20) is dominated by seafood and shellfish, but includes gourmet burgers and wood-fired oven pizzas too.

Finally, *The Square* (☎ 01326-573911, 🖥 thesquareatporthleven.co.uk; food daily 11am-9pm), 7 Fore St, also offers some splendid comestibles. Evening mains cost £14-20 but there's also the option of a set menu (Mon-Thur; 2/3 courses, £20.50/24.50).

Transport

[See also pp52-6] First Kernow's U4 **bus** service operates to Penzance and Helston.

PORTHLEVEN TO MULLION COVE [MAPS 79-82]

This is an enjoyable **6-mile (10km, 2-2½hrs)** walk with lots of diversity. You leave Porthleven past the iconic clock tower, over which heavy seas sometimes crash in winter storms, and climb the hill past all the holiday cottages to the open spaces high above Western Tye beach.

Next you come to **Loe Bar**, a shingle bank that cuts off the sea from the fresh water lagoon known as The Loe (see box p220); keen birdwatchers passing in winter will want to spend some time here; it is possible to walk around the lagoon. It was on Loe Bar that *HMS Anson* (see box below) was wrecked in 1807; this is commemorated by a bright, white-painted cross which you pass as you climb up onto the cliffs again. The coastal path then meanders along to the tiny beach at **Gunwalloe** where the church of St Winwaloe (see p221) huddles in the dunes. You'll soon reach **Halzephron Cove**.

After **Dollar Cove** you come to **Poldhu Cove** which has historic significance in the development of radio signals (see box p224). There's also a good café here, *Poldhu Beach Café* (☎ 01326-240530, 🖥 poldhu.com; daily 9.30am-6pm, limited hours out of peak season); on Fridays they serve stonebaked pizzas to 7pm. First Kernow's No 37 **bus** service (see pp52-6) calls at the cove.

Then it's **Polurrian Cove** which boasts the fine *Polurrian Bay Hotel* (Map 82; ☎ 01326-240421, 🖥 polurrianhotel.com; 41D or T; WI-FI; 🐾; £60-150pp) before the huge edifice of Mullion Cove Hotel announces your arrival at perhaps the quintessential Cornish harbour, **Mullion Cove**. The coast path doesn't go into **Mullion village**, which is about a mile inland, but it's worth the diversion if you need food, accommodation or general supplies.

> ❏ **Grylls' Act**
> Passed in 1808, Grylls' Act, drafted by local solicitor Thomas Grylls allowed bodies washed up by the sea to be buried in the nearest consecrated ground. Before this all bodies were buried on the cliff tops as it was not possible to distinguish between Christians and non-Christians. The memorial (see Map 79, p216) marks the passing of this Act, which was prompted by the wrecking of the 44-gun frigate *HMS Anson* the previous year, in which 130 people drowned.

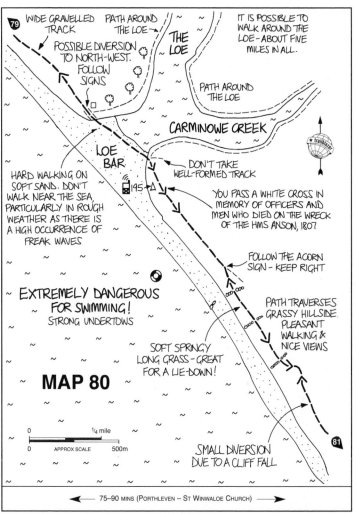

79 WIDE GRAVELLED TRACK

PATH AROUND THE LOE →

THE LOE

IT IS POSSIBLE TO WALK AROUND THE LOE - ABOUT FIVE MILES IN ALL.

POSSIBLE DIVERSION TO NORTH-WEST. FOLLOW SIGNS

PATH AROUND THE LOE

CARMINOWE CREEK

LOE BAR

DON'T TAKE WELL-FORMED TRACK

HARD WALKING ON SOFT SAND. DON'T WALK NEAR THE SEA, PARTICULARLY IN ROUGH WEATHER AS THERE IS A HIGH OCCURRENCE OF FREAK WAVES

195

YOU PASS A WHITE CROSS IN MEMORY OF OFFICERS AND MEN WHO DIED ON THE WRECK OF THE HMS ANSON, 1807

FOLLOW THE ACORN SIGN - KEEP RIGHT

EXTREMELY DANGEROUS FOR SWIMMING! STRONG UNDERTOWS

PATH TRAVERSES GRASSY HILLSIDE. PLEASANT WALKING & NICE VIEWS

SOFT SPRINGY LONG GRASS - GREAT FOR A LIE-DOWN!

MAP 80

0   ¼ mile
0   500m
APPROX SCALE

81

SMALL DIVERSION DUE TO A CLIFF FALL

← 75–90 MINS (PORTHLEVEN – ST WINWALOE CHURCH) →

ROUTE GUIDE AND MAPS

❑ **Warning [Map 80]**

Although the sea may look innocuous on a calm day there are powerful undertows here and the geology of the sea floor on Mount's Bay causes unusually high numbers of freak waves to occur; please **don't consider swimming**. In rough weather it is not advisable to even walk near the sea.

❏ **The Loe**   **[Map 80, p219]**
The Loe is Cornwall's largest natural freshwater lake. Originally the Loe was the estuary of the river Cober but it was dammed by the shingle bar around 800 years ago. The National Trust owns all the land surrounding the Loe and it has been designated a Site of Special Scientific Interest (see box p66).
    It is mostly known for its bird population and over-wintering wildfowl but such a place inevitably attracts legends of its own, one of which is that Sir Bedivere cast Excalibur, the sword of the dying King Arthur, into this lake.
    The walk around the Loe is about five miles (8km), mostly along the water's edge. The path is easy to follow but it can get muddy on the eastern side.

HALZEPHRON   [MAP 81]

Right on the cliffs the path passes a wonderful white building. *Halzephron House* (☎ 07899-925816 or ☎ 01326-240517, 🖥 halzephronhouse.co.uk; 2T/2D/1F; ✒; £55-65pp, sgl occ from £80) is designed mainly with self-catering groups in mind. However, when the house is not booked they offer B&B: It isn't cheap, but such an outstanding setting makes it well worth considering. Five minutes away is the charming 15th-century, *Halzephron Inn* (☎ 01326-240406, 🖥 halzephron-inn.co.uk; 2D; from £50pp, sgl occ £65; food daily noon-2pm & 6-9pm), with excellent food and rooms.

MULLION COVE   [MAP 82, p223]

One of the more unusual attractions round here is *The Chocolate Factory* (☎ 01326 241311, 🖥 the-chocolatefactory.co.uk; daily 10am-5pm), between Mullion Cove and Mullion Village. Cornish chocolate is hand made here, and there's a chocolate and gift **shop** and an excellent **café**, too.

    The plushest place to stay in the area is *Mullion Cove Hotel* (☎ 01326-240328, 🖥 mullion-cove.co.uk; 12T/15D/3F; ✒; WI-FI; 🐾; £58-148pp, best rates online) with an unsurpassable location and a reputation for hospitality; it would be a great place for a special break. They run some courses from the hotel including a Coastal Walking week in October with daily walks to places like the Lizard and Porthleven led by an experienced guide; a good introduction for anyone nervous about tackling the coast path. Food is available in the hotel's two restaurants.

    There is also a seasonal café: *Porthmellin Café* (☎ 01326-240941; 10.30am-5pm) that has cream teas, pasties and all-day breakfasts amongst many tempting offerings. A **kiosk** next door has the same opening hours and sells ice-creams and cold drinks.

MULLION   [map p222]

Mullion Mini Market **convenience store** (daily summer 7am-8pm, winter 7am-7pm) on Nansmellyon Rd is well stocked and has a **cash machine** . The **post office** is nearby in the Co-op (daily 7am-11pm), outside which there is another free-to-use **ATM**.

    Nearer to the centre of the village is a Spar **shop** (daily 6am-9pm) which also has a **cash machine** and a **bakery** with a lovely selection of warm pasties, freshly baked bread and fresh coffee. There's also a **pharmacy** (Mon-Fri 9am-6pm, Sat 9am-5.30pm).

Where to stay

Campers should head for the National Trust-managed *Tenerife Farm Caravan and Camping Park* (Map 83; ☎ 01326-240293; hiker & small tent £6-10; Mar-Jan) about a mile beyond Mullion Cove. They also have

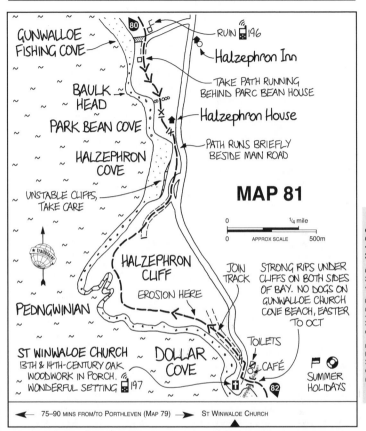

GUNWALLOE ~ FISHING COVE

80

RUIN 📱196

Halzephron Inn

TAKE PATH RUNNING BEHIND PARC BEAN HOUSE

Halzephron House

PATH RUNS BRIEFLY BESIDE MAIN ROAD

BAULK ~ HEAD

PARK BEAN COVE

HALZEPHRON COVE

MAP 81

0   ¼ mile

0   APPROX SCALE   500m

UNSTABLE CLIFFS, TAKE CARE

★ trailblazer

HALZEPHRON CLIFF

EROSION HERE

JOIN TRACK

STRONG RIPS UNDER CLIFFS ON BOTH SIDES OF BAY. NO DOGS ON GUNWALLOE CHURCH COVE BEACH, EASTER TO OCT

PEDNGWINIAN

ST WINWALOE CHURCH
13TH & 14TH-CENTURY OAK WOODWORK IN PORCH.
WONDERFUL SETTING 📱197

DOLLAR COVE

TOILETS

CAFÉ

82

🚩 ☀ SUMMER HOLIDAYS

ROUTE GUIDE AND MAPS

← 75–90 MINS FROM/TO PORTHLEVEN (MAP 79) →   ST WINWALOE CHURCH

❑ St Winwaloe Church, Gunwalloe   [Map 81]

The present church has been restored over the generations but there has been a church here since the 14th century or even earlier. Some of the carved woodwork in the porch has been dated to the 13th century although storms have caused havoc periodically resulting in restoration work by the community determined to keep the faith alive in this inhospitable spot. The burial registers dating from 1716 record shipwrecks and drownings along the coast – a Spanish ship with a cargo of silver dollars was wrecked just to the north in the 1780s – and these have been the object of many searches ever since, so far without success. Dollar Cove (also known as Jangye Ryn) preserves the legend, or truth, of the incident.

St Winwaloe, whose statue greets the visitor to the church, was an abbot who came from Brittany, France, in the 6th century and founded the first sacred place on this site which has come to be known as the Church of the Storms.

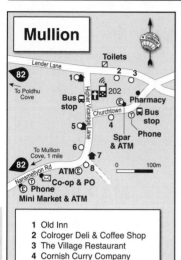

Mullion

To Poldhu Cove

82

Lender Lane

Bus stop

Higher Vicarage Lane

Churchtown

Pharmacy

Bus stop

Spar & ATM

Phone

To Mullion Cove, 1 mile

82

Nansmellyon Rd

ATM

Co-op & PO

Phone

Mini Market & ATM

Toilets

202

0   100m

1 Old Inn
2 Colroger Deli & Coffee Shop
3 The Village Restaurant
4 Cornish Curry Company
5 Mounts Bay Inn
6 The Galleon Fish & Chips
7 Old Vicarage B&B
8 Crafty Slice Coffee Shop

camping pods for two adults (£30-45) and up to four adults (same price).

B&B choices include the spacious *Old Vicarage* (☎ 01326-240898, ☐ bandbmullion@hotmail.com; 2D/2F; £43-45pp, sgl occ £43-50), a lovely old house in the heart of the village, which welcomes walkers and accepts single-night bookings. It is said that Sir Arthur Conan Doyle stayed here and the house is mentioned in the Sherlock Holmes story *The Devil's Foot*.

The two pubs here also do B&B; rooms at *Old Inn* (☎ 01326-240240, ☐ oldinnmullion.co.uk; 2T/3D; from £37.50pp, sgl occ from £60) are light and airy; while *Mounts Bay Inn* (☎ 01326-240221, ☐ mountsbaymullion.co.uk; 1T/

3D/1F; WI-FI; from £42.50pp, sgl occ from £70) has sea views.

Where to eat and drink
The two pubs in Mullion both do food. *Mounts Bay Inn* (see Where to stay; food Mon-Sat noon-2pm & 6-9pm, Sun noon-2.30pm & 6-9.30pm) is a lively place with a beer garden, and is popular with both locals and holidaymakers. Mains include steaks and burgers (£10-20) but there are also vegetarian options and specials. *Old Inn* (see Where to stay; daily noon-2.30pm & 6-9pm) is equally busy and has an interesting menu of daily specials including grilled mackerel for starters. Beers on tap include St Austell's Tribute, HSD, Proper Job and IPA.

Crafty Slice Coffee Shop (☎ 01326-240381; Mon, Tue & Thur 9.30am-5pm, Fri to 4.30pm, Wed to 9pm, Sat 10am-4pm) has homemade desserts and weekly specials as well as a pizza night (all pizzas eat-in £8.50, takeaway £7.50) on a Wednesday. *Colroger Deli & Coffee Shop* (☎ 01326-240833; ✾; Easter-Sep Mon-Sat 9.30am-4pm) is a traditional café which will do you a picnic for the trail; if you ring in advance they can prepare one for you to collect. They are also refreshingly dog-friendly. The wonderfully named *The Village Restaurant* (☎ 01326-241007, ☐ thevillagerestaurantmullion.co.uk; Tue-Sat 6.30-9pm) specialises in fresh fish, seafood and steaks. Evening mains cost £14.50-20.50.

The village also boasts an excellent fish & chip restaurant: *The Galleon* (Mon-Sat 11am-9pm) does all-day breakfasts and proper coffee as well as chip-shop fair. For homemade takeaway curries *Cornish Curry Company* (☎ 01326-240016; Tue-Thur 5.30-8pm) serves five types of curry (chicken or prawn £6.50, veg £6) plus a special.

Transport
First's No 37 **bus** stops here (see pp52-6).

❑ Where to stay: the details
Unless specified, B&B-style accommodation is either en suite or has private facilities; ✿ means at least one room has a bath; ✾ signifies that dogs are welcome in at least one room but always by prior arrangement, an additional charge may also be payable (see pp336-8); WI-FI means wi-fi is available. See also p79.

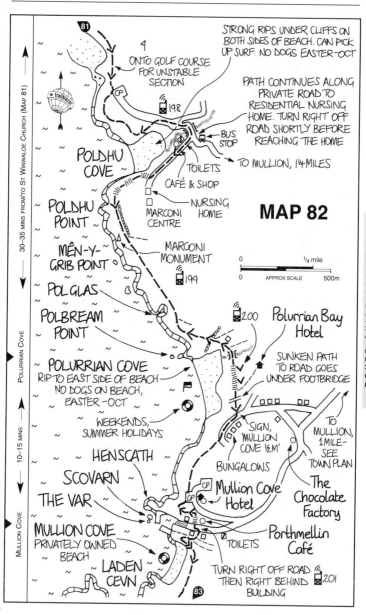

81

ONTO GOLF COURSE
FOR UNSTABLE
SECTION

CP

📱198

STRONG RIPS UNDER CLIFFS ON
BOTH SIDES OF BEACH. CAN PICK
UP SURF. NO DOGS EASTER-OCT

PATH CONTINUES ALONG
PRIVATE ROAD TO
RESIDENTIAL NURSING
HOME. TURN RIGHT OFF
ROAD SHORTLY BEFORE
REACHING THE HOME

BUS
STOP

TO MULLION, 1¼ MILES

POLDHU
COVE

TOILETS

CAFÉ & SHOP

NURSING
HOME

MARCONI
CENTRE

MAP 82

POLDHU
POINT

MÊN-Y-
GRIB POINT

MARCONI
MONUMENT

📱199

POL GLAS

0   ¼ mile

0   500m
APPROX SCALE

POLBREAM
POINT

📱200

Polurrian Bay
Hotel

POLURRIAN COVE
RIP TO EAST SIDE OF BEACH
NO DOGS ON BEACH,
EASTER-OCT

SUNKEN PATH
TO ROAD GOES
UNDER FOOTBRIDGE

WEEKENDS,
SUMMER HOLIDAYS

SIGN,
'MULLION
COVE ½M'

TO
MULLION,
1 MILE-
SEE
TOWN PLAN

HENSCATH

BUNGALOWS

SCOVARN

Mullion Cove
Hotel

The
Chocolate
Factory

THE VAR

CP
CP

MULLION COVE
PRIVATELY OWNED
BEACH

Porthmellin
Café

TOILETS

LADEN
CEVN

TURN RIGHT OFF ROAD
THEN RIGHT BEHIND
BUILDING

📱201

83

30-35 MINS FROM/TO ST WINWALOE CHURCH (MAP 81)

POLURRIAN COVE

10-15 MINS

MULLION COVE

ROUTE GUIDE AND MAPS

❏ **The Marconi monument**   **[Map 82, p223]**

Walkers passing the stone obelisk on the cliffs near Poldhu might do well to pause and consider what it commemorates. Guglielmo Marconi chose this spot from which to transmit the very first message ever to cross the Atlantic by wireless. On December 12th 1901, a morse signal sent from a station on Angrouse Cliff was received by Marconi in Newfoundland. Twenty years later the world's first short-wave beam signals were transmitted from the same spot and history was made. Poldhu became a research centre and when it closed in 1934 Marconi gave the site to the National Trust (NT) and erected the memorial.

The other significant radio station, Marconi's Lizard Wireless Station (see Map 86, p229) was also bought by the NT and can be seen along the coast path just north of the Lizard lighthouse.

MULLION COVE TO LIZARD POINT   [MAPS 82-86]

The next **6 miles (10km, 2½-3¼hrs)** are along exposed cliff tops giving some of the best coastal walking in South Cornwall with superb views of the treacherous rocks on which so many ships have been wrecked. The terrain underfoot can get boggy at times due to poor drainage.

You might spot the New Forest ponies brought in by the National Trust to crop the gorse, clearing the ground to allow unique and fragile plant species to come through.

Kynance Cove is a delightful spot where the intrusion of summer visitors has not spoiled a unique cove that deserves a longer stay than most walkers allow it. *Kynance Café* (see Map 85, p227) is open in the main season.

As you get nearer to Lizard Point the coastline becomes increasingly spectacular and if this is your first visit it's hard not to be impressed by its wildness and beauty. The Lizard has been called Cornwall's big toe dipped into the ocean. Rare clovers and heathers grow here and nowhere else, and some exotics such as gunneras and tree ferns flourish in the sub-tropical conditions.

After **Pentreath Beach** several paths lead away from the coast to Lizard Village (see below) where you may have decided to spend the night or get a pasty. The temptation is to take the first path in and the last path out but this would mean missing **Lizard Point.** The shortest route into **Lizard Village** is from Housel Cove but it's only about 15 minutes along the path from near Shag Rock. Alternatively, there's a pretty walk from Church Cove past thatched-roofed houses.

LIZARD VILLAGE   [Map p228]

Lizard Village has a somewhat Bohemian feel to it, making the passing traveller feel very much at home. You'll see brightly painted buildings dotted around the place, home-made sculptures on front lawns and, if you stay at Henry's Campsite (see p226), broods of chickens running about the place.

The distinctive, 260-year-old twin towers of *Lizard Lighthouse* (☎ 01326-

290222, 🖳 trinityhouse.co.uk; Apr-Oct Sun-Thur 11am-5pm; Heritage Centre £3.50, plus Lighthouse Tour £8) mark the most southerly point of mainland Britain, where there is a heritage centre for visitors, who can also sign up for a guided tour of the complex.

Lizard Village has all the services you are likely to need. There is a **post office**

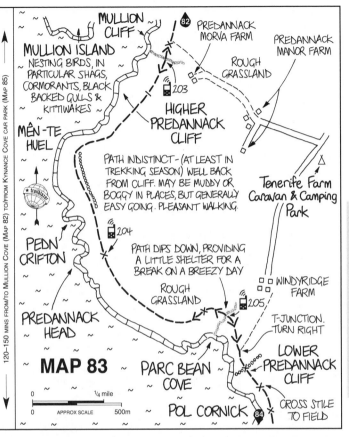

MULLION CLIFF

82 PREDANNACK MORVA FARM

PREDANNACK MANOR FARM

MULLION ISLAND

NESTING BIRDS, IN PARTICULAR SHAGS, CORMORANTS, BLACK BACKED GULLS & KITTIWAKES

ROUGH GRASSLAND

203

HIGHER PREDANNACK CLIFF

MÊN-TE HUEL

trailblazer

PATH INDISTINCT - (AT LEAST IN TREKKING SEASON) WELL BACK FROM CLIFF. MAY BE MUDDY OR BOGGY IN PLACES, BUT GENERALLY EASY GOING. PLEASANT WALKING.

Tenerife Farm Caravan & Camping Park

204

PEDN CRIFTON

PATH DIPS DOWN, PROVIDING A LITTLE SHELTER FOR A BREAK ON A BREEZY DAY

ROUGH GRASSLAND

WINDYRIDGE FARM

205

PREDANNACK HEAD

T-JUNCTION. TURN RIGHT

MAP 83

PARC BEAN COVE

LOWER PREDANNACK CLIFF

0   1/4 mile

0   500m
APPROX SCALE

POL CORNICK

84

CROSS STILE TO FIELD

120-150 MINS FROM/TO MULLION COVE (MAP 82) TO/FROM KYNANCE COVE CAR PARK (MAP 85)

ROUTE GUIDE AND MAPS

❏ **Geology of The Lizard**

Even the most ungeologically minded can't miss the colourful serpentine rock around the Lizard; great streaks of green cliffs reminiscent of a snake's skin giving the stone its name. Spanning 20 square miles, this is the largest outcrop of serpentine in mainland Britain. It is actually part of the Earth's mantle, which would normally be about 20km, on average, below the surface. Local sculptors still carve ornaments from the serpentine rock which reached their height of popularity during the Victorian era, although they're probably a little too heavy to carry away in your pack.

Lizard Point isn't just famed as the most southerly point of mainland Britain. The offshore islets from Lizard Point are 500 million years old, a leftover crumb of the collision between the super-continents of Gondwanaland and Euramerica.

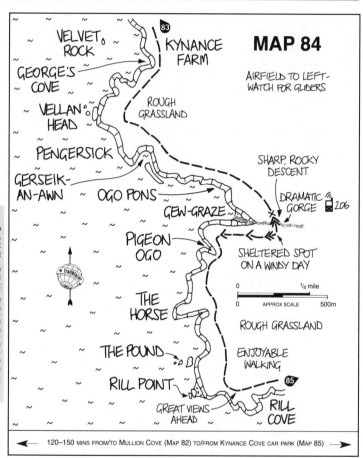

MAP 84

VELVET ROCK

GEORGE'S COVE

VELLAN HEAD

PENGERSICK

GERSEIK-AN-AWN

OGO PONS

KYNANCE FARM

83

ROUGH GRASSLAND

AIRFIELD TO LEFT - WATCH FOR GLIDERS

SHARP, ROCKY DESCENT

DRAMATIC GORGE 206

GEW-GRAZE

PIGEON OGO

SHELTERED SPOT ON A WINDY DAY

THE HORSE

ROUGH GRASSLAND

ENJOYABLE WALKING

THE POUND

RILL POINT

GREAT VIEWS AHEAD

RILL COVE

85

0   ¼ mile
0   APPROX SCALE   500m

trailblaze

ROUTE GUIDE AND MAPS

← 120–150 MINS FROM/TO MULLION COVE (MAP 82) TO/FROM KYNANCE COVE CAR PARK (MAP 85) →

(Mon-Thur 9am-noon & 1-5pm, Fri 9am-noon, Sat 9am-12.30pm), while Steps **convenience store** (Mon-Fri 8.15am-7.30pm, Sat from 9am, Sun 10am-7.30pm) is the main grocery shop and also has a **cash machine** (£1.50 charge). There's a nice **deli-cum-greengrocers**, C&E Retallack (Mon-Fri 8am-5pm, Sat 8am-1pm), although everyone gets their pasties up the road from Ann Muller at *Ann's Pasties* (☎ 01326-290889, 🖳 annspasties.co.uk; Mon-Sat 9am-5pm).

Where to stay

Campers need look no further than *Henry's Campsite* (☎ 01326-290596, 🖳 henryscampsite.co.uk; WI-FI; 🐾; hiker & tent £10), still our favourite campsite on the whole of the Cornwall Coast Path. Like staying in a small farmyard commune, there's a wonderful atmosphere: pigs, chickens, goats and alpacas keep the kids amused, while parents home in on the fresh coffee and croissants served for breakfast, or the bottles of real ale and Cornish cider sold in the well-stocked shop. You can buy firewood and rent fire braziers, and there's a communal fire pit for everyone to share. Oh, and the sea-view sunsets are stunning. Don't forget to say you're a walker when you call ahead; they almost always find room for walkers even if the campsite is otherwise full.

Occupying the buildings of a former Victorian hotel, at **YHA Lizard** (see Map 86; ☎ 01326-291145, 🖳 www.yha.org .uk/hostel/lizard-point; 28 beds, from £25pp; Mar-Dec only) there is a huge self-catering kitchen and oodles of space throughout. Booking ahead is recommended, although there are usually one or two dorm beds available.

For **B&B The Caerthillian** (☎ 01326-290019, 🖳 thecaerthillian.co.uk; 1S/1T/ 3D; ☞; WI-FI; 🐾; from £33pp, sgl occ from £45) is a lovely blue and white painted house in the heart of the village. Alternatively, enjoy panoramic sea views, and freshly baked bread for breakfast, at **Hellarcher Farm** (☎ 01326-291188, 🖳 hellarcherfarm.co.uk; 1S/2D; £28-40pp); they welcome one-night-stay walkers.

The Top House Inn (☎ 01326-290974, 🖳 thetophouselizard.co.uk; 5D/ 2T/1F; WI-FI; from £50pp, sgl occ rate on request) is a friendly local pub with very comfortable B&B rooms.

Where to eat and drink

For pub food, head to **The Top House Inn** (see Where to stay; food daily noon-8pm, Fri & Sat to 8.30pm) which does good-value

MAP 85

0 — 1/4 mile
0 — 500m APPROX SCALE

GREAT VIEWS OF THE ISLAND

AT HIGH TIDE WHEN YOU CAN'T CROSS THE BEACH, TAKE THE ROAD - IT'S ONLY A SHORT DIVERSION

KYNANCE CLIFF

Kynance Café (SEASONAL)

TOILETS

84

GRAVELLED PATH

★ trailblazer

THE BELLOWS

CP 207

ASPARAGUS ISLAND

GREAT VIEWS

NANTIVET ROCK
LOOK FOR GREEN SERPENTINE ROCK

GULL ROCK

KYNANCE COVE

86

THE BISHOP

ENYS YEAN

LION ROCK

AT LOW TIDE IT'S POSSIBLE TO EXPLORE THE ISLANDS AND CAVES. ALWAYS BE AWARE OF THE INCOMING TIDE, PARTICULARLY IF ON THIS SIDE - CAN HAVE VERY DANGEROUS SURF & RIPS

NO DOGS ON BEACH EASTER-OCT

← 120-150 MINS FROM/TO MULLION COVE (MAP 82) | KYNANCE COVE CAR PARK | 35-45 MINS TO/FROM LIZARD POINT (MAP 86) →

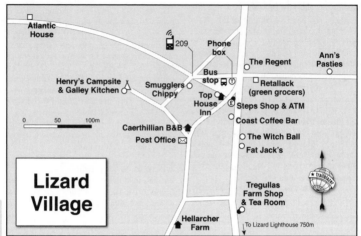

Lizard Village

pub grub and has Tribute and Proper Job on tap. Nearby, *Smugglers* (☎ 01326-290763; Mon-Sat 1-8pm, Sun 1-7pm) is the place to go for fish & chips.

Also close by, you'll find plenty of outdoor seating at *Coast Coffee Bar* (daily 9.30am-11.30am & noon-7pm); good for breakfasts, cream teas and sandwiches, but with a decent evening menu too.

The Regent (☎ 01326-290483; daily 9.30am-7pm) serves an extensive reasonably priced menu including cream teas (£5.25); the homemade cake portions are probably the largest along the whole Cornish coast. Between village and coast *Tregullas Farm Shop and Tea Rooms* (☎ 01326-290122) dishes up some fabulous Cornish breakfasts (9-11am; £7.50).

The Witchball (☎ 01326-290662, 🖳 witchball.co.uk; Mar-Dec daily noon-3pm & 6-9.30pm, Jan & Feb Thur-Sun noon-3pm & 7-9pm, booking advised) is an unusual place serving imaginative dishes on a changing menu. If you like things spicy, don't miss the Voodoo Burger (£14.50). They also serve Cadgwith Crabber Ale, brewed by Cornish Chough Brewery right here in the village.

In case you were wondering, a 'witch ball' is a hollow sphere of glass hung in a cottage window to ward off evil spirits. Next door, *Fat Jack's* is a café serving sandwiches, ice-cream and coffee.

Galley Kitchen (daily 6-9pm) at Henry's campsite (see Where to stay) has a new menu everyday which may include Indian-style curries (£10), or spicy chicken, or Quorn noodles (£10). They also have pizzas and burgers and drinks can be bought from the campsite shop. For something a little different this is the place to go.

The most southerly café on mainland Britain, *Polpeor Café* (see Map 86; ☎ 01326-290939; summer daily 10am-7.30pm or earlier if quiet, winter 11am-3pm) at Lizard Point has one of the best terraces anywhere, with a view over the rocks and sea that is second to none. Table service is on the menu as is a 'bring your own wine' policy in the evenings. Come here to catch the last rays of the setting sun; you'd be hard-pressed to imagine anywhere more evocative.

Transport

[See also pp52-6] First Kernow's No 37 **bus** service calls here.

For a **taxi**, ring Mullion Taxis (☎ 07415-773773).

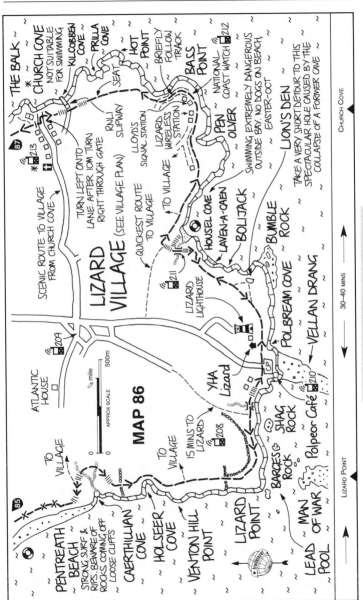

MAP 86

APPROX SCALE

¼ mile

0   500m

PENTREATH BEACH
STRONG SURF & RIPS. BEWARE OF ROCKS COMING OFF LOOSE CLIFFS

85

TO VILLAGE

CAERTHILLIAN COVE

HOLSEER COVE

VENTON HILL POINT

LIZARD POINT

LEAD POOL

MAN OF WAR

BARGES ROCK

SHAG ROCK

Polpeor Café

15 MINS TO LIZARD

208

YHA Lizard

CP

210

VELLAN DRANG

POLBREAM COVE

BUMBLE ROCK

TO VILLAGE

LIZARD LIGHTHOUSE

209

ATLANTIC HOUSE

SCENIC ROUTE TO VILLAGE FROM CHURCH COVE

LIZARD VILLAGE
(SEE VILLAGE PLAN)

TURN LEFT ONTO LANE AFTER 10M TURN RIGHT THROUGH GATE

QUICKEST ROUTE TO VILLAGE

211

TO VILLAGE

LLOYD'S SIGNAL STATION

LIZARD WIRELESS STATION

RNLI SLIPWAY

SEAT

213

87

THE BALK

CHURCH COVE
NOT SUITABLE FOR SWIMMING

KILCOBBEN COVE

PRILLA COVE

HOT POINT

BRIEFLY FOLLOW TRACK

BASS POINT

NATIONAL COAST WATCH 212

PEN OLVER

HOUSEL COVE

LAVEN-A-CAEN

BOLJACK

SWIMMING EXTREMELY DANGEROUS OUTSIDE BAY. NO DOGS ON BEACH EASTER–OCT

LION'S DEN

TAKE A VERY SHORT DETOUR TO THIS SPECTACULAR HOLE CAUSED BY THE COLLAPSE OF A FORMER CAVE

LIZARD POINT TO CADGWITH COVE [MAPS 86-87]

This **4-mile (6km, 1½-1¾hrs)** stretch is quite popular and no wonder, given the superb views back to the lighthouse. The blue-ish serpentine rock can be seen on the path and on the slabs used for the stiles. It becomes quite slippery when wet, and even on dry days it is easy to slip where there has been constant polishing by boots. Serpentine provides the craftsmen with the raw material for their ash-trays and lighthouse ornaments that you can buy in the gift shops in the area and in Lizard Village you can watch them at work.

CADGWITH [MAP 87]

This tiny village is a collection of lobster pots, fishing floats and boats clustered around the one pub, *Cadgwith Cove Inn* (☎ 01326-290513, 🖳 cadgwithcoveinn.com; 1S/2D/2D or T/1Tr, some en suite; WI-FI; 🐾; £30.35-50pp) an intriguing survivor from a simpler age, with newly refurbished B&B rooms. On a Friday you could be in for a sing-song since the Cadgwith Singers meet to work on their sea shanties. The food (daily noon-9pm) includes standard pub fare, plus dishes such as moules marinière, seafood massaman curry and Cadgwith crab sandwiches. The beers are Betty Stoggs, Doom Bar and Otter.

Next door, down the hill, fish is also the speciality at *The Old Cellars* (☎ 01326-290727; Easter-Oct Mon-Sat 11.30am-3pm & 6-8.30pm, Sun 11am-4pm), perhaps

unsurprisingly given its proximity to the harbour. You can also enjoy cakes, cream teas and coffee outside the usual food-serving hours, as you sit amongst the hanging baskets and nesting swallows of the courtyard.

If you just fancy grabbing a snack on the go, you can buy takeaway pasties, crois-sants, cake and ice-cream at *The Watch House* (🖳 thewatchhouse.co.uk), which also serves tea and coffee as well as sou-venirs, from what is the village's 200-year-old former customs and excise house.

The nearest campsite is two miles fur-ther on at Kennack Sands (see p232).

The **bus** doesn't visit Cadgwith; instead, walk half a mile inland to **Ruan Minor** and get First's No 37 (The Lizard to Helston) bus. [See also pp52-6].

CADGWITH COVE TO COVERACK [MAPS 87-91]

The next **7 miles (11km, 2½-3hrs)** are over a mixed terrain that makes for var-ied walking from quite dull to exhilarating. After you leave Cadgwith the cliffs are relatively low-lying and the path traverses country thick with blackthorn, gorse and bracken. You'll soon pass the ruins of the **Serpentine works**, a once-thriving Victorian serpentine rock factory. Later you cross the beach at **Kennack Sands** (see p232), which has two beach cafés, before continuing with a sharp descent at **Downas Cove** followed by the inevitable climb up out of it.

A further descent has to be tackled at **Beagles Hole**, from where it's a skip around **Chynhalls Point** followed by an easy amble into the secretive little har-bour village of Coverack.

❏ **Important note – walking times**
Unless otherwise specified, **all times in this book refer only to the time spent walk-ing**. You will need to add 20-30% to allow for rests, photography, checking the map, drinking water etc. When planning the day's hike count on 5-7 hours' actual walking.

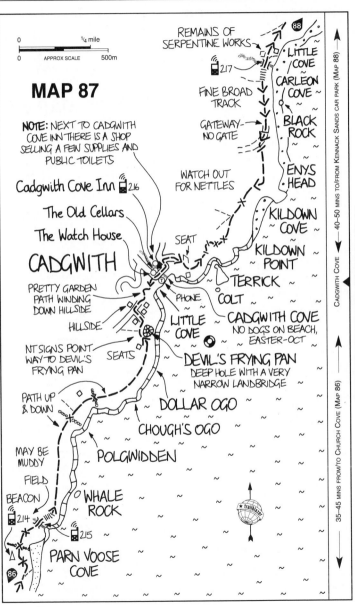

40–50 MINS TO/FROM KENNACK SANDS CAR PARK (MAP 88) →

CADGWITH COVE

35–45 MINS FROM/TO CHURCH COVE (MAP 86)

REMAINS OF SERPENTINE WORKS

88

LITTLE COVE

217

CARLEON COVE

FINE BROAD TRACK

GATEWAY — NO GATE

BLACK ROCK

WATCH OUT FOR NETTLES

ENYS HEAD

MAP 87

NOTE: NEXT TO CADGWITH COVE INN THERE IS A SHOP SELLING A FEW SUPPLIES AND PUBLIC TOILETS

Cadgwith Cove Inn 216

The Old Cellars

The Watch House

CADGWITH

PRETTY GARDEN PATH WINDING DOWN HILLSIDE

HILLSIDE

NT SIGNS POINT WAY TO DEVIL'S FRYING PAN

PATH UP & DOWN

MAY BE MUDDY

FIELD

BEACON

214

215

PARN VOOSE COVE

86

KILDOWN COVE

KILDOWN POINT

SEAT

TERRICK

PHONE

COLT

LITTLE COVE

CADGWITH COVE

NO DOGS ON BEACH, EASTER–OCT

SEATS

DEVIL'S FRYING PAN

DEEP HOLE WITH A VERY NARROW LANDBRIDGE

DOLLAR OGO

CHOUGH'S OGO

POLGWIDDEN

WHALE ROCK

0   ¼ mile

0   APPROX SCALE   500m

★ trailblazer

KENNACK SANDS   [MAP 88]

The beach here is popular with surfers.

At **Silver Sands Camp Site** (☎ 01326-290631, 🖥 silversandsholidaypark.co.uk; 2 people & small tent £13-20; early Apr to mid Sep; 🐾) coastal walkers are always

welcome and you can exercise dogs in the campsite's one-acre field.

There's also **The Beach Hut** (Easter-Oct; daily 8.30am-7pm) and **Kennack Sands Beach Café** (daily 9am-6pm) with teacakes, scones and other Cornish delights.

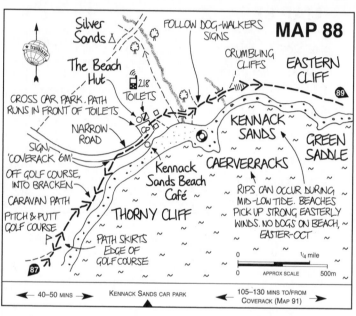

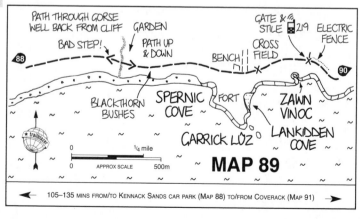

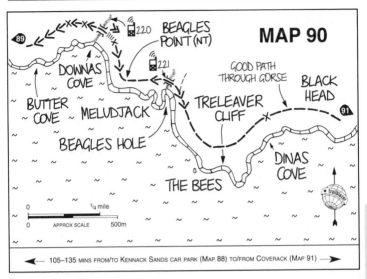

COVERACK [MAP 91, p234]

The foreshore at Coverack has an unusual claim to fame as one of only three places in Britain where you can see exposed *Moho*, the geological boundary between the Earth's crust and the Earth's mantle. The rocks you see at the surface here would have been 5km underground 380 million years ago. The Serpentine rocks to the south of the beach were the deepest, and once formed part of the Earth's mantle. The Gabbro rocks to the north of the beach once formed part of the Earth's crust, above the mantle. The beach is effectively the transition zone between the two – the *Moho* – and contains a jumble of intermingling rocks from both the mantle and the crust. Unsurprisingly perhaps, Coverack goes about its business in blissful ignorance of such matters, concerning itself more with coping with the huge influx of holidaymakers in the summer. It is one of the nicest little villages in the whole of this part of the coast – one with a great community spirit – and has avoided the seaside commercialisation of many other places.

Coverack Village Stores (Mon-Sat 8.30am-5pm, except Wed to 12.30pm) is good for sandwiches, snacks and general supplies.

Where to stay

You can find accommodation listings, and other information and news about the village on the community-run website 🖳 coverack.org.uk.

YHA Coverack (☎ 01326-280687, 🖳 yha.org.uk/hostel/coverack; 33 beds, in dorms & private rooms; from £25pp; Apr-Oct) is a splendid Victorian country house, high up on School Hill; it's well-run and welcoming with a bar, self-catering kitchen and laundry area. There is space for **camping** (£14) in the orchard behind. Campers have separate shower and kitchen facilities, but can use the main house too. They also have two bell tents (£99; sleeps 5) although these will need to be booked months in advance. If the YHA campsite is full, the nearest **campsite** is a mile further up the road at *Little Trevothan* (off Map 91; ☎ 01326-280260, 🖳 littletrevothan.co.uk; hiker and tent £8.50; Easter-Oct).

For **B&B**, and you may even get a welcome gin and tonic on arrival, consider

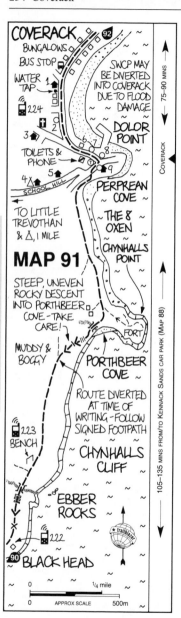

COVERACK – MAP KEY

Where to stay
1 The Bay Hotel
3 Fernleigh
4 YHA Coverack
5 Boak House
9 Paris Hotel

Where to eat and drink
2 Harbour Lights Café
7 Archie's Loft
8 The Lifeboat House
9 Paris Hotel

Other
6 Coverack Village Stores

swish **Boak House** (☎ 01326-280329, 🖳 bridgetyoung@hotmail.co.uk; 3D/1T; 🗪; WI-FI; 🐾; from £40pp, sgl occ £50, plus £5 for one-night stays). The rooms are light and bright and the view from the front of the house is fantastic.

Fernleigh (☎ 01326-280626, 🖳 fernleighcoverack.co.uk; 1T/2D; 🗪; WI-FI; 🐾; from £37.50pp, sgl occ £50), on Chymbloth Way, is a nicely appointed establishment with the added appeal of an evening meal (£13.95 for two courses), if requested in advance. The owners are very welcoming.

You can also stay at the only pub in the village, **Paris Hotel** (☎ 01326-280258, 🖳 pariscoverack.com; 2T/2D/2Tr; WI-FI; 🐾; £30-45pp, sgl occ £40-60), named after the ocean liner, the *SS Paris*, which was wrecked on the headland in 1899.

At the top end of the scale, overlooking the beach, is the charming **Bay Hotel** (☎ 01326-280464, 🖳 thebayhotel.co.uk; 12D, 2 suites; Mar-Nov; 🗪; WI-FI; 🐾; £60-165pp, sgl occ 20% discount from room rate) where comfort and a good welcome are assured.

Where to eat and drink
Food-wise, there are several places in town but Coverack's humble chippy is the best known. The award-winning **Lifeboat House**

(☎ 01326-281400, 🖥 thelifeboathouse.co
.uk; restaurant Tue-Sat 10am-8pm, Sun
10am-4pm, takeaway Mon-Fri noon-8pm,
Sun noon-4pm) is as good as ever; the haddock & chips are fantastic, and the sea
views are sublime. You can sit in at the
restaurant, which has its own bar with
Cornish ales on tap, or grab a takeaway and
sit on the rocks outside.

Paris Hotel (see Where to stay; daily
noon-2.30pm & 6.45am-9pm) is also a nice
place to eat, with lovely sea views from its
restaurant extension. The menu changes
regularly but seafood is pre-eminent,
amongst other pub-grub standards.

Archie's Loft (10am-7.30pm, limited
hours out of season) is a tiny tea room with

Roskilly's ice-cream, toasted sandwiches,
pizzas and fresh coffee; ideal for a quick
snack before hitting the trail.

Further along is a pleasant café: the
excellent *Harbour Lights* (☎ 01326-
280612, 🖥 harbourlightscafecoverack.co
.uk; Tue-Sat 10am-5pm, Sun-4pm, hours
may differ depending on the season). The
owner and head chef is a local Coverack
girl who tries to source as much produce as
possible from the immediate area.

Transport
[See also p52-6] First Kernow's No 36 **bus**
service calls at Coverack. The bus turns at
the bend north of the village, right on the
coast path.

COVERACK TO PORTHALLOW   [MAPS 91-94]

This **5-mile (8km, 1¾-2¼hrs)** section leaves Coverack along a lane lined with
bungalows with gardens full of sub-tropical plants that you won't see at home.
You then follow the shore through fields to the monstrous obstacle that is **Dean
Quarry**. The way through the quarry is well signposted; be sure to follow the
signs carefully. Once past the quarry the path is taken inland; the former official
route was abandoned to avoid more of the quarry's workings as well as some
extensive flood damage.

Porthoustock (Map 93) has no services other than toilets but there's an
excellent café (Fat Apples) and a pleasant pub (Five Pilchards Inn) waiting for
you at **Porthallow**.

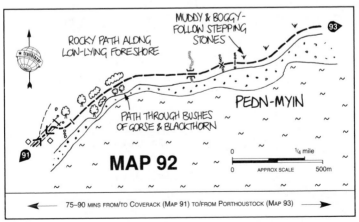

MUDDY & BOGGY-
FOLLOW STEPPING
STONES

ROCKY PATH ALONG
LOW-LYING FORESHORE

★ trailblazer

PEDN-MYIN

PATH THROUGH BUSHES
OF GORSE & BLACKTHORN

MAP 92

0 _____ ¼ mile
0 _____ 500m
APPROX SCALE

←——— 75-90 MINS FROM/TO COVERACK (MAP 91) TO/FROM PORTHOUSTOCK (MAP 93) ———→

ROUTE GUIDE AND MAPS

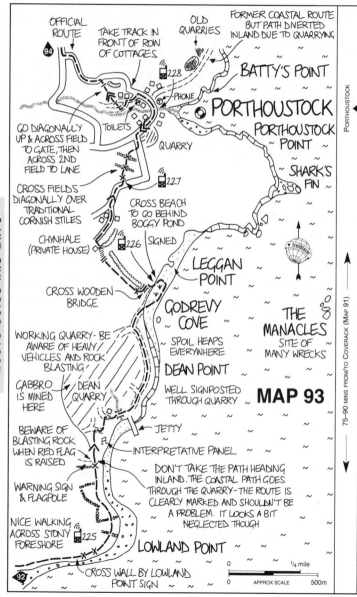

ROUTE GUIDE AND MAPS

OFFICIAL ROUTE

94

TAKE TRACK IN FRONT OF ROW OF COTTAGES

OLD QUARRIES

FORMER COASTAL ROUTE BUT PATH DIVERTED INLAND DUE TO QUARRYING

BATTY'S POINT

228

PHONE

PORTHOUSTOCK

TOILETS

PORTHOUSTOCK POINT

QUARRY

GO DIAGONALLY UP & ACROSS FIELD TO GATE, THEN ACROSS 2ND FIELD TO LANE

SHARK'S FIN

227

CROSS FIELDS DIAGONALLY OVER TRADITIONAL CORNISH STILES

CROSS BEACH TO GO BEHIND BOGGY POND

CHYNHALE (PRIVATE HOUSE)

226 SIGNED

CROSS WOODEN BRIDGE

LEGGAN POINT

GODREVY COVE

THE MANACLES SITE OF MANY WRECKS

WORKING QUARRY- BE AWARE OF HEAVY VEHICLES AND ROCK BLASTING

SPOIL HEAPS EVERYWHERE

DEAN POINT

GABBRO IS MINED HERE

DEAN QUARRY

WELL SIGNPOSTED THROUGH QUARRY

MAP 93

BEWARE OF BLASTING ROCK WHEN RED FLAG IS RAISED

JETTY

INTERPRETATIVE PANEL

DON'T TAKE THE PATH HEADING INLAND. THE COASTAL PATH GOES THROUGH THE QUARRY- THE ROUTE IS CLEARLY MARKED AND SHOULDN'T BE A PROBLEM. IT LOOKS A BIT NEGLECTED THOUGH

WARNING SIGN & FLAGPOLE

NICE WALKING ACROSS STONY FORESHORE

225

LOWLAND POINT

92

CROSS WALL BY LOWLAND POINT SIGN

0   1/4 mile

0   APPROX SCALE   500m

PORTHOUSTOCK

75-90 MINS FROM/to COVERACK (MAP 91)

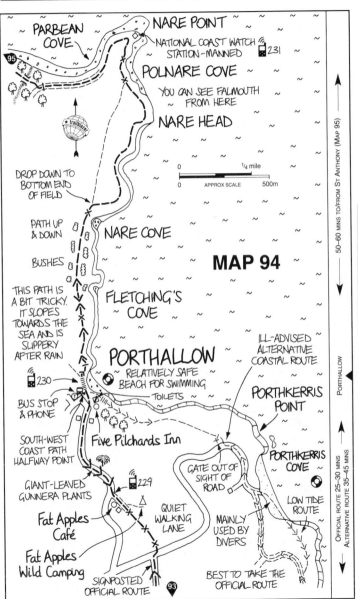

PARBEAN COVE

NARE POINT

NATIONAL COAST WATCH STATION - MANNED 📱 231

POLNARE COVE

YOU CAN SEE FALMOUTH FROM HERE

NARE HEAD

0   ¼ mile

0   APPROX SCALE   500m

DROP DOWN TO BOTTOM END OF FIELD

PATH UP & DOWN

NARE COVE

BUSHES

THIS PATH IS A BIT TRICKY. IT SLOPES TOWARDS THE SEA AND IS SLIPPERY AFTER RAIN

FLETCHING'S COVE

MAP 94

📱 230

BUS STOP & PHONE

SOUTH-WEST COAST PATH HALFWAY POINT

GIANT-LEAVED GUNNERA PLANTS

Fat Apples Café

Fat Apples Wild Camping

SIGNPOSTED OFFICIAL ROUTE

PORTHALLOW

RELATIVELY SAFE BEACH FOR SWIMMING

TOILETS

Five Pilchards Inn

📱 229

QUIET WALKING LANE

ILL-ADVISED ALTERNATIVE COASTAL ROUTE

PORTHKERRIS POINT

PORTHKERRIS COVE

GATE OUT OF SIGHT OF ROAD

LOW TIDE ROUTE

MAINLY USED BY DIVERS

BEST TO TAKE THE OFFICIAL ROUTE

93

95

trailblazer

50-60 MINS TO/FROM St ANTHONY (MAP 95)

PORTHALLOW

OFFICIAL ROUTE 25-30 MINS

ALTERNATIVE ROUTE 35-45 MINS

ROUTE GUIDE AND MAPS

❏ **The Manacles** [Map 93, p236]

This treacherous reef lies a mile out to sea from Dean Quarry, dangerously close to the shipping lanes in and out of Falmouth. Hundreds of people have lost their lives here. In 1809 two ships were wrecked on the same night: *HMS Dispatch*, which was carrying troops, and *HMS Primrose*; only eight survived the tragedy. Many shipwreck victims are buried in the churchyard at St Keverne.

More positively, The Manacles provide good fishing grounds for boats from Porthallow and Porthoustock who mainly use handlines to catch bass here.

PORTHALLOW [MAP 94, p237]

Porthallow may seem to have little of interest to the visitor. However, for coastal walkers the place holds a very special significance, for here is a sculpture, unveiled in 2009, to celebrate the halfway point on the South-West Coast Path – it's 315 miles (517km) from here to Minehead in Somerset, and 315 miles to South Haven Point near Poole in Dorset. On one side of the sculpture is a list of flora and fauna that may be seen on the path, from orchids to oystercatchers, while on the other side is a poem, *Fading Voices*, by writer Stephen Hall, which commemorates the life of Pralla (aka Porthallow) and coastal Cornwall in general.

On the approach into the village, you'll pass the wonderful *Fat Apples Café* (☎ 01326-281559, 🖳 fatapplescafe@gmail .com; Easter to end Oct 9.30am-5pm), which does breakfasts, fresh coffee, sandwiches and homemade cakes. They also offer **wild camping** (£7 per tent) in a forested area nearby. There are plans to introduce basic dormitory-style accommodation in one of the barns.

In the village itself, *The Five Pilchards Inn* (☎ 01326-280256, or ☎ 01326-280751, 🖳 thefivepilchards.co.uk; 3D or T; from £40pp, sgl occ £55), serves good pub **food** (noon-2pm & 6-9pm) and does **B&B**.

PORTHALLOW TO HELFORD [MAPS 94-96]

The next **7¼ miles (11.75km, 1¾-2¼hrs)** are fairly straightforward, though the path can be slippery after rain. Once past **Nare Point**, where there is a National Coastwatch Station manned by volunteers, the path encounters a new obstacle, the inlet of **Gillan Creek**. Here you are faced with a choice. Since the creek can only be forded one hour either side of low tide you will either have to wait for the tide to go out or take the path round the estuary, a walk of 40-45 mins. There is one other possibility. An enterprising boatman in **St Anthony-in-Meneage** offers to ferry people across for £3 per person (minimum £5 per trip) between 9am and 6pm.

Across the creek, St Anthony is simply some cottages, mostly holiday lets, grouped round the church but it gives you something to aim for when wading across. A small gift shop opposite the church sells confectionery and ice-creams.

Beyond **Dennis Head** the sweep of the Helford River offers great views across to Falmouth. Large ships can be seen standing off until a berth becomes available in the docks. The path meanders through some lovely little wooded stretches, passes **Ponsence Cove** and **Bosahan Cove** and enters the riverside village of Helford by the back door, through a car park.

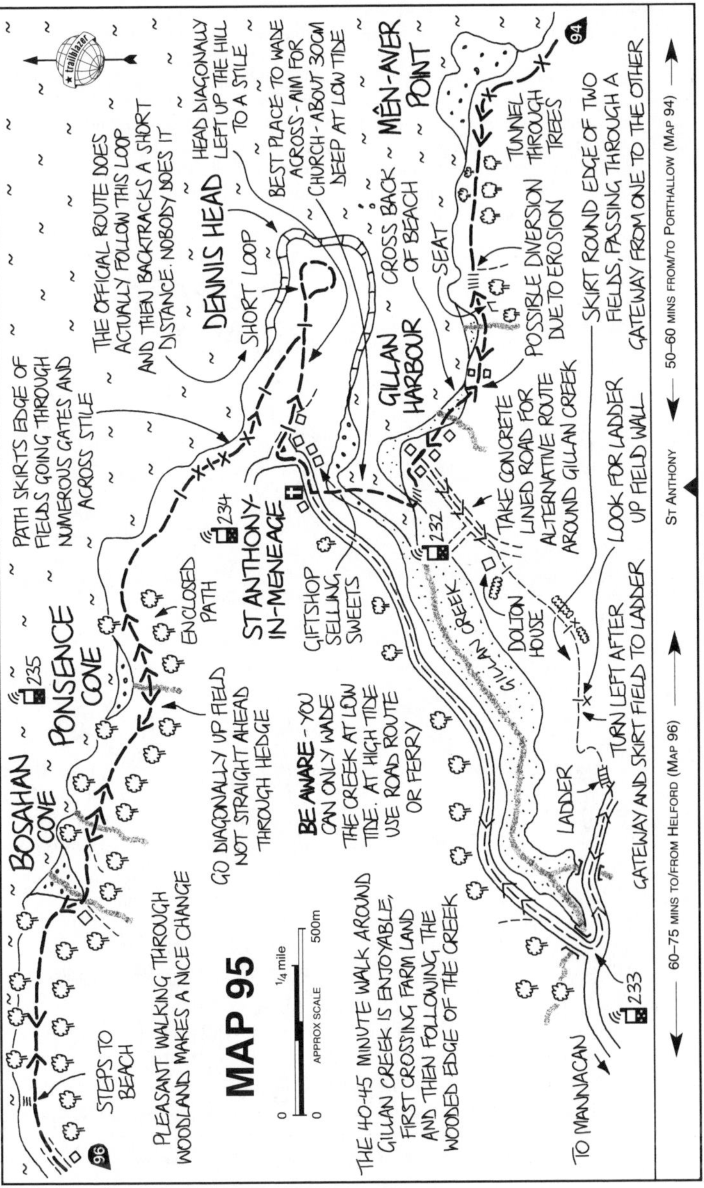

MAP 95

1/4 mile

APPROX SCALE

0 ... 500m

THE 40-45 MINUTE WALK AROUND GILLAN CREEK IS ENJOYABLE, FIRST CROSSING FARM LAND AND THEN FOLLOWING THE WOODED EDGE OF THE CREEK

PLEASANT WALKING THROUGH WOODLAND MAKES A NICE CHANGE

STEPS TO BEACH

BOSAHAN COVE

PONSENCE COVE

📻 235

📻 234

📻 233

GO DIAGONALLY UP FIELD NOT STRAIGHT AHEAD THROUGH HEDGE

BE AWARE - YOU CAN ONLY WADE THE CREEK AT LOW TIDE. AT HIGH TIDE USE ROAD ROUTE OR FERRY

ENCLOSED PATH

ST ANTHONY-IN-MENEAGE

GIFTSHOP SELLING SWEETS

PATH SKIRTS EDGE OF FIELDS GOING THROUGH NUMEROUS GATES AND ACROSS STILE

THE OFFICIAL ROUTE DOES ACTUALLY FOLLOW THIS LOOP AND THEN BACKTRACKS A SHORT DISTANCE. NOBODY DOES IT

DENNIS HEAD

SHORT LOOP

HEAD DIAGONALLY LEFT UP THE HILL TO A STILE

BEST PLACE TO WADE ACROSS - AIM FOR CHURCH - ABOUT 30CM DEEP AT LOW TIDE

CROSS BACK ~ MÊN-AVER POINT

SEAT

GILLAN HARBOUR

POSSIBLE DIVERSION DUE TO EROSION

TUNNEL THROUGH TREES

SKIRT ROUND EDGE OF TWO FIELDS, PASSING THROUGH A GATEWAY FROM ONE TO THE OTHER

🏴 94

TAKE CONCRETE LINED ROAD FOR ALTERNATIVE ROUTE AROUND GILLAN CREEK

DOLTON HOUSE

GILLAN CREEK

LOOK FOR LADDER UP FIELD WALL

TURN LEFT AFTER GATEWAY AND SKIRT FIELD TO LADDER

LADDER

TO MANNACAN

📻 132

60-75 MINS TO/FROM HELFORD (MAP 96)

ST ANTHONY

50-60 MINS FROM/TO PORTHALLOW (MAP 94)

📻 96

HELFORD   [MAP 96]

Helford is a picture-postcard village beside an inlet of the Helford River, which drains completely at low tide. **Helford Village Stores** (daily 9am-5pm) sells pasties, a few baked goods and other groceries. They'll also fill water bottles for walkers.

The café just before the footbridge, *The Holy Mackerel* (☎ 01326-231008; Sat-Thur 11am-4pm; 🐾), serves light lunches,

cream teas, ploughman's and crab sandwiches and also has Cornish craft ales, cider and lager. The pub, *Shipwright's Arms* (☎ 01326-231235, 🖥 shipwright shelford.co.uk; daily noon-3pm & 6-9pm, but may differ depending on season; 🐾) is a lovely old inn with a thatched roof and a garden right beside the creek. The food is good-quality pub grub, plus pasties.

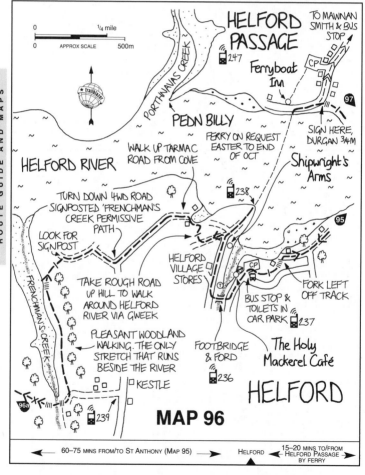

MAP 96

HELFORD TO HELFORD PASSAGE [MAPS 96 & 96a-d]

The most convenient crossing of the Helford River is by **Helford Ferry** (☎ 01326-250770, 🖳 helford-river-boats.co.uk; Apr-Jun & Sep-Oct daily 9.30am-5.30pm, Jul & Aug daily 9.30am-9.30pm; £4) which runs all day, apart from an hour either side of low tide when all you can do is wait; a tide table is handy and is on sale in post offices, many shops and some pubs (or get tide times online at 🖳 tidetimes.org.uk/helford-river-entrance-tide-times). The ferry operates on request and if you arrive at the slipway with no sign of it you have to display a yellow disc erected on the jetty for the purpose of alerting the ferryman. See below for details of how to get around Helford River if walking the coast path out of season.

GETTING AROUND THE HELFORD RIVER IN WINTER (ON FOOT)

On foot (Map 96 and 96a-96d, pp242-5) It is a **10-mile (16km, 3-4hrs)** walk around Helford River. The walk starts off promisingly along the wooded Frenchman's Creek but from Mudgeon Farm to Gweek it's all on tarmac with only tantalising glimpses of the river. However, in winter there won't be many cars and the pretty country lanes may provide some enjoyable walking away from the sea. *Gear Farm* (Map 96a, p242; ☎ 07968-778631, 🖳 campinghelfordriver .co.uk), owned by a welcoming elderly couple, offers **camping** (£9pp; June-Sep). Also small and friendly, *Helford River Camping* (☎ 07971-540644, 🖳 helfordrivercamping.co.uk; tents £13-16) is right across the road. The next village, **Mawgan**, has a pub, *The Ship Inn* (☎ 01326-221240, 🖳 shipinnmaw gan.co.uk), that does food (Tue-Sat 6-9pm) in the evening, and **Mawgan Stores** (Mon-Sat 7am-7pm, Sun 9am-6pm), which is well stocked with groceries.

Gweek (see below) is a pleasant halfway point. If you are tired of walking it is possible to go by **bus** (First's No 35; p54) to Helford Passage (p246).

Between Gweek and Helford Passage there are a few shortcuts across fields taking you briefly off the roads. You pass through **Nancenoy** (see p244; Map 96c) with a popular pub (Trengilly Wartha Inn) right on the route.

You rarely see the river but instead are teased every now and again by a steep descent down to a connecting creek and an equally steep climb away from it; the two creeks are Polwheveral and Porth Navas before you reach **Helford Passage**.

Or by taxi If you decide this option, try Autocabs (☎ 01326-573773, or ☎ 01326-573131) or Telstar (☎ 01326-221007, or ☎ 0800-999 2477).

GWEEK [MAP 96b, p243]

Gweek can provide some rest and relaxation although the services are limited. Those who failed to spot a single seal on their coastal wanderings may like to visit the **National Seal Sanctuary** (☎ 01326-221361, 🖳 sealsanctuary.co.uk; daily summer 10am-5pm, winter to 4pm; adults £10.85, children £8.75). There's a Premier **shop** and **post office** (daily 8am-8pm, Sun 9am-6pm) with sandwiches and bakery goods. Across the road, *The Black Swan* (☎ 01326-221502, 🖳 theblackswangweek .co.uk; 4D; from £42.50pp, sgl occ £70) has a wide selection of real ales, some decent pub **food** (noon-9pm), and **rooms**.

First Kernow's No 35 **bus** service between Falmouth and Helston stops here. See also p52-6.

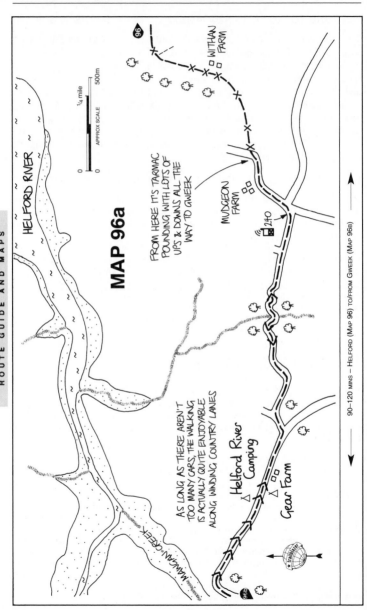

HELFORD RIVER

MAP 96a

WITHAN FARM

500m
¼ mile
0
0
APPROX SCALE

FROM HERE IT'S TARMAC POUNDING WITH LOTS OF UP'S & DOWNS ALL THE WAY TO GWEEK

MUDGEON FARM

240

AS LONG AS THERE AREN'T TOO MANY CARS, THE WALKING IS ACTUALLY QUITE ENJOYABLE ALONG WINDING COUNTRY LANES

MANGAN CREEK

Helford River Camping

Gear Farm

90–120 MINS – HELFORD (MAP 96) TO/FROM GWEEK (MAP 96B)

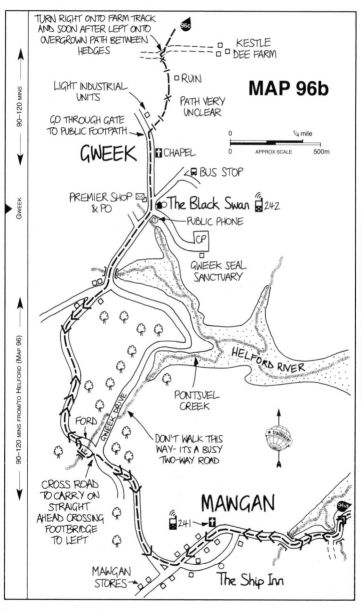

TURN RIGHT ONTO FARM TRACK
AND SOON AFTER LEFT ONTO
OVERGROWN PATH BETWEEN
HEDGES

96c

KESTLE
DEE FARM

RUIN

MAP 96b

LIGHT INDUSTRIAL
UNITS

PATH VERY
UNCLEAR

GO THROUGH GATE
TO PUBLIC FOOTPATH

0   ¼ mile
0   APPROX SCALE   500m

GWEEK   ✝ CHAPEL

BUS STOP

PREMIER SHOP
& PO

The Black Swan 242

PUBLIC PHONE

CP

GWEEK SEAL
SANCTUARY

HELFORD RIVER

PONTSUEL
CREEK

FORD

GWEEK DRIVE

DON'T WALK THIS
WAY- IT'S A BUSY
TWO-WAY ROAD

★ trailblazer

CROSS ROAD
TO CARRY ON
STRAIGHT
AHEAD CROSSING
FOOTBRIDGE
TO LEFT

MAWGAN

241 ✝

96a

MAWGAN
STORES

The Ship Inn

90-120 MINS

GWEEK

90-120 MINS FROM/to HELFORD (MAP 96)

ROUTE GUIDE AND MAPS

NANCENOY   [MAP 96c]

You might like to drop in at *Trengilly Wartha Inn* (☎ 01326-340332, 🖳 trengilly.co.uk; food daily noon-2.15pm & 6-9.30pm; bar 11am-3.15pm & 6-11pm), well-known and a favourite locally. The menu includes 8oz sirloin steak and open crab sandwich with mayonnaise, tabasco & lemon on home-made granary bread, served with a salad garnish. They also offer **B&B** (8D/1T/2Tr; 🛏; WI-FI; 🐾; £42-54.50pp, sgl occ £75-77).

> ❑ **Trebah and Glendurgan Gardens**   **(Map 97, p246)**
>
> For garden and plant lovers there are two beautiful gardens slightly inland between Helford Passage and Mawnan Smith which would make an exceptionally pleasant and relaxing day of gentle wandering. Both can be reached by walking up the lane from Helford Passage. First Kernow's No 35 (see pp52-6) bus stops here.
>
> ● **Trebah Garden** (☎ 01326-252200, 🖳 trebahgarden.co.uk; daily 10am-5pm; £10) descends 200ft down a steeply wooded ravine to a private beach. The stream meanders through ponds containing giant Koi (carp) and runs through two acres of blue and white hydrangeas before spilling onto the beach. There's also a licensed restaurant that sells lunches and cream teas.
>
> ● **Glendurgan Garden** (☎ 01326-252020; mid Feb to end Oct Tue-Sun 10.30am-5.30pm, plus Mon in August; £9.50, free for NT members) is owned by the National Trust. The valley garden was created in the 1820s and is rich in fine trees and rare and exotic plants and also features a maze. Spring time brings outstanding displays of magnolias and camellias.

ROUTE GUIDE AND MAPS

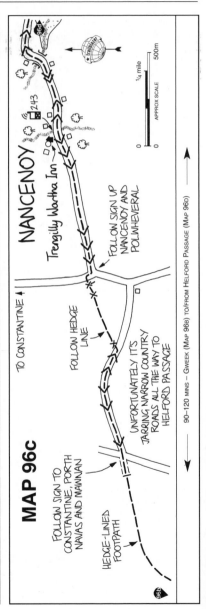

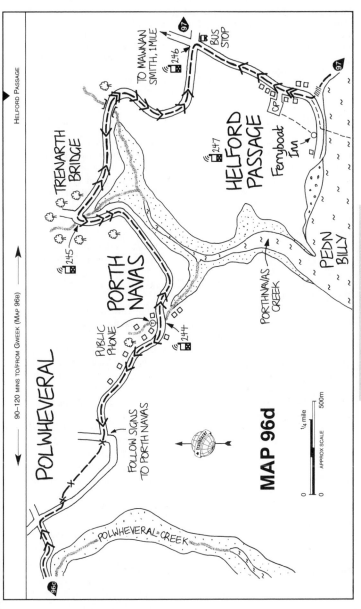

HELFORD PASSAGE   [MAP 97]

Helford Passage is directly opposite Helford on the north bank of the wide river-mouth. It is alive with the boating set in summer but rather dead out of season.

The only amenity is the *Ferryboat Inn* (☎ 01326-250625, 🖳 ferryboatcornwall.co .uk; food noon-3pm & 5-9pm). The menu

(mains £12-20) consists of your typical pub classics, plus some local specials such as Helford River mussels.

First Kernow's No 35 **bus** calls here. [See also pp52-6]. You can also try one of the local **taxi** companies such as Autocabs (see p241).

HELFORD PASSAGE TO FALMOUTH   [MAPS 97-100]

The **10 miles (16km, 2-2¾hrs)** to Falmouth provide wonderful gentle walking. On leaving the foreshore at Helford Passage the path climbs a grassy bank to lead by narrow ways to **Trebah Beach** where American troops embarked for the D-Day landings. **Trebah Gardens** (see box p244) come right down to the shore and the path passes below them as it does **Glendurgan Gardens** a little further on. There are wide views across the mouth of the picturesque Helford River. At Durgan, you'll pass *The Fish Cellar*, run by the National Trust, although you'll get little more than an ice-cream or soft drink.

Before the rocky promontory of **Toll Point** there are a couple of paths leading inland to **Mawnan Smith** (see below): after Toll Point the path enters steep woodland and another path leads inland to **Mawnan** which has an interesting church dedicated to St Maunanus, a Celtic saint. Then it loops out to **Rosemullion Head**, a superb viewpoint.

A series of little beaches follows, including **Gatamala Cove** and **Bream Cove** before the lovely expanse of **Maenporth Beach** (see p248) where there's a café and a smarter restaurant.

From Maenporth the path is well travelled. At the family-friendly beach, **Swanpool**, there's a popular restaurant, *Hooked on the Rocks* (☎ 01326-311866, 🖳 hookedontherocksfalmouth.com; daily noon-2.30pm & 6-9pm), with a seaview terrace and a menu of tapas and seafood.

After Gyllyngvase Beach suburban pavements take you all the way around **Pendennis Point** and past Falmouth Docks, a popular spot to lean on the fence for a while and watch the boats being repaired below. About 20 fishing boats work from this port of which half either trawl for whitefish or dredge for scallops. There is a native oyster fishery situated in the River Fal.

Then on through the streets of **Falmouth** jostling for space with the shoppers. There are plenty of pubs and restaurants here where you can celebrate your achievement so far.

MAWNAN SMITH   [map p248]

This village used to have four blacksmiths so acquired the name to distinguish it from nearby Mawnan. The 200-year-old **Old Smithy Workshops** (Mon-Fri 10am-5.30pm, Sat 11am-4pm) is the only one of the four still in operation, and offers a very

rare opportunity to see a fully functioning traditional blacksmith's.

Mawnan Smith isn't actually on the coast path but it can easily be reached by walking from Helford Passage (25-30 mins), Durgan (15-20 mins), or Mawnan

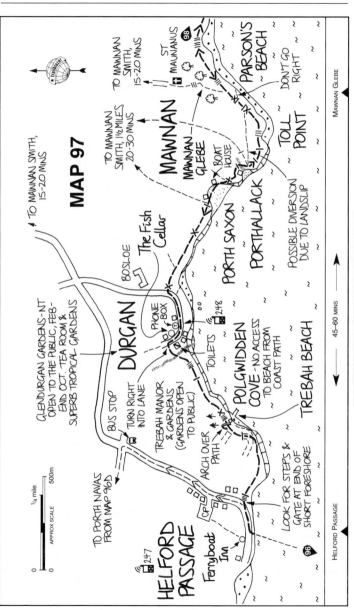

(15-20 mins). The **post office** (Mon-Fri 9am-1pm & 2-5.30pm except Wed morning, Sat 9am-12.30pm) is in the **general stores** (Mon-Fri 8am-1pm & 2-5.30pm, Sat 8am-1pm & 2-4pm, Sun 9-11am) which has all the usual groceries including sandwiches, fruit and crisps.

Trevarn B&B (☎ 01326-251245, 💻 trevarn.co.uk; 2D/1T private bathrooms; £42.50-47.50pp, sgl occ from £60) is small but bright and comfortable. The owners are friendly and helpful.

Gold Martin (☎ 01326-250666, 💻 goldmartin.co.uk; 1T or D/1D; £42.50-45pp, sgl occ from £60), Carlidnak Rd, is a beautiful late 18th-century house with a lounge, conservatory and garden. Contact them regarding pick up from/drop off to the trail.

The *Red Lion* (☎ 01326-250026, 💻 redlioncornwall.com; WI-FI; food noon-2.30pm & 6-9pm) is a pub to spend time in; a true beauty with real ales such as Old Speckled Hen and Doom Bar. The food is excellent and if you try no other crab bisque (soup; £5.25) in Cornwall, try it here.

Just across the road, *Cornish Maid* (9am-6pm; WI-FI) is a pleasant café serving breakfasts, coffee and cream teas.

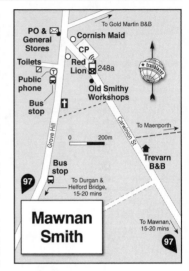

Mawnan Smith

Transport

[See also pp52-6] Mawnan Smith is on First Kernow's No 35 **bus** route between Falmouth and Helston.

MAENPORTH [MAP 98]

The beach here is a real gem.

Campers should head to *Pennance Mill Farm* (Map 99; ☎ 01326-317431, 💻 pennancemill.co.uk; hiker & tent £13-15; Easter-Oct). It's best accessed from here or from Swanpool beach: phone for directions.

Apart from its café, *Life's a Beach* (☎ 01326-251209, 💻 maenporthbeach.co.uk; daily summer 9am-6pm, winter 10am-3pm), which does burgers, baguettes, ciabattas and very, very good ice-cream, Maenporth also has an upmarket beach restaurant, *The Cove* (☎ 01326-251136, 💻 thecovemaenporth.co.uk; daily noon-9.30pm), where you can sit out on the deck and have coffee or sample the tapas for lunch. Evening mains (£15-26) may include duck and lobster.

FALMOUTH [MAP 100, p253]

Falmouth is a working port and holiday resort rolled into one. Just a small fishing village in the 17th century, it was developed by the Killigrew family who made their money from privateering and piracy, a lucrative trade in those days. Falmouth is still defined by the sea and the ships that sail in thanks to its large expanse of sheltered water. It is said that an entire navy can anchor safely in Carrick Roads, the body of

water between Falmouth and St Mawes. One of Britain's major yachting centres, it is often the first port of call for trans-Atlantic sailors, and the Tall Ships (large, traditionally rigged sailing vessels) regularly visit, bringing out the crowds in their tens of thousands. Two festivals worth attending are **Falmouth Regatta Week** and the **Oyster Festival** (see p16). The entrance to Carrick Roads is guarded by two castles

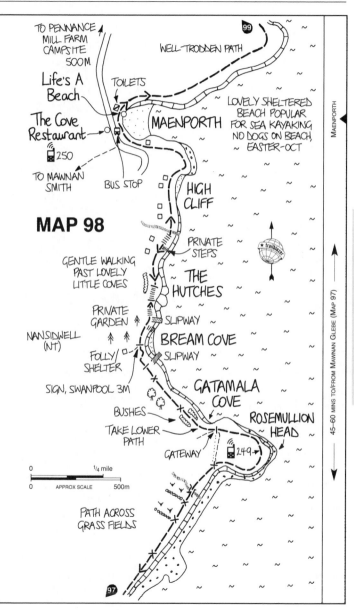

TO PENNANCE MILL FARM CAMPSITE 500M

WELL-TRODDEN PATH

99

TOILETS

Life's A Beach

The Cove Restaurant
📱 250

MAENPORTH

LOVELY SHELTERED BEACH POPULAR FOR SEA KAYAKING NO DOGS ON BEACH, ~ EASTER-OCT

TO MAWNAN SMITH

BUS STOP

MAP 98

HIGH CLIFF

PRIVATE STEPS

GENTLE WALKING PAST LOVELY LITTLE COVES

THE HUTCHES

PRIVATE GARDEN

SLIPWAY

NANSIDWELL (NT)

BREAM COVE

FOLLY/ SHELTER

SLIPWAY

SIGN, SWANPOOL 3M

GATAMALA COVE

BUSHES

ROSEMULLION HEAD

TAKE LOWER PATH

GATEWAY
📱 249

0   ¼ mile
0   APPROX SCALE   500m

PATH ACROSS GRASS FIELDS

97

MAENPORTH

45-60 MINS TO/FROM MAWNAN GLEBE (MAP 97)

ROUTE GUIDE AND MAPS

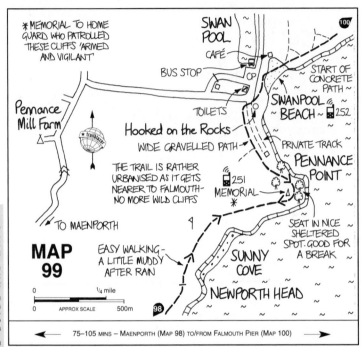

* MEMORIAL TO HOME GUARD WHO PATROLLED THESE CLIFFS 'ARMED AND VIGILANT'

SWAN POOL

CAFÉ

BUS STOP

CP

START OF CONCRETE PATH

Pennance Mill Farm

TOILETS

SWANPOOL BEACH 252

Hooked on the Rocks

WIDE GRAVELLED PATH

PRIVATE TRACK

THE TRAIL IS RATHER URBANISED AS IT GETS NEARER TO FALMOUTH — NO MORE WILD CLIFFS

251 MEMORIAL *

PENNANCE POINT

TO MAENPORTH

MAP 99

EASY WALKING — A LITTLE MUDDY AFTER RAIN

SEAT IN NICE SHELTERED SPOT. GOOD FOR A BREAK

SUNNY COVE

0 ¼ mile
0 APPROX SCALE 500m

98

NEWPORTH HEAD

75–105 MINS – MAENPORTH (MAP 98) TO/FROM FALMOUTH PIER (MAP 100)

ROUTE GUIDE AND MAPS

built by Henry VIII, Pendennis Castle on the western promontory and the other across the water at St Mawes (see p255). **Pendennis Castle** (☎ 01326-316594, 🖥 english-heritage.org.uk; late Mar to end Sep daily 10am-6pm, Oct daily to 5pm, Nov to mid Feb Sat & Sun 10am-4pm, mid Feb to mid Mar daily 10am-4pm; £10.50) is well worth a visit.

The **National Maritime Museum** (☎ 01326-313388, 🖥 nmmc.co.uk; daily 10am-5pm; £13.50), on Discovery Quay, has plenty of interesting displays telling the stories of Cornwall's nautical past. Don't miss The Lookout Tower, with panoramic views across the harbour, and The Tidal Zone, where you can see the underwater world changing with the tides from below the water line through two (immensely thick) windows.

Falmouth Art Gallery (☎ 01326-313863, 🖥 www.falmouthartgallery.com; Mon-Sat 10am-5pm; admission free), on The Moor, has a permanent collection of work by mainly Cornish artists with several visiting exhibitions throughout the year; the gallery is in the Municipal Buildings and is above the **library**. The independent **Poly Cinema** (☎ 01326-319461, 🖥 the poly.org), on Church St, shows art-house films. The box office is open Monday-Saturday 10am-5pm.

Services
The staff at the **visitor centre** (☎ 01326-741194, 🖥 falmouth.co.uk or 🖥 falriver.co.uk; Mon-Sat 10am-3pm, Sun 10am-2pm), on Prince of Wales Pier, are volunteers and very helpful. The **post office** (Mon-Fri 9am-5.15pm, Sat 8am-1pm) is in a branch

of Spar supermarket (8am-midnight). The **library** (Mon-Fri 9.30am-5pm, Sat 10am-1pm; WI-FI) provides **internet access** (£1.80/30mins).

The main High Street **banks** are along Market St, all with **ATMs** (no charge) and there's a Tesco Express **supermarket** (6am-midnight) at Discovery Quay which has an ATM outside it. The nearest **launderette** is Bubbles (Mon-Sat 8.30am-5pm), up Killigrew St. The **medical centre** Westover Surgery (☎ 01326-212120; Mon-Fri 8am-1pm & 2-6pm) is on Western Terrace. There is a Boots **pharmacy** (Mon-Sat 9am-5.30pm, Sun 10.30am-4.30pm) on Market St. You can find **camping equipment** at Mountain Warehouse (Mon-Fri 9am-5.30pm, Sat 9am-6pm, Sun 11am-5pm). Nearby, there's a branch of the **newsagent/stationer** WH Smith (Mon-Sat 8.45am-5.30pm, Sun 11am-4pm).

Where to stay

Campsites and hostels Those wanting to **camp** will have to go to *Pennance Mill Farm* (see Maenporth p248 & Map 99). The only **hostel** in town is the very welcoming *Falmouth Backpackers* (☎ 01326-319996, 🖳 falmouthbackpackers.co.uk; 18 dorm beds, 1D/1F; WI-FI; from £19pp, sgl occ £40), at 9 Gyllyngvase Terrace, with clean, decent-sized rooms, friendly staff and a simple toast-and-coffee breakfast.

B&Bs and guesthouses The following is just a selection from Falmouth's huge choice of B&B accommodation; in terms of quality there is not a lot to choose between them. In summer, and for events such as the Tall Ships' gathering (see p248), the town can get booked up so keep this in mind when planning your trip.

B&Bs are plentiful in the Melvill Rd/ Avenue Rd area. At the half-timbered *Rosemullion* (☎ 01326-314690, 🖳 rose mullionhotel.co.uk; 1S/3T/9D; ✆; WI-FI; £40-50pp) they can arrange luggage transfer. Opposite this, at 54 Melvill Rd, is *Eden Lodge* (☎ 01326-212989, 🖳 edenlodgefal mouth.co.uk; ✆; 🐾; WI-FI; 1S/3D or T/1 suite; £15-75pp, sgl £30-45), one of Falmouth's cheapest B&Bs. They offer

lunch and evening meals by prior arrangement and there is an indoor swimming pool. On the same road are two guesthouses side by side: *Melvill House* (☎ 01326-316645, 🖳 melvill-house-falmouth.co.uk; 2T/3D/2F; ✆; WI-FI; £35-45pp), at 52 Melvill Rd; and the very welcoming *Dolvean* (☎ 01326-313658, 🖳 dolvean .co.uk; 2S/2T/6D; ✆; WI-FI; 🐾; £50-62.50pp, sgl £60-70), at No 50, which has a licensed bar.

On the corner of Gyllyngvase Rd and Melville Rd, the attractive *Gyllyngvase House Hotel* (☎ 01326-312956, 🖳 gyllyn gvase.co.uk; 3S/2T/7D/1F, some en suite; ✆; WI-FI; £40-50pp) has a restaurant and bar. *Camelot* (☎ 01326-312480, 🖳 camelot falmouth.com; 2S/1T/5D; WI-FI; £50-60pp, sgl occ from £70) is at No 5 Avenue Rd. *Braemar* (☎ 01326-311285, 🖳 braemar guesthousefalmouth.co.uk; 1S/3T/4D/1F; ✆; WI-FI; 🐾; from £37.50pp) is at No 9.

At 22 Gyllyngvase Terrace, a quiet side road, *The Rosemary* (☎ 01326-314669, 🖳 therosemary.co.uk; 1S/2D/2D or T/2F; ✆; WI-FI; 🐾 in low season only; £39.50-81pp, sgl/sgl occ £50-67) is a stylish and highly rated guesthouse which takes credit cards. On the corner of Killigrew St and Western Terrace, is *The Observatory Guesthouse* (☎ 01326-314509, 🖳 theobser vatoryguesthouse.co.uk; 3D/2Tr; from £35pp, sgl occ from £40), a friendly family-run B&B housed in an 1884 former observatory. Next door, at 17 Western Terrace, is the highly recommended *Lyonesse Guesthouse* (☎ 01326-313017, 🖳 lyonesse falmouth.co.uk; 1D/2D or T; from £28pp, sgl occ from £40), also family run.

Hotels If you're in need of pampering, *St Michael's Hotel & Spa* (☎ 01326-369785, 🖳 stmichaelshotel.co.uk; 61 rooms; from £35pp), near Gyllyngvase Beach, is a smart, 4-star hotel in leafy grounds. Non-residents can use the **pool** and **spa** too. Check online for special offers.

Less plush, but with plenty of character, *Merchant's Manor* (☎ 01326-312734, 🖳 merchantsmanor.com; 39 rooms; from £42.50pp) is a 1913 manor house with small but stylish rooms, plus a pool and gym.

ROUTE GUIDE AND MAPS

Where to eat and drink

Falmouth is packed with places to eat, ranging from fish & chip joints and low-key cafés through to intimate bistros and fine-dining restaurants. Naturally enough seafood predominates.

Discovery Quay is the most buzzing part of town on a summer's evening, and events are often held on the square, which is surrounded by restaurants, cafés and bars.

Cafés *De Wynns* (☎ 01326-319259; Apr-Oct Mon-Sat 10am-5pm, Sun 11am-4pm; Nov-Mar Mon-Fri 10am-4pm, Sat 10am-5pm), at 55 Church St, is a lovely 30-year-old coffee house and tearoom that does pleasant lunches and breakfasts. Dishes include a fine Cornish rarebit and a decent selection of teas and coffees.

It's tough to resist the smell of roasted coffee beans that wafts across the pavement as you walk past *Espressini* (8am-5.30pm),

a modern Italian-style café with fabulous coffee, plus healthier-than-usual breakfasts (eggs Benedict, avocado on toast, smoked haddock potato cakes etc). Another modern café with a great choice of breakfasts is *Fuel* (daily 8am to late) on Arwenack St.

Gylly Beach Café (daily 9-11.30am, noon-4pm & 6-9pm) has a nice perch above the ever-popular Gyllyngvase Beach, and does excellent food for a beach café, accompanied by live music on Sunday evenings.

Pasty fans should look no further than the much-loved *Oggy Oggy Pasty Company* (daily 9.30am-5.30pm). It also does sandwiches and coffee, and you can eat in or takeaway.

Pubs Traditional pubs that serve food include the 17th-century *Chain Locker* (food daily noon-9pm; WI-FI; 🐾), on Quay Hill, which has quayside seating out back. Also on the quay here, *The Front*

FALMOUTH – MAP KEY

Where to stay
12 The Observatory Guesthouse
13 Lyonesse Guesthouse
15 Merchant's Manor
36 Braemar
37 Camelot
38 Dolvean House
39 Melvill House
40 Eden Lodge
41 Rosemullion
42 Gyllyngvase House
43 Falmouth Backpackers
44 The Rosemary
45 St Michael's Hotel & Spa

Where to eat & drink
8 Nepalese Gurkha
9 Pennycomequick
10 Espressini
16 The Grapes
17 Beerwolf Books
18 De Wynns
19 Ming's Garden
21 Cribbs
22 Fuel
23 The Seafood Bar
24 Ploi Thai
25 Oggy Oggy Pasty Co
26 The Chain Locker

Where to eat & drink (cont'd)
27 The Stable
28 The Front
29 Harbour Lights
32 The Shed
33 The Ranch
34 Rick Stein's Fish
35 5 Degrees West
46 Gylly Beach Café

Other
1 Spar & Post Office
2 Visitor Centre
3 Mountain Warehouse
4 Boots
5 WH Smith
6 Tesco Metro
7 Art Gallery, Library & Internet Access
11 Launderette
14 Medical Centre
17 Beerwolf Books
20 Poly Cinema
30 Tesco Express
31 National Maritime Museum

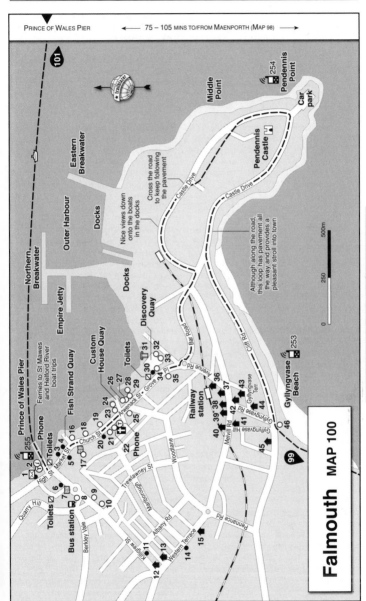

ROUTE GUIDE AND MAPS

Falmouth MAP 100

(11am-11pm) is a real-ale pub that doesn't do food but does allow drinkers to eat their own takeaways on its tables outside on the quay.

Nearby, *The Grapes* (☎ 01326-314704, 🖥 grapesalehouse.co.uk; food daily noon-3pm & 6-9pm, hours may differ slightly in winter), at 64 Church St, is an old alehouse that does fine pub food, including plenty of seafood specials.

Closer to the railway station, *5 Degrees West* (☎ 01326-311288, 🖥 fivewest.co; daily noon-10pm) has a good range of beers and food, including veggie and vegan options. Near the bus station, meanwhile, *Pennycomequick* (☎ 01326-311912, 🖥 pennycomequick.co.uk; food Mon-Sat noon-3pm & 6-9pm, Sun noon-5pm; WI-FI) is St Austell Brewery's offering in town.

Literary real ale enthusiasts may be interested in visiting *Beerwolf Books* (☎ 01326-618474, 🖥 beerwolfbooks.com; Mon-Sat 10am-midnight, Sun noon-11pm, WI-FI; 🐾) where you can indulge in numerous ales and lagers and peruse their book shop. It's tucked away in Bells Court just off Market St.

Asian Cuisine Housed inside the splendid 18th-century Grade II-listed building known as Bank House, *Ming's Garden Restaurant* (☎ 01326-314413; Sun-Tue 5-10.30pm, Wed-Thur noon-2pm & 5-10.30pm, Fri-Sat noon-2pm & 5-11pm) is perhaps less grand than it should be, but still a decent place to come for Chinese food.

For Thai cuisine, try *Ploi Thai* (☎ 01326-210333; Wed-Mon 5-9.30pm) on Quay St. And for something more unusual, head to *Nepalese Gurkha* (☎ 01326-311483, 🖥 opendining.co.uk/gurkhafalmouth; daily 5.30-11pm), at 2a The Moor, to sample some high-quality Nepalese curries.

Seafood For a great-value fish & chips experience, you can't beat *Harbour Lights* (☎ 01326-316934, 🖥 harbourlights.co.uk; daily 11.30am-9.30pm; WI-FI), where you can get quality fish & chips for £7-10, and enjoy a view of the harbour while you eat.

Surprisingly affordable, *Rick Stein's Fish* (🖥 rickstein.com; restaurant Sun-Fri

noon-3pm & 5-9pm, Sat noon-9pm, takeaway daily 11.30am-9.30pm) is on Discovery Quay.

Secreted away down a small lane leading to the harbour, *The Seafood Bar* (☎ 01326-315129; daily 7-9pm) is an intimate independent restaurant specialising in locally caught fish and shellfish, as well as homemade desserts.

Restaurants Two restaurants that spill out onto Discovery Quay are *The Ranch* (☎ 01326-210989, 🖥 theranchfalmouth.co.uk; noon-3pm & 6-9pm), Falmouth's standout steakhouse, and *The Shed* (☎ 01326-318502; food daily 9.30am-10pm), which also does an excellent sirloin steak (£19.50), as well as good mussels (£13.95).

Up towards Church St, *The Stable* (food 11.30am-10pm, kitchen closed 3.30-4.30pm) offers pizza, pies and cider. It's family friendly and has a very attractive try-before-you-buy cider-sampling policy. There's also a vegan menu.

Close by, *Cribbs* (🖥 cribbscornwall.co.uk; 10am-3pm & 6-9.30pm) is a funky restaurant specialising in Caribbean food. There's plenty of rum-based drinks to choose from, plus alcohol-free 'mocktails'.

Transport

[See also pp52-6] First Kernow has bus services to Truro (U1) and to Mawnan Smith, Gweek, Helford Passage & Helston (35). Trains, operated by GWR, go to Truro hourly.

The NX315 coach service (see box p50) also operates here.

Ferry from Falmouth to St Mawes

The ferry service (☎ 01872-861910, 🖥 falriver.co.uk/frl/ferries/st_mawes_ferry) between bustling Falmouth and sleepy St Mawes runs year-round and takes just 20 minutes. The service departs from the Prince of Wales dock in the heart of Falmouth, operating approximately hourly (half-hourly in high season) from about 8.30am to 5pm. There is a second ferry in summer from Custom House Quay in Falmouth, again hourly. A single from either dock to St Mawes costs £7.

FALMOUTH TO PORTSCATHO [MAPS 100-103]

This 6¼-mile (10km; 2-2½hrs) jaunt is a relatively easy one that is full of interesting sights and attractions. The journey begins with a couple of **ferries**: the one
from Falmouth to St Mawes runs all year (see opposite), while the other links St
Mawes with the tiny settlement of Place (see below). There's a pretty – and easy
– walk from St Mawes to Place round Trethem Creek if the ferries aren't operating; see below for details.

ST MAWES [MAP 101, p257]

Though less than a mile separates Falmouth
from St Mawes, the latter is more than just
a suburb of the former and it's a shame for
most coastal walkers that they don't experience more of this town than the harbour,
where the ferry to Falmouth docks and from
where a second ferry, to Place, sets sail.

St Mawes, named after the 5th-century
Celtic saint Maudez, is the gateway to, and
largest town on, the Roseland Peninsula and
was once a busy fishing port, though these
days tourism is its economic mainstay.

Facilities in town include **Roseland
Visitor Centre** (☎ 01326-270440, 🖳
stmawesandtheroseland.co.uk;   Mon-Sat
10am-4pm), a Co-op **supermarket** (daily
7am-10pm), and a **post office** (Mon-Fri
8am-5.30pm, Sat 9am-noon).

Where to stay and eat

For a fabulous **B&B**, walk up the lane
beside The Watchhouse restaurant, then turn
right up the very steep Grove Hill and you'll
soon see, on your right, the entrance to the
exquisite *Braganza* (☎ 01326-270281, 🖳
bragan za-stmawes.co.uk; 1S/4D or T; WI-
FI; 🐾; £57.50-62.50pp, sgl £60-65), a beautifully decorated period building with stunning harbour views. There are no one-night
stays on Fridays and Saturdays during peak
season, but otherwise they are very accommodating to passing walkers.

Back down at the harbour, *The Rising
Sun* (☎ 01326-270233, 🖳 risingsunst
mawes.co.uk; 1S/3D/2T/2F; ❤; WI-FI; 🐾;
£61-81pp, sgl £69-85; food daily 8.30-10am
& noon-9pm) does standard pub food, but
also has eight beautiful rooms, some of
which have panoramic sea views. Nearby
Idle Rocks Hotel (☎ 01326-270270, 🖳 idle
rocks.co.uk; 2S/1T/3D or T/7D; ❤; WI-FI;
🐾; £99-175pp) is proper gorgeous, but
proper expensive! *The Rising Sun* (see
above) is best for pub grub, while for more
formal dining there's *The Watchhouse* (☎
01326-270038, 🖳 watchhousestmawes.co.uk;
daily noon-3pm & 6-9pm); mains £14-
24.50. For pasties and other pastry delights
head to *St Mawes Bakery* (☎ 01326-
270292, 🖳 st-mawes-bakery.co.uk; Mon-
Sat 8am-4/5pm) on the quay.

Transport

[See also pp52-6] First Kernow's No 50
bus runs to Portscatho & Truro.

Ferry from St Mawes to Place

The ferry (☎ 01326-741194; 9am-5.30pm
every 30 mins; journey time 10 mins;
£5.40) between St Mawes and Place runs in
summer only. So before Good Friday or
after the end of October you'll need to
either rely on the local bus services or take
the walk described below.

ST MAWES TO PLACE VIA THE INLAND ROUTE

Those who need to, or simply wish to take this route will find it's a lovely
stroll; nice and flat, full of interest, and in parts quite beautiful. Highlights
include a castle that dates back to Henry VIII, a gorgeous 13th-century church
and some delightful ambling through woods lining the creek. The only part
that is in any way 'difficult' is the central section as you cross from the banks
of the Carrick Roads (separating Falmouth from St Mawes) to Gerrans. This is
not because it's physically arduous (although there are a couple of small hills),
but because you're not on the national trail now, so the clearly marked path

with all its waymarks, signposts, information boards and landmarks is conspicuous in its absence. As a result, it *can* be slightly tricky finding your way. But follow the directions in this guide closely and it shouldn't be too demanding.

St Mawes Castle (Map 101a; ☎ 01326-270526, ⌨ english-her itage.org.uk; Apr-Sep Sun-Fri 10am-5pm, Jul & Aug to 6pm, Oct daily 10am-4pm, Nov-Mar Sat & Sun only 10am-4pm; £6) lies just to the west of St Mawes looking towards Falmouth. A superior example of Henry VIII's artillery castles, of which you will encounter several on the coast path, the fortifications are built in a

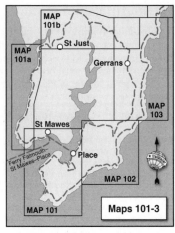

Maps 101-3

clover-leaf shape. Despite its utilitarian purpose, the castle is not without decoration including inscriptions in Latin praising the king and his son Edward VI.

A succession of sometimes-muddy cattle fields and a somnolent harbour leads from the castle to the next attraction, the beautiful 13th-century **Church of St Just** (Map 101b), surrounded by palm trees and set in some of the prettiest semi-tropical gardens of any church. The path passes through the gardens, and rounds the church, where you'll see *Miss V's Cornish Cream Tea* (May-Oct 10.30am-5pm), a tiny café by the church car park. Continuing to skirt the edge of the church grounds opposite the café, you then drop down to the small natural spring or fountain where, just beyond, the path takes a sharp right up the hill through the trees to the road. More fields are crossed before another road is reached, which you follow down past *Trethem Mill Touring Park* (☎ 01872-580504, ⌨ trethem.com; Easter-Oct; tent & two people £22-34), an award-winning campsite with a lovely rural setting. At the end of this stretch of road, turn left across the bridge, then immediately right, up a path off the road, before crossing more fields until another road is joined. Turn right here, then follow the road to Polhendra Cottage, where you turn left through the second gate and drop down towards a stream. There's no discernible path through this field, but try aiming for the line of trees on the slopes opposite. Follow that line of trees, keeping them on your left as you climb up to a track that crosses two fields before emerging on a lane leading to **Gerrans Church** (Map 103). Those who have taken the bus (First Kernow's 50; see p54) will be dropped off here. There's another excellent campsite here, and a village pub – see p260.

At this point a choice is available: take the road left after the church and a five-minute descent will bring you to Portscatho. Alternatively, those who want to follow the coast path religiously should continue by taking the track (Treloan Lane) by the Royal Standard pub and follow this all the way down to a road, where you should turn right. Leave the road on the left by the bridge to follow Porth Creek and the Percuil River that will eventually lead you to the ferry launch at Place – and a reunion with the coast path.

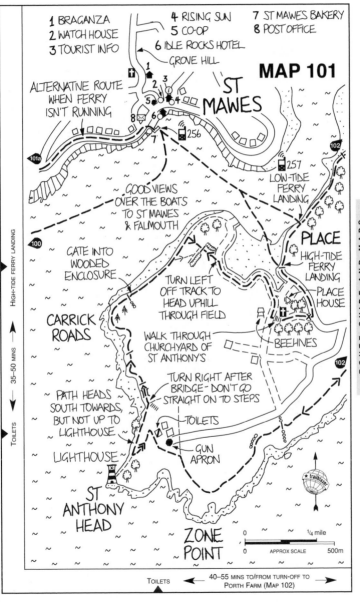

1 BRAGANZA
2 WATCH HOUSE
3 TOURIST INFO

4 RISING SUN
5 CO-OP
6 IDLE ROCKS HOTEL
GROVE HILL

7 ST MAWES BAKERY
8 POST OFFICE

MAP 101

ST MAWES

ALTERNATIVE ROUTE
WHEN FERRY
ISN'T RUNNING

101a

256

257
LOW-TIDE
FERRY
LANDING

PLACE

HIGH-TIDE
FERRY
LANDING

PLACE
HOUSE

~ GOOD VIEWS
~ OVER THE BOATS
~ TO ST MAWES ~
~ & FALMOUTH ~

100

GATE INTO
WOODED
ENCLOSURE

TURN LEFT
OFF TRACK TO
HEAD UPHILL
THROUGH FIELD

CARRICK
ROADS

WALK THROUGH
CHURCHYARD OF
ST ANTHONY'S

BEEHIVES

TURN RIGHT AFTER
BRIDGE – DON'T GO
STRAIGHT ON TO STEPS

~ PATH HEADS
~ SOUTH TOWARDS,
~ BUT NOT UP TO
~ LIGHTHOUSE

TOILETS

GUN
APRON

LIGHTHOUSE ~

102

ST ~
ANTHONY ~
HEAD ~

ZONE
POINT

0   1/4 mile
0   500m
APPROX SCALE

TOILETS ← 40–55 MINS TO/FROM TURN-OFF TO → PORTH FARM (MAP 102)

HIGH-TIDE FERRY LANDING

35–50 MINS

TOILETS

ROUTE GUIDE AND MAPS

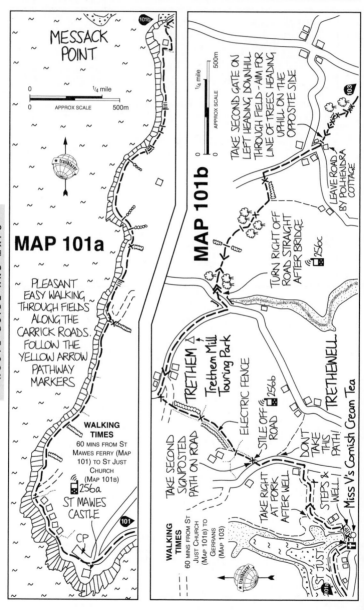

MESSACK POINT

1/4 mile

APPROX SCALE   500m

trailblazer

MAP 101a

~ PLEASANT
EASY WALKING
THROUGH FIELDS
~ ALONG THE
CARRICK ROADS.
FOLLOW THE
~ YELLOW ARROW
PATHWAY
~ MARKERS

**WALKING
TIMES**
60 MINS FROM ST
MAWES FERRY (MAP
101) TO ST JUST
CHURCH
(MAP 101B)
📱256a
ST MAWES
CASTLE
CP

TAKE SECOND GATE ON
LEFT HEADING DOWNHILL
THROUGH FIELD – AIM FOR
LINE OF TREES HEADING
UPHILL ON THE
OPPOSITE SIDE

1/4 mile

APPROX SCALE   500m

MAP 101b

LEAVE ROAD
BY POLHENDRA
COTTAGE

TURN RIGHT OFF
ROAD STRAIGHT
AFTER BRIDGE
📱256c

TRETHEM
Trethem Mill
Touring Park

ELECTRIC FENCE

STILE OFF
ROAD 📱256b

TRETHEWELL

DON'T
TAKE
THIS
PATH!

Miss V's Cornish Cream Tea

TAKE SECOND SIGNPOSTED
PATH ON ROAD

TAKE RIGHT
AT FORK
AFTER WELL

STEPS &
WELL

**WALKING
TIMES**
60 MINS FROM ST
JUST CHURCH
(MAP 101B) TO
GERRANS
(MAP 103)

ST JUST

trailblazer

ROUTE GUIDE AND MAPS

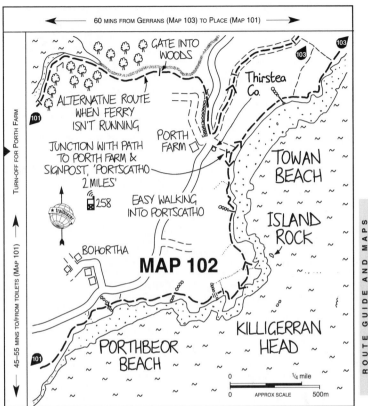

60 MINS FROM GERRANS (MAP 103) TO PLACE (MAP 101)

TURN-OFF FOR PORTH FARM

45-55 MINS TO/FROM TOILETS (MAP 101)

103

103

GATE INTO WOODS

Thirstea Co.

ALTERNATIVE ROUTE WHEN FERRY ISN'T RUNNING

PORTH FARM

JUNCTION WITH PATH TO PORTH FARM & SIGNPOST, 'PORTSCATHO 2 MILES'

★ trailblazer

258

EASY WALKING INTO PORTSCATHO

TOWAN BEACH

ISLAND ROCK

BOHORTHA

MAP 102

101

PORTHBEOR BEACH

KILLIGERRAN HEAD

0   1/4 mile

0   APPROX SCALE   500m

ROUTE GUIDE AND MAPS

Assuming you're starting at **Place**, where the ferry docks, the path begins with a saunter around picturesque **Place House** to the neighbouring church and from there up to the top of the ridge with lovely views of St Mawes Harbour and, in the distance, Falmouth itself. **St Anthony Head**, the southernmost tip of the **Roseland Peninsula**, with its historic lighthouse, is the next destination (though the path actually turns off east before reaching the lighthouse). All around the point are the silent remnants of defensive fortifications such as a WWII gun battery as well as earlier, 19th-century relics. The whole Head is owned by the National Trust and there are toilets here. From here the path squeezes between the old military road and the sea, high above the sailors, surfers and jet-skiers. The landmarks of **Killigerran Head** and **Greeb Point** are ticked off without too much difficulty. Between the two, you can get **refreshments** at *The Thirstea Company* (Map 102; ☎ 01872-581898, 🖳 thethirsteacompany.co.uk; Apr-Oct,

Sat-Thur 11am-5pm; daily in summer holidays) which provides pasties, snacks, drinks and cream teas, from Earl, their Citroen van, conveniently parked above Towan Beach. After Greeb Point, the path passes a memorial to those who fell in Burma during WWII, then rounds the small geographical pimple of **Pencabe** that shelters the former pilchard-fishing harbour of **Portscatho**.

PORTSCATHO & GERRANS
[MAP 103]

Portscatho's history is typical of this part of Cornwall. A former fishing village that once survived on the seemingly endless supplies of pilchards that flourished in the balmy waters here, it now relies on tourism, with a bare remnant of the fishing industry still clinging on gamely. Around 5-10 minutes up the hill is the neighbouring village of **Gerrans**, home to a lovely old 13th-century church dedicated to the obscure St Gerendus. The centre of Portscatho is a square where you'll find a decent restaurant, a well-stocked store and a busy pub. The **store** is Ralph's (☎ 01872-580702; daily 7am-7pm), which serves the odd pasty and snack and has the village's **post office** (same hours) inside it. *The Boathouse* (☎ 01872-580326; Tue-Sat 11am-5pm & 6.30-9pm, Sun 11am-5pm) has a quality menu that includes plenty of freshly caught fish. The menu at *Plume of Feathers* (☎ 01872-580321, 🖥 plumeof feathers-roseland.com; noon-9pm, Sat & Sun 9am-noon for breakfast) changes daily (evening starters £5-7, mains £10-20) and they also have **rooms** (3D/2D or T; £40-65pp, sgl occ rate on request). Up the hill in Gerrans is the 18th-century *Royal Standard*

(☎ 01872-580271, 🖥 royalstandard-ger rans.co.uk; food summer daily noon-2pm & 6-9pm, to 11pm Fri & Sat; winter closed Mon lunchtime; WI-FI; 🐾), a lovely old pub, but a word of warning – ask permission before using the plug sockets to recharge your phone!

There is an excellent **campsite** here called *Treloan* (☎ 01872-580989, 🖥 coas talfarmholidays.co.uk; 🐾), which is often busy, but always makes room for coast-path walkers... and only charges them £5! They also have a wooden 'Snug' (sleeps 2, £21) and a yurt (sleeps 3, £23-24pp) which can be rented by the night outside the school summer holidays.

The nearest B&B, about a mile north of Portscatho, is *Trewithian Farm* (Map 104; ☎ 01872-580293, 🖥 trewithian-farm.co.uk; 2D/2T/2F; 🐾; from £37.50pp, sgl occ from £55), a 400-year-old stone farmhouse with spacious rooms. To get here, take the lane running north from Porthcurnick Beach (see Map 103), past Rosevine, then turn left at the sign for St Mawes and Truro, and walk to the end of the lane.

First Kernow's 50 **bus** passes through Gerrans and Portscatho en route between St Mawes and Truro. [See also pp52-6].

PORTSCATHO TO PORTLOE
[MAPS 103-106]

Things get a little trickier after Portscatho on this **7½-mile (12km; 2½-3hrs)** stage. The path initially describes an arc bending eastwards around sizeable **Gerrans Bay**, passing some lovely little beaches such as at Porthcurnick (where you could seek out *The Hidden Hut* café; 🖥 hiddenhut.co.uk; Mar-Oct daily 10am-5pm, lunch served noon-3pm), Pendower and neighbouring Carne (which at low tide unite to form one huge, very inviting expanse of sand). You could stop at the luxury *Nare Hotel* (Map 105; ☎ 01872-501111, 🖥 narehotel.co.uk; 36 rooms; low season from £147.50pp, sgl £158, double that in the summer) but you probably won't want to blow your entire holiday budget on one of their rooms.

Nare Head provides the stage's first real test, the path undulating ever more severely before culminating in a steep al-fresco staircase that soars up to the

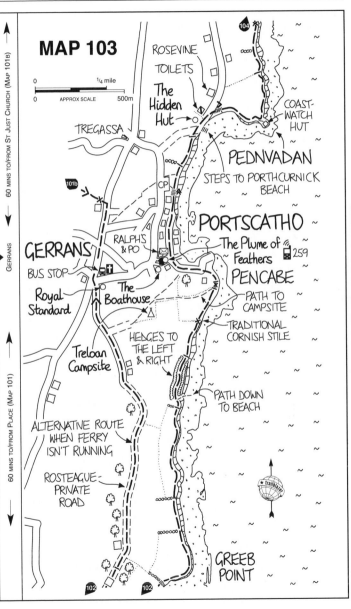

MAP 103

60 MINS TO/FROM ST JUST CHURCH (MAP 101B)

GERRANS

60 MINS TO/FROM PLACE (MAP 101)

ROSEVINE
TOILETS

The
Hidden
Hut

TREGASSA

COAST-
WATCH
HUT

PEDNVADAN

STEPS TO PORTHCURNICK
BEACH

CP

PORTSCATHO

RALPH'S
& PO

The Plume of
Feathers   259

GERRANS

PENCABE

BUS STOP

Royal
Standard

The Boathouse

PATH TO
CAMPSITE

TRADITIONAL
CORNISH STILE

HEDGES TO
THE LEFT
& RIGHT

Treloan
Campsite

PATH DOWN
TO BEACH

ALTERNATIVE ROUTE
WHEN FERRY
ISN'T RUNNING

ROSTEAGUE -
PRIVATE
ROAD

GREEB
POINT

ROUTE GUIDE AND MAPS

1/4 mile

APPROX SCALE   500m

Head. From here, the path becomes kinder as it drops gently through fields into the slumbering fishing village of Portloe.

PORTLOE   [MAP 106, p265]

Yet another pretty little fishing harbour, this one is tinier and even more tranquil than most. The centre of life in the village lies a short jaunt up the road from the harbour at *The Ship Inn* (☎ 01872-501356; 2D/1T; WI-FI; from £40pp, sgl occ £60), with rooms and food (daily noon-2pm & 6-9pm). It has a relaxing beer garden across the road. Back down on the path, the upmarket *Lugger*

Hotel (☎ 01872-501322, 🖳 luggerhotel .com; 23D; ☕; WI-FI; 🐾; £60-84pp, sgl occ from £110pp; food daily 12.30-2pm & 7-9pm) has a lovely location on the water's edge and is open for morning coffee. It doesn't take single-night bookings at weekends, though.

A more affordable option is *Carradale* (☎ 01872-501508, 🖳 carradale-bnb.co.uk;

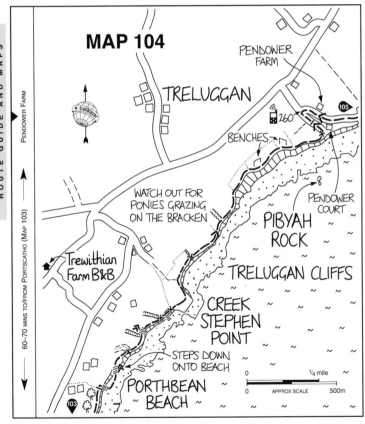

MAP 104

PENDOWER FARM

TRELUGGAN

🖳 260

105

BENCHES

WATCH OUT FOR PONIES GRAZING ON THE BRACKEN

PENDOWER COURT

PIBYAH ROCK

Trewithian Farm B&B

TRELUGGAN CLIFFS

CREEK STEPHEN POINT

STEPS DOWN ONTO BEACH

PORTHBEAN BEACH

103

0   ¼ mile
0   APPROX SCALE   500m

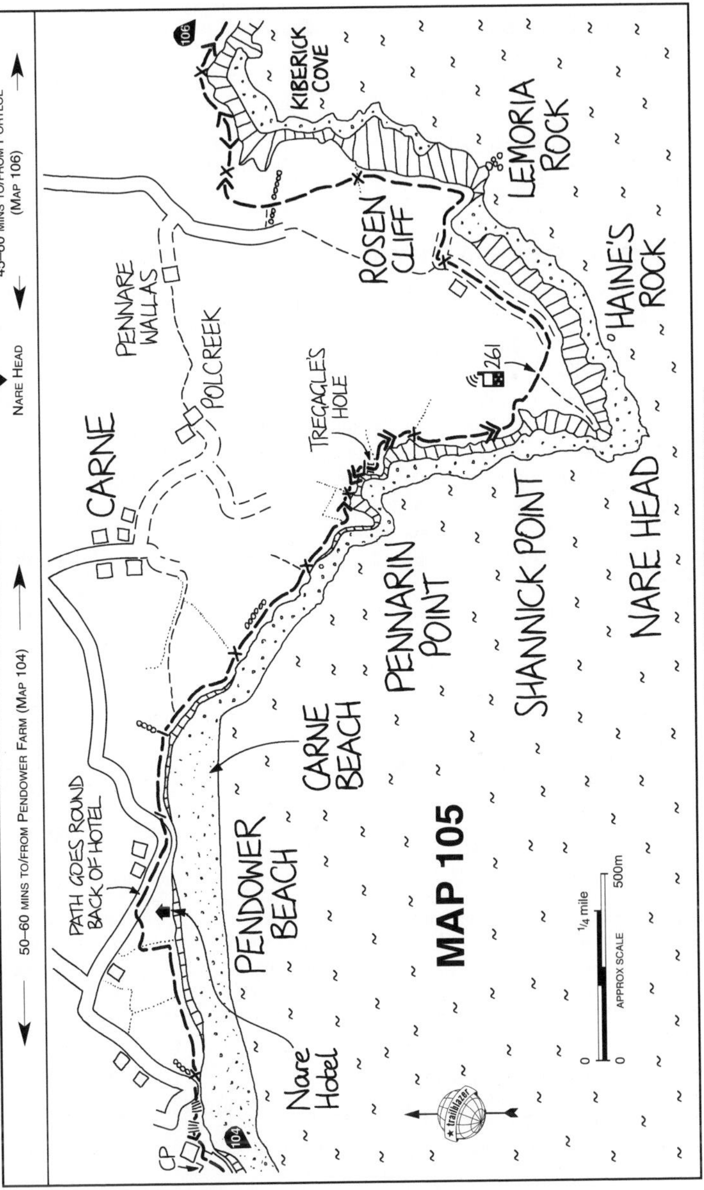
50–60 MINS TO/FROM PENDOWER FARM (MAP 104)
NARE HEAD
45–60 MINS TO/FROM PORTLOE (MAP 106)
104
106
CP
PATH GOES ROUND BACK OF HOTEL
Nare Hotel
PENDOWER BEACH
CARNE BEACH
CARNE
PENNARE WALLAS
POLCREEK
TREGAGLE'S HOLE
PENNARIN POINT
SHANNICK POINT
NARE HEAD
261
ROSEN CLIFF
HAINE'S ROCK
LEMORIA ROCK
KIBERICK COVE
MAP 105
0
1/4 mile
0
500m
APPROX SCALE
trailblazer

2D; WI-FI; 🐾; from £42pp, sgl occ £56), run by a very welcoming couple and set in its own spacious garden, 200 yards beyond the pub.

Right on the coast path, just before the village, B&B is available at the grand Georgian clifftop *Broom Parc* (☎ 01872-501803, 🖥 broomparc.co.uk; 1D/2T; £45-52.50pp) which is something of a local landmark, having been the setting for the 1992 television adaptation of Mary Wesley's novel *The Camomile Lawn*.

Portloe United Church (☎ 01872-320103) sometimes has a **pop-up tea shop** (11am-5pm) serving teas, pasties and sandwiches at very reasonable prices.

First Kernow's No 51 **bus** is Portloe's link to the outside world. To get to Portscatho you would need to transfer onto the No 50 at Tregony. [See also pp52-6].

PORTLOE TO GORRAN HAVEN   [MAPS 106-110]

This relatively easy **9-mile** (**14.5km; 2-3hrs**) stage is one of the prettiest in southern Cornwall. A fairly uneventful stretch of clifftop marching, broken up by a couple of stiff gradients, brings you eventually to the twin hamlets of **West** and **East Portholland**. You may well need some sustenance at the **Porthluney Cove** beach café (Map 108, *YHA Boswinger* is also on this map with details on p269) in preparation for the hike up to Dodman Point, which is embellished with a large stone cross that was erected at the end of the 19th century as a navigational aid. **Dodman Point** was actually once the location of a huge Iron Age fort, the biggest in the South West. Reasons as to why early Britons should have chosen to build their fortifications here quickly become obvious on a clear day, with views to Lizard Point in one direction and Berry Head in the other. It's a lovely spot for a rest.

After Dodman, the path follows a fairly gentle course down to the peaceful village of **Gorran Haven**.

WEST & EAST PORTHOLLAND   [MAP 107, p266]

Both Porthollands combined may only have around forty residents and form part of the gorgeous estate of **Caerhays Castle** (☎ 01872-501310, 🖥 caerhays.co.uk; gardens open mid Feb to mid June daily 10am-4pm; castle open only for guided tours, mid Mar to mid June Mon-Fri at noon, 1.30pm & 3pm; £9 garden or castle, £15 for both), which peers above the trees to your left on reaching **Porthluney Cove** (Map 108). The castle itself was designed by Georgian architect John Nash, most famous as the man behind Buckingham Palace, Marble Arch and much of Regency London.

East Portholland boasts the delightfully cute *Pebbles Café and Crafts* (☎ 01872-501036, 🖥 pebblescafeandcrafts.com; Easter-Sep daily 10.30am-4.30pm), and the cosy, self-contained *Seaspray Cottage B&B* (☎ 01872-501187, 🖥 seaspraycornwall.co.uk; 1D & sitting room; £40pp; min 2-night stay preferred).

At Porthluney Cove, the seasonal *café* (Map 108; 11am-5pm) next to the car park is an excellent one. It's set back from the beach without sea views, but there are views of the castle, and the food is very good. They open later than usual some summer evenings, and they occasionally have live music.

❏ **Important note – walking times**
Unless otherwise specified, **all times in this book refer only to the time spent walking**. You will need to add 20-30% to allow for rests, photography, checking the map, drinking water etc. When planning the day's hike count on 5-7 hours' actual walking.

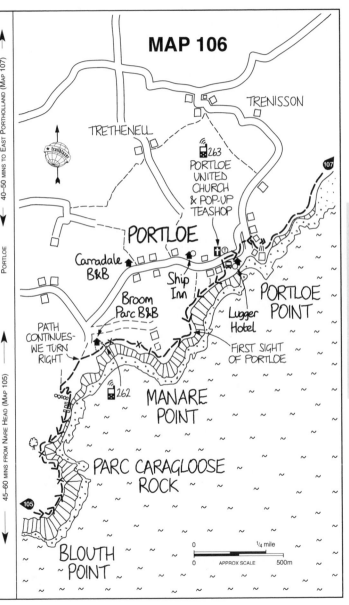

MAP 106

TRENISSON

TRETHENELL

★ trailblazer

▯263
PORTLOE
UNITED
CHURCH
& POP-UP
TEASHOP

PORTLOE

Carradale
B&B

Ship
Inn

PORTLOE
POINT

Broom
Parc B&B

Lugger
Hotel

FIRST SIGHT
OF PORTLOE

PATH
CONTINUES—
WE TURN
RIGHT

▯262
MANARE
POINT

PARC CARAGLOOSE
ROCK

BLOUTH
POINT

0   ¼ mile
0   APPROX SCALE   500m

40–50 MINS TO EAST PORTHOLLAND (MAP 107)

PORTLOE

45–60 MINS FROM NARE HEAD (MAP 105)

107

105

ROUTE GUIDE AND MAPS

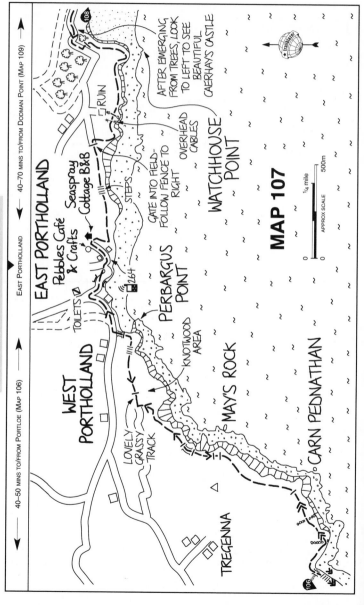

MAP 107

← 40-50 MINS TO/FROM PORTLOE (Map 106) →   EAST PORTHOLLAND   ← 40-70 MINS TO/FROM DODMAN POINT (Map 109) →

← 40-70 MINS TO/FROM DODMAN POINT (MAP 109) →

WEST PORTHOLLAND

EAST PORTHOLLAND

Pebbles Café & Crafts

Seaspray Cottage B&B

TOILETS

LOVELY GRASSY TRACK

KNOTWOOD AREA

PERBARGUS POINT

MAY'S ROCK

CARN PEDNATHAN

TREGENNA

RUIN

AFTER EMERGING FROM TREES, LOOK TO LEFT TO SEE BEAUTIFUL CAERHAYS CASTLE

OVERHEAD CABLES

GATE INTO FIELD – FOLLOW FENCE TO RIGHT

STEPS

WATCHHOUSE POINT

APPROX SCALE
0   500m
0   ¼ mile

108

106

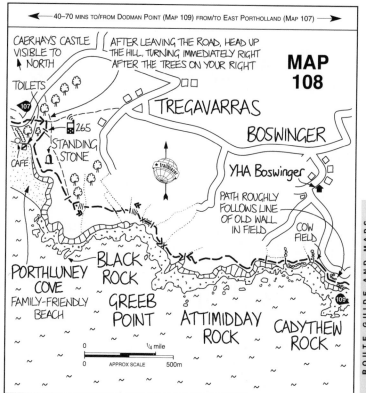

CAERHAYS CASTLE VISIBLE TO NORTH

AFTER LEAVING THE ROAD, HEAD UP THE HILL, TURNING IMMEDIATELY RIGHT AFTER THE TREES ON YOUR RIGHT

MAP 108

TOILETS

107

265

STANDING STONE

CAFE

TREGAVARRAS

BOSWINGER

★ trailblazer

YHA Boswinger

PATH ROUGHLY FOLLOWS LINE OF OLD WALL IN FIELD

COW FIELD

PORTHLUNEY COVE

FAMILY-FRIENDLY BEACH

BLACK ROCK

GREEB POINT

ATTIMIDDAY ROCK

CADYTHEW ROCK

109

0   ¼ mile
APPROX SCALE
0   500m

ROUTE GUIDE AND MAPS

GORRAN HAVEN   [MAP 110, p269]

Sheltered from the wind by Dodman Point, Gorran Haven is a popular spot, particularly for families who can enjoy the sandy beaches that are amongst the safest in the county. It's a location, however, that Gorran Haven seems reluctant to exploit: not only is there no tourist office (visitors can instead consult the village's website, 🖥 gorranhaven.org.uk), but nor is there – perhaps uniquely for Cornwall – a pub.

Other facilities are thin on the ground too, though the very friendly folks at **Cakebreads shop** (Mon-Sat 8am-7pm, Sun 8.45am-5pm) have both a bakery and the village **post office** (Mon-Fri 9am-5pm,

Sat 9am-4pm). Alongside it is *Cakebreads Café* (summer 8am-6pm, winter to 4pm), a licensed café in a marquee, which does a hearty full English breakfast. Note that hours may differ depending on the season.

Camping in Gorran Haven can be found roughly three-quarters of a mile from the path at *Trelispen* (☎ 01726-843501, 🖥 trelispen.co.uk; 🐾; 2 people & tent £10-12). To get here turn left at the end of Church St and walk along Chute Lane. Arriving at Trewollock Lane, turn right and follow this until you reach a T-junction; turn left here and continue; the campsite is on your right. Hikers don't need to reserve

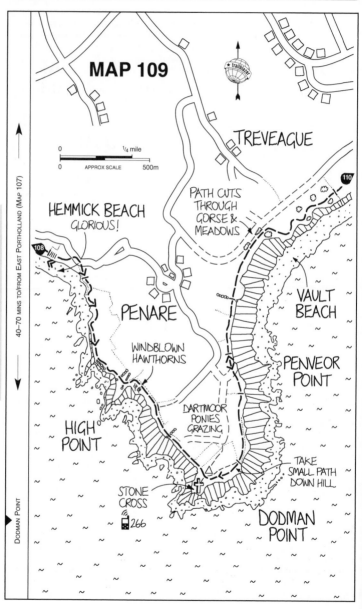

MAP 109

TREVEAGUE

HEMMICK BEACH
GLORIOUS!

PATH CUTS
THROUGH
GORSE &
MEADOWS

PENARE

VAULT
BEACH

WINDBLOWN
HAWTHORNS

PENVEOR
POINT

HIGH
POINT

DARTMOOR
PONIES
GRAZING

STONE
CROSS

📱266

TAKE
SMALL PATH
DOWN HILL

DODMAN
POINT

ROUTE GUIDE AND MAPS

40–70 MINS TO/FROM EAST PORTHOLLAND (Map 107)

DODMAN POINT

a pitch, although calling ahead won't hurt. The nearest budget accommodation is back over the side of Dodman Point, at *YHA Boswinger* (Map 108; ☎ 0345-371 9107, 💻 yha.org.uk/hostel/boswinger; 40 beds including some private rooms; WI-FI; £16-25pp). Walking via Penare (Map 109) is quickest, if you're going west.

The very welcoming *Swiftshore B&B* (☎ 01726-844847, 💻 swiftshore.co.uk; 1Tr; 🐾; WI-FI; from £40pp) has a self-contained annexe. *The Llawnroc* (☎ 01726-843461, 💻 thellawnrochotel.co.uk; 18 rooms; 🍺;

WI-FI; £60-125pp, sgl occ rate on request), Gorran Haven's only hotel, is a large modern place with plenty of luxuries, although it's far from cheap. The hotel's *Gwineas Bar & Bistro* (food daily noon-9.30pm, bar Mon-Sat 11am-11pm, Sun noon-10.30pm; mains £11.50-20) is the closest thing Gorran Haven has to a pub, and you're welcome to just pop in for a pint. In case you haven't spotted it, 'Llawnroc' is 'Cornwall' backwards!

The Haven Fish & Chips (Easter-Aug noon-9pm) is a popular chippy, but the

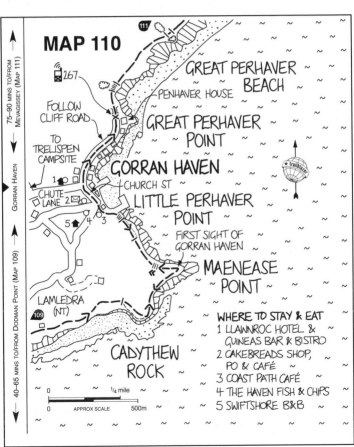

MAP 110

75-90 MINS TO/FROM MEVAGISSEY (MAP 111)

GORRAN HAVEN

40-65 MINS TO/FROM DODMAN POINT (MAP 109)

📱267

FOLLOW CLIFF ROAD

TO TRELISPEN CAMPSITE

GREAT PERHAVER BEACH

PENHAVER HOUSE

GREAT PERHAVER POINT

GORRAN HAVEN

CHURCH ST

LITTLE PERHAVER POINT

FIRST SIGHT OF GORRAN HAVEN

★ trailblazer

MAENEASE POINT

CHUTE LANE

LAMLEDRA (NT)

109

CADYTHEW ROCK

WHERE TO STAY & EAT
1 LLAWNROC HOTEL & GUINEAS BAR & BISTRO
2 CAKEBREADS SHOP, PO & CAFÉ
3 COAST PATH CAFÉ
4 THE HAVEN FISH & CHIPS
5 SWIFTSHORE B&B

0 ¼ mile
0 500m
APPROX SCALE

standout place for some light food is lovely community-run *Coast Path Café* (Tue & Wed 2-4.30pm, Thur-Sat 10.30am-4.30pm, Sun 12.30-4.30pm), staffed entirely by volunteers (hence the limited opening hours) who serve homemade cakes, sandwiches, tea and coffee from their perch right on the coast path.

For **buses**, the invaluable but limited Gorran and District Community Bus's G1, G3 & G4 (☎ 01726-844933; reservations recommended). [See also pp52-6].

GORRAN HAVEN TO MEVAGISSEY [MAPS 110-111]

A relatively easy **3½-mile (5.5km; 1¼-1½hrs)** amble across a small headland separates Gorran Haven from Mevagissey, a picturesque stroll that takes in the lovely cottages at **Chapel Point**, built in the 1930s (using stone quarried from the point itself) and which featured in Daphne du Maurier's novel *The House on the Strand*. The point is preceded on the trail by a clifftop meadow known as **Bodrugan's Leap**, named after Sir Henry Bodrugan who is said to have successfully leapt off the cliffs to a waiting boat in the cove below in his efforts to evade his pursuer, Sir Richard Edgcumbe of Cothele, during the War of the Roses in the 15th century.

Soon afterwards you reach the Mevagissey suburb of **Portmellon**, where the local, 17th-century pub, *The Rising Sun* (Map 111; ☎ 01726-843235, 🖥 theris ingsuninn.com; 1S/1T/2D/1F; WI-FI; from £40pp; food 12.30-2.30pm & 6-8pm) serves good-value food (mains £8.50-16.50), fine Cornish ales, and has rooms available for B&B. The path then follows the road into Mevagissey itself.

MEVAGISSEY [map p272]

Named after two saints, Meva and Issey, the busy, bustling working harbour of Mevagissey is one of the highlights of the south Cornish Coast. It also has all that the walker needs, including some great pubs and restaurants and several decent B&Bs.

There is believed to have been a settlement on this site as early as the Bronze Age and it was mentioned in records that date back to the early 14th century (though it was called Porthhilly then). The town only truly thrived, however, with the rise of the pilchard industry. The fish provided both a source of nutrition *and* a source of power, a power station having been built in the village in 1895 that ran on pilchard oil! As a result, Mevagissey claims to be the first village in England to have had electric street lighting.

Today there is plenty to warrant you spending at least a morning here, and if you're not too pushed for time a day of gentle meandering and munching can be enjoyably passed. Sights are few, though the **Museum** (☎ 01726-843568, 🖥 mevagissey museum.com; Easter-Oct 11am-4pm, July & Aug 10am-5pm), set between harbour and sea, is interesting, and free to visit. Housed in a building that dates back to the 1740s, it's a cute little place with some interesting curios including a £1 note from the Bank of Mevagissey, and photos of the village from the 19th and 20th centuries.

Services
Visitor Information can be found in Hurley Books (☎ 01726-842200; daily 10am-4pm) on Jetty St. The **post office** is in the Premier **shop** (Mon-Sat 7am-8pm, Sun to 7pm) just off Market Sq on River St. Boots **pharmacy** (Mon-Fri 9am-6pm, Sat 9am-5pm, Sun 10am-4pm) is on Fore St.

Where to stay
If you don't mind staying above a pub and wish to be right in the centre, *The Ship Inn* (☎ 01726-843324, 🖥 theshipinnmeva.co .uk; 3D/2F; ➤; WI-FI; from £40pp, sgl occ £60-75), on Fore St, is an old-fashioned

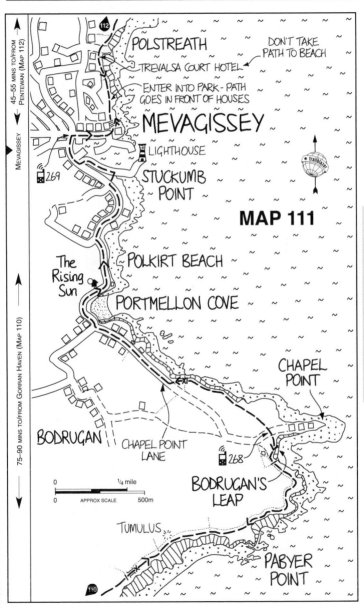

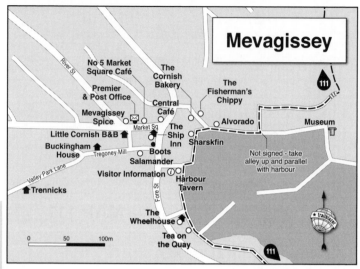

Cornish fisherman's pub with low ceilings and decent rooms. Another pub with accommodation, *The Wheelhouse Restaurant and Guesthouse* (☎ 01726-339029, 🖳 wheelhouserestaurant.co.uk; 3D; WI-FI; £33-40pp, sgl occ room rate), sits right on the harbourfront, and has rooms with – naturally – great harbour views.

One of the cutest **B&Bs** is *The Little Cornish B&B* (☎ 01726-842563, 🖳 lit tlecornishbandb.co.uk; 3D; WI-FI; £35-45pp, sgl occ from £40), at 1-2 River Terrace. It's a quirky, friendly place with helpful hosts and a fine breakfast; booking directly will get you the best price.

The elegant and spacious *Buckingham House* (☎ 01726-843375, 🖳 bucking hamhousemevagissey.co.uk; 4D or F; ☛; WI-FI; 🐾; from £37.50pp, sgl occ £70-85) is at 17 Tregoney Hill.

A short distance from the centre is *Trennicks* (☎ 01726-842235, 🖳 trennicks guesthouse.co.uk; 3D; WI-FI; £42.50-47.50pp, sgl occ from £70), on Valley Park Lane. Its elevated position makes for some wonderful harbour and sea views – enjoy them whilst eating salmon for breakfast, or after a lazy dip in the outdoor pool.

Where to eat and drink
No 5 Market Square Café (9am-3pm & 6-8pm) is a lovely eatery that serves up gourmet burgers as well as old classics like fish and chips. In tune with the times they also now offer tapas.

You'll find the usual collection of lovely pubs with good menus in the town. *The Ship Inn* (see Where to stay; daily summer noon-9pm; winter noon-3pm & 6-9pm) has varied and locally caught fish on the specials board each day – their prices will depend on the cost of the catch. *The Wheelhouse* (see Where to stay; food daily Mar-Oct 9am-9pm, Nov-Feb to 4pm) is one of the larger places on the waterfront, and one of the oldest too, with the building said to date back to the early 19th century. It was a net loft in a previous incarnation, where it is said the Methodist John Wesley preached his first sermon. These days the inn has opted for a pirate theme, with several life-sized swashbucklers gazing down upon you as you dine. Food consists of breakfasts, a gastro lunch menu, and evening meals (6-9pm) in summer, including a fish grill. *Harbour Tavern* (food 10am-9pm) does food throughout the day including breakfast in two sizes. Further along, *The Sharksfin* (☎ 01726-842969; food noon-3pm & 5-9pm), has daily fish specials but fairly standard pub food otherwise.

Also on the waterfront, *Alvorado* (☎ 01726-842055; Tue-Sun noon-2pm & 6.30 to late; mains £13.50-19.50) is an authentic Portuguese seafood restaurant that's been going for more than 20 years.

Arguably the best restaurant in Mevagissey, however, is *Salamander* (☎ 01726-842254, 🖳 salamander-restaurant .co.uk; Tue-Sat 6-9.30pm, daily in summer), a lovely little place serving local produce where possible from a tastebud-tantalising menu featuring choices such as Cornish chicken fillet stuffed with hogs pudding and Helford blue cheese wrapped in Parma ham and roasted, and served with pink pepper sauce. A two- or three-course meal costs a set £21 or £26.

For something spicier, *Mevagissey Spice* (☎ 01726-844701 or ☎ 01726-843373; Mon-Sat 5.30-11pm, Sun noon-10pm), at 3-4 River St, is the town's local Indian restaurant. For cheaper bites there are several options including *Fisherman's Chippy* (☎ 01726-842209; summer daily noon-9pm, winter weekends only); fish & chips costs approximately £7. Opposite that, *The Cornish Bakery* (daily 9am-9.30pm, to 4.30pm out of season) does the best pasties in town.

Central Café (9am-5pm; 🐾) is a no-frills café; good for all-day breakfasts (£5.95-8.25) and the like. For something more refined, try *Tea on the Quay* (9am-5pm, Sun to 4.30pm), a cute harbour-side café; perfect for cream teas (£5.25).

Transport

[See also pp52-6] For **buses**, First Kernow's service No 24 will transport you to Fowey via Pentewan, St Austell, Charleston and Par.

For Gorran Haven there's Travel Cornwall's 471, and Gorran and District Community Bus's G1, G3 & G4 (☎ 01726-844933; seat reservation recommended).

MEVAGISSEY TO CHARLESTOWN [MAPS 111-114]

This 7¼-mile (11.75km; 2¾-3¾hrs) stage is one of the toughest on the Cornish south coast, superseded perhaps only by the later stretch between Polruan and Polperro.

It starts gently enough, with a straightforward stroll to **Pentewan** (see p274), a small and unassuming village squashed hard by coast and caravan park. However, things get decidedly more dramatic as the path tackles the often sharp ascents leading to Black Head, the route seeming to take an almost perverse pleasure in finding gradients to climb. A secluded woodland valley decorated here and there with wooden statues provides some distraction from the sweat-inducing slopes as you approach **Black Head**, which was yet another location for an Iron Age fort. The path doesn't visit the head itself, preferring instead to take a sharp left by a large stone memorial to the Cornish poet and historian AL Rowse – the stone at least providing you with an excuse to tarry awhile before tackling more of the path.

A couple of climbs later and you find yourself entering into the Cornish nature reserve of **Ropehaven** – famed for its fulmars which nest on ledges in the cliff-face – alas, not visible from the trail itself.

A few more steep gradients separate you from the beach at **Porthpean**. Note, periodic cliff erosion in recent years means that the coastal path on the final stretch into **Charlestown** (see p276), is sometimes diverted inland along Porthpean Beach Rd (Map 114). Follow the signpost instructions.

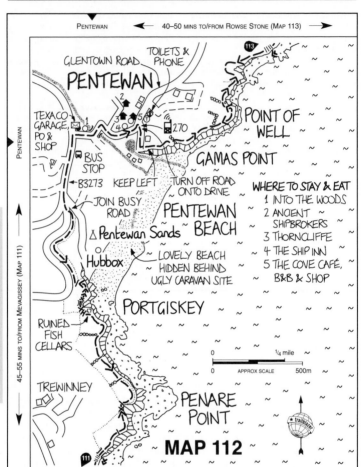

GLENTOWN ROAD
TOILETS & PHONE
PENTEWAN
TEXACO GARAGE, PO & SHOP
BUS STOP
B3273 KEEP LEFT
JOIN BUSY ROAD
△ Pentewan Sands
Hubbox
RUINED FISH CELLARS
TREWINNEY

POINT OF WELL
GAMAS POINT
TURN OFF ROAD ONTO DRIVE
PENTEWAN BEACH
LOVELY BEACH HIDDEN BEHIND UGLY CARAVAN SITE
PORTGISKEY
PENARE POINT

WHERE TO STAY & EAT
1 INTO THE WOODS
2 ANCIENT SHIPBROKERS
3 THORNCLIFFE
4 THE SHIP INN
5 THE COVE CAFÉ, B&B & SHOP

0 ¼ mile
0 APPROX SCALE 500m

★ trailblazer

MAP 112

PENTEWAN [MAP 112]

The name Pentewan comes from the Cornish 'Pen', meaning headland, and 'Towan', which means sand dunes. As with most headlands on this stretch there was once an Iron Age fort here, and in the 19th century the town was a major port for the china clay industry, big enough to rival nearby Charlestown and to handle about a third of all the china clay produced in the country. Since the 1950s, however, the village has been better known for – and dwarfed by – the huge caravan site that you probably just walked past.

Services aren't particularly comprehensive in the village. There's no tourist office, for example, though the village website (🖳 pentewan.com) is surprisingly informative given the size of the place. On

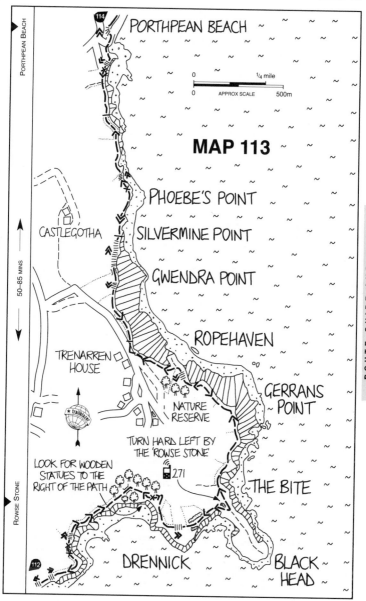

PORTHPEAN BEACH

0 ___ 1/4 mile
0 ___ APPROX SCALE ___ 500m

MAP 113

PHOEBE'S POINT

SILVERMINE POINT

CASTLEGOTHA

GWENDRA POINT

ROPEHAVEN

GERRANS POINT

TRENARREN HOUSE

NATURE RESERVE

TURN HARD LEFT BY THE 'ROWSE STONE'

271

THE BITE

LOOK FOR WOODEN STATUES TO THE RIGHT OF THE PATH

DRENNICK

BLACK HEAD

PORTHPEAN BEACH

50–85 MINS

ROWSE STONE

ROUTE GUIDE AND MAPS

the village's outskirts is a Texaco garage which has a **shop** (Mon-Sat 8am-8pm, to 6pm in winter, Sun 9am-4pm, to 2pm in winter) and also houses the **post office** (Mon-Fri 9am-5.30pm, Sat to 12.30pm).

Where to stay
It's not everyone's cup of tea, and it's hideously expensive in July and August, but you can **camp** at the large beachside holiday park, *Pentewan Sands* (☎ 01726-843485, ☐ pentewan.co.uk; tents £14.30-£35.20).

Otherwise, accommodation is limited to the few B&Bs in the village, all of which lie within a stone's throw of the path. The short row of traditional Cornish granite terraces leads on to Higher West End where you will find *Thorncliffe* (☎ 01726-843583, ☐ pentewanbedandbreakfast.co.uk; 1D/1T shared facilities; WI-FI; from £30pp); a large board on the corner as you climb the hill advertises the establishment's sea view. At No 1, *Ancient Shipbrokers* (☎ 01726-843370, ☐ pentewanbedandbreakfast.com; 1D/2D or T; WI-FI; from £36pp) is another welcoming option with lovely views.

Above its namesake (see Where to eat and drink) is *The Cove* (☎ 01726-843781, ☐ pentewanbandb.co.uk; 1T/3D; ✸; WI-FI; from £42.50pp, sgl occ £45). Relax in the guests' lounge and warm your feet by the wood-burner whilst considering which variety of breakfast you might require: both continental and Turkish (!) are options.

Where to eat and drink
Hubbox (☎ 01726-844189, ☐ hubbox.co .uk; 11.30am-9pm) is a popular beach shack with indoor and outdoor seating, serving gourmet burgers and hotdogs as well as beer on tap.

The family-run café, *The Cove* (Easter to Oct 10am-5pm) does tea, coffee, tea-cakes and sandwiches, while the adjoining *Cove Shop* (Apr-Sep daily 10am-5pm) sells cold drinks and ice-creams.

The Ship Inn (☎ 01726-842855, ☐ theshipinnpentewan.co.uk; food daily 10am-9pm, winter hours vary; WI-FI; ✸) serves fairly standard pub grub (fish & chips, steak & ale pie, vegetable lasagne) at decent prices (mains £8-17), as well as more expensive steaks.

On your way into the village, *Into the Woods* (☎ 01726-844639; bar noon-11.45pm; food daily noon-9pm, hours may vary out of season) is a family-run bar and restaurant serving Cornish ales and lagers amongst other drinks. The food is decent enough and there's a pleasant beer garden to sit in.

Transport
[See also pp52-6] First Kernow's No 24 & Travel Cornwall's 471 **bus** services connect the village with the surrounding area. Gorran and District Community Bus's G1, G3 & G4 also pass through (☎ 01726-844933; seat reservation recommended).

CHARLESTOWN [MAP 114]
One of the lovelier spots on the whole path, the unspoilt harbour village of Charlestown was partly developed by – and named after – local landowner Charles Rashleigh in the late 18th century as a port for the booming china clay industry. Once a thriving dock, its history is celebrated at the **Shipwreck and Heritage Centre** (☎ 01726-69897, ☐ ship wreckcharlestown.com; Mar-Oct 10am-5pm; WI-FI; ✸) which claims to have the biggest collection of artefacts recovered from shipwrecks anywhere in the UK.

There are no small grocery stores in the village. The nearest **supermarket** is Tesco (open 24hrs, free **ATM**), half a mile out of town; turn right along Church Rd, then left at the small roundabout. In the village itself, there's an ATM (£1.50 charge) in The Rashleigh Arms.

Where to stay
There is a splendid **campsite** on the eastern edge of the village. As well as having above-standard facilities, *Broadmeadow House* (☎ 01726-76636, ☐ broadmeadow house.com; WI-FI; ✸; hiker & tent £10) is run by a knowledgeable local lady with lots of useful tips on the surrounding area. There is a 'Camp and Breakfast' deal where, having spent a night under canvas,

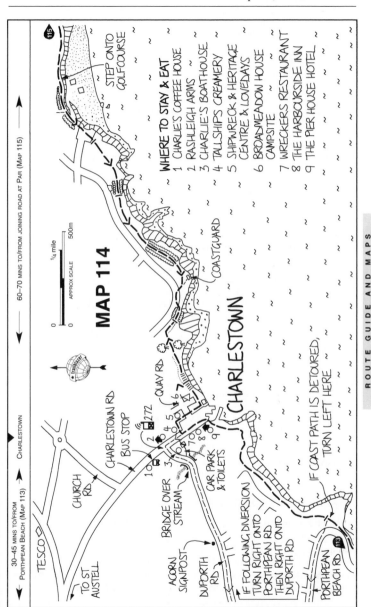

30-45 MINS TO/FROM Porthpean Beach (Map 113) ▶ Charlestown ▶ 60-70 MINS TO/FROM JOINING ROAD AT PAR (MAP 115)

TESCO

CHURCH RD

TO ST AUSTELL

CHARLESTOWN RD

BUS STOP

★ Trailblazer

MAP 114

APPROX SCALE
0   1/4 mile
0   500m

STEP ONTO GOLFCOURSE

115

COASTGUARD

QUAY RD

CHARLESTOWN

BRIDGE OVER STREAM

272

CAR PARK & TOILETS

ACORN SIGNPOST

DUPORTH RD

IF FOLLOWING DIVERSION
TURN RIGHT ONTO
PORTHPEAN RD
THEN RIGHT ONTO
DUPORTH RD

IF COAST PATH IS DETOURED, TURN LEFT HERE

PORTHPEAN BEACH RD

113

WHERE TO STAY & EAT
1 CHARLIES COFFEE HOUSE
2 RASHLEIGH ARMS
3 CHARLIE'S BOATHOUSE
4 TALLSHIPS CREAMERY
5 SHIPWRECK & HERITAGE CENTRE & LOVEDAYS
6 BROADMEADOW HOUSE CAMPSITE
7 WRECKERS RESTAURANT
8 THE HARBOURSIDE INN
9 THE PIER HOUSE HOTEL

you can look forward to your pre-ordered breakfast basket (£7). It's one of the best little campsites on the path, but it only has 12 pitches, so if possible book in advance for August. If it is full, head to *Carlyon Bay Camping Park* (Map 115; ☎ 01726-812735, 🖳 carlyonbay.net; WI-FI; hiker & tent £10-12), a large but friendly holiday park which never turns away walkers. They have a *café* (8-10am & 6-8pm), a shop, and even a heated outdoor pool! Walk across the golf course between here and Par, and under the railway bridge.

The Rashleigh Arms (☎ 01726-73635, 🖳 rashleigharms.co.uk; 18 rooms; ▼; WI-FI; from £42pp, sgl occ from £64; check online for offers), on Charlestown Rd, is a 150-year-old pub with rooms, eight of which are in an attached annexe. There are glimpses of the harbour, and the tall ships which sometimes frequent it, from some of the upper rooms.

Built in 1794, *The Pier House Hotel* (☎ 01726-67955, 🖳 pierhousehotel.com; 5S/19D/3F; ▼; WI-FI; from £37pp, sgl occ from £64) on the harbour-front represents Charlestown's most expensive and luxurious accommodation. Note that none of the single rooms has a sea view.

B&Bs are now operating in Charlestown via Airbnb (🖳 airbnb.co.uk).

Where to eat and drink

If simply passing through, *Tallships Creamery* (summer 10am-8pm, winter 11am-5pm) is right by the trail and can supply you with a drink, a pasty or a slice of cake. There's no indoor seating but there are benches outside to sit on.

Congenial *Charlie's Coffeehouse* (☎ 01726-67421; May-Sep Mon-Fri 9am-5pm, Sat & Sun 9am-4pm, Oct-Apr closed Mon), at 79 Charlestown Rd, has an emphasis on local non-fried food such as their smoked salmon breakfast (£6.95), paninis (around £5) and homemade cakes. Down the hill a little is their sister property *Charlie's Boathouse* (10am-9pm), which is more of a bar and bistro, with burgers and pizza on the menu.

The Rashleigh Arms (see Where to stay; food daily noon-9pm) does standard pub fare but with the occasional surprise, such as Cornish whiting goujons.

Another option is *Loveday's* (☎ 01726-67618, 🖳 shipwreckcharlestown.com/love days; Mar-Oct Mon-Wed 9.30am-9pm, Thur-Sat 9.30am-11pm, Sun 9.30am-5pm) situated above the Shipwreck and Heritage Centre. The menu is impressive and includes seafood chowder (£8.95) and fish of the day (£12.95).

For a gastro lunch or dinner head to *Wreckers* (☎ 01726-879053, 🖳 wreckers .me.uk; daily 10am-5pm & 6pm-9pm), also a good spot for a cream tea; the evening menu includes St Austell Bay mussels (£16).

Sister-inn to The Pier House Hotel (see Where to stay), *The Harbourside Inn* (food noon-9pm; WI-FI) is a St Austell Brewery pub with all-day food and a good selection of real⁺ ales. The **restaurant** adjoining *The Pier House Hotel* (see Where to stay) is another option (mains £10-20). Alongside seafood there are veggie and vegan options on offer.

Transport

[See also pp52-6] First Kernow's No 24 and 25 **bus** services stop here.

CHARLESTOWN TO FOWEY   [MAPS 114-117]

After the exertions of the previous stage these **11½ miles** (**18.5km; 3-4hrs**) are positively gentle. Unfortunately, there is a price to pay for this leniency, the path taking you firstly beside a golf course and then around the back of **Par Docks**. True, the docks and the china-clay plant that they serve do have some history, having been established back in the 19th century; but that does little to make them, or the section of road walking you have to undertake to circumvent them, any more attractive. Indeed, it's one of those stages that the coast path throws up

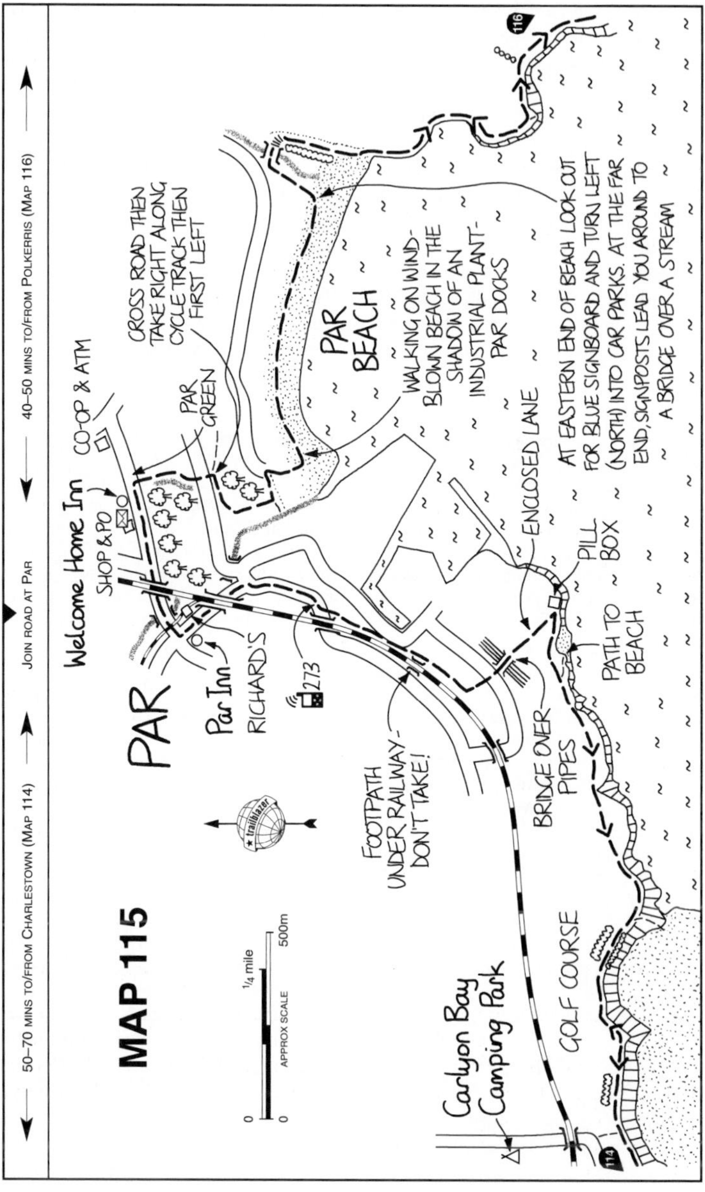

50–70 MINS TO/FROM CHARLESTOWN (MAP 114)

JOIN ROAD AT PAR

40–50 MINS TO/FROM POLKERRIS (MAP 116)

MAP 115

¼ mile

500m

APPROX SCALE

Carlyon Bay Camping Park

GOLF COURSE

FOOTPATH UNDER RAILWAY – DON'T TAKE!

BRIDGE OVER PIPES

PAR

Par Inn

RICHARD'S

273

Welcome Home Inn

CO-OP & ATM

SHOP & PO

PAR GREEN

CROSS ROAD THEN TAKE RIGHT ALONG CYCLE TRACK THEN FIRST LEFT

PILL BOX

ENCLOSED LANE

PATH TO BEACH

WALKING ON WIND-BLOWN BEACH IN THE SHADOW OF AN INDUSTRIAL PLANT – PAR DOCKS

PAR BEACH

AT EASTERN END OF BEACH LOOK OUT FOR BLUE SIGNBOARD AND TURN LEFT (NORTH) INTO CAR PARKS. AT THE FAR END, SIGNPOSTS LEAD YOU AROUND TO A BRIDGE OVER A STREAM

116

114

occasionally to remind walkers that they are still in the real world. Still, the beach at the end of **Par** is nice enough and backed by some interesting dunes that actually form a nature reserve – though with the industrial plant so close, you may want to save your swimming for later.

Climbing away from the sands, the path is fairly straightforward to **Polkerris** and its lovely little enclosed beach. From Polkerris the path continues its relatively gentle way to the red and white tower, or **daymark**, at **Gribbin Head**, built in 1832 as a navigational aid to help sailors distinguish this promontory from neighbouring Dodman Point and St Anthony Head. From here the gradients get a little more severe as you descend to **Polridmouth** – the house here providing the inspiration for the beach house in Daphne du Maurier's novel *Rebecca* (the author used to live just up the valley; see p286) – then round **Southground Point** before passing the remains of **St Catherine's Castle**, another one of Henry VIII's many Cornish coastal fortifications, on your way into lovely Fowey.

PAR [MAP 115, p279]

Most walkers scuttle fairly quickly through Par, though there are some facilities which you may find useful. *Richard's* (8am-5pm) is a long-standing family **grocer**, and a great place to pick up fresh fruit. Over the other side of the railway line is a **shop** (Mon-Sat 6.30am-5.30pm, Sun to 1pm) which contains a **bakery** and the **post office** (Mon-Fri 7am-5.30pm, Sat 7am-4pm, Sun 8-11am). Further along there's an

ATM at the Co-op (daily 7am-10pm). *The Welcome Home Inn* (☎ 01726-816894; WI-FI; 🐾) serves **food** (daily noon-2pm & 5-8pm) and *The Par Inn* (☎ 01726-815695; WI-FI; 🐾) is good for a drink. Both are owned by St Austell Brewery.

First Kernow's No 24 & 25 **bus** services stop in Par en route between St Austell and Fowey. Par is also a stop on several of GWR's **train** services. [See also pp52-6.]

POLKERRIS [MAP 116]

Watersports are the focus for many who visit this sandy little beach. Most walkers, however, will be far more interested in the calories and liquids they can consume whilst watching those windsurfing and sailing.

The Rashleigh Inn (☎ 01726-813991, 🖳 therashleighinnpolkerris.co.uk; food daily summer noon-9pm, winter noon-3pm & 6-9pm; 🐾) serves up some great food including a mouthwatering 8oz Cornish Sirloin (£13.95) and plenty of fresh local fish (including hake and plaice). To wash all the protein and carbs down there are half a dozen real ales on tap, including

those from Skinners, St Austell brewery and Timothy Taylor. There are also ciders by both Stowford Press and Addlestones.

Sam's on the Beach (☎ 01726-812255, 🖳 samscornwall.co.uk; food noon-9pm; WI-FI; 🐾 on terrace) is next door to the pub and has a terrace overlooking the beach. Their menu includes stone-baked pizza (£8-15) and mussels (£14.95) plus an extensive wine list. You may need to reserve a table for an evening meal on summer weekends. With outside seating and friendly staff, *The Hungry Sailor* (Easter-Oct daily 9am-5pm) does coffee and light meals.

❏ Where to stay – the details

Unless specified, B&B-style accommodation is either en suite or has private facilities; 🛁 means at least one room has a bath; 🐾 signifies that dogs are welcome in at least one room but always by prior arrangement, an additional charge may also be payable (see pp336-8); WI-FI means wi-fi is available. See also p79.

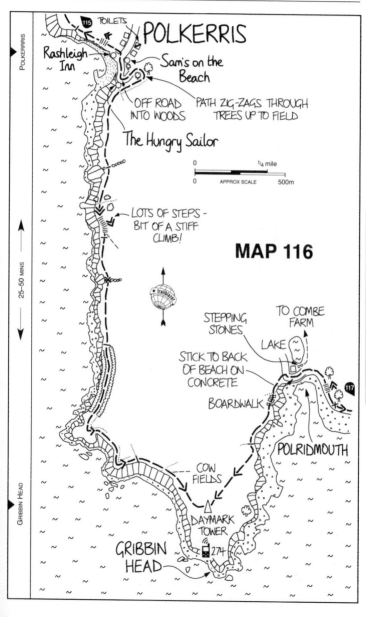

POLKERRIS

TOILETS

Rashleigh Inn

Sam's on the Beach

OFF ROAD INTO WOODS

PATH ZIG-ZAGS THROUGH TREES UP TO FIELD

The Hungry Sailor

0   ¼ mile
0   APPROX SCALE   500m

LOTS OF STEPS - BIT OF A STIFF CLIMB!

MAP 116

trailblazer

STEPPING STONES

TO COMBE FARM

LAKE

STICK TO BACK OF BEACH ON CONCRETE

BOARDWALK

POLRIDMOUTH

COW FIELDS

DAYMARK TOWER

274

GRIBBIN HEAD

POLKERRIS

25-50 MINS

GRIBBIN HEAD

ROUTE GUIDE AND MAPS

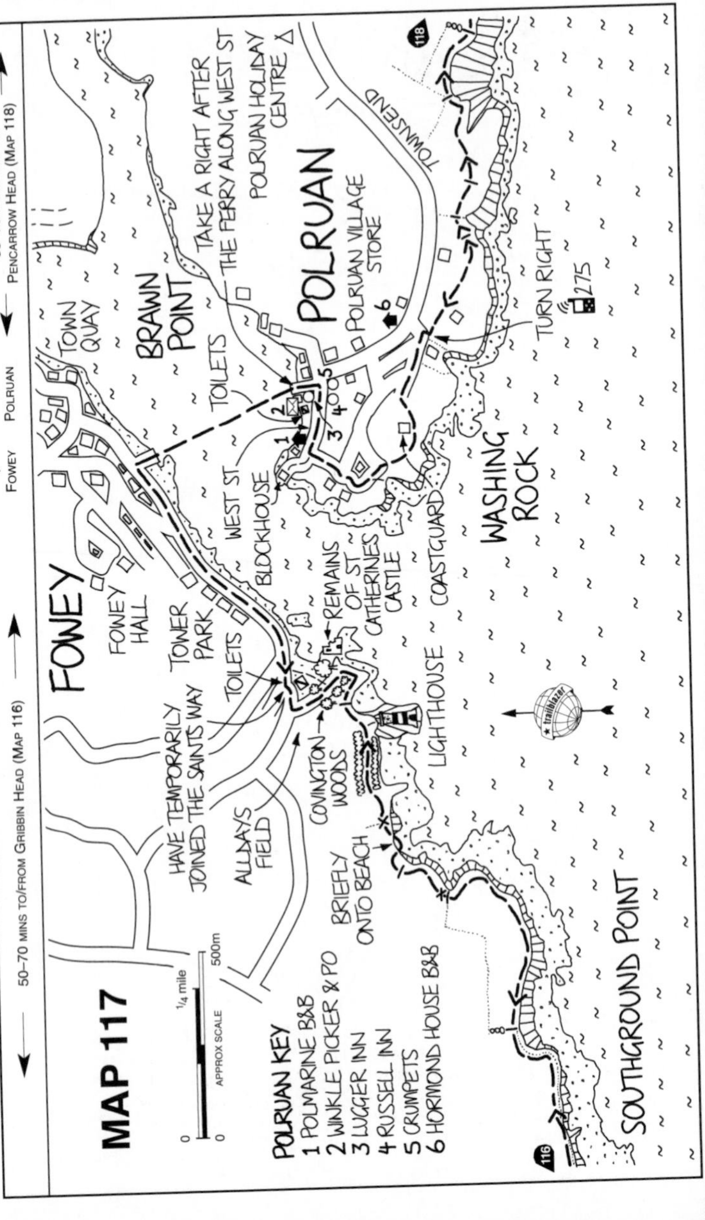

ROUTE GUIDE AND MAPS

MAP 117

0 — 500m
0 — 1/4 mile
APPROX SCALE

50-70 MINS TO/FROM GRIBBIN HEAD (MAP 116)

55-70 MINS TO/FROM PENCARROW HEAD (MAP 118)

Fowey ▶ Polruan ▶

FOWEY

FOWEY HALL

TOWER PARK

TOILETS

HAVE TEMPORARILY JOINED THE SAINTS WAY

ALLAYS FIELD

BRIEFLY ONTO BEACH

COVINGTON WOODS

REMAINS OF ST CATHERINES CASTLE

WEST ST

BLOCKHOUSE

TOWN QUAY

BRAWN POINT

TAKE A RIGHT AFTER THE FERRY ALONG WEST ST

POLRUAN HOLIDAY CENTRE △

POLRUAN

POLRUAN VILLAGE STORE

TOWNSEND

TURN RIGHT

275

WASHING ROCK

COASTGUARD

LIGHTHOUSE

trailblazer

SOUTHGROUND POINT

HORMOND HOUSE B&B

POLRUAN KEY
1 POLMARINE B&B
2 WINKLE PICKER & PO
3 LUGGER INN
4 RUSSELL INN
5 CRUMPETS
6 HORMOND HOUSE B&B

FOWEY [map p284]

It seems strange to think that what now seems an incredibly quaint, laid back and serene little Cornish town – one of the most attractive on the whole coast path – was once a major trading and industrial port. The medieval defences that you walk past on your way into the town, however, such as **St Catherine's Castle** and the two **blockhouses** that stand on either side of the river at the harbour entrance, provide an indication of just how important, commercially, this town was in the 15th and 16th centuries. Unfortunately for Fowey (pronounced 'Foy'), Plymouth's fortune was to be largely at Fowey's expense and the locals returned to fishing and smuggling to make a living. The town enjoyed a renaissance in the 19th century owing to the rise of the china clay industry. Initially, the town had to watch while other harbours at Charlestown, Par and Pentewan were established and took the lion's share of the trade. However, once it was developed, in 1869, its natural deep-water anchorage immediately gave it a considerable advantage over the shallower artificial harbours of neighbours, even though it was further from the tin mines and clay works that produced the cargo to be shipped. The beacon tower at Gribben Head also helped to improve navigation into Fowey which further increased its popularity.

While some china clay is still exported from the harbour, the mines have all now shut and the old cargo boats and steamers have largely been replaced by the yachts and pleasure craft of the amateur sailor. Indeed, it is estimated that around 7000 yachts visit in any one season, swelling the large numbers of visiting tourists that throng the main street in summer.

Services

Enjoy! Fowey Visitor Information (Mon-Sat 10.30am-4.30pm, Sun 11am-4pm) at 5 South St, is pretty limited when it actually comes to any information; the website (⌨ fowey.co.uk) is good, though. For **supplies**, Fowey Mini-market (Mon-Sat 7am-8pm, Sun 7.30am-6pm), which also houses the **post office** (Mon-Fri 9am-5.30pm, Sat 9am-12.30pm), is on the main drag, Fore St. So too is a branch of Boots **pharmacy** (Mon-Sat 9am-5.30pm, Sun 10.30am-4pm) and a **bookshop**, Bookends (⌨ bookendsoffowey .com; Mon-Sat 9.30am-5.30pm, Sun 11am-4pm), which stocks pretty much every book that was ever written by, or about, Daphne du Maurier. You'll pass a **newsagent** (8am-7pm) along the Esplanade.

❏ St Catherine's Castle and the fortifications around Fowey

When walking east from Polkerris, it is quite striking to note just how many fortifications have been built to defend Fowey down the centuries. The town was once a fairly major port and following Henry VIII's perceived attack on the Catholic Church after the Reformation and dissolution of the monasteries, it was decided that the fortifications around Britain's southern coastline needed boosting, with (largely Catholic) France and Spain threatening. The D-shaped St Catherine's Castle was built on the highest available point, with good views that encompassed the estuary as well as out to sea. Indeed, such were the strategic advantages of the site that it was utilised for defensive purposes up until the end of WWII, when it was used as a gun battery and observation point.

St Catherine's Castle, however, was not the earliest fortification protecting Fowey and its river. Prior to the castle, two **blockhouses** stood on either side of the river – medieval fortifications between which, at one time, a chain would have stretched across the river to prevent access to the harbour by invading French warships and, on occasion, rapacious pirates. The blockhouse on the Fowey side is now, alas, in a parlous state but that on the Polruan side is in reasonable condition and can be visited by taking a small detour off the coast path as you walk out of the village.

For **camping supplies** there's a Mountain Warehouse (Mon-Sat 9am-5.30pm, Sun 10am-4.30pm) on Fore St. For **internet access** use the library (Tue, Thur & Fri 9.30am-5pm; WI-FI; internet £3.60/hr or £1.80 with library card from home) on Passage Lane at the northern end of the village. There's an **ATM** near the museum.

Small and sweet little *Fowey Aquarium* (☎ 07815-840467, 🖳 fowey aquarium.co.uk; Apr-May 10.30am-4pm, Jun-Aug 10am-5pm, Sep-Oct 10.30am-4pm; £4) is located on land that was previously part of the covered market. *Fowey Museum* (Easter-Sep Mon-Fri 10.30am-4.30pm; £1) celebrates the history of Fowey and has some unusual exhibits including, oddly, a cloak that once belonged to Italian hero General Garibaldi.

Where to stay

The nearest **campsite** is across the Fowey River, above Polruan (see p287).

Looking for **B&Bs** as you come into the centre, at 12 Lostwithiel St you'll find *Foye Old Exchange* (☎ 07711-901650, 🖳 foye-old-exchange.co.uk; 3D; from £40pp, sgl occ from £75).

More central, *The Well House* (☎ 01726-833832, 🖳 wellhousefowey.co.uk; 3D; ▼; WI-FI; 🐾; £37.50-42.50pp, sgl occ £50-70), at 31-35 Fore St, is in a gorgeous old building with low ceilings and period decor. They're very friendly and welcoming towards hikers here.

The Dwelling House (☎ 01726-833662; 1D; ▼; WI-FI; from £45pp, sgl occ rate on request) has one double room in a Grade II Georgian townhouse above a

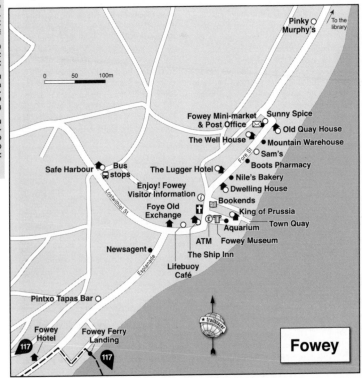

Fowey

tearoom (see below). Quaint and quirky, it's run by charming hosts.

Two olde-worlde **pubs** offer accommodation: *The Ship Inn* (☎ 01726-832230, 🖥 shipfowey.co.uk; 2D/1T; WI-FI; 🐕; from £50pp, sgl occ rate on request), which dates from 1570; and the 17th-century *King of Prussia* (☎ 01726-833694, 🖥 kingofprussiafowey.co.uk; 4D or T/2D; 🛏; WI-FI; £60-65pp, sgl occ from £90), which overlooks the water and all rooms face the front. The name is believed to have come from the smuggler John Carter, who resided at the inn in the 1780s and was nicknamed the 'King of Prussia' (see p213). *Safe Harbour* (☎ 01726-833379, 🖥 thesafeharbourinn.com; 3S/3D/1Tr/1F; 🛏; WI-FI; 🐕; £35-55pp, sgl occ rate on request) is also a pub with rooms. It's a short climb up Lostwithiel St, at No 58, and has views over the town and the river.

If you prefer **hotel** accommodation, *Old Quay House* (☎ 01726-833302, 🖥 theoldquayhouse.com; 13D; 🛏; WI-FI; from £75pp, sgl occ £120) is an ultra-modern, super-swish, boutique hotel with prices to match its swankiness. For something more traditional, *Fowey Hotel* (☎ 01726 832551, 🖥 thefoweyhotel.co.uk; 37 rooms; 🛏; WI-FI; 🐕; from £54.50pp, sgl occ rate on request) dates back to 1882 and is all class.

Where to eat and drink

For simple food on the go, *Nile's Bakery* (daily 8.30am-5pm) won't let you down.

Away from the crowds, on a quiet lane out towards the library, *Pinky Murphy's* (☎ 01726-832512, 🖥 pinkymurphys.co.uk; 9.30am-4.30pm), is a very relaxed, friendly café. Decor is colourful (although, surprisingly, not pink) and there are river views from the tables on the small front terrace.

Equally pleasant, although much busier thanks to its central location on Lostwithiel St, *Lifebuoy Café* (☎ 07715-075869, 🖥 thelifebuoycafe.co.uk/fowey; 9am-5pm, closed Nov) does a range of breakfasts and light lunches, plus cakes, coffee and cream teas.

If you're looking for a more traditional place for a cream tea head either to *The Dwelling House* (see Where to stay;

Wed-Mon 10am-6pm), or the similarly delightful *Well House* (see Where to stay; 10am-5pm). If you prefer a pub, *The Lugger Hotel* (☎ 01726-833435; food daily noon-2.30pm & 6-9pm) is one of several old taverns on Fore St; the food is traditional pub fare. Right on the front, *King of Prussia* (see Where to stay; food daily noon-9.30pm) serves hearty and tasty meals, including a slow-cooked pork belly. *The Ship Inn* (see Where to stay; food 9am-9.30pm) is unpretentious and friendly, and opens for breakfast.

You might remember *Sam's* (☎ 01726-832273, 🖥 samsfowey.co.uk; food daily noon-9.30pm) from Polkerris Beach. This Fowey branch is equally lively and includes a menu that lists 12 different types of burgers (£10-18) as well as plenty of fresh fish dishes.

For something approaching fine dining, *Old Quay House* (see Where to stay; Wed-Mon 12.30-9pm, Tue 4-9pm) has a lovely al-fresco area overlooking the water. The menu changes frequently and you can expect to pay £37.50/£45 for two or three courses respectively.

Indian to eat in or takeaway can be found at *Sunny Spice* (☎ 01726-833594; daily 5-11pm), 39A Fore St, while *Pintxo* (☎ 01726-337450, 🖥 pintxo.co.uk; Tue-Sat noon-9pm, Sun noon-5pm, 38 Esplanade, dishes up some tremendous tapas (£2.30-8) – which may be a very welcome sight if you're entering town hungry from the south.

Transport

[See also pp52-6] First Kernow's No 24 (to Mevagissey) & 25 (to Newquay) **bus** services also call at Par and Charlestown.

The official South-West Coast Path now takes the **ferry** (every 15 mins; 9.45am-11.30pm; £1.80) across the Fowey River to Polruan. Make sure you have your camera ready when you board – it's a lovely crossing when the sun's shining. Daytime ferries (9.45am & 5.15pm) leave from **Fowey Ferry Landing**, on Esplanade. Evening ferries (5.30-11.30pm) leave from **Town Quay**, near King of Prussia pub.

ROUTE GUIDE AND MAPS

FOWEY TO POLPERRO [MAPS 117-120]

From the Fowey ferry landing-point, this strenuous 7¼-mile (11.75km; 2½-3½hrs) stage begins with a meander through pretty **Polruan**. Emerging by the Coastguard lookout at the top of the village, the path then leads you on a jaunt eastwards around **Lantic Bay** and its popular beach. At the end, a stiff climb brings you out above **Pencarrow Head**, with its lovely clear-day views all the way back to the Lizard. Prepare yourself: this is just the first of several steep ascents, the path unrelenting as it struggles up and down along the cliff edge at the eastern end of **Lantivet Bay**. An unusual white stone cone – yet another navigational aid for seafarers – and the natural rock arch at **Blackybale Point** provide distractions from your aching legs: this is a pretty tough section. The reward for your exertions, however, is the lovely **Polperro**; more than worth the effort.

Be sure to stock up on drinks and snacks for this stretch as there's nowhere to buy anything between Polruan and Polperro.

POLRUAN [MAP 117, p282]

Polruan is for those who like their experience of the Fowey River to be quieter and more serene. Indeed, surrounded on three sides by water, and hidden from the fourth by the steep hill, it feels like one of the more isolated settlements on the path, though Fowey is only 10 minutes away by ferry. The main sight in the village is the

---

❏ Cornwall's literary giants

Maybe it's the gorgeous scenery, the wild coastline, the spectacular weather – or simply something in the water. For whatever reason, this stretch of the southern Cornish shoreline has produced its fair share of literary talents.

Perhaps the author most identified with this corner of the UK is **Daphne du Maurier**, which is curious as she only moved here in 1943, long after she had already achieved a level of fame and renown for her works. However, the claim that Du Maurier is a Cornish author is not a fatuous one: she had actually been visiting Cornwall since her parents bought a holiday home, Ferryside, just north of Fowey, and both wrote and set many of her best-known works in the county. The first of these, *The Loving Spirit*, concerning the lives of Cornish boat builders, moved a Major Tommy Browning so much that he set sail for Cornwall with the specific intention of meeting her. They were married the next year at Llanteglos Church. *Jamaica Inn* (a real inn, situated on Bodmin Moor) and *Rebecca*, perhaps her two most famous novels, were both set at least partly in Cornwall. Indeed, the famous opening lines of *Rebecca* ('Last night I dreamt I went to Manderley again') were inspired by a 17th-century mansion, Menabilly, overlooking the sea and owned by the Rashleigh family (after which several pubs in the area, such as those at Charlestown and Polkerris, are named). She managed to secure a 25-year lease on the property in 1943 and stayed there until 1965 and the death of Major Browning, when she moved to another Rashleigh property, Kilmarth, which was immortalised in another novel, *The House on the Strand*. She died in 1989, having been made a dame 20 years earlier; her ashes were scattered on the cliffs near her home.

Another distinctive Cornish voice – indeed, he is celebrated on his memorial as the Voice of Cornwall – is **AL Rowse**. Though not as famous as Du Maurier, during his lifetime Rowse (1903-1997) published more than 100 books, his best-known works being histories of Elizabethan England and a book of poetry about Cornwall.

blockhouse, far more complete than its twin across the water. The town's few facilities lie at the bottom end of the main street close to the ferry point. The **post office** (Mon-Fri 9am-4.30pm, Sat 9am-1pm) is in a shop called **The Winkle Picker** (daily 8.30am-around 6pm). There's also Polruan Village **Store** (Mon-Sat 7am-5pm, Sun to 12.30pm) with an **ATM** (£1.95).

For **camping**, head to *Polruan Holiday Centre* (☎ 01726-870263, 🖳 polruanholidays.com; one adult & tent £7-10; 🐾), a pretty and well-run site; follow Fore St (which becomes Townsend) for half a mile up a very steep hill out of town and you'll find the site shortly after Ocean View on your left. It does get booked up in summer, so be sure to call ahead. For **B&B**, there are two choices: *Hormond House* (☎ 01726-870853, 🖳 hormondhouse.com; 1S/1D or T/1F; 🛁; WI-FI; 🐾; £40-55pp) is a pleasant family-run place on the main Fore St (No 55) with cracking views over the

harbour; *Polmarine* (☎ 01726-870459, 🖳 polmarine.com; 1T/1D; 🛁; from £50pp; Easter-Oct) is a lovely place right by the waterside, with a wonderful breakfast conservatory, but they don't take single-night bookings in the high season.

There are several **food** options here too. For pub grub, *Lugger Inn* (☎ 01726-870007; noon-2pm & 6-8.30pm; WI-FI; 🐾; mains £10-12.50) has the best location in the village, overlooking the harbour. Behind it sits *The Russell Inn* (☎ 01726-870707, 🖳 russellinn.co.uk; food daily noon-2.30pm & 6-8.30pm; WI-FI; 🐾) which serves real ale and bar meals including pizzas (£10). On the corner is small, simple *Crumpets Tearoom* (Mon-Sat summer 9am-5pm, winter 9am-2pm), just back from the harbour.

Travel Cornwall's No 481 **bus** links Polruan with Polperro & Looe. The No 482 goes to Bodmin via Polperro. Note, neither runs at the weekend. [See also pp52-6].

If he is known at all today, however – other than for his rather lovely memorial on Black Head, right by the coast path – it is for his rather acerbic criticism of the works of others. One who clearly enjoyed his reputation as an intellectual heavyweight (he was a graduate from Oxford and enjoyed renown as one of the foremost English scholars of his generation), he was quick to dismiss the efforts of others, memorably describing (admittedly, merely in pencil in his own copy of a magazine) John Middleton Murry's poem *In Memory of Katherine Mansfield* as 'Sentimental gush on the part of JMM. And a bad poem. A.L.R'. Though his relationship with the county wasn't as straightforward as his reputation would suggest, he did return to live out his remaining days here following his retirement in 1973, living at Trenarren House near Black Head. His bestseller, *A Cornish Childhood*, the first part of his autobiography and published in 1942, served to cement his reputation as 'The Voice of Cornwall', a title that he officially took in 1968 when made a Bard of Gorseth Kernow. His ashes are buried in the Charlestown cemetery.

One of Rowse's main influences was **Arthur Quiller-Couch**, who was born in Bodmin of two very ancient Cornish families, and returned after university to settle in Fowey in 1891. Like Rowse, he was also honoured with the title Bard of Gorseth Kernow and, also like Rowse, is perhaps best known for his critiques, reviews and anthologies of the literary efforts of others, including *Studies in Literature* (1918), *On the Art of Reading* (1920) and the impressively comprehensive *Oxford Book Of English Verse 1250-1900* (1900). All of these were published under the sobriquet, 'Q'.

Curiously, Quiller-Couch was cited by **Kenneth Grahame** as the inspiration for the character Ratty in his best-known work, *Wind in the Willows*. Though he was born in Scotland (in 1859) and spent most of his life in Cookham in Berkshire, Grahame was married in Fowey, spent his honeymoon in St Ives, and it is widely claimed that the inspiration for the first chapter of *Wind in the Willows*, in which Ratty and Mole enjoy a boat trip, came after a similar trip taken by Grahame along the Fowey River.

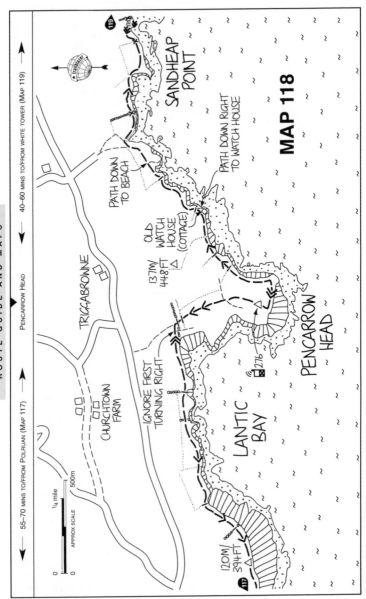

← 55-70 MINS TO/FROM POLRUAN (MAP 117) → PENCARROW HEAD ← 40-60 MINS TO/FROM WHITE TOWER (MAP 119) →

TRIGGABRONNE

CHURCHTOWN FARM

IGNORE FIRST TURNING RIGHT

PATH DOWN TO BEACH

OLD WATCH HOUSE (COTTAGE)

137M/ 448FT

PATH DOWN RIGHT TO WATCH HOUSE

SANDHEAP POINT

MAP 118

PENCARROW HEAD

LANTIC BAY

120M/ 394FT

TRUMARTIN

APPROX SCALE
¼ mile
500m

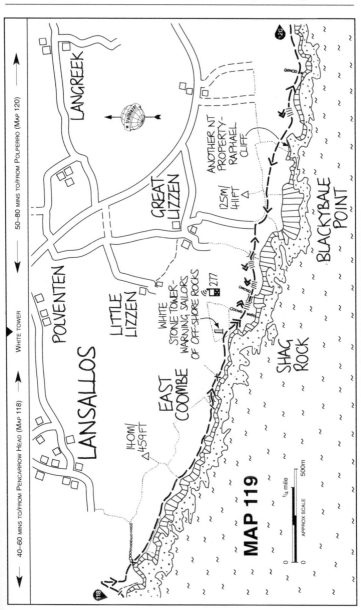

← 40–60 MINS TO/FROM PENCARROW HEAD (MAP 118) →   WHITE TOWER   ← 50–80 MINS TO/FROM POLPERRO (MAP 120) →

LANSALLOS

POLVENTEN

LANCREEK

GREAT LIZZEN

LITTLE LIZZEN

EAST COOMBE

ANOTHER NT PROPERTY-RAPHAEL CLIFF

125M/ 41IFT

WHITE STONE TOWER-WARNING SAILORS OF OFF-SHORE ROCKS

277

SHAG ROCK

BLACKYBALE POINT

140M/ 459FT

MAP 119

¼ mile

500m

APPROX SCALE

118

120

POLPERRO [map p292]

Polperro is one of the more idiosyncratic towns on the entire coast path. Maybe it's the location, squeezed between high hills that, bearded with pine forests, give it a vaguely alpine feel. Maybe it's the unusual layout, the town strung along a couple of parallel roads that stretch back for almost a mile from the harbour to **Crumplehorn**. Or maybe it's the presence of a 'tram' (£1.10 single, £1.90 return) – actually an electric cart – that ferries people to and from the town centre and Crumplehorn. Whatever it is, Polperro is one of the more unusual – and likeable – towns on the route.

The town has an interesting history. Originally a fishing village its isolated location, sheltered by those high hills to the east and west, gave it a significant advantage as a centre for various illegal activities, foremost amongst which were smuggling and privateering. Tea, gin, brandy and tobacco were the mainstays of the smuggling industry, mostly shipped over from Guernsey. Indeed, so all-pervasive was the trade that John Wesley remarked when visiting: '*An accursed thing among them: well nigh one and all bought or sold uncustomed goods.*'

Polperro's heyday coincided with the arrival of Zephaniah Job (1749-1822). Job probably did more than anyone to ensure the town's prosperity, organising the smuggling trade, acting as accountant to the inhabitants and establishing a bank in town. He also rebuilt the harbour following a terrible storm in 1817. Privateering brought further wealth, the Admiralty giving license to the boats of Polperro to attack French craft and keep the cargo. Thereafter, the coastguard slowly became more organised and smuggling declined in the town, to be replaced in the 19th century by tourism.

That history is recounted in the local **museum** (Easter-Oct 10am-4.30pm; £2) down by the harbour, just past an eccentric private home, dubbed 'Shell House', the façade of which is almost entirely covered with seashells.

Services

There are a few facilities in town, mostly on Fore St, including a **post office** (Mon-Fri 9am-5pm, Sat 9am-1pm) with an **ATM** (£1.85 charge). There's also Roberts **pharmacy** (☎ 01503-272250; Mon 8.30am-5.30pm, Tue & Fri 9am-5.30pm, Wed & Thur 9am-6pm, Sat 9am-5pm, Sun 10am-5pm; winter closed Sat pm and Sun) and a **newsagent**, Polperro News (Mon-Fri 7.30am-5pm, Sat 8am-5pm, Sun 8am-noon).

Where to stay

For **camping**, there's *Great Kellow Farm* (off Map 120; ☎ 01503-272387, ⌨ great kellowfarm.co.uk; hiker & tent £6; 🐾; Mar to early Jan) which never turns walkers away. It is a basic, but very friendly campsite with a small shower block on a working beef cattle farm with great views back over Polperro Bay, although the half-mile climb uphill to get here is quite a slog; turn left at the roundabout after Milly's, then take the first right (signposted to the campsite) and keep going.

Fore St and its continuation, The Coombe, is the main place to look for **B&B**. Several are right in the heart of the action including the 16th-century *House on the Props* (☎ 01503-272310, ⌨ houseon theprops.co.uk; 2D/1T; 🐾; £40-45pp, sgl occ £55-65), which is built on props or stilts taken from a ship, *Maverine*, that foundered in the harbour back in around 1700. The rooms are some of the only ones in Polperro with views over the harbour – which you can view through the lovely old leaded windows. It's a friendly place, and staying for one night only is not a problem. *Claremont Hotel* (☎ 01503-272241, ⌨ the claremonthotel.co.uk; 1S/9D/1T/1F; ✎; WI-FI; £35-50pp, sgl occ from £90) is further up near where Fore St turns into The Coombes and has come a long way since its origins as a fisherman's cottage in the 17th century. It's now a smart and large B&B.

Just up the road but still very much in the middle of it all, *The Cottage* (☎ 01503-272217, ⌨ polperrobedandbreakfast.co .uk; 6D; WI-FI; £42.50-46pp) is a 400-year-old building with timber-beamed ceilings. Further along is large country-house style *Penryn House Hotel* (☎ 01503-272157, ⌨ penrynhouse.co.uk; 1S/2T/9D; ✎; WI-FI;

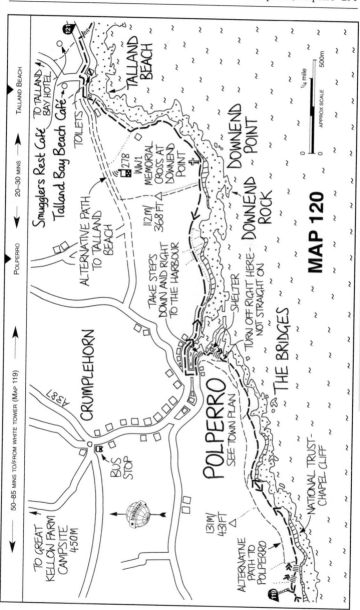

🐾; from £42.50pp, sgl £50, sgl occ £55), followed by friendly *Natal House* (☎ 01503-273011, 🖳 natalhouse.co.uk; 2D/ 2F; ♥; 🐾; from £42.50pp, sgl occ £65), though there's a minimum three-night booking policy in the school holidays.

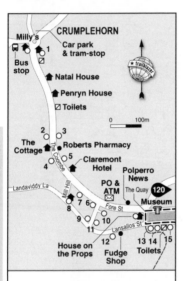

Polperro

Where to eat and drink
1 Crumplehorn Inn
2 The Kitchen Restaurant
3 Polmary Restaurant
4 Plantation Tearooms
5 Bean & Scone
6 Polperro Bakery
7 Ship Inn
8 The Old Millhouse Inn
9 Couch's Great House
10 Michelle's
11 Nelson's Restaurant
12 The Chip Ahoy
13 Wheelhouse Restaurant
14 The Three Pilchards
15 The Blue Peter Inn

There are two further options at the top of The Coombe, a short walk (or tram ride) from the centre. *Milly's* (☎ 01503-272492, 🖳 millysbandb.co.uk; 3D; WI-FI; from £42.50pp) has perfectly pleasant rooms and a restaurant attached. They will not always take one-night bookings in advance, though. Opposite that, *Crumplehorn Inn & Mill* (☎ 01503-272348, 🖳 crumplehorn-inn .co.uk; 3D or T; WI-FI; from £37.50pp) is a very popular pub with great food (see opposite) and three B&B rooms, two of which have attached living rooms.

Another pub option, in a good location on Mill Hill – close to everything yet away from the main hubbub of Fore St – is *The Old Millhouse Inn* (☎ 01503-272362, 🖳 theoldmillhouseinn.co.uk; 7D; WI-FI; 🐾; £45-47.50pp), where there is plenty to amuse you of an evening with live entertainment on some summer nights.

Where to eat and drink
Eating is one of the main pastimes in Polperro – there's plenty of choice.

If you're after a simple sugar fix, right on the harbour is *Corner Cottage Fudge Shop* (Easter-Oct 10am-6pm, summer hols 10am-9pm). For Cornish pasties and the like, try *Polperro Bakery* (daily 8.30am-6pm, winter 8.30am-4pm; WI-FI) with a nice patio at the rear. There's also a fish & chip shop, *The Chip Ahoy*, near the harbour, where you can eat in or take away.

On The Coombe, *Plantation Tea Rooms* (☎ 01503-272223; daily 10am-5pm & Thur-Sun 6.30pm to late) is a large place that does main meals too. Nearby, *Bean and Scone* (Sun-Tue 10am-5.30pm, Wed-Sat 10am-8.30pm) is very friendly and has some outdoor seating – lovely if the sun's out. Right on the path and the harbour is *The House on the Props* (see Where to stay; food Mon-Sat 9.30am-4pm & 6.30-8.30pm, Sun 9.30am-4pm only; WI-FI), which has played a central role in the town's story of smuggling (it even once had secret stairs leading from the river) but is now more renowned for its cakes and cream teas.

Unsurprisingly for an old smuggling village, **pubs** are not in short supply. The first one you come to as you enter town is *The Blue Peter Inn* (☎ 01503-272743, 🖥 thebluepeterinn.com; food daily noon-9pm) at the end of Quay Rd. It is known for its fresh seafood including its fish 'n' chips, and also serves real ales as well as hosting regular live entertainment. A few doors down *The Three Pilchards* (☎ 01503-272233, 🖥 threepilchardspolperro.co.uk; food daily noon-9pm), also on Quay Rd, serves decent meals and uses locally sourced produce wherever possible. Their pies are much lauded: try the 'famous' fish one (£13.95). On Fore St, *Ship Inn* (food daily noon-9pm) offers a fairly classic pub menu and is useful if you want to watch the football on Sky.

Away from Fore St and open all day, *The Old Millhouse Inn* (see Where to stay) serves breakfasts (8.30-10am) for non residents earlier than many of the village's cafés. They then offer sandwiches and cream teas throughout the day before switching to an evening menu.

Crumplehorn Inn & Mill (see Where to stay; food daily 8.30-9.30am & noon-9pm) serves very good food, including breakfasts. They do light lunches (sandwiches, cream teas) throughout the afternoon, before pulling out an excellent evening menu of homemade delights such as Crumplehorn Curry (£10.95-13.50), pork and chorizo pie (£11.95), and falafel fritters (£10.25).

In the **restaurant** line, across the road from Crumplehorn, *Milly's* (see Where to stay; Mon-Sat 6-9pm) specialises in tapas and fine wines, but is also open for breakfast at 9.30am (Mon-Sat).

For more formal dining the *Wheelhouse Restaurant* (☎ 07702-115992;

food served peak times daily 9am-9pm, winter 10am-3pm, normally 9.30am-5pm) is located on The Quay in the stable of an old house, and dishes up all home-cooked food including the ubiquitous Cornish crab sandwich.

Also worth a look is *Couch's Great House* (☎ 01503-272554, 🖥 couchspolperro.com; Mon-Sat 6.30pm to late, opening days vary out of season); the executive chef honed his skills alongside Gordon Ramsay! They offer three- and five-course set menus (£35 & £45).

Opposite, *Nelson's Restaurant* (☎ 01503-272366, 🖥 polperro.co.uk/nelsons-restaurant; Tue-Sun from 6.30pm) does a selection of quality seafood and steaks (mains £20-30). Nearby, *Michelle's* (6pm to late, closed Wed) is a lovely seafood restaurant (mains £12-17) that throws in a selection of Thai curries for good measure.

Further up the hill, *Polmary Restaurant* (☎ 01503-272828; summer daily noon-9pm; winter hours vary & may close) has a good choice of seafood dishes.

Opposite that, *The Kitchen* (☎ 01503-272812, 🖥 thekitchenpolperro.com; Tue-Sun 6.30-9pm) has morphed from a humble tearoom into a multi-award-winning licensed restaurant (mains £14-22).

Transport

[See also pp52-6] To get a **bus** it's best to walk (or get the 'tram', see p290) to Crumplehorn, though a few services go to the village centre.

Plymouth City Bus's No 73 travels to Liskeard via Looe. Travel Cornwall's No 481 links Crumplehorn with Polruan & Looe and the (Wed only) 482 goes to Bodmin and Polruan.

POLPERRO TO LOOE [MAPS 120-122]

These **5 miles (8km; 1¼hr-2hrs)** provide a gratifyingly gentle contrast to the severity of the previous stage. From Polperro the path climbs out of the village towards the war memorial at **Downend Point**.

After Downend Point the original coast path takes a more northerly direction for the descent to **Talland Beach**, home to a car park and two lovely cafés; the stylish *Talland Bay Beach Café* (☎ 01503-272088, 🖥 tallandbay beachcafe.co.uk; mid Mar to end Oct daily 9am-5.30pm) and *The Smuggler's*

ROUTE GUIDE AND MAPS

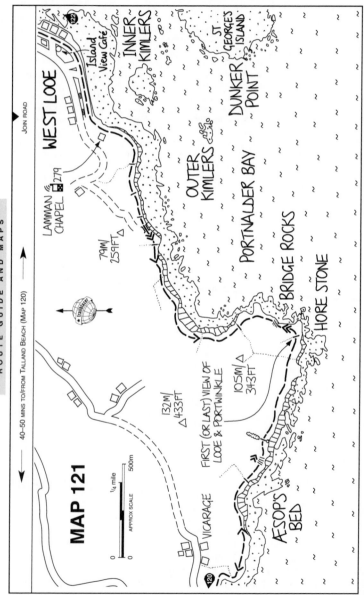

MAP 121

1/4 mile

APPROX SCALE

500m

← 40–50 MINS TO/FROM TALLAND BEACH (MAP 120) →

JOIN ROAD

WEST LOOE

Island View Café

INNER KIMLERS

ST GEORGES ISLAND

DUNKER POINT

LAWHAN CHAPEL 279

OUTER KIMLERS

PORTNADLER BAY

79M/ 259FT

132M/ 433FT

105M/ 343FT

BRIDGE ROCKS

HORE STONE

FIRST (OR LAST) VIEW OF LOOE & PORTWINKLE

VICARAGE

AESOP'S BED

120

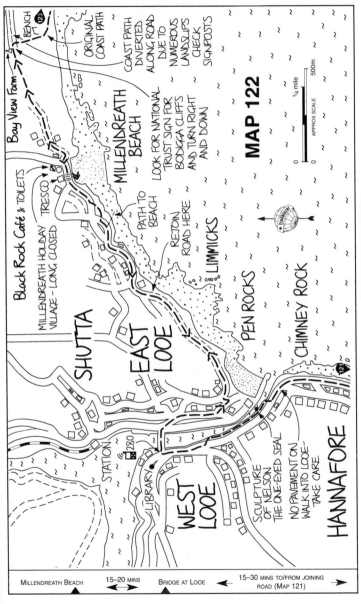

BENCH

Bay View Farm

ORIGINAL COAST PATH

COAST PATH DIVERTED ALONG ROAD DUE TO NUMEROUS LANDSLIPS CHECK SIGNPOSTS

Black Rock Café & TOILETS

TRESCO

MILLENDREATH HOLIDAY VILLAGE - LONG CLOSED

MILLENDREATH BEACH

LOOK FOR NATIONAL TRUST SIGN FOR BODIGGA CLIFFS AND TURN RIGHT AND DOWN

PATH TO BEACH

REJOIN ROAD HERE

MAP 122

¼ mile

APPROX SCALE

0   500m

LIMMICKS

PEN ROCKS

CHIMNEY ROCK

SHUTTA

EAST LOOE

STATION

LIBRARY

WEST LOOE

SCULPTURE OF NELSON THE ONE-EYED SEAL

NO PAVEMENT ON WALK INTO LOOE - TAKE CARE

HANNAFORE

ROUTE GUIDE AND MAPS

| MILLENDREATH BEACH | ◄ 15–20 MINS ► | BRIDGE AT LOOE | ◄ 15–30 MINS TO/FROM JOINING ROAD (MAP 121) ► |

Rest (☎ 01503-272259; Easter to Nov 10am-5.30pm), with patio seating and great sea views. Curiously, Talland Bay was dubbed the Playground of Plymouth in the 19th century owing to its popularity with daytripping Victorian city-dwellers.

A further jaunt out to the point brings you the first glimpses of **St George's Island** (aka **Looe Island**) which you can actually walk to a couple of times a year when the tide is particularly low. According to local legend, Jesus of Nazareth visited Looe Island with Joseph of Arimathea in order to buy tin – though presumably he didn't need to wait for the tide in order to walk out. Soon after you spy the island the town itself comes into view, and is eventually reached after a steady but longwinded stroll through fields and the suburb of **Hannafore**.

LOOE

Looe is a medium-sized Cornish coastal town divided – East Looe and West Looe – by the river of the same name and united by an old stone Victorian bridge. It was mentioned in the *Domesday Book* and enjoyed brief prosperity in the 14th century as a boatbuilding town and commercial port, but only really grew in the 19th century with the Victorians' insatiable appetite for seaside holidays. Nevertheless, Looe still has a fishing industry and is known as a national centre for shark angling.

The town, like many in the county, pretty much falls asleep in winter, though it's renowned for its New Year celebrations when many of the local residents don fancy dress to party in the streets.

As with many of these Cornish coastal towns, there are few official attractions as such though the **Old Guildhall**, right in the heart of East Looe, is one of the oldest buildings here (it was constructed around 1450) and now houses the **Museum** (Sun-Fri 11am-4pm, Sat 11am-1.30pm; £2), providing a quick run-through of this historic port's lengthy past.

Services

The **tourist information centre** (☎ 01503-262072, 🖥 looeguide.co.uk; Easter-Sep Mon-Sat 10am-3pm, Oct to 2pm, winter unstaffed but open mornings for leaflets) is in the heart of East Looe, just off the main Fore St. As well as being very helpful and friendly they also provide **internet** (£1.50/30mins) – which is slightly cheaper than at the **library** (Map 122; ☎ 0300-123 4111, 🖥 cornwall.gov.uk/library; Tue 9.30am-6.30pm, Wed & Thur 9.30am-5pm,

Fri 9.30am-1.30pm, Sat 10am-1pm; WI-FI; internet £1.80/30mins), across the water at Millpool in West Looe.

Services on East Looe's Fore St include Boots **pharmacy** (Mon-Sat 9am-5.30pm), a Co-op **supermarket** (Mon-Sat 8am-8pm, Sun 9am-6pm), and more than one **ATM**. For **camping** gear, there's a **Mountain Warehouse** (Mon-Sat 9am-5pm, Sun 10am-5pm) on Fore St.

Where to stay

The nearest **campsite** to Looe is *Bay View Farm* (Map 122; ☎ 01503-265922, 🖥 looe baycaravans.co.uk; 2 people & tent £17-26; 🐾) which overlooks Looe Bay and St George's Island from a peaceful perch right by the coast path. As well as normal tent pitches they also rent out wooden 'camping snugs' (sleep 2-4) for £35-50.

In central Looe, there's accommodation on both sides of the river.

West Looe There are a few **B&B** options near the bus station. Two of the better ones are *Tidal Court* (☎ 01503-263695; 2S/1T/3D/4Tr; ➽; WI-FI; £25-30pp, sgl £35-45pp), at 3 Church St, and *The Old Malthouse* (☎ 01503-264976, 🖥 oldmalt houselooe.com; 3D; WI-FI; from £65pp, sgl occ £110) on West Looe Hill.

Nearby, and one of several places that claim to be the oldest pub in Looe, *Ye Olde Jolly Sailor Inn* (☎ 01503-263387, 🖥 jolly sailorlooe.co.uk; 3D/2T; ➽; WI-FI; £25-40pp), built in 1516, has low-beamed ceilings and bags of character.

Nearer to the bridge – and thus with great river views – are *Little Mainstone*

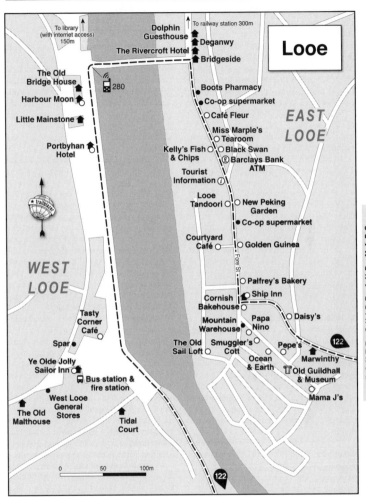

Looe

To library (with internet access) 150m

To railway station 300m

Dolphin Guesthouse

Deganwy

The Rivercroft Hotel

Bridgeside

The Old Bridge House

Harbour Moon

Little Mainstone

Portbyhan Hotel

280

Boots Pharmacy

Co-op supermarket

Café Fleur

EAST LOOE

Miss Marple's Tearoom

Kelly's Fish & Chips

Black Swan

Barclays Bank ATM

Tourist Information

Looe Tandoori

New Peking Garden

Co-op supermarket

Courtyard Café

Golden Guinea

Fore St

Palfrey's Bakery

Ship Inn

Cornish Bakehouse

WEST LOOE

Mountain Warehouse

Papa Nino

Daisy's

Tasty Corner Café

The Old Sail Loft

Smuggler's Cott

Pepe's

Spar

Ocean & Earth

Marwinthy

Ye Olde Jolly Sailor Inn

Old Guildhall & Museum

Bus station & fire station

Mama J's

West Looe General Stores

The Old Malthouse

Tidal Court

122

0   50   100m

122

ROUTE GUIDE AND MAPS

(☎ 01503-262983, 🖳 littlemainstone-looe .com; 1T/4D; £29-31pp; Jan-Nov) and *The Old Bridge House* (☎ 01503-263159, 🖳 theoldbridgehousehotel.co.uk; 2S/5D/2T; WI-FI; £40.50-67pp, sgl £48-59), who prefer two-night minimum stays in summer.

Next to those two is *Harbour Moon* (☎ 01503-265600, 🖳 info@theharbour moon.co.uk; 1S/3D/1T; ☞; WI-FI; from £30pp, sgl from £50), a very friendly bar and bistro with rooms.

A **hotel** worth considering is the modern *Portbyhan Hotel* (☎ 01503-262071, 🖳 portbyhan.com; 4S/18D/12T/10F; ☞; £35-110pp) which charges more for rooms with a riverside view.

East Looe By the bridge on this side of the river is the appropriately named *Bridgeside* (☎ 01503-263113, 🖳 bridge side.cornwall.uk.net; 1S/1T/4D/2F; WI-FI; 🐾; £28-35pp, sgl occ £50-60), Fore St. Neighbours with Bridgeside are *Deganwy* (☎ 01503-262984, 🖳 deganwyhotel.co.uk; 6D/1D or T/1Tr; WI-FI; £35-40pp, sgl occ £45-55) and *Dolphin Guesthouse* (☎ 01503-262578, 🖳 dolphin-house.co.uk; 6D/1T; ➡; WI-FI; 🐾; £40-45pp, sgl occ from £60); both with high-spec rooms. Next door to them is *The Rivercroft Hotel* (☎ 01503-262251, 🖳 rivercrofthotel.co.uk; 1S/11D; ➡; WI-FI; £40-52.50pp, sgl occ £45-80), which has a restaurant and bar.

Further down on Fore St, *Ship Inn* (☎ 01503-263124; ➡; 1S/1D/6T; from £40pp) is a rival to Ye Olde Jolly Sailor (see p296), if not in age then certainly in character and atmosphere. Up the hill, away from the crowds, *Marwinthy* (☎ 01503-264382 or ☎ 07491-961609, 🖳 marwinthy.co.uk; 2D en suite/2F share bathroom; WI-FI; 🐾; £25-40pp) is a friendly B&B with sea views.

Where to eat and drink

Most of the action, in terms of shopping, dining and drinking, happens in East Looe.

West Looe You can get pasties and other picnic supplies at *West Looe General Stores* (Mon-Sat 8am-8pm, Sun 10am-8pm), which also has a delicatessen. There's also a small Spar **supermarket** (Mon-Sat 7.30am-10pm, Sun 8am-10pm) on this side.

Nearby, *Tasty Corner Café and Takeaway* (☎ 0797-366 0995; summer 8.30am-6pm, winter to 4pm; WI-FI) is a no-frills café with plenty of breakfast and lunch options (mains £7-9).

Across the road, *Ye Olde Jolly Sailor Inn* (See Where to stay) doesn't do food, which allows thirsty punters to give their full undivided attention to the real ales.

For a sit-down evening meal, snag one of the seats on the terrace overlooking the river at *Harbour Moon* (see Where to stay; food daily noon-8pm). *Portbyhan Hotel* (see Where to stay) also has a riverside restaurant (Mon-Sat noon-9pm, Sun to 8pm; mains £8-16).

East Looe Half the buildings on this side of the river seem to be eateries of one sort or another. Places with **pasties** include *Cornish Bakehouse* (☎ 01503-265524; daily summer 8.30am-9pm, winter 9am-4pm) and *Palfrey's Bakery* (☎ 01503-262945; Mon-Sat 8.30am-5pm, Sun 9.30am-5pm; WI-FI) which also does cakes, sandwiches and coffee, and has some seating indoors.

Amongst the **takeaway** options are the hugely popular *Kelly's Fish & Chips* (Mon-Sat 8am-10pm; eat in or takeaway); and *New Peking Garden* (☎ 01503-264500; Mon-Sat noon-2pm, daily 5-11pm), a classic Chinese restaurant and takeaway with an extensive menu (mains £6-10). Spicy subcontinental suppers are on offer at *Looe Tandoori Restaurant* (☎ 01503-265372; daily noon-2.30pm & 5.30pm-midnight), while tantalising Thai tucker (curries from £6.50) is available at *Ocean and Earth* (☎ 01503-263080; daily 5.30-11pm) on Higher Market St.

Cafés of all shapes, sizes and characters are particularly prevalent. Popular *Café Fleur* (☎ 01503-265734; daily 9am-5pm) does cheap breakfast baps, as well as light lunches, while *Miss Marple's Tearoom* (☎ 01503-263157; summer Mon-Sat 9.30am-6pm, Sun 10am-6pm, winter 9.30am-4.30pm, closed in Jan) has comfortingly dated décor and equally traditional home-made cakes, as well as an award-wining sweetshop. Further down towards the sea, *Courtyard Café* (☎ 01503-264494; 11.30am-9pm) provides a lovely little sanctuary away from the hubbub on Fore St. It serves some great food too including Fowey River Mussels (£8.95/17.95) and Looe Crab (£17.95), and has an impressive wine list.

However, the undisputed king of cafés in Looe is *Daisy's* (☎ 07988-803315; Mon-Sat 9am-4pm; 🐾), up the hill a few metres on Castle St but right on the path. It's a treat for walkers – they even advertise that both dogs and muddy boots are welcome – and they do some sizeable food too, including pasties, doorstep toasties and fabulous breakfasts.

There's a cluster of lovely old **pubs** on this side of the river, most of which do food. The oldest of the lot is *Smuggler's Cott* (☎ 01503-262397, 🖥 looerestaurants .co.uk; food daily 6.30-8.50pm; carvery Sun: sittings noon & 1.30pm, also Fri from 6.30pm), built in 1430 and restored in 1595 with, so it is said, timbers salvaged from the Spanish Armada! The bar is still styled on a nautical theme with ropes and riggin'. In the cellar you can still see the entrance to a genuine smugglers' tunnel that led down to the quayside. Food-wise, their renowned rib roast Sunday carvery (£10.25) packs in the punters, though their regular restaurant isn't to be ignored either, particularly their fresh lemon sole (£16.50) and their coalfish cooked 'en papillote' (£17.50).

Nearby on Fore St there's *Ship Inn* (see Where to stay; food daily noon-3pm & 6-9pm), with good baguettes (£5.95) and some generous mains (£9.25-21.95) served in the evening; and the handsome *Golden Guinea* (☎ 01503-262780; noon-9pm), with its extensive pub-grub menu including griddled tuna (£13.95). *Black Swan* (☎ 01503-263002, 🖥 blackswanlooe.com; noon-9pm) is another pub option.

In terms of **restaurants**, *Papa Nino* (☎ 01503-264231; Mon-Sat 6-11pm) is a great little Italian with a wide breadth of dishes (mains £8-16). For a more modern take on Italian cuisine, head to *Mama J's* (☎ 01503-262787, 🖥 mamajsitalian.com; daily 5-9pm), a colourful, family-friendly pizzeria (pizzas £9-13.50).

Pepe's Tex-Mex Kitchen (☎ 01503-165832; daily from 5.30pm, hours vary out of season) is where to go for fajitas (£10.50-13.50) and burritos (£11.50-11.95). *The Old Sail Loft* (☎ 01503-262131, 🖥 the oldsailloftrestaurant.com; Sun-Tue 5.30-9pm, Thur-Sat 11.30am-9pm; mains £14-30) serves some mouthwatering fish and steak dishes from its 16th-century premises on Quay St.

Transport

[See also pp52-6] Looe railway station is on the East Looe side (see Map 122). **Trains** on Looe Valley Line (GWR 37 service) run to Liskeard where you can connect to services for Truro & Plymouth.

Plymouth City Bus's No 72 **bus** calls at West & East Looe and will get you to Plymouth; their No 73 service visits East Looe en route between Polperro & Liskeard. Travel Cornwall's 481 links both West & East Looe with Polperro & Polruan.

Taxi firms include Looe Taxis (☎ 01503-262405, 🖥 looetaxis.org.uk) and Killigarth Private Hire (☎ 01503-272818).

LOOE TO PORTWRINKLE [MAPS 122-125]

The 7¾ **miles** (**12.5km; 2¼-3hrs**) separating the two harbours of Looe and Portwrinkle are dotted with little settlements that break up the sometimes monotonous walking, much of which is done on roads without pavements (though there is the option of taking to the sands between Seaton and Downderry).

Leaving Looe, the first of these settlements is **Millendreath**, where you'll find a toilet, and *Black Rock Café* (daily 10am-4pm), but little else.

On the other side of the bay, the original coast path goes back towards the sea and **Bodigga Cliffs**, which along with the woods above it are in the care of the National Trust. Passing a small **labyrinth** (🖥 windsworth.org.uk) cut into the grass, it enters into the woods above **Keveral Beach** before descending along the steps to more National Trust property at **Struddicks**, where the path undulates until descending on steps through a pine plantation to the road at **Seaton** (see p300). However, owing to a number of landslips in this area, you may be diverted along a road for the last mile-and-a-half into Seaton. Be sure to pay attention to the signposts by Bay View Farm (Map 122).

After Seaton, a not-entirely-safe stretch of road walking (no pavement) takes you to the village of **Downderry**. The **beach alternative route** at low tide – which rejoins the main path just after The Inn on the Shore – is attractive. The path then continues along the road to a hairpin bend, where it finally leaves the tarmac for a climb up to and alongside farmland, negotiating a couple of sharp gradients, and a small diversion due to cliff fall, as it leads into **Portwrinkle**, which plays host to a golf course, a café... and a famous ghost (see below).

SEATON [MAP 123]

There are some places to stop for a bite here, plus a place to stay. **Rooms** (without breakfast) are available on the far eastern side of Seaton at *The Smugglers Inn* (☎ 01503-250923, 🖳 thesmugglersinnseaton.co.uk; 2D; ➥; 🐾; WI-FI; £30-50pp), a traditional, family-friendly pub. They also do decent **food** (summer Mon-Sat noon-4pm & 5.30-8.30pm, Sun noon-3.30pm; winter limited hours; mains £9-17). At the beginning of the bay and actually on the sand

there's *Seaton Beach Café* (☎ 01503-250621; Mon-Thur 9am-6.30pm, Fri & Sat to 8pm, Sun to 6pm; bring your own alcohol), a large glass-fronted beach café with plenty of outdoor seating and an impressive menu. *Waves Bar* (☎ 01503-250065, 🖳 wavesbar.co.uk; food daily 9am-9pm, bar to 11pm; WI-FI) is more upmarket; mains (noon-9pm) cost £10-20. Close by there's a **shop** (Easter to Oct Mon-Sat 8am-5.30pm, Sun 9am-5.30pm) that sells basics.

DOWNDERRY [MAP 124, p302]

Downderry **stores** (Mon-Sat 8am-7pm, Sun 9am-6pm) is well-stocked although the **post office** hours are now limited (Tue & Fri 1-3pm). *Summinck Different* (☎ 01503-250311; Fri-Wed 9am-4pm) on Broads Yard Rd, does great coffee, tea and

cake and has vegan options. On the next corner, *Blue Plate* (☎ 01503-250308, 🖳 blueplatecornwall.com; Tue-Sat 10am-9pm, Sun 11am-6pm) has a **delicatessen** and **café**, as well as an evening **restaurant**. Nice sun terrace too.

> ### ❏ The legend of Finnygook
>
> **Silas Finny** was a notorious smuggler who lived in and around **Portwrinkle** in the 18th century. He was part of a gang of successful lawbreakers who exploited the rather threadbare state of the Coastguard and law enforcement in the region to import alcohol, tobacco and lace into England. A very lucrative little operation it turned out to be, too, until one day Silas got into an argument with his fellow smugglers over where to land a particular consignment. In a fit of anger, Silas went to the Excise men to reveal to them where the smuggled goods were going to land. As a result of the information provided, several of the gang members were arrested, sentenced and deported to Australia. Of course, Silas Finny was a marked man after this and it wasn't long before he was bludgeoned to death by persons unknown – presumably friends and relatives of the exiled men, and other smugglers who wanted to make an example of Silas to show what happens if you betray them.
>
> The story, however, doesn't end there, for in the subsequent couple of centuries Silas's ghost, or 'gook', has been making a nuisance of itself – to the extent that there are some local families who keep away from the hill between Portwrinkle and Crafthole after dark.
>
> Whether his spirit actually lives on in the village is, of course, a moot point. His fame and legend, however, certainly do, with the lovely nearby pub named after him.

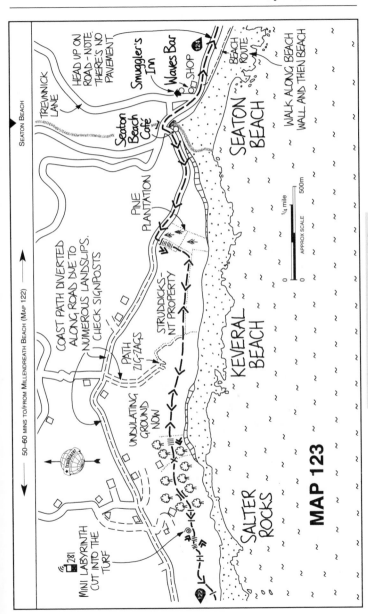

SEATON BEACH

HEAD UP ON ROAD - NOTE. THERE'S NO PAVEMENT.

TREVNNICK LANE

Smuggler's Inn

Waves Bar

124

SHOP

Seaton Beach Café

BEACH ROUTE

SEATON BEACH

WALK ALONG BEACH WALL AND THEN BEACH

PINE PLANTATION

STRUDDICKS - NT PROPERTY

COAST PATH DIVERTED ALONG ROAD DUE TO NUMEROUS LANDSLIPS. CHECK SIGNPOSTS

50-60 MINS TO/FROM MILLENDREATH BEACH (MAP 122)

PATH ZIG-ZAGS

UNDULATING GROUND NOW

KEVERAL BEACH

SALTER ROCKS

MAP 123

MINI LABYRINTH CUT INTO THE TURF

281

122

¼ mile

500m

APPROX SCALE

0

0

* trailblazer

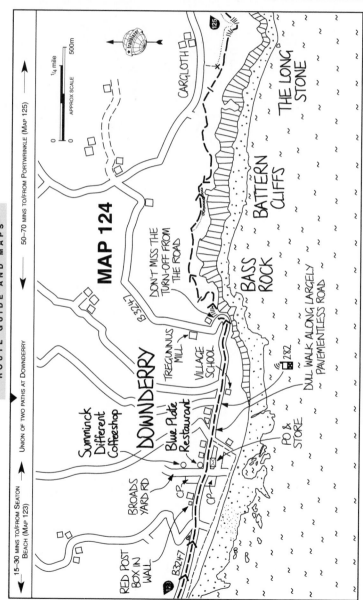

15-30 MINS TO/FROM SEATON BEACH (MAP 123)

UNION OF TWO PATHS AT DOWNDERRY

50-70 MINS TO/FROM PORTWRINKLE (MAP 125)

MAP 124

RED POST BOX IN WALL

B3247

BROADS YARD RD

CP

CP

Sumink Different Coffeeshop

DOWNDERRY

Blue Plate Restaurant

PO & STORE

TREGUNNUS MILL

VILLAGE SCHOOL

B3247

DON'T MISS THE TURN-OFF FROM THE ROAD

CARGLOTH

125

DULL WALK ALONG LARGELY PAVEMENTLESS ROAD

BASS ROCK

BATTERN CLIFFS

THE LONG STONE

1/4 mile

APPROX SCALE

0   500m

282

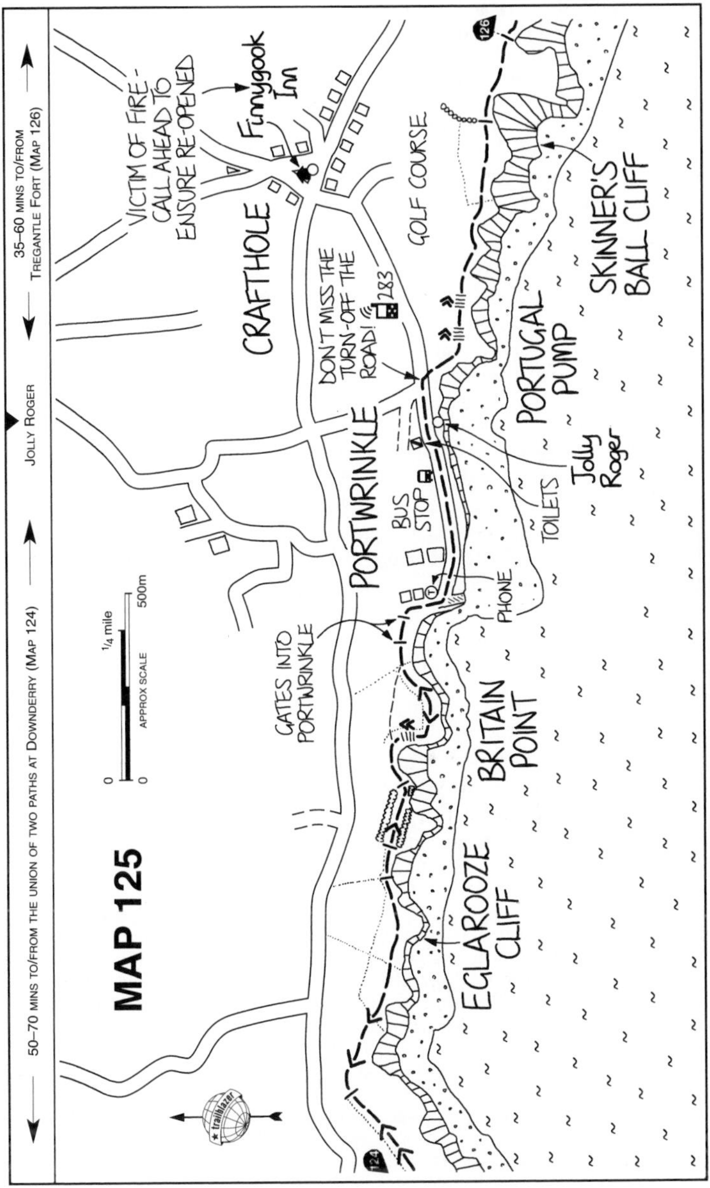
MAP 125
50–70 MINS TO/FROM THE UNION OF TWO PATHS AT DOWNDERRY (MAP 124)
35–60 MINS TO/FROM TREGANTLE FORT (MAP 126)
JOLLY ROGER
0
0
APPROX SCALE
1/4 mile
500m
CRAFTHOLE
VICTIM OF FIRE - CALL AHEAD TO ENSURE RE-OPENED
Finnygook Inn
GOLF COURSE
DON'T MISS THE TURN-OFF THE ROAD!
283
PORTWRINKLE
BUS STOP
TOILETS
Jolly Roger
PHONE
GATES INTO PORTWRINKLE
BRITAIN POINT
PORTUGAL PUMP
SKINNER'S BALL CLIFF
EGLAROOZE CLIFF
124
126
trailblazer

PORTWRINKLE   **[MAP 125, p303]**

Jolly Roger (daily 10am-5pm) is a lovely spot for a break, providing shelter when the weather's against you, and with a large outdoor seating area for when the sun's out. Their café menu is standard fare (breakfasts, sandwiches, burgers) and the coffee's good. There were plans at the time of research, to rebuild the lovely *Finnygook Inn* (☎ 01503-230338, 🖥 finnygook.co.uk) following a devastating fire. Check the website. Otherwise there's nowhere to stay between Seaton and Cawsend.

Plymouth City Bus's No 70B **bus** service stops here. (see pp52-6).

PORTWRINKLE TO PLYMOUTH   [MAPS 125-130]

The path continues to hug the clifftops after Portwrinkle at the beginning of this lengthy **13¼-mile/21.25km stage** (to Cremyll Ferry only; add another **2½ miles/4km** to reach the Mayflower Steps; **4¼-5¾hrs** to Cremyll Ferry, **plus 1hr** to Mayflower Steps). Initially passing through a golf course then fields of sheep and cattle, the first excitement of the day is only really encountered at the military firing ranges of **Tregantle Fort** (military area). A red flag here indicates that the alternative path along the road must be followed. If the red flag isn't flying, however, a superior cliffside tramp through the grounds can be enjoyed, a path that leads up to the Napoleonic fort.

Reuniting with the roadside route, the path then flirts with the tarmac for much of the next mile before actually joining it by Sharrow Point. The Point is home to **Sharrow Grotto** (Map 126), which is the work of one man, James Lugger, a Naval purser, who completed his task in 1784. Mr Lugger actually began the work in an attempt to cure his gout; as the poem inscribed on an interior wall makes clear:

> *But, as thou walk'st should sudden storms arise,*
> *Red lightnings flash, or thunder shake the skies,*
> *To Sharrows friendly grot in haste retreat,*
> *And find safe shelter and a rocky seat.*
> *By this, and exercise, here oft endured*
> *The gout itself for many years was cured.*

Back on the tarmac, the path now brings you to the conjoined villages of **Freathy** and **Tregonhawke** (Map 127), an elongated expanse of small holiday bungalows. It's a bit of an uninteresting schlep along the road and when the path

---

❏ **Tregantle Fort**   **[Map 126]**

Tregantle Fort is just one of several fortifications built in the 1860s to deter the French from attacking Plymouth's naval base. The fort at Cawsand, and the batteries at Mt Edgcumbe Park and Penlee Point, are further examples of these fortifications built on the orders of the then prime minister, Lord Palmerston, following a review by the Royal Commission on the Defence of the United Kingdom in 1859 that highlighted some of the weaknesses in the UK's defences.

Tregantle was actually one of the larger constructions, with a capacity of one thousand personnel and over thirty large guns. However, by the early 20th century it was being used more for training than defensive purposes, and since WWII has largely been renowned for and utilised for its rifle ranges, a couple of which you walk past if taking the route through the fort.

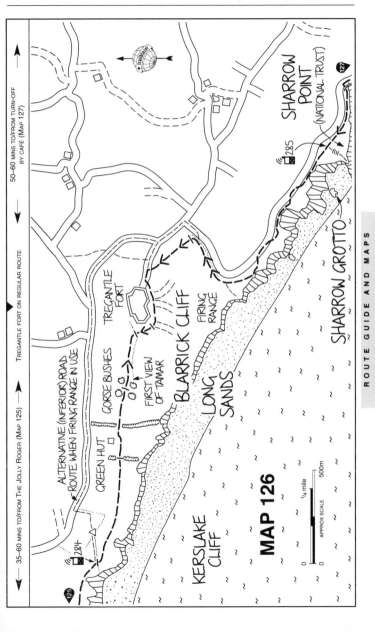

MAP 126

← 35–60 MINS TO/FROM THE JOLLY ROGER (MAP 125) → TREGANTLE FORT ON REGULAR ROUTE

← 50–60 MINS TO/FROM TURN-OFF BY CAFÉ (MAP 127) →

ALTERNATIVE (INFERIOR) ROAD ROUTE WHEN FIRING RANGE IN USE

GREEN HUT

GORSE BUSHES

FIRST VIEW OF TAMAR

TREGANTLE FORT

BLARRICK CLIFF

FIRING RANGE

SHARROW POINT (NATIONAL TRUST)

KERSLAKE CLIFF

LONG SANDS

SHARROW GROTTO

¼ mile

500m

0

APPROX SCALE

ROUTE GUIDE AND MAPS

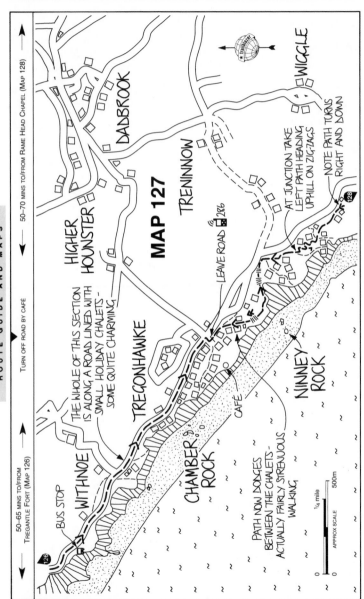

50–65 MINS TO/FROM Tregantle Fort (MAP 126)

TURN OFF ROAD BY CAFÉ

50–70 MINS TO/FROM RAME HEAD CHAPEL (MAP 128)

WIGGLE

DABBROOK

HIGHER HOUNSTER

TRENINNOW

MAP 127

AT JUNCTION TAKE LEFT PATH HEADING UPHILL ON ZIG-ZAGS

NOTE PATH TURNS RIGHT AND DOWN

128

LEAVE ROAD P 286

TRECONHAWKE

THE WHOLE OF THIS SECTION IS ALONG A ROAD LINED WITH SMALL HOLIDAY CHALETS – SOME QUITE CHARMING

WITHNOE

BUS STOP

126

CAFÉ

NINNEY ROCK

CHAMBER ROCK

PATH NOW DODGES BETWEEN THE CHALETS – ACTUALLY FAIRLY STRENUOUS WALKING

¼ mile

500m

APPROX SCALE

does finally leave it (just after a sign for a café) to dodge between the chalets on the cliffside, the numerous rises and falls do little to lighten the mood. Finally, however, the path relents and begins the gentle march to the lovely old chapel at **Rame Head** (Map 128). The building, dedicated to St Michael, actually dates back to the end of the 14th century and was built on the site of an even earlier

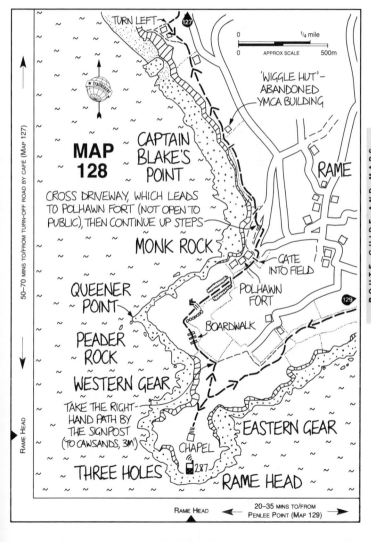

ROUTE GUIDE AND MAPS

Celtic hermitage. A priest would stay here and keep a beacon burning for passing ships. As with other promontories on this coastline, the headland was once the location of an Iron Age fort.

The gradients become more gentle now as you wend your way via farmland and forest, round **Penlee Battery Nature Reserve**, past the ruined **Folly Tower** – built in the 19th century for Princess Adelaide (wife of William IV, and the woman after whom Adelaide in South Australia is named) – and on to the twin villages of Cawsand and Kingsand.

CAWSAND & KINGSAND [MAP 129]

The twin villages of Cawsand and Kingsand offer a peaceful alternative to a night staying in Plymouth, and are linked to the city via a 30-minute ferry ride. The villages' narrow streets and alleyways have plenty of character and a surprisingly good choice of pubs and accommodation.

Curiously, despite their proximity, before 1844 the two villages were in different counties; a house on Garrett St bears the name Devon-Corn and stands on the old boundary between Devon (to which Kingsand belonged) and Cawsand (which has always been in Cornwall). Today the twins provide a quaint and friendly resort with a few amenities – though with the lure of Plymouth beckoning from just around the next headland, it's a rare walker who stays overnight.

Those amenities include **The Shop In The Square** (☎ 01752-822505; daily 10am-6pm, hours differ depending on season) in Cawsand, which sells takeaway food including pizzas and cod 'n' chips, hot drinks and general supplies, and a Premier **convenience store** (daily 7am-7pm) at 55 Fore St, in Kingsand. The **post office** (Mon, Wed-Fri 9am-1pm & 2-5.30pm, Tue 9am-1pm, Sat 9am-12.30pm) is in Kingsand.

For those who aren't following the coast path religiously, **Cawsand Ferry** (see p310) makes an enjoyable alternative route into Plymouth.

Where to stay

If you want to **camp**, *Maker Heights* (☎ 01752-823888, 🖳 makercamp.org.uk; hiker & tent £8-10; 🐾), run by Rame Conservation Trust (🖳 rameconservation trust.org.uk) is your nearest option. It's a

site full of character and also has a small restaurant/café and a shop. To get to the site follow Jackman's Meadow Rd out of Kingsand as far as a T-junction where you turn right on the B3247. Follow this up the hill until the campsite is signed off to the right. Alternatively follow the network of paths that begins at the top of Devonport Hill.

For **accommodation** in Cawsand, the newly renovated *Amal Amor* (☎ 01752-822229, 🖳 cawsandbedandbreakfast.co.uk; 1T/1D; WI-FI; 🐾; from £40pp; closed July & Aug) is a sunny house with great views out over the bay; it's also the closest place to the ferry slipway.

On the way to Kingsand, *The Old Bakery* (☎ 01752-656215, 🖳 theoldbak ery-cawsand.co.uk; 2D; WI-FI; from £45pp, sgl occ £80) is a standout café (see below) that also has a couple of nice rooms available for B&B.

Actually in Kingsand on the corner of Fore St, *Halfway House Inn* (☎ 01752-822279, 🖳 halfwayinnkingsand.co.uk; 1S/ 4D/1T; 🛥; WI-FI; 🐾; £45-55, sgl £50-60) is a comfortable pub with rooms.

Where to eat

The Old Bakery (See Where to stay; summer daily 9am-4pm, winter closed Thur) is the most pleasant place to eat in town, although it isn't open in the evening other than for takeaway pizza on Mondays (5.30-8pm; but you need to pre-order on the Sunday). It's a modern café, serving excellent breakfasts, soups, sandwiches and homemade cakes, plus fresh coffee, locally grown tea and a good selection of beers and wine.

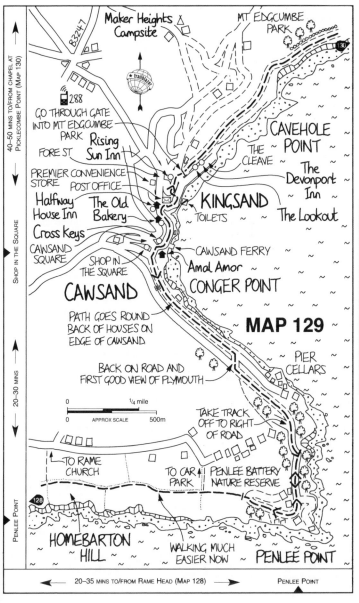

Maker Heights Campsite

MT EDGCUMBE PARK

B3247

★ trailblazer

288

GO THROUGH GATE INTO MT EDGCUMBE PARK

FORE ST

Rising Sun Inn

THE CLEAVE

CAVEHOLE POINT

The Devonport Inn

PREMIER CONVENIENCE STORE

POST OFFICE

KINGSAND

Halfway House Inn

The Old Bakery

TOILETS

The Lookout

Cross Keys

CAWSAND SQUARE

SHOP IN THE SQUARE

CAWSAND FERRY

Amal Amor

CONGER POINT

CAWSAND

PATH GOES ROUND BACK OF HOUSES ON EDGE OF CAWSAND

MAP 129

PIER CELLARS

BACK ON ROAD AND FIRST GOOD VIEW OF PLYMOUTH

0 ¼ mile

0 APPROX SCALE 500m

TAKE TRACK OFF TO RIGHT OF ROAD

TO RAME CHURCH

TO CAR PARK

PENLEE BATTERY NATURE RESERVE

128

HOMEBARTON HILL

WALKING MUCH EASIER NOW

PENLEE POINT

20–35 MINS TO/FROM RAME HEAD (MAP 128)

PENLEE POINT

40–50 MINS TO/FROM CHAPEL AT PICKLECOMBE POINT (MAP 130)

SHOP IN THE SQUARE

20–30 MINS

PENLEE POINT

ROUTE GUIDE AND MAPS

If you want a sea view, though, head to *The Lookout* (9am-4pm), a no-frills café with some outdoor seating overlooking the beach. For pub food, *The Cross Keys Inn* (☎ 01752-822706, 🖳 crosskeyscawsand.co .uk; food daily noon-2pm & 7-9pm), in Cawsand, does pretty standard pub-grub (£10-15) with a good selection of vegetarian options.

In Kingsand, *Halfway House Inn* (see Where to stay; food daily noon-2pm & 6-9pm) serves reasonable food in modern surroundings. On The Cleave, *The Devonport Inn* (☎ 01752-822869, 🖳 devonportinn.com; food Mon-Sat noon-2.30pm & 6-9.30pm, Sun noon-3pm) does some wonderful seafood including grilled Looe scallops. They also serve afternoon tea – perfect on the little terrace overlooking the sea. The smallest pub in the village, *The Rising Sun Inn* (☎ 01752-822840; food daily noon-2.30pm & 6.30-9pm, closed Mon in winter) receives rave reviews for its seasonal dishes including its 'famous' fish soup.

Transport

[See also pp52-6] A-Line Coaches' No 32 **bus** service connects Cawsand with Cremyll via Millbrook Quay. Plymouth Citybus's 70/70A also call here.

The small **Cawsand Ferry** (one-way £4) makes the 30-minute crossing to The Barbican in Plymouth six times a day (9.30am, 11am, 12.30pm, 2pm, 3.30pm & 5pm).

A final, glorious stretch is all that separates you now from the end of the walk. Leaving Kingsand opposite The Rising Sun pub, you enter the grounds of lovely **Mount Edgcumbe Park**, dotted here and there with lakes and follies, grottoes and chapels, before passing into the Formal Gardens and on, via the 18th-century *Orangery* (summer daily 10am-4pm, winter weekends only) – a charming spot for your final Cornish cream tea – to the monumental gates leading to the Cremyll Ferry.

The popular *Edgcumbe Arms* (☎ 01752-822294, 🖳 edgcumbearms.co.uk; food 10am-9pm) is conveniently located here for a pitstop before catching the ferry.

Once across **Plymouth Sound**, the city itself is reached. For most, a B&B in the city or a train back home is the next and final destination. For those who seek a more monumental end to their monumental journey, however, we have chosen as our final stop on the path the **Mayflower Steps** by the old part of Plymouth, an area known as the Barbican. Not only does this take you along Plymouth's attractive and historic waterfront, but it also seems an appropriate place to end your journey in lands of the far west – given that the Pilgrim Fathers (see p318) were looking to start a new chapter with their own occidental odyssey when they set sail from here almost 400 years ago.

❏ Cremyll Ferry
The ferry (☎ 01752-253153, 🖳 plymouthboattrips.co.uk/ferries/cremyll-ferry; £2) crosses the Tamar every 30 minutes – on the hour and half-hour – from Cremyll on Rame Head to Admiral's Hard, Stonehouse, in Plymouth. The journey takes just five minutes. In summer, the last boat leaves Cremyll at 9pm during the week, and at 9.30pm or 10pm at weekends (earlier in winter).

Plymouth Citybus's Nos 70/70A/70B (see pp52-6) connect with the ferry and also travel to Plymouth by land (1hr 40 mins).

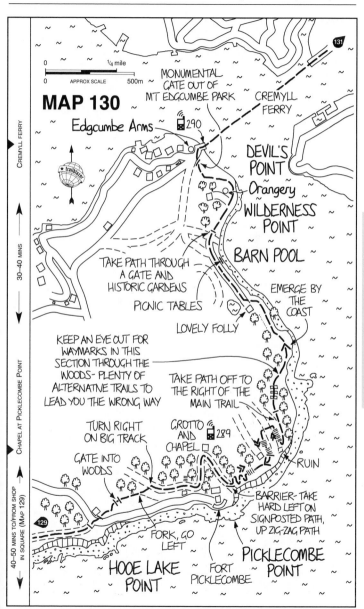

MAP 130

0 — 1/4 mile
0 — APPROX SCALE — 500m

★ trailblazer

CREMYLL FERRY

30-40 MINS

CHAPEL AT PICKLECOMBE POINT

40-50 MINS TO/FROM SHOP
IN SQUARE (MAP 129)

MONUMENTAL GATE OUT OF MT EDGCUMBE PARK

Edgcumbe Arms 📱290

CREMYLL FERRY

DEVIL'S POINT

Orangery

WILDERNESS POINT

BARN POOL

TAKE PATH THROUGH A GATE AND HISTORIC GARDENS

PICNIC TABLES

EMERGE BY THE COAST

LOVELY FOLLY

KEEP AN EYE OUT FOR WAYMARKS IN THIS SECTION THROUGH THE WOODS- PLENTY OF ALTERNATNE TRAILS TO LEAD YOU THE WRONG WAY

TAKE PATH OFF TO THE RIGHT OF THE MAIN TRAIL

TURN RIGHT ON BIG TRACK

GATE INTO WOODS

GROTTO AND CHAPEL 📱289

RUIN

BARRIER- TAKE HARD LEFT ON SIGNPOSTED PATH, UP ZIG-ZAG PATH

129

FORK, GO LEFT

HOOE LAKE POINT

FORT PICKLECOMBE

PICKLECOMBE POINT

131

ROUTE GUIDE AND MAPS

PLYMOUTH   [MAP 131, p315]

'Plymouth is indeed a town of considera-
tion, and of great importance to the public.
The situation of it between two very large
inlets of the sea, and in the bottom of a
large bay [...] is very remarkable for the
advantage of navigation.'

Daniel Defoe, *A Tour through the*
Whole Island of Great Britain

Lying between the mouths of the rivers
Plym and Tamar, Plymouth is a modern city
with a rich and eventful past. The city's
growth and prosperity are forever indebted
to her proximity to – and relationship with
– the sea. Not just as the famous departure
point of the Pilgrim Fathers but also as a
hub for trade (the commercial dockyards
are amongst the largest in Europe) and,
foremost, as a vital naval base; with a tradition that dates back to the very inception of
the Royal Navy, there is much to see and do
in this historic and thriving metropolis.

The first record of habitation in the
area, Sudtone (Saxon for 'South Farm'),
situated on the site of the present-day

Barbican, can be found in the Domesday
Book (1086). Initially just a small fishing
village, its strategically important location
soon brought prosperity and despite bouts
of plague, cholera and smallpox trimming
the ever-burgeoning population – as well as
a concerted attempt at destruction by the
Luftwaffe during the Plymouth Blitz – the
town has continued to swell in size.

Much of this success is down to its situation at the mouths of two rivers, a crucial
location that the nascent Royal Navy in the
17th century was quick to recognise. Her
Majesty's Naval Base (HMNB) Devonport
opened in 1690, with further docks being
built in 1727, 1762 and 1795. Isambard
Kingdom Brunel then designed the Great
Western Docks (1844-1850) and in 1854 the
Keynham Steam Yard, built for the construc-
tion of steam ships, was also completed.
Hardly surprising, then, that most of the
town's defining moments are sea based,
from the defeat of the Spanish Armada
(1588) to the sailing of the Mayflower
(1620) as well as the heroic resistance the

❑ The coast path through Plymouth

Initially this **2¾-mile** (4.5km) trail from the Cremyll Ferry through Plymouth is a little confusing, the lack of coast path signs not helping. If you fancy some refreshment,
the much-loved **Elvira's Café** (daily 8am-2.30pm; cash only) is right in front of you
as you disembark from the ferry. Their breakfasts are particularly good. Close by you
come to the **Codeword Pavement**, where messages between sailors and their loved
ones at home were carved into the pavement in a kind of shorthand.

Take a right onto Strand St and then a left and a right onto Cremyll St. This leads
you past **Ede Vinegar Works** (owned by the same family for six generations) to
Royal William Yard. Named after King William IV (who stands overlooking the
entrance), the yard was built, mostly on reclaimed land, to supply the navy with beef,
biscuits and beer – with a brewery, bakery and slaughterhouse on site. Recently, the
official coast path was re-directed into the yard, so you can now explore the historic
buildings here before emerging from it again at the **Artillery Tower**, built to protect
the harbour and yard but now a restaurant.

From here, make your way past the smart Georgian terraces of Durnford St,
where Sir Arthur Conan Doyle worked as a doctor – which explains the **Sherlock
Holmes/ quotes** in the pavement.

A hard right after Stonehouse Barracks leads you onto Barrack Place, which
becomes Millbay Rd, with Millbay Docks on the right; at the next roundabout is the
Wall of Stars – Bing Crosby and Judy Garland to name but two – celebrating the
famous figures who have arrived in the dock on the cruise ships that still call in here.

city showed in WW2 when, despite enduring 59 German bombing sorties, it still played a full part in the Battle of the Atlantic and was a major embarkation point on D-Day.

Unfortunately, where the Luftwaffe flattened Plymouth numerous ugly, concrete buildings have sprouted, and a large chunk of the town is run-down and devoid of charm. Thankfully, the seafront route to the Mayflower Steps remains one of the more interesting and attractive corners of Plymouth; the area around the steps, known as the Barbican, is one of Plymouth's oldest, prettiest and most vibrant, with plenty of bars and restaurants in which to toast your achievements on the path. For this reason, while most people will probably want to cross the Cremyll and finish their trek as soon as they dock, if you have an extra hour or so on your hands – not to mention stamina – we suggest finishing up at the Mayflower Steps (see box p317 for route), a suitably impressive finale to your Cornwall Coast Path odyssey – and the place where many before you, centuries ago, began their own incredible journeys.

What to see and do

The Hoe The green expanse that separates the modern-day city centre from the sea, The Hoe is most famous for playing host to Francis Drake's game of bowls in 1588, when, with the Spanish Armada fast approaching, he resolved to finish his game and wait for the tide to change before exchanging pleasantries with the enemy. It is also the place where, during the Plymouth Blitz of WWII, Nancy Astor, MP for the city and great friend of TE Lawrence (of Arabia) danced with servicemen, defiantly proclaiming that the city would go on despite the bombing.

Lighthouse lovers will be impressed by **Smeaton's Tower** (🖥 plymhearts.org/smeatons-tower; daily 10am-5pm; £4). Originally the third lighthouse to be put on Eddystone Rocks, which lie 14km southwest of Rame Head, it was dismantled in 1882 and the upper portions of the tower were rebuilt on The Hoe. John Smeaton, incidentally, after whom the tower is named, was the original builder of the tower way back in 1759.

Immediately past this, also on your right, is the **Ingot Sculpture**, a squat block of dozens of bars of gold bullion, created to celebrate the flow of British bullion that used to pass through the docks almost daily. This sculpture, alas, is made of iron and merely painted gold.

Moving to the next roundabout, to return to the waterfront you need to turn right onto West Hoe Rd. The road leads you past the **Wall of Industrial Memories**, celebrating the heritage of the Millbay area.

You now join Hoe Road, which you follow all the way to the Barbican, passing the lovely **Tinside Lido**, on your right, and The Hoe (see above) and The Citadel (see p314) on the left.

There are still some quirky little sights on the way, including a cross in the pavement to celebrate the total eclipse of the sun that occurred in 1999, and a **marble scallop shell** in the wall near the start of The Barbican, celebrating the fact that Plymouth was one of only two ports licensed by the king from which pilgrims were allowed to embark when heading to Santiago de Compostella on the Way of St James. The shell is the symbol of St James, the patron saint of pilgrims. Another patron saint is celebrated in the same wall a little further down: **Stella Maris, the Virgin, Star of the Sea**, patron saint of seafarers, was rescued from a lost cargo of marble and now sits illuminated by the pole star shining above. Pilgrims would pray to these saints for protection during their journeys. For you, however, the journey is over; a few metres on, you'll reach the **Mayflower Steps**, marking the end of your almighty trek along Cornwall's magnificent coast path.

ROUTE GUIDE AND MAPS

Other notable sites on The Hoe include a three-tier **belvedere** (a structure that has been deliberately designed to command a view) built in 1891, and the **Drake Statue** (1884), sculpted by one of the Victorian era's most pre-eminent producers of commemorative statues, Joseph Boehm. Many **war memorials** also adorn the area, fittingly so when one considers the number of servicemen and women to have departed from (and hopefully returned to) the city on various campaigns and missions over the years.

Finally, overlooked by the Smeaton Tower is **Tinside Lido** (☎ 01752-261915, 💻 everyoneactive.com/centre/Tinside-Lido; May-Sep noon-6pm, in school holidays 10am-6pm; adults £4, children £3), an Art Deco outdoor swimming pool that opened in 1935. Following years of neglect the

pool became a Grade II-listed building before being renovated and reopened in 2005.

The Citadel At The Hoe's eastern end is the Royal Citadel (☎ 07876-402728, 💻 english-heritage.org.uk). A large and impressive limestone fort, it was built in the late 1660s on the orders of Charles II in response to the second Dutch War (1664-67). Encompassing a previous fort that Drake had requested to be built in the 16th century, its guns bear down on the town as well as out to sea, most likely as a reaction to Plymouth's Parliamentarian leanings during the English Civil War.

Still militarily operational today, guided tours are available three times per week (May-Sep Tue, Thur, Sun 2.30pm; £6) and on bank holiday Mondays. Note that as The

PLYMOUTH – MAP KEY

Where to stay
3 Plymouth Backpackers Hotel
4 Duke of Cornwall Hotel
5 Travelodge
8 The Firs
9 Caraneal
11 Athenaeum Lodge
12 Caledonia Guesthouse
13 The Kynance
14 Invicta Hotel
15 The Bowling Green Hotel
17 Hashtag Hotels
18 The Pub On The Hoe
19 George Guest House
28 Casa Mia Guesthouse
29 Four Seasons Guesthouse
30 Mayflower Guesthouse

Where to stay (*cont'd*)
31 Seymour Guesthouse

Where to eat & drink
1 Elvira's Café
2 Artillery Tower
10 By the Park Deli-Café
18 The Pub On The Hoe
21 Yukisan
22 Favourite Foods
24 Eastern Eye
25 Arribas
26 The Thai House
27 Barbican Steakhouse
32 Plymouth Gin Distillery & Barbican Kitchen
33 Hakka
34 Barbican Pasty Co
35 The Ship
36 Rakuda's Kitchen
37 The Village
38 The Navy Inn

Where to eat & drink (*cont'd*)
40 The Flower Café
42 Jacka Bakery
43 Harbourside
44 Monty's Café
46 B-Bar

Other
6 Millets
7 Trespass
16 Tesco Express
20 Co-op
23 Hoegate Laundromat
39 Co-op & post office
41 Elizabethan House
45 Tourist Office & Mayflower Exhibition
46 Barbican Theatre

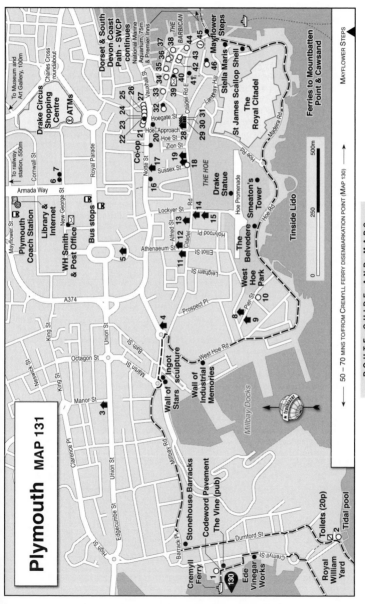

ROUTE GUIDE AND MAPS

Citadel is still a working fort, tours may be cancelled without notice and that photography is also prohibited.

The Barbican The Barbican is the old harbour area of the city and the heart of the old town. Fortuitously escaping much of the bombing inflicted on Plymouth during the war, the mazes of narrow **cobbled streets** (reputed to be the most extensive collection of cobbled thoroughfares in the UK) still exist in the originally medieval layout of what was then the town of Sutton.

The former location of Plymouth's fish market, the area is now more of a draw to those seeking art, antiques and alcohol.

Speaking of the latter, if you feel that a celebratory tipple is in order, the venerable **Plymouth Gin Distillery** (☎ 01752-665292, 🖳 plymouthgin.com), on Southside St, has been knocking out grade-A booze to discerning punters for over 200 years (since 1793 to be precise) and runs distillery tours (daily 10.30am-4.30pm; £7) round its building, which originally dates back to the mid 15th century. The building,

> ❏ **Sir Francis Drake and the Spanish Armada**
> The Elizabethan era was a time of turmoil. The major European powers were often at war, with religion frequently the cause. The two main protagonists at this time were Protestant England and Catholic Spain. The latter controlled the Netherlands where Protestant ideals were popular. England, as was their wont, aided the Dutch Protestants who were being hunted by the Spanish Inquisition, and it was this deci-sion – as well as the beheading of the Catholic Mary Queen of Scots, ordered by the Protestant Queen Elizabeth I in 1587 – that led to King Philip II of Spain's decision to defend Catholicism by invading England.
> One of Queen Elizabeth I's most feared seamen was Sir Francis Drake. A buc-caneering adventurer and hero to the English, the Spanish considered him a menace and he was a constant thorn in their side. Conducting his own personal Protestant cru-sade, by 1588 he had already harassed and harried many Spanish boats in the West Indies, occupied the ports of Cadiz and Corunna, destroying 37 Spanish ships as he did so, and plundered the treasures of Spain wherever he found them, describing his wish to 'singe the king of Spain's beard.'
> King Philip II's Spanish Armada set sail from Lisbon in May 1588. Their ships were harassed by English and Dutch boats throughout their journey. The huge flotil-la struggling through, the Spanish were eventually spotted off the Lizard and the news of their arrival swiftly reached Plymouth, where the English navy was waiting. Famously, Drake purportedly scoffed on being told of the arrival of the Armada, and chose to finish his game of bowls instead, claiming he could do so *and* defeat the Spanish. A much debated incident, if it did actually happen it is possible that Drake would have known that the tide of the Tamar was against him – so preventing his boats from accessing the Channel until it turned – and thus recognised that he had ample time to complete his game.
> History doesn't record whether Drake won his game of bowls. The outcome of the battle, however, is well known. Fighting between the Spanish and English navies went on for eight days before the Spaniards finally had to admit defeat, their navy beaten, burnt and scattered. Rubbing sea salt into the wounds, owing to westerly winds many of the defeated boats couldn't return straight home, but instead had to sail around the tip of Scotland and down the coast of Ireland where they were fur-ther battered by storms – as well as being executed by the English in Ireland. Drake meanwhile sailed home a hero, his legend forever cemented in English naval histo-ry for establishing England's dominance of the Atlantic – and refusing to end a game of bowls.

incidentally, and more than a little ironically, was also where the Puritan Pilgrim Fathers supposedly spent their last night before embarking for America.

Only a couple of minutes' away, **Elizabethan House** (☎ 01752-304774, 🖳 plymhearts.org/elizabethan-house) retains much of its original structure. Closed for refurbishment at the time of research (but scheduled to reopen in 2020), it's worth checking the website to see if you can squeeze a visit into your SWCP schedule.

Next to the pedestrian walkway which crosses Sutton Harbour, **The Mayflower Steps** commemorate the Pilgrim Fathers' departure for the New World in 1620. The steps consist of a portico that was built in 1934 and a platform hanging out over the water's edge. Nearby, above the tourist information office you will find **Plymouth Mayflower Exhibition** (Apr-Oct Mon-Sat 9.30am-5pm, Sun 10.30am-4pm, Nov-Mar Mon-Fri 9.30am-5pm, Sat 10.30am-4pm; £3), covering three floors and telling the story of the Pilgrim Fathers. It also has a balcony from which you can gaze out over the bustle below.

Not technically part of the Barbican but just across the walkway from the Mayflower Steps is the **National Marine Aquarium** (☎ 0844-893 7938, 🖳 national-aquarium.co.uk; daily 10am-5pm; £16.95, £15.25 if bought online in advance). The UK's largest, it houses a tank that contains 2.5 million litres of water! Truly unmissable, the Atlantic Ocean display, as it is known, is home not only to ragged tooth sharks, stingrays and barracuda but also a full-sized replica of a WWII plane. There are regular talks and feedings as well as a 4D cinema.

The intriguing **Plymouth Museum and Art Gallery** (☎ 01752-304774, 🖳 plymhearts.org/pcmag; Tue-Fri 10am-5.30pm, Sat & bank holiday Mon 10am-5pm, Sun & Mon closed; free admission) is on Drake Circus, just a few minutes' walk north of the Barbican. Highlights here include effects belonging to two of the city's heroes: a side drum (the oldest in the UK) that once belonged to Francis Drake; and a pair of skis owned and used by

Robert Falcon Scott in his 1902 Antarctic expedition.

Services
As you'd expect, Plymouth has just about every amenity you need. The **tourist information centre** (☎ 01752-306330, 🖳 visit plymouth.co.uk; Apr-Oct Mon-Sat 9am-5pm, Sun 10am-4pm, Nov-Mar Mon-Fri 9am-5pm, Sat 10am-4pm) is handily placed right by the Mayflower Steps on the Barbican and is one of the friendliest and most helpful on the entire walk. There's a Co-op **supermarket** (7am-10pm), which also contains a **sub post office** (Mon-Fri 9am-5.30pm, Sat 9am-12.30pm), nearby at 49-50 Southside St. The main branch (Mon-Sat 9am-5.30pm) is on 5 Saint Andrew's Cross Roundabout, about 10 minutes' away. There's also a handy Tesco Express **supermarket** (6am-11pm) on Notte St and another Co-op (6am-11pm, Sun from 7am).

At 167-171 Armada Way, the Central **library** (☎ 01752-305901, 🖳 plymouth .gov.uk/libraries; Mon-Fri 8.30am-6pm, Thur to 8pm, Sat 9am-5pm; WI-FI) has **internet** access (£1/15 mins).

For **camping/trekking** supplies head to nearby New George St, north-west of the Saint Andrew's Cross Roundabout, where you'll find Millets (Mon-Sat 9am-6pm, Sun 10.30am-4.30pm) at No 40 and Trespass at No 34. There are plenty of **ATMs** near here too, in the largely pedestrianised shopping zone.

Back nearer the waterfront, the most convenient of Plymouth's **launderettes** is Hoegate Laundromat (☎ 01752-223031; Mon-Fri 8.30am-6pm) at 55 Notte St.

Where to stay
Hostels and budget accommodation
Plymouth Backpackers Hotel (☎ 01752-213033, ☎ 01752-269333, or ☎ 07745-589361, 🖳 plymouthbackpackershotel .co.uk; dorm from £16pp, private twin rooms from £39 per room; WI-FI), 102 Union St, has a mixture of dorm beds and private rooms, some are en suite and some share facilities. They offer packed lunches, evening meals and are pet-friendly.

Plymouth has two relatively central *Premier Inns* (🖥 premierinn.com; Lockyers Quay ☎ 0871-527 8880; and Sutton Rd ☎ 0871-527 8882); both are located on the other side of Sutton Harbour behind the National Marine Aquarium. A branch of *Travelodge* (☎ 0871-984 6251, 🖥 travelodge.co.uk; Derry's Cross) and a central *#Hotels* (🖥 hashtag-hotels.com) are on Notte St. Best prices for all of them can be found online.

B&Bs There are B&Bs aplenty in Plymouth; a useful resource is 🖥 visitply mouth.co.uk/accommodation. Many of them are well situated for both the path and the city sights. Two of the most convenient for the Cremyll ferry are *The Firs* (☎ 01752-262870, 🖥 thefirsinplymouth.co .uk; 3S/1D/1T/1D or T/2Tr, some en suite; WI-FI; 🐾; from £27.50pp, sgl/sgl occ from £35), at 13 Pier St; and *The Caraneal* (☎ 01752-663589, 🖥 caranealplymouth.co.uk; 8D/2T; WI-FI; 🐾; from £27.50pp, sgl occ from £35), at 12-14 Pier St.

Those more central are generally based along **Citadel Rd**. Facing Hoe Park is *The George Guesthouse* (☎ 01752-661517, 🖥 georgeguesthouse.com; 1S/5T/4F; WI-FI; 🐾; from £20pp, sgl £30), at No 161. Also along this stretch of Citadel Rd, at No 159, is *The Pub On The Hoe*

❑ The Mayflower and the Pilgrim Fathers

Most visitors to Plymouth – and probably just about every American tourist in the city – are aware that amongst the first, and certainly the most famous, Europeans to settle in America (a group now celebrated as the Pilgrim Fathers) set sail from Plymouth in 1620. What is less well known, perhaps, is the background to their emigration and why they felt compelled to head for the New World in the first place.

The pilgrimage had its roots in Henry VIII's rejection of the Catholic Church back in 1534, an act that led to England becoming a Protestant country for the first time. Puritanism, the ideology followed by the Pilgrim Fathers, emerged soon afterwards during the reign of Henry VIII's daughter, Elizabeth I. As the name suggests, the Puritans felt that Henry VIII's Church of England was neither strict nor pious enough for their rather fanatical tastes. This stance angered both Elizabeth and her successor, James I, and before long the Puritans were being persecuted for their beliefs.

In 1609 a number of Puritans headed for Leiden in the Netherlands to seek a land where they could practise their faith in peace. Unfortunately, whilst the persecutions were less common, they were still unhappy with the tolerance and levity of their Dutch hosts; more worrying still for the Puritans was the way their offspring were being assimilated into Dutch culture. There seemed to be only one solution: to build their own community, away from the persecution and profanity (as they saw it) of Europe, in the New World.

Plymouth's role in their story is actually both fortuitous and fairly minor. Setting sail from Southampton in *The Mayflower* and *The Speedwell* in August 1620, they only docked in Plymouth due to a storm that damaged the already old and leaking boats as they navigated The Channel. Fully stocked with and the decision made to leave *The Speedwell* behind, a total of 102 passengers and crew (not all of whom were Puritans) finally left the city on 6 September 1620, reaching Cape Cod 66 days later to found the community they had dreamed of in Massachusetts.

The Pilgrim Fathers' travails didn't end there, though. Weakened by their journey and unprepared for winter, half of them died within the first four months of landing. However, those who did live owed their survival to the natives, a relationship cemented in the Pilgrims' first harvest of 1621 – a ceremony which would go on to become the basis for the American festival of Thanksgiving.

(☎ 01752-202405, 🖳 thepubonthehoe.co
.uk; 4 rooms; WI-FI; 🐾; from £30pp).

Towards the western end of Citadel Rd,
there are more options such as *The Kynance*
(☎ 01752-266821, 🖳 kynancehouse.co.uk;
6S/18D or T/2F; 🛏; WI-FI; 🐾; from £30pp,
sgl from £36), at 107-11, and, on Athenaeum
St, *Caledonia Guesthouse* (☎ 01752-
229052; 1S/5D/4T; WI-FI; from £22pp, sgl
£28), at No 27; and *Athenaeum Lodge* (☎
01752-665005; 3D/4F; WI-FI; from £28, sgl
occ from £32) at No 4.

Closer to The Barbican, but still on
Citadel Rd, at its eastern end, there is
another selection of guesthouses including
Seymour (☎ 01752-667002, 🖳 seymour
guesthouse.co.uk; 2S/2D/3T, some en suite;
WI-FI; from £31pp) at No 211; *Mayflower*
(☎ 01752-667496, 🖳 mayflowerguest
house.co.uk; 2S/7D or T; WI-FI; from
£32.50pp, sgl £37) at No 209; *Four
Seasons* (☎ 01752-223591, 🖳 fourseasons
guesthouse.co.uk; 2S/3D/2D or T; WI-FI;
🐾; £27.50-34pp, sgl £30-35) at No 207,
where there is a choice of breakfast including veggie or gluten-free; and *Casa Mia* (☎
01752-265742, 🖳 casamiaguesthouse.co
.uk; 2S/2D or T/3D; WI-FI; from £33.50pp,
sgl £43), No 201, also a purveyor of the
vegetarian breakfast.

Hotels The closest hotel to the Cremyll
Ferry is the grand, 150-year-old *Duke of
Cornwall Hotel* (☎ 01752-275850, 🖳 the
dukeofcornwall.co.uk; 72 rooms; 🛏; WI-FI;
from £38pp) on Millbay Rd. Check online
for their best offers. Closer to The Hoe are
The Bowling Green Hotel (☎ 01752-
209090, 🖳 thebowlinggreenplymouth
.com; 1S/2T/8D/1F; 🛏; WI-FI; £35-50pp),
9-10 Osborne Place, which is used by a
number of walking companies; and *Invicta
Hotel* (☎ 01752-664997, 🖳 invictahotel.
co.uk; 4S/8D/6D or T/4F; 🛏; WI-FI; 🐾;
£40-70pp), 11/12 Osborne Place.

Where to eat and drink
The Barbican is the place to go for food or
a drink.

Snacks & takeaways For **pasties**, head
to *Barbican Pasty Co* (☎ 01752-262462),

on Southside St. They do 12 different vari-
eties, including traditional Cornish. Get
your **fish & chips** fix at *Harbourside* (daily
11am-10.30/11pm), at 35 Southside St.

B-Bar (☎ 01752-242021, 🖳 b-bar
.co.uk; food noon-9pm; eat in or takeaway)
is a **Thai** noodle bar inside Barbican
Theatre on Castle St. Their scrumptious
Thai noodle boxes start at £7.50.

Another takeaway option is *Favourite
Foods* (☎ 01752-222232; daily 4.30pm-
1am), a fast-food joint on Notte St, serving
kebabs for around £5.

Cafés The coffee's good at *Jacka
Bakery* (9am-4pm), an unassuming gem
of a café at 38 Southside St, but it's the
fresh breads, all baked on the premises,
that really steal the show. You won't find
better bread anywhere in the city. A few
steps away, at 13 The Barbican, *Monty's
Café* (☎ 01752-252877, 🖳 montyscafe
plymouth.co.uk; 9am-5.30pm) does equally good coffee, plus standout all-day
breakfasts, as well as sandwiches and ciabattas for less than a fiver. The other side
of Jacka Bakery, further up Southside St at
No 46, is *The Flower Café* (9.45am-
5.30pm), a cute and friendly little place,
perfect for tea and cake and with a small
back garden to boot.

Further from the centre, but just a short
diversion off the coast path as you enter the
city is the small deli-café *By The Park*
(Tue-Fri 9.30am-4.30pm, Sat & Sun
9.30am-5pm, closed Mon) at 26 Pier St.
They do wonderful cakes and cream teas as
well as lunches and hot and cold drinks.

Pubs & bars On Southside St, *The Navy
Inn* (☎ 01752-301812; food noon-9pm) has
won awards for its food. It's nothing flash –
just a traditional pub with a seemingly ordi-
nary pub-grub menu – but the results are
excellent, and the atmosphere always lively. An added bonus is the terrace on the first
floor with views along the waterfront.

Opening out onto the waterfront, *The
Ship* (☎ 01752-667604, 🖳 theshipply
mouth.co.uk; food Mon-Fri noon-3pm &
5.30-9pm, Sat noon-9pm, Sun noon-8pm)
is owned by St Austell Brewery. Mains,

including vegetarian options are around the £10-15 mark.

Practically next door, *Racuda's Kitchen* (11.30am-9pm) is more of a bar-restaurant than a pub, but with the same great outdoor seating spot as The Ship. Food wise, it's burgers, grilled meats, fish and pasta. For drinks, it's all about cocktails.

Away from the tourists, *The Pub On The Hoe* (see Where to stay; food served 10am-9pm) has a regularly changing selection of real ales, and good honest pub grub (bangers & mash, cod & chips, steak & ale pie etc). It also opens early to serve good-value breakfasts and serves vegan and gluten-free dishes.

Restaurants Next door to The Navy Inn, *The Village* (☎ 01752-667688, 🖳 thevillagerestaurantplymouth.co.uk; Mon-Sat 11.30am-2pm & 5.30-10.15pm, Sun 11.30am-10.15pm), at No 32 Southside St, is an excellent seafood restaurant which also does a terrific roast beef on Sundays.

Also on Southside St, *Barbican Kitchen* (☎ 01752-604448, 🖳 barbicankitchen.com; Mon-Thur noon-2.30pm & 6-9.30pm, Fri-Sat noon-2.30pm & 5-10pm) is located in Plymouth Gin Distillery. The menu is very eclectic, including dishes from Japan to Italy, though they also do lovely sausages & mash with onion gravy.

A short walk away, on Notte St, *Barbican Steakhouse* (☎ 01752-222214; Mon-Thur 5-10.30pm, Fri 5-11pm, Sat noon-11pm, Sun noon-10pm) does a mouth-watering smothered fillet steak for £19.95.

For **Indian** cuisine, try *The Eastern Eye* (☎ 01752-262948, 🖳 easterneyeplymouth.com; Sun-Thur 6pm-midnight, Fri & Sat 6pm-2am).

For **Thai** food, head to *Thai House* (☎ 01752-661600, 🖳 thethaihouse.co.uk; Sun-Thur 6-10pm, Fri & Sat to 10.30pm). And for **Mexican**, try *Arribas* (☎ 01752-603303, 🖳 arribasmexican.co.uk; daily 5-10pm).

There are plenty of **Chinese** options, including *Hakka* (☎ 01752-224777; noon-3pm & 6-9.30pm; mains £8-12), a Cantonese joint with the only home-made dim sum in Devon. On Notte St, meanwhile,

Yukisan (☎ 01752-250240, 🖳 yukisan.co.uk; Mon-Thur 11.30am-2.30pm & 5-10pm, Fri-Sat 11.30am-10.30pm, Sun noon-10pm) is the only Japanese restaurant in town. The sushi's good, of course, but try the *yakitori* (grilled meat/ veg skewers in a Japanese barbecue sauce) too. If you can't decide, go for one of the set menus (£18-26).

Further afield, but worth the walk, *Artillery Tower* (☎ 01752-257610, 🖳 artillerytower.co.uk; Wed-Sat 7.15-9.30pm), is one of the more discreet places in the city; indeed, you may well have walked right past it on the way into the centre from the Cremyll ferry. Evening meals are set at £48.50 for three courses, but include mains such as roast duck with marinated cherries, or peppered loin of venison with quince & chestnuts. The restaurant is located in a 15th-century defensive tower on the sea wall and overlooks Plymouth Sound. Booking is recommended.

Transport

[See also pp52-6] The most convenient place to board buses for local services are the bus stops along Royal Parade. Numerous services leave from here. First's 70/70A/70B **buses** go to Torpoint Ferry and Plymouth Citybus's 12/12B travel to Bude via Launceston; their 72 operates to Looe and their 48 to Wembury. Stagecoach's No 3 heads to Dartmouth. Gorran and District Community Bus G4 runs to St Austell, Mevagissey & Gorran Haven.

National Express coaches leave from **Plymouth Coach Station** (☎ 0871-781 8181), Armada Way, with direct or connecting services to pretty much every city in mainland Britain. Plymouth is a stop on GWR's regular **train** services between London (Paddington) and Penzance. The railway station is an easy 10-minute walk north of Royal Parade.

For a **taxi**, try Excel Cabs (☎ 01752-666699) or Armada Cabs (☎ 01752-666222).

Cawsand Ferry leaves from The Barbican daily at 9am, 10.30am, noon, 1.30pm, 3pm & 4.30pm. It costs £4 and takes 30 minutes to reach Cawsand (p308).

APPENDIX A: HARTLAND QUAY TO BUDE

HARTLAND QUAY TO BUDE [MAPS 48x-54x]

The following section, the route from Hartland Quay in Devon over the border into Cornwall and on to Bude, is from *Exmoor & North Devon Coast Path*, the first book in the series. It's included for completeness, so that every inch of the path within Cornwall is covered in this book.

This **15½-mile (24.9km; 8½hrs)** part is actually the hardest section on the entire South-West Coast Path! It's across soaring summit and plunging combe that includes, by our reckoning, ten *major* ascents and descents as you scramble across valley after valley, with no refreshments along the way until right near the end (though it's possible to divert off the path to Morwenstow where there is both a wonderful tea room and a marvellous pub).

Thankfully, the rewards are manifold: the views along the way, especially the panorama at Higher Sharpnose Point, the vista south from Steeple Point and the aspect from Yeolmouth Cliff back to Devil's Hole, are little short of magnificent. If surveying the scenery is difficult due to inclement conditions you can find shelter in the huts of writers Rev Stephen Hawker, near Morwenstow, and Ronald Duncan, above the border with Cornwall. While if the weather is good, it seems churlish not to pay a visit to the endless stretch of sand before Bude, the perfect place to cool one's corns and paddle in the sea. All this, and we haven't even mentioned the waterfalls (with a particularly fine example at Speke's Mill Mouth), Iron Age forts, Roman sites, a branch of GCHQ ... and the sheer joy of being on one of the remotest and most beautiful stretches of coastline this country can offer.

HARTLAND QUAY [MAP 48x, p322]

In Tudor times this was a major port but a storm in 1887 destroyed the quay, and now there's only a small modern slipway and *Hartland Quay Hotel* (☎ 01237-441218, 🖥 hartlandquayhotel.co.uk; 3S/3T/4D/7F; 🛏; WI-FI; from £52.50pp, sgl occ from £70). It has its own museum, with photos and mementoes of various local shipwrecks. (They've plenty of raw material to choose from, for it's said that this coastline has about ten shipwrecks per mile!). The hotel's bar serves food daily noon-2.30pm & 6-9pm plus 3-5.30pm in summer.

The route

Despite the fearsome reputation of this stage, the beginning of the walk is rather gentle as you leave Hartland Point to head towards the triangular promontory of **St Catherine's Tor**. The path ignores the scramble up the Tor (which is believed to have had a Roman villa on its summit), preferring instead to follow Wargery Water upstream, a waterway that ends its journey in impressive fashion by plummeting over the cliffs to the north of the Tor. Those who miss this waterfall (which, after all, is not actually on the path) needn't be too concerned, for the next valley, **Speke's Mill Mouth**, has, if anything, an even more spectacular version, and one that is easily visible just a few metres from the path.

Climbing out of the combe – the first of many calf-popping ascents – up Swansford Hill and past the turn-off to Elmscott Youth Hostel, the path is

MAP 48x

rather uneventful to **Nabor Point**, even joining a road at one point, and only gets exciting again at **Embury Beacon**, where the path runs alongside the defensive earthwork of an Iron Age fort. Yet another vertiginous descent follows, this time at **Welcombe Mouth**, where the path crosses the stream on stepping stones. It's a beautiful spot surpassed in its noteworthiness for walkers only, perhaps, by the next laceration in the surface of the land: **Marsland Valley**. Another steep combe, it is here on its northern slopes that you'll find the **hut of Ronald Duncan**. Author, poet, playwright and pacifist, Duncan is perhaps best known for writing the libretto of Benjamin's Britten's opera *The Rape of Lucretia*, but also for this lovely hut that he constructed so he could have views over the sea while writing. On the walls inside are some examples of his work.

ELMSCOTT   [off MAP 49x, p324]

Elmscott is an easy, short walk from the path and the accommodation is rather pleasant. *Elmscott Youth Hostel* (☎ 01237-441367, 🖳 elmscott.org.uk; 32 beds: 1T/three 4-bed dorms/three 6-bed dorms; £20-24pp) is one such, originally built as a school in Victorian times and now a cosy (YHA accredited) hostel with a small shop (Easter to Oct) and good kitchen facilities (which is just as well as meals aren't provided and there's nowhere to eat around here). The farm on which it is set is also a B&B: *Elmscott Farm* (☎ 01237-441276, 🖳 elmscott.org.uk; 2D/1T; ☛; from £35pp) lies about 400m from the path.

Struggle down the steps to the floor of the valley and you cross the **border into Cornwall**, the exact boundary marked by a bridge and a signpost welcoming you to 'Kernow' (as they call it round here). But while the county might have changed, the path remains as challenging as ever as you traverse yet more stamina-sapping undulations at **Litter Mouth** and **Yeol Mouth** and around **St Morwenna's Well** – so easy to write, so exhausting to hike.

Thankfully, soon after the latter, it's possible to get off the rollercoaster for a while by taking the short diversion to the hamlet of **Morwenstow**.

MORWENSTOW   [MAP 51x, p326]

There's little more to this ancient settlement than a church, a tearoom and a pub. All three, however, are full of character. The church is dedicated to St Morwenna and St John the Baptist, and while the earliest part of the current church is Norman, there is believed to have been a church on this site since Anglo-Saxon times. The Rev Hawker, of Hawker's Hut fame (see p320), was one of the vicars here.

Opposite sits the award-winning *Rectory Farm Tearoom* (☎ 01288-331251, 🖳 rectory-tearooms.co.uk; week before Easter to end Oct daily 11am-5pm, possibly later in peak season; winter hours variable), part of a charming 13th-century farm that's been serving cream-topped scones to hungry walkers for over 50 years now. To the south, the 13th-century *Bush Inn* (☎ 01288-331242, 🖳 thebushinnmorwenstow.com; 2D/2T; ☛; wi-fi; 🐾; from £45pp, sgl occ £65-75) provides B&B and serves food (daily noon-8pm; most mains £11-13). Ask the owners to point out some of the ancient features of the inn, including the lepers' squint, through which the diseased of the parish were fed scraps, and a monastic cross carved into a flagstone in the floor.

Although the *Old Vicarage* (☎ 01288-331369, 🖳 rshawker.co.uk; 1S/1D/1T; ☛; wi-fi; from £58pp, one-night stay £60pp) is a wonderful place to stay, a minimum two-night stay is preferred in high season and at weekends.

(cont'd on p329)

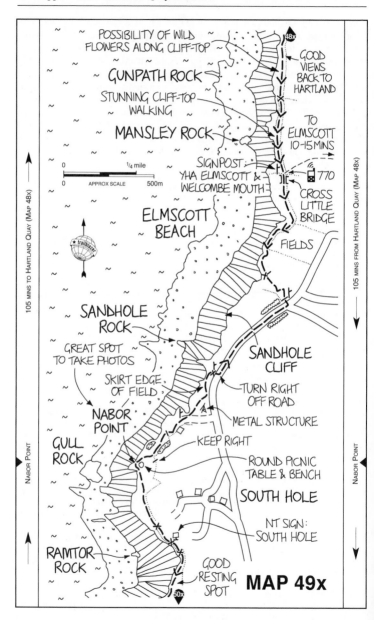

POSSIBILITY OF WILD FLOWERS ALONG CLIFF-TOP

GUNPATH ROCK

STUNNING CLIFF-TOP WALKING

MANSLEY ROCK

GOOD VIEWS BACK TO HARTLAND

TO ELMSCOTT 10-15 MINS

SIGNPOST: YHA ELMSCOTT & WELCOMBE MOUTH

770

CROSS LITTLE BRIDGE

ELMSCOTT BEACH

FIELDS

SANDHOLE ROCK

GREAT SPOT TO TAKE PHOTOS

SKIRT EDGE OF FIELD

SANDHOLE CLIFF

TURN RIGHT OFF ROAD

METAL STRUCTURE

NABOR POINT

GULL ROCK

KEEP RIGHT

ROUND PICNIC TABLE & BENCH

SOUTH HOLE

NT SIGN: SOUTH HOLE

RAMTOR ROCK

GOOD RESTING SPOT

MAP 49x

48x

50x

0 ¼ mile
APPROX SCALE
0 500m

★ trailblazer

105 MINS TO HARTLAND QUAY (MAP 48x)

105 MINS FROM HARTLAND QUAY (MAP 48x)

NABOR POINT

NABOR POINT

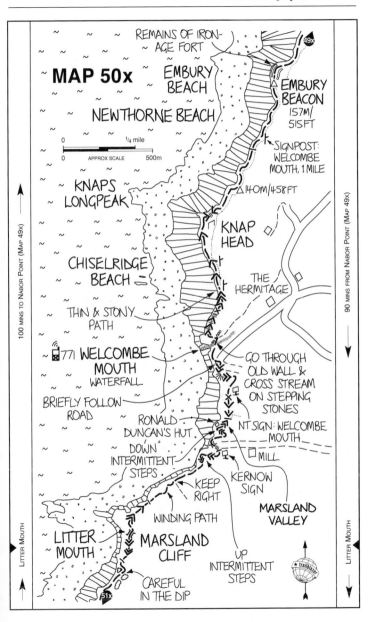

MAP 50x

REMAINS OF IRON-AGE FORT
EMBURY BEACH
NEWTHORNE BEACH
EMBURY BEACON 157M/515FT
SIGNPOST: WELCOMBE MOUTH, 1 MILE
△140M/458FT
KNAPS LONGPEAK
KNAP HEAD
THE HERMITAGE
CHISELRIDGE BEACH
THIN & STONY PATH
771 WELCOMBE MOUTH WATERFALL
GO THROUGH OLD WALL & CROSS STREAM ON STEPPING STONES
BRIEFLY FOLLOW ROAD
RONALD DUNCAN'S HUT
NT SIGN: WELCOMBE MOUTH
DOWN INTERMITTENT STEPS
MILL
KERNOW SIGN
MARSLAND VALLEY
KEEP RIGHT
WINDING PATH
LITTER MOUTH
MARSLAND CLIFF
UP INTERMITTENT STEPS
CAREFUL IN THE DIP
51x

0   ¼ mile
APPROX SCALE
0   500m

100 MINS TO NABOR POINT (MAP 49x)
LITTER MOUTH

90 MINS FROM NABOR POINT (MAP 49x)
LITTER MOUTH

49x

trailblazer

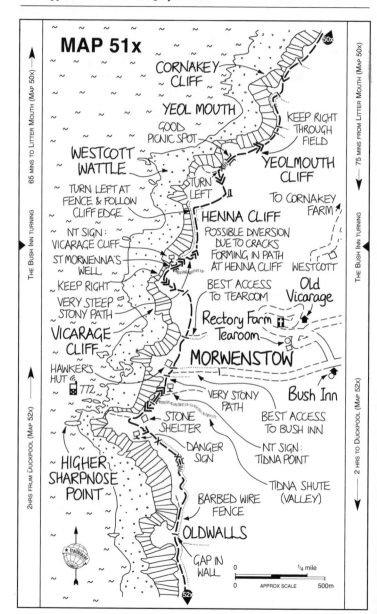

MAP 51x

CORNAKEY CLIFF

YEOL MOUTH

GOOD PICNIC SPOT

50x

KEEP RIGHT THROUGH FIELD

WESTCOTT WATTLE

TURN LEFT AT FENCE & FOLLOW CLIFF EDGE

TURN LEFT

YEOLMOUTH CLIFF

NT SIGN: VICARAGE CLIFF

ST MORWENNA'S WELL

HENNA CLIFF

POSSIBLE DIVERSION DUE TO CRACKS FORMING IN PATH AT HENNA CLIFF

TO CORNAKEY FARM

WESTCOTT

KEEP RIGHT

VERY STEEP STONY PATH

BEST ACCESS TO TEAROOM

Old Vicarage

VICARAGE CLIFF

Rectory Farm Tearoom

MORWENSTOW

HAWKER'S HUT

772

VERY STONY PATH

Bush Inn

STONE SHELTER

DANGER SIGN

BEST ACCESS TO BUSH INN

NT SIGN: TIDNA POINT

HIGHER SHARPNOSE POINT

BARBED WIRE FENCE

TIDNA SHUTE (VALLEY)

OLDWALLS

GAP IN WALL

trailblazer

0   ¼ mile

0   500m
APPROX SCALE

52x

65 MINS TO LITTER MOUTH (MAP 50x)

THE BUSH INN TURNING

2HRS FROM DUCKPOOL (MAP 52x)

75 MINS FROM LITTER MOUTH (MAP 50x)

THE BUSH INN TURNING

2 HRS TO DUCKPOOL (MAP 52x)

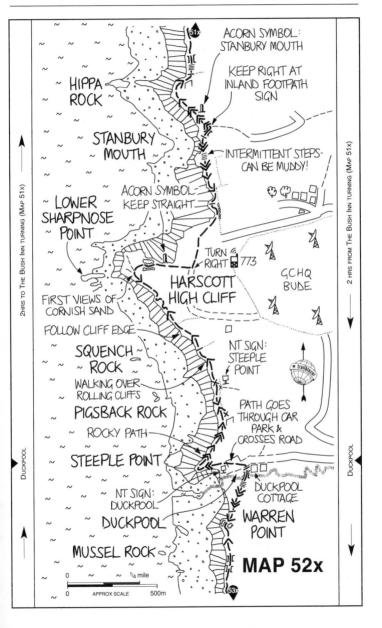

2HRS TO THE BUSH INN TURNING (MAP 51x)

2 HRS FROM THE BUSH INN TURNING (MAP 51x)

ACORN SYMBOL: STANBURY MOUTH

KEEP RIGHT AT INLAND FOOTPATH SIGN

HIPPA ROCK

STANBURY MOUTH

INTERMITTENT STEPS - CAN BE MUDDY!

LOWER SHARPNOSE POINT

ACORN SYMBOL KEEP STRAIGHT

TURN RIGHT 773

HARSCOTT HIGH CLIFF

GCHQ BUDE

FIRST VIEWS OF CORNISH SAND

FOLLOW CLIFF EDGE

SQUENCH ROCK

NT SIGN: STEEPLE POINT

WALKING OVER ROLLING CLIFFS

PIGSBACK ROCK

PATH GOES THROUGH CAR PARK & CROSSES ROAD

ROCKY PATH

STEEPLE POINT

NT SIGN: DUCKPOOL

DUCKPOOL COTTAGE

WARREN POINT

DUCKPOOL

MUSSEL ROCK

MAP 52x

0   ¼ mile
APPROX SCALE   500m

DUCKPOOL

DUCKPOOL

trailblazer

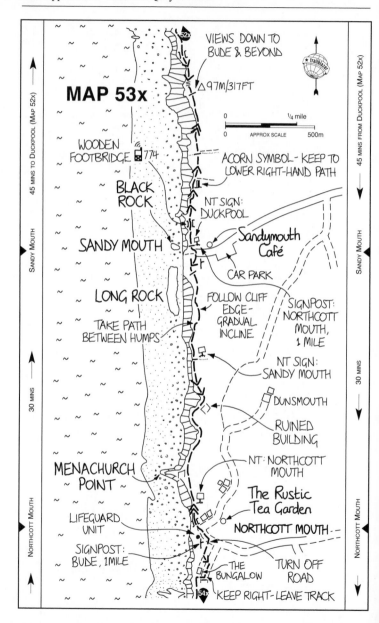

(*cont'd from p323*) Those who forego the delights of Morwenstow will instead continue along **Vicarage Cliff**, in time coming to the cliff-face path to **Hawker's Hut** (easy to miss but if you're following the path right by the cliff you'll see the sign near it), built from the timbers of shipwrecked craft by the eccentric vicar of Morwenstow, the Reverend Stephen Hawker.

Still the relentless gradients of the path continue as you clamber in and out of the valleys of **Tidna Shute** and **Stanbury**, the latter seemingly the steepest of all today's climbs. Your reward at the top is **GCHQ (Bude)** and its enormous satellite dishes from where, at its southern end, there are views of Bude.

Another steep valley, **Duckpool**, follows, where in July at dusk you can see the rare spectacle of glow worms. Duckpool is also the last serious challenge on this stage. The gradients finally relent now and the path, though still long and undulating, is more merciful than it has been previously on this stage. Cafés start to appear on the route too, including *Sandymouth Café* (Map 53x; ☎ 01288-354286, 💻 sandymouth.com; Easter to Oct daily 9am-6pm, Wed-Sun only in winter) and the lovely eatery, *Margaret's Rustic Tea Garden* (which has actually been here since the '40s when Margaret's mum ran the place), with outside seating by the stream at **Northcott Mouth**, and wonderful cream teas served from an old green mobile home. But by now even this idyllic place may not be enough to halt your determined march to **Bude** (see p79) which you should reach about 2-2½ hours after leaving Duckpool.

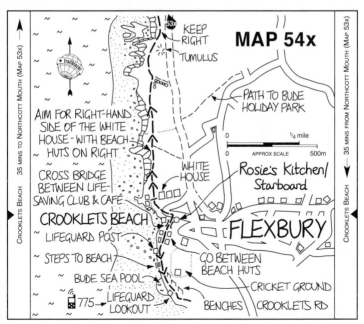

APPENDIX B: GPS WAYPOINTS

MAP	REF	GPS WAYPOINTS		DESCRIPTION
Map 1	001	50 49 601	04 32 803	Falcon Hotel, Bude
Map 1	002	50 49 685	04 33 330	Compass tower
Map 1	003	50 49 427	04 33 380	trig point
Map 1	004	50 48 861	04 33 242	Upton
Map 2	005	50 48 006	04 33 514	stone seat
Map 2	006	50 47 224	04 33 342	Black Rock Café
Map 3	007	50 46 769	04 33 519	junction with road
Map 3	008	50 46 257	04 34 494	Millook
Map 4	009	50 45 632	04 35 924	trig point
Map 4	010	50 45 425	04 36 795	footbridge, Lower Tresmorn
Map 5	011	50 44 809	04 37 815	footbridge
Map 5	012	50 44 446	04 37 911	Crackington Haven
Map 5	013	50 44 287	04 38 742	boardwalk, Cambeak
Map 6	014	50 43 562	04 38 723	turning to car park
Map 6	015	50 43 039	04 38 957	bench at highest point
Map 6	016	50 42 661	04 39 303	bench
Map 7	017	50 42 458	04 39 721	boardwalk
Map 7	018	50 42 215	04 40 615	gap in hedge
Map 8	019	50 41 826	04 40 942	boardwalk
Map 8	020	50 41 717	04 40 688	stile
Map 8	021	50 41 530	04 41 669	Flagstaff, Penally
Map 8	022	50 41 403	04 41 645	Boscastle Bridge
Map 9	023	50 41 030	04 42 489	steps by ruin
Map 9	024	50 41 000	04 43 286	Lady's Window rock arch
Map 10	025	50 40 372	04 43 693	Rocky Valley
Map 10	026	50 40 201	04 44 213	path to beach
Map 10	027	50 40 315	04 44 440	bench
Map 11	028	50 40 058	04 45 399	café at castle
Map 11	029	50 39 854	04 45 277	footbridge
Map 11	030	50 39 553	04 45 777	YHA Tintagel
Map 11	031	50 39 280	04 45 707	gate
Map 11	032	50 39 038	04 45 396	bench
Map 12	033	50 38 651	04 45 574	Trebarwith Strand
Map 12	034	50 38 365	04 45 818	stream crossing
Map 12	035	50 38 053	04 45 987	gate
Map 12	036	50 37 450	04 45 974	path to Tregardock Beach
Map 13	037	50 37 794	04 46 517	path to Tregragon Farm
Map 13	038	50 36 430	04 46 939	stream crossing
Map 13	039	50 36 209	04 47 190	stepping stones
Map 14	040	50 35 974	04 47 456	stile
Map 14	041	50 35 736	04 48 404	boardwalk
Map 14	042	50 35 609	04 49 200	road at Headlands Hotel, Port Gaverne
Map 15	043	50 35 778	04 50 880	stile at Varley Sand
Map 15	044	50 35 617	04 51 254	bench at Scarnor Point
Map 15	045	50 35 655	04 52 062	bench, Kellan Head
Map 16	046	50 35 437	04 52 187	bench in memory of Sgt Roberts
Map 16	047	50 35 308	04 51 998	stile, Doyden Point
Map 16	048	50 35 097	04 52 795	Trevan Point
Map 16	049	50 34 996	04 53 930	path to Pentireglaze
Map 17	050	50 35 249	04 55 011	path to Pentire Farm

MAP	REF	GPS WAYPOINTS		DESCRIPTION
Map 17	051	50 35 477	04 55 477	stone seat, The Rumps
Map 17	052	50 35 188	04 55 988	Pentire Point
Map 18	053	50 34 770	04 54 940	Pentireglaze Haven
Map 18	054	50 34 414	04 54 989	junction with road, Polzeath
Map 18	055	50 33 838	04 55 769	Trebetherick Point
Map 18	056	50 33 679	04 55 491	steps to Daymer Beach
Map 19	057	50 32 722	04 55 496	Rock car park
Map 19	058	50 32 646	04 55 384	Blue Tomato Café, Rock
Map 21	059	50 32 808	04 56 040	War Memorial, Padstow
Map 21	060	50 33 204	04 56 957	junction with track
Map 22	061	50 33 570	04 56 892	Hawker's Cove
Map 22	062	50 34 052	04 57 090	tower
Map 22	063	50 33 415	04 57 988	path to road
Map 23	064	50 32 681	04 58 601	Trevone Beach steps
Map 23	065	50 32 344	04 59 632	Harlyn Bridge
Map 23	066	50 32 728	05 00 213	bench at viewpoint
Map 24	067	50 32 581	05 00 889	junction with path
Map 24	068	50 32 892	05 02 018	Trevose Head
Map 24	069	50 32 422	05 01 489	first house in Booby's Bay
Map 24	070	50 31 851	05 01 318	beach exit south
Map 25	071	50 31 491	05 01 307	steps up from beach, Constantine Bay
Map 25	072	50 31 015	05 01 571	steps
Map 25	073	50 30 521	05 01 208	bridge at Porthcothan
Map 25	074	50 30 168	05 01 998	footbridge
Map 26	075	50 29 870	05 02 409	cairn
Map 26	076	50 28 830	05 01 861	National Trust shop, Carnewas
Map 27	077	50 27 866	05 01 834	Mawgan Porth
Map 27	078	50 27 586	05 02 163	path to Bre Pen Farm
Map 28	079	50 26 622	05 02 472	Watergate Bay
Map 29	080	50 25 522	05 03 134	bridge at Porth Beach
Map 29	081	50 25 033	05 04 236	path junction with road
Map 30	082	50 25 141	05 05 408	war memorial, Headland
Map 31	083	50 25 104	05 05 779	Fistral Blu
Map 31	084	50 24 720	05 06 060	Esplanade toilets, Fistral Beach
Map 31	085	50 24 420	05 05 883	Penpol footbridge
Map 31	086	50 24 341	05 06 699	Beach Café
Map 31a	087	50 24 319	05 04 641	Laurie Bridge
Map 32	088	50 24 253	05 07 616	Crantock Beach Steps
Map 32	089	50 24 041	05 08 972	footbridge, Porth Joke
Map 33	090	50 23 333	05 08 560	exit from beach, Holywell Bay
Map 33	091	50 23 172	05 08 358	bus stop by Treguth Inn
Map 33	092	50 22 788	05 08 979	stile by isolated farm
Map 33	093	50 22 459	05 08 653	top of path to beach
Map 34	094	50 20 694	05 09 209	Beach Rd, Perranporth
Map 35	095	50 20 336	05 10 704	quarry, Cligga Head
Map 36	096	50 19 577	05 11 383	airstrip
Map 36	097	50 19 253	05 11 505	Blue Hills Tin Mine
Map 36	098	50 19 108	05 12 062	WC, Trevaunance Cove
Map 37	099	50 19 057	05 13 888	St Agnes Head
Map 37	100	50 18 027	05 13 926	chimney, Wheal Coates
Map 37	101	50 17 976	05 14 011	Chapel Porth
Map 38	102	50 17 231	05 14 417	Porthtowan Beach

MAP	REF	GPS WAYPOINTS		DESCRIPTION
Map 38	103	50 16 755	05 15 319	chimney
Map 39	104	50 16 578	05 15 513	stream crossing, Nancekuke
Map 39	105	50 16 353	05 16 526	concrete shelter
Map 40	106	50 15 821	05 17 019	car park, Portreath
Map 40	107	50 15 645	05 17 517	Portreath beach
Map 41	108	50 15 528	05 18 117	gate opposite The Horse
Map 41	109	50 15 312	05 18 466	stream, Porthcadjack Cove
Map 41	110	50 14 915	05 18 765	car park exit
Map 42	111	50 14 408	05 19 807	car park, Deadman's Cove
Map 43	112	50 14 196	05 21 639	Hell's Mouth
Map 43	113	50 14 471	05 22 687	trig point, The Knavocks
Map 44	114	50 13 803	05 23 226	Godrevy Café
Map 44	115	50 13 233	05 23 084	Gwithian
Map 45	116	50 12 287	05 24 715	Phillack Towans
Map 46	117	50 11 278	05 25 276	Hayle tidal gate
Map 46	118	50 11 033	05 25 211	Hayle Viaduct
Map 47	119	50 10 651	05 26 484	Path leaves car park at Lelant Saltings
Map 47	120	50 11 271	05 26 129	St Uny Church
Map 48	121	50 11 804	05 27 714	road at Carbis Bay
Map 48	122	50 12 312	05 28 239	shelter, Porthminster Point
Map 48	123	50 12 538	05 28 612	Porthminster Station
Map 49	124	50 12 856	05 28 707	St Ives post office
Map 50	125	50 12 949	05 29 300	shelter
Map 50	126	50 12 862	05 30 674	stream crossing
Map 51	127	50 12 775	05 31 345	stone circle
Map 51	128	50 12 779	05 32 168	trig point, Carn Naun Point
Map 51	129	50 12 613	05 32 534	stream, River Cove
Map 51	130	50 12 143	05 33 246	stream crossing
Map 52	131	50 11 742	05 34 421	turn for Zennor
Map 52	132	50 11 839	05 34 553	Zennor Head
Map 52	133	50 11 697	05 34 375	gap in hedge
Map 52	134	50 11 473	05 34 002	Tinner's Arms, Zennor
Map 52	135	50 11 669	05 34 485	stream, Pendour Cove
Map 52	136	50 11 385	05 35 028	stream, Porthglaze Cove
Map 53	137	50 11 300	05 35 864	path junction to Gurnard's Head
Map 53	138	50 10 817	05 36 269	stream, Porthmeor Cove
Map 54	139	50 10 503	05 37 096	Bosigran Castle
Map 54	140	50 10 397	05 37 009	stone bridge, Porthmoina Cove
Map 54	141	50 09 924	05 37 839	stream crossing, Trevowhan Cliff
Map 55	142	50 09 935	05 38 345	stile, Morvah Cliff
Map 55	143	50 09 799	05 39 328	buoyancy aid, Portheras Cove
Map 56	144	50 09 823	05 40 178	car park, Pendeen Watch
Map 56	145	50 09 567	05 40 280	stream, Enys Zawn
Map 56	146	50 09 304	05 40 699	footbridge, Geevor
Map 57	147	50 08 654	05 41 465	trig point, Botallack Head
Map 57	148	50 08 071	05 41 667	gate and stone stile
Map 57	149	50 07 926	05 41 953	change of direction to right
Map 58	150	50 07 591	05 42 224	Cape Cornwall car park
Map 58	151	50 07 325	05 42 106	trig point Ballowal Barrow
Map 58	152	50 07 049	05 41 590	junction in path
Map p183	152a	50 07 431	05 40 721	St Just Square
Map 59	153	50 06 892	05 41 843	turn in path

MAP	REF	GPS WAYPOINTS		DESCRIPTION
Map 59	154	50 06 289	05 41 742	stream crossing, Maen Dower
Map 60	155	50 05 874	05 41 699	rocky outcrop
Map 60	156	50 05 273	05 41 237	lifeguard station
Map 60	157	50 04 796	05 41 401	junction with path inland
Map 61	158	50 04 635	05 42 091	car park, Sennen Cove
Map 61	159	50 04 634	05 42 263	toilets, Sennen Cove
Map 61	160	50 04 059	05 42 859	Land's End
Map 61	161	50 03 320	05 42 207	Trevilley Cliff
Map 62	162	50 03 197	05 41 470	Nanjizal
Map 62	163	50 02 211	05 40 545	black and white tower
Map 62	164	50 02 235	05 40 283	Porthgwarra
Map 63	165	50 02 333	05 39 575	Carn Scathe
Map 63	166	50 02 599	05 39 059	Porthcurno
Map 63	167	50 02 654	05 38 011	stream crossing, Gamper
Map 64	168	50 02 831	05 37 704	Penberth Cove
Map 64	169	50 03 048	05 37 107	stream, Porth Guarnon
Map 64	170	50 03 024	05 36 363	sign on rock
Map 65	171	50 03 118	05 36 066	Cove Cottage, St Loy
Map 66	172	50 03 201	05 34 887	metal gate
Map 66	173	50 03 319	05 34 096	path junction, Carn Barges
Map 66	174	50 03 657	05 33 788	Lamorna Cove
Map 67	175	50 03 639	05 33 216	steps, Carn-Du
Map 67	176	50 04 207	05 32 616	bench
Map 68	177	50 04 596	05 32 453	road junction
Map 68	178	50 04 977	05 32 283	war memorial, Mousehole
Map 69	179	50 06 366	05 32 907	Newlyn Bridge
Map 70	180	50 06 881	05 31 901	Jubilee Pool, Penzance
Map 70	181	50 07 266	05 31 888	bus station, Penzance
Map 72	182	50 07 388	05 28 424	Godolphin Arms, Marazion
Map 73	183	50 07 398	05 27 485	path leaves road, Marazion
Map 73	184	50 06 756	05 26 496	Perran Sands
Map 74	185	50 05 950	05 25 525	Cudden Point
Map 75	186	50 06 050	05 25 063	steps to beach, Bessy's Cove
Map 75	187	50 06 194	05 24 179	stream crossing, Pestreath Cove
Map 76	188	50 06 217	05 23 484	road by Sandbar Café, Praa Sands
Map 76	189	50 06 053	05 22 860	beach exit, Praa Sands
Map 77	190	50 05 703	05 22 061	car park, Porthcew
Map 77	191	50 05 428	05 21 269	Grey Stone Mine
Map 78	192	50 05 477	05 20 209	stream crossing, Tremearne Cliff
Map 79	193	50 05 053	05 19 370	Grylls' Act Memorial
Map 79	194	50 05 085	05 18 911	Porthleven Harbour
Map 80	195	50 04 034	05 17 433	HMS Anson Memorial
Map 81	196	50 03 270	05 16 601	Gunwalloe Beach Café
Map 81	197	50 02 402	05 16 130	Gunwalloe Church
Map 82	198	50 02 005	05 15 507	Poldhu Cove
Map 82	199	50 01 704	05 15 707	Marconi Monument
Map 82	200	50 01 418	05 15 279	steps, Polurrian Cove
Map 82	201	50 00 893	05 15 385	Mullion Cove
Map 82a	202	50 01 613	05 14 488	Mullion Church
Map 83	203	50 00 515	05 15 594	stream, Mullion Cliff
Map 83	204	50 00 045	05 15 816	stile, Predannack Head
Map 83	205	49 59 860	05 15 273	stream, Parc Bean Cove

MAP	REF	GPS WAYPOINTS		DESCRIPTION
Map 84	206	49 59 008	05 14 471	gorge, Gew-Graze
Map 85	207	49 58 487	05 13 818	Kynance Cove
Map 86	208	49 57 583	05 12 541	footpath to Lizard Village
Map 86	209	49 58 092	05 12 165	Lizard Green
Map 86	210	49 57 506	05 12 308	most southerly point
Map 86	211	49 57 803	05 11 800	Housel Cove
Map 86	212	49 57 769	05 11 139	National Coast Watch, Nare Point
Map 86	213	49 58 227	05 11 267	Church Cove
Map 87	214	49 58 372	05 11 332	beacon
Map 87	215	49 58 476	05 11 209	stream crossing, Parn Voose Cove
Map 87	216	49 59 218	05 10 714	Cadgwith Cove
Map 87	217	49 59 832	05 10 337	bridge, Little Cove
Map 88	218	50 00 300	05 09 750	Kennack Sands West
Map 89	219	50 00 535	05 07 610	gate and stile, Zawn Vinoc
Map 90	220	50 00 530	05 07 306	stream, Downas Cove
Map 90	221	50 00 405	05 06 872	stream, Meludjack
Map 91	222	50 00 285	05 06 088	concrete hut
Map 91	223	50 00 751	05 05 906	bench, Chynhall's Cliff
Map 91	224	50 01 436	05 05 791	Coverack Harbour
Map 93	225	50 02 094	05 04 073	Lowland Point
Map 93	226	50 02 849	05 04 018	stream, Godrevy Cove
Map 93	227	50 03 100	05 04 092	path leaves lane
Map 93	228	50 03 333	05 03 926	Porthoustock
Map 93	229	50 03 766	05 04 609	junction with road
Map 94	230	50 04 023	05 04 703	Porthallow
Map 94	231	50 05 087	05 04 551	Nare Point
Map 95	232	50 05 188	05 06 020	steps, Gillan Creek
Map 95	233	50 04 771	05 07 509	path to Manaccan
Map 95	234	50 05 335	05 06 018	St Anthony-in-Meneage
Map 95	235	50 05 558	05 06 496	Ponsense Cove
Map 96	236	50 05 454	05 08 083	ford, Helford
Map 96	237	50 05 512	05 08 000	bus stop, car park, Helford
Map 96	238	50 05 701	05 07 978	ferry landing, Helford
Map 96	239	50 05 184	05 08 475	Kestle
Map 96a	240	50 04 755	05 09 806	crossroads, Mudgeon Farm
Map 96b	241	50 04 851	05 12 114	Mawgan Church
Map 96b	242	50 05 791	05 12 422	Gweek Inn
Map 96c	243	50 06 634	05 10 356	Trengilly Wartha pub
Map 96d	244	50 06 405	05 08 645	Porth Navas
Map 96d	245	50 06 671	05 08 196	Trenarth Bridge
Map 96d	246	50 06 331	05 07 421	crossroads
Map 96d	247	50 05 986	05 07 660	Helford Passage
Map 97	248	50 06 202	05 06 884	Durgan
Map p248	248a	50 06 966	05 06 497	Red Lion, Mawnan Smith
Map 98	249	50 06 587	05 04 958	Rosemullion Head
Map 99	250	50 07 477	05 05 615	Maenporth Beach
Map 99	251	50 08 039	05 04 417	Home Guard Memorial
Map 100	252	50 08 423	05 04 512	beach exit, Swanpool Beach
Map 100	253	50 08 646	05 04 035	Gyllyngvase Beach
Map 100	254	50 08 780	05 02 862	Pendennis Point
Map 100	255	50 09 351	05 04 180	tourist information, Falmouth
Map 101	256	50 09 464	05 00 834	ferry point St Mawes

MAP	REF	GPS WAYPOINTS		DESCRIPTION
Map 101	257	50 09 152	05 00 257	low-tide ferry landing
Map 101a	256a	50 09 354	05 01 375	St Mawes Castle
Map 101b	256b	50 11 197	05 00 579	stile off road
Map 101b	256c	50 11 331	04 59 853	turn off road
Map 102	258	50 09 432	04 59 012	junction with path to Porth Farm
Map 103	259	50 10 739	04 58 457	Plume of Feathers, Portscatho
Map 104	260	50 12 309	04 57 173	top of alleyway by Pendower Farm
Map 105	261	50 11 840	04 55 122	junction with path from Nare Head
Map 106	262	50 12 832	04 54 057	gate into Broom Parc B&B
Map 106	263	50 13 090	04 53 495	church at Portloe
Map 107	264	50 14 118	04 51 632	East Portholland
Map 108	265	50 14 219	04 50 342	gate behind trees
Map 109	266	50 13 169	04 48 122	stone cross at Dodman Point
Map 110	267	50 14 632	04 47 128	gate and bridge before Penhaver House
Map 111	268	50 15 351	04 46 197	track to Chapel Point
Map 111	269	50 16 185	04 47 137	road junction by Mevagissey Harbour
Map 112	270	50 17 537	04 46 785	turn-off road out of Pentewan
Map 113	271	50 18 011	04 45 309	Rowse Stone
Map 114	272	50 19 964	04 45 463	junction of Charlestown Rd & Duporth Rd
Map 115	273	50 20 607	04 42 442	join road leading into Par
Map 116	274	50 19 020	04 40 391	Daymark Tower
Map 117	275	50 19 582	04 37 978	right turn outside Polruan
Map 118	276	50 19 512	04 35 992	Pencarrow Head
Map 119	277	50 19 677	04 33 501	white stone tower
Map 120	278	50 19 873	04 30 151	Cross at Downend Point
Map 121	279	50 20 652	04 27 478	Lamman Chapel
Map 122	280	50 21 362	04 27 395	bridge at Looe
Map 123	281	50 21 850	04 25 054	Labyrinth
Map 124	282	50 21 689	04 21 908	junction with beach route
Map 125	283	50 21 741	04 18 417	turn off from road
Map 126	284	50 21 559	04 17 369	junction of two paths
Map 126	285	50 20 899	04 15 463	path above Sharrow Point
Map 127	286	50 20 397	04 14 168	path leaves road
Map 128	287	50 18 820	04 13 389	Chapel at Rame Head
Map 129	288	50 20 075	04 12 045	gate into Edgcumbe Park
Map 130	289	50 20 749	04 10 397	grotto and chapel
Map 130	290	50 21 627	04 10 492	Cremyll Ferry

Appendix A: Hartland Quay to Bude

Map 48x	769	N50 59.631 W4 31.968	Hartland Quay
Map 49x	770	N50 58.069 W4 31.795	turn-off to YHA Elmscott (Elmscott Youth Hostel
Map 50x	771	N50 55.988 W4 32.624	Welcombe Mouth
Map 51x	772	N50 54.389 W4 33.720	Hawker's Hut
Map 52x	773	N50 53.129 W4 33.531	right turn by radio station
Map 53x	774	N50 51.659 W4 33.224	wooden footbridge at Sandy Mouth
Map 54x	775	N50 50.121 W4 33.129	lifeguard lookout

APPENDIX C: TAKING A DOG ALONG THE PATH

The South-West Coast Path is a dog-friendly path and many are the rewards that await those prepared to make the extra effort required to bring their best friend along the trail. However, you shouldn't underestimate the amount of work involved in bringing your pooch to the path. Indeed, just about every decision you make will be influenced by the fact that you've got a dog: how you plan to travel to the start of the trail, where you're going to stay, how far you're going to walk each day, where you're going to rest and where you're going to eat in the evening etc etc.

The decision-making begins well before you've set foot on the trail. For starters, you have to ask – and be honest with – yourself: can your dog really cope with walking 10+ miles (16+km) a day, day after day, week after week? And just as importantly, will he or she actually enjoy it?

If you think the answer is yes to both, you need to start preparing accordingly. For one thing, extra thought also needs to go into your itinerary. The best starting point is to study the Village & Town Facilities table on pp36-9 (and the advice below), and plan where to stop, where to eat, where to buy food for your mutt.

Looking after your dog

To begin with, you need to make sure that your own dog is fully **inoculated** against the usual doggy illnesses, and also up to date with regard to **worm pills** (eg Drontal) and **flea preventatives** such as Frontline – they are, after all, following in the pawprints of many a dog before them, some of whom may well have left fleas or other parasites on the trail that now lie in wait for their next meal to arrive. **Pet insurance** is also a very good idea; if you've already got insurance, do check that it will cover a trip such as this.

On the subject of looking after your dog's health, perhaps the most important implement you can take with you is the **plastic tick remover**, available from vets for a couple of quid. Ticks are a real problem on the SWCP, as they hide in the long grass waiting for unsuspecting victims to trot past. These removers, while fiddly, help you to remove the tick safely (ie without leaving its head buried under the dog's skin).

Being in unfamiliar territory also makes it more likely that you and your dog could become separated. All dogs now have to be **microchipped**, but make sure your dog also has a **tag with your contact details on it** (a mobile phone number would be best if you are carrying one with you).

Dogs on beaches

There is no general rule regarding whether dogs are allowed on beaches or not. Some of the beaches on the SWCP are open to dogs all year; some allow them on the beach only outside the summer season (Easter or 1 May to 30 September); while a few beaches don't allow dogs at all. (Guide dogs, by the way, are usually excluded from any bans.) If in doubt, look for the noticeboards that tell you the exact rules. A useful website for further details is 🖳 cornwall-beaches.co.uk/dog-friendly. Where dogs are banned from a beach there will usually be an alternative path that you can take that avoids the sands. If there isn't an alternative, and you have no choice but to cross the beach even though dogs are officially banned, you are permitted to do so as long as you cross the beach as speedily as possible, follow the line of the path (which is usually well above the high-water mark) and keep your dog tightly under control.

Whatever the rules of access are for the beach, remember that your dog shouldn't disturb other beach-users – and you must always **clean up after your dog**.

Finally, remember that you need to bring drinking water with you on the beach as dogs can over-heat with the lack of shade.

When to keep your dog on a lead
● **On cliff tops** It's a sad fact that, every year, a few dogs lose their lives falling over the edge of the cliffs. It usually occurs when they are chasing rabbits (which know where the cliff-edge is and are able, unlike your poor pooch, to stop in time).
● **When crossing farmland**, particularly in the lambing season (around May) when your dog can scare the sheep, causing them to lose their young. Farmers are allowed by law to shoot at and kill any dogs that they consider are worrying their sheep. During lambing, most farmers would prefer it if you didn't bring your dog at all. The exception to the keep-your-dog-on-a-lead-advice is if your dog is being attacked by cows (see box p74); almost every year in the UK at least one or two walkers are trampled to death by cows, usually as they try to rescue their dogs from the attentions of cattle. The advice in this instance is to let go of the lead, head speedily to a position of safety (usually the other side of the field gate or stile) and call your dog to you.
● **On National Trust land**, where it is compulsory to keep your dog on a lead.
● **Around ground-nesting birds** It's important to keep your dog under control when crossing an area where certain species of birds nest on the ground. Most dogs love foraging around in the woods but make sure you have permission to do so; some woods are used as 'nurseries' for game birds and dogs are only allowed through them if they are on a lead.

What to pack
You've already got a good idea of what to bring to keep your dog alive and happy, but the following is a checklist:
● **Food/water bowl** Foldable cloth bowls are popular with walkers, being light and take up little room in the rucksack. You can also get a water-bottle-and-bowl combination, where the bottle folds into a 'trough' from which the dog can drink.
● **Lead and collar** An extendable one is probably preferable for this sort of trip. Make sure both lead and collar are in good condition – you don't want either to snap on the trail, or you may end up carrying your dog through sheep fields until a replacement can be found.
● **Medication** You'll know if you need to bring any lotions or potions.
● **Tick remover** See opposite
● **Bedding** A simple blanket may suffice, or you can opt for something more elaborate if you aren't carrying your own luggage.
● **Poo bags** Essential.
● **Hygiene wipes** For cleaning your dog after it's rolled in stuff.
● **A favourite toy** Helps prevent your dog from pining for the entire walk.
● **Food/water** Remember to bring treats as well as regular food to keep up the mutt's morale. That said, if your dog is anything like mine the chances are they'll spend most of the walk dining on rabbit droppings and sheep poo anyway.
● **Corkscrew stake** Available from camping or pet shops, this will help you to keep your dog secure in one place while you set up camp/doze.
● **Raingear** It can rain a lot!
● **Old towels** For drying your dog after the deluge.

How to pack
When it comes to packing, I always leave an exterior pocket of my rucksack empty so I can put used poo bags in there (for deposit at the first bin I come to). I always like to keep all the dog's kit together and separate from the other luggage (usually inside a plastic bag inside my rucksack). I have also seen several dogs sporting their own 'doggy rucksack', so they can carry their own food, water, poo etc – which certainly reduces the burden on their owner!

Cleaning up after your dog
It is extremely important that dog owners behave in a responsible way when walking the path. Dog excrement should be cleaned up. In towns, villages and fields where animals graze

or which will be cut for silage, hay etc, you need to pick up and bag the excrement. In other places you can possibly get away with merely flicking it with a nearby stick into the undergrowth, thus ensuring there is none left on the path to decorate the boots of others.

Staying with your dog

In this guide we have used the symbol 🐕 to denote where a hotel, pub or B&B welcomes dogs. However, this always needs to be arranged in advance and some places may charge extra. Hostels (both YHA and independent) do not permit them unless they are an assistance (guide) dog; smaller campsites tend to accept them, but some of the larger holiday parks do not. Before you turn up always double check whether the place you would like to stay accepts dogs and whether there is space for them; many places have only one or two rooms suitable for people with dogs.

When it comes to eating, most landlords allow dogs in at least a section of their pubs, though few restaurants do. Make sure you always ask first and ensure your dog doesn't run around the pub but is secured to your table or a radiator.

Henry Stedman

INDEX

Page references in bold type refer to maps

Maps 1-5, Bude to Crackington Haven
10 miles/16km – 4-5hrs

NOTE: Add 20-30% to these times
to allow for stops

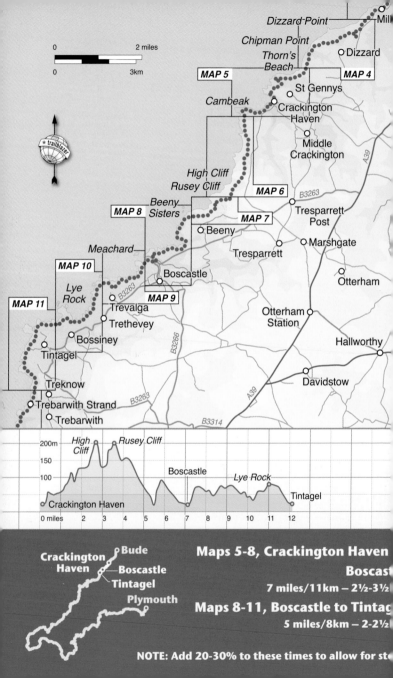

Dizzard Point
Chipman Point
Thorn's Beach
Mill
Dizzard
MAP 5
MAP 4
Cambeak
St Gennys
Crackington Haven
Middle Crackington

High Cliff
Rusey Cliff
MAP 6
B3263
Tresparrett Post

Beeny Sisters
MAP 7
Beeny
Tresparrett
Marshgate

Meachard
MAP 8
MAP 10
Boscastle
Otterham

Lye Rock
MAP 9
Trevalga
B3263
Trethevey
Otterham Station

MAP 11
Bossiney
Tintagel
Hallworthy

Treknow
Davidstow

Trebarwith Strand
B3263
Trebarwith
B3314

0   2 miles
0   3km

High Cliff   Rusey Cliff
200m
150
100   Boscastle   Lye Rock
Crackington Haven   Tintagel
0 miles   2   3   4   5   6   7   8   9   10   11   12

Bude
Crackington Haven
Boscastle
Tintagel
Plymouth

Maps 5-8, Crackington Haven
Boscas
7 miles/11km – 2½-3½

Maps 8-11, Boscastle to Tintag
5 miles/8km – 2-2½

NOTE: Add 20-30% to these times to allow for ste

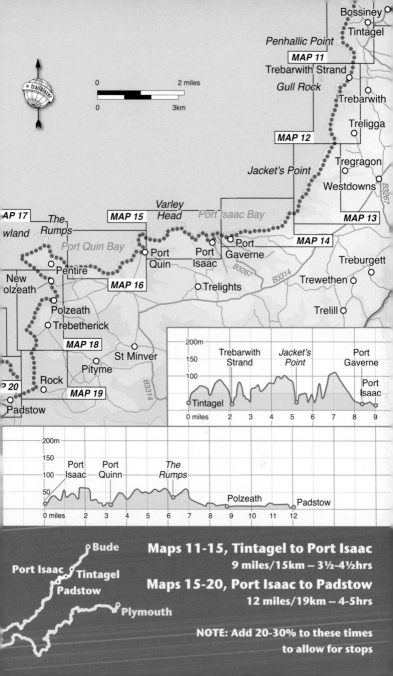

Bossiney

Penhallic Point

Tintagel

MAP 11

Trebarwith Strand

Gull Rock

Trebarwith

Treligga

MAP 12

Tregragon

Jacket's Point

Westdowns

B3267

Varley Head

Port Isaac Bay

MAP 13

MAP 15

MAP 14

AP 17

The Rumps

wland

Port Quin Bay

Port Quin

Port Isaac

Port Gaverne

Treburgett

Pentire

MAP 16

B3267

B3314

Trewethen

New olzeath

Trelights

Trelill

Polzeath

Trebetherick

MAP 18

St Minver

Pityme

B3314

2 20

Rock

MAP 19

Padstow

200m
150
100

Trebarwith Strand

Jacket's Point

Port Gaverne

Port Isaac

Tintagel

0 miles   2   3   4   5   6   7   8   9

200m
150
100
50

Port Isaac

Port Quinn

The Rumps

Polzeath

Padstow

0 miles   2   3   4   5   6   7   8   9   10   11   12

Bude

Port Isaac

Tintagel

Padstow

Plymouth

Maps 11-15, Tintagel to Port Isaac
9 miles/15km – 3½-4½hrs

Maps 15-20, Port Isaac to Padstow
12 miles/19km – 4-5hrs

**NOTE: Add 20-30% to these times
to allow for stops**

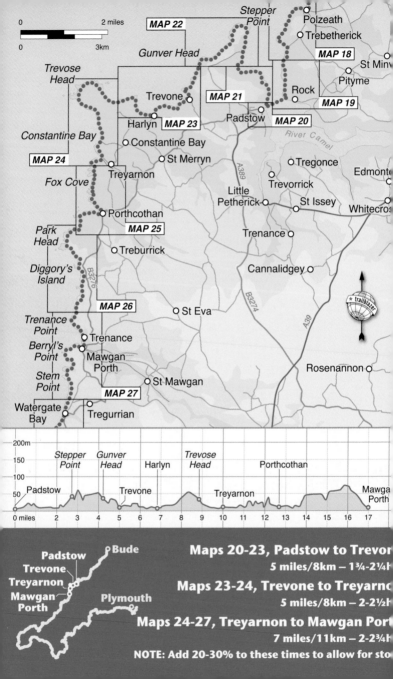

MAP 22

MAP 18

MAP 21

MAP 19

MAP 20

MAP 23

MAP 24

MAP 25

MAP 26

MAP 27

Stepper Point Polzeath
Trebetherick

St Minv

Gunver Head Pityme

Rock

Trevose Head Trevone

Padstow

Harlyn River Camel

Constantine Bay

Tregonce

Edmonte

St Merryn Trevorrick

St Issey

Fox Cove Treyarnon Little Petherick Whitecros

Park Head Porthcothan Trenance

Diggory's Island Treburrick

Cannalidgey

Trenance Point St Eva

Berryl's Point Trenance

Mawgan Porth

Stem Point St Mawgan

Watergate Bay Tregurrian

Rosenannon

Stepper Point | Gunver Head | | Harlyn | | Trevose Head | | Porthcothan

Padstow | | Trevone | | | Treyarnon | | | | | Mawga Porth

0 miles 2 3 4 5 6 7 8 9 10 11 12 13 14 15 16 17

Padstow **Bude** **Maps 20-23, Padstow to Trevor**
Trevone 5 miles/8km – 1¾-2¼h
Treyarnon
Mawgan **Plymouth** **Maps 23-24, Trevone to Treyarno**
Porth 5 miles/8km – 2-2½h

Maps 24-27, Treyarnon to Mawgan Port
7 miles/11km – 2-2¾h
NOTE: Add 20-30% to these times to allow for sto

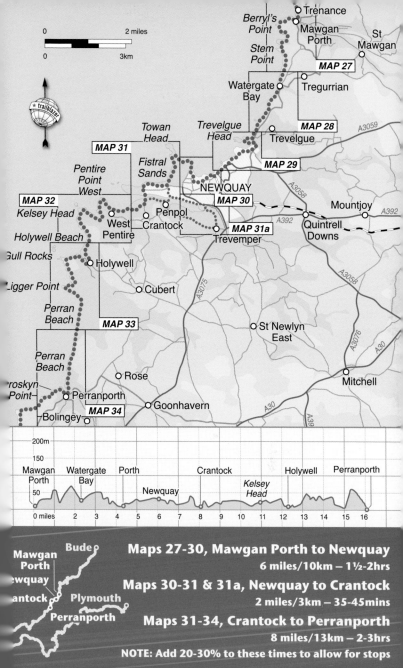

MAP 27

Trenance

Berry's
Point

Mawgan
Porth

Stem
Point

St
Mawgan

Watergate
Bay

Tregurrian

MAP 28

Towan
Head

Trevelgue
Head

Trevelgue

MAP 31

MAP 29

Fistral
Sands

Pentire
Point
West

MAP 30

NEWQUAY

A3059

MAP 32

Kelsey Head

Penpol

Crantock

MAP 31a

Mountjoy

A392

Holywell Beach

West
Pentire

Trevemper

A392

Quintrell
Downs

Gull Rocks

Holywell

Ligger Point

Cubert

A3075

A3058

Perran
Beach

St Newlyn
East

A3076

A30

MAP 33

Perran
Beach

Rose

Mitchell

roskyn
Point

Perranporth

Goonhavern

A30

A39

Bolingey

MAP 34

Scale: 0 — 2 miles / 0 — 3km

Elevation profile:
200m — 150 — 50

Mawgan Porth · Watergate Bay · Porth · Newquay · Crantock · *Kelsey Head* · Holywell · Perranporth

0 miles 1 2 3 4 5 6 7 8 9 10 11 12 13 14 15 16

Bude

Mawgan
Porth

Newquay

Crantock

Plymouth

Perranporth

Maps 27-30, Mawgan Porth to Newquay
6 miles/10km – 1½-2hrs

Maps 30-31 & 31a, Newquay to Crantock
2 miles/3km – 35-45mins

Maps 31-34, Crantock to Perranporth
8 miles/13km – 2-3hrs
NOTE: Add 20-30% to these times to allow for stops

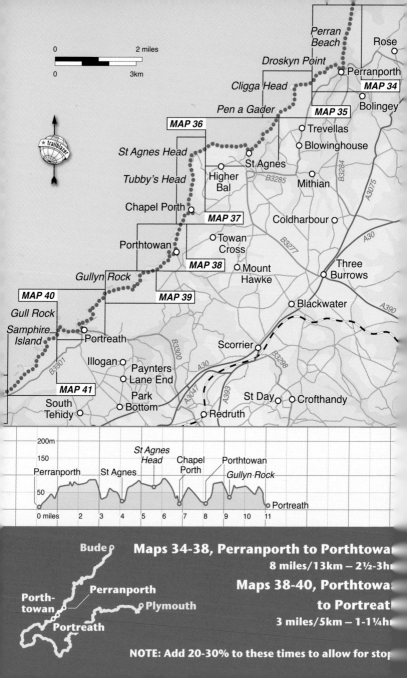

Perran Beach
Rose
Droskyn Point
Perranporth
MAP 34
Cligga Head
MAP 35
Bolingey
Pen a Gader
MAP 36
Trevellas
St Agnes Head
Blowinghouse
Higher Bal
St Agnes
B3285
Mithian
Tubby's Head
Chapel Porth
MAP 37
Coldharbour
A30
A3075
Porthtowan
Towan Cross
MAP 38
Three Burrows
Gullyn Rock
Mount Hawke
B3277
MAP 40
MAP 39
Gull Rock
Blackwater
A390
Samphire Island
Portreath
Scorrier
B3298
Illogan
Paynters Lane End
B3300
A30
St Day
Croolandy
MAP 41
Park Bottom
A3047
A393
South Tehidy
Redruth

0   2 miles
0   3km

200m
150
St Agnes Head
Perranporth   St Agnes   Chapel Porth   Porthtowan
50   Gullyn Rock
                                                                              Portreath
0 miles   2   3   4   5   6   7   8   9   10   11

Bude
Porthtowan
Perranporth
Porthtowan
Plymouth
Portreath

Maps 34-38, Perranporth to Porthtowan
8 miles/13km – 2½-3hr

Maps 38-40, Porthtowan to Portreath
3 miles/5km – 1-1¼hr

NOTE: Add 20-30% to these times to allow for stop

Maps 40-44, Portreath to Gwithian
8 miles/13km – 2-2¾hrs

Maps 44-46, Gwithian to Hayle
4 miles/6km – 1-1¼hrs

NOTE: Add 20-30% to these times
to allow for stops

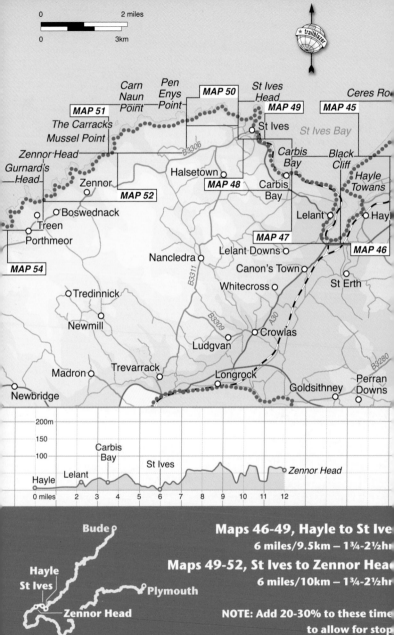

0 | 2 miles
0 | 3km

Carn Naun Point
Pen Enys Point
MAP 51
MAP 50
St Ives Head
MAP 49
Ceres Ro
MAP 45

The Carracks
Mussel Point
○ St Ives
St Ives Bay

Zennor Head
B3306
Carbis Bay
Black Cliff

Gurnard's Head
Halsetown ○
MAP 48
Carbis Bay
Hayle Towans

○ Zennor
MAP 52
Lelant ○
○ Hay

○ Boswednack
MAP 47
○ Treen
Porthmeor
MAP 46

MAP 54
Lelant Downs ○

Nancledra ○
Canon's Town ○
St Erth ○

○ Tredinnick
Whitecross ○

○ Newmill
B3311
B3309
○ Crowlas
B3280

Trevarrack ○
Ludgvan ○

Madron ○
Longrock ○
Goldsithney ○
Perran Downs ○
○ Newbridge

200m
150
100
Carbis Bay
St Ives
Zennor Head
Hayle | Lelant
0 miles 2 3 4 5 6 7 8 9 10 11 12

Bude ○

Hayle
St Ives
○ Plymouth

Zennor Head

Maps 46-49, Hayle to St Ive
6 miles/9.5km – 1¾-2½hr

Maps 49-52, St Ives to Zennor Hea
6 miles/10km – 1¾-2½hr

NOTE: Add 20-30% to these time
to allow for stop

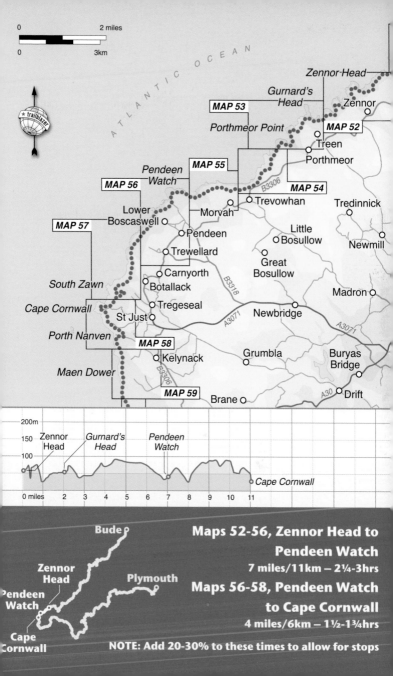

Maps 52-56, Zennor Head to
Pendeen Watch
7 miles/11km – 2¼-3hrs
Maps 56-58, Pendeen Watch
to **Cape Cornwall**
4 miles/6km – 1½-1¾hrs

NOTE: Add 20-30% to these times to allow for stops

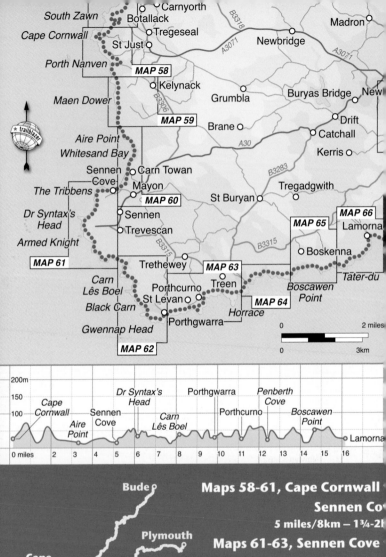

South Zawn
Botallack
Carnyorth
Madron
Cape Cornwall
Tregeseal
St Just
Newbridge
B3318
A3071
A307.1
Porth Nanven
MAP 58
Kelynack
Grumbla
Buryas Bridge
New
B3306
Maen Dower
MAP 59
Brane O
Drift
A30
Catchall
Aire Point
Kerris O
Whitesand Bay
B3283
Sennen
Carn Towan
Cove
Mayon
Tregadgwith
The Tribbens
MAP 60
St Buryan O
MAP 66
Dr Syntax's
Sennen
MAP 65
Lamorna
Head
Trevescan
Boskenna O
Armed Knight
B3315
B3315
MAP 61
Trethewey
MAP 63
Tater-du
Carn
Treen
Lês Boel
Porthcurno
MAP 64
Boscawen
Black Carn
St Levan O
Point
Horrace
Gwennap Head
Porthgwarra
0   2 miles
MAP 62
0   3km

200m
150
100   Dr Syntax's   Porthgwarra
Cape   Head   Penberth
Cornwall   Sennen   Cove
Aire   Cove   Carn   Porthcurno   Boscawen
Point   Lês Boel   Point
Lamorna
0 miles   2   3   4   5   6   7   8   9   10   11   12   13   14   15   16

Bude
Maps 58-61, Cape Cornwall
Sennen Co
Plymouth
5 miles/8km – 1¾-2h
Maps 61-63, Sennen Cove
Cape
Porthcurr
Cornwall
Sennen
6 miles/9.5km – 1¾-2½h
Cove
Maps 63-66, Porthcurno
Porthcurno
Lamorna
Lamor
5 miles/8km – 2-2½h
NOTE: Add 20-30% to these times to allow for sto

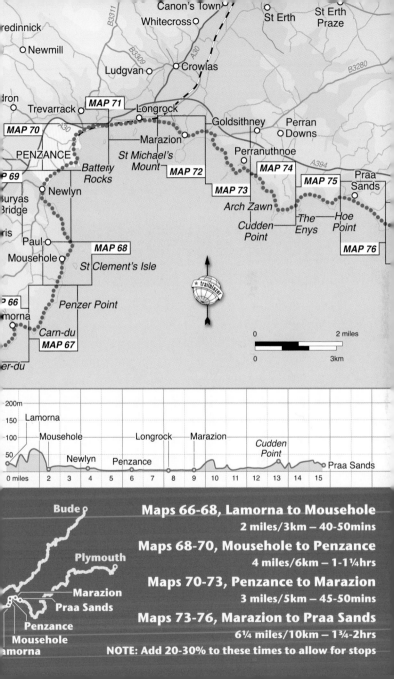

Maps 66-68, Lamorna to Mousehole
2 miles/3km – 40-50mins

Maps 68-70, Mousehole to Penzance
4 miles/6km – 1-1¼hrs

Maps 70-73, Penzance to Marazion
3 miles/5km – 45-50mins

Maps 73-76, Marazion to Praa Sands
6¼ miles/10km – 1¾-2hrs

NOTE: Add 20-30% to these times to allow for stops

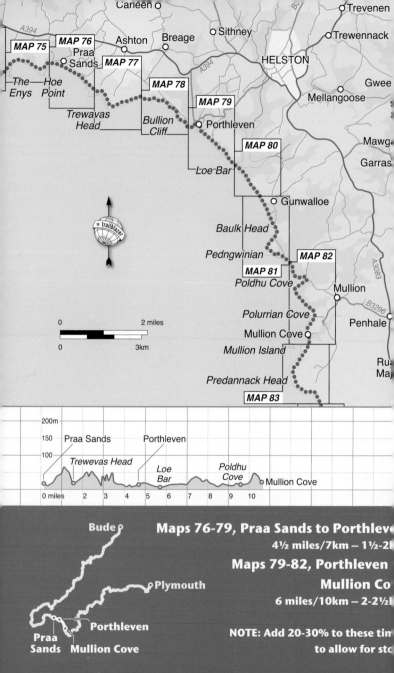

MAP 75

MAP 76

MAP 77

MAP 78

MAP 79

MAP 80

MAP 81

MAP 82

MAP 83

Carleen

Sithney

Trevenen

Trewennack

A394

Ashton

Breage

HELSTON

Praa
Sands

Gwee

Mellangoose

The
Enys

Hoe
Point

Trewavas
Head

Bullion
Cliff

Porthleven

Mawg

Garras

Loe Bar

Gunwalloe

Baulk Head

Pedngwinian

Poldhu Cove

Mullion

A3083

Polurrian Cove

Mullion Cove

Penhale

B3296

Mullion Island

Predannack Head

Ru
Ma

trailblazer

0   2 miles

0   3km

200m

150   Praa Sands   Porthleven

100

Trewevas Head   Loe   Poldhu
                          Bar   Cove

                                                    Mullion Cove

0 miles   2   3   4   5   6   7   8   9   10

Bude

Plymouth

Praa
Sands   Porthleven

          Mullion Cove

Maps 76-79, Praa Sands to Porthleve
4½ miles/7km – 1½-2h

Maps 79-82, Porthleven
Mullion Co
6 miles/10km – 2-2½h

NOTE: Add 20-30% to these tim
to allow for sto

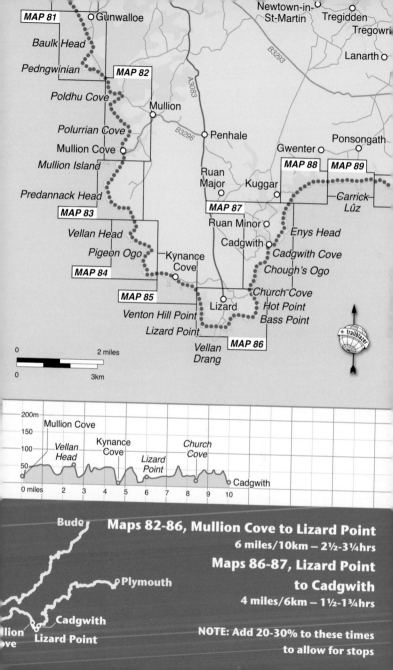

MAP 81

Gunwalloe

Baulk Head

Pedngwinian

MAP 82

Poldhu Cove

Mullion

Polurrian Cove

Mullion Cove

Mullion Island

Predannack Head

MAP 83

Vellan Head

Pigeon Ogo

MAP 84

MAP 85

Kynance Cove

Venton Hill Point

Lizard Point

Lizard

Vellan Drang

MAP 86

Newtown-in-St-Martin

Tregidden

Tregowri

Lanarth

B3293

A3083

B3296

Penhale

Ruan Major

Kuggar

Gwenter

Ponsongath

MAP 88

MAP 89

Carrick Lûz

MAP 87

Ruan Minor

Cadgwith

Enys Head

Cadgwith Cove

Chough's Ogo

Church Cove

Hot Point

Bass Point

trailblazer

0 — 2 miles

0 — 3km

200m
150
100
50

Mullion Cove

Vellan Head

Kynance Cove

Lizard Point

Church Cove

Cadgwith

0 miles 2 3 4 5 6 7 8 9 10

Bude

Plymouth

Cadgwith

Lizard Point

llion ve

Maps 82-86, Mullion Cove to Lizard Point
6 miles/10km – 2½-3¼hrs

Maps 86-87, Lizard Point to Cadgwith
4 miles/6km – 1½-1¾hrs

NOTE: Add 20-30% to these times to allow for stops

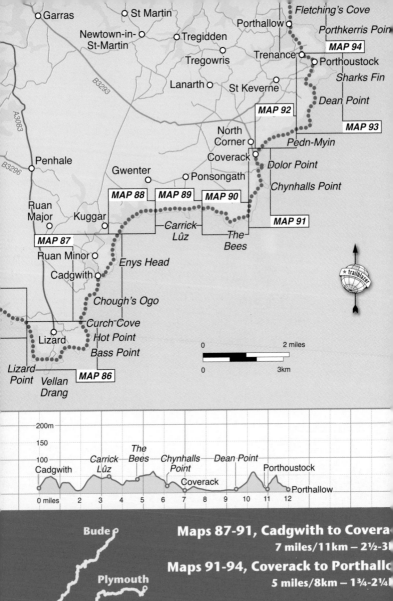

Garras St Martin
Newtown-in- Tregidden
St-Martin
Tregowris
Lanarth St Keverne

Fletching's Cove
Porthallow Porthkerris Poin
MAP 94
Trenance Porthoustock
Sharks Fin
Dean Point
MAP 93

MAP 92
North
Corner Pedn-Myin
Coverack Dolor Point
Gwenter Ponsongath Chynhalls Point
MAP 88 **MAP 89** **MAP 90**
Penhale
Ruan
Major Kuggar Carrick- **MAP 91**
Lûz
MAP 87 The
Bees
Ruan Minor
Enys Head
Cadgwith
Chough's Ogo
Curch Cove
Lizard Hot Point
Bass Point
Lizard **MAP 86**
Point Vellan
Drang

| 0 | | 2 miles |
| 0 | | 3km |

200m
150
100 The
Carrick Bees Chynhalls Dean Point
Lûz Point Porthoustock
Cadgwith Coverack Porthallo
0 miles 2 3 4 5 6 7 8 9 10 11 12

Bude **Maps 87-91, Cadgwith to Covera**
7 miles/11km – 2½-3I

Plymouth **Maps 91-94, Coverack to Porthallo**
5 miles/8km – 1¾-2¼I

Porthallow **NOTE: Add 20-30% to these tim**
Coverack to allow for st
Cadgwith

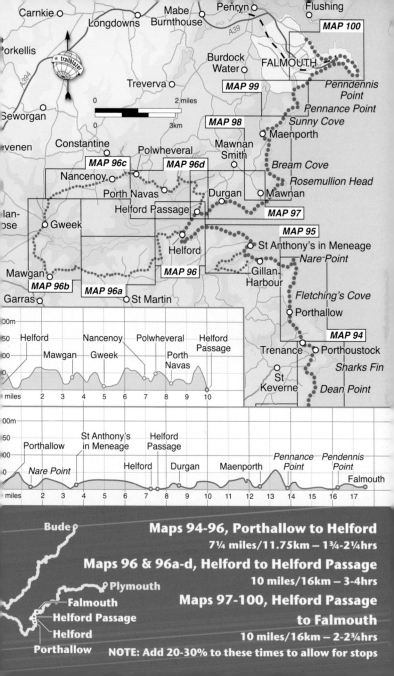

Maps 94-96, Porthallow to Helford
7¼ miles/11.75km — 1¾-2¼hrs

Maps 96 & 96a-d, Helford to Helford Passage
10 miles/16km — 3-4hrs

Maps 97-100, Helford Passage to Falmouth
10 miles/16km — 2-2¾hrs

NOTE: Add 20-30% to these times to allow for stops

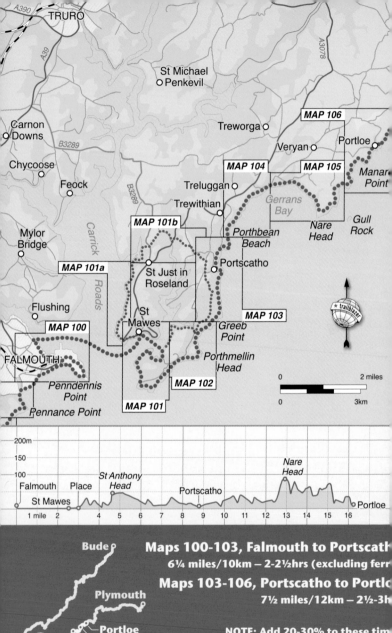

TRURO

St Michael
O Penkevil

Carnon
O Downs

Chycoose

Feock

Mylor
Bridge

Flushing

MAP 100

FALMOUTH

Penndennis
Point

Pennance Point

MAP 101a

MAP 101b

St Just in
Roseland

St
Mawes

MAP 101

MAP 102

Treworga O

Veryan O

Portloe O

Manare
Point

MAP 104

MAP 105

MAP 106

Treluggan O

Trewithian

MAP 103

Porthbean
Beach

Portscatho

Greeb
Point

Porthmellin
Head

Gerrans
Bay

Nare
Head

Gull
Rock

0   2 miles

0   3km

200m
150
100   St Anthony
Falmouth Place Head   Nare
                                          Head
St Mawes   Portscatho
                                                    Portloe
1 mile 2   3   4   5   6   7   8   9   10   11   12   13   14   15   16

Bude

Plymouth

Portloe
Portscatho
Falmouth

Maps 100-103, Falmouth to Portscath
6¼ miles/10km – 2-2½hrs (excluding ferr

Maps 103-106, Portscatho to Portlo
7½ miles/12km – 2½-3h

NOTE: Add 20-30% to these tim
to allow for sto

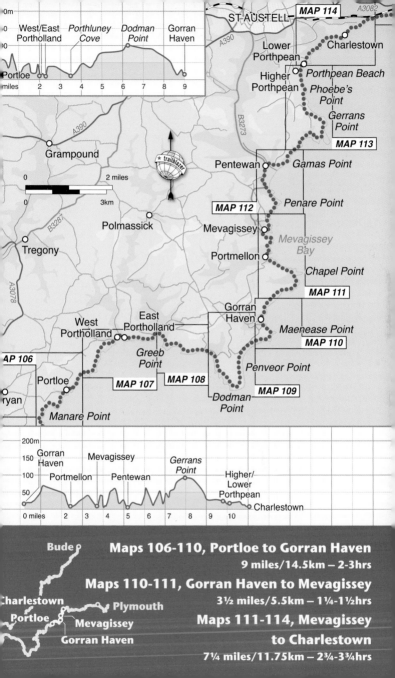

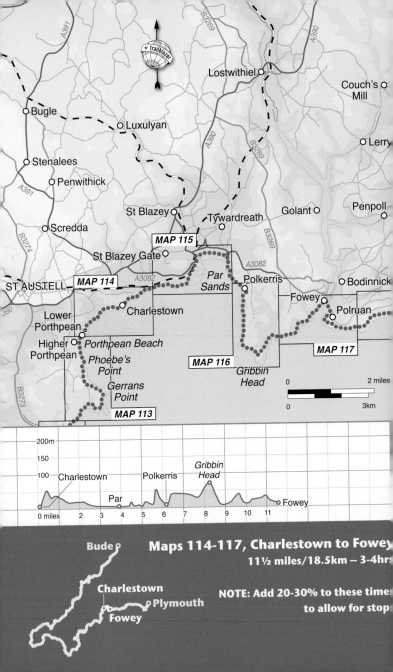

North ★ trailblazer

Lostwithiel

Couch's Mill

Bugle

Luxulyan

Lerry

Stenalees

Penwithick

Penpoll

St Blazey

Tywardreath

Golant

Scredda

MAP 115

ST AUSTELL

St Blazey Gate

MAP 114

Par Sands

Polkerris

Bodinnick

Charlestown

Fowey

Polruan

Lower Porthpean

Higher Porthpean

Porthpean Beach

MAP 116

MAP 117

Phoebe's Point

Gribbin Head

Gerrans Point

MAP 113

| 0 | 2 miles |

| 0 | 3km |

200m
150
100 — Charlestown   *Gribbin Head*
                Polkerris
              Par   Fowey

0 miles   2   3   4   5   6   7   8   9   10   11

Bude

Maps 114-117, Charlestown to Fowey
11½ miles/18.5km – 3-4hrs

Charlestown
              Plymouth
Fowey

**NOTE: Add 20-30% to these times
to allow for stops**

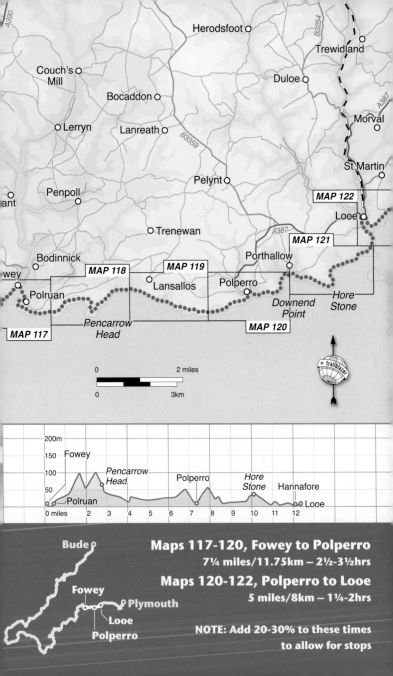

Herodsfoot ○

Trewidland ○

Couch's ○
Mill

Bocaddon ○

Duloe ○

Morval ○

Lerryn ○

Lanreath ○

B3359

St Martin ○

Pelynt ○

Penpoll ○

MAP 122

ant ○

Trenewan ○

A387

Looe ○

MAP 121

Bodinnick ○

MAP 118

MAP 119

Porthallow

wey ○

Polruan ○

Lansallos ○

Polperro ○

*Hore
Stone*

*Downend
Point*

MAP 117

*Pencarrow
Head*

MAP 120

| 0 | | | 2 miles |
| 0 | | 3km | |

★ trailblazer

200m
150 — Fowey
100 — *Pencarrow Head*   Polperro   *Hore Stone*   Hannafore
50 — Polruan   Looe
0 miles 1 2 3 4 5 6 7 8 9 10 11 12

Bude ○

Maps 117-120, Fowey to Polperro
7¼ miles/11.75km – 2½-3½hrs

Fowey ○

Plymouth ○

Maps 120-122, Polperro to Looe
5 miles/8km – 1¼-2hrs

Looe ○
Polperro ○

**NOTE: Add 20-30% to these times
to allow for stops**

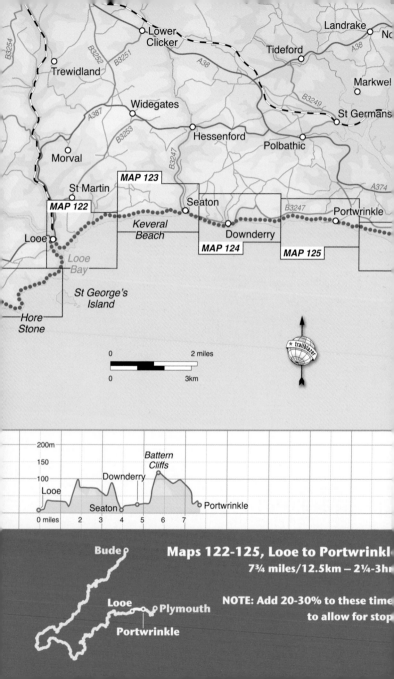

Lower Clicker

Landrake

No

Tideford

Markwel

St Germans

B3254

B3252

Trewidland

B3251

A38

Widegates

B3249

B3253

Morval

A387

Hessenford

Polbathic

St Martin

MAP 123

Seaton

A374

B3247

Portwrinkle

MAP 122

Keveral Beach

Downderry

B3247

Looe

Looe Bay

MAP 124

MAP 125

St George's Island

Hore Stone

| 0 | | 2 miles |
| 0 | | 3km |

200m
150
100

Battern Cliffs

Downderry

Looe

Seaton

Portwrinkle

0 miles 2 3 4 5 6 7

Bude

Looe ○ ○ Plymouth

Portwrinkle

Maps 122-125, Looe to Portwrinkl
7¾ miles/12.5km – 2¼-3hr

**NOTE: Add 20-30% to these time
to allow for stop**

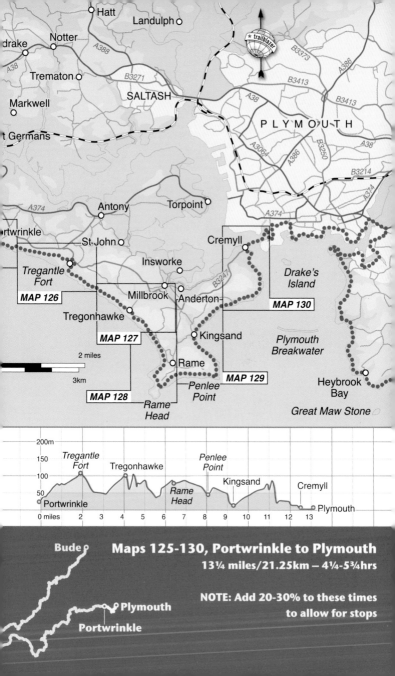

TRAILBLAZER'S LONG-DISTANCE PATH (LDP) WALKING GUIDES

We've applied to destinations which are closer to home Trailblazer's proven formula for publishing definitive practical route guides for adventurous travellers. Britain's network of long-distance trails enables the walker to explore some of the finest landscapes in the country's best walking areas. These are guides that are user-friendly, practical, informative and environmentally sensitive.

● **Unique mapping features** In many walking guidebooks the reader has to read a route description then try to relate it to the map. Our guides are much easier to use because walking directions, tricky junctions, places to stay and eat, points of interest and walking times are all written onto the maps themselves in the places to which they apply. With their uncluttered clarity, these are not general-purpose maps but fully edited maps drawn by walkers for walkers.

'The same attention to detail that distinguishes its other guides has been brought to bear here'.
THE SUNDAY TIMES

● **Largest-scale walking maps** At a scale of just under 1:20,000 (8cm or 3¹/₈ inches to one mile) the maps in these guides are bigger than even the most detailed British walking maps currently available in the shops.

● **Not just a trail guide – includes where to stay, where to eat and public transport** Our guidebooks cover the complete walking experience, not just the route. Accommodation options for all budgets are provided (pubs, hotels, B&Bs, campsites, bunkhouses, hostels) as well as places to eat. Detailed public transport information for all access points to each trail means that there are itineraries for all walkers, for hiking the entire route as well as for day or weekend walks.

Cleveland Way *Henry Stedman*, 1st edn, ISBN 978-1-905864-91-1, 208pp, 58 maps
Coast to Coast *Henry Stedman*, 8th edn, ISBN 978-1-905864-96-6, 268pp, 110 maps
Cornwall Coast Path (SW Coast Path Pt 2) *Stedman & Newton*, 6th edn, ISBN 978-1-912716-05-0, 352pp, 142 maps
Cotswold Way *Tricia & Bob Hayne*, 4th edn, ISBN 978-1-912716-04-3, 204pp, 53 maps,
Dales Way *Henry Stedman*, 1st edn, ISBN 978-1-905864-78-2, 192pp, 50 maps
Dorset & South Devon (SW Coast Path Pt 3) *Stedman & Newton*, 2nd edn, ISBN 978-1-905864-94-2, 336pp, 88 maps
Exmoor & North Devon (SW Coast Path Pt I) *Stedman & Newton*, 2nd edn, ISBN 978-1-905864-86-7, 224pp, 68 maps
Great Glen Way *Jim Manthorpe*, 1st edn, ISBN 978-1-905864-80-5, 192pp, 55 maps
Hadrian's Wall Path *Henry Stedman*, 5th edn, ISBN 978-1-905864-85-0, 224pp, 60 maps
Norfolk Coast Path & Peddars Way *Alexander Stewart*, 1st edn, ISBN 978-1-905864-98-0, 224pp, 75 maps,
North Downs Way *Henry Stedman*, 2nd edn, ISBN 978-1-905864-90-4, 240pp, 98 maps
Offa's Dyke Path *Keith Carter*, 5th edn, ISBN 978-1-912716-03-6, 256pp, 98 maps
Pembrokeshire Coast Path *Jim Manthorpe*, 5th edn, ISBN 978-1-905864-84-3, 236pp, 96 maps
Pennine Way *Stuart Greig*, 5th edn, ISBN 978-1-912716-02-9, 272pp, 138 maps
The Ridgeway *Nick Hill*, 4th edn, ISBN 978-1-905864-79-9, 208pp, 53 maps
South Downs Way *Jim Manthorpe*, 6th edn, ISBN 978-1-905864-93-5, 204pp, 60 maps
Thames Path *Joel Newton*, 2nd edn, ISBN 978-1-905864-97-3, 256pp, 99 maps
West Highland Way *Charlie Loram*, 7th edn, ISBN 978-1-912716-01-2, 218pp, 60 maps

'The Trailblazer series stands head, shoulders, waist and ankles above the rest.
They are particularly strong on mapping ...'
THE SUNDAY TIMES

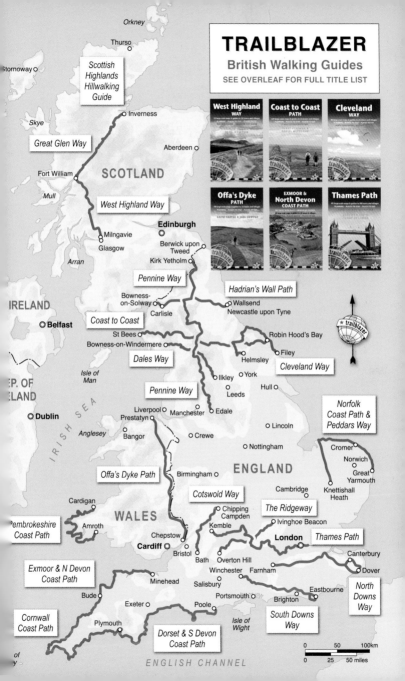

TRAILBLAZER TITLE LIST

For more information about Trailblazer and our
expanding range of guides, for guidebook updates or
for credit card mail order sales visit our website:

www.trailblazer-guides.com

Cornwall Coast Path

SOUTH-WEST COAST PATH – PART 2

(12 = MAP NUMBER – SEE KEY OVERLEAF FOR PAGE NUMBER)

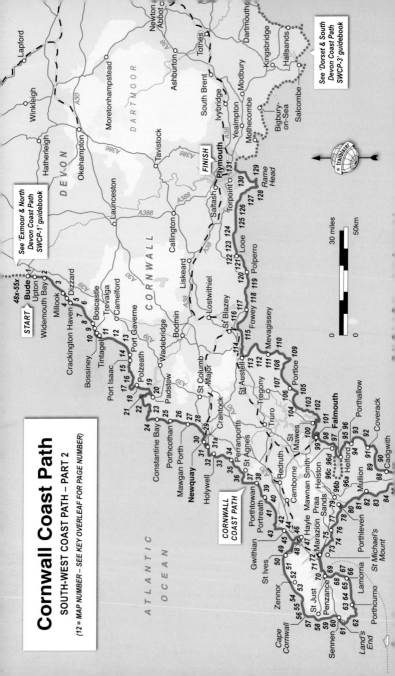

See 'Exmoor & North Devon Coast Path SWCP-1' guidebook

See 'Dorset & South Devon Coast Path SWCP-3' guidebook

48x–55x START Bude 1

Upton 2
Widemouth Bay 2
Millook 3
Dizzard 3
Crackington Haven 4
Boscastle 6
Trevalga 7
8 9
Bossiney 10 9
Tintagel 11
12 13
Port Gaverne
Port Isaac 14
15 16
17 18
Polzeath 19
20
21 22
23
Constantine Bay 24
Porthcothan 25
26
Mawgan Porth 27
28
Holywell 30 31
31a
Newquay 32 33 34
Perranporth 35 36
St Agnes 37 38
Porthtowan 39
Portreath 40
41
42
43 44
45
46
47
Gwithian
St Ives 50 49 48
51
52
53
54 55
56 57
58
St Just 59
60
Sennen 61
62
Land's End
Porthcurno 63 64 65 66
67
Lamorna 68 69
Penzance 70
71 72 73
Marazion 74 75 76
Praa Sands 77 78 79
80
81
Porthleven 82
83
Mullion 84
88 89
90
91 92
Coverack 93
94 95 96
Porthallow
97 98 99
Falmouth 100 101
102
103
104
105
Portloe 106 107
108 109
110
Mevagissey 111 112
113
114
115
Fowey 116 117
118 119
Polperro 120 121
122 123 124
Looe 125 126
127
128 Rame Head
129
130
131
FINISH Plymouth
Torpoint
Saltash

CORNWALL COAST PATH

CORNWALL

DEVON

DARTMOOR

ATLANTIC OCEAN

Cape Cornwall
Zennor

St Michael's Mount
Helston
Camborne
Redruth
Truro
St Mawes
St Austell
St Blazey
Lostwithiel
Bodmin
Wadebridge
St Columb Major
Crantock
Padstow
Camelford
Liskeard
Callington
Launceston
Okehampton
Hatherleigh
Winkleigh
Lapford
Tavistock
Moretonhampstead
Ashburton
South Brent
Ivybridge
Yealmpton
Modbury
Kingsbridge
Salcombe
Bigbury-on-Sea
Hallsands
Dartmouth
Totnes
Newton Abbot

St Mawes
Mawnan Smith
Hayle
Helford
Mylor

30 miles
0   50km
0

trailblazer